THE POLITICAL
ECONOMY
READER

MARKETS AS INSTITUTIONS

THE POLITICAL ECONOMY READER

MARKETS AS INSTITUTIONS

Edited by
Naazneen H. Barma and Steven K. Vogel

Routledge
Taylor & Francis Group
New York   London

Routledge
Taylor & Francis Group
270 Madison Avenue
New York, NY 10016

Routledge
Taylor & Francis Group
2 Park Square
Milton Park, Abingdon
Oxon OX14 4RN

© 2008 by Taylor & Francis Group, LLC
Routledge is an imprint of Taylor & Francis Group, an Informa business

International Standard Book Number-13: 978-0-415-95493-8 (Softcover) 978-0-415-95492-1 (Hardcover)

Library of Congress Cataloging-in-Publication Data

The political economy reader : markets as institutions / Naazneen H. Barma and Steven K. Vogel, editors.
   p. cm.
  ISBN 978-0-415-95492-1 (alk. paper) -- ISBN 978-0-415-95493-8 (alk. paper)
   1. International economic relations. 2. Capitalism. I. Barma, Naazneen. II. Vogel, Steven Kent.

HF1359.P6556 2007
330--dc22
                                               2007001183

**Visit the Taylor & Francis Web site at
http://www.taylorandfrancis.com**

**and the Routledge Web site at
http://www.routledge.com**

Contents

Preface

This reader began as a collaboration between a course instructor and a graduate student instructor for a course at the University of California, Berkeley (The Varieties of Capitalism: The Political-Economic Systems of the World). Eric Nelson of Routledge spotted the course syllabus on the Internet and asked Vogel if he would be interested in editing a reader based on the course reading list.

We feel that this reader fills a major gap among course readers and course texts on political economy. Although there are some excellent course books on international political economy, there is much less available for comparative political economy. Moreover, most course readers in the field are grounded in a single social science discipline, so they are unable to capture its interdisciplinary nature. Hence in this reader we have chosen to introduce work from four core disciplines: economics, sociology, political science, and history. We recognize that political economy is a broad field, and no single volume could possibly do justice to the full range of perspectives and topics. Some readers of this collection will inevitably be disappointed or frustrated by the particular choices we have made, but we have tried to assemble selections that will appeal to a wide range of readers.

In this reader we present what we view as an emerging consensus across several disciplines—which we term the "market-institutional" perspective on political economy—and delineate the variations within this broad camp. We introduce core theoretical works in Part I, framing this section as a debate between the liberal paradigm and market-institutional perspectives from four disciplines. Then in Part II we focus on market reforms in advanced industrial, postcommunist, and developing countries and conclude with selections on globalization and the information technology revolution. We frame these readings as a series of debates as well: Seldon versus Vogel, for example, then Sachs versus Stiglitz, Lal versus Chaudhry, Friedman versus Newman and Zysman, and Strange versus Gilpin. We hope that readers will enjoy engaging in these intellectual and real-world policy debates for themselves.

We are indebted to the students of Political Science 138E for trying out many of the selections in this reader, offering us their impressions, and teaching us about political economy while we tried to teach them. We benefited enormously from input from the other graduate student instructors who have taught the course: Jennifer Bussell, Mark Dallas, Lee Drutman, Albert Hahn, and Tobias Schulze-Cleven. Anonymous reviewers provided critical feedback on our proposal and the selection of readings. Richard Abrams, Mark Bevir, Jennifer Bussell, Neil Fligstein, Abraham Newman,

Ezra Vogel, Nicholas Ziegler, and John Zysman offered valuable comments on our introductions. Several authors of the reading selections assisted in securing copyright permissions. Vogel wants to acknowledge his intellectual debt to several key mentors: Peter Hall, Kenneth Jowitt, Peter Katzenstein, David Soskice, Harold Wilensky, and John Zysman. Barma wants to acknowledge Peter Evans, Andrew Janos, Steven Weber, Margaret Weir, Nicholas Ziegler, and John Zysman. Robert Tempio guided the review process, Michael Kerns steered the project from review through publication, Felisa Salvago-Keyes assisted with permissions and editing; Jennifer Smith served as project editor; Nicole Hirschman was the copy editor; and Nathalie Martinez was the proofreader.

Introduction

In this reader, we advocate a particular approach to studying political economy. We do not attempt to cover all the various schools of political economy, but rather we focus primarily on the market-institutional perspective that is increasingly prevalent across the social science disciplines. This perspective contends that markets should be viewed as institutions embedded in a particular social and political context and makes the study of these specific institutions its central mission. We contend that this perspective not only is relevant to academic debates but also has major ramifications for policy debates in advanced industrial countries, transitional economies, and developing countries today. There is nothing controversial about the proposition that markets are institutions in its most stripped-down form. Theorists diverge considerably, however, in what they mean by this. Classical liberals acknowledge that markets require some basic rules of the game. The government must establish and enforce laws; create the infrastructure for a modern economy, such as a monetary system; and provide certain public goods, such as national defense. Yet scholars have increasingly stressed that modern market systems are embedded in a far more extensive web of institutions. Institutional economists, for example, view "transaction costs" (such as the costs of obtaining information or enforcing contracts) as the friction in the market system, and property rights, broadly defined, as the means to reduce these costs. They move beyond the basic legal and financial infrastructure to study institutions such as the modern corporation, corporate governance systems, and long-term business contracts. Economic sociologists define market institutions even more broadly, including social networks and cultural norms. Political scientists emphasize how market systems reflect power relationships and how market and political institutions are inextricably linked. In this volume our definition of market institutions includes both formal institutions, such as corporate laws, and informal institutions, such as customary business practices, and it spans from the global, such as the international monetary system, to the local, such as the village bazaar.

Theorists first used the term *political economy* in the eighteenth century to refer to the management of the economic affairs of the state. The classical political economists—such as Adam Smith and later John Stuart Mill—challenged the earlier primacy of religion and tradition and embraced an empirical, pragmatic, and utilitarian approach to studying political and social institutions.[1] For our purposes, we define political economy simply as the study of real-world market systems, including local, sectoral, national, and global markets. We dispense with the fiction of perfect markets, in which buyers and sellers are instantly and costlessly matched, and focus on the complex institutions that sustain, impede, and structure markets. In this spirit, this reader includes both classical works in political economy and contemporary research from several academic disciplines that addresses how markets are embedded in politics and society. We do not include, however, one important branch in the contemporary study of political economy, which uses the analytical tools of modern economics to study issues, such as politics or social behavior, that lie outside the main substantive concerns of economics.[2]

Some scholars have positioned an institutional perspective as a frontal attack on mainstream economics, arguing that most research in economics builds on unrealistic assumptions about perfect markets. We concur that these assumptions are unrealistic, but we stop short of arguing that it cannot be useful to make them. Economists often assume perfect markets for the purposes of devising a model or making an argument, and there is nothing inherently wrong with that. They have made some of their greatest theoretical breakthroughs and presented some of their most useful prescriptions by making precisely this sort of simplifying assumption. However, they are engaged in a different enterprise from the one we take up here: that of studying real-word market systems and their variation across time, space, and fields (such as industrial sectors). Likewise, some economists may make a useful analytical distinction between the economic system and politics and society, yet the real-world economy is inextricably tied to politics and society. In this reader we focus precisely on the nature of this interaction.

We can introduce the market-institutional perspective—and how it differs from both classical liberal views and contemporary mainstream economics—by way of Karl Polanyi's critique of Adam Smith. Smith argues that people have a natural propensity to exchange. As people engage in voluntary exchange, a powerful organizing principle is born: the market. People individually make rational economic decisions based on their material self-interest, and the multitude of their expressed preferences is then communicated through the price mechanism. The market thus provides a system of want satisfaction that is regulated neither by the family nor by the state but rather by the famous "invisible hand" of the price mechanism. The market also provides a powerful incentive for innovation, because people seek to develop better ways of producing goods or services. Over time the market becomes more efficient as the division of labor becomes more sophisticated and extends further across space.

In contrast, Polanyi stresses that people are not necessarily motivated by self-interest and they do not have an inherent propensity to trade for profit. People are motivated more by social standing than by material wealth, so they are driven to maximize wealth only within a social order that attaches status to wealth. In other words, Polanyi suggests that economic rationality is culturally conditioned and market cultures may vary considerably across time and space. Polanyi makes this case by discussing primitive societies in which people do not maximize their own self-interest but engage in other types of economic relations, including what he calls "reciprocity" (mutual gift-giving) and "redistribution" (pooling goods and then distributing them).

Polanyi also offers a distinctive interpretation of the evolution from feudalism to market society in nineteenth-century Europe. He contends that the market system did not spontaneously arise but that governments had to actively create national markets. Governments organized long-distance trade; broke down local barriers to trade; established the basic infrastructure of a market, including property rights, currency, and competition rules; and regulated the economy enough to buffer society from some of the worst ravages of an unbridled market. As Polanyi says in his famous phrase, "While *laissez-faire* economy was the product of deliberate state action, subsequent restrictions on *laissez-faire* started in a spontaneous way. *Laissez-faire* was planned; planning was not."[3] Polanyi stresses that markets undermine the existing social fabric because they turn labor, land, and money—which are part of society—into commodities. Yet society inevitably fights back against the market with regulation. Polanyi refers to this interaction as a "double movement": the trading classes promote economic liberalism to foster a self-regulating market, but the working and landed classes push for social protection aimed at conserving man and nature.

In essence the market-institutional perspective claims that markets are social and political constructions, which must be actively created and governed. The process of market development and market reform is therefore a positive endeavor of building market institutions rather than a negative endeavor of removing obstacles to market activity.

Contending Perspectives: Four Disciplines

An increasing number of scholars now stress the institutional side of market development, yet they differ considerably in how they approach the study of market institutions. Here we briefly review some of the reigning paradigms within economics, sociology, political science, and history that will be represented in this reader.[4]

The New Institutional Economics

The New Institutional Economics (NIE) is a relatively coherent school of thought in that practitioners share a common intellectual lineage, language, and core concepts and identify themselves as working within a paradigm.[5] NIE scholars strive to be more theoretical in their approach than the "old" institutional economists, such as Thorstein Veblen and John Commons. They embrace the neoclassical assumption of utility maximization, yet they criticize standard economics for its failure to address economic institutions. As Douglass North puts it, the "neoclassical formulation appears to beg all the interesting questions. The world with which it is concerned is a frictionless one in which institutions do not exist and all change occurs through perfectly operating markets."[6]

The NIE theorists build on the study of transaction costs first introduced by Ronald Coase. They define transaction costs literally in the sense of anything that makes a transaction costly: that is, anything that impedes the costless matching of buyers and sellers. They divide transaction costs into two basic categories: information costs, such as the cost of obtaining information about a firm or a product, and enforcement costs, such as the cost of monitoring and enforcing contracts. If information costs are high, then buyers may not find sellers, or workers may not find employers, or borrowers may not find lenders—even though these sellers or employers or lenders may be out there somewhere. Or consumers may not have enough information to decide about a purchase or an investment. If enforcement costs are high, then market actors may not have the confidence to make an exchange because they lack the backing of a legal system that enforces deals. A market system requires effective third-party enforcement to operate beyond the level of personal exchange. Institutional economists see systems of property rights as solutions to transaction cost problems.

Douglass North uses transaction cost economics to analyze the historical evolution of economic institutions. Throughout much of history, transaction costs were sufficiently high to prevent most transactions from taking place. As property rights developed, however, transaction costs declined and market systems became more efficient. North stresses that well-defined property rights spur innovation. In a simple economic system, entrepreneurs do not have an incentive to innovate because the private return to innovation (their own profit) is miniscule relative to the social return (the benefit to society as a whole). That is, the innovator cannot reap the rewards of his or her invention. A more developed system of property rights raises the private return to innovation, strengthening the incentive to innovate. North argues that people reform economic institutions because of exogenous shocks (such as technological change) that alter relative prices, thereby shifting incentives. He takes a more "functionalist" line in his earlier work in that he implies that people develop better institutional solutions over time.[7] In later work, however, he depicts institutional change as a more open-ended process in which politics and ideology weigh heavily and changes may or may not constitute improvements.[8]

Coase first introduced transaction cost economics in an article in which he focused on one critical market institution: the firm. He asked, Why do we have firms? He argued that businesses create firms (corporate organizations) to reduce transaction costs.[9] That is, businesses choose to perform certain services and to produce certain parts for themselves rather than to purchase them on the open market. They do so because transaction costs in the marketplace are high, so it is more efficient to keep these functions out of the market and to conduct them in-house. He used this logic to theorize about where the firm would end and where the market would begin: firms would expand to the point where returns disappear (i.e., where the benefits of further expansion do not exceed the costs). Coase thus demonstrated how the concept of transaction costs could be applied to the study of economic institutions. Institutional economists have built on this logic to study a growing range of economic institutions, from types of corporate organization to forms of contracts. Oliver Williamson, for example, examines forms of contracts, corporate governance, franchise bidding, and antitrust enforcement.[10] Masahiko Aoki applies institutional economics to Japan, arguing that companies use institutions such as lifetime employment, the main bank system, and supplier networks to reduce transaction costs.[11]

Economic Sociology

Like institutional economics, economic sociology represents a relatively coherent school of thought in that practitioners view themselves as working within a common paradigm.[12] Following Polanyi, they believe that markets are governed by shared beliefs, customs, and norms. They particularly stress that markets are embedded in social relations, such as relations between retailers and their customers or manufacturers and their suppliers. They tend to differentiate their approach more sharply from standard economics than from institutional economics. They stress that their approach is more realistic, more historically informed, more oriented toward empirical research, and better equipped to analyze the diversity in markets across time, space, and sectors.[13] They eschew the methodological individualism of standard economics, identifying collective actors—such as groups or even social systems—as important units of analysis. Some sociologists, such as Powell and DiMaggio, reject the assumption of utility maximization, arguing that people are as likely to follow a logic of appropriateness in their actions as they are to adhere to a logic of utility.[14] Others, such as Mark Granovetter, prefer to expand the scope of rationality to incorporate social and economic goals.[15] For example, managers may fail to maximize a firm's profits because they are trying to enhance their status within a business network or to augment their power within a political coalition. As Victor Nee puts it, sociologists stress that rationality is bound by its context. What is rational in one society may be irrational in another.[16] Economic sociologists study in their empirical work everything from global agreements to local trade guilds. Many focus on the institutions of a particular industrial sector, such as the automobile market or the software market.[17]

Economic sociologists share more common ground with institutional economists than with mainstream economists, yet they maintain clear differences. We can bring these differences into relief by reviewing two articles in which major figures within the two paradigms address each other directly: North's critique of Polanyi and Granovetter's critique of Williamson. North agrees with Polanyi that the nineteenth-century emergence of market systems was a unique event in history and that mainstream economists fail to explain this shift. North even suggests that Polanyi's challenge could be taken further: How do we account for other substitutes for price-making markets, such as families, firms, guilds, manors, unions, or cooperatives? North points out that even today price-making markets do not dominate resource allocation but share that role with households, voluntary organizations, and governments. He then critiques Polanyi, however, by suggesting that this has also been the case historically: markets existed earlier as well. He disagrees with Polanyi that early exchange and trade does not reflect economic motivation. He contends that transaction cost economics can account for the primitive transactional modes Polanyi describes, but only better. What Polanyi calls "reciprocity" and "redistribution," for example, are really just least-cost trading and allocation arrangements for an environment of high transaction costs (with no system of enforcing the terms of exchange). These institutions evolved as ways to reduce transaction costs. North concludes that institutional economics provides a better way to develop and test hypotheses and to account for institutional change.[18]

Mark Granovetter develops his argument about the embeddedness of markets with a critique of Williamson. He argues that perfect competition would require atomized individuals, but in fact business relations are linked to personal relations. Williamson sees order within firms (the hierarchy of the corporate structure) and disorder between firms (the anarchy of the market). Yet Granovetter contends that social relations generate some order even in markets, and this enhances trust and limits opportunism. The balance of order and disorder in markets depends not just on firms' decisions about what to produce within the firm and what to purchase on the market but also on the specific nature of social relations in the sector or country in question. So a company will have less need for vertical integration (producing its own parts and subsystems) if it operates in a context of stable social relations in which it can rely on high levels of trust and good communications with its suppliers. Toyota needs less vertical integration than General Motors, for example, because it can rely on denser social relations throughout its supply chain. Granovetter concludes, "Williamson's perspective … may appear to have more kinship to a sociological perspective than the usual economic arguments. But the main thrust of the 'new institutional economists' is to deflect the analysis of institutions from sociological, historical, and legal argumentation and show instead that they arise as the efficient solution to economic problems. This mission and the pervasive functionalism it implies discourage the detailed analysis of social structure that I argue here is the key to understanding how existing institutions arrived at their present state."[19]

We conclude that research in economic sociology tends to be more accurate than that within the NIE school in that it provides a fuller and richer depiction of human motivation and interaction. Some NIE theorists adhere too rigidly to the assumption of human rationality or adopt an overly functionalist view of institutional change by assuming that changes proceed toward more rational forms. The logic of the NIE proceeds backward in the sense that it moves from perfect markets to institutions. That is, NIE theorists ask, What is impeding perfect markets? They refer to the impediments as "transaction costs," and they see economic institutions as mechanisms to reduce these costs. Yet real-life history has proceeded in the opposite direction. Social institutions came first, and the market system evolved upon their foundation. There is something perverse about seeing the family as the response to a transaction-cost problem (or as a "substitute" for the market, in North's language). At the same time, however, we concur with North that the NIE approach tends to be more useful analytically in that it is more amenable to generating specific research questions and testable hypotheses.

Political Science

Political scientists have a strong research tradition in political economy, yet they do not have a core research paradigm as coherent as that of institutional economics or economic sociology. They are first divided along the lines described previously, between those who use the analytical tools of economics to study politics and those who focus on substantive areas that bridge economics and politics. And even those in the latter camp adopt many different approaches, from the political analysis of economic policy to the integration of political and economic variables into causal models. In general, political scientists naturally focus more on power relationships than economists or sociologists do, and they stress that markets are linked to political institutions.

Many political scientists have focused on the role of the state and its relationship to the economy. Chalmers Johnson, for example, argues that the Japanese state enjoyed relative autonomy from the demands of particular social groups plus a competent and powerful bureaucracy, and this enabled the government to formulate and implement pro-growth economic policies designed to shift the industrial structure toward higher-value-added sectors. He extends this argument to other East Asian developmental states, such as South Korea and Taiwan, while also noting variations among these.[20] Likewise, experts on Latin America contend that "bureaucratic authoritarian" regimes in these countries were relatively insulated from short-term political pressures and thereby able to enact long-term economic growth strategies.[21]

Others have subsequently sought to flesh out the industry side of the government–industry relationship. Peter Katzenstein and his collaborators, for example, developed a typology that combines a spectrum from organized to less organized societies with one from strong to weak states.[22] John Zysman explicitly links the state, microlevel market institutions, and policy profiles. He focuses especially on financial systems, demonstrating a connection between strong states, credit-based financial systems, and industrial policies in France and Japan, on one hand, and weak states, equity-based financial systems, and more market-based adjustment strategies in Britain and the United States, on the other.[23] Peter Hall includes an even wider range of market institutions, including labor relations systems and product market structures.[24] Peter Evans links state strength not so much to autonomy from society but rather to the state's penetration of (or collaboration with) society.[25]

In recent years, Peter Hall and David Soskice and their collaborators have attempted a further integration of the study of political and market institutions in their work on the varieties of capitalism. The varieties of capitalism literature builds on earlier traditions in comparative political economy but gives greater attention to the microlevel of the firm.[26] It adopts the basic logic of institutional economics and also embraces a wider range of political and sociological factors. Hall and Soskice focus especially on the dichotomy between liberal market economies and coordinated market economies, arguing that these constitute alternative models with distinctive logics. They emphasize the complementarities between the various components of national models and suggest that partial deviations from these two models are likely to be less stable and less successful than more internally consistent versions. Critics of the Hall and Soskice approach suggest that their typology is less useful for "hybrid" cases such as France or Italy, that it goes too far in moving from a state-centric perspective to an industry-centric perspective, that it overstates the complementarities among the components of the models, and that it focuses too much on national models at the expense of variations across industrial sectors and regions within countries.[27]

History

Like political scientists, historians do not have a single paradigm that dominates the study of political economy within the discipline. As a rule they are more interested in understanding the particularities of political–economic systems than in making generalizations across cases. They almost inevitably adopt a market-institutional perspective, as defined here, because they are interested in real-world markets and their evolution over time. They are less prone to identify one or two core causal factors than to combine a multiplicity of factors—including politics, culture, and key events—into less parsimonious yet richer explanations.[28] Economic historians have especially stressed several core themes that have been overlooked by mainstream economics:

entrepreneurship, innovation, personal leadership, and the evolution of economic institutions. We cannot possibly do justice to the range of perspectives among economic historians here, but we can introduce several leading figures as illustrative examples.

Eric Hobsbawm combines a daunting array of factors into his influential account of the British Industrial Revolution. He acknowledges climate, geography, population, overseas discovery, and the Protestant Reformation as possible contributing factors. Yet he stresses the growth of domestic markets, enabled by improvements in transportation, and the availability of export markets, fueled by the expansion of the British Empire. The British government spurred industrial growth and technological innovation by building up its navy, and it decimated rival countries' industry and created a virtual monopoly on colonies. Like other economic historians, Hobsbawm challenges the classical economists by problematizing technological innovation. He contends that business people seek profits, not innovation, and in practice they often favor profits at the expense of innovation. They will view industrial investment as profitable only if the potential market is large and the risk is manageable. The growth in domestic and export markets in eighteenth-century England provided just these conditions, and this fostered the Industrial Revolution.[29]

Alexander Gerschenkron's argument about the timing of industrialization has been particularly influential in political economy research across disciplines. He contends that late-industrializing countries face fundamentally different challenges from Britain, the first country to industrialize. His approach contrasts to Walter Rostow's more biological model of stages of growth. Although Rostow inserts some important qualifications, he still depicts a remarkably uniform growth process: all countries evolve through the same stages, albeit at different times and different speeds. In contrast Gerschenkron stresses that late-industrializing countries confront a huge technological gap, so they do not have the luxury of industrializing slowly. They must make massive investments to shift rapidly into heavy industry. This requires large-scale financing, an institutional mechanism for channeling the funds, and a powerful ideology to motivate the mobilization effort. Industrial banks provided the institutional mechanism in Germany, whereas the state played this role in Russia. Gerschenkron was particularly troubled by the political ramifications of late industrialization. Late industrializing would require a more powerful state because of the larger technological gap, and this might well take the form of a totalitarian state, as in the Soviet case.

Alfred Chandler also addresses the relationship between institutions and innovation, but he focuses on firms rather than on states or banks. Chandler addresses some of the same substantive questions addressed by Williamson—such as why firms vertically integrate—but he approaches them as a historian rather than as an economist; that is, whereas Williamson offers models, Chandler provides detailed historical narrative. To his credit, Williamson read Chandler's work quite carefully, and he incorporated some of Chandler's insights into his models.[30] Like other theorists surveyed here, Chandler frames his work as a critique of Adam Smith and standard economic theory. He argues that beginning in the late nineteenth century in the United States, the "visible hand" of the modern business enterprise replaced the invisible hand of the market. The modern firm took over the market functions of coordinating the flow of goods and allocating resources to future production and distribution. It did so when the volume of economic activity reached a level that made administrative coordination more efficient than market coordination. And it did so by creating a managerial hierarchy that allowed it to internalize the activities of many business units within a single enterprise. In the process, the modern business enterprise became the most powerful institution in the U.S. economy.[31]

Contemporary Debates: Three Types of Market Reform

The market-institutional perspective not only represents an emerging consensus within some scholarly circles but also has specific implications for policy debates. We can illustrate this by providing concrete examples of three types of market reform: incremental reforms designed to enhance market competition in the advanced industrial countries, the fundamental transition from a command economy to a market system in the former communist states, and the effort to create modern market institutions in developing countries. These three types of market reform are sometimes referred to as deregulation, privatization, and liberalization, respectively, but we shall see that this language obscures more than it clarifies. In the latter half of this reader, we present readings that focus specifically on these three transitions. In essence, we pose a very basic question: What does it take to make a market? Our first answer is that it is not easy! If market activity were natural and separate from society and politics, then making a market should be straightforward. Market reform would simply mean removing constraints on market activity. If markets are complex institutions intertwined with politics and society, however, then market reform should be a painstaking process of building institutions.

Market Reform in the Advanced Industrial Countries

We can apply this logic to the advanced industrial countries by looking at the deregulation movement of the past three decades. Many analysts view it as part of a global trend among industrial countries, propelled by reforms under Margaret Thatcher in Britain and Ronald Reagan in the United States in the 1980s, that fundamentally reduced the role of the government and enhanced the role of the market.[32] Debates about economic issues generally presuppose a zero-sum relationship between governments and markets; that is, more government means less market and less government means more market. In fact, many commentators use the term *deregulation* in a way that belies this assumption. They assume that deregulation refers to less government regulation and more market competition, as if the two were naturally associated. Yet government regulation and market competition are more complementary than contradictory. The general trend has been not freer markets and fewer rules but rather freer markets and more rules—and in fact there is a clear logical connection between the two. Freer markets require more rules of at least three varieties: a more sophisticated market infrastructure, including the legal and financial systems; more regulation to sustain competition, such as antitrust policy; and more social regulation to buffer society from negative externalities, including health, safety, and environmental regulation (Vogel reading). If the goal is to maximize competition, therefore, then the policy should be not simply to reduce government regulation, or simply to increase it, but rather to enhance regulation that creates, promotes, and sustains competition and to reduce regulation that impedes it. In sum, debates about market reform in these countries are less about liberating markets from the government than about recalibrating market design.[33]

Market Transition in Eastern Europe and China

If regulatory reform in industrial countries is the most subtle of the three types of market reform, then the market transition of formerly planned economies is the most radical. Market transition in these countries gives us the opportunity to view the process of creating market institutions in real time. We can see what types of institutions are necessary to create viable market systems and how variations in reform policies shape market development. How does a country make the transition from plan to market? Is dismantling the old system enough? What new institutions and values are required? Given the scale of the transformation, the institution-building side of the process is less likely to be overlooked than it is with more limited market reforms in the industrial countries. Even so, there is a lively debate in the field between those who stress the negative side of the reform process—dismantling the old institutions as quickly as possible and then allowing markets to flourish—and those who stress the positive side—the painstaking process of building new market institutions.

This debate is typically framed in terms of "shock therapy" versus "gradualism." We can grasp the logic of the positions with two common metaphors. In one view, market transition is like switching from driving on the right side of the road to driving on the left: you have to make the change as quickly and thoroughly as possible. You do not want to tell drivers that they have an interim period in which they can drive on whichever side they like. In the other view, market transition is more like building a bridge from an old structure to a new one: you have to be sure that the new structure is sound before you abandon the old one, and you want to pay particular attention to designing an effective bridge between the two.

The experts also differ on the proper political strategy for economic reform. Those who advocate shock therapy contend that the government must act quickly to seize the initial window of opportunity before opponents of reform have a chance to mobilize.[34] Those who favor a more gradual process suggest that leaders should orchestrate reforms carefully to contain political and social upheaval. The leaders who initiated the reform processes in the Soviet Union and China, Mikhail Gorbachev and Deng Xiaoping, respectively, had very different philosophies about how political reform and economic reform interact. Gorbachev felt that he needed to promote political reform to facilitate economic reform because it would empower the advocates of reform and undermine the opponents. Deng felt that he needed to limit democracy and maintain central authority to implement economic reform.[35]

The actual debate among the experts is more subtle than the stark juxtaposition of shock therapy versus gradualism implies. Those who advocate shock therapy tend to focus more on the mechanics of monetary stabilization, whereas those who favor gradualism stress the construction of market infrastructure. And most serious scholars concur that these countries need both short-term stabilization and longer-term institutional development. In this reader we sample two leading figures in the debate: Jeffrey Sachs and Joseph Stiglitz. Neither can be neatly pigeonholed as a simple-minded shock therapist or gradualist, and yet there are clear differences in their diagnoses and their prescriptions. Sachs recognizes the need to cultivate market institutions, yet he stresses the negative side of the process—the removal of government intervention—and highlights the need for speed. He sees the market transition as a seamless web, a complex variety of measures that are more effective if they are implemented together. Stiglitz stresses that the transition process takes time and that the sequence of reforms is critical. The government should not privatize, for example, without first building a regulatory structure that promotes competition. Otherwise, privatization leads simply to asset stripping, whereby new owners sell off assets, rather than retain the productive capacity of the company, and take their profits abroad—as many did in Russia.

Both sides cite country case examples to bolster their argument, but the reality is sufficiently complex to leave plenty of room for rival interpretations. Some cite Poland as an example of successful shock therapy because the government acted swiftly, for example, whereas others categorize it as a case of gradualism because it built on a relatively long history of market institutions. Sachs emphasizes that the Soviet Union tried gradualism under Gorbachev and it failed, whereas Stiglitz stresses that Russia tried shock therapy under Boris Yeltsin and that did not work either.

For Stiglitz, China's approach to reform offers a promising alternative to the Russian model. For Sachs, however, China is so fundamentally different from Russia that the lessons do not apply. China was primarily an agricultural economy at the onset of reform, whereas Russia was already an industrial economy. This meant that China could achieve substantial growth simply by modernizing the agricultural sector. Russia, meanwhile, had to confront the much more daunting problem of industrial reform right from the beginning.

Given China's relatively successful experience with a gradualist approach to economic reform, there are fewer advocates of a shock therapy approach among those who study China. In an illuminating head-to-head debate, however, Wing Thye Woo argues that the benefits from reform come as government is supplanted by the market as a mechanism of allocating resources. Therefore Chinese slowness was not a virtue—it was just plain slow. Thomas Rawski counters that the Chinese have combined market reforms with institutional legacies from the prereform era in ways that have facilitated a successful transition. For example, the Chinese model has benefited from town and village enterprises, which compete in the market place yet build on the prereform institutions of common ownership and village community.[36]

Market Development in Developing Countries

The market-institutional perspective suggests that developing countries are not suffering from too much government interference in markets so much as from the government's failure to develop market institutions. Samuel Huntington has argued that developing country governments have not too much authority but too little. They are authoritarian, that is, precisely because they lack political authority, in terms of both the legitimacy of the regime and the institutions of government.[37] We can make an analogous argument about the economy: the state is not too strong but too weak. The state lacks the capacity to develop the legal system, the financial system, and other core market infrastructure, and it lacks the ability to regulate market competition. It resorts to the direct provision of goods and services and other authoritative approaches to allocating resources precisely because it lacks the capacity to provide an infrastructure to perform these functions and to monitor competition between private companies (see Chaudhry in this volume). In other words, these countries suffer from underdeveloped political and economic institutions, and this fosters authoritarian politics and statist economic policies.

Debates about the political economy of development are often framed as a competition between the Washington consensus and its opponents. Commentators coined the term "Washington consensus" to refer to what they viewed as the mainstream view at the World Bank and the International Monetary Fund, two international financial institutions based in Washington, D.C. These institutions often imposed certain conditions on loans or aid to developing countries, such as balancing the government budget or liberalizing the economy. The critics of the Washington consensus stressed that rapid economic liberalization was not appropriate for these countries and that developing countries should focus first on building up local agriculture and industry and cultivating market institutions.

As with shock therapy and gradualism, however, the actual contours of the debate are more subtle. In fact, one institution at the heart of the consensus—the World Bank—has undergone a gradual evolution toward a more market-institutional perspective on market reform. In the 1980s, the Japanese government commissioned a study of the East Asian economic miracle. Japanese officials were unhappy that their own views on development were not better reflected in the Bank's policies, given that Japan was second only to the United States as a financial contributor. They felt that Bank policies should better reflect Japan's own development experience. After all, Japan was the first country to rise from developing-country status to an industrial power in the twentieth century. The Japanese advocated a stronger emphasis on building institutions—including a competent bureaucracy and a sound banking system—and less of an ideological commitment to free trade policies. The East Asian miracle project generated an intense debate within the Bank yet resulted in a relatively bland compromise between U.S.-trained economists and Japanese sponsors.[38] The Bank did not abruptly change its position in response to this report, but it has gradually adopted a more nuanced view of market development over time. The Bank's 1997 World Development Report focused on the role of the state in the economy, and its 2002 report turned to our core theme of building market institutions. The latter built on the literature in the New Institutional Economics in particular, proposing concrete measures to strengthen market institutions in developing countries.[39]

Hernando de Soto, the renowned Chilean economist, has popularized this line of argument with his thesis that the single biggest problem in developing countries is the lack of property rights. De Soto stresses property rights in the most literal sense: title to land. He contends that if poor people had title to their land, then they would have capital with which to obtain a loan or start a venture. Without it, however, they are stuck in a poverty trap. Many scholars in institutional economics and economic sociology agree on the importance of property rights, but they prefer a broader definition of property rights that encompasses the legal system and even social norms.[40] Some focus more on the political side, stressing that peace, national identity, state autonomy, regime legitimacy, and administrative capacity are all pre-requisites to the development of modern market institutions.[41]

Whither Market Institutions?

If we take markets-as-institutions seriously, then we inevitably have to confront the question of how current events are reshaping these institutions. Is globalization fundamentally altering national political–economic systems? Is the information technology (IT) revolution generating new possibilities for more perfect, or less embedded, markets? Addressing these two challenges provides a useful way to rethink the approach to the study of political economy we have introduced here.

Globalization

In the current period we are deluged with generalizations about globalization, but too frequently this discussion lacks precision about what globalization means and what it is and is not changing. To move beyond this morass, we must unpack globalization into its component parts and specify the mechanisms of change and the limits to change. Finance has become more global as capital flows across borders have surged and financial markets and financial institutions have become more international. Trade has become more global as the flow of goods and services across national borders has increased. Production has become more global as companies, products, and production networks have become less tied to a single national origin. There is considerable controversy on whether multinational companies are truly global, however, or whether they offer products or services that are uniform throughout the world.[42] Likewise, international supply chains and even regional production networks generally remain linked to a specific national economy. The globalization of finance, trade, and production has strengthened pressure on governments to adjust their policies and to harmonize regulation across borders. Globalization also has a more political dimension, in which international institutions—from the World Trade Organization to private sector accounting boards—develop and enforce common rules. The United States and other major powers also use their political and economic leverage to impose their preferred rules on the international community. And of course globalization has a cultural element, including the diffusion of popular culture, ideas, and norms across national borders. This facet of globalization is neither altogether new nor all-powerful, but it does suggest that the study of discrete market cultures should be combined with an analysis of how market cultures diffuse across space, how they interact with each other, and how they blend in practice.

These varieties of globalization suggest that we should reconsider our core unit of analysis, the nation-state. As noted previously, important research in political economy shifts downward to the subnational level of localities, industrial sectors, and individual firms, but it must also shift upward to the regional and global level as well. Susan Strange contends that global markets have fundamentally shifted power away from the nation-state. If markets are institutions, however, then governments would inevitably play a part in enhancing competition in international markets, and they would certainly play a part in governing these markets. To the extent that globalization is happening—one might quip, following Polanyi—then much of it has been planned. Robert Gilpin confronts Strange's challenge directly, arguing that although economic globalization has affected state capabilities, it has not imposed any clear net loss on these abilities. Economic globalization is partial and uneven, and it has eroded state power in some regions and some sectors, while it has augmented that power in others.[43]

Globalization may not have obliterated the nation-state, but has it forced national market systems to converge toward a common model? Scholars of comparative political economy tend to stress the continuing diversity of institutions despite the pressures of globalization. The countries of the world may face a common set of pressures that fall within the broad rubric of "globalization," but they retain considerable leeway to respond to these pressures in their own distinct ways. And precisely because of their differential institutional legacies, they vary in how they respond.[44]

The Information Technology Revolution

We began this introduction with the assertion that the market-institutional perspective rejects the possibility of perfect markets. But does the IT revolution change all that? Does it generate the possibility of near-perfect markets? In one selection in this reader, Thomas Friedman notes that the Internet offers the closest thing to a perfectly competitive market in the world: there are no barriers to entry, no protection from failure for unprofitable firms, and everyone (consumers and producers) has easy access to information. Consider eBay, the popular Internet marketplace. Is it not awfully close to a perfect market? Transaction costs are extremely low, information disseminates easily, and buyers and sellers are almost instantly matched. And what about business-to-business transactions? Does not electronic commerce "disembed" transactions from society? After all, companies can compare suppliers from around the world without relying on face-to-face transactions.

Our short answer is that the IT revolution affects the nature of market institutions but it does not obliterate them or challenge the basic logic of the argument presented thus far. After all, electronic markets are practical for only certain types of goods and certain types of transactions. They work best for standardized goods, when price is the dominant factor. The more multidimensional the qualities of the product, the less amenable it is to electronic trade. In addition, many consumers and businesses still prefer face-to-face transactions. They conduct business this way because they have to make too many complicated judgments about product or service quality or because they have to engage in complex negotiations with the other party. If we follow Polanyi's logic that all markets are embedded in society, moreover, then we must recognize that this is true of electronic markets as well. As Newman and Zysman demonstrate, even cybermarkets require rules to govern property, exchange, and market structure, and governments have actively intervened to shape these rules. Even eBay has a fairly sophisticated set of formal rules and informal guidelines that govern transactions. Participants in the market rely on reputational scores from third parties in the place of face-to-face trust gleaned over a long period of time. And eBay transactions ultimately rely on the larger property rights regime as a fallback option in the case of disputes. In other words, eBay has a market culture and an institutional structure, even if the culture and the structure are different from those of previous marketplaces. And eBay is still linked to the broader market system.

In sum, globalization and the IT revolution are dramatically altering the nature of market institutions, but they are not making these markets any less embedded in social and political institutions.

Notes

1. James A. Caporaso and David P. Levine, *Theories of Political Economy* (Cambridge: Cambridge University Press, 1992), 1–2, 33–46; Peter Gourevitch, "Political Economy," in Joel Krieger, ed., *The Oxford Companion to Politics of the World* (Oxford: Oxford University Press, 1993), 715–719.

2. This branch includes the social choice, public choice, and rational choice schools. For an overview, including definitions of the various schools, see Kristin Renwick Monroe, *The Economic Approach to Politics: A Critical Reassessment of the Theory of Rational Action* New York: HarperCollins, 1991), especially 1–31. Elisabeth Gerber proposes that the subfield of political economy should be defined as "the study of political phenomena using the tools of economic analysis" for the purposes of organizing the Political Economy Section of the American Political Science Association (APSA): "What is Political Economy?," *The Political Economist* 11 (Fall 2003), 1, 3. We agree that this definition identifies an important subfield within American political science, but we do not concur that this subfield should usurp the term "political economy" from the likes of Andrew Shonfield or Peter Katzenstein, not to mention Adam Smith and Karl Marx.

3. Karl Polanyi, *The Great Transformation: The Political and Economic Origins of Our Time* (Boston: Beacon Press, 1944), 141.

4. Our selection of academic disciplines that address political economy is by no means exhaustive. We have not included, for example, major works from anthropology, geography, business administration, or law.

5. See Douglass C. North, "The New Institutional Economics," *Journal of Institutional and Theoretical Economics* 142 (1986): 230–37; and Oliver Williamson, "The New Institutional Economics: Taking Stock, Looking Ahead," *Journal of Economic Literature* 38 (September 2000): 595–613. Anthologies of NIE scholarship include Oliver E. Williamson and Scott E. Master, *Transaction Cost Economics,* 2 vols. (Aldershot: Edward Elgar, 1995); Claude Menard, ed., *The International Library of New Institutional Economics,* 7 vols. (Cheltenham: Edward Elgar, 2004); and Claude Menard and Mary M. Shirley, eds., *Handbook of New Institutional Economics* (Dordrecht: Springer, 2005).

6. Douglass C. North, *Structure and Change in Economic History* (New York: W.W. Norton, 1981), 5.

7. Ibid.

8. Douglass C. North, *Institutions, Institutional Change and Economic Performance* (Cambridge: Cambridge University Press, 1990).

9. Ronald Coase, "The Nature of the Firm," *Economica* 4 (1937): 386–405.

10. Oliver Williamson, *The Economic Institutions of Capitalism* (New York: Free Press, 1985).

11. Masahiko Aoki, *Information, Incentives, and Bargaining in the Japanese Economy* (Cambridge: Cambridge University Press, 1988); and *Toward a Comparative Institutional Analysis* (Cambridge: MIT Press, 2001).

12. Anthologies presenting work in this subfield include Nicole W. Biggart, ed., *Readings in Economic Sociology* (Oxford: Blackwell, 2002); Frank Dobbin, ed., *The New Economic Sociology: A Reader* (Princeton: Princeton University Press, 2004); Neil J. Smelser and Richard Swedberg, eds., *The Handbook of Economic Sociology,* 2nd ed. (Princeton: Princeton University Press, 2005); and Victor Nee and Richard Swedberg, eds., *The Economic Sociology of Capitalism* (Princeton: Princeton University Press, 2005).

13. Nicole W. Biggart, *Readings in Economic Sociology.*

14. Walter W. Powell and Paul J. DiMaggio, eds., *The New Institutionalism in Organizational Analysis* (Chicago: University of Chicago Press, 1991), 1–38.

15. Mark Granovetter, "Economic Action and Social Structure: The Problem of Embeddedness," *American Journal of Sociology* 91 (1985): 481–510.

16. Victor Nee, "The New Institutionalisms in Economics and Sociology," in *The Handbook of Economic Sociology,* 49–74.

17. Neil Fligstein, *The Architecture of Markets: An Economic Sociology of Twenty-first Century Capitalist Societies* (Princeton: Princeton University Press, 2001). John L. Campbell, J. Rogers Hollingsworth, and Leon N. Lindberg illustrate the broad range of market institutions with their typology of "governance mechanisms": Campbell, Hollingsworth, and Lindberg, eds., *Governance of the American Economy* (Cambridge: Cambridge University Press, 1991), 14.

18. Douglass C. North, "Market and Other Allocation Systems in History: The Challenge of Karl Polanyi," *Journal of European Economic History* 6(3) (Winter 1977): 703–16.

19. Mark Granovetter, "Economic Action and Social Structure," 505. Williamson counters that the embeddedness argument "is consistent with, and much of it has been anticipated by, transaction cost reasoning": *The Mechanisms of Governance* (Oxford: Oxford University Press, 1996), 230.

20. Chalmers Johnson, "Political Institutions and Economic Performance: The Government-Business Relationship in Japan, South Korea, and Taiwan," in *The Political Economy of the New Asian Industrialism,* ed. Frederic Deyo (Ithaca: Cornell University Press, 1987), 136–64.

21. Guillermo A. O'Donnell, *Modernization and Bureaucratic Authoritarianism* (Berkeley: Institute of International Studies, University of California, 1973); and David Collier, ed., *The New Authoritarianism in Latin America* (Princeton: Princeton University Press, 1979).

22. Peter Katzenstein, ed., *Between Power and Plenty: Foreign Economic Policies of Advanced Industrial States* (Madison: University of Wisconsin Press, 1978), especially pp. 323–24.

23. John Zysman, *Governments, Markets and Growth: Financial Systems and the Politics of Industrial Change* (Ithaca: Cornell University Press, 1983).

24. Peter Hall, *Governing the Economy: The Politics of State Intervention in Britain and France* (New York: Oxford University Press, 1986).

25. Also see Atul Kohli. *State-Directed Development: Political Power and Industrialization in the Global Periphery.* (Cambridge: Cambridge University Press, 2004).

26. A substantial body of work on the varieties of capitalism predates the Hall and Soskice volume. For example, Andrew Shonfield, *Modern Capitalism: The Changing Balance of Public and Private Power* (New York: Oxford University Press, 1965); J. Rogers Hollingsworth, Philippe C. Schmitter, and Wolfgang Streeck, eds., *Governing Capitalist*

Economies: Performance and Control of Economic Sectors (New York: Oxford University Press, 1994); and Colin Crouch and Wolfgang Streeck, eds., *Political Economy of Modern Capitalism* (London: Sage, 1997).

27. Jonah Levy, ed., *The State after Statism: New State Activities in the Age of Liberalization* (Cambridge, MA: Harvard University Press, 2006); and Steven K. Vogel, *Japan Remodeled: How Government and Industry Are Transforming Japanese Capitalism* (Ithaca: Cornell University Press, 2006), 12–13.

28. David S. Landes, "Introduction: On Technology and Growth," in *Favorites of Fortune: Technology, Growth, and Economic Development since the Industrial Revolution,* ed. Patrice Higonnet, David S. Landes, and Henry Rosovsky (Cambridge, MA: Harvard University Press, 1991), especially p. 5.

29. Eric J. Hobsbawm, *Industry and Empire: An Economic History of Britain since 1750* (London: Weidenfeld and Nicolson, 1968), 1–39.

30. William Lazonick argues that Williamson's transaction cost approach, unlike Chandler's historical approach, cannot explain key features of U.S. business history: *Business Organization and the Myth of the Market Economy* (Cambridge: Cambridge University Press, 1991), 228–61.

31. Alfred Chandler, *The Visible Hand: The Managerial Revolution in American Business* (Cambridge: Belknap Press, 1977), 1–8.

32. Daniel Yergin and Joseph Stanislaw, *The Commanding Heights: The Battle between Government and the Marketplace That Is Remaking the Modern World* (New York: Simon & Schuster, 1998), especially 9–17, 92–124, 325–63.

33. See Marc K. Landy, Martin A. Levin, and Martin Shapiro, eds., *Creating Competitive Markets: The Politics of Regulatory Reform* (Washington, DC: Brookings Institution Press, 2007).

34. Jeffrey Sachs, "Poland and Eastern Europe: What Is to Be Done?" in *Foreign Economic Liberalization: Transformations in Socialist and Market Economies,* ed. Andras Koves and Paul Marer (Boulder, CO: Westview, 1991), 235–46.

35. See William Overholt, *The Rise of China: How Economic Reform Is Creating a New Superpower* (New York: W.W. Norton, 1993), especially 118–31.

36. Wing Thye Woo, "The Real Reasons for China's Growth," and Thomas Rawski, "Reforming China's Economy: What Have We Learned?" *China Journal* 41 (January 1999): 115–56. Also see the exchange between Woo and Yu-Shan Wu: Yu-Shan Wu, "Chinese Economic Reform in a Comparative Perspective: Asia vs. Europe," *Issues and Studies* 38 (December 2002–March 2003): 93–138; and Wing Thye Woo, "A United Front for the Common Objective to Understand China's Economic Growth: A Case of Nonantagonistic Contradiction, Wu vs. Woo," and Yu Shan-Wu, "Institutions and Policies Must Bear the Responsibility: Another Case of Nonantagonistic Contradiction," *Issues and Studies* 39 (June 2003): 1–40.

37. Samuel Huntington, *Political Order in Changing Societies* (New Haven: Yale University Press, 1968), 1–2.

38. World Bank, *The East Asian Miracle: Economic Growth and Public Policy* (Oxford: Oxford University Press, 1993); and Robert Wade, "Japan, the World Bank, and the Art of Paradigm Maintenance: *The East Asian Miracle* in Political Perspective," *New Left Review* 217 (May–June 1996): 3–36.

39. World Bank, *World Development Report 1997: The State in a Changing World* (Oxford: Oxford University Press, 1997), and *World Development Report 2002: Building Institutions for Markets* (Oxford: Oxford University Press, 2002). Joseph Stiglitz critiques

International Monetary Fund policies in *Globalization and Its Discontents* (New York: W.W. Norton, 2002), and Kenneth Rogoff counters in "The IMF Strikes Back," *Foreign Policy* 134 (January–February 2003): 39–46.

40. The *World Development Report 2002* (p. 12) stresses that formal title to land is not sufficient. Frank Upham charges that the property rights literature does not give sufficient attention to informal institutions, including broader social norms: "Mythmaking in the Rule of Law Orthodoxy" (working paper, Carnegie Endowment for International Peace, 2002).

41. Peter Evans, *Embedded Autonomy: States and Industrial Transformation* (Princeton: Princeton University Press, 1995); and Atul Kohli, *State-Directed Development: Political Power and Industrialization in the Global Periphery* (Cambridge: Cambridge University Press, 2004).

42. Paul N. Doremus, William W. Keller, Louis W. Pauly, and Simon Reich, *The Myth of the Global Corporation* (Princeton: Princeton University Press, 1998).

43. Also see Peter Evans, "The Eclipse of the State? Reflections on Stateness in an Era of Globalization," *World Politics* 50 (October 1997): 62–87.

44. Suzanne Berger and Ronald Dore, eds., *National Diversity and Global Capitalism* (Ithaca: Cornell University Press, 1996); Steven K. Vogel, *Freer Markets, More Rules: Regulatory Reform in Advanced Industrial Countries* (Ithaca: Cornell University Press, 1996); Herbert Kitschelt et al., eds., *Continuity and Change in Contemporary Capitalism* (Cambridge: Cambridge University Press, 1999); and Peter Hall and David Soskice, eds., *Varieties of Capitalism: The Institutional Foundations of Comparative Advantage* (Oxford: Oxford University Press, 2001)

Part I

Contending Perspectives: Four Disciplines

1

The Classics

Political economy is a relatively new discipline, and its classic works are both fairly recent and clearly identifiable. Yet even from the beginning, distinct approaches to the study of political economy and views on the nature of markets emerged. The three classical theorists considered here, for example, differ on the relationship between politics and economics in the functioning of the market and the capitalist system, and on the role of the state in relation to the economy. The three perspectives are representatives of the capitalist, communist, and mercantilist approaches to political economy. Together they cover the theoretical poles of debates on political economy and provide much insight into the political–economic traditions of the modern world.

Adam Smith is considered by many to be the father of modern political economy. One of a group of scholars known as the Scottish moral philosophers, Smith treated explicitly the linkages between politics and economics. Moreover, he was one of the first theorists of the capitalist system, breaking down how its component parts, such as the production process, markets, and the international trade system, function. Adam Smith is still remembered today for these insights into the working of markets. His analysis left lasting legacies for the subsequent discipline of economics and in more general prevailing worldviews about the nature of economic freedom.

Smith's *Inquiry into the Nature and Causes of the Wealth of Nations*, published in 1776, was one of the earliest attempts to study industry and commerce in England, the nation where the Industrial Revolution began. The selection presented here includes insights that have had a lasting effect on the way we think about markets. The phrase most commonly associated with Adam Smith is probably the "invisible hand" through which an unorganized and potentially chaotic market system creates the amount and variety of goods desired by society. Economic liberals today continue to believe that markets are self-regulating and that failures are introduced externally rather than being inherent in markets. Equally influential is Smith's concept of the "division of labor," elaborated through his pin factory example. He demonstrates explicitly the mechanisms through which the division of labor increases the productivity of labor and notes that society functions as a well-oiled machine, with pieces fitting together seamlessly to provide man with all his needs.

In Smith's analysis, this well-functioning system of production and trade is not, however, constructed artificially but is rather the "consequence of a certain propensity in human nature ... the propensity to truck, barter, and exchange."[1] That propensity, in turn, is encouraged by self-interest, which Smith views as a natural phenomenon that consistently motivates human behavior and interaction. He argues that a system in which self-interest is allowed to function achieves the highest collective good.[2] Thus, a free market, animated by the pursuit of self-interest, through a series of unintended consequences known as the "invisible hand," begets a system of economic relations and social organization that surpasses any based on altruism in the production of both economic output and social harmony. This philosophy has had a lasting impact into today: free market liberals (see **Friedrich Hayek** and **Milton Friedman** in this volume, for example) go even further than Smith in arguing both that self-interest-driven behavior is a natural human trait and that the most effective and efficient way to maximize collective social welfare and the public interest is to allow individuals to act in their self-interest.

Smith also mounts a defense of the functioning of free markets in international trade. The practice of and scholarship on foreign policy in the seventeenth and eighteenth centuries were predominantly within a framework of ideas that came to be known as mercantilism.[3] *The Wealth of Nations* represented Smith's impassioned plea to the British Parliament to cease its counterproductive mercantilist strategy, which attempted to increase national wealth by enlarging reserves of gold and silver bullion. Smith explained that foreign trade actually increases national wealth by exporting surplus production and importing needed goods in return. His analysis of the benefits of free trade continue to form the basis of pro–free trade logic today.[4] One of the major inefficiencies of managed trade, according to Smith, is that the individual can better judge the most valuable use of his capital than can the state.

Smith argues more generally that any attempt by the state to direct economic activity—such as through trade barriers or industrial incentives—actually subverts those goals it hopes to achieve by tampering with the efficient functioning of the invisible hand. This analysis leaves the state with only three major functions to play: the defense of national security, the provision of a framework for and administration of the just rule of law (including antitrust regulation to prevent the formation of either public or private monopolies), and the provision of public goods that would not be provided by the market. In this respect, the state ideally conducts a laissez-faire policy with respect to markets, leaving them to regulate themselves and acting in the capitalist system only where markets cannot. The laissez-faire perspective has proved to have lasting staying power since Smith wrote *The Wealth of Nations*.

Karl Marx's analysis of capitalism and his school of thought provide the classic counterpoint to Adam Smith's liberal philosophy. Together the two schools of thought represent the polar extremes of political economy theory and practice. Yet Smith and Marx share a number of interesting analytical similarities. Both saw markets as natural systems rather than as constructed institutions. Both present materialist views of history, in which economics—the mode of production and the division of labor—drives social change and history. Both also saw a natural unilinear dynamic in history, with society moving through stages of production and the different associated social orders. Yet whereas Smith saw capitalism as an equilibrium state for society, Marx was more teleological, conceiving of capitalism as a stage through which societies must pass on their way to the inexorable endpoint of communism. Each of the theorists saw the human alienation in the division of labor. Smith, as we have seen, considered that a necessary cost in achieving greater wealth for everyone. For Marx, however, the division of labor represented the crux of his critique of capitalism: that capitalists reap the benefits of the system through the exploitation of labor and that labor is alienated by its own work and by the very system. In Marxist thought, market relations embody power relationships and are thus not on the equal terms of exchange that the classical and neoliberal economists claim. In emphasizing the power and social relationships embedded in markets, **Karl Polanyi** and **Charles Lindblom** (this volume) are heirs to some of Marx's insights.

Marxist thought holds that the capitalist system contains the seeds of its own destruction. In a dialectical relationship between the two classes associated with capital and labor, the continuous social upheaval entailed as the bourgeois class continually revolutionizes the means of production eventually leads to the proletarian revolution and the communist stage. Whereas Smith recognized that the state could indeed be in thrall to special interests (such as the mercantilists), Marx saw the relationship as more insidious, calling the state the executive committee of the bourgeoisie or the "instrument of the ruling class." Furthermore, the bourgeoisie, according to Marx, has stripped away all social relations and reduced them to economic relations and uses ideology, such as "liberalism," to legitimate its own rule. Marx elaborated his theory of the capitalist mode of production, including particularly his labor theory of value and his thinking on surplus value and exploitation, in his landmark 1867 work *Das Kapital.*

The Communist Manifesto, cowritten by **Karl Marx and Friedrich Engels** is a famous and stirring critique of capitalism. It was published in February 1848, intended as a clear formulation of the principles of the recently formed Communist League. Although the document contained no new ideas, its force of expression remains striking, and Marx and Engels saw it for many years as the classic expression of their views.[5] They theorized in the pamphlet the dynamics through which the proletarian revolution would occur and provided the inspiration for it, but they left no real guidelines for the process. In theory, by exploiting the proletariat class upon which its prosperity rests, the bourgeoisie deterministically unleashes a set of economic and political forces that become too powerful for it to control. In practice, however, there was a big gap between Marxist theory and twentieth-century communist reality, as the formation of class consciousness required some voluntarist action.

Marxism had a theorist but no statesman until Lenin. He became the great voluntarist Marxist, intervening to tip the scales of history by theorizing that the vanguard of the proletariat must create class consciousness and revolution. Marxism's legacy in praxis rested in the system of political economy that we know as communism (defined by Marx as the abolition of private property and its conversion into common property), which persisted from the Bolshevik Revolution in October 1917 in Russia until the fall of the Berlin Wall in 1989 and the subsequent collapse of the Soviet Union. In China, Mao Zedong also claimed to be an intellectual heir to Marx, arguing that peasants, in addition to workers, could play an important role in the communist revolution, even in countries that had yet to go through the capitalist stage of production. Marxist theory remains important today, with successors in the field of political economy in the forms of neo-Marxist theories of the state, which consider the state an agent of the capitalist classes, and dependency theory, which applies class analysis to the international political economy.

The final theorist presented in this section, **Friedrich List,** is a representative of the mercantilist school of thought, which Adam Smith so inveighed against. Born in 1789 in Germany, List had the luxury, in 1841, of writing after Smith and thus taking him on directly. He developed much of his thought after a stay in the United States, inspired by the works of Alexander Hamilton, the first treasury secretary of the United States and a leading mercantilist thinker. Whereas Smith and Marx were primarily developing theoretical perspectives on political economy, List's viewpoint may be the classical view most reflected in real practice, both past and current, and produces a set of arguments for deviation from free trade principles.

List was concerned primarily with national power and prosperity, and he emphasized that the national interest should be paramount in determining the political–economic system. He challenged both Smith's "cosmopolitanism" and his individualism, charging that the classical liberals ignored the principles of nationality and national interest and thereby misguidedly emphasized free trade and wrongly conflated individual economy with national economy. In his view, the national interest and the collective welfare needs national direction and cannot be achieved by individuals focusing on their self-interest as Smith and the liberal school claim. For List, the prosperity of a nation depends not on the degree to which it has amassed wealth but rather on how it has developed its powers of production. In his view, productive powers, which produce wealth, are more essential to individual and collective well-being than is wealth. Thus, the nation must guide economic activity to build productive powers, even at the expense of immediate material prosperity or individual interests, to ensure future national prosperity. One of the core principles underlying List's theory of productive powers is that nations must develop all sectors, and manufacturing in particular must be emphasized rather than relying solely on comparative advantage in agriculture.

Contrary to the liberal view that emphasizes the mutual benefit possible through the positive-sum game of international trade, List saw interaction between nations as conflictual and zero-sum. In his view, the state is both justified and bound to impose regulations on economic activity that are in the interests of the nation. He outlined the basic contours of many of the protectionist arguments against free trade that have become so prevalent in contemporary international political economy, such as describing the social dislocation that accompanies the freeing up of trade. List also argued that nations have different requirements and optimal strategies based on their circumstances and levels of development. His arguments were hence the precursor to later policy stances such as the import-substitution industrialization strategy pursued by Latin American countries to protect their domestic infant industries from external competition and to build productive powers at home. Japan and the East Asian newly industrializing countries—particularly South Korea and Taiwan—pursued the same strategy very successfully in transitioning to cheaper domestic production and then moving to an export-oriented strategy. Theorists of these developmental state strategies have since built on List's viewpoint in arguing that nations can have very different strategies concerning the role of government in development and that the premises of liberalism are not self-evident truths but rather a set of choices to be made.[6]

Notes

1. Adam Smith, this volume, p. 32.
2. Smith did not think that people are solely motivated by self-interest. In his earlier *Theory of Moral Sentiments*, he also drew a role for morals and propounded the broader ethical and philosophical basis on which his later works rest. Adam Smith, *The Theory of Moral Sentiments* (Cambridge: Cambridge University Press, 2002).
3. Jacob Viner, "Power versus Plenty as Objectives of Foreign Policy in the Seventeenth and Eighteenth Centuries," *World Politics* 1 (1948): 1.
4. David Ricardo, Smith's successor, is also a central figure in classical economics, particularly in the free trade camp. He elaborated the theory of comparative advantage, which holds that nations can always benefit from free trade if they specialize in producing the goods in which they have a comparative cost advantage in production. See David Ricardo, *On the Principles of Political Economy and Taxation* (London: John Murray, 1821).
5. David McLellan, ed., *Karl Marx: Selected Writings* (Oxford: Oxford University Press, 2000), 245.
6. See **Chalmers Johnson** in this volume for the Japanese viewpoint on the reality of economic nationalism in developmental state industrial policy and an industrial structure policy that actively manages the proportions of agriculture, manufacturing, and services in the nation's production. See also, for example, James Fallows, *Looking at the Sun: The Rise of the New East Asian Economic and Political System* (New York: Random House, 1994).

Adam Smith,
An Inquiry into the Nature and Causes of the Wealth of Nations (1776)*

Book One: Of the Causes of Improvement in the Productive Powers of Labour, And of the Order according to which its Produce is Naturally Distributed among the Different Ranks of the People.

Chapter I: Of the Division of Labour

The greatest improvement in the productive powers of labour, and the greater part of the skill, dexterity, and judgment with which it is anywhere directed, or applied, seem to have been the effects of the division of labour.

The effects of the division of labour, in the general business of society, will be more easily understood by considering in what manner it operates in some particular manufactures. It is commonly supposed to be carried furthest in some very trifling ones; not perhaps that it really is carried further in them than in others of more importance: but in those trifling manufactures which are destined to supply the small wants of but a small number of people, the whole number of workmen must necessarily be small; and those employed in every different branch of the work can often be collected into the same workhouse, and placed at once under the view of the spectator. In those great manufactures, on the contrary, which are destined to supply the great wants of the great body of the people, every different branch of the work employs so great a number of workmen that it is impossible to collect them all into the same workhouse. We can seldom see more, at one time, than those employed in one single branch. Though in such manufactures, therefore, the work may really be divided into a much greater number of parts than in those of a more trifling nature, the division is not near so obvious, and has accordingly been much less observed.

To take an example, therefore, from a very trifling manufacture; but one in which the division of labour has been very often taken notice of, the trade of the pin-maker; a workman not educated to this business (which the division of labour has rendered a distinct trade), nor acquainted with the use of the machinery employed in it (to the invention of which the same division of labour has probably given occasion), could scarce, perhaps, with his utmost industry, make one pin in a day, and certainly could not make twenty. But in the way in which this business is now carried on, not only the whole work is a peculiar trade, but it is divided into a number of branches, of which

---

* Excerpts from: *An Inquiry into the Nature and Causes of the Wealth of Nations* (1776). Material in the public domain.

the greater part are likewise peculiar trades. One man draws out the wire, another straights it, a third cuts it, a fourth points it, a fifth grinds it at the top for receiving, the head; to make the head requires two or three distinct operations; to put it on is a peculiar business, to whiten the pins is another; it is even a trade by itself to put them into the paper; and the important business of making a pin is, in this manner, divided into about eighteen distinct operations, which, in some manufactories, are all performed by distinct hands, though in others the same man will sometimes perform two or three of them. I have seen a small manufactory of this kind where ten men only were employed, and where some of them consequently performed two or three distinct operations. But though they were very poor, and therefore but indifferently accommodated with the necessary machinery, they could, when they exerted themselves, make among them about twelve pounds of pins in a day. There are in a pound upwards of four thousand pins of a middling size. Those ten persons, therefore, could make among them upwards of forty-eight thousand pins in a day. Each person, therefore, making a tenth part of forty-eight thousand pins, might be considered as making four thousand eight hundred pins in a day. But if they had all wrought separately and independently, and without any of them having been educated to this peculiar business, they certainly could not each of them have made twenty, perhaps not one pin in a day; that is, certainly, not the two hundred and fortieth, perhaps not the four thousand eight hundredth part of what they are at present capable of performing, in consequence of a proper division and combination of their different operations.

In every other art and manufacture, the effects of the division of labour are similar to what they are in this very trifling one; though, in many of them, the labour can neither be so much subdivided, nor reduced to so great a simplicity of operation. The division of labour, however, so far as it can be introduced, occasions, in every art, a proportionable increase of the productive powers of labour. The separation of different trades and employments from one another seems to have taken place in consequence of this advantage. This separation, too, is generally called furthest in those countries which enjoy the highest degree of industry and improvement; what is the work of one man in a rude state of society being generally that of several in an improved one. In every improved society, the farmer is generally nothing but a farmer; the manufacturer, nothing but a manufacturer. The labour, too, which is necessary to produce any one complete manufacture is almost always divided among a great number of hands. How many different trades are employed in each branch of the linen and woollen manufactures from the growers of the flax and the wool, to the bleachers and smoothers of the linen, or to the dyers and dressers of the cloth! The nature of agriculture, indeed, does not admit of so many subdivisions of labour, nor of so complete a separation of one business from another, as manufactures. It is impossible to separate so entirely the business of the grazier from that of the corn-farmer as the trade of the carpenter is commonly separated from that of the smith. The spinner is almost always a distinct person from the weaver; but the ploughman, the harrower, the sower of the seed, and the reaper of the corn, are often the same. The occasions for those different sorts of labour returning with the different seasons of the year, it is impossible that one man should be constantly employed in any one of them. This impossibility of making so complete and entire a separation of all the different branches of labour employed in agriculture is perhaps the reason why the improvement of the productive powers of labour in this art does not always keep pace with their improvement in manufactures. The most opulent nations, indeed, generally excel all their neighbours in agriculture as well as in manufactures; but they are commonly more distinguished by their superiority in the latter than in the former. Their lands are in general better cultivated, and having more labour and expense bestowed upon them, produce more in proportion to the extent and natural fertility of the ground. But this superiority of produce is seldom much more than in proportion to the superiority of labour and expense. In agriculture, the labour of the rich country is not always much more productive than that of the poor; or, at least, it is never so much more productive as it commonly is in manufactures. The corn of the rich country, therefore, will not always, in the same degree of goodness, come cheaper to market than that of the poor. The corn of Poland, in the same degree of goodness, is as cheap as that of France, notwithstanding the superior opulence and improvement of the latter country. The corn of France is, in the corn provinces, fully as good, and in most years nearly about the same price with the corn of England, though, in opulence and improvement, France is perhaps inferior to England. The corn-lands of England, however, are better cultivated than those of France, and the corn-lands of France are said to be much better cultivated than those of Poland. But though the poor country, notwithstanding the inferiority of its cultivation, can, in some measure, rival the rich in the cheapness and goodness of its corn, it can pretend to no such competition in its manufactures; at least if those manufactures suit the soil, climate, and situation of the rich country. The silks of France are better and cheaper than those of England, because the silk manufacture, at least under the present high duties upon the importation of raw silk, does not so well suit the climate of England as that of France. But the hardware and the coarse woollens of England are beyond all comparison superior to those of France, and much cheaper too in the same degree of goodness. In Poland there are said to be scarce any manufactures of any kind, a few of those coarser household manufactures excepted, without which no country can well subsist.

This great increase of the quantity of work which, in consequence of the division of labour, the same number of people are capable of performing, is owing to three different circumstances; first, to the increase of dexterity in every particular workman; secondly, to the saving of the time which is commonly lost in passing from one species of work to another; and lastly, to the invention of a great number of machines which facilitate and abridge labour, and enable one man to do the work of many.

First, the improvement of the dexterity of the workman necessarily increases the quantity of the work he can perform; and the division of labour, by reducing every man's business to some one simple operation, and by making this operation the sole employment of his life, necessarily increased very much dexterity of the workman. A common smith, who, though accustomed to handle the hammer, has never been used to make nails, if upon some particular occasion he is obliged to attempt it, will scarce, I am assured, be able to make above two or three hundred nails in a day, and those too very bad ones. A smith who has been accustomed to make nails, but whose sole or principal business has not been that of a nailer, can seldom with his utmost diligence make more than eight hundred or a thousand nails in a day. I have seen several boys under twenty years of age who had never exercised any other trade but that of making nails, and who, when they exerted themselves, could make, each of them, upwards of two thousand three hundred nails in a day. The making of a nail, however, is by no means one of the simplest operations. The same person blows the bellows, stirs or mends the fire as there is occasion, heats the iron, and forges every part of the nail: in forging the head too he is obliged to change his tools. The different operations into which the making of a pin, or of a metal button, is subdivided, are all of them much more simple, and the dexterity of the person, of whose life it has been the sole business to perform them, is usually much greater. The rapidity with which some of the operations of those manufacturers are performed, exceeds what the human hand could, by those who had never seen them, be supposed capable of acquiring.

Secondly, the advantage which is gained by saving the time commonly lost in passing from one sort of work to another is much greater than we should at first view be apt to imagine it. It is impossible to pass very quickly from one kind of work to another that is carried on in a different place and with quite different tools. A country weaver, who cultivates a small farm, must lose a good deal of time in passing from his loom to the field, and from the field to his loom. When the two trades can be carried on in the same workhouse, the loss of time is no doubt much less. It is even in this case, however, very considerable. A man commonly saunters a little in turning his hand from one sort of employment to another. When he first begins the new work he is seldom very keen and hearty; his mind, as they say, does not go to it, and for some time he rather trifles than applies to good purpose. The habit of sauntering and of indolent careless application, which is naturally, or rather necessarily acquired by every country workman who is obliged to change his work and his tools every half hour, and to apply his hand in twenty different ways almost every day of his life, renders him almost always slothful and lazy, and incapable of any vigorous application even on the most pressing occasions. Independent, therefore, of his deficiency in point of dexterity, this cause alone must always reduce considerably the quantity of work which he is capable of performing.

Thirdly, and lastly, everybody must be sensible how much labour is facilitated and abridged by the application of proper machinery. It is unnecessary to give any example. I shall only observe, therefore, that the invention of all those machines by which labour is so much facilitated and abridged seems to have been originally owing to the division of labour. Men are much more likely to discover easier and readier methods of attaining any object when the whole attention of their minds is directed towards that single object than when it is dissipated among a great variety of things. But in consequence of the division of labour, the whole of every man's attention comes naturally to be directed towards some one very simple object. It is naturally to be expected, therefore, that some one or other of those who are employed in each particular branch of labour should soon find out easier and readier methods of performing their own particular work, wherever the nature of it admits of such improvement. A great part of the machines made use of in those manufactures in which labour is most subdivided, were originally the inventions of common workmen, who, being each of them employed in some very simple operation, naturally turned their thoughts towards finding out easier and readier methods of performing it. Whoever has been much accustomed to visit such manufactures must frequently have been shown very pretty machines, which were the inventions of such workmen in order to facilitate and quicken their particular part of the work. In the first fire-engines, a boy was constantly employed to open and shut alternately the communication between the boiler and the cylinder, according as the piston either ascended or descended. One of those boys, who loved to play with his companions, observed that, by tying a string from the handle of the valve which opened this communication to another part of the machine, the valve would open and shut without his assistance, and leave him at liberty to divert himself with his playfellows. One of the greatest improvements that has been made upon this machine, since it was first invented, was in this manner the discovery of a boy who wanted to save his own labour.

All the improvements in machinery, however, have by no means been the inventions of those who had occasion to use the machines. Many improvements have been made by the ingenuity of the makers of the machines, when to make them became the business of a peculiar trade; and some by that of those who are called philosophers or men of speculation, whose trade it is not to do anything, but to observe everything; and who, upon that account, are often capable of combining together the powers of the most distant and dissimilar objects. In the progress of society, philosophy or speculation becomes, like every other employment, the principal or sole trade and occupation of a particular class of citizens. Like every other employment too, it is subdivided into a great number of different branches, each of which affords occupation to a peculiar tribe or class of philosophers; and this subdivision of employment in philosophy, as well as in every other business, improves dexterity, and saves time. Each individual becomes more expert in his own peculiar branch, more work is done upon the whole, and the quantity of science is considerably increased by it.

It is the great multiplication of the productions of all the different arts, in consequence of the division of labour, which occasions, in a well-governed society, that universal opulence which extends itself to the lowest ranks of the people. Every workman has a great quantity of his own work to dispose of beyond what he himself has occasion for; and every other workman being exactly in the same situation, he is enabled to exchange a great quantity of his own goods for a great quantity, or, what comes to the same thing, for the price of a great quantity of theirs. He supplies them abundantly with what they have occasion for, and they accommodate him as amply with what he has occasion for, and a general plenty diffuses itself through all the different ranks of the society.

Observe the accommodation of the most common artificer or day-labourer in a civilised and thriving country, and you will perceive that the number of people of whose industry a part, though but a small part, has been employed in procuring him this accommodation, exceeds all computation. The woollen coat, for example, which covers the day-labourer, as coarse and rough as it may appear, is the produce of the joint labour of a great multitude of workmen. The shepherd, the sorter of the wool, the wool-comber or carder, the dyer, the scribbler, the spinner, the weaver, the fuller, the dresser, with many others, must all join their different arts in order to complete even this homely production. How many merchants and carriers, besides, must have been employed in transporting the materials from some of those workmen to others who often live in a very distant part of the country! How much commerce and navigation in particular, how many ship-builders, sailors, sail-makers, rope-makers, must have been employed in order to bring together the different drugs made use of by the dyer, which often come from the remotest corners of the world! What a variety of labour, too, is necessary in order to produce the tools of the meanest of those workmen! To say nothing of such complicated machines as the ship of the sailor, the mill of the fuller, or even the loom of the weaver, let us consider only what a variety of labour is requisite in order to form that very simple machine, the shears with which the shepherd clips the wool. The miner, the builder of the furnace for smelting the ore, the seller of the timber, the burner of the charcoal to be made use of in the smelting-house, the brickmaker, the brick-layer, the workmen who attend the furnace, the mill-wright, the forger, the smith, must all of them join their different arts in order to produce them. Were we to examine, in the same manner, all the different parts of his dress and household furniture, the coarse linen shirt which he wears next to his skin, the shoes which cover his feet, the bed which he lies on, and all the different parts which compose it, the kitchen-grate at which he prepares his victuals, the coals which he makes use of for that purpose, dug from the bowels of the earth, and brought to him perhaps by a long sea and a long land carriage, all the other utensils of his kitchen, all the furniture of his table, the knives and forks, the earthen or pewter plates upon which he serves up and divides his victuals, the different hands employed in preparing his bread and his beer, the glass window which lets in the heat and the light, and keeps out the wind and the rain, with all the knowledge and art requisite for preparing that beautiful and happy invention, without which these northern parts of the world could scarce have afforded a very comfortable habitation, together with the tools of all the different workmen employed in producing those different conveniences; if we examine, I say, all these things, and consider what a variety of labour is employed about each of them, we shall be sensible that, without the assistance and co-operation of many thousands, the very meanest person in a civilised country could not be provided, even according to what we very falsely imagine the easy and simple manner in which he is commonly accommodated. Compared, indeed, with the more extravagant luxury of the great, his accommodation must no doubt appear extremely simple and easy; and yet it may be true, perhaps, that the accommodation of a European prince does not always so much exceed that of an industrious and frugal peasant as the accommodation of the latter exceeds that of many an African king, the absolute master of the lives and liberties of ten thousand naked savages.

Chapter II: Of the Principle which gives Occasion to the Division of Labour

This division of labour, from which so many advantages are derived, is not originally the effect of any human wisdom, which foresees and intends that general opulence to which it gives occasion. It is the necessary, though very slow and gradual consequence of a certain propensity in human nature which has in view no such extensive utility; the propensity to truck, barter, and exchange one thing for another.

Whether this propensity be one of those original principles in human nature of which no further account can be given; or whether, as seems more probable, it be the necessary consequence of the faculties of reason and speech, it belongs not to our present subject to inquire. It is common to all men, and to be found in no other race of animals, which seem to know neither this nor any other species of contracts. Two greyhounds, in running down the same hare, have sometimes the appearance of acting in some sort of concert. Each turns her towards his companion, or endeavours to intercept her when his companion turns her towards himself. This, however, is not the effect of any contract, but of the accidental concurrence of their passions in the same object at that particular time. Nobody ever saw a dog make a fair and deliberate exchange of one bone for another with another dog. Nobody ever saw one animal by its gestures and natural cries signify to another, this is mine, that yours; I am willing to give this for that. When an animal wants to obtain something either of a man or of another animal, it has no other means of persuasion but to gain the favour of those whose service it requires. A puppy fawns upon its dam, and a spaniel endeavours by a thousand attractions to engage the attention of its master who is at dinner, when it wants to be fed by him. Man sometimes uses the same arts with his brethren, and when he has no other means of engaging them to act according to his inclinations, endeavours by every servile and fawning attention to obtain their good will. He has not time, however, to do this upon every occasion. In civilised society he stands at all times in need of the cooperation and assistance of great multitudes, while his whole life is scarce sufficient to gain the friendship of a few persons. In almost every other race of animals each individual, when it is grown up to maturity, is entirely independent, and in its natural state has occasion for the assistance of no other living creature. But man has almost constant occasion for the help of his brethren, and it is in vain for him to expect it from their benevolence only. He will be more likely to prevail if he can interest their self-love in his favour, and show them that it is for their own advantage to do for him what he requires of them. Whoever offers to another a bargain of any kind, proposes to do this. Give me that which I want, and you shall have this which you want, is the meaning of every such offer; and it is in this manner that we obtain from one another the far greater part of those good offices which we stand in need of. It is not from the benevolence of the butcher, the brewer, or the baker that we expect our dinner, but from their regard to their own interest. We address ourselves, not to their humanity but to their self-love, and never talk to them of our own necessities but of their advantages. Nobody but a beggar chooses to depend chiefly upon the benevolence of his fellow-citizens. Even a beggar does not depend upon it entirely. The charity of well-disposed people, indeed, supplies him with the whole fund of his subsistence. But though this principle ultimately provides him with all the necessaries of life which he has occasion for, it neither does nor can provide him with them as he has occasion for them. The greater part of his occasional wants are supplied in the same manner as those of other people, by treaty, by barter, and by purchase. With the money which one man gives him he purchases food. The old clothes which another bestows upon him he exchanges for other old clothes which suit him better, or for lodging, or for food, or for money, with which he can buy either food, clothes, or lodging, as he has occasion.

As it is by treaty, by barter, and by purchase that we obtain from one another the greater part of those mutual good offices which we stand in need of, so it is this same trucking disposition which originally gives occasion to the division of labour. In a tribe of hunters or shepherds a particular person makes bows and arrows, for example, with more readiness and dexterity than any other. He frequently exchanges them for cattle or for venison with his companions; and he finds at last that he can in this manner get more cattle and venison than if he himself went to the field to catch them. From a regard to his own interest, therefore, the making of bows and arrows grows to be his chief business, and he becomes a sort of armourer. Another excels in making the frames and covers of their little huts or movable houses. He is accustomed to be of use in this way to his neighbours, who reward him in the same manner with cattle and with venison, till at last he finds it his interest to dedicate himself entirely to this employment, and to become a sort of house-carpenter. In the same manner a third becomes a smith or a brazier, a fourth a tanner or dresser of hides or skins, the principal part of the nothing of savages. And thus the certainty of being able to exchange all that surplus part of the produce of his own labour, which is over and above his own consumption, for such parts of the produce of other men's labour as he may have occasion for, encourages every man to apply himself to a particular occupation, and to cultivate and bring to perfection whatever talent or genius he may possess for that particular species of business.

The difference of natural talents in different men is, in reality, much less than we are aware of; and the very different genius which appears to distinguish men of different professions, when grown up to maturity, is not upon many occasions so much the cause as the effect of the division of labour. The difference between the most dissimilar characters, between a philosopher and a common street porter, for example, seems to arise not so much from nature as from habit, custom, and education. When they came into the world, and for the first six or eight years of their existence, they were perhaps very much alike, and neither their parents nor playfellows could perceive any remarkable difference. About that age, or soon after, they come to be employed in very different occupations. The difference of talents comes then to be taken notice of, and widens by degrees, till at last the vanity of the philosopher is willing to acknowledge scarce any resemblance. But without the disposition to truck, barter, and exchange, every man must have procured to himself every necessary and conveniency of life which he wanted. All must have had the same duties to perform, and the same work to do, and there could have been no such difference of employment as could alone give occasion to any great difference of talents.

As it is this disposition which forms that difference of talents, so remarkable among men of different professions, so it is this same disposition which renders that difference useful. Many tribes of animals acknowledged to be all of the same species derive from nature a much more remarkable distinction of genius, than what, antecedent to custom and education, appears to take place among men. By nature a philosopher is not in genius and disposition half so different from a street porter, as a mastiff is from a greyhound, or a greyhound from a spaniel, or this last from a shepherd's dog. Those different tribes of animals, however, though all of the same species, are of scarce any use to one another. The strength of the mastiff is not, in the least, supported either by the swiftness of the greyhound, or by the sagacity of the spaniel, or by the docility of the shepherd's dog. The effects of those different geniuses and talents, for want of the power or disposition to barter and exchange, cannot be brought into a common stock, and do not in the least contribute to the better accommodation and conveniency of the species. Each animal is still obliged to support and defend itself, separately and independently, and derives no sort of advantage from that variety of talents with which nature has distinguished its fellows. Among men, on the contrary, the most dissimilar geniuses are of use to one another; the different produces of their respective talents, by the general disposition to truck, barter, and exchange, being brought, as it were, into a common stock, where every man may purchase whatever part of the produce of other men's talents he has occasion for.

Book Four: Of Systems of Political Economy

Chapter II: Of Restraints upon the Importation from Foreign Countries of Such Goods as can be Produced at Home

By restraining, either by high duties or by absolute prohibitions, the importation of such goods from foreign countries as can be produced at home, the monopoly of the home market is more or less secured to the domestic industry employed in producing them. Thus the prohibition of importing either live cattle or salt provisions from foreign countries secures to the graziers of Great Britain the monopoly of the home market for butcher's meat. The high duties upon the importation of corn, which in times of moderate plenty amount to a prohibition, give a like advantage to the growers of that commodity. The prohibition of the importation of foreign woollens is equally favourable to the woollen manufacturers. The silk manufacture, though altogether employed upon foreign materials, has lately obtained the same advantage. The linen manufacture has not yet obtained it, but is making great strides towards it. Many other sorts of manufacturers have, in the same manner, obtained in Great Britain, either altogether or very nearly, a monopoly against their countrymen. The variety of goods of which the importation into Great Britain is prohibited, either absolutely, or under certain circumstances, greatly exceeds what can easily be suspected by those who are not well acquainted with the laws of the customs.

That this monopoly of the home market frequently gives great encouragement to that particular species of industry which enjoys it, and frequently turns towards that employment a greater share of both the labour and stock of the society than would otherwise have gone to it, cannot be doubted. But whether it tends either to increase the general industry of the society, or to give it the most advantageous direction, is not, perhaps, altogether so evident.

The general industry of the society never can exceed what the capital of the society can employ. As the number of workmen that can be kept in employment by any particular person must bear a certain proportion to his capital, so the number of those that can be continually employed by all the members of a great society must bear a certain proportion to the whole capital of that society, and never can exceed that proportion. No regulation of commerce can increase the quantity of industry in any society beyond what its capital can maintain. It can only divert a part of it into a direction into which it might not otherwise have gone; and it is by no means certain that this artificial direction is likely to be more advantageous to the society than that into which it would have gone of its own accord.

Every individual is continually exerting himself to find out the most advantageous employment for whatever capital he can command. It is his own advantage, indeed, and not that of the society, which he has in view. But the study of his own advantage naturally, or rather necessarily, leads him to prefer that employment which is most advantageous to the society.

First, every individual endeavours to employ his capital as near home as he can, and consequently as much as he can in the support of domestic industry; provided always that he can thereby obtain the ordinary, or not a great deal less than the ordinary profits of stock.

Thus, upon equal or nearly equal profits, every wholesale merchant naturally prefers the home trade to the foreign trade of consumption, and the foreign trade of consumption to the carrying trade. In the home trade his capital is never so long out of his sight as it frequently is in the foreign trade of consumption. He can know better the character and situation of the persons whom he trusts, and if he should happen to be deceived, he knows better the laws of the country from which he must seek redress. In the carrying trade, the capital of the merchant is, as it were, divided between two foreign countries, and no part of it is ever necessarily brought home, or placed under his own immediate view and command. The capital which an Amsterdam merchant employs in carrying corn from Konigsberg to Lisbon, and fruit and wine from Lisbon to Konigsberg, must generally be the one half of it at Konigsberg and the other half at Lisbon. No part of it need ever come to Amsterdam. The natural residence of such a merchant should either be at Konigsberg or Lisbon, and it can only be some very particular circumstances which can make him prefer the residence of Amsterdam. The uneasiness, however, which he feels at being separated so far from his capital generally determines him to bring part both of the Konigsberg goods which he destines for the market of Lisbon, and of the Lisbon goods which he destines for that of Konigsberg, to Amsterdam: and though this necessarily subjects him to a double charge of loading and unloading, as well as to the payment of some duties and customs, yet for the sake of having some part of his capital always under his own view and command, he willingly submits to this extraordinary charge; and it is in this manner that every country which has any considerable share of the carrying trade becomes always the emporium, or general market, for the goods of all the different countries whose trade it carries on. The merchant, in order to save a second loading and unloading, endeavours always to sell in the home market as much of the goods of all those different countries as he can, and thus, so far as he can, to convert his carrying trade into a foreign trade of consumption. A merchant, in the same manner, who is engaged in the foreign trade of consumption, when he collects goods for foreign markets, will always be glad, upon equal or nearly equal profits, to sell as great a part of them at home as he can. He saves himself the risk and trouble of exportation, when, so far as he can, he thus converts his foreign trade of consumption into a home trade. Home is in this manner the centre, if I may say so, round which the capitals of the inhabitants of every country are continually circulating, and towards which they are always tending, though by particular causes they may sometimes be driven off and repelled from it towards more distant employments. But a capital employed in the home trade, it has already been shown, necessarily puts into motion a greater quantity of domestic industry, and gives revenue and employment to a greater number of the inhabitants of the country, than an equal capital employed in the foreign trade of consumption: and one employed in the foreign trade of consumption has the same advantage over an equal capital employed in the carrying trade. Upon equal, or only nearly equal profits, therefore, every individual naturally inclines to employ his capital in the manner in which it is likely to afford the greatest support to domestic industry, and to give revenue and employment to the greatest number of people of his own country.

Secondly, every individual who employs his capital in the support of domestic industry, necessarily endeavours so to direct that industry that its produce may be of the greatest possible value.

The produce of industry is what it adds to the subject or materials upon which it is employed. In proportion as the value of this produce is great or small, so will likewise be the profits of the employer. But it is only for the sake of profit that any man employs a capital in the support of industry; and he will always, therefore, endeavour to employ it in the support of that industry of which the produce is likely to be of the greatest value, or to exchange for the greatest quantity either of money or of other goods.

But the annual revenue of every society is always precisely equal to the exchangeable value of the whole annual produce of its industry, or rather is precisely the same thing with that exchangeable value. As every individual, therefore, endeavours as much as he can both to employ his capital in the support of domestic industry, and so to direct that industry that its produce may be of the greatest value; every individual necessarily labours to render the annual revenue of the society as great as he can. He generally, indeed, neither intends to promote the public interest, nor knows how much he is promoting it. By preferring the support of domestic to that of foreign industry, he intends only his own security; and by directing that industry in such a manner as its produce may be of the greatest value, he intends only his own gain, and he is in this, as in many other cases, led by an invisible hand to promote an end which was no part of his intention. Nor is it always the worse for the society that it was no part of it. By pursuing his own interest he frequently promotes that of the society more effectually than when he really intends to promote it. I have never known much good done by those who affected to trade for the public good. It is an affectation, indeed, not very common among merchants, and very few words need be employed in dissuading them from it.

What is the species of domestic industry which his capital can employ, and of which the produce is likely to be of the greatest value, every individual, it is evident, can, in his local situation, judge much better than any statesman or lawgiver can do for him. The statesman who should attempt to direct private people in what manner they ought to employ their capitals would not only load himself with a most unnecessary attention, but assume an authority which could safely be trusted, not only to no single person, but to no council or senate whatever, and which would nowhere be so dangerous as in the hands of a man who had folly and presumption enough to fancy himself fit to exercise it.

To give the monopoly of the home market to the produce of domestic industry, in any particular art or manufacture, is in some measure to direct private people in what manner they ought to employ their capitals, and must, in almost all cases, be either a useless or a hurtful regulation. If the produce of domestic can be brought there as cheap as that of foreign industry, the regulation is evidently useless. If it cannot, it must generally be hurtful. It is the maxim of every prudent master of a family never to attempt to make at home what it will cost him more to make than to buy. The tailor does not attempt to make his own shoes, but buys them of the shoemaker. The shoemaker does not attempt to make his own clothes, but employs a tailor. The farmer attempts to make neither the one nor the other, but employs those different artificers. All of them find it for their interest to employ their whole industry in a way in which they have some advantage over their neighbours, and to purchase with a part of its produce, or what is the same thing, with the price of a part of it, whatever else they have occasion for.

What is prudence in the conduct of every private family can scarce be folly in that of a great kingdom. If a foreign country can supply us with a commodity cheaper than we ourselves can make it, better buy it of them with some part of the produce of our own industry employed in a way in which we have some advantage. The general industry of the country, being always in proportion to the capital which employs it, will not thereby be diminished, no more than that of the above-mentioned artificers; but only left to find out the way in which it can be employed with the greatest advantage. It is certainly not employed to the greatest advantage when it is thus directed towards an object which it can buy cheaper than it can make. The value of its annual produce is certainly more or less diminished when it is thus turned away from producing commodities evidently of more value than the commodity which it is directed to produce. According to the supposition, that commodity could be purchased from foreign countries cheaper than it can be made at home. It could, therefore, have been purchased with a part only of the commodities, or, what is the same thing, with a part only of the price of the commodities, which the industry employed by an equal capital would have produced at home, had it been left to follow its natural course. The industry of the country, therefore, is thus turned away from a more to a less advantageous employment, and the exchangeable value of its annual produce, instead of being increased, according to the intention of the lawgiver, must necessarily be diminished by every such regulation.

By means of such regulations, indeed, a particular manufacture may sometimes be acquired sooner than it could have been otherwise, and after a certain time may be made at home as cheap or cheaper than in the foreign country. But though the industry of the society may be thus carried with advantage into a particular channel sooner than it could have been otherwise, it will by no means follow that the sum total, either of its industry, or of its revenue, can ever be augmented by any such regulation. The industry of the society can augment only in proportion as its capital augments, and its capital can augment only in proportion to what can be gradually saved out of its revenue. But the immediate effect of every such regulation is to diminish its revenue, and what diminishes its revenue is certainly not very likely to augment its capital faster than it would have augmented of its own accord had both capital and industry been left to find out their natural employments.

Chapter IX: Of the Agricultural Systems, or of those Systems of Political Economy, which Represent the Produce of Land, as either the Sole or the Principal, Source of the Revenue and Wealth of Every Country

The greatest and most important branch of the commerce of every nation, it has already been observed, is that which is carried on between the inhabitants of the town and those of the country. The inhabitants of the town draw from the country the rude produce which constitutes both the materials of their work and the fund of their subsistence; and they pay for this rude produce by sending back to the country a certain portion of it manufactured and prepared for immediate use. The trade which is carried on between these two different sets of people consists ultimately in a certain quantity of rude produce exchanged for a certain quantity of manufactured produce. The dearer the latter, therefore, the cheaper the former; and whatever tends in any country to raise the price of manufactured produce tends to lower that of the rude produce of the land, and thereby to discourage agriculture. The smaller the quantity of manufactured produce which in any given quantity of rude produce, or, what comes to the same thing, which the price of any given quantity of rude produce is capable of purchasing, the smaller the exchangeable value of that given quantity of rude produce, the smaller the encouragement which either the landlord has to increase its quantity by improving or the farmer by cultivating the land. Whatever, besides, tends to diminish in any country the number of artificers and manufacturers, tends to diminish the home market, the most important of all markets for the rude produce of the land, and thereby still further to discourage agriculture.

Those systems, therefore, which, preferring agriculture to all other employments, in order to promote it, impose restraints upon manufactures and foreign trade, act contrary to the very end which they propose, and indirectly discourage that very species of industry which they mean to promote. They are so far, perhaps, more inconsistent than even the mercantile system. That system, by encouraging manufactures and foreign trade more than agriculture, turns a certain portion of the capital of the society from supporting a more advantageous, to support a less advantageous species of industry. But still it really and in the end encourages that species of industry which it means to promote. Those agricultural systems, on the contrary, really and in the end discourage their own favourite species of industry.

It is thus that every system which endeavours, either by extraordinary encouragements to draw towards a particular species of industry a greater share of the capital of the society than what would naturally go to it, or, by extraordinary restraints, force from a particular species of industry some share of the capital which would otherwise be employed in it, is in reality subversive of the great purpose which it means to promote. It retards, instead of accelerating, the progress of the society towards real wealth and greatness; and diminishes, instead of increasing, the real value of the annual produce of its land and labour.

All systems either of preference or of restraint, therefore, being thus completely taken away, the obvious and simple system of natural liberty establishes itself of its own accord. Every man, as long as he does not violate the laws of justice, is left perfectly free to pursue his own interest his own way, and to bring both his industry and capital into competition with those of any other man, or order of men. The sovereign is completely discharged from a duty, in the attempting to perform which he must always be exposed to innumerable delusions, and for the proper performance of which no human wisdom or knowledge could ever be sufficient; the duty of superintending the industry of private people, and of directing it towards the employments most suitable to the interest of the society. According to the system of natural liberty, the sovereign has only three duties to attend to; three duties of great importance, indeed, but plain and intelligible to common understandings: first, the duty of protecting the society from violence and invasion of other independent societies; secondly, the duty of protecting, as far as possible, every member of the society from the injustice or oppression of every other member of it, or the duty of establishing an exact administration of justice; and, thirdly, the duty of erecting and maintaining certain public works and certain public institutions which it can never be for the interest of any individual, or small number of individuals, to erect and maintain; because the profit could never repay the expense to any individual or small number of individuals, though it may frequently do much more than repay it to a great society.

Karl Marx and Friedrich Engels,
The Communist Manifesto (1848)*

A spectre is haunting Europe—the spectre of communism. All the powers of old Europe have entered into a holy alliance to exorcise this spectre: Pope and Tsar, Metternich and Guizot, French Radicals and German police-spies.

Where is the party in opposition that has not been decried as communistic by its opponents in power? Where is the opposition that has not hurled back the branding reproach of communism, against the more advanced opposition parties, as well as against its reactionary adversaries?

Two things result from this fact:

I. Communism is already acknowledged by all European powers to be itself a power.
II. It is high time that Communists should openly, in the face of the whole world, publish their views, their aims, their tendencies, and meet this nursery tale of the spectre of communism with a manifesto of the party itself.

To this end, Communists of various nationalities have assembled in London and sketched the following manifesto, to be published in the English, French, German, Italian, Flemish and Danish languages.

I. Bourgeois and Proletarians

The history of all hitherto existing society is the history of class struggles.

Freeman and slave, patrician and plebian, lord and serf, guild-master and journeyman, in a word, oppressor and oppressed, stood in constant opposition to one another, carried on an uninterrupted, now hidden, now open fight, a fight that each time ended, either in a revolutionary reconstitution of society at large, or in the common ruin of the contending classes.

In the earlier epochs of history, we find almost everywhere a complicated arrangement of society into various orders, a manifold gradation of social rank. In ancient Rome we have patricians, knights, plebians, slaves; in the Middle Ages, feudal lords, vassals, guild-masters, journeymen, apprentices, serfs; in almost all of these classes, again, subordinate gradations.

The modern bourgeois society that has sprouted from the ruins of feudal society has not done away with class antagonisms. It has but established new classes, new conditions of oppression, new forms of struggle in place of the old ones.

---

* *The Communist Manifesto* (1848). Material in the public domain.

Our epoch, the epoch of the bourgeoisie, possesses, however, this distinct feature: it has simplified class antagonisms. Society as a whole is more and more splitting up into two great hostile camps, into two great classes directly facing each other—bourgeoisie and proletariat.

From the serfs of the Middle Ages sprang the chartered burghers of the earliest towns. From these burgesses the first elements of the bourgeoisie were developed.

The discovery of America, the rounding of the Cape, opened up fresh ground for the rising bourgeoisie. The East-Indian and Chinese markets, the colonisation of America, trade with the colonies, the increase in the means of exchange and in commodities generally, gave to commerce, to navigation, to industry, an impulse never before known, and thereby, to the revolutionary element in the tottering feudal society, a rapid development.

The feudal system of industry, in which industrial production was monopolized by closed guilds, now no longer suffices for the growing wants of the new markets. The manufacturing system took its place. The guild-masters were pushed aside by the manufacturing middle class; division of labor between the different corporate guilds vanished in the face of division of labor in each single workshop.

Meantime, the markets kept ever growing, the demand ever rising. Even manufacturers no longer sufficed. Thereupon, steam and machinery revolutionized industrial production. The place of manufacture was taken by the giant, Modern Industry; the place of the industrial middle class by industrial millionaires, the leaders of the whole industrial armies, the modern bourgeois.

Modern industry has established the world market, for which the discovery of America paved the way. This market has given an immense development to commerce, to navigation, to communication by land. This development has, in turn, reacted on the extension of industry; and in proportion as industry, commerce, navigation, railways extended, in the same proportion the bourgeoisie developed, increased its capital, and pushed into the background every class handed down from the Middle Ages.

We see, therefore, how the modern bourgeoisie is itself the product of a long course of development, of a series of revolutions in the modes of production and of exchange.

Each step in the development of the bourgeoisie was accompanied by a corresponding political advance in that class. An oppressed class under the sway of the feudal nobility, an armed and self-governing association of medieval commune: here independent urban republic (as in Italy and Germany); there taxable "third estate" of the monarchy (as in France); afterward, in the period of manufacturing proper, serving either the semi-feudal or the absolute monarchy as a counterpoise against the nobility, and, in fact, cornerstone of the great monarchies in general—the bourgeoisie has at last, since the establishment of Modern Industry and of the world market, conquered for itself, in the modern representative state, exclusive political sway. The executive of the modern state is but a committee for managing the common affairs of the whole bourgeoisie.

The bourgeoisie, historically, has played a most revolutionary part.

The bourgeoisie, wherever it has got the upper hand, has put an end to all feudal, patriarchal, idyllic relations. It has pitilessly torn asunder the motley feudal ties that bound man to his "natural superiors," and has left no other nexus between people than naked self-interest, than callous "cash payment." It has drowned out the most heavenly ecstacies of religious fervor, of chivalrous enthusiasm, of philistine sentimentalism, in the icy water of egotistical calculation. It has resolved personal worth into exchange value, and in place of the numberless indefeasible chartered freedoms, has set up that single, unconscionable freedom—Free Trade. In one word, for exploitation, veiled by religious and political illusions, it has substituted naked, shameless, direct, brutal exploitation.

The bourgeoisie has stripped of its halo every occupation hitherto honored and looked up to with reverent awe. It has converted the physician, the lawyer, the priest, the poet, the man of science, into its paid wage laborers.

The bourgeoisie has torn away from the family its sentimental veil, and has reduced the family relation into a mere money relation.

The bourgeoisie has disclosed how it came to pass that the brutal display of vigor in the Middle Ages, which reactionaries so much admire, found its fitting complement in the most slothful indolence. It has been the first to show what man's activity can bring about. It has accomplished wonders far surpassing Egyptian pyramids, Roman aqueducts, and Gothic cathedrals; it has conducted expeditions that put in the shade all former exoduses of nations and crusades.

The bourgeoisie cannot exist without constantly revolutionizing the instruments of production, and thereby the relations of production, and with them the whole relations of society. Conservation of the old modes of production in unaltered form, was, on the contrary, the first condition of existence for all earlier industrial classes. Constant revolutionizing of production, uninterrupted disturbance of all social conditions, everlasting uncertainty and agitation distinguish the bourgeois epoch from all earlier ones. All fixed, fast frozen relations, with their train of ancient and venerable prejudices and opinions, are swept away, all new-formed ones become antiquated before they can ossify. All that is solid melts into air, all that is holy is profaned, and man is at last compelled to face with sober senses his real condition of life and his relations with his kind.

The need of a constantly expanding market for its products chases the bourgeoisie over the entire surface of the globe. It must nestle everywhere, settle everywhere, establish connections everywhere.

The bourgeoisie has, through its exploitation of the world market, given a cosmopolitan character to production and consumption in every country. To the great chagrin of reactionaries, it has drawn from under the feet of industry the national ground on which it stood. All old-established national industries have been destroyed or are daily being destroyed. They are dislodged by new industries, whose introduction becomes a life and death question for all civilized nations, by industries that no longer work up indigenous raw material, but raw material drawn from the remotest zones; industries whose products are consumed, not only at home, but in every quarter of the globe. In place of the old wants, satisfied by the production of the country, we find new wants, requiring for their satisfaction the products of distant lands and climes. In place of the old local and national seclusion and self-sufficiency, we have intercourse in every direction, universal inter-dependence of nations. And as in material, so also in intellectual production. The intellectual creations of individual nations become common property. National one-sidedness and narrow-mindedness become more and more impossible, and from the numerous national and local literatures, there arises a world literature.

The bourgeoisie, by the rapid improvement of all instruments of production, by the immensely facilitated means of communication, draws all, even the most barbarian, nations into civilization. The cheap prices of commodities are the heavy artillery with which it forces the barbarians' intensely obstinate hatred of foreigners to capitulate. It compels all nations, on pain of extinction, to adopt the bourgeois mode of production; it compels them to introduce what it calls civilization into their midst, i.e., to become bourgeois themselves. In one word, it creates a world after its own image.

The bourgeoisie has subjected the country to the rule of the towns. It has created enormous cities, has greatly increased the urban population as compared with the rural, and has thus rescued a considerable part of the population from the idiocy of rural life. Just as it has made the country dependent on the towns, so it has made barbarian and semi-barbarian countries dependent on the civilized ones, nations of peasants on nations of bourgeois, the East on the West.

The bourgeoisie keeps more and more doing away with the scattered state of the population, of the means of production, and of property. It has agglomerated population, centralized the means of production, and has concentrated property in a few hands. The necessary consequence of this was political centralization. Independent, or but loosely connected provinces, with separate interests, laws, governments, and systems of taxation, became lumped together into one nation, with one government, one code of laws, one national class interest, one frontier, and one customs tariff.

The bourgeoisie, during its rule of scarce one hundred years, has created more massive and more colossal productive forces than have all preceding generations together. Subjection of nature's forces to man, machinery, application of chemistry to industry and agriculture, steam navigation, railways, electric telegraphs, clearing of whole continents for cultivation, canalization or rivers, whole populations conjured out of the ground—what earlier century had even a presentiment that such productive forces slumbered in the lap of social labor?

We see then: the means of production and of exchange, on whose foundation the bourgeoisie built itself up, were generated in feudal society. At a certain stage in the development of these means of production and of exchange, the conditions under which feudal society produced and exchanged, the feudal organization of agriculture and manufacturing industry, in one word, the feudal relations of property became no longer compatible with the already developed productive forces; they became so many fetters. They had to be burst asunder; they were burst asunder.

Into their place stepped free competition, accompanied by a social and political constitution adapted in it, and the economic and political sway of the bourgeois class.

A similar movement is going on before our own eyes. Modern bourgeois society, with its relations of production, of exchange and of property, a society that has conjured up such gigantic means of production and of exchange, is like the sorcerer who is no longer able to control the powers of the nether world whom he has called up by his spells. For many a decade past, the history of industry and commerce is but the history of the revolt of modern productive forces against modern conditions of production, against the property relations that are the conditions for the existence of the bourgeois and of its rule. It is enough to mention the commercial crises that, by their periodical return, put the existence of the entire bourgeois society on its trial, each time more threateningly. In these crises, a great part not only of the existing products, but also of the previously created productive forces, are periodically destroyed. In these crises, there breaks out an epidemic that, in all earlier epochs, would have seemed an absurdity—the epidemic of over-production. Society suddenly finds itself put back into a state of momentary barbarism; it appears as if a famine, a universal war of devastation, had cut off the supply of every means of subsistence; industry and commerce seem to be destroyed. And why? Because there is too much civilization, too much means of subsistence, too much industry, too much commerce. The productive forces at the disposal of society no longer tend to further the development of the conditions of bourgeois property; on the contrary, they have become too powerful for these conditions, by which they are fettered, and so soon as they overcome these fetters, they bring disorder into the whole of bourgeois society, endanger the existence of bourgeois property. The conditions of bourgeois society are too narrow to comprise the wealth created by them. And how does the bourgeoisie get over these crises? On the one hand, by enforced destruction of a mass of productive forces; on the other, by the conquest of new markets, and by the more thorough exploitation of the old ones. That is to say, by paving the way for more extensive and more destructive crises, and by diminishing the means whereby crises are prevented.

The weapons with which the bourgeoisie felled feudalism to the ground are now turned against the bourgeoisie itself.

But not only has the bourgeoisie forged the weapons that bring death to itself; it has also called into existence the men who are to wield those weapons—the modern working class—the proletarians.

In proportion as the bourgeoisie, i.e., capital, is developed, in the same proportion is the proletariat, the modern working class, developed—a class of laborers, who live only so long as they find work, and who find work only so long as their labor increases capital. These laborers, who must sell themselves piecemeal, are a commodity, like every other article of commerce, and are consequently exposed to all the vicissitudes of competition, to all the fluctuations of the market.

Owing to the extensive use of machinery, and to the division of labor, the work of the proletarians has lost all individual character, and, consequently, all charm for the workman. He becomes an appendage of the machine, and it is only the most simple, most monotonous, and most easily acquired knack, that is required of him. Hence, the cost of production of a workman is restricted, almost entirely, to the means of subsistence that he requires for maintenance, and for the propagation of his race. But the price of a commodity, and therefore also of labor, is equal to its cost of production. In proportion, therefore, as the repulsiveness of the work increases, the wage decreases. What is more, in proportion as the use of machinery and division of labor increases, in the same proportion the burden of toil also increases, whether by prolongation of the working hours, by the increase of the work exacted in a given time, or by increased speed of machinery, etc.

Modern Industry has converted the little workshop of the patriarchal master into the great factory of the industrial capitalist. Masses of laborers, crowded into the factory, are organized like soldiers. As privates of the industrial army, they are placed under the command of a perfect hierarchy of officers and sergeants. Not only are they slaves of the bourgeois class, and of the bourgeois state; they are daily and hourly enslaved by the machine, by the overlooker, and, above all, in the individual bourgeois manufacturer himself. The more openly this despotism proclaims gain to be its end and aim, the more petty, the more hateful and the more embittering it is.

The less the skill and exertion of strength implied in manual labor, in other words, the more modern industry becomes developed, the more is the labor of men superseded by that of women. Differences of age and sex have no longer any distinctive social validity for the working class. All are instruments of labor, more or less expensive to use, according to their age and sex.

No sooner is the exploitation of the laborer by the manufacturer, so far at an end, that he receives his wages in cash, than he is set upon by the other portion of the bourgeoisie, the landlord, the shopkeeper, the pawnbroker, etc.

The lower strata of the middle class—the small tradespeople, shopkeepers, and retired tradesmen generally, the handicraftsmen and peasants—all these sink gradually into the proletariat, partly because their diminutive capital does not suffice for the scale on which Modern Industry is carried on, and is swamped in the competition with the large capitalists, partly because their specialized skill is rendered worthless by new methods of production. Thus, the proletariat is recruited from all classes of the population.

The proletariat goes through various stages of development. With its birth begins its struggle with the bourgeoisie. At first, the contest is carried on by individual laborers, then by the work of people of a factory, then by the operative of one trade, in one locality, against the individual bourgeois who directly exploits them. They direct their attacks not against the bourgeois condition of production, but against the instruments of production themselves; they destroy imported wares that compete with their labor, they smash to pieces machinery, they set factories ablaze, they seek to restore by force the vanished status of the workman of the Middle Ages.

At this stage, the laborers still form an incoherent mass scattered over the whole country, and broken up by their mutual competition. If anywhere they unite to form more compact bodies, this is not yet the consequence of their own active union, but of the union of the bourgeoisie, which class, in order to attain its own political ends, is compelled to set the whole proletariat in motion, and is moreover yet, for a time, able to do so. At this stage, therefore, the proletarians do not fight their enemies, but the enemies of their enemies, the remnants of absolute monarchy, the landowners, the non-industrial bourgeois, the petty bourgeois. Thus, the whole historical movement is concentrated in the hands of the bourgeoisie; every victory so obtained is a victory for the bourgeoisie.

But with the development of industry, the proletariat not only increases in number; it becomes concentrated in greater masses, its strength grows, and it feels that strength more. The various interests and conditions of life within the ranks of the proletariat are more and more equalized, in proportion as machinery obliterates all distinctions of labor, and nearly everywhere reduces wages to the same low level. The growing competition among the bourgeois, and the resulting commercial crises, make the wages of the workers ever more fluctuating. The increasing improvement of machinery, ever more rapidly developing, makes their livelihood more and more precarious; the collisions between individual workmen and individual bourgeois take more and more the character of collisions between two classes. Thereupon, the workers begin to form combinations (trade unions) against the bourgeois; they club together in order to keep up the rate of wages; they found permanent associations in order to make provision beforehand for these occasional revolts. Here and there, the contest breaks out into riots.

Now and then the workers are victorious, but only for a time. The real fruit of their battles lie not in the immediate result, but in the ever expanding union of the work-ers. This union is helped on by the improved means of communication that are cre-ated by Modern Industry, and that place the workers of different localities in contact with one another. It was just this contact that was needed to centralize the numerous local struggles, all of the same character, into one national struggle between classes. But every class struggle is a political struggle. And that union, to attain which the burghers of the Middle Ages, with their miserable highways, required centuries, the modern proletarian, thanks to railways, achieve in a few years.

This organization of the proletarians into a class, and, consequently, into a politi-cal party, is continually being upset again by the competition between the workers themselves. But it ever rises up again, stronger, firmer, mightier. It compels legislative recognition of particular interests of the workers, by taking advantage of the divi-sions among the bourgeoisie itself. Thus, the Ten-Hours Bill in England was carried.

Altogether, collisions between the classes of the old society further in many ways the course of development of the proletariat. The bourgeoisie finds itself involved in a constant battle. At first with the aristocracy; later on, with those portions of the bourgeoisie itself, whose interests have become antagonistic to the progress of industry; at all time with the bourgeoisie of foreign countries. In all these battles, it sees itself compelled to appeal to the proletariat, to ask for help, and thus to drag it into the political arena. The bourgeoisie itself, therefore, supplies the proletariat with its own elements of political and general education, in other words, it furnishes the proletariat with weapons for fighting the bourgeoisie.

Further, as we have already seen, entire sections of the ruling class are, by the advance of industry, precipitated into the proletariat, or are at least threatened in their conditions of existence. These also supply the proletariat with fresh elements of enlightenment and progress.

Finally, in times when the class struggle nears the decisive hour, the progress of dissolution going on within the ruling class, in fact within the whole range of old society, assumes such a violent, glaring character, that a small section of the ruling class cuts itself adrift, and joins the revolutionary class, the class that holds the future in its hands. Just as, therefore, at an earlier period, a section of the nobility went over to the bourgeoisie, so now a portion of the bourgeoisie goes over to the proletariat, and in particular, a portion of the bourgeois ideologists, who have raised themselves to the level of comprehending theoretically the historical movement as a whole.

Of all the classes that stand face to face with the bourgeoisie today, the proletariat alone is a genuinely revolutionary class. The other classes decay and finally disappear in the face of Modern Industry; the proletariat is its special and essential product.

The lower middle class, the small manufacturer, the shopkeeper, the artisan, the peasant, all these fight against the bourgeoisie, to save from extinction their existence as fractions of the middle class. They are therefore not revolutionary, but conservative. Nay, more, they are reactionary, for they try to roll back the wheel of history. If, by chance, they are revolutionary, they are only so in view of their impending transfer into the proletariat; they thus defend not their present, but their future interests; they desert their own standpoint to place themselves at that of the proletariat.

The "dangerous class," the social scum, that passively rotting mass thrown off by the lowest layers of the old society, may, here and there, be swept into the movement by a proletarian revolution; its conditions of life, however, prepare it far more for the part of a bribed tool of reactionary intrigue.

In the condition of the proletariat, those of old society at large are already virtually swamped. The proletarian is without property; his relation to his wife and children has no longer anything in common with the bourgeois family relations; modern industry labor, modern subjection to capital, the same in England as in France, in America as in Germany, has stripped him of every trace of national character. Law, morality, religion, are to him so many bourgeois prejudices, behind which lurk in ambush just as many bourgeois interests.

All the preceding classes that got the upper hand sought to fortify their already acquired status by subjecting society at large to their conditions of appropriation. The proletarians cannot become masters of the productive forces of society, except by abolishing their own previous mode of appropriation, and thereby also every other previous mode of appropriation. They have nothing of their own to secure and to fortify; their mission is to destroy all previous securities for, and insurances of, individual property.

All previous historical movements were movements of minorities, or in the interest of minorities. The proletarian movement is the self-conscious, independent movement of the immense majority, in the interest of the immense majority. The proletariat, the lowest stratum of our present society, cannot stir, cannot raise itself up, without the whole superincumbent strata of official society being sprung into the air.

Though not in substance, yet in form, the struggle of the proletariat with the bourgeoisie is at first a national struggle. The proletariat of each country must, of course, first of all settle matters with its own bourgeoisie.

In depicting the most general phases of the development of the proletariat, we traced the more or less veiled civil war, raging within existing society, up to the point where that war breaks out into open revolution, and where the violent overthrow of the bourgeoisie lays the foundation for the sway of the proletariat.

Hitherto, every form of society has been based, as we have already seen, on the antagonism of oppressing and oppressed classes. But in order to oppress a class, certain conditions must be assured to it under which it can, at least, continue its slavish existence. The serf, in the period of serfdom, raised himself to membership in the commune, just as the petty bourgeois, under the yoke of the feudal absolutism, managed to develop into a bourgeois. The modern laborer, on the contrary, instead of rising with the process of industry, sinks deeper and deeper below the conditions of existence of his own class. He becomes a pauper, and pauperism develops more rapidly than population and wealth. And here it becomes evident that the bourgeoisie is unfit any longer to be the ruling class in society, and to impose its conditions of existence upon society as an overriding law. It is unfit to rule because it is incompetent to assure an existence to its slave within his slavery, because it cannot help letting him sink into such a state, that it has to feed him, instead of being fed by him. Society can no longer live under this bourgeoisie, in other words, its existence is no longer compatible with society.

The essential conditions for the existence and for the sway of the bourgeois class is the formation and augmentation of capital; the condition for capital is wage labor. Wage labor rests exclusively on competition between the laborers. The advance of industry, whose involuntary promoter is the bourgeoisie, replaces the isolation of the laborers, due to competition, by the revolutionary combination, due to association. The development of Modern Industry, therefore, cuts from under its feet the very foundation on which the bourgeoisie produces and appropriates products. What the bourgeoisie therefore produces, above all, are its own grave-diggers. Its fall and the victory of the proletariat are equally inevitable.

II. Proletarians and Communists

In what relation do the Communists stand to the proletarians as a whole?

The Communists do not form a separate party opposed to the other working-class parties.

They have no interests separate and apart from those of the proletariat as a whole.

They do not set up any sectarian principles of their own, by which to shape and mold the proletarian movement.

The Communists are distinguished from the other working-class parties by this only: (1) In the national struggles of the proletarians of the different countries, they point out and bring to the front the common interests of the entire proletariat, independently of all nationality. (2) In the various stages of development which the struggle of the working class against the bourgeoisie has to pass through, they always and everywhere represent the interests of the movement as a whole.

The Communists, therefore, are on the one hand practically, the most advanced and resolute section of the working-class parties of every country, that section which pushes forward all others; on the other hand, theoretically, they have over the great mass of the proletariat the advantage of clearly understanding the lines of march, the conditions, and the ultimate general results of the proletarian movement.

The immediate aim of the Communists is the same as that of all other proletarian parties: Formation of the proletariat into a class, overthrow of the bourgeois supremacy, conquest of political power by the proletariat.

The theoretical conclusions of the Communists are in no way based on ideas or principles that have been invented, or discovered, by this or that would-be universal reformer.

They merely express, in general terms, actual relations springing from an existing class struggle, from a historical movement going on under our very eyes. The abolition of existing property relations is not at all a distinctive feature of communism.

All property relations in the past have continually been subject to historical change consequent upon the change in historical conditions.

The French Revolution, for example, abolished feudal property in favor of bourgeois property.

The distinguishing feature of communism is not the abolition of property generally, but the abolition of bourgeois property. But modern bourgeois private property is the final and most complete expression of the system of producing and appropriating products that is based on class antagonisms, on the exploitation of the many by the few.

In this sense, the theory of the Communists may be summed up in the single sentence: Abolition of private property.

We Communists have been reproached with the desire of abolishing the right of personally acquiring property as the fruit of a man's own labor, which property is alleged to be the groundwork of all personal freedom, activity and independence.

Hard-won, self-acquired, self-earned property! Do you mean the property of petty artisan and of the small peasant, a form of property that preceded the bourgeois form? There is no need to abolish that; the development of industry has to a great extent already destroyed it, and is still destroying it daily.

Or do you mean the modern bourgeois private property?

But does wage labor create any property for the laborer? Not a bit. It creates capital, i.e., that kind of property which exploits wage labor, and which cannot increase except upon conditions of begetting a new supply of wage labor for fresh exploitation. Property, in its present form, is based on the antagonism of capital and wage labor. Let us examine both sides of this antagonism.

To be a capitalist, is to have not only a purely personal, but a social STATUS in production. Capital is a collective product, and only by the united action of many members, nay, in the last resort, only by the united action of all members of society, can it be set in motion.

Capital is therefore not only personal; it is a social power.

When, therefore, capital is converted into common property, into the property of all members of society, personal property is not thereby transformed into social property. It is only the social character of the property that is changed. It loses its class character.

Let us now take wage labor.

The average price of wage labor is the minimum wage, i.e., that quantum of the means of subsistence which is absolutely requisite to keep the laborer in bare existence as a laborer. What, therefore, the wage laborer appropriates by means of his labor merely suffices to prolong and reproduce a bare existence. We by no means intend to abolish this personal appropriation of the products of labor, an appropriation that is made for the maintenance and reproduction of human life, and that leaves no surplus wherewith to command the labor of others. All that we want to do away with is the miserable character of this appropriation, under which the laborer lives merely to increase capital, and is allowed to live only in so far as the interest of the ruling class requires it.

In bourgeois society, living labor is but a means to increase accumulated labor. In communist society, accumulated labor is but a means to widen, to enrich, to promote the existence of the laborer.

In bourgeois society, therefore, the past dominates the present; in communist society, the present dominates the past. In bourgeois society, capital is independent and has individuality, while the living person is dependent and has no individuality.

And the abolition of this state of things is called by the bourgeois, abolition of individuality and freedom! And rightly so. The abolition of bourgeois individuality, bourgeois independence, and bourgeois freedom is undoubtedly aimed at.

By freedom is meant, under the present bourgeois conditions of production, free trade, free selling and buying.

But if selling and buying disappears, free selling and buying disappears also. This talk about free selling and buying, and all the other "brave words" of our bourgeois about freedom in general, have a meaning, if any, only in contrast with restricted selling and buying, with the fettered traders of the Middle Ages, but have no meaning when opposed to the communist abolition of buying and selling, or the bourgeois conditions of production, and of the bourgeoisie itself.

You are horrified at our intending to do away with private property. But in your existing society, private property is already done away with for nine-tenths of the population; its existence for the few is solely due to its non-existence in the hands of those nine-tenths. You reproach us, therefore, with intending to do away with a form of property, the necessary condition for whose existence is the non-existence of any property for the immense majority of society.

In one word, you reproach us with intending to do away with your property. Precisely so; that is just what we intend.

From the moment when labor can no longer be converted into capital, money, or rent, into a social power capable of being monopolized, i.e., from the moment when individual property can no longer be transformed into bourgeois property, into capital, from that moment, you say, individuality vanishes.

You must, therefore, confess that by "individual" you mean no other person than the bourgeois, than the middle-class owner of property. This person must, indeed, be swept out of the way, and made impossible.

Communism deprives no man of the power to appropriate the products of society; all that it does is to deprive him of the power to subjugate the labor of others by means of such appropriations.

It has been objected that upon the abolition of private property, all work will cease, and universal laziness will overtake us.

According to this, bourgeois society ought long ago to have gone to the dogs through sheer idleness; for those who acquire anything, do not work. The whole of this objection is but another expression of the tautology: There can no longer be any wage labor when there is no longer any capital.

All objections urged against the communistic mode of producing and appropriating material products, have, in the same way, been urged against the communistic mode of producing and appropriating intellectual products. Just as to the bourgeois, the disappearance of class property is the disappearance of production itself, so the disappearance of class culture is to him identical with the disappearance of all culture.

That culture, the loss of which he laments, is, for the enormous majority, a mere training to act as a machine.

But don't wrangle with us so long as you apply, to our intended abolition of bourgeois property, the standard of your bourgeois notions of freedom, culture, law, etc. Your very ideas are but the outgrowth of the conditions of your bourgeois production and bourgeois property, just as your jurisprudence is but the will of your class made into a law for all, a will whose essential character and direction are determined by the economical conditions of existence of your class.

The selfish misconception that induces you to transform into eternal laws of nature and of reason the social forms stringing from your present mode of production and form of property—historical relations that rise and disappear in the progress of production—this misconception you share with every ruling class that has preceded you. What you see clearly in the case of ancient property, what you admit in the case of feudal property, you are of course forbidden to admit in the case of your own bourgeois form of property.

Abolition of the family! Even the most radical flare up at this infamous proposal of the Communists.

On what foundation is the present family, the bourgeois family, based? On capital, on private gain. In its completely developed form, this family exists only among the bourgeoisie. But this state of things finds its complement in the practical absence of the family among proletarians, and in public prostitution.

The bourgeois family will vanish as a matter of course when its complement vanishes, and both will vanish with the vanishing of capital.

Do you charge us with wanting to stop the exploitation of children by their parents? To this crime we plead guilty.

But, you say, we destroy the most hallowed of relations, when we replace home education by social.

And your education! Is not that also social, and determined by the social conditions under which you educate, by the intervention direct or indirect, of society, by means of schools, etc.? The Communists have not intended the intervention of society in education; they do but seek to alter the character of that intervention, and to rescue education from the influence of the ruling class.

The bourgeois claptrap about the family and education, about the hallowed correlation of parents and child, becomes all the more disgusting, the more, by the action of Modern Industry, all the family ties among the proletarians are torn asunder, and their children transformed into simple articles of commerce and instruments of labor.

But you Communists would introduce community of women, screams the bourgeoisie in chorus.

The bourgeois sees his wife a mere instrument of production. He hears that the instruments of production are to be exploited in common, and, naturally, can come to no other conclusion that the lot of being common to all will likewise fall to the women.

He has not even a suspicion that the real point aimed at is to do away with the status of women as mere instruments of production.

For the rest, nothing is more ridiculous than the virtuous indignation of our bourgeois at the community of women which, they pretend, is to be openly and officially established by the Communists. The Communists have no need to introduce community of women; it has existed almost from time immemorial.

Our bourgeois, not content with having wives and daughters of their proletarians at their disposal, not to speak of common prostitutes, take the greatest pleasure in seducing each other's wives.

Bourgeois marriage is, in reality, a system of wives in common and thus, at the most, what the Communists might possibly be reproached with is that they desire to introduce, in substitution for a hypocritically concealed, an openly legalized system of free love. For the rest, it is self-evident that the abolition of the present system of production must bring with it the abolition of free love springing from that system, i.e., of prostitution both public and private.

The Communists are further reproached with desiring to abolish countries and nationality.

The workers have no country. We cannot take from them what they have not got. Since the proletariat must first of all acquire political supremacy, must rise to be the leading class of the nation, must constitute itself *the* nation, it is, so far, itself national, though not in the bourgeois sense of the word.

National differences and antagonism between peoples are daily more and more vanishing, owing to the development of the bourgeoisie, to freedom of commerce, to the world market, to uniformity in the mode of production and in the conditions of life corresponding thereto.

The supremacy of the proletariat will cause them to vanish still faster. United action of the leading civilized countries at least is one of the first conditions for the emancipation of the proletariat.

In proportion as the exploitation of one individual by another will also be put an end to, the exploitation of one nation by another will also be put an end to. In proportion as the antagonism between classes within the nation vanishes, the hostility of one nation to another will come to an end.

The charges against communism made from a religious, a philosophical and, generally, from an ideological standpoint, are not deserving of serious examination.

Does it require deep intuition to comprehend that man's ideas, views, and conception, in one word, man's consciousness, changes with every change in the conditions of his material existence, in his social relations and in his social life?

What else does the history of ideas prove, than that intellectual production changes its character in proportion as material production is changed? The ruling ideas of each age have ever been the ideas of its ruling class.

When people speak of the ideas that revolutionize society, they do but express that fact that within the old society the elements of a new one have been created, and that the dissolution of the old ideas keeps even pace with the dissolution of the old conditions of existence.

When the ancient world was in its last throes, the ancient religions were overcome by Christianity. When Christian ideas succumbed in the eighteenth century to rationalist ideas, feudal society fought its death battle with the then revolutionary bourgeoisie. The ideas of religious liberty and freedom of conscience merely gave expression to the sway of free competition within the domain of knowledge.

"Undoubtedly," it will be said, "religious, moral, philosophical, and juridicial ideas have been modified in the course of historical development. But religion, morality, philosophy, political science, and law, constantly survived this change."

"There are, besides, eternal truths, such as Freedom, Justice, etc., that are common to all states of society. But communism abolishes eternal truths, it abolishes all religion, and all morality, instead of constituting them on a new basis; it therefore acts in contradiction to all past historical experience."

What does this accusation reduce itself to? The history of all past society has consisted in the development of class antagonisms, antagonisms that assumed different forms at different epochs.

But whatever form they may have taken, one fact is common to all past ages, viz., the exploitation of one part of society by the other. No wonder, then, that the social consciousness of past ages, despite all the multiplicity and variety it displays, moves within certain common forms, or general ideas, which cannot completely vanish except with the total disappearance of class antagonisms.

The communist revolution is the most radical rupture with traditional relations; no wonder that its development involved the most radical rupture with traditional ideas.

But let us have done with the bourgeois objections to communism.

We have seen above that the first step in the revolution by the working class is to raise the proletariat to the position of ruling class to win the battle of democracy.

The proletariat will use its political supremacy to wrest, by degree, all capital from the bourgeoisie, to centralize all instruments of production in the hands of the state, i.e., of the proletariat organized as the ruling class; and to increase the total productive forces as rapidly as possible.

Of course, in the beginning, this cannot be effected except by means of despotic inroads on the rights of property, and on the conditions of bourgeois production; by means of measures, therefore, which appear economically insufficient and untenable, but which, in the course of the movement, outstrip themselves, necessitate further inroads upon the old social order, and are unavoidable as a means of entirely revolutionizing the mode of production.

These measures will, of course, be different in different countries.

Nevertheless, in most advanced countries, the following will be pretty generally applicable.

1. Abolition of property in land and application of all rents of land to public purposes.
2. A heavy progressive or graduated income tax.
3. Abolition of all rights of inheritance.
4. Confiscation of the property of all emigrants and rebels.
5. Centralization of credit in the banks of the state, by means of a national bank with state capital and an exclusive monopoly.
6. Centralization of the means of communication and transport in the hands of the state.
7. Extension of factories and instruments of production owned by the state; the bringing into cultivation of waste lands, and the improvement of the soil generally in accordance with a common plan.
8. Equal obligation of all to work. Establishment of industrial armies, especially for agriculture.
9. Combination of agriculture with manufacturing industries; gradual abolition of all the distinction between town and country by a more equable distribution of the populace over the country.
10. Free education for all children in public schools. Abolition of children's factory labor in its present form. Combination of education with industrial production, etc.

When, in the course of development, class distinctions have disappeared, and all production has been concentrated in the hands of a vast association of the whole nation, the public power will lose its political character. Political power, properly so called, is merely the organized power of one class for oppressing another. If the proletariat during its contest with the bourgeoisie is compelled, by the force of circumstances, to organize itself as a class; if, by means of a revolution, it makes itself the ruling class, and, as such, sweeps away by force the old conditions of production, then it will, along with these conditions, have swept away the conditions for the existence of class antagonisms and of classes generally, and will thereby have abolished its own supremacy as a class.

In place of the old bourgeois society, with its classes and class antagonisms, we shall have an association in which the free development of each is the condition for the free development of all.

III. Socialist and Communist Literature

1. Reactionary Socialism

(a) *Feudal Socialism*. Owing to their historical position, it became the vocation of the aristocracies of France and England to write pamphlets against modern bourgeois society. In the French Revolution of July 1830, and in the English reform agitation, these aristocracies again succumbed to the hateful upstart. Thenceforth, a serious political struggle was altogether out of the question. A literary battle alone remained possible. But even in the domain of literature, the old cries of the restoration period had become impossible.

In order to arouse sympathy, the aristocracy was obliged to lose sight, apparently, of its own interests, and to formulate its indictment against the bourgeoisie in the interest of the exploited working class alone. Thus, the aristocracy took their revenge by singing lampoons on their new masters and whispering in his ears sinister prophesies of coming catastrophe.

In this way arose feudal socialism: half lamentation, half lampoon; half an echo of the past, half menace of the future; at times, by its bitter, witty and incisive criticism, striking the bourgeoisie to the very heart's core, but always ludicrous in its effect, through total incapacity to comprehend the march of modern history.

The aristocracy, in order to rally the people to them, waved the proletarian alms-bag in front for a banner. But the people, so often as it joined them, saw on their hindquarters the old feudal coats of arms, and deserted with loud and irreverent laughter. One section of the French Legitimists and "Young England" exhibited this spectacle:

In pointing out that their mode of exploitation was different to that of the bourgeoisie, the feudalists forget that they exploited under circumstances and conditions that were quite different and that are now antiquated. In showing that, under their rule, the modern proletariat never existed, they forget that the modern bourgeoisie is the necessary offspring of their own form of society.

For the rest, so little do they conceal the reactionary character of their criticism that their chief accusation against the bourgeois amounts to this: that under the bourgeois regime a class is being developed which is destined to cut up, root and branch, the old order of society.

What they upbraid the bourgeoisie with is not so much that it creates a proletariat as that it creates a revolutionary proletariat.

In political practice, therefore, they join in all corrective measures against the working class; and in ordinary life, despite their high falutin' phrases, they stoop to pick up the golden apples dropped from the tree of industry, and to barter truth, love, and honor, for traffic in wool, beetroot-sugar, and potato spirits.

As the parson has ever gone hand in hand with the landlord, so has clerical socialism with feudal socialism.

Nothing is easier than to give Christian asceticism a socialist tinge. Has not Christianity declaimed against private property, against marriage, against the state? Has it not preached in the place of these, charity and poverty, celibacy and mortification of the flesh, monastic life and Mother Church? Christian socialism is but the holy water with which the priest consecrates the heart-burnings of the aristocrat.

(b) *Petty-Bourgeois Socialism*. The feudal aristocracy was not the only class that was ruined by the bourgeoisie, not the only class whose conditions of existence pined and perished in the atmosphere of modern bourgeois society. The medieval burgesses and the small peasant proprietors were the precursors of the modern bourgeoisie. In those countries which are but little developed, industrially and commercially, these two classes still vegetate side by side with the rising bourgeoisie.

In countries where modern civilization has become fully developed, a new class of petty bourgeois has been formed, fluctuating between proletariat and bourgeoisie, and ever renewing itself a supplementary part of bourgeois society. The individual members of this class, however, as being constantly hurled down into the proletariat by the action of competition, and, as Modern Industry develops, they even see the moment approaching when they will completely disappear as an independent section of modern society, to be replaced in manufactures, agriculture and commerce, by overlookers, bailiffs and shopmen.

In countries like France, where the peasants constitute far more than half of the population, it was natural that writers who sided with the proletariat against the bourgeoisie should use, in their criticism of the bourgeois regime, the standard of the peasant and petty bourgeois, and from the standpoint of these intermediate classes, should take up the cudgels for the working class. Thus arose petty-bourgeois socialism. Sismondi was the head of this school, not only in France but also in England.

This school of socialism dissected with great acuteness the contradictions in the conditions of modern production. It laid bare the hypocritical apologies of economists. It proved, incontrovertibly, the disastrous effects of machinery and division of labor; the concentration of capital and land in a few hands; overproduction and crises; it pointed out the inevitable ruin of the petty bourgeois and peasant, the misery of the proletariat, the anarchy in production, the crying inequalities in the distribution of wealth, the industrial war of extermination between nations, the dissolution of old moral bonds, of the old family relations, of the old nationalities.

In its positive aims, however, this form of socialism aspires either to restoring the old means of production and of exchange, and with them the old property relations, and the old society, or to cramping the modern means of production and of exchange within the framework of the old property relations that have been, and were bound to be, exploded by those means. In either case, it is both reactionary and Utopian.

Its last words are: corporate guilds for manufacture; patriarchal relations in agriculture.

Ultimately, when stubborn historical facts had dispersed all intoxicating effects of self-deception, this form of socialism ended in a miserable hangover.

(c) *German or "True" Socialism.* The socialist and communist literature of France, a literature that originated under the pressure of a bourgeoisie in power, and that was the expressions of the struggle against this power, was introduced into Germany at a time when the bourgeoisie in that country had just begun its contest with feudal absolutism.

German philosophers, would-be philosophers, and beaux esprits (men of letters), eagerly seized on this literature, only forgetting that when these writings immigrated from France into Germany, French social conditions had not immigrated along with them. In contact with German social conditions, this French literature lost all its immediate practical significance and assumed a purely literary aspect. Thus, to the German philosophers of the eighteenth century, the demands of the first French Revolution were nothing more than the demands of "Practical Reason" in general, and the utterance of the will of the revolutionary French bourgeoisie signified, in their eyes, the laws of pure will, of will as it was bound to be, of true human will generally.

The work of the German literati consisted solely in bringing the new French ideas into harmony with their ancient philosophical conscience, or rather, in annexing the French ideas without deserting their own philosophic point of view.

This annexation took place in the same way in which a foreign language is appropriated, namely, by translation.

It is well known how the monks wrote silly lives of Catholic saints over the manuscripts on which the classical works of ancient heathendom had been written. The German literati reversed this process with the profane French literature. They wrote their philosophical nonsense beneath the French original. For instance, beneath the French criticism of the economic functions of money, they wrote "alienation of humanity," and beneath the French criticism of the bourgeois state they wrote "dethronement of the category of the general," and so forth.

The introduction of these philosophical phrases at the back of the French historical criticisms, they dubbed "Philosophy of Action," "True Socialism," "German Science of Socialism," "Philosophical Foundation of Socialism," and so on.

The French socialist and communist literature was thus completely emasculated. And, since it ceased, in the hands of the German, to express the struggle of one class with the other, he felt conscious of having overcome "French one-sidedness" and of representing, not true requirements, but the requirements of truth; not the interests of the proletariat, but the interests of human nature, of man in general, who belongs to no class, has no reality, who exists only in the misty realm of philosophical fantasy.

This German socialism, which took its schoolboy task so seriously and solemnly, and extolled its poor stock-in-trade in such a mountebank fashion, meanwhile gradually lost its pedantic innocence.

The fight of the Germans, and especially of the Prussian bourgeoisie, against feudal aristocracy and absolute monarchy, in other words, the liberal movement, became more earnest.

By this, the long-wished for opportunity was offered to "True" Socialism of confronting the political movement with the socialistic demands, of hurling the traditional anathemas against liberalism, against representative government, against bourgeois competition, bourgeois freedom of the press, bourgeois legislation, bourgeois liberty and equality, and of preaching to the masses that they had nothing to gain, and everything to lose, by this bourgeois movement. German socialism forgot, in the nick of time, that the French criticism, whose silly echo it was, presupposed the existence of modern bourgeois society, with its corresponding economic conditions of existence, and the political constitution adapted thereto, the very things whose attainment was the object of the pending struggle in Germany.

To the absolute governments, with their following of parsons, professors, country squires, and officials, it served as a welcome scarecrow against the threatening bourgeoisie.

It was a sweet finish, after the bitter pills of flogging and bullets, with which these same governments, just at that time, dosed the German working-class risings.

While this "True" Socialism thus served the government as a weapon for fighting the German bourgeoisie, it, at the same time, directly represented a reactionary interest, the interest of German philistines. In Germany, the petty-bourgeois class, a relic of the sixteenth century, and since then constantly cropping up again under the various forms, is the real social basis of the existing state of things.

To preserve this class is to preserve the existing state of things in Germany. The industrial and political supremacy of the bourgeoisie threatens it with certain destruction—on the one hand, from the concentration of capital; on the other, from the rise of a revolutionary proletariat. "True" Socialism appeared to kill these two birds with one stone. It spread like an epidemic.

The robe of speculative cobwebs, embroidered with flowers of rhetoric, steeped in the dew of sickly sentiment, this transcendental robe in which the German Socialists wrapped their sorry "eternal truths," all skin and bone, served to wonderfully increase the sale of their goods amongst such a public.

And on its part German socialism recognized, more and more, its own calling as the bombastic representative of the petty-bourgeois philistine.

It proclaimed the German nation to be the model nation, and the German petty philistine to be the typical man. To every villainous meanness of this model man, it gave a hidden, higher, socialistic interpretation, the exact contrary of its real character. It went to the extreme length of directly opposing the "brutally destructive" tendency of communism, and of proclaiming its supreme and impartial contempt of all class struggles. With very few exceptions, all the so-called socialist and communist publications that now (1847) circulate in Germany belong to the domain of this foul and enervating literature.

2. Conservative or Bourgeois Socialism

A part of the bourgeoisie is desirous of redressing social grievances in order to secure the continued existence of bourgeois society.

To this section belong economists, philanthropists, humanitarians, improvers of the condition of the working class, organizers of charity, members of societies for the prevention of cruelty to animals, temperance fanatics, hole-and-corner reformers of every imaginable kind. This form of socialism has, moreover, been worked out into complete systems.

We may cite Proudhon's *Philosophy of Poverty* as an example of this form.

The socialistic bourgeois want all the advantages of modern social conditions without the struggles and dangers necessarily resulting therefrom. They desire the existing state of society, minus its revolutionary and disintegrating elements. They wish for a bourgeoisie without a proletariat. The bourgeoisie naturally conceives the world in which it is supreme to be the best; and bourgeois socialism develops this comfortable conception into various more or less complete systems. In requiring the proletariat to carry out such a system, and thereby to march straightway into the social New Jerusalem, it but requires in reality that the proletariat should remain within the bounds of existing society, but should cast away all its hateful ideas concerning the bourgeoisie.

A second, and more practical, but less systematic, form of this socialism sought to depreciate every revolutionary movement in the eyes of the working class by showing that no mere political reform, but only a change in the material conditions of existence, in economical relations, could be of any advantage to them. By changes in the material conditions of existence, this form of socialism, however, by no means understands abolition of the bourgeois relations of production, an abolition that can be affected only by a revolution, but administrative reforms, based on the continued existence of these relations; reforms, therefore, that in no respect affect the relations between capital and labor, but, at the best, lessen the cost, and simplify the administrative work of bourgeois government.

Bourgeois socialism attains adequate expression when, and only when, it becomes a mere figure of speech.

Free trade: for the benefit of the working class. Protective duties: for the benefit of the working class. Prison reform: for the benefit of the working class. This is the last word and the only seriously meant word of bourgeois socialism.

It is summed up in the phrase: the bourgeois is a bourgeois—for the benefit of the working class.

3. Critical-Utopian Socialism and Communism

We do not here refer to that literature which, in every great modern revolution, has always given voice to the demands of the proletariat, such as the writings of Babeuf and others.

The first direct attempts of the proletariat to attain its own ends, made in times of universal excitement, when feudal society was being overthrown, necessarily failed, owing to the then undeveloped state of the proletariat, as well as to the absence of the economic conditions for its emancipation, conditions that had yet to be produced, and could be produced by the impending bourgeois epoch alone. The revolutionary literature that accompanied these first movements of the proletariat had necessarily a reactionary character. It inculcated universal asceticism and social levelling in its crudest form.

The socialist and communist systems, properly so called, those of Saint-Simon, Fourier, Owen, and others, spring into existence in the early undeveloped period, described above, of the struggle between proletariat and bourgeoisie (see Section 1. Bourgeois and Proletarians).

The founders of these systems see, indeed, the class antagonisms, as well as the action of the decomposing elements in the prevailing form of society. But the proletariat, as yet in its infancy, offers to them the spectacle of a class without any historical initiative or any independent political movement.

Since the development of class antagonism keeps even pace with the development of industry, the economic situation, as they find it, does not as yet offer to them the material conditions for the emancipation of the proletariat. They therefore search after a new social science, after new social laws, that are to create these conditions.

Historical action is to yield to their personal inventive action; historically created conditions of emancipation to fantastic ones; and the gradual, spontaneous class organization of the proletariat to an organization of society especially contrived by these inventors. Future history resolves itself, in their eyes, into the propaganda and the practical carrying out of their social plans.

In the formation of their plans, they are conscious of caring chiefly for the interests of the working class, as being the most suffering class. Only from the point of view of being the most suffering class does the proletariat exist for them.

The undeveloped state of the class struggle, as well as their own surroundings, causes Socialists of this kind to consider themselves far superior to all class antagonisms. They want to improve the condition of every member of society, even that of the most favored. Hence, they habitually appeal to society at large, without the distinction of class; nay, by preference, to the ruling class. For how can people when once they understand their system, fail to see in it the best possible plan of the best possible state of society?

Hence, they reject all political, and especially all revolutionary action; they wish to attain their ends by peaceful means, necessarily doomed to failure, and by the force of example, to pave the way for the new social gospel.

Such fantastic pictures of future society, painted at a time when the proletariat is still in a very undeveloped state and has but a fantastic conception of its own position, correspond with the first instinctive yearnings of that class for a general reconstruction of society.

But these socialist and communist publications contain also a critical element. They attack every principle of existing society. Hence, they are full of the most valuable materials for the enlightenment of the working class. The practical measures proposed in them—such as the abolition of the distinction between town and country, of the family, of the carrying on of industries for the account of private individuals, and of the wage system, the proclamation of social harmony, the conversion of the function of the state into a more superintendence of production—all these proposals point solely to the disappearance of class antagonisms which were, at that time, only just cropping up, and which, in these publications, are recognized in their earliest indistinct and undefined forms only. These proposals, therefore, are of a purely utopian character.

The significance of critical-utopian socialism and communism bears an inverse relation to historical development. In proportion as the modern class struggle develops and takes definite shape, this fantastic standing apart from the contest, these fantastic attacks on it, lose all practical value and all theoretical justifications. Therefore, although the originators of these systems were, in many respects, revolutionary, their disciples have, in every case, formed mere reactionary sects. They hold fast by the original views of their masters, in opposition to the progressive historical development of the proletariat. They, therefore, endeavor, and that consistently, to deaden the class struggle and to reconcile the class antagonisms. They still dream of experimental realization of their social utopias, of founding isolated *phalansteres,* of establishing "Home Colonies," or setting up a "Little Icaria"—pocket editions of the New Jerusalem—and to realize all these castles in the air, they are compelled to appeal to the feelings and purses of the bourgeois. By degrees, they sink into the category of the reactionary conservative socialists depicted above, differing from these only by more systematic pedantry, and by their fanatical and superstitious belief in the miraculous effects of their social science.

They, therefore, violently oppose all political action on the part of the working class; such action, according to them, can only result from blind unbelief in the new gospel.

The Owenites in England, and the Fourierists in France, respectively, oppose the Chartists and the Reformistes.

IV. Position of the Communists in Relation to the Various Existing Opposition Parties

Section II has made clear the relations of the Communists to the existing working-class parties, such as the Chartists in England and the Agrarian Reformers in America.

The Communists fight for the attainment of the immediate aims, for the enforcement of the momentary interests of the working class; but in the movement of the present, they also represent and take care of the future of that movement. In France, the Communists ally with the Social Democrats against the conservative and radical bourgeoisie, reserving, however, the right to take up a critical position in regard to phases and illusions traditionally handed down from the Great Revolution.

In Switzerland, they support the Radicals, without losing sight of the fact that this party consists of antagonistic elements, partly of Democratic Socialists, in the French sense, partly of radical bourgeois.

In Poland, they support the party that insists on an agrarian revolution as the prime condition for national emancipation, that party which fomented the insurrection of Krakow in 1846.

In Germany, they fight with the bourgeoisie whenever it acts in a revolutionary way, against the absolute monarchy, the feudal squirearchy, and the petty-bourgeoisie.

But they never cease, for a single instant, to instill into the working class the clearest possible recognition of the hostile antagonism between bourgeoisie and proletariat, in order that the German workers may straightway use, as so many weapons against the bourgeoisie, the social and political conditions that the bourgeoisie must necessarily introduce along with its supremacy, and in order that, after the fall of the reactionary classes in Germany, the fight against the bourgeoisie itself may immediately begin.

The Communists turn their attention chiefly to Germany, because that country is on the eve of a bourgeois revolution that is bound to be carried out under more advanced conditions of European civilization and with a much more developed proletariat than that of England was in the seventeenth, and France in the eighteenth century, and because the bourgeois revolution in Germany will be but the prelude to an immediately following proletarian revolution.

In short, the Communists everywhere support every revolutionary movement against the existing social and political order of things.

In all these movements, they bring to the front, as the leading question in each, the property question, no matter what its degree of development at the time.

Finally, they labor everywhere for the union and agreement of the democratic parties of all countries.

The Communists disdain to conceal their views and aims. They openly declare that their ends can be attained only by the forcible overthrow of all existing social conditions. Let the ruling classes tremble at a communist revolution. The proletarians have nothing to lose but their chains. They have a world to win.

PROLETARIANS OF ALL COUNTRIES, UNITE!

Friedrich List,
The National System of Political Economy (1841)*

Chapter XII: The Theory of the Powers of Production and the Theory of Values

Adam Smith's celebrated work is entitled, 'The Nature and Causes of the Wealth of Nations.' The founder of the prevailing economical school has therein indicated the double point of view from which the economy of nations, like that of private separate individuals, should be regarded.

The causes of wealth are something totally different from *wealth itself*. A person may possess wealth, i.e. exchangeable value; if, however, he does not possess the power of producing objects of more value than he consumes, he will become poorer. A person may be poor; if he, however, possesses the power of producing a larger amount of valuable articles than he consumes, he becomes rich.

The power of producing wealth is therefore infinitely more important than *wealth itself*; it insures not only the possession and the increase of what has been gained, but also the replacement of what has been lost. This is still more the case with entire nations (who cannot live out of mere rentals) than with private individuals. Germany has been devastated in every century by pestilence, by famine, or by civil or foreign wars; she has, nevertheless, always retained a great portion of her powers of production, and has thus quickly re-attained some degree of prosperity; while rich and mighty but despot- and priest-ridden Spain, notwithstanding her comparative enjoyment of internal peace, has sunk deeper into poverty and misery. The same sun still shines on the Spaniards, they still possess the same area of territory, their mines are still as rich, they are still the same people as before the discovery of America, and before the introduction of the Inquisition; but that nation has gradually lost her powers of production, and has therefore become poor and miserable. The War of Independence of the United States of America cost that nation hundreds of millions, but her powers of production were immeasurably strengthened by gaining independence, and it was for this reason that in the course of a few years after the peace she obtained immeasurably greater riches than she had ever possessed before. If we compare the state of France in the year 1809 with that of the year 1839, what a difference in favour of the latter! Nevertheless, France has in the interim lost her sovereignty over a large portion of the European continent; she has suffered two devastating invasions, and had to pay milliards of money in war contributions and indemnities.

---

* List, Friedrich. Excerpts from: *The National System of Political Economy* (1841). Material in the public domain.

It was impossible that so clear an intellect as Adam Smith possessed could alto-gether ignore the difference between wealth and its causes and the overwhelming influence of these causes on the condition of nations. In the introduction to his work, he says in clear words in effect: 'Labour forms the fund from which every nation derives its wealth, and the increase of wealth depends first on the *productive power* of labour, namely, on the degree of skill, dexterity, and judgment with which the labour of the nation is generally applied, and secondly, on the proportion between the number of those employed productively and the number of those who are not so employed.' From this we see how clearly Smith in general perceived that the condi-tion of nations is principally dependent on the sum of their *productive powers*.

It does not, however, appear to be the plan of nature that complete sciences should spring already perfected from the brain of individual thinkers. It is evident that Smith was too exclusively possessed by the cosmopolitical idea of the physiocrats, 'universal freedom of trade,' and by his own great discovery, 'the division of labour,' to follow up the idea of the importance to a nation of its *powers of production*. However much science may be indebted to him in respect of the remaining parts of his work, the idea 'division of labour' seemed to him his most brilliant thought. It was calculated to secure for his book a name, and for himself posthumous fame.

He had too much worldly wisdom not to perceive that whoever wishes to sell a precious jewel does not bring the treasure to market most profitably by burying it in a sack of wheat, however useful the grains of wheat may be, but better by exposing it at the forefront. He had too much experience not to know that a *debutant* (and he was this as regards political economy at the time of the publication of his work) who in the first act creates a *furore* is easily excused if in the following ones he only occasion-ally raises himself above mediocrity; he had every motive for making the introduc-tion to his book, the doctrine of division of labour. Smith has not been mistaken in his calculations; his first chapter has made the fortune of his book, and founded his authority as an economist.

However, we on our part believe ourselves able to prove that just this zeal to put the important discovery *'division of labour'* in an advantageous light, has hindered Adam Smith from following up the idea *'productive power'* (which has been expressed by him in the introduction, and also frequently afterwards, although merely inciden-tally) and from exhibiting his doctrines in a much more perfect form. By the great value which he attached to his idea *'division of labour'* he has evidently been misled into representing labour itself as the 'fund' of all the wealth of nations, although he himself clearly perceives and also states that the productiveness of labour principally depends on the degree of skill and judgment with which the labour is performed. We ask, can it be deemed scientific reasoning if we assign as the cause of a phenomenon that which in itself is the result of a number of deeper lying causes? It cannot be doubted that all wealth is obtained by means of mental and bodily exertions (labour), but yet from that circumstance no reason is indicated from which useful conclusions may be drawn; for history teaches that whole nations have, in spite of the exertions and of the thrift of their citizens, fallen into poverty and misery. Whoever desires to know and investigate how one nation from a state of poverty and barbarism has attained to one of wealth and prosperity, and how another has fallen from a condition of wealth and well-being into one of poverty and misery, has always, after receiving the information that labour is the cause of wealth and idleness the cause of poverty (a remark which King Solomon made long before Adam Smith), to put the further question, what are the causes of labour, and what the causes of idleness?

It would be more correct to describe the limbs of men (the head, hands, and feet) as the causes of wealth (we should thus at least approach far nearer to the truth), and the question then presents itself, what is it that induces these heads, arms, and hands to produce, and calls into activity these exertions? What else can it be than the spirit which animates the individuals, the social order which renders their energy fruitful, and the powers of nature which they are in a position to make use of? The more a man perceives that he must provide for the future, the more his intelligence and feelings incite him to secure the future of his nearest connections, and to promote their well-being; the more he has been from his youth accustomed to forethought and activity, the more his nobler feelings have been developed, and body and mind cultivated, the finer examples that he has witnessed from his youth, the more opportunities he has had for utilising his mental and bodily powers for the improvement of his condition, also the less he has been restrained in his legitimate activity, the more successful his past endeavours have been, and the more their fruits have been secured to him, the more he has been able to obtain public recognition and esteem by orderly conduct and activity, and the less his mind suffers from prejudices, superstition, false notions, and ignorance, so much the more will he exert his mind and limbs for the object of production, so much the more will he be able to accomplish, and so much the better will he make use of the fruits of his labour. However, most depends in all these respects on the conditions of the society in which the individual has been brought up, and turns upon this, whether science and arts flourish, and public institutions and laws tend to promote religious character, morality and intelligence, security for person and for property, freedom and justice; whether in the nation all the factors of material prosperity, agriculture, manufactures, and trade, have been equally and harmoniously cultivated; whether the power of the nation is strong enough to secure to its individual citizens progress in wealth and education from generation to generation, and to enable them not merely to utilise the natural powers of their own country to their fullest extent, but also, by foreign trade and the possession of colonies, to render the natural powers of foreign countries serviceable to their own.

Adam Smith has on the whole recognised the nature of these powers so little, that he does not even assign a productive character to the mental labours of those who maintain laws and order, and cultivate and promote instruction, religion, science, and art. His investigations are limited to that human activity which creates material values. With regard to this, he certainly recognises that its productiveness depends on the 'skill and judgment' with which it is exercised; but in his investigations as to the causes of this skill and judgment, he does not go farther than the division of labour, and that he illustrates solely by exchange, augmentation of material capital, and extension of markets. His doctrine at once sinks deeper and deeper into materialism, particularism, and individualism. If he had followed up the idea 'productive power' without allowing his mind to be dominated by the idea of 'value,' 'exchangeable value,' he would have been led to perceive that an independent theory of the 'productive power,' must be considered by the side of a 'theory of values' in order to explain the economical phenomena. But he thus fell into the mistake of explaining mental forces from material circumstances and conditions, and thereby laid the foundation for all the absurdities and contradictions from which his school (as we propose to prove) suffers up to the present day, and to which alone it must be attributed that the doctrines of political economy are those which are the least accessible to the most intelligent minds. That Smith's school teaches nothing else than the theory of values, is not only seen from the fact that it bases its doctrine everywhere on the conception of 'value of exchange,' but also from the definition which it gives of its doctrine. It is (says J.B. Say) that science which teaches how riches, or exchangeable values, are produced, distributed, and consumed. This is undoubtedly not the science which teaches how the *productive powers* are awakened and developed, and how they become depressed and destroyed. M'Culloch calls it explicitly *'the science of values,'* and recent English writers *'the science of exchange.'*

Examples from private economy will best illustrate the difference between the theory of productive powers and the theory of values.

Let us suppose the case of two fathers of families, both being landed proprietors, each of whom saves yearly 1,000 thalers and has five sons. The one puts out his savings at interest, and keeps his sons at common hard work, while the other employs his savings in educating two of his sons as skillful and intelligent landowners, and in enabling the other three to learn a trade after their respective tastes; the former acts according to the theory of values, the latter according to the theory of productive powers. The first at his death may prove much richer than the second in mere exchangeable value, but it is quite otherwise as respects productive powers. The estate of the latter is divided into two parts, and every part will by the aid of improved management yield as much total produce as the whole did before; while the remaining three sons have by their talents obtained abundant means of maintenance. The landed property of the former will be divided into five parts, and every part will be worked in as bad a manner as the whole was heretofore. In the latter family a mass of different mental forces and talents is awakened and cultivated, which will increase from generation to generation, every succeeding generation possessing more power of obtaining material wealth than the preceding one, while in the former family stupidity and poverty must increase with the diminution of the shares in the landed property. So the slaveholder increases by slave-breeding the sum of his values of exchange, but he ruins the productive forces of future generations. All expenditure in the instruction of youth, the promotion of justice, defence of nations, &c. is a consumption of present values for the behoof of the productive powers. The greatest portion of the consumption of a nation is used for the education of the future generation, for promotion and nourishment of the future national productive powers.

The Christian religion, monogamy, abolition of slavery and of vassalage, hereditability of the throne, invention of printing, of the press, of the postal system, of money weights and measures, of the calendar, of watches, of police, the introduction of the principle of freehold property, of means of transport, are rich sources of productive power. To be convinced of this, we need only compare the condition of the European states with that of the Asiatic ones. In order duly to estimate the influence which liberty of thought and conscience has on the productive forces of nations, we need only read the history of England and then that of Spain. The publicity of the administration of justice, trial by jury, parliamentary legislation, public control of

State administration, self-administration of the commonalties and municipalities, liberty of the press, liberty of association for useful purposes, impart to the citizens of constitutional states, as also to their public functionaries, a degree of energy and power which can hardly be produced by other means. We can scarcely conceive of any law or any public legal decision which would not exercise a greater or smaller influence on the increase or decrease of the productive power of the nation.

If we consider merely bodily labour as the cause of wealth, how can we then explain why modern nations are incomparably richer, more populous, more powerful, and prosperous than the nations of ancient times? The ancient nations employed (in proportion to the whole population) infinitely more hands, the work was much harder, each individual possessed much more land, and yet the masses were much worse fed and clothed than is the case in modern nations. In order to explain these phenomena, we must refer to the progress which has been made in the course of the last thousand years in sciences and arts, domestic and public regulations, cultivation of the mind and capabilities of production. The present state of the nations is the result of the accumulation of all discoveries, inventions, improvements, perfections, and exertions of all generations which have lived before us; they form the mental capital of the present human race, and every separate nation is productive only in the proportion in which it has known how to appropriate these attainments of former generations and to increase them by its own acquirements, in which the natural capabilities of its territory, its extent and geographical position, its population and political power, have been able to develop as completely and symmetrically as possible all sources of wealth within its boundaries, and to extend its moral, intellectual, commercial, and political influence over less advanced nations and especially over the affairs of the world.

The popular school of economists would have us believe that politics and political power cannot be taken into consideration in political economy. So far as it makes only values and exchange the subjects of its investigations, this may be correct; we can define the ideas of value and capital, profit, wages, and rent; we can resolve them into their elements, and speculate on what may influence their rising or falling, &c. without thereby taking into account the political circumstances of the nation. Clearly, however, these matters appertain as much to private economy as to the economy of whole nations. We have merely to consider the history of Venice, of the Hanseatic League, of Portugal, Holland, and England, in order to perceive what reciprocal influence material wealth and political power exercise on each other.

The school also always falls into the strangest inconsistencies whenever this reciprocal influence forces itself on their consideration. Let us here only call to mind the remarkable dictum of Adam Smith on the English Navigation Laws.

The popular school, inasmuch as it does not duly consider the nature of the powers of production, and does not take into account the conditions of nations in their aggregate, disregards especially the importance of developing in an equal ratio agriculture, manufactures and commerce, political power and internal wealth, and disregards especially the value of a manufacturing power belonging specially to the nation and fully developed in all its branches. It commits the error of placing manufacturing power in the same category with agricultural power, and of speaking of labour, natural power, capital, &c. in general terms without considering the differences which exist between them. It does not perceive that between a State devoted merely to agriculture and a State possessing both agriculture and manufactures, a much greater difference exists than between a pastoral State and an agricultural one. In a condition of merely agricultural industry, caprice and slavery, superstition and ignorance, want of means of culture, of trade, and of transport, poverty and political weakness exist. In the merely agricultural State only the least portion of the mental and bodily powers existing in the nation is awakened and developed, and only the least part of the powers and resources placed by nature at its disposal can be made use of, while little or no capital can be accumulated.

Let us compare Poland with England: both nations at one time were in the same stage of culture; and now what a difference. Manufactories and manufactures are the mothers and children of municipal liberty, of intelligence, of the arts and sciences, of internal and external commerce, of navigation and improvements in transport, of civilisation and political power. They are the chief means of liberating agriculture from its chains, and of elevating it to a commercial character and to a degree of art and science, by which the rents, farming profits, and wages are increased, and greater value is given to landed property. The popular school has attributed this civilising power to foreign trade, but in that it has confounded the mere exchanger with the originator. Foreign manufactures furnish the goods for the foreign trade, which the latter conveys to us, and which occasion consumption of products and raw materials which we give in exchange for the goods in lieu of money payments.

If, however, trade in the manufactures of far distant lands exercises admittedly so beneficial an influence on our agricultural industry, how much more beneficial must the influence be of those manufactures which are bound up with us locally, commercially, and politically, which not only take from us a small portion, but the largest portion of their requirements of food and of raw materials, which are not made dearer to us by great costs of transport, our trade in which cannot be interrupted by the chance of foreign manufacturing nations learning to supply their own wants themselves, or by wars and prohibitory import duties?

We now see into what extraordinary mistakes and contradictions the popular school has fallen in making material wealth or value of exchange the sole object of its investigations, and by regarding mere bodily labour as the sole productive power.

The man who breeds pigs is, according to this school, a productive member of the community, but he who educates men is a mere non-productive. The maker of bagpipes or jews-harps for sale is a productive, while the great composers and virtuosos are non-productive simply because that which they play cannot be brought into the market. The physician who saves the lives of his patients does not belong to the productive class, but on the contrary the chemist's boy does so, although the values of exchange (viz. the pills) which he produces may exist only for a few minutes before they pass into a valueless condition. A Newton, a Watt, or a Kepler is not so productive as a donkey, a horse, or a draught-ox (a class of labourers who have been recently introduced by M'Culloch into the series of the productive members of human society).

We must not believe that J.B. Say has remedied this defect in the doctrine of Adam Smith by his fiction of 'immaterial goods' or products; he has thus merely somewhat varnished over the folly of its results, but not raised it out of its intrinsic absurdity. The mental (immaterial) producers are merely productive, according to his views, because they are remunerated with values of exchange, and because their attainments have been obtained by sacrificing values of exchange, and not because they produce productive powers. They merely seem to him an accumulated capital. M'Culloch goes still further; he says that man is as much a product of labour as the machine which he produces, and it appears to him that in all economical investigations he must be regarded from this point of view. He thinks that Smith comprehended the correctness of this principle, only he did not deduce the correct conclusion from it. Among other things he draws the conclusion that eating and drinking are productive occupations. Thomas Cooper values a clever American lawyer at 3,000 dollars, which is about three times as much as the value of a strong slave.

The errors and contradictions of the prevailing school to which we have drawn attention, can be easily corrected from the standpoint of *the theory of the productive powers.* Certainly those who fatten pigs or prepare pills are productive, but the instructors of youths and of adults, virtuosos, musicians, physicians, judges, and administrators, are productive in a much higher degree. The former *produce values of exchange,* and the latter *productive powers,* some by enabling the future generation to become producers, others by furthering the morality and religious character of the present generation, a third by ennobling and raising the powers of the human mind, a fourth by preserving the productive powers of his patients, a fifth by rendering human rights and justice secure, a sixth by constituting and protecting public security, a seventh by his art and by the enjoyment which it occasions fitting men the better to produce values of exchange. In the doctrine of mere values, these *producers of the productive powers* can of course only be taken into consideration so far as their services are rewarded by values of exchange; and this manner of regarding their services may in some instances have its practical use, as e.g. in the doctrine of public taxes, inasmuch as these have to be satisfied by values of exchange. But whenever our consideration is given to the nation (as a whole and in its international relations) it is utterly insufficient, and leads to a series of narrow-minded and false views.

The prosperity of a nation is not, as Say believes, greater in the proportion in which it has amassed more wealth (i.e. values of exchange), but in the proportion in which it has more *developed its powers of production.* Although laws and public institutions do not produce immediate values, they nevertheless produce productive powers, and Say is mistaken if he maintains that nations have been enabled to become wealthy under all forms of government, and that by means of laws no wealth can be created. The foreign trade of a nation must not be estimated in the way in which individual merchants judge it, solely and only according to the theory of values (i.e. by regarding merely the gain at any particular moment of some material advantage); the nation is bound to keep steadily in view all these conditions on which its present and future existence, prosperity, and power depend.

The nation must sacrifice and give up a measure of material property in order to gain culture, skill, and powers of united production; it must sacrifice some present advantages in order to insure to itself future ones. If, therefore, a manufacturing power developed in all its branches forms a fundamental condition of all higher advances in civilisation, material prosperity, and political power in every nation (a fact which, we think, we have proved from history); if it be true (as we believe we can prove) that in the present conditions of the world a new unprotected manufacturing power cannot possibly be raised up under free competition with a power which has long since grown in strength and is protected on its own territory; how can anyone possibly undertake to prove by arguments only based on the mere theory of values, that a nation ought to buy its goods like individual merchants, at places where they are to be had the cheapest—that we act foolishly if we manufacture anything at all which can be got cheaper from abroad—that we ought to place the industry of the nation at the mercy of the self-interest of individuals—that protective duties constitute monopolies, which are granted to the individual home manufacturers at the expense of the nation? It is true that protective duties at first increase the price of manufactured goods; but it is just as true, and moreover acknowledged by the prevailing economical school, that in the course of time, by the nation being enabled to build up a completely developed manufacturing power of its own, those goods are produced more cheaply at home than the price at which they can be imported from foreign parts. If, therefore, a sacrifice of *value* is caused by protective duties, it is made good by the gain of a *power of production,* which not only secures to the nation an infinitely greater amount of material goods, but also industrial independence in case of war. Through industrial independence and the internal prosperity derived from it the nation obtains the means for successfully carrying on foreign trade and for extending its mercantile marine; it increases its civilisation, perfects its institutions internally, and strengthens its external power. A nation capable of developing a manufacturing power, if it makes use of the system of protection, thus acts quite in the same spirit as that landed proprietor did who by the sacrifice of some material wealth allowed some of his children to learn a productive trade.

Into what mistakes the prevailing economical school has fallen by judging conditions according to the mere theory of values which ought properly to be judged according to the theory of powers of production, may be seen very clearly by the judgment which J.B. Say passes upon the bounties which foreign countries sometimes offer in order to facilitate exportation; he maintains that *'these are presents made to our nation.'* Now if we suppose that France considers a protective duty of twenty-five per cent sufficient for her not yet perfectly developed manufactures, while England were to grant a bounty on exportation of thirty per cent, what would be the consequence of the 'present' which in this manner the English would make to the French? The French consumers would obtain for a few years the manufactured articles which they needed much cheaper than hitherto, but the French manufactories would be ruined, and millions of men be reduced to beggary or obliged to emigrate, or to devote themselves to agriculture for employment. Under the most favourable circumstances, the present consumers and customers of the French agriculturists would be converted into competitors with the latter, agricultural production would be increased, and the consumption lowered. The necessary consequence would be diminution in value of the products, decline in the value of property, national poverty and national weakness in France. The English 'present' in mere value would be dearly paid for in loss of power; it would seem like the present which the Sultan is wont to make to his pashas by sending them valuable *silken cords.*

Since the time when the Trojans were 'presented' by the Greeks with a wooden horse, the acceptance of 'presents' from other nations has become for the nation which receives them a very questionable transaction. The English have given the

Continent presents of immense value in the form of subsidies, but the Continental nations have paid for them dearly by the loss of power. These subsidies acted like a bounty on exportation in favour of the English, and were detrimental to the German manufactories. If England bound herself to-day to supply the Germans gratuitously for years with all they required in manufactured articles, we could not recommend them to accept such an offer. If the English are enabled through new inventions to produce linen forty per cent cheaper than the Germans can by using the old process, and if in the use of their new process they merely obtain a start of a few years over the Germans, in such a case, were it not for protective duties, one of the most important and oldest branches of Germany's industry will be ruined. It will be as if a limb of the body of the German nation had been lost. And who would be consoled for the loss of an arm by knowing that he had nevertheless bought his shirts forty per cent cheaper?

If the English very often find occasion to offer presents to foreign nations, very different are the forms in which this is done; it is not unfrequently done against their will; always does it behove foreign nations well to consider whether or not the present should be accepted. Through their position as the manufacturing and commercial monopolists of the world, their manufactories from time to time fall into the state which they call 'glut,' and which arises from what they call 'overtrading.' At such periods everybody throws his stock of goods into the steamers. After the elapse of eight days the goods are offered for sale in Hamburg, Berlin, or Frankfort, and after three weeks in New York, at fifty per cent under their real value. The English manufacturers suffer for the moment, but they are saved, and they compensate themselves later on by better prices. The German and American manufacturers receive the blows which were deserved by the English—they are ruined. The English nation merely sees the fire and hears the report of the explosion; the fragments fall down in other countries, and if their inhabitants complain of bloody heads, the intermediate merchants and dealers say, 'The crisis has done it all!' If we consider how often by such crises the whole manufacturing power, the system of credit, nay the agriculture, and generally the whole economical system of the nations who are placed in free competition with England, are shaken to their foundations, and that these nations have afterwards notwithstanding richly to recompense the English manufacturers by higher prices, ought we not then to become very sceptical as to the propriety, of the commercial conditions of nations being regulated according to the mere theory of values and according to cosmopolitical principles? The prevailing economical school has never deemed it expedient to elucidate the causes and effects of such commercial crises.

The great statesmen of all modern nations, almost without exception, have comprehended the great influence of manufactures and manufactories on the wealth, civilisation, and power of nations, and the necessity of protecting them. Edward III comprehended this like Elizabeth; Frederick the Great like Joseph II; Washington like Napoleon. Without entering into the depths of the industry theory, their foreseeing minds comprehended the nature of in its entirety, and appreciated it correctly. It was reserved for the school of physiocrats to regard this nature from another point of view in consequence of a sophistical line of reasoning. Their castle in the air has disappeared; the more modern economical school itself has destroyed it; but even the latter has also not disentangled itself from the original errors, but has merely advanced somewhat farther from them. Since it did not recognise the difference between productive power and mere values of exchange, and did not investigate the former independently of the latter, but subordinated it to the theory of values of exchange, it was impossible for that school to arrive at the perception how greatly the nature of the agricultural productive power differs from the nature of the manufacturing productive power. It does not discern that through the development of a manufacturing industry in an agricultural nation a mass of mental and bodily powers, of natural powers and natural resources, and of instrumental powers too (which latter the prevailing school terms 'capital'), is brought to bear, and brought into use, which had not previously been active, and would never have come into activity but for the formation and development of an internal manufacturing power; it imagines that by the establishment of manufacturing industry these forces must be taken away from agriculture, and transferred to manufacture, whereas the latter to a great extent is a perfectly new and additional power, which, very far indeed from increasing at the expense of the agricultural interest, is often the means of helping that interest to attain a higher degree of prosperity and development.

Chapter XIII: The National Division of Commercial Operations and the Confederation of the National Productive Forces

The school is indebted to its renowned founder for the discovery of that natural law which it calls '*division of labour*,' but neither Adam Smith nor any of his successors have thoroughly investigated its essential nature and character, or followed it out to its most important consequences.

The expression '*division of labour*' is an indefinite one, and must necessarily produce a false or indefinite idea.

It is '*division of labour*' if one savage on one and the same day goes hunting or fishing, cuts down wood, repairs his wigwam, and prepares arrows, nets, and clothes; but it is also '*division of labour*' if (as Adam Smith mentions as an example) ten different persons share in the different occupations connected with the manufacture of a pin: the former is an objective, and the latter a subjective division of labour; the former hinders, the latter furthers production. The essential difference between both is, that in the former instance one person divides his work so as to produce *various* objects, while in the latter *several* persons share in the production of a single object.

Both operations, on the other hand, may be called with equal correctness a *union of labour*; the savage unites various tasks in his person, while in the case of the pin manufacture various persons are united in one work of production in common.

The essential character of the natural law from which the popular school explains such important phenomena in social economy, is evidently not merely a *division of labour*, but *a division of different commercial operations between several individuals*, and at the same time *a confederation or union of various energies, intelligences, and powers on behalf of a common production*. The cause of the productiveness of these operations is not merely that *division*, but essentially this *union*. Adam Smith well perceives this himself when he states, 'The necessaries of life of the lowest members of society are a product of *joint* labour and of the co-operation of a number of individuals.' What a pity that he did not follow out this idea (which he so clearly expresses) of *united labour.*

If we continue to consider the example of the pin manufacture adduced by Adam Smith in illustration of the advantages of division of labour, and seek for the causes of the phenomenon that ten persons united in that manufacture can produce an infinitely larger number of pins than if every one carried on the entire pin manufacture separately, we find that the division of commercial operations without *combination of the productive powers towards one common object* could but little further this production.

In order to create such a result, the different individuals must co-operate bodily as well as mentally, and work together. The one who makes the heads of the pins must be certain of the co-operation of the one who makes the points if he does not want to run the risk of producing pin heads in vain. The labour operations of all must be in the proper proportion to one another, the workmen must live as near to one another as possible, and their co-operation must be insured. Let us suppose e.g. that every one of these ten workmen lives in a different country; how often might their co-operation be interrupted by wars, interruptions of transport, commercial crises, &c.; how greatly would the cost of the product be increased, and consequently the advantage of the division of operation diminished; and would not the separation or secession of a single person from the union, throw all the others out of work?

The popular school, because it has regarded the division of operation alone as the essence of this natural law, has committed the error of applying it merely to the separate manufactory or farm; it has not perceived that the same law extends its action especially over the *whole manufacturing* and *agricultural power,* over *the whole economy of the nation.*

As the pin manufactory only prospers by the confederation of the productive force of the individuals, so does every kind of manufacture prosper only by the confederation of its productive forces with those of all other kinds of manufacture. For the success of a machine manufactory, for instance, it is necessary that the mines and metal works should furnish it with the necessary materials, and that all the hundred different sorts of manufactories which require machines, should buy their products from it. Without machine manufactories, a nation would in time of war be exposed to the danger of losing the greater portion of its manufacturing power.

In like manner the entire manufacturing industry of a State in connection with its agricultural interest, and the latter in connection with the former, will prosper the more the nearer they are placed to one another, and the less they are interrupted in their mutual exchanges with one another. The advantages of their confederation under one and the same political Power in times of war, of national differences, of commercial crises, failure of crops, &c., are not less perceptible than are the advantages of the union of the persons belonging to a pin manufactory under one and the same roof.

Smith affirms that the division of labour is less applicable to agriculture than to manufactures. Smith had in view only the separate manufactory and the separate farm. He has, however, neglected to extend his principle over whole districts and provinces. Nowhere has the division of commercial operations and the confederation of the productive powers greater influence than where every district and every province is in a position to devote itself exclusively, or at least chiefly, to those branches of agricultural production for which they are mostly fitted by nature. In one district corn and hops chiefly thrive, in another vines and fruit, in a third timber production and cattle rearing, &c. If every district is devoted to all these branches of production, it is clear that its labour and its land cannot be nearly so productive as if every separate district were devoted mainly to those branches of production for which it is specially adapted by nature, and as if it exchanged the surplus of its own special products for the surplus produce of those provinces which in the production of other necessaries of life and raw materials possess a natural advantage equally peculiar to themselves. This division of commercial operations, this confederation of the productive forces occupied in agriculture, can only take place in a country which has attained the greatest development of all branches of manufacturing industry; for in such a country only can a great demand for the greatest variety of products exist, or the demand for the surplus of agricultural productions be so certain and considerable that the producer can feel certain of disposing of any quantity of his surplus produce during this or at least during next year at suitable prices; in such a country only can considerable capital be devoted to speculation in the produce of the country and holding stocks of it, or great improvements in transport, such as canals and railway systems, lines of steamers, improved roads, be carried out profitably; and only by means of thoroughly good means of transport can every district or province convey the surplus of its peculiar products to all other provinces, even to the most distant ones, and procure in return supplies of the peculiar products of the latter. Where everybody supplies himself with what he requires, there is but little opportunity for exchange, and therefore no need for costly facilities of transport.

We may notice how the augmentation of the powers of production in consequence of the separation of occupations and the co-operation of the powers of individuals begins in the separate manufactory and extends to the united nation. The manufactory prospers so much the more in proportion as the commercial operations are divided, the more closely the workmen are united, and the more the co-operation of each person is insured for the whole. The productive powers of every separate manufactory are also increased in proportion as the whole manufacturing power of the country is developed in all its branches, and the more intimately it is united with all other branches of industry. The agricultural power of production is so much greater the more intimately a manufacturing power developed in all its branches is united locally, commercially, and politically with agriculture. In proportion as the manufacturing power is thus developed will the division of the commercial operations and the co-operation of the productive powers in agriculture also develop themselves and be raised to the highest stage of perfection. That nation will therefore possess most productive power, and will consequently be the richest, which has cultivated manufacturing industry in all branches within its territory to the highest perfection, and whose territory and agricultural production is large enough to supply its manufacturing population with the largest part of the necessaries of life and raw materials which they require.

Let us now consider the opposite side of this argument. A nation which possesses merely agriculture, and merely the most indispensable industries, is in want of the first and most necessary division of commercial operations among its inhabitants, and of the most important half of its productive powers, indeed it is in want of a useful division of commercial operations even in the separate branches of agriculture itself. A nation thus imperfect will not only be merely half as productive as a perfect nation, but with an equal or even with a much larger territory, with an equal or a much larger population, it will perhaps scarcely obtain a fifth, probably scarcely a tenth, part of that material wealth which a perfect nation is able to procure; and this for the same reason owing to which in a very complicated manufactory ten persons produce not merely ten times more, but perhaps thirty times more, than one person, or a man with one arm cannot merely work half as little, but infinitely less, than a man with two arms. This loss in productive power will be so much greater, the more that the manufacturing operations can be furthered by machinery, and the less that machinery can be applied in agriculture. A part of the productive power which the agricultural nation thus loses, will fall to the lot of that nation which exchanges its manufactured goods for agricultural products. This will, however, be a positive loss only in case the agricultural nation has already reached that stage of civilisation and political development which is necessary for the establishment of a manufacturing power. If it has not yet attained that stage, and still remains in a barbarous or half-civilised state, if its agricultural power of production has not yet developed itself even from the most primitive condition, if by the importation of foreign fabrics and the exportation of raw products its prosperity nevertheless increases considerably from year to year, and its mental and social powers continue to be awakened and increased, if such commerce as it can thus carry on is not interrupted by foreign prohibition of importation of raw products, or by wars, or if the territory of the agricultural nation is situated in a tropical climate, the gain on both sides will then be equal and in conformity with the laws of nature, because under the influence of such an exchange of the native products for foreign fabrics, a nation so situated will attain to civilisation and development of its productive powers more quickly and safely than when it has to develop them entirely out of its resources. If, however, the agricultural nation has already reached the culminating point of its agricultural development, as far as that can be attained by the influence of foreign commerce, or if the manufacturing nation refuses to take the products of the agricultural nation in exchange for its manufactured goods, and if nevertheless, owing to the successful competition of the manufacturing nation in the markets of the agricultural nation, no manufactures can spring up in the latter, in such a case the agricultural productive power of the agricultural nation is exposed to the danger of being crippled.

By *a crippled state of agriculture* we mean that state of things in which, from want of a powerful and steadily developing manufacturing industry, the entire increase of population tends to throw itself on agriculture for employment, consumes all the surplus agricultural production of the country, and as soon as it has considerably increased either has to emigrate or share with the agriculturists already in existence the land immediately at hand, till the landed property of every family has become so small that it produces only the most elementary and necessary portion of that family's requirements of food and raw materials, but no considerable surplus which it might exchange with the manufacturers for the manufactured products which it requires. Under a normal development of the productive powers of the State, the greater part of the increase of population of an agricultural nation (as soon as it has attained a certain degree of culture) should transfer itself to manufacturing industry, and the excess of the agricultural products should partly serve for supplying the manufacturing population with provisions and raw materials, and partly for procuring for the agriculturists the manufactured goods, machines, and utensils which they require for their consumption, and for the increase of their own production.

If this state of things sets in at the proper time, agricultural and industrial productive power will increase reciprocally, and indeed *ad infinitum*. The demand for agricultural products on the part of the industrial population will be so great, that no greater number of labourers will be diverted to agriculture, nor any greater division of the existing land be made, than is necessary to obtain the greatest possible surplus produce from it. In proportion to this surplus produce the population occupied in agriculture will be enabled to consume the products of the workmen employed in manufacturing. A continuous increase of the agricultural surplus produce will occasion a continuous increase of the demand for manufacturing workmen. The excess of the agricultural population will therefore continually find work in the manufactories, and the manufacturing population will at length not only equal the agricultural population in numbers, but will far exceed it. This latter is the condition of England; that which we formerly described is that of part of France and Germany. England was principally brought to this natural division of industrial pursuits between the two great branches of industry, by means of her flocks of sheep and woollen manufactures, which existed there on a large scale much sooner than in other countries. In other countries agriculture was crippled mainly by the influence of feudalism and arbitrary power. The possession of land gave influence and power, merely because by it a certain number of retainers could be maintained which the feudal proprietor could make use of in his feuds. The more vassals he possessed, so many more warriors he could muster. It was besides impossible, owing to the rudeness of those times, for the landed proprietor to consume his income in any other manner than by keeping a large number of servants, and he could not pay these better and attach them to his own person more surely than by giving them a bit of land to cultivate under the condition of rendering him personal service and of paying a smaller tax in produce. Thus the foundation for excessive division of the soil was laid in an artificial manner; and if in the present day the Government seeks by artificial means to alter that system, in so doing it is merely restoring the original state of things.

In order to restrain the continued depreciation of the agricultural power of a nation, and gradually to apply a remedy to that evil in so far as it is the result of previous institutions, no better means exists (apart from the promotion of emigration) than to establish an internal manufacturing power, by which the increase of population may be gradually drawn over to the latter, and a greater demand created for agricultural produce, by which consequently the cultivation of larger estates may be rendered more profitable, and the cultivator induced and encouraged to gain from his land the greatest possible amount of surplus produce.

The productive power of the cultivator and of the labourer in agriculture will always be greater or smaller according to the degree in which the exchange of agricultural produce for manufactures and other products of various kinds can proceed more or less readily. That in this respect the foreign trade of any nation which is but little advanced can prove in the highest degree beneficial, we have shown in another chapter by the example of England. But a nation which has already made considerable advances in civilisation, in possession of capital, and in population, will find the development of a manufacturing power of its own infinitely more beneficial to its agriculture than the most flourishing foreign trade can be without such manufactures, because it thereby secures itself against all fluctuations to which it may be exposed by war, by foreign restrictions on trade, and by commercial crises, because it thereby saves the greatest part of the costs of transport and commercial charges incurred in exporting its own products and in importing manufactured articles, because it derives the greatest advantages from the improvements in transport which are called into existence by its own manufacturing industry, while from the same cause a mass of personal and natural powers hitherto unemployed will be developed, and *especially because the reciprocal exchange between manufacturing power and agricultural power is so much greater, the closer the agriculturist and manufacturer are placed to one another, and the less they are liable to be interrupted in the exchange of their various products by accidents of all kinds.*

In my letters to Mr. Charles J. Ingersoll, President of the Society for Promoting Arts and Industries in Philadelphia, of the year 1828 (entitled, 'Outlines of a New System of Political Economy'), I tried to explain the advantages of a union of the manufacturing power with agriculture in one and the same country, and under one and the same political power, in the following manner. Supposing you did not understand the art of grinding corn, which has certainly been a great art in its time; supposing further that the art of baking bread had remained unknown to you, as (according to Anderson) the real art of salting herrings was still unknown to the English in the seventeenth century; supposing, therefore, that you had to send your corn to England to be ground into flour and baked into bread, how large a quantity of your corn would not the English retain as pay for the grinding and baking; how much of it would the carters, seamen, and merchants consume, who would have to be employed in exporting the corn and importing the bread; and how much would come back into the hands of those who cultivated the corn? There is no doubt that by such a process the foreign trade would receive a considerable impetus, but it is very doubtful whether this intercourse would be specially advantageous to the welfare and independence of the nation. Consider only in case of a war breaking out between your country (the United States) and Great Britain, what would be the situation of those who produced corn for the English mills and bakehouses, and on the other hand the situation of those who had become accustomed to the taste of the English bread. Just as, however, the economical prosperity of the corn-cultivating interest requires that the corn millers should live in its vicinity, so also does the prosperity of the farmer especially require that the manufacturer should live close to him, so also does the prosperity of a flat and open country require that a prosperous and industrial town should exist in its centre, and so does the prosperity of the whole agriculture of a country require that its own manufacturing power should be developed in the highest possible degree.

Let us compare the condition of agriculture in the vicinity of a populous town with its condition when carried on in distant provinces. In the latter case the farmer can only cultivate for sale those products which can bear a long transport, and which cannot be supplied at cheaper prices and in better quality from districts lying nearer to those who purchase them. A larger portion of his profits will be absorbed by the costs of transport. He will find it difficult to procure capital which he may employ usefully on his farm. From want of better examples and means of education he will not readily be led to avail himself of new processes, of better implements, and of new methods of cultivation. The labourer himself, from want of good example, of stimulus to exertion, and to emulation in the exercise of his productive powers, will only develop those powers inefficiently, and will indulge himself in loitering about and in idleness.

On the other hand, in the proximity of the town, the farmer is in a position to use every patch of land for those crops which best suit the character of the soil. He will produce the greatest variety of things to the best advantage. Garden produce, poultry, eggs, milk, butter, fruit, and especially articles which the farmer residing at a distance considers insignificant and secondary things, will bring to the farmer near the town considerable profit. While the distant farmer has to depend mainly on the mere breeding of cattle, the other will make much better profits from fattening them, and will thereby be led to perfect his cultivation of root crops and fodder. He can utilise with much profit a number of things which are of little or no use to the distant farmer; e.g. stone, sand, water power, &c. The most numerous and best machines and implements as well as all means for his instruction, are close at hand. It will be easy for him to accumulate the capital necessary for the improvement of his farm. Landed proprietors and workmen, by the means of recreation which the town affords, the emulation which it excites among them, and the facility of making profits, will be incited to exert all their mental and bodily powers for the improvement of their condition. And precisely the same difference exists between a nation which unites agriculture and manufactures on its own territory, and a nation which can only exchange its own agricultural products for foreign manufactured goods.

The whole social state of a nation will be chiefly determined *by the principle of the variety and division of occupations and the cooperation of its productive powers.* What the pin is in the pin manufactory, that the national well-being is to the large society which we term 'the nation.' *The most important division of occupations in the nation is that between the mental and material ones.* Both are mutually dependent on one another. The more the mental producers succeed in promoting morality, religion, enlightenment, increase of knowledge, extension of liberty and of perfection of political institutions—security of persons and property within the State, and the independence and power of the nation externally—so much greater will be the production of material Wealth. On the other hand, the more goods that the material producers produce, the more will *mental production be capable of being promoted.*

The most important division of occupations, and the most important co-operation of productive powers in material production, is that of agriculture and manufacture. Both depend mutually upon one another, as we have shown.

As in the pin manufactory, so also in the nation does the productiveness of every individual—of every separate branch of production—and finally of the whole nation depend on the exertions of all individuals standing in proper relation to one another. We call this relation the *balance* or the *harmony of the productive powers.* It is possible for a nation to possess too many philosophers, philologers, and literati, and too few skilled artisans, merchants, and seamen. This is the consequence of highly advanced and learned culture which is not supported by a highly advanced manufacturing power and by an extensive internal and external trade; it is as if in a pin manufactory far more pin heads were manufactured than pin points. The surplus pin heads in such a nation are: a mass of useless books, subtle theoretical systems, and learned controversies, through which the mind of the nation is more obscured than cultivated, and is withdrawn from useful occupations; consequently its productive powers are retarded in their progress almost as much as if it possessed too many priests and too few instructors of youth, too many soldiers and too few politicians, too many administrators and too few judges and defenders of justice and right.

A nation which only carries on agriculture, is an individual who in his material production lacks one arm. Commerce is merely the medium of exchange between the agricultural and the manufacturing power, and between their separate branches. A nation which exchanges agricultural products for foreign manufactured goods is an individual with one arm, which is supported by a foreign arm. This support may be useful to it, but not so useful as if it possessed two arms itself, and this because its activity is dependent on the caprice of the foreigner. In possession of a manufacturing power of its own, it can produce as much provisions and raw materials as the home manufacturers can consume; but if dependent upon foreign manufacturers, it can merely produce as much surplus as foreign nations do not care to produce for themselves, and which they are obliged to buy from another country.

As between the different districts of one and the same country, so does the division of labour and the co-operation of the productive powers operate between the various nations of the earth. The former is conducted by internal or national, the latter by international commerce. The international co-operation of productive powers is, however, a very imperfect one, inasmuch as it may be frequently interrupted by wars, political regulations, commercial crises, &c. Although it is the most important in one sense, inasmuch as by it the various nations of the earth are connected with one another, it is nevertheless the least important with regard to the prosperity of any separate nation which is already far advanced in civilisation. This is admitted by writers of the popular school, who declare that the home market of a nation is without comparison more important than its foreign market. It follows from this, that it is the interest of every great nation to make the *national* confederation of its productive powers the main object of its exertions, and to consider their *international* confederation as second in importance to it.

Both *international* and *national division of labour* are chiefly determined by climate and by Nature herself. We cannot produce in every country tea as in China, spices as in Java, cotton as in Louisiana, or corn, wool, fruit, and manufactured goods as in the countries of the temperate zone. It would be folly for a nation to attempt to supply itself by means of national division of labour (i.e. by home production) with articles for the production of which it is not favoured by nature, and which it can procure better and cheaper by means of international division of labour (i.e. through foreign commerce). And just as much does it betoken a want of national intelligence or national industry if a nation does not employ all the natural powers which it possesses in order to satisfy its own internal wants, and then by means of the surplus of its own productions to purchase those necessary articles which nature has forbidden it to produce on its own territory.

The countries of the world most favoured by nature, with regard to both national and international division of labour, are evidently those whose soil brings forth the most common necessaries of life of the best quality and in the largest quantity, and whose climate is most conducive to bodily and mental exertion, and these are *the countries of the temperate zone;* for in these countries the manufacturing power especially prospers, by means of which the nation not merely attains to the highest degree of mental and social development and of political power, but is also enabled to make the countries of tropical climates and of inferior civilisation tributary in a certain measure to itself. The countries of the temperate zone therefore are above all others called upon to bring their own national division of labour to the highest perfection, and to use the international division of labour for their enrichment.

Chapter XIV: Private Economy and National Economy

We have proved historically that the unity of the nation forms the fundamental condition of lasting national prosperity; and we have shown that only where the interest of individuals has been subordinated to those of the nation, and where successive generations have striven for one and the same object, the nations have been brought to harmonious development of their productive powers, and how little private industry can prosper without the united efforts both of the individuals who are living at the time, and of successive generations directed to one common object. We have further tried to prove in the last chapter how the law of union of powers exhibits its beneficial operation in the individual manufactory, and how it acts with equal power on the industry of whole nations. In the present chapter we have now to demonstrate how the popular school has concealed its misunderstanding of the national interests and of the effects of national union of powers, by confounding the principles of private economy with those of national economy.

'What is prudence in the conduct of every private family,' says Adam Smith, 'can scarce be folly in that of a great kingdom.' Every individual in pursuing his own interests necessarily promotes thereby also the interests of the community. It is evident that every individual, inasmuch as he knows his own local circumstances best and pays most attention to his occupation, is far better able to judge than the statesman or legislator how his capital can most profitably be invested. He who would venture to give advice to the people how to invest their capital would not merely take upon himself a useless task, but would also assume to himself an authority which belongs solely to the producer, and which can be entrusted to those persons least of all who consider themselves equal to so difficult a task. Adam Smith concludes from this: 'Restrictions on trade imposed on the behalf of the internal industry of a country, are mere folly; every nation, like every individual, ought to buy articles where they can be procured the cheapest; in order to attain to the highest degree of national prosperity, we have simply to follow the maxim of letting things alone (laisser faire et laisser aller).' Smith and Say compare a nation which seeks to promote its industry by protective duties, to a tailor who wants to make his own boots, and to a bootmaker who would impose a toll on those who enter his door, in order to promote his prosperity. As in all errors of the popular school, so also in this one does Thomas Cooper go to extremes in his book which is directed against the American system of protection. 'Political economy,' he alleges, 'is almost synonymous with the private economy of all individuals; *politics* are no essential ingredient of *political economy;* it is folly to suppose that the community is something quite different from the individuals of whom it is composed. Every individual knows best how to invest his labour and his capital. The wealth of the community is nothing else than the aggregate of the wealth of all its individual members; and if every individual can provide best for himself, that nation must be the richest in which every individual is most left to himself.' The adherents of the American system of protection had opposed themselves to this argument, which had formerly been adduced by importing merchants in favour of free trade; the American navigation laws had greatly increased the carrying trade, the foreign commerce, and fisheries of the United States; and for the mere protection of their mercantile marine millions had been annually expended on their fleet; according to his theory those laws and this expense also would be as reprehensible as protective duties. ' In any case,' exclaims Mr. Cooper, 'no commerce by sea is worth a naval war; the merchants may be left to protect themselves.'

Thus the popular school, which had begun by ignoring the principles of nationality and national interests, finally comes to the point of altogether denying their existence, and of leaving individuals to defend them as they may solely by their own individual powers.

How? Is the wisdom of private economy, also wisdom in national economy? Is it in the nature of individuals to take into consideration the wants of future centuries, as those concern the nature of the nation and the State? Let us consider only the first beginning of an American town; every individual left to himself would care merely for his own wants, or at the most for those of his nearest successors, whereas all individuals united in one community provide for the convenience and the wants of the most distant generations; they subject the present generation for this object to privations and sacrifices which no reasonable person could expect from individuals. Can the individual further take into consideration in promoting his private economy, the defence of the country, public security and the thousand other objects which can only be attained by the aid of the whole community? Does not the State require individuals to limit their private liberty according to what these objects require? Does it not even require that they should sacrifice for these some part of their earnings, of their mental and bodily labour, nay, even their own life? We must first root out, as Cooper does, the very ideas of 'State' and 'nation' before this opinion can be entertained.

No; that may be wisdom in national economy which would be folly in private economy, and vice versâ; and owing to the very simple reason, that a tailor is no nation and a nation no tailor, that one family is something very different from a community of millions of families, that one house is something very different from a large national territory. Nor does the individual merely by understanding his own interests best, and by striving to further them, if left to his own devices, always further the interests of the community. We ask those who occupy the benches of justice, whether they do not frequently have to send individuals to the tread-mill on account of their excess of inventive power, and of their all too great industry. Robbers, thieves, smugglers, and cheats know their own local and personal circumstances and conditions extremely well, and pay the most active attention to their business; but it by no means follows therefrom, that society is in the best condition where such individuals are least restrained in the exercise of their private industry.

In a thousand cases the power of the State is compelled to impose restrictions on private industry. It prevents the shipowner from taking on board slaves on the west coast of Africa, and taking them over to America. It imposes regulations as to the building of steamers and the rules of navigation at sea, in order that passengers and sailors may not be sacrificed to the avarice and caprice of the captains. In England certain rules have recently been enacted with regard to shipbuilding, because an infernal union between assurance companies and shipowners has been brought to light, whereby yearly thousands of human lives and millions in value were sacrificed to the avarice of a few persons. In North America millers are bound under a penalty to pack into each cask not less than 198 lbs. of good flour, and for all market goods market inspectors are appointed, although in no other country is individual liberty more highly prized. Everywhere does the State consider it to be its duty to guard the public against danger and loss, as in the sale of necessaries of life, so also in the sale of medicines, &c.

But the cases which we have mentioned (the school will reply) concern unlawful damages to property and to the person, not the honourable exchange of useful objects, not the harmless and useful industry of private individuals; to impose restrictions on these latter the State has no right whatever. Of course not, so long as they remain harmless and useful; that which, however, is harmless and useful in itself, in general commerce with the world, can become dangerous and injurious in national internal commerce, and vice versâ. In time of peace, and considered from a cosmopolitan point of view, privateering is an injurious profession; in time of war, Governments favour it. The deliberate killing of a human being is a crime in time of peace, in war it becomes a duty. Trading in gunpowder, lead, and arms in time of peace is allowed; but whoever provides the enemy with them in time of war, is punished as a traitor.

For similar reasons the State is not merely justified in imposing, but bound to impose, certain regulations and restrictions on commerce (which is in itself harmless) for the best interests of the nation. By prohibitions and protective duties it does not give directions to individuals how to employ their productive powers and capital (as the popular school sophistically alleges); it does not tell the one, 'You must invest your money in the building of a ship, or in the erection of a manufactory;' or the other, 'You must be a naval captain or a civil engineer;' it leaves it to the judgment of every individual how and where to invest his capital, or to what vocation he will devote himself. It merely says, 'It is to the advantage of our nation that we manufacture these or the other goods ourselves; but as by free competition with foreign countries we can never obtain possession of this advantage, we have imposed restrictions on that competition, so far as in our opinion is necessary, to give those among us who invest their capital in these new branches of industry, and those who devote their bodily and mental powers to them, the requisite guarantees that they shall not lose their capital and shall not miss their vocation in life; and further to stimulate foreigners to come over to our side with their productive powers. In this manner, it does not in the least degree restrain private industry; on the contrary, it secures to the personal, natural, and moneyed powers of the nation a greater and wider field of activity. It does not thereby do something which its individual citizens could understand better and do better than it; on the contrary it does something which the individuals, even if they understood it, would not be able to do for themselves.

The allegation of the school, that the system of protection occasions unjust and anti-economical encroachments by the power of the State against the employment of the capital and industry of private individuals, appears in the least favourable light if we consider that it is the *foreign* commercial regulations which allow such encroachments on *our* private industry to take place, and that only by the aid of the system of protection are we enabled to counteract those injurious operations of the foreign commercial policy. If the English shut out our corn from their markets, what else are they doing than compelling our agriculturists to grow so much less corn than they would have sent out to England under systems of free importation? If they put such heavy duties on our wool, our wines, or our timber, that our export trade to England wholly or in great measure ceases, what else is thereby effected than that the power of the English nation restricts proportionately our branches of production? In these cases a direction is evidently given by *foreign legislation* to *our* capital and *our* personal productive powers, which but for the regulations made by it they would scarcely have followed. It follows from this, that were we to disown giving, by means of *our* own legislation, a direction to our own national industry in accordance with our own national interests, we could not prevent foreign nations from regulating our national industry after a fashion which corresponds with their own real or presumed advantage, and which in any case operates disadvantageously to the development of our own productive powers. But can it possibly be wiser on our part, and more to the advantage of those who nationally belong to us, for us to allow our private industry to be regulated by a foreign national Legislature, in accordance with foreign national interests, rather than regulate it by means of our own Legislature and in accordance with our own interests? Does the German or American agriculturist feel himself less restricted if he has to study every year the English Acts of Parliament, in order to ascertain whether that body deems it advantageous to encourage or to impose restrictions on his production of corn or wool, than if his own Legislature imposes certain restrictions on him in respect of foreign manufactured goods, but at the same time insures him a market for all his products, of which he can never again be deprived by foreign legislation?

If the school maintains that protective duties secure to the home manufacturers a monopoly to the disadvantage of the home consumers, in so doing it makes use of a weak argument. For as every individual in the nation is free to share in the profits of the home market which is thus secured to native industry, this is in no respect a private monopoly, but a privilege, secured to all those who belong to our nation, as against those who nationally belong to foreign nations, and which is the more righteous and just inasmuch as those who nationally belong to foreign nations possess themselves the very same monopoly, and those who belong to us are merely thereby put on the same footing with them. It is neither a privilege to the exclusive advantage of the producers, nor to the exclusive disadvantage of the consumers; for if the producers at first obtain higher prices, they run great risks, and have to contend against those considerable losses and sacrifices which are always connected with all beginnings in manufacturing industry. But the consumers have ample security that these extraordinary profits shall not reach unreasonable limits, or become perpetual, by means of the competition at home which follows later on, and which, as a rule, always lowers prices further than the level at which they had steadily ranged under the free competition of the foreigner. If the agriculturists, who are the most important consumers to the manufacturers, must also pay higher prices, this disadvantage will be amply repaid to them by increased demands for agricultural products, and by increased prices obtained for the latter.

It is a further sophism, arrived at by confounding the theory of mere values with that of the powers of production, when the popular school infers from the doctrine, '*that the wealth of the nation is merely the aggregate of the wealth of all individuals in it, and that the private interest of every individual is better able than all State regulations to incite to production and accumulation of wealth,*' the conclusion that the national industry would prosper best if only every individual were left undisturbed in the occupation of accumulating wealth. That doctrine can be conceded without the conclusion resulting from it at which the school desires thus to arrive; for the point in question is not (as we have shown in a previous chapter) that of immediately increasing by commercial restrictions the amount of *the values of exchange* in the nation, but of increasing *the amount of its productive powers*. But that the aggregate of the productive powers of the nation is not synonymous with the aggregate of the productive powers of all individuals, each considered separately—that the total amount of these powers depends chiefly on social and Political conditions, but especially on the degree in which the nation has rendered effectual the division of labour and the confederation of the powers of production within itself—we believe we have sufficiently demonstrated in the preceding chapters.

This system everywhere takes into its consideration only individuals who are in free unrestrained intercourse among themselves, and who are contented if we leave everyone to pursue his own private interests according to his own private natural inclination. This is evidently not a system of national economy, but a system of the private economy of the human race, as that would constitute itself were there no interference on the part of any Government, were there no wars, no hostile foreign tariff restrictions. Nowhere do the advocates of that system care to point out by what means those nations which are now prosperous have raised themselves to that stage of power and prosperity which we see them maintain, and from what causes others have lost that degree of prosperity and power which they formerly maintained. We can only learn from it how in private industry, natural ability, labour and capital, are combined in order to bring into exchange valuable products, and in what manner these latter are distributed among the human race and consumed by it. But what means are to be adopted in order to bring the natural powers belonging to any individual nation into activity and value, to raise a poor and weak nation to prosperity and power, cannot be gathered from it, because the school totally ignoring politics, ignores the special conditions of the nation, and concerns itself merely about the prosperity of the whole human race. Wherever international commerce is in question, the native individual is throughout simply pitted against the foreign individual; examples from the private dealings of separate merchants are throughout the only ones adduced—goods are spoken of in general terms (without considering whether the question is one of raw products or of manufactured articles)—in order to prove that it is equally for the benefit of the nation whether its exports and imports consist of money, of raw materials, or of manufactured goods, and whether or not they balance one another. If we, for example, terrified at the commercial crises which prevail in the United States of North America like native epidemics, consult this theory as to the means of averting or diminishing them, it leaves us utterly without comfort or instruction; nay, it is indeed impossible for us to investigate these phenomena scientifically, because, under the penalty of being taken for muddleheads and ignoramuses, we must not even utter the term '*balance of trade*,' while this term is, notwithstanding, made use of in all legislative assemblies, in all bureaux of administration, on every exchange. For the sake of the welfare of humanity, the belief is inculcated on us that exports always balance themselves spontaneously by imports; notwithstanding that we read in public accounts how the Bank of England comes to the assistance of the nature of things; notwithstanding that corn laws exist, which make it somewhat difficult for the agriculturist of those countries which deal with England to pay with his own produce for the manufactured goods which he consumes.

The school recognises no distinction between nations which have attained a higher degree of economical development, and those which occupy a lower stage. Everywhere it seeks to exclude the action of the power of the State; everywhere, according to it, will the individual be so much better able to produce, the less the power of the State concerns itself for him. In fact, according to this doctrine savage nations ought to be the most productive and wealthy of the earth, for nowhere is the individual left more to himself than in the savage state, nowhere is the action of the power of the State less perceptible.

Statistics and history, however, teach, on the contrary, that the necessity for the intervention of legislative power and administration is everywhere more apparent, the further the economy of the nation is developed. As individual liberty is in general a good thing so long only as it does not run counter to the interests of society, so is it reasonable to hold that private industry can only lay claim to unrestricted action so long as the latter consists with the well-being of the nation. But whenever the enterprise and activity of individuals does not suffice for this purpose, or in any case where these might become injurious to the nation, there does private industry rightly require support from the whole power of the nation, there ought it for the sake of its own interests to submit to legal restrictions.

If the school represents the free competition of all producers as the most effectual means for promoting the prosperity of the human race, it is quite right from the point of view which it assumes. On the hypothesis of a universal union, every restriction on the honest exchange of goods between various countries seems unreasonable and injurious. But so long as other nations Subordinate the interests of the human race as a whole to their national interests, it is folly to speak of free competition among the individuals of various nations. The arguments of the school in favour of free competition are thus only applicable to the exchange between those who belong to one and the same nation. Every great nation, therefore, must endeavour to form an aggregate within itself, which will enter into commercial intercourse with other similar aggregates so far only as that intercourse is suitable to the interests of its own special community. These interests of the community are, however, infinitely different from the private interests of all the separate individuals of the nation, if each individual is to be regarded as existing for himself alone and not in the character of a member of the

national community, if we regard (as Smith and Say do) individuals as mere producers and consumers, not citizens of states or members of nations; for as such, mere
individuals do not concern themselves for the prosperity of future generations—they
deem it foolish (as Mr. Cooper really demonstrates to us) to make certain and present
sacrifices in order to endeavour to obtain a benefit which is as yet uncertain and lying
in the vast field of the future (if even it possess any value at all); they care but little
for the continuance of the nation—they would expose the ships of their merchants
to become the prey of every bold pirate—they trouble themselves but little about the
power, the honour, or the glory of the nation, at the most they can persuade themselves to make some material sacrifices for the education of their children, and to give
them the opportunity of learning a trade, provided always that after the lapse of a few
years the learners are placed in a position to earn their own bread.

Indeed, according to the prevailing theory, so analogous is national economy to
private economy that J.B. Say, where (exceptionally) he allows that internal industry
may be protected by the State, makes it a condition of so doing, that every probability must exist that after the lapse of a *few years* it will attain independence, just as a
shoemaker's apprentice is allowed only a few years' time in order to perfect himself
so far in his trade as to do without parental assistance.

2

The Liberal Paradigm

Economic liberals today build on **Adam Smith's** notions of the invisible hand, self-regulating markets, and the pursuit of self-interest leading efficiently to the collective interest, and they also echo his prescriptions for the role of government in relation to economic activity and society more broadly. The word *liberal* is used in this reader to refer to free market or economic liberals. In this sense, it refers to a philosophy with primarily European origins, as represented in the work of **Friedrich Hayek**.[1] Hayek was a leading twentieth-century pro-free market theorist who built on the traditions of the Austrian School of economics, particularly on the teachings of his mentor Ludwig von Mises. Many of today's most famous liberals hail from what is known as "the Chicago School of economics," named after the University of Chicago where a number of them were trained and carry out research. **Milton Friedman** is a paragon of the Chicago School[2]—he stands out as a leading liberal voice in both the scholarly and policy debates on markets and government in the latter part of the twentieth century.

Friedrich Hayek was born in Vienna, Austria, in 1899. He was trained at the University of Vienna, spent the early part of his intellectual career at the London School of Economics, and moved finally to the University of Chicago's Committee on Social Thought. His interests spanned from economics and political philosophy to psychology and cognitive science, but the body of work for which he is renowned mounts a defense of liberal democracy and capitalism against the socialist and collectivist thought that was influential in Europe in the mid-twentieth century. In the 1930s, although Hayek enjoyed a reputation as a leading economic theorist, his views were not always popular at the time, because mainstream European economic thought in the 1930s through the early 1960s was dominated by the Keynesian approach.[3] In 1974, however, Hayek shared the Nobel Prize in Economics, which prompted a revival of interest in his economic theory and the Austrian School.

This renewed intellectual focus coincided with a global economic environment in which Keynesian government policy seemed no longer able to manage inflation and unemployment. The Reagan–Thatcher revolution in the 1980s drew heavily from the liberal perspective in its emphasis on getting government out of the economy. By the time of Hayek's death in 1992, he was considered the father of neoliberalism and was an inspiration for the Reagan–Thatcher pursuit of deregulation and privatization.[4] Margaret Thatcher, the Conservative British prime minister (1979–90), was a self-avowed disciple of Hayek; her economic philosophy, known as "Thatcherism," drew heavily from Hayek and his followers.[5] On the other side of the Atlantic, Hayek also exerted an influence on some advisors of U.S. president Ronald Reagan (1980–88), including Milton Friedman. The latter played a central role in the Reagan Administration as a leading advocate of the monetarist school of economic thought[6] and a limited government role in the economy, two cornerstones of "Reaganomics." Friedman also won a Nobel Prize in Economics (1976) and was central in building the intellectual community that came to be known as the Chicago School.

The selections presented here demonstrate how modern-day liberals are descendants of Adam Smith. Friedrich Hayek's *Road to Serfdom* (1944) is animated by the politics of the time, as he argues that all forms of collectivism—be they Hitler's National Socialism or Stalin's Communism—lead inevitably to tyranny by the faulty logic of central economic planning. Yet Hayek reminds the reader that his view is not a dogmatic laissez-faire standpoint. Building on Smith's self-interest principle, Hayek argues that a competitive framework, underpinned by legal rules, in which individuals can make rational decisions is superior to a planned system. He emphasizes one of the tenets of neoclassical economic theory in maintaining that competition spontaneously and efficiently coordinates economic activity through price signals. Hayek argues that mixing competition and planning, which was in vogue in postwar Europe, is a problematic policy because it relies on contradictory principles. He believes that the "great liberal principle" is the rule of law, which safeguards individual equality before government by preventing government from acting in an ad hoc manner. Hayek agrees with Smith in arguing that the core role of the state must be to set up and administer the legal framework, one that facilitates competition, and that a second crucial role for the state is to provide public goods where the contribution to social welfare is large.

Milton Friedman is a classic liberal in terms of his view that the government's role in economic activity, even in guiding the economy, should be extremely limited. His views on this are more strident even than Smith's and Hayek's. He underlines the importance of the price system as a coordination mechanism, again demonstrating the liberal link with neoclassical economics. In his view, the government is a major source of price distortion, thwarting individuals as they attempt to play their economic roles as producers, consumers, owners, and workers, and thus government failure is as much of a problem as the "market failure" that it seeks to correct. He is even cautious on antitrust, backing away from one of Smith's core roles for government. Friedman elevates the primacy of the self-interest principle introduced by Smith; he argues that economic freedom is in fact a necessary condition for political freedom, that individual needs are primary and the individual is the ultimate entity, and that government must exist only to serve the individual.

The debate about the appropriate role of government in the economy continues to be one of the defining fault lines of contemporary political discourse around the world. The liberal viewpoint will continue to be represented throughout the reader, particularly by **Arthur Seldon** in the debate about market reform in rich democracies and by **Deepak Lal** on market development in poor countries. In contrast, whereas Adam Smith and subsequent economic liberals argue that the state has a few circumscribed roles to play in the economy, the market-institutional perspective illuminated through other selections in the reader maintains that the state is more actively engaged in building and sustaining markets.

Notes

1. Beginning in the late nineteenth century, social liberalism in the United States took on a different view of the desirability of state facilitation of preferred functions of the market, a viewpoint covered later in this reader by **Charles Lindblom**.
2. Some of Friedman's fellow Chicago School theorists include George Stigler, Gary Becker, and Robert Lucas.
3. Named after John Maynard Keynes, a British economist, the Keynesian perspective advocated, in direct opposition to laissez-faire economics, an interventionist government approach to the economy to manage macroeconomic phenomena such as unemployment, recession, and inflation. Keynesianism also supported a mixed economy, where both the state and private sectors had important, complementary roles to play in economic activity. This was a very popular school of thought and practice in the Great Depression and on into the postwar period in both Europe and the United States.
4. Fred Block, "Introduction," in *The Great Transformation: The Political and Economic Origins of Our Time*, ed. Karl Polanyi (Boston: Beacon Press, 2001), xx.
5. Shortly after becoming party leader, Thatcher wielded a copy of Hayek's *The Constitution of Liberty* to announce to other party members, "This is what we believe."
6. Monetarism, largely formulated and subsequently influenced by Milton Friedman, maintains that inflation should be controlled by the government's management of the supply of money in the national economy. This is a direct rejection of Keynesian, "demand-side," fiscal management of the economy. It is interesting that Friedman began his career as a Keynes devotee but later reversed his views.

Friedrich A. Hayek,
The Road to Serfdom (1944)*

III: Individualism and Collectivism

The socialists believe in two things which are absolutely different and perhaps even contradictory: freedom and organization.

—Élie Halévy.

Before we can progress with our main problem, an obstacle has yet to be surmounted. A confusion largely responsible for the way in which we are drifting into things which nobody wants must cleared be up. This confusion concerns nothing less than the concept of socialism itself. It may mean, and is often used to describe, merely the ideals of social justice, greater equality, and security, which are the ultimate aims of socialism. But it means also the particular method by which most socialists hope to attain these ends and which many competent people regard as the only methods by which they can be fully and quickly attained. In this sense socialism means the abolition of private enterprise, of private ownership of the means of production, and the creation of a system of "planned economy" in which the entrepreneur working for profit is replaced by a central planning body.

There are many people who call themselves socialists, although they care only about the first, who fervently believe in those ultimate aims of socialism but neither care nor understand how they can be achieved, and who are merely certain that they must be achieved, whatever the cost. But to nearly all those to whom socialism is not merely a hope but an object of practical politics, the characteristic methods of modern socialism are as essential as the ends themselves. Many people, on the other hand, who value the ultimate ends of socialism no less than the socialists refuse to support socialism because of the dangers to other values they see in the methods proposed by the socialists. The dispute about socialism has thus become largely a dispute about means and not about ends—although the question whether the different ends of socialism can be simultaneously achieved is also involved.

This would be enough to create confusion. And the confusion has been further increased by the common practice of denying that those who repudiate the means value the ends. But this is not all. The situation is still more complicated by the fact that the same means, the "economic planning" which is the prime instrument of socialist reform, can be used for many other purposes. We must centrally direct economic activity if we want to make the distribution of income conform to current ideas of social justice. "Planning," therefore, is wanted by all those who demand that "production for use" be substituted for production for profit. But such planning is no less indispensable if the distribution of incomes is to be regulated in a way which to us appears to be the opposite of just. Whether we should wish that more of the good things of this world should go to some racial élite, the Nordic men, or the members of a party or an aristocracy, the methods which we shall have to employ are the same as those which could insure an equalitarian distribution.

It may, perhaps, seem unfair to use the term "socialism" to describe its methods rather than its aims, to use for a particular method a term which for many people stands for an ultimate ideal. It is probably preferable to describe the methods which can be used for a great variety of ends as collectivism and to regard socialism as a species of that genus. Yet, although to most socialists only one species of collectivism will represent true socialism, it must always be remembered that socialism is a species of collectivism and that therefore everything which is true of collectivism as such must apply also to socialism. Nearly all the points which are disputed between socialists and liberals concern the methods common to all forms of collectivism and not the particular ends for which socialists want to use them; and all the consequences with which we shall be concerned in this book follow from the methods of collectivism irrespective of the ends for which they are used. It must also not be forgotten that socialism is not only by far the most important species of collectivism or "planning" but that it is socialism which has persuaded liberal-minded people to submit once more to that regimentation of economic life which they had overthrown because, in the words of Adam Smith, it puts governments in a position where "to support themselves they are obliged to be oppressive and tyrannical."[1]

The difficulties caused by the ambiguities of the common political terms are not yet over if we agree to use the term "collectivism" so as to include all types of "planned economy," whatever the end of planning. The meaning of this term becomes somewhat more definite if we make it clear that we mean that sort of planning which is necessary to realize any given distributive ideals. But, as the idea of central economic planning owes its appeal largely to this very vagueness of its meaning, it is essential that we should agree on its precise sense before we discuss its consequences.

"Planning" owes its popularity largely to the fact that everybody desires, of course, that we should handle our common problems as rationally as possible and that, in so doing, we should use as much foresight as we can command. In this sense everybody who is not a complete fatalist is a planner, every political act is (or ought to be) an act of planning, and there can be differences only between good and bad, between wise and foresighted and foolish and shortsighted planning. An economist, whose whole task is the study of how men actually do and how they might plan their affairs, is the last person who could object to planning in this general sense. But it is not in this sense that our enthusiasts for a planned society now employ this term, nor merely in this sense that we must plan if we want the distribution of income or wealth to conform to some particular standard. According to the modern planners, and for their purposes, it is not sufficient to design the most rational permanent framework within which the various activities would be conducted by different persons according to their individual plans. This liberal plan, according to them, is no plan—and it is, indeed, not a plan designed to satisfy particular views about who should have what. What our planners demand is a central direction of all economic activity according to a single plan, laying down how the resources of society should be "consciously directed" to serve particular ends in a definite way.

The dispute between the modern planners and their opponents is, therefore, *not* a dispute on whether we ought to choose intelligently between the various possible organizations of society; it is not a dispute on whether we ought to employ foresight and systematic thinking in planning our common affairs. It is a dispute about what is the best way of so doing. The question is whether for this purpose it is better that the holder of coercive power should confine himself in general to creating conditions under which the knowledge and initiative of individuals are given the best scope so that *they* can plan most successfully; or whether a rational utilization of our resources requires *central* direction and organization of all our activities according to some consciously constructed "blueprint." The socialists of all parties have appropriated the term "planning" for planning of the latter type, and it is now generally accepted in this sense. But though this is meant to suggest that this is the only rational way of handling our affairs, it does not, of course, prove this. It remains the point on which the planners and the liberals disagree.

It is important not to confuse opposition against this kind of planning with a dogmatic laissez faire attitude. The liberal argument is in favor of making the best possible use of the forces of competition as a means of co-ordinating human efforts, not an argument for leaving things just as they are. It is based on the conviction that, where effective competition can be created, it is a better way of guiding individual efforts than any other. It does not deny, but even emphasizes, that, in order that competition should work beneficially, a carefully thought-out legal framework is required and that neither the existing nor the past legal rules are free from grave defects. Nor does it deny that, where it is impossible to create the conditions necessary to make competition effective, we must resort to other methods of guiding economic activity. Economic liberalism is opposed, however, to competition's being supplanted by inferior methods of co-ordinating individual efforts. And it regards competition as superior not only because it is in most circumstances the most efficient method known but even more because it is the only method by which our activities can be adjusted to each other without coercive or arbitrary intervention of authority. Indeed, one of the main arguments in favor of competition is that it dispenses with the need for "conscious social control" and that it gives the individuals a chance to decide whether the prospects of a particular occupation are sufficient to compensate for the disadvantages and risks connected with it.

The successful use of competition as the principle of social organization precludes certain types of coercive interference with economic life, but it admits of others which sometimes may very considerably assist its work and even requires certain kinds of government action. But there is good reason why the negative requirements, the points where coercion must not be used, have been particularly stressed. It is necessary in the first instance that the parties in the market should be free to sell and buy at any price at which they can find a partner to the transaction and that anybody should be free to produce, sell, and buy anything that may be produced or sold at all. And it is essential that the entry into the different trades should be open to all on equal terms and that the law should not tolerate any attempts by individuals or groups to restrict this entry by open or concealed force. Any attempt to control prices or quantities of particular commodities deprives competition of its power of bringing about an effective co-ordination of individual efforts, because price changes then cease to register all the relevant changes in circumstances and no longer provide a reliable guide for the individual's actions.

This is not necessarily true, however, of measures merely restricting the allowed methods of production, so long as these restrictions affect all potential producers equally and are not used as an indirect way of controlling prices and quantities. Though all such controls of the methods or production impose extra costs (i.e., make it necessary to use more resources to produce a given output), they may be well worth while. To prohibit the use of certain poisonous substances or to require special precautions in their use, to limit working hours or to require certain sanitary arrangements, is fully compatible with the preservation of competition. The only question here is whether in the particular instance the advantages gained are greater than the social costs which they impose. Nor is the preservation of competition incompatible with an extensive system of social services—so long as the organization of these services is not designed in such a way as to make competition ineffective over wide fields.

It is regrettable, though not difficult to explain, that in the past much less attention has been given to the positive requirements of a successful working of the competitive system than to these negative points. The functioning of a competition not only requires adequate organization of certain institutions like money, markets, and channels of information—some of which can never be adequately provided by private enterprise—but it depends, above all, on the existence of an appropriate legal system, a legal system designed both to preserve competition and to make it operate as beneficially as possible. It is by no means sufficient that the law should recognize the principle of private property and freedom of contract; much depends on the precise definition of the right of property as applied to different things. The systematic study of the forms of legal institutions which will make the competitive system work efficiently has been sadly neglected; and strong arguments can be advanced that serious shortcomings here, particularly with regard to the law of corporations and of patents, not only have made competition work much less effectively than it might have done but have even led to the destruction of competition in many spheres.

There are, finally, undoubted fields where no legal arrangements can create the main condition on which the usefulness of the system of competition and private property depends: namely, that the owner benefits from all the useful services rendered by his property and suffers for all the damages caused to others by its use. Where, for example, it is impracticable to make the enjoyment of certain services dependent on the payment of a price, competition will not produce the services; and the price system becomes similarly ineffective when the damage caused to others by certain uses of property cannot be effectively charged to the owner of that property. In all these instances there is a divergence between the items which enter into private calculation and those which affect social welfare; and, whenever this divergence becomes important, some method other than competition may have to be found to supply the services in question. Thus neither the provision of signposts on the roads nor, in most circumstances, that of the roads themselves can be paid for by every individual user. Nor can certain harmful effects of deforestation, of some methods of farming, or of the smoke and noise of factories be confined to the owner of the property in question or to those who are willing to submit to the damage for an agreed compensation. In such instances we must find some substitute for the regulation by the price mechanism. But the fact that we have to resort to the substitution of direct regulation by authority where the conditions for the proper working of competition cannot be created does not prove that we should suppress competition where it can be made to function.

To create conditions in which competition will be as effective as possible, to supplement it where it cannot be made effective, to provide the services which, in the words of Adam Smith, "though they may be in the highest degree advantageous to a great society, are, however, of such a nature, that the profit could never repay the expense to any individual or small number of individuals"—these tasks provide, indeed, a wide and unquestioned field for state activity. In no system that could be rationally defended would the state just do nothing. An effective competitive system needs an intelligently designed and continuously adjusted legal framework as much as any other. Even the most essential prerequisite of its proper functioning, the prevention of fraud and deception (including exploitation of ignorance), provides a great and by no means yet fully accomplished object of legislative activity.

The task of creating a suitable framework for the beneficial working of competition had, however, not yet been carried very far when states everywhere turned from it to that of supplanting competition by a different and irreconcilable principle. The question was no longer one of making competition work and of supplementing it but of displacing it altogether. It is important to be quite clear about this: the modern movement for planning is a movement against competition as such, a new flag under which all the old enemies of competition have rallied. And although all sorts of interests are now trying to reestablish under this flag privileges which the liberal era swept away, it is socialist propaganda for planning which has restored to respectability among liberal-minded people opposition to competition and which has effectively lulled the healthy suspicion which any attempt to smother competition used to arouse.[2] What in effect unites the socialists of the Left and the Right is this common hostility to competition and their common desire to replace it by a directed economy. Though the terms "capitalism" and "socialism" are still generally used to describe the past and the future forms of society, they conceal rather than elucidate the nature of the transition through which we are passing.

Yet, though all the changes we are observing tend in the direction of a comprehensive central direction of economic activity, the universal struggle against competition promises to produce in the first instance something in many respects even worse, a state of affairs which can satisfy neither planners nor liberals: a sort of syndicalist or "corporative" organization of industry, in which competition is more or less suppressed but planning is left in the hands of the independent monopolies of the separate industries. This is the inevitable first result of a situation in which the people are united in their hostility to competition but agree on little else. By destroying competition in industry after industry, this policy puts the consumer at the mercy of the joint monopolist action of capitalists and workers in the best organized industries. Yet, although this is a state of affairs which in wide fields has already existed for some time, and although much of the muddled (and most of the interested) agitation for planning aims at it, it is not a state which is likely to persist or can be rationally justified. Such independent planning by industrial monopolies would, in fact, produce effects opposite to those at which the argument for planning aims. Once this stage is reached, the only alternative to a return to competition is the control of the monopolies by the state—a control which, if it is to be made effective, must become progressively more complete and more detailed. It is this stage we are rapidly approaching. When, shortly before the war, a weekly magazine pointed out that there were many signs that British leaders, at least, were growing accustomed to thinking in terms of national development by controlled monopolies, this was probably a true estimate of the position as it then existed. Since then this process has been greatly accelerated by the war, and its grave defects and dangers will become increasingly obvious as time goes on.

The idea of complete centralization of the direction of economic activity still appalls most people, not only because of the stupendous difficulty of the task, but even more because of the horror inspired by the idea of everything being directed from a single center. If we are, nevertheless, rapidly moving toward such a state, this is largely because most people still believe that it is must be possible to find some middle way between "atomistic" competition and central direction. Nothing, indeed, seems at first more plausible, or is more likely to appeal to reasonable people, than the idea that our goal must be neither the extreme decentralization of free competition nor the complete centralization of a single plan but some judicious mixture of the two methods. Yet mere common sense proves a treacherous guide in this field. Although competition can bear some admixture of regulation, it cannot be combined with planning to any extent we like without ceasing to operate as an effective guide to production. Nor is "planning" a medicine which, taken in small doses, can produce the effects for which one might hope from its thoroughgoing application. Both competition and central direction become poor and inefficient tools if they are incomplete; they are alternative principles used to solve the same problem, and a mixture of the two means that neither will really work and that the result will be worse than if either system had been consistently relied upon. Or, to express it differently, planning and competition can be combined only by planning for competition but not by planning against competition.

It is of the utmost importance to the argument of this book for the reader to keep in mind that the planning against which all our criticism is directed is solely the planning against competition—the planning which is to be substituted for competition. This is the more important, as we cannot, within the scope of this book, enter into a discussion of the very necessary planning which is required to make competition as effective and beneficial as possible. But as in current usage "planning" has become almost synonymous with the former kind of planning, it will sometimes be inevitable for the sake of brevity to refer to it simply as planning, even though this means leaving to our opponents a very good word meriting a better fate.

VI: Planning and the Rule of Law

Recent studies in the sociology of law once more confirm that the fundamental principle of formal law by which every case must be judged according to general rational precepts, which have as few exceptions as possible and are based on logical subsumptions, obtains only for the liberal competitive phase of capitalism.

—Karl Mannheim

Nothing distinguishes more clearly conditions in a free country from those in a country under arbitrary government than the observance in the former of the great principles known as the Rule of Law. Stripped of all technicalities, this means that government in all its actions is bound by rules fixed and announced beforehand—rules which make it possible to foresee with fair certainty how the authority will use its coercive powers in given circumstances and to plan one's individual affairs on the basis of this knowledge.[3] Though this ideal can never be perfectly achieved, since legislators as well as those to whom the administration of the law is intrusted are fallible men, the essential point, that the discretion left to the executive organs wielding coercive power should be reduced as much as possible, is clear enough. While every law restricts individual freedom to some extent by altering the means which people may use in the pursuit of their aims, under the Rule of Law the government is prevented from stultifying individual efforts by *ad hoc* action. Within the known rules of the game the individual is free to pursue his personal ends and desires, certain that the powers of government will not be used deliberately to frustrate his efforts.

The distinction we have drawn before between the creation of a permanent framework of laws within which the productive activity is guided by individual decisions and the direction of economic activity by a central authority is thus really a particular case of the more general distinction between the Rule of Law and arbitrary government. Under the first the government confines itself to fixing rules determining the conditions under which the available resources may be used, leaving to the individuals the decision for what ends they are to be used. Under the second the government directs the use of the means of production to particular ends. The first type of rules can be made in advance, in the shape of *formal rules* which do not aim at the wants and needs of particular people. They are intended to be merely instrumental in the pursuit of people's various individual ends. And they are, or ought to be, intended for such long periods that it is impossible to know whether they will assist particular people more than others. They could almost be described as a kind of instrument of production, helping people to predict the behavior of those with whom they must collaborate, rather than as efforts toward the satisfaction of particular needs.

Economic planning of the collectivist kind necessarily involves the very opposite of this. The planning authority cannot confine itself to providing opportunities for unknown people to make whatever use of them they like. It cannot tie itself down in advance to general and formal rules which prevent arbitrariness. It must provide for the actual needs of people as they arise and then choose deliberately between them. It must constantly decide questions which cannot be answered by formal principles only, and, in making these decisions, it must set up distinctions of merit between the needs of different people. When the government has to decide how many pigs are to be raised or how many busses are to be run, which coal mines are to operate, or at what prices shoes are to be sold, these decisions cannot be deduced from formal principles or settled for long periods in advance. They depend inevitably on the circumstances of the moment, and, in making such decisions, it will always be necessary to balance one against the other the interests of various persons and groups. In the end somebody's views will have to decide whose interests are more important; and these views must become part of the law of the land, a new distinction of rank which the coercive apparatus of government imposes upon the people.

The distinction we have just used between formal law or justice and substantive rules is very important and at the same time most difficult to draw precisely in practice. Yet the general principle involved is simple enough. The difference between the two kinds of rules is the same as that between laying down a Rule of the Road, as in the Highway Code, and ordering people where to go; or, better still, between providing signposts and commanding people which road to take. The formal rules tell people in advance what action the state will take in certain types of situation, defined in general terms, without reference to time and place or particular people. They refer to typical situations into which anyone may get and in which the existence of such rules will be useful for a great variety of individual purposes. The knowledge that in such situations the state will act in a definite way, or require people to behave in a certain manner, is provided as a means for people to use in making their own plans. Formal rules are thus merely instrumental in the sense that they are expected to be useful to yet unknown people, for purposes for which these people will decide to use for them, and in circumstances which cannot be foreseen in detail. In fact, that we do *not* know their concrete effect, that we do *not* know what particular ends these rules will further, or which particular people they will assist, that they are merely given the form most likely on the whole to benefit all the people affected by them, is the most important criterion of formal rules in the sense in which we here use this term. They do not involve a choice between particular ends or particular people, because we just cannot know beforehand by whom and in what way they will be used.

In our age, with its passion for conscious control of everything, it may appear paradoxical to claim as a virtue that under one system we shall know less about the particular effect of the measures the state takes than would be true under most other systems and that a method of social control should be deemed superior because of our ignorance of its precise results. Yet this consideration is in fact the rationale of the great liberal principle of the Rule of Law. And the apparent paradox dissolves rapidly when we follow the argument a little further.

This argument is twofold; the first is economic and can here only briefly be stated. The state should confine itself to establishing rules applying to general types of situations and should allow the individuals freedom in everything which depends on the circumstances of time and place, because only the individuals concerned in each instance can fully know these circumstances and adapt their actions to them. If the individuals are to be able to use their knowledge effectively in making plans, they must be able to predict actions of the state which may affect these plans. But if the actions of the state are to be predictable, they must be determined by rules fixed independently of the concrete circumstances which can be neither foreseen nor taken into account beforehand: and the particular effects of such actions will be unpredictable. If, on the other hand, the state were to direct the individual's actions so as to achieve particular ends, its action would have to be decided on the basis of the full circumstances of the moment and would therefore be unpredictable. Hence the familiar fact that the more the state "plans," the more difficult planning becomes for the individual.

The second, moral or political, argument is even more directly relevant to the point under discussion. If the state is precisely to foresee the incidence of its actions, it means that it can leave those affected no choice. Wherever the state can exactly foresee the effects on particular people of alternative courses of action, it is also the state which chooses between the different ends. If we want to create new opportunities open to all, to offer chances of which people can make what use they like, the precise results cannot be foreseen. General rules, genuine laws as distinguished from specific orders, must therefore be intended to operate in circumstances which cannot be foreseen in detail, and, therefore, their effect on particular ends or particular people cannot be known beforehand. It is in this sense alone that it is at all possible for the legislator to be impartial. To be impartial means to have no answer to certain questions—to the kind of questions which, if we have to decide them, we decide by tossing a coin. In a world where everything was precisely foreseen, the state could hardly do anything and remain impartial.

Where the precise effects of government policy on particular people are known, where the government aims directly at such particular effects, it cannot help knowing these effects, and therefore it cannot be impartial. It must, of necessity, take sides, impose its valuations upon people and, instead of assisting them in the advancement of their own ends, choose the ends for them. As soon as the particular effects are foreseen at the time a law is made, it ceases to be a mere instrument to be used by the people and becomes instead an instrument used by the lawgiver upon the people and for his ends. The state ceases to be a piece of utilitarian machinery intended to help individuals in the fullest development of their individual personality and becomes a "moral" institution—where "moral" is not used in contrast to immoral but describes an institution which imposes on its members its views on all moral questions, whether these views be moral or highly immoral. In this sense the Nazi or any other collectivist state is "moral," while the liberal state is not.

Perhaps it will be said that all this raises no serious problem because in the kind of questions which the economic planner would have to decide he need not and should not be guided by his individual prejudices but could rely on the general conviction of what is fair and reasonable. This contention usually receives support from those who have experience of planning in a particular industry and who find that there is no insuperable difficulty about arriving at a decision which all those immediately interested will accept as fair. The reason why this experience proves nothing is, of course, the selection of the "interests" concerned when planning is confined to a particular industry. Those most immediately interested in a particular issue are not necessarily the best judges of the interests of society as a whole. To take only the most characteristic case: when capital and labor in an industry agree on some policy of restriction and thus exploit the consumers, there is usually no difficulty about the division of the spoils in proportion to former earnings or on some similar principle. The loss which is divided between thousands or millions is usually either simply disregarded or quite inadequately considered. It we want to test the usefulness of the principle of "fairness" in deciding the kind of issues which arise in economic planning, we must apply it to some question where the gains and the losses are seen equally clearly. In such instances it is readily recognized that no general principle such as fairness can provide an answer. When we have to choose between higher wages for nurses or doctors and more extensive services for the sick, more milk for children and better wages for agricultural workers, or between employment for the unemployed or better wages for those already employed, nothing short of a complete system of values in which every want of every person or group has a definite place is necessary to provide an answer.

In fact, as planning becomes more and more extensive, it becomes regularly necessary to qualify legal provisions increasingly by reference to what is "fair" or "reasonable"; this means that it becomes necessary to leave the decision of the concrete case more and more to the discretion of the judge or authority in question. One could write a history of the decline of the Rule of Law, the disappearance of the *Rechtsstaat*, in terms of the progressive introduction of these vague formulas into legislation and jurisdiction, and of the increasing arbitrariness and uncertainty of, and the consequent disrespect for, the law and the judicature, which in these circumstances could not but become an instrument of policy. It is important to point out once more in this connection that this process of the decline of the Rule of Law had been going on steadily in Germany for some time before Hitler came into power and that a policy well advanced toward totalitarian planning had already done a great deal of the work which Hitler completed.

There can be no doubt that planning necessarily involves deliberate discrimination between particular needs of different people, and allowing one man to do what another must be prevented from doing. It must lay down by a legal rule how well off particular people shall be and what different people are to be allowed to have and do. It means in effect a return to the rule of status, a reversal of the "movement of progressive societies" which, in the famous phrase of Sir Henry Maine, "has hitherto been a movement from status to contract." Indeed, the Rule of Law, more than the rule of contract, should probably be regarded as the true opposite of the rule of status. It is the Rule of Law, in the sense of the rule of formal law, the absence of legal privileges of particular people designated by authority, which safeguards that equality before the law which is the opposite of arbitrary government.

A necessary, and only apparently paradoxical, result of this is that formal equality before the law is in conflict, and in fact incompatible, with any activity of the government deliberately aiming at material or substantive equality of different people, and that any policy aiming directly at a substantive ideal of distributive justice must lead to the destruction of the Rule of Law. To produce the same result for different people, it is necessary to treat them differently. To give different people the same objective opportunities is not to give them the same subjective chance. It cannot be denied that the Rule of Law produces economic inequality—all that can be claimed for it is that this inequality is not designed to affect particular people in a particular way. It is very significant and characteristic that socialists (and Nazis) have always protested against "merely" formal justice, that they have always objected to a law which had no views on how well off particular people ought to be,[4] and that they have always demanded a "socialization of the law," attacked the independence of judges, and at the same time given their support to all such movements as the *Freirechtsschule* which undermined the Rule of Law.

It may even be said that for the Rule of Law to be effective it is more important that there should be a rule applied always without exceptions than what this rule is. Often the content of the rule is indeed of minor importance, provided the same rule is universally enforced. To revert to a former example: it does not matter whether we all drive on the left- or on the right-hand side of the road so long as we all do the same. The important thing is that the rule enables us to predict other people's behavior correctly, and this requires that it should apply to all cases—even if in a particular instance we feel it to be unjust.

The conflict between formal justice and formal equality before the law, on the one hand, and the attempts to realize various ideals of substantive justice and equality, on the other, also accounts for the widespread confusion about the concept of "privilege" and its consequent abuse. To mention only the most important instance of this abuse—the application of the term "privilege" to property as such. It would indeed be privilege if, for example, as has sometimes been the case in the past, landed property were reserved to members of the nobility. And it is privilege if, as is true in our time, the right to produce or sell particular things is reserved to particular people designated by authority. But to call private property as such, which all can acquire under the same rules, a privilege, because only some succeed in acquiring it, is depriving the word "privilege" of its meaning.

The unpredictability of the particular effects, which is the distinguishing characteristic of the formal laws of a liberal system, is also important because it helps us to clear up another confusion about the nature of this system: the belief that its characteristic attitude is inaction of the state. The question whether the state should or should not "act" or "interfere" poses an altogether false alternative, and the term "laissez faire" is a highly ambiguous and misleading description of the principles on which a liberal policy is based. Of course, every state must act and every action of the state interferes with something or other. But that is not the point. The important question is whether the individual can foresee the action of the state and make use of this knowledge as a datum in forming his own plans, with the result that the state cannot control the use made of its machinery and that the individual knows precisely how far he will be protected against interference from others, or whether the state is in a position to frustrate individual efforts. The state controlling weights and measures (or preventing fraud and deception in any other way) is certainly acting, while the state permitting the use of violence, for example, by strike pickets, is inactive. Yet it is in the first case that the state observes liberal principles and in the second that it does not. Similarly with respect to most of the general and permanent rules which the state may establish with regard to production, such as building regulations or factory laws: these may be wise or unwise in the particular instance, but they do not conflict with liberal principles so long as they are intended to be permanent and are not used to favor or harm particular people. It is true that in these instances there will, apart from the long-run effects which cannot be predicted, also be short-run effects on particular people which may be clearly known. But with this kind of laws the short-run effects are in general not (or at least ought not to be) the guiding consideration. As these immediate and predictable effects become more important compared with the long-run effects, we approach the border line where the distinction, however clear in principle, becomes blurred in practice.

The Rule of Law was consciously evolved only during the liberal age and is one of its greatest achievements, not only as a safeguard but as the legal embodiment of freedom. As Immanuel Kant put it (and Voltaire expressed it before him in very much the same terms), "Man is free if he needs to obey no person but solely the laws." As a vague ideal it has, however, existed at least since Roman times, and during the last few centuries it has never been so seriously threatened as it is today. The idea that there is no limit to the powers of the legislator is in part a result of popular sovereignty and democratic government. It has been strengthened by the belief that, so long as all actions of the state are duly authorized by legislation, the Rule of Law will be preserved. But this is completely to misconceive the meaning of the Rule of Law. This rule has little to do with the question whether all actions of government are legal in the juridical sense. They may well be and yet not conform to the Rule of Law. The fact that someone has full legal authority to act in the way he does gives no answer to the question whether the law gives him power to act arbitrarily or whether the law prescribes unequivocally how he has to act. It may well be that Hitler has obtained his unlimited powers in a strictly constitutional manner and that whatever he does is therefore legal in the juridical sense. But who would suggest for that reason that the Rule of Law still prevails in Germany?

To say that in a planned society the Rule of Law cannot hold is, therefore, not to say that the actions of the government will not be legal or that such a society will necessarily be lawless. It means only that the use of the government's coercive powers will no longer be limited and determined by pre-established rules. The law can, and to make a central direction of economic activity possible must, legalize what to all intents and purposes remains arbitrary action. If the law says that such a board or authority may do what it pleases, anything that board or authority does is legal—but its actions are certainly not subject to the Rule of Law. By giving the government unlimited powers, the most arbitrary rule can be made legal; and in this way a democracy may set up the most complete despotism imaginable.[5]

If, however, the law is to enable authorities to direct economic life, it must give them powers to make and enforce decisions in circumstances which cannot be foreseen and on principles which cannot be stated in generic form. The consequence is that, as planning extends, the delegation of legislative powers to divers boards and authorities becomes increasingly common. When before the last war, in a case to which the late Lord Hewart has recently drawn attention, Mr. Justice Darling said that "Parliament had enacted only last year that the Board of Agriculture in acting as they did should be no more impeachable than Parliament itself," this was still a rare thing. It has since become an almost daily occurrence. Constantly the broadest powers are conferred on new authorities which, without being bound by fixed rules, have almost unlimited discretion in regulating this or that activity of the people.

The Rule of Law thus implies limits to the scope of legislation: it restricts it to the kind of general rules known as formal law and excludes legislation either directly aimed at particular people or at enabling anybody to use the coercive power of the state for the purpose of such discrimination. It means, not that everything is regulated by law, but, on the contrary, that the coercive power of the state can be used only in cases defined in advance by the law and in such a way that it can be foreseen how it will be used. A particular enactment can thus infringe the Rule of Law. Anyone ready to deny this would have to contend that whether the Rule of Law prevails today in Germany, Italy, or Russia depends on whether the dictators have obtained their absolute power by constitutional means.[6]

Whether, as in some countries, the main applications of the Rule of Law are laid down in a bill of rights or in a constitutional code, or whether the principle is merely a firmly established tradition, matters comparatively little. But it will readily be seen that, whatever form it takes, any such recognized limitations of the powers of legislation imply the recognition of the inalienable right of the individual, inviolable rights of man.

It is pathetic but characteristic of the muddle into which many of our intellectuals have been led by the conflicting ideals in which they believe that a leading advocate of the most comprehensive central planning like H.G. Wells should at the same time write an ardent defense of the rights of man. The individual rights which Mr. Wells hopes to preserve would inevitably obstruct the planning which he desires. To some extent he seems to realize the dilemma, and we find therefore the provisions of his proposed "Declaration of the Rights of Man" so hedged about with qualifications that they lose all significance. While, for instance, his declaration proclaims that every man "shall have the right to buy and sell without any discriminatory restrictions anything which may be lawfully bought and sold," which is admirable, he immediately proceeds to make the whole provision nugatory by adding that it applies only to buying and selling "in such quantities and with such reservations as are compatible with the common welfare." But since, of course, all restrictions ever imposed upon buying or selling anything are supposed to be necessary in the interest of the "common welfare," there is really no restriction which this clause effectively prevents and no right of the individual that is safeguarded by it.

Or, to take another basic clause, the declaration states that every man "may engage in any lawful occupation" and that "he is entitled to paid employment and to a free choice whenever there is any variety of employment open to him." It is not stated, however, who is to decide whether a particular employment is "open" to a particular person, and the added provision that "he may suggest employment for himself and have his claim publicly considered, accepted or dismissed," shows that Mr. Wells is thinking in terms of an authority which decides whether a man is "entitled" to a particular position—which certainly means the opposite of free choice of occupation. And how in a planned world "freedom of travel and migration" is to be secured when not only the means of communication and currencies are controlled but also the location of industries planned, or how the freedom of the press is to be safeguarded when the supply of paper and all the channels of distribution are controlled by the planning authority, are questions to which Mr. Wells provides as little answer as any other planner.

In this respect much more consistency is shown by the more numerous reformers who, ever since the beginning of the socialist movement, have attacked the "metaphysical" idea of individual rights and insisted that in a rationally ordered world there will be no individual rights but only individual duties. This, indeed, has become the much more common attitude of our so-called "progressives," and few things are more certain to expose one to the reproach of being a reactionary than if one protests against a measure on the grounds that it is a violation of the rights of the individual. Even a liberal paper like the *Economist* was a few years ago holding up to us the example of the French, of all people, who had learned the lesson that "democratic government no less than dictatorship must always [*sic*] have plenary powers *in posse*, without sacrificing their democratic and representative character. There is no restrictive penumbra of individual rights that can never be touched by government in administrative matters whatever the circumstances. There is no limit to the power of ruling which can and should be taken by a government freely chosen by the people and can be fully and openly criticised by an opposition."

This may be inevitable in wartime, when, of course, even free and open criticism is necessarily restricted. But the "always" in the statement quoted does not suggest that the *Economist* regards it as a regrettable wartime necessity. Yet as a permanent institution this view is certainly incompatible with the preservation of the Rule of Law, and it leads straight to the totalitarian state. It is, however, the view which all those who want the government to direct economic life must hold.

How even a formal recognition of individual rights, or of the equal rights of minorities, loses all significance in a state which embarks on a complete control of economic life, has been amply demonstrated by the experience of the various Central European countries. It has been shown there that it is possible to pursue a policy of ruthless discrimination against national minorities by the use of recognized instruments of economic policy without ever infringing the letter of the statutory protection of minority rights. This oppression by means of economic policy was greatly facilitated by the fact that particular industries or activities were largely in the hands of a national minority, so that many a measure aimed ostensibly against an industry or class was in fact aimed at a national minority. But the almost boundless possibilities for a policy of discrimination and oppression provided by such apparently innocuous principles as "government control of the development of industries" have been amply demonstrated to all those desirous of seeing how the political consequences of planning appear in practice.

Notes

1. Quoted in Dugald Stewart's *Memoir of Adam Smith* from a memorandum written by Smith in 1755.
2. Of late, it is true, some academic socialists, under the spur of criticism and animated by the same fear of the extinction of freedom in a centrally planned society, have devised a new kind of "competitive socialism" which they hope will avoid the difficulties and dangers of central planning and combine the abolition of private property with the full retention of individual freedom. Although some discussion of this new kind of socialism has taken place in learned journals, it is hardly likely to recommend itself to practical politicians. If it ever did, it would not be difficult to show (as the author has attempted elsewhere—see *Economica*, 1940) that these plans rest on a delusion and suffer from

an inherent contradiction. It is impossible to assume control over all the productive resources without also deciding for whom and by whom they are to be used. Although under this so-called "competitive socialism" the planning by the central authority would take somewhat more roundabout forms, its effects would not be fundamentally different, and the element of competition would be little more than a sham.

3. According to the classical exposition by A.V. Dicey in *The Law of the Constitution* (8th ed.), p. 198, the Rule of Law "means, in the first place, the absolute supremacy or predominance of regular law as opposed to the influence of arbitrary power, and excludes the existence of arbitrariness, of prerogative, or even of wide discretionary authority on the part of government." Largely as a result of Dicey's work the term has, however, in England acquired a narrower technical meaning which does not concern us here. The wider and older meaning of the concept of the rule or reign of law, which in England had become an established tradition which was more taken for granted than discussed, has been most fully elaborated, just because it raised what were new problems there, in the early nineteenth-century discussion in Germany about the nature of the *Rechtsstaat*.

4. It is therefore not altogether false when the legal theorist of National Socialism, Carl Schmitt, opposes to the liberal *Rechststaat* (i.e. the Rule of Law) the National Socialist ideal of the *gerechte Staat* ("the just state")—only that the sort of justice which is opposed to formal justice necessarily implies discrimination between persons.

5. The conflict is thus *not*, as it has often been misconceived in nineteenth-century discussions, one between liberty and law. As John Locke had already made clear, there can be no liberty without law. The conflict is between different kinds of law—law so different that it should hardly be called by the same name: one is the law of the Rule of Law, general principles laid down beforehand, the "rules of the game" which enable individuals to foresee how the coercive apparatus of the state will be used, or what he and his fellow-citizens will be allowed to do, or made to do, in stated circumstances. The other kind of law gives in effect the authority power to do what it thinks fit to do. Thus the Rule of Law could clearly not be preserved in a democracy that undertook to decide every conflict of interests not according to rules previously laid down but "on its merits."

6. Another illustration of an infringement of the Rule of Law by legislation is the case of the bill of attainder, familiar in the history of England. The form which the Rule of Law takes in criminal law is usually expressed by the Latin tag *nulla poena sine lege*—no punishment without a law expressly prescribing it. The essence of this rule is that the law must have existed as a general rule before the individual case arose to which it is to be applied. Nobody would argue that, when in a famous case in Henry VIII's reign Parliament resolved with respect to the Bishop of Rochester's cook that "the said Richard Rose shall be boiled to death without having the advantage of his clergy," this act was performed under the Rule of Law. But while the Rule of Law had become an essential part of criminal procedure in all liberal countries, it cannot be preserved in totalitarian regimes. There, as E.B. Ashton has well expressed it, the liberal maxim is replaced by the principles *nullum crimen sine poena*—no "crime" must remain without punishment, whether the law explicitly provides for it or not. "The rights of the state do not end with punishing law breakers. The community is entitled to whatever may seem necessary to the protection of its interests—of which observance of the law, as it stands, is only one of the more elementary requirements" (E.B. Ashton, *The Fascist, His State and Mind* [1937], p. 119). What is an infringement of "the interests of the community" is, of course, decided by the authorities.

Milton Friedman,
Capitalism and Freedom (1962)*

Chapter II: The Role of Government in a Free Society

A common objection to totalitarian societies is that they regard the end as justifying the means. Taken literally, this objection is clearly illogical. If the end does not justify the means, what does? But this easy answer does not dispose of the objection; it simply shows that the objection is not well put. To deny that the end justifies the means is indirectly to assert that the end in question is not the ultimate end, that the ultimate end is itself the use of the proper means. Desirable or not, any end that can be attained only by the use of bad means must give way to the more basic end of the use of acceptable means.

To the liberal, the appropriate means are free discussion and voluntary co-operation, which implies that any form of coercion is inappropriate. The ideal is unanimity among responsible individuals achieved on the basis of free and full discussion. This is another way of expressing the goal of freedom emphasized in the preceding chapter.

From this standpoint, the role of the market, as already noted, is that it permits unanimity without conformity; that it is a system of effectively proportional representation. On the other hand, the characteristic feature of action through explicitly political channels is that it tends to require or to enforce substantial conformity. The typical issue must be decided "yes" or "no"; at most, provision can be made for a fairly limited number of alternatives. Even the use of proportional representation in its explicitly political form does not alter this conclusion. The number of separate groups that can in fact be represented is narrowly limited, enormously so by comparison with the proportional representation of the market. More important, the fact that the final outcome generally must be a law applicable to all groups, rather than separate legislative enactments for each "party" represented, means that proportional representation in its political version, far from permitting unanimity without conformity, tends toward ineffectiveness and fragmentation. It thereby operates to destroy any consensus on which unanimity with conformity can rest.

There are clearly some matters with respect to which effective proportional representation is impossible. I cannot get the amount of national defense I want and you, a different amount. With respect to such indivisible matters we can discuss, and argue, and vote. But having decided, we must conform. It is precisely the existence of such

* From: *Capitalism and Freedom*, Milton Friedman, Copyright © 1962, 1982, 2002 The University of Chicago. (pp. 22–36) Reproduced by permission of The University of Chicago Press and Milton Friedman.

indivisible matters—protection of the individual and the nation from coercion are clearly the most basic—that prevents exclusive reliance on individual action through the market. If we are to use some of our resources for such indivisible items, we must employ political channels to reconcile differences.

The use of political channels, while inevitable, tends to strain the social cohesion essential for a stable society. The strain is least if agreement for joint action need be reached only on a limited range of issues on which people in any event have common views. Every extension of the range of issues for which explicit agreement is sought strains further the delicate threads that hold society together. If it goes so far as to touch an issue on which men feel deeply yet differently, it may well disrupt the society. Fundamental differences in basic values can seldom if ever be resolved at the ballot box; ultimately they can only be decided, though not resolved, by conflict. The religious and civil wars of history are a bloody testament to this judgment.

The widespread use of the market reduces the strain on the social fabric by rendering conformity unnecessary with respect to any activities it encompasses. The wider the range of activities covered by the market, the fewer are the issues on which explicitly political decisions are required and hence on which it is necessary to achieve agreement. In turn, the fewer the issues on which agreement is necessary, the greater is the likelihood of getting agreement while maintaining a free society.

Unanimity is, of course, an ideal. In practice, we can afford neither the time nor the effort that would be required to achieve complete unanimity on every issue. We must perforce accept something less. We are thus led to accept majority rule in one form or another as an expedient. That majority rule is an expedient rather than itself a basic principle is clearly shown by the fact that our willingness to resort to majority rule, and the size of the majority we require, themselves depend on the seriousness of the issue involved. If the matter is of little moment and the minority has no strong feelings about being overruled, a bare plurality will suffice. On the other hand, if the minority feels strongly about the issue involved, even a bare majority will not do. Few of us would be willing to have issues of free speech, for example, decided by a bare majority. Our legal structure is full of such distinctions among kinds of issues mat require different kinds of majorities. At the extreme are those issues embodied in the Constitution. These are the principles that are so important that we are willing to make minimal concessions to expediency. Something like essential consensus was achieved initially in accepting them, and we require something like essential consensus for a change in them.

The self-denying ordinance to refrain from majority rule on certain kinds of issues that is embodied in our Constitution and in similar written or unwritten constitutions elsewhere, and the specific provisions in these constitutions or their equivalents prohibiting coercion of individuals, are themselves to be regarded as reached by free discussion and as reflecting essential unanimity about means.

I turn now to consider more specifically, though still in very broad terms, what the areas are that cannot be handled through the market at all, or can be handled only at so great a cost that the use of political channels may be preferable.

Government as Rule-Maker and Umpire

It is important to distinguish the day-to-day activities of people from the general customary and legal framework within which these take place. The day-to-day activities
are like the actions of the participants in a game when they are playing it; the framework, like the rules of the game they play. And just as a good game requires acceptance by the players both of the rules and of the umpire to interpret and enforce them,
so a good society requires that its members agree on the general conditions that will
govern relations among them, on some means of arbitrating different interpretations
of these conditions, and on some device for enforcing compliance with the generally
accepted rules. As in games, so also in society, most of the general conditions are the
unintended outcome of custom, accepted unthinkingly. At most, we consider explicitly only minor modifications in them, though the cumulative effect of a series of
minor modifications may be a drastic alteration in the character of the game or of the
society. In both games and society also, no set of rules can prevail unless most participants most of the time conform to them without external sanctions; unless that is,
there is a broad underlying social consensus. But we cannot rely on custom or on this
consensus alone to interpret and to enforce the rules; we need an umpire. These then
are the basic roles of government in a free society: to provide a means whereby we can
modify the rules, to mediate differences among us on the meaning of the rules, and
to enforce compliance with the rules on the part of those few who would otherwise
not play the game.

The need for government in these respects arises because absolute freedom is
impossible. However attractive anarchy may be as a philosophy, it is not feasible in a
world of imperfect men. Men's freedoms can conflict, and when they do, one man's
freedom must be limited to preserve another's—as a Supreme Court Justice once put
it, "My freedom to move my fist must be limited by the proximity of your chin."

The major problem in deciding the appropriate activities of government is how to
resolve such conflicts among the freedoms of different individuals. In some cases, the
answer is easy. There is little difficulty in attaining near unanimity to the proposition that one man's freedom to murder his neighbor must be sacrificed to preserve
the freedom of the other man to live. In other cases, the answer is difficult. In the
economic area, a major problem arises in respect of the conflict between freedom
to combine and freedom to compete. What meaning is to be attributed to "free" as
modifying "enterprise"? In the United States, "free" has been understood to mean
that anyone is free to set up an enterprise, which means that existing enterprises are
not free to keep out competitors except by selling a better product at the same price or
the same product at a lower price. In the continental tradition, on the other hand, the
meaning has generally been that enterprises are free to do what they want, including
the fixing of prices, division of markets, and the adoption of other techniques to keep
out potential competitors. Perhaps the most difficult specific problem in this area
arises with respect to combinations among laborers, where the problem of freedom to
combine and freedom to compete is particularly acute.

A still more basic economic area in which the answer is both difficult and important is the definition of property rights. The notion of property, as it has developed
over centuries and as it is embodied in our legal codes, has become so much a part

of us that we tend to take it for granted, and fail to recognize the extent to which just what constitutes property and what rights the ownership of property confers are complex social creations rather than self-evident propositions. Does my having title to land, for example, and my freedom to use my property as I wish, permit me to deny to someone else the right to fly over my land in his airplane? Or does his right to use his airplane take precedence? Or does this depend on how high he flies? Or how much noise he makes? Does voluntary exchange require that he pay me for the privilege of flying over my land? Or that I must pay him to refrain from flying over it? The mere mention of royalties, copyrights, patents; shares of stock in corporations; riparian rights, and the like, may perhaps emphasize the role of generally accepted social rules in the very definition of property. It may suggest also that, in many cases, the existence of a well specified and generally accepted definition of property is far more important than just what the definition is.

Another economic area that raises particularly difficult problems is the monetary system. Government responsibility for the monetary system has long been recognized. It is explicitly provided for in the constitutional provision which gives Congress the power "to coin money, regulate the value thereof, and of foreign coin." There is probably no other area of economic activity with respect to which government action has been so uniformly accepted. This habitual and by now almost unthinking acceptance of governmental responsibility makes thorough understanding of the grounds for such responsibility all the more necessary, since it enhances the danger that the scope of government will spread from activities that are, to those that are not, appropriate in a free society, from providing a monetary framework to determining the allocation of resources among individuals.

In summary, the organization of economic activity through voluntary exchange presumes that we have provided, through government, for the maintenance of law and order to prevent coercion of one individual by another, the enforcement of contracts voluntarily entered into, the definition of the meaning of property rights, the interpretation and enforcement of such rights, and the provision of a monetary framework.

Action through Government on Grounds of Technical Monopoly and Neighborhood Effects

The role of government just considered is to do something that the market cannot do for itself, namely, to determine, arbitrate, and enforce the rules of the game. We may also want to do through government some things that might conceivably be done through the market but that technical or similar conditions render it difficult to do in that way. These all reduce to cases in which strictly voluntary exchange is either exceedingly costly or practically impossible. There are two general classes of such cases: monopoly and similar market imperfections, and neighborhood effects.

Exchange is truly voluntary only when nearly equivalent alternatives exist. Monopoly implies the absence of alternatives and thereby inhibits effective freedom of exchange. In practice, monopoly frequently, if not generally, arises from government support or from collusive agreements among individuals. With respect to these, the problem is either to avoid governmental fostering of monopoly or to stimulate the effective enforcement of rules such as those embodied in our anti-trust laws. However, monopoly may also arise because it is technically efficient to have a single producer or enterprise. I venture to suggest that such cases are more limited than is supposed but they unquestionably do arise. A simple example is perhaps the provision of telephone services within a community. I shall refer to such cases as "technical" monopoly.

When technical conditions make a monopoly the natural outcome of competitive market forces, there are only three alternatives that seem available: private monopoly, public monopoly, or public regulation. All three are bad so we must choose among evils. Henry Simons, observing public regulation of monopoly in the United States, found the results so distasteful that he concluded public monopoly would be a lesser evil. Walter Eucken, a noted German liberal, observing public monopoly in German railroads, found the results so distasteful that he concluded public regulation would be a lesser evil. Having learned from both, I reluctantly conclude that, if tolerable, private monopoly may be the least of the evils.

If society were static so that the conditions which give rise to a technical monopoly were sure to remain, I would have little confidence in this solution. In a rapidly changing society, however, the conditions making for technical monopoly frequently change and I suspect that both public regulation and public monopoly are likely to be less responsive to such changes in conditions, to be less readily capable of elimination, than private monopoly.

Railroads in the United States are an excellent example. A large degree of monopoly in railroads was perhaps inevitable on technical grounds in the nineteenth century. This was the justification for the Interstate Commerce Commission. But conditions have changed. The emergence of road and air transport has reduced the monopoly element in railroads to negligible proportions. Yet we have not eliminated the ICC. On the contrary, the ICC, which started out as an agency to protect the public from exploitation by the railroads, has become an agency to protect railroads from competition by trucks and other means of transport, and more recently even to protect existing truck companies from competition by new entrants. Similarly, in England, when the railroads were nationalized, trucking was at first brought into the state monopoly. If railroads had never been subjected to regulation in the United States, it is nearly certain that by now transportation, including railroads, would be a highly competitive industry with little or no remaining monopoly elements.

The choice between the evils of private monopoly, public monopoly, and public regulation cannot, however, be made once and for all, independently of the factual circumstances. If the technical monopoly is of a service or commodity that is regarded as essential and if its monopoly power is sizable, even the short-run effects of private unregulated monopoly may not be tolerable, and either public regulation or ownership may be a lesser evil.

Technical monopoly may on occasion justify a *de facto* public monopoly. It cannot by itself justify a public monopoly achieved by making it illegal for anyone else to compete. For example, there is no way to justify our present public monopoly of the post office. It may be argued that the carrying of mail is a technical monopoly and that a government monopoly is the least of evils. Along these lines, one could perhaps justify a government post office but not the present law, which makes it illegal for anybody else to carry mail. If the delivery of mail is a technical monopoly, no one will be able to succeed in competition with the government. If it is not, there is no reason why the government should be engaged in it. The only way to find out is to leave other people free to enter.

The historical reason why we have a post office monopoly is because the Pony Express did such a good job of carrying the mail across the continent that, when the government introduced transcontinental service, it couldn't compete effectively and lost money. The result was a law making it illegal for anybody else to carry the mail. That is why the Adams Express Company is an investment trust today instead of an operating company. I conjecture that if entry into the mail-carrying business were open to all, there would be a large number of firms entering it and this archaic industry would become revolutionized in short order.

A second general class of cases in which strictly voluntary exchange is impossible arises when actions of individuals have effects on other individuals for which it is not feasible to charge or recompense them. This is the problem of "neighborhood effects." An obvious example is the pollution of a stream. The man who pollutes a stream is in effect forcing others to exchange good water for bad. These others might be willing to make the exchange at a price. But it is not feasible for them, acting individually, to avoid the exchange or to enforce appropriate compensation.

A less obvious example is the provision of highways. In this case, it is technically possible to identify and hence charge individuals for their use of the roads and so to have private operation. However, for general access roads, involving many points of entry and exit, the costs of collection would be extremely high if a charge were to be made for the specific services received by each individual, because of the necessity of establishing toll booths or the equivalent at all entrances. The gasoline tax is a much cheaper method of charging individuals roughly in proportion to their use of the roads. This method, however, is one in which the particular payment cannot be identified closely with the particular use. Hence, it is hardly feasible to have private enterprise provide the service and collect the charge without establishing extensive private monopoly.

These considerations do not apply to long-distance turnpikes with high density of traffic and limited access. For these, the costs of collection are small and in many cases are now being paid, and there are often numerous alternatives, so that there is no serious monopoly problem. Hence, there is every reason why these should be privately owned and operated. If so owned and operated, the enterprise running the highway should receive the gasoline taxes paid on account of travel on it.

Parks are an interesting example because they illustrate the difference between cases that can and cases that cannot be justified by neighborhood effects, and because almost everyone at first sight regards the conduct of National Parks as obviously a valid function of government. In fact, however, neighborhood effects may justify a city park; they do not justify a national park, like Yellowstone National Park or the Grand Canyon. What is the fundamental difference between the two? For the city park, it is extremely difficult to identify the people who benefit from it and to charge them for the benefits which they receive. If there is a park in the middle of the city, the houses on all sides get the benefit of the open space, and people who walk through it or by it also benefit. To maintain toll collectors at the gates or to impose annual charges per window overlooking the park would be very expensive and difficult. The entrances to a national park like Yellowstone, on the other hand, are few; most of the people who come stay for a considerable period of time and it is perfectly feasible to set up toll gates and collect admission charges. This is indeed now done, though the charges do not cover the whole costs. If the public wants this kind of an activity enough to pay for it, private enterprises will have every incentive to provide such parks. And, of course, there are many private enterprises of this nature now in existence. I cannot myself conjure up any neighborhood effects or important monopoly effects that would justify governmental activity in this area.

Considerations like those I have treated under the heading of neighborhood effects have been used to rationalize almost every conceivable intervention. In many instances, however, this rationalization is special pleading rather than a legitimate application of the concept of neighborhood effects. Neighborhood effects cut both ways. They can be a reason for limiting the activities of government as well as for expanding them. Neighborhood effects impede voluntary exchange because it is difficult to identify the effects on third parties and to measure their magnitude; but this difficulty is present in governmental activity as well. It is hard to know when neighborhood effects are sufficiently large to justify particular costs in overcoming them and even harder to distribute the costs in an appropriate fashion. Consequently, when government engages in activities to overcome neighborhood effects, it will in part introduce an additional set of neighborhood effects by failing to charge or to compensate individuals properly. Whether the original or the new neighborhood effects are the more serious can only be judged by the facts of the individual case, and even then, only very approximately. Furthermore, the use of government to overcome neighborhood effects itself has an extremely important neighborhood effect which is unrelated to the particular occasion for government action. Every act of government intervention limits the area of individual freedom directly and threatens the preservation of freedom indirectly for reasons elaborated in the first chapter.

Our principles offer no hard and fast line how far it is appropriate to use government to accomplish jointly what it is difficult or impossible for us to accomplish separately through strictly voluntary exchange. In any particular case of proposed intervention, we must make up a balance sheet, listing separately the advantages and disadvantages. Our principles tell us what items to put on the one side and what items on the other and they give us some basis for attaching importance to the different items. In particular, we shall always want to enter on the liability side of any proposed government intervention, its neighborhood effect in threatening freedom, and give this effect considerable weight. Just how much weight to give to it, as to other items, depends upon the circumstances. If, for example, existing government intervention is minor, we shall attach a smaller weight to the negative effects of additional government intervention. This is an important reason why many earlier liberals, like Henry Simons, writing at a time when government was small by today's standards, were willing to have government undertake activities that today's liberals would not accept now that government has become so overgrown.

Action through Government on Paternalistic Grounds

Freedom is a tenable objective only for responsible individuals. We do not believe in freedom for madmen or children. The necessity of drawing a line between responsible individuals and others is inescapable, yet it means that there is an essential ambiguity in our ultimate objective of freedom. Paternalism is inescapable for those whom we designate as not responsible.

The clearest case, perhaps, is that of madmen. We are willing neither to permit them freedom nor to shoot them. It would be nice if we could rely on voluntary activities of individuals to house and care for the madmen. But I think we cannot rule out the possibility that such charitable activities will be inadequate, if only because of the neighborhood effect involved in the fact that I benefit if another man contributes to the care of the insane. For this reason, we may be willing to arrange for their care through government.

Children offer a more difficult case. The ultimate operative unit in our society is the family, not the individual. Yet the acceptance of the family as the unit rests in considerable part on expediency rather than principle. We believe that parents are generally best able to protect their children and to provide for their development into responsible individuals for whom freedom is appropriate. But we do not believe in the freedom of parents to do what they will with other people. The children are responsible individuals in embryo, and a believer in freedom believes in protecting their ultimate rights.

To put this in a different and what may seem a more callous way, children are at one and the same time consumer goods and potentially responsible members of society. The freedom of individuals to use their economic resources as they want includes the freedom to use them to have children—to buy, as it were, the services of children as a particular form of consumption. But once this choice is exercised, the children have a value in and of themselves and have a freedom of their own that is not simply an extension of the freedom of the parents.

The paternalistic ground for governmental activity is in many ways the most troublesome to a liberal; for it involves the acceptance of a principle—that some shall decide for others—which he finds objectionable in most applications and which he rightly regards as a hallmark of his chief intellectual opponents, the proponents of collectivism in one or another of its guises, whether it be communism, socialism, or a welfare state. Yet there is no use pretending that problems are simpler than in fact they are. There is no avoiding the need for some measure of paternalism. As Dicey wrote in 1914 about an act for the protection of mental defectives, "The Mental Deficiency Act is the first step along a path on which no sane man can decline to enter, but which, if too far pursued, will bring statesmen across difficulties hard to meet without considerable interference with individual liberty."[1] There is no formula that can tell us where to stop. We must rely on our fallible judgment and, having reached a judgment, on our ability to persuade our fellow men that it is a correct judgment, or their ability to persuade us to modify our views. We must put our faith, here as elsewhere, in a consensus reached by imperfect and biased men through free discussion and trial and error.

Conclusion

A government which maintained law and order, defined property rights, served as a means whereby we could modify property rights and other rules of the economic game, adjudicated disputes about the interpretation of the rules, enforced contracts, promoted competition, provided a monetary framework, engaged in activities to counter technical monopolies and to overcome neighborhood effects widely regarded as sufficiently important to justify government intervention, and which supplemented private charity and the private family in protecting the irresponsible, whether madman or child—such a government would clearly have important functions to perform. The consistent liberal is not an anarchist.

Yet it is also true that such a government would have clearly limited functions and would refrain from a host of activities that are now undertaken by federal and state governments in the United States, and their counterparts in other Western countries. Succeeding chapters will deal in some detail with some of these activities, and a few have been discussed above, but it may help to give a sense of proportion about the role that a liberal would assign government simply to list, in closing this chapter, some activities currently undertaken by government in the U.S., that cannot, so far as I can see, validly be justified in terms of the principles outlined above:

1. Parity price support programs for agriculture.
2. Tariffs on imports or restrictions on exports, such as current oil import quotas, sugar quotas, etc.
3. Governmental control of output, such as through the farm program, or through prorationing of oil as is done by the Texas Railroad Commission.
4. Rent control, such as is still practiced in New York, or more general price and wage controls such as were imposed during and just after World War II.
5. Legal minimum wage rates, or legal maximum prices, such as the legal maximum of zero on the rate of interest that can be paid on demand deposits by commercial banks, or the legally fixed maximum rates that can be paid on savings and time deposits.
6. Detailed regulation of industries, such as the regulation of transportation by the Interstate Commerce Commission. This had some justification on technical monopoly grounds when initially introduced for railroads; it has none now for any means of transport. Another example is detailed regulation of banking.
7. A similar example, but one which deserves special mention because of its implicit censorship and violation of free speech, is the control of radio and television by the Federal Communications Commission.
8. Present social security programs, especially the old-age and retirement programs compelling people in effect (a) to spend a specified fraction of their income on the purchase of retirement annuity, (b) to buy the annuity from a publicly operated enterprise.
9. Licensure provisions in various cities and states which restrict particular enterprises or occupations or professions to people who have a license, where the license is more than a receipt for a tax which anyone who wishes to enter the activity may pay.
10. So-called "public-housing" and the host of other subsidy programs directed at fostering residential construction such as F.H.A. and V.A. guarantee of mortgage, and the like.

11. Conscription to man the military services in peacetime. The appropriate free market arrangement is volunteer military forces; which is to say, hiring men to serve. There is no justification for not paying whatever price is necessary to attract the required number of men. Present arrangements are inequitable and arbitrary, seriously interfere with the freedom of young men to shape their lives, and probably are even more costly than the market alternative. (Universal military training to provide a reserve for war time is a different problem and may be justified on liberal grounds.)
12. National parks, as noted above.
13. The legal prohibition on the carrying of mail for profit.
14. Publicly owned and operated toll roads, as noted above.

This list is far from comprehensive.

Note

1. A.V. Dicey, *Lectures on the Relation between Law and Public Opinion in England during the Nineteenth Century* (2d. ed.; London: Macmillan & Co., 1914), p. li.

3

Economic Sociology

Karl Polanyi is one of the forefathers of the school of economic sociology. His work provides a counterpoint to the economic liberal school of thought, represented in this reader by **Adam Smith, Friedrich Hayek,** and **Milton Friedman.**[1] Polanyi first encountered and directly challenged the arguments of Ludwig von Mises and Friedrich Hayek as a student in Vienna in the 1920s. In writing his landmark work, *The Great Transformation,* as the Second World War drew to a close, Polanyi launched a searing critique of economic liberalism and its utopian myth of the self-regulating market. The foundation of his argument is the observation that only under market liberalism is society subjugated to the economy and run as an adjunct to the market. This is contrary to traditional forms of human organization, where markets and the economy are an integrated part of society and economic motives are submerged in social principles such as reciprocity and redistribution. At the crux of the economic sociology paradigm are the insights that markets are inherently social phenomena embedded in sociopolitical structures and hence that economic and social life are inherently interconnected.

According to Polanyi's critique of economic liberalism, the notion of the self-regulating market contains its own contradiction: the inevitable disruption of social order based on its principles. Polanyi introduces the famous "double movement" to illuminate how this paradox is resolved in practice. Economic liberalism is inevitably accompanied by the forces of social protectionism as various classes in society react to protect themselves against the unbearable sociopolitical dislocations introduced by self-regulating markets. Thus two primary organizing principles in political economy—the laissez-faire movement and the protective countermovement—interact to slow the overall rate of transformation and keep each moving forward. Economic liberalism, in Polanyi's view, adopts a mystical readiness to accept the social consequences of economic advancement, instead of understanding that if the transformation wrought by economic change is too fast, it should be slowed down to guard the welfare of the community. In reality, Polanyi argues, government responds to societal demands for protection, slowing down the rate of change and allowing a process of social adjustment to take place. He demonstrates the double movement through the enclosures example: the enclosure movement was essential to economic improvement and the Industrial Revolution, but without the antienclosure movement, which did not stop enclosures but slowed down the rate of change, the pace of progress might have been ruinous rather than constructive.

Polanyi turns the logic of economic liberalism on its head by emphasizing the core insight of the market-institutional perspective: that state intervention is central in creating and maintaining markets. In the economic liberal school of thought, from Adam Smith on, markets arise naturally, whereas state intervention in the economy is misguided and reactionary and prevents the market from self-regulating to correct its own short-term failures. In his history of the social transformation accompanying the Industrial Revolution, Polanyi attacks this logic by arguing that markets and regulation grew up together. He argues that the construction and maintenance of the laissez-faire economy was not natural but the product of deliberate state action and that the great variety of forms the social protection countermovement took resulted not from deliberate antiliberalism but spontaneously from the broad range of social interests affected by the destructive pressures of the market mechanism as it expanded. Without society's protective countermoves, exercised through state involvement in the role of managing the three fictitious commodities, the progress of an unchecked self-regulating market mechanism would have proved too destructive to society to continue to exist.

Economic sociologists have built on Polanyi's insights, continuing to see economic principles not as universal precepts necessary to market societies but rather as economic conventions, traditions, and practices rooted in history and society.[2] Scholars in the field of economic sociology emphasize that capitalism is a constructed and continually reconstructed system, rather than a natural system that can be articulated only through one set of rules.[3] Economic liberalism and Marxism see only two possible political–economic outcomes for societies: capitalism or communism. Polanyi, in contrast, suggests that a range of alternatives in political economy are possible, because markets can be embedded in a range of different ways.[4] Many varieties of political economy developed as a result of different social and political choices implemented through state intervention. Polanyi's concept of the "embeddedness" of the economy in society has thus come to be central to the economic sociology paradigm.[5] For economic sociologists, furthermore, the social relationships surrounding economic activity—such as social networks, for example—are phenomena to be problematized and studied. This contrasts with the functionalist approach of the new institutional economics, which assumes that institutional and social relationships exist to reduce transaction costs.

Neil Fligstein's research is an important example of a contemporary economic sociological analysis of markets. In the selection presented here, he lays out a "theory of fields." Sociologists use the term *fields* to refer to arenas of activity that have an identity as a coherent issue-area or locus of activity, with social structures that go along with them. Examples of a field include neoclassical economics, a sports league, and human rights law. In Fligstein's view, a sectoral market (such as the American automobile industry) is such a field, which encompasses a set of vertical institutions—

that is, firms—and horizontal institutions—relationships among firms, consumers, and the state, among other societal actors.

A distinctive feature of this analysis is that sectoral markets have social structures, which in turn affect market behavior in predictable ways. One of the core insights that emerges from Fligstein's perspective of markets as fields is that firms try to produce a stable environment for themselves, so the ultimate motive of firms in this conception of markets is not always profit but also stability or survival. Another key insight is that market activity plays out as a series of power struggles both within and among firms, where dominant actors, such as large incumbent firms, produce rules and meanings that allow them to maintain their advantage. A market, in this view, is a socio-organizational construct intended to establish stability in exchange relationships, and firms generate that stability by creating social structure in the form of status hierarchies. In other words, within a market there are dominant firms, incumbents, and challengers, and dominant firms create the social relations of the market to ensure their continued advantage. Examples of such behavior include Microsoft's successive attempts to maintain its market share in the software market and Coca-Cola's attempts to stay on top in the beverage industry.

Fligstein's framework also includes an expansive definition of the institutions relevant to an analysis of markets. Rather than viewing institutions as the functional outcomes of an efficient process as does the new institutional economics, Fligstein argues that market institutions are cultural and historical products, specific to each industry in a given society, that have evolved through a continuous, contested process. These institutions have intersubjective meanings, that is, they depend intricately on how social actors perceive them and are not constructs that are separable from their embeddedness in society. Following Polanyi, Fligstein emphasizes that the state plays a crucial role in creating markets as institutions. The entry of a country into capitalism pushes states to develop rules that market actors cannot create themselves. States are also the focal points for economic and social actors during crisis and so are central in enforcing market institutions and sustaining markets through change. The manner and extent to which they do so depends on what type of state they are (interventionist versus regulatory) and their capacity. The initial definition of the social structure in markets produces a cultural template that determines the mode of social organization for production. In a comparative sense, furthermore, the configuration of rules and institutions within markets and the nature of social relationships between economic actors accounts for persistent differences in national political–economic systems.

Notes

1. Polanyi's insights are related in content, but not in conclusion, to those of **Karl Marx**, who saw the mode of production—which constitutes both production processes and social relations—as driving economic history.
2. Nicole W. Biggart, ed., *Readings in Economic Sociology* (Oxford: Blackwell, 2002), xiii.
3. Fred Block, "Rethinking Capitalism," in *Readings in Economic Sociology*, ed. Nicole Biggart (Oxford: Blackwell, 2002), 223.

4. Fred Block, "Introduction," in *The Great Transformation: The Political and Economic Origins of Our Time,* Karl Polanyi (Boston: Beacon Press, 2001), xxix.

5. See, in particular, Mark Granovetter, "Economic Action and Social Structure: The Problem of Embeddedness," *American Journal of Sociology* 91 (1985): 481–510. This article reintroduced an evolved definition of the concept of the embeddedness of markets into the economic sociology paradigm. It is discussed in brief in the introduction to this volume.

Karl Polanyi,
The Great Transformation (1944)*

I. Satanic Mill

Chapter 3: "Habitation versus Improvement"

At the heart of the Industrial Revolution of the eighteenth century there was an almost miraculous improvement in the tools of production, which was accompanied by a catastrophic dislocation of the lives of the common people.

We will attempt to disentangle the factors that determined the forms of this dislocation, as it appeared at its worst in England about a century ago. What "satanic mill" ground men into masses? How much was caused by the new physical conditions? How much by the economic dependencies, operating under the new conditions? And what was the mechanism through which the old social tissue was destroyed and a new integration of man and nature so unsuccessfully attempted?

Nowhere has liberal philosophy failed so conspicuously as in its understanding of the problem of change. Fired by an emotional faith in spontaneity, the common-sense attitude toward change was discarded in favor of a mystical readiness to accept the social consequences of economic improvement, whatever they might be. The elementary truths of political science and statecraft were first discredited, then forgotten. It should need no elaboration that a process of undirected change, the pace of which is deemed too fast, should be slowed down, if possible, so as to safeguard the welfare of the community. Such household truths of traditional statesmanship, often merely reflecting the teachings of a social philosophy inherited from the ancients, were in the nineteenth century erased from the thoughts of the educated by the corrosive of a crude utilitarianism combined with an uncritical reliance on the alleged self-healing virtues of unconscious growth.

Economic liberalism misread the history of the Industrial Revolution because it insisted on judging social events from the economic viewpoint. For an illustration of this we shall turn to what may at first seem a remote subject: to enclosures of open fields and conversions of arable land to pasture during the earlier Tudor period in England, when fields and commons were hedged by the lords, and whole counties were threatened by depopulation. Our purpose in thus evoking the plight of the people brought about by enclosures and conversions will be on the one hand to demonstrate

* From: *The Great Transformation: The Political and Economic Origins of Our Time*, Karl Polanyi, Copyright © 1944, 1957, 2001 by Karl Polanyi. Boston, Mass.: Beacon Press, 2001. (pp. 35–80) Reprinted by permission of Kari Polanyi Levitt.

the parallel between the devastations caused by the ultimately beneficial enclosures and those resulting from the Industrial Revolution, and on the other hand—and more broadly—to clarify the alternatives facing a community which is in the throes of unregulated economic improvement.

Enclosures were an obvious improvement *if* no conversion to pasture took place. Enclosed land was worth double and treble the unenclosed. Where tillage was maintained, employment did not fall off, and the food supply markedly increased. The yield of the land manifestly increased, especially where the land was let.

But even conversion of arable land to sheep runs was not altogether detrimental to the neighborhood in spite of the destruction of habitations and the restriction of employment it involved. Cottage industry was spreading by the second half of the fifteenth century, and a century later it began to be a feature of the countryside. The wool produced on the sheep farm gave employment to the small tenants and landless cottagers forced out of tillage, and the new centers of the woolen industry secured an income to a number of craftsmen.

But—this is the point—only in a market economy can such compensating effects be taken for granted. In the absence of such an economy the highly profitable occupation of raising sheep and selling their wool might ruin the country. The sheep which "turned sand into gold" could well have turned the gold into sand as happened ultimately to the wealth of seventeenth century Spain whose eroded soil never recovered from the overexpansion of sheep farming.

An official document of 1607, prepared for the use of the Lords of the Realm, set out the problem of change in one powerful phrase: "The poor man shall be satisfied in his end: Habitation; and the gentleman not hindered in his desire: Improvement." This formula appears to take for granted the essence of purely economic progress, which is to achieve improvement at the price of social dislocation. But it also hints at the tragic necessity by which the poor man clings to his hovel, doomed by the rich man's desire for a public improvement which profits him privately.

Enclosures have appropriately been called a revolution of the rich against the poor. The lords and nobles were upsetting the social order, breaking down ancient law and custom, sometimes by means of violence, often by pressure and intimidation. They were literally robbing the poor of their share in the common, tearing down the houses which, by the hitherto unbreakable force of custom, the poor had long regarded as theirs and their heirs'. The fabric of society was being disrupted; desolate villages and the ruins of human dwellings testified to the fierceness with which the revolution raged, endangering the defenses of the country, wasting its towns, decimating its population, turning its overburdened soil into dust, harassing its people and turning them from decent husbandmen into a mob of beggars and thieves. Though this happened only in patches, the black spots threatened to melt into a uniform catastrophe.[1] The King and his Council, the Chancellors, and the Bishops were defending the welfare of the community and, indeed, the human and natural substance of society against this scourge. With hardly any intermittence, for a century and a half—from the 1490's, at the latest, to the 1640's—they struggled against depopulation. Lord Protector Somerset lost his life at the hands of the counterrevolution which wiped the enclosure laws from the statute book and established the dictatorship of the grazier lords, after Kett's Rebellion was defeated with several thousand peasants slaughtered in the process. Somerset was accused, and not without truth, of having given encouragement to the rebellious peasants by his staunch denunciation of enclosures.

It was almost a hundred years later when a second trial of strength came between the same opponents, but by that time the enclosers were much more frequently wealthy country gentlemen and merchants rather than lords and nobles. High politics, lay and ecclesiastical, were now involved in the Crown's deliberate use of its prerogative to prevent enclosures and in its no less deliberate use of the enclosure issue to strengthen its position against the gentry in a constitutional struggle, which brought death to Strafford and Laud at the hands of Parliament. But their policy was not only industrially but politically reactionary; furthermore, enclosures were now much more often than before intended for tillage, and not for pasture. Presently the tide of the Civil War engulfed Tudor and early Stuart public policy forever.

Nineteenth century historians were unanimous in condemning Tudor and early Stuart policy as demagogic, if not as outright reactionary. Their sympathies lay, naturally, with Parliament and that body had been on the side of the enclosers. H. de B. Gibbins, though an ardent friend of the common people, wrote: "Such protective enactments were, however, as protective enactments generally be, utterly vain."[2] Innes was even more definite: "The usual remedies of punishing vagabondage and attempting to force industry into unsuited fields and to drive capital into less lucrative investments in order to provide employment failed—as usual."[3] Gairdner had no hesitation in appealing to free trade notions as "economic law": "Economic laws were, of course, not understood," he wrote, "and attempts were made by legislation to prevent husbandmen's dwellings from being thrown down by landlords, who found it profitable to devote arable land to pasture to increase the growth of wool. The frequent repetition of these Acts only show how ineffective they were in practice."[4] Recently an economist like Heckscher emphasizes his conviction that mercantilism should, in the main, be explained by an insufficient understanding of the complexities of economic phenomena, a subject which the human mind obviously needed another few centuries to master.[5] In effect, anti-enclosure legislation never seemed to have stopped the course of the enclosure movement, nor even to have obstructed it seriously. John Hales, second to none in his fervor for the principles of the Commonwealth men, admitted that it proved impossible to collect evidence against the enclosers, who often had their servants sworn upon the juries, and such was the number "of their retainers and hangers-on that no jury could be made without them." Sometimes the simple expedient of driving a single furrow across the field would save the offending lord from a penalty.

Such an easy prevailing of private interests over justice is often regarded as a certain sign of the ineffectiveness of legislation, and the victory of the vainly obstructed trend is subsequently adduced as conclusive evidence of the alleged futility of "a reactionary interventionism." Yet such a view seems to miss the point altogether. Why should the ultimate victory of a trend be taken as a proof of the ineffectiveness of the efforts to slow down its progress? And why should the purpose of these measures not be seen precisely in that which they achieved, *i.e.*, in the slowing down of the rate of change? That which is ineffectual in stopping a line of development altogether is not, on that account, altogether ineffectual. The rate of change is often of no less importance than the direction of the change itself; but while the latter frequently does not depend upon our volition, it is the rate at which we allow change to take place which well may depend upon us.

A belief in spontaneous progress must make us blind to the role of government in economic life. This role consists often in altering the rate of change, speeding it up or slowing it down as the case may be; if we believe that rate to be unalterable—or even worse, if we deem it a sacrilege to interfere with it—then, of course, no room is left for intervention. Enclosures offer an example. In retrospect nothing could be clearer than the Western European trend of economic progress which aimed at eliminating an artificially maintained uniformity of agricultural technique, intermixed strips, and the primitive institution of the common. As to England, it is certain that the development of the woolen industry was an asset to the country, leading, as it did, to the establishment of the cotton industry—that vehicle of the Industrial Revolution. Furthermore, it is clear that the increase of domestic weaving depended upon the increase of a home supply of wool. These facts suffice to identify the change from arable land to pasture and the accompanying enclosure movement as the trend of economic progress. Yet, but for the consistently maintained policy of the Tudor and early Stuart statesmen, the rate of that progress might have been ruinous, and have turned the process itself into a degenerative instead of a constructive event. For upon this rate, mainly, depended whether the dispossessed could adjust themselves to changed conditions without fatally damaging their substance, human and economic, physical and moral; whether they would find new employment in the fields of opportunity indirectly connected with the change; and whether the effects of increased imports induced by increased exports would enable those who lost their employment through the change to find new sources of sustenance.

The answer depended in every case on the relative rates of change and adjustment. The usual "long-run" considerations of economic theory are inadmissible; they would prejudge the issue by assuming that the event took place in a market economy. However natural it may appear to us to make that assumption, it is unjustified: market economy is an institutional structure which, as we all too easily forget, has been present at no time except our own, and even then it was only partially present. Yet apart from this assumption "long-run" considerations are meaningless. If the immediate effect of a change is deleterious, then, until proof to the contrary, the final effect is deleterious. If conversion of arable land to pasture involves the destruction of a definite number of houses, the scrapping of a definite amount of employment, and the diminution of the supplies of locally available food provisions, then these effects must be regarded as final, until evidence to the contrary is produced. This does not exclude the consideration of the possible effects of increased exports on the income of the landowners; of the possible chances of employment created by an eventual increase in the local wool supply; or of the uses to which the land-owners might put their increased incomes, whether in the way of further investments or of luxury expenditure. The time-rate of change compared with the time-rate of adjustment will decide what is to be regarded as the net effect of the change. But in no case can we assume the functioning of market laws unless a self-regulating market is shown to exist. Only in the institutional setting of market economy are market laws relevant; it was not the statesmen of Tudor England who strayed from the facts, but the modern economists, whose strictures upon them implied the prior existence of a market system.

England withstood without grave damage the calamity of the enclosures only because the Tudors and the early Stuarts used the power of the Crown to slow down the process of economic improvement until it became socially bearable—employing the power of the central government to relieve the victims of the transformation, and attempting to canalize the process of change so as to make its course less devastating. Their chancelleries and courts of prerogative were anything but conservative in outlook; they represented the scientific spirit of the new statecraft, favoring the immigration of foreign craftsmen, eagerly implanting new techniques, adopting statistical methods and precise habits of reporting, flouting custom and tradition, opposing prescriptive rights, curtailing ecclesiastical prerogatives, ignoring Common Law. If innovation makes the revolutionary, they were the revolutionaries of the age. Their commitment was to the welfare of the commonalty, glorified in the power and grandeur of the sovereign; yet the future belonged to constitutionalism and Parliament. The government of the Crown gave place to government by a class—the class which led in industrial and commercial progress. The great principle of constitutionalism became wedded to the political revolution that dispossessed the Crown, which by that time had shed almost all its creative faculties, while its protective function was no longer vital to a country that had weathered the storm of transition. The financial policy of the Crown now restricted the power of the country unduly, and began to constrain its trade; in order to maintain its prerogatives the Crown abused them more and more, and thereby harmed the resources of the nation. Its brilliant administration of labor and industry, its circumspect control of the enclosure movement, remained its last achievement. But it was the more easily forgotten as the capitalists and employers of the rising middle class were the chief victims of its protective activities. Not till another two centuries had passed did England enjoy again a social administration as effective and well ordered as that which the Commonwealth destroyed. Admittedly, an administration of this paternalistic kind was now less needed. But in one respect the break wrought infinite harm, for it helped to obliterate from the memory of the nation the horrors of the enclosure period and the achievements of government in overcoming the peril of depopulation. Perhaps this helps to explain why the real nature of the crisis was not realized when, some 150 years later, a similar catastrophe in the shape of the Industrial Revolution threatened the life and well-being of the country.

This time also the event was peculiar to England; this time also sea-borne trade was the source of a movement which affected the country as a whole; and this time again it was improvement on the grandest scale which wrought unprecedented havoc with the habitation of the common people. Before the process had advanced very far, the laboring people had been crowded together in new places of desolation, the so-called industrial towns of England; the country folk had been dehumanized into slum dwellers; the family was on the road to perdition; and large parts of the country were rapidly disappearing under the slack and scrap heaps vomited forth from the "satanic mills." Writers of all views and parties, conservatives and liberals, capitalists and socialists invariably referred to social conditions under the Industrial Revolution as a veritable abyss of human degradation.

No quite satisfactory explanation of the event has yet been put forward. Contemporaries imagined they had discovered the key to damnation in the iron regularities governing wealth and poverty, which they called the law of wages and the law of population; they have been disproved. Exploitation was put forth as another explanation both of wealth and of poverty; but this was unable to account for the fact that wages in the industrial slums were higher than those in any other areas and on the whole continued to rise for another century. More often a convolute of causes was adduced, which again was hardly satisfactory.

Our own solution is anything but simple; it actually fills the better part of this book. We submit that an avalanche of social dislocation, surpassing by far that of the enclosure period, came down upon England; that this catastrophe was the accompaniment of a vast movement of economic improvement; that an entirely new institutional mechanism was starting to act on Western society; that its dangers, which cut to the quick when they first appeared, were never really overcome; and that the history of nineteenth century civilization consisted largely in attempts to protect society against the ravages of such a mechanism. The Industrial Revolution was merely the beginning of a revolution as extreme and radical as ever inflamed the minds of sectarians, but the new creed was utterly materialistic and believed that all human problems could be resolved given an unlimited amount of material commodities.

The story has been told innumerable times: how the expansion of markets, the presence of coal and iron as well as a humid climate favorable to the cotton industry, the multitude of people dispossessed by the new eighteenth century enclosures, the existence of free institutions, the invention of the machines, and other causes interacted in such a manner as to bring about the Industrial Revolution. It has been shown conclusively that no one single cause deserves to be lifted out of the chain and set apart as *the* cause of that sudden and unexpected event.

But how shall this Revolution itself be defined? What was its basic characteristic? Was it the rise of the factory towns, the emergence of slums, the long working hours of children, the low wages of certain categories of workers, the rise in the rate of population increase, or the concentration of industries? We submit that all these were merely incidental to one basic change, the establishment of market economy, and that the nature of this institution cannot be fully grasped unless the impact of the machine on a commercial society is realized. We do not intend to assert that the machine caused that which happened, but we insist that once elaborate machines and plant were used for production in a commercial society, the idea of a self-regulating market was bound to take shape.

The use of specialized machines in an agrarian and commercial society must produce typical effects. Such a society consists of agriculturalists and of merchants who buy and sell the produce of the land. Production with the help of specialized, elaborate, expensive tools and plants can be fitted into such a society only by making it incidental to buying and selling. The merchant is the only person available for the undertaking of this, and he is fitted to do so as long as this activity will not involve him in a loss. He will sell the goods in the same manner in which he would otherwise sell goods to those who demand them; but he will procure them in a different way, namely, not by buying them ready-made, but by purchasing the necessary labor and raw material. The two put together according to the merchant's instructions, plus some waiting which he might have to undertake, amount to the new product. This is not a description of domestic industry or "putting out" only, but of any kind of industrial capitalism, including that of our own time. Important consequences for the social system follow.

Since elaborate machines are expensive, they do not pay unless large amounts of goods are produced.[6] They can be worked without a loss only if the vent of the goods is reasonably assured and if production need not be interrupted for want of the primary goods necessary to feed the machines. For the merchant this means that all factors involved must be on sale, that is, they must be available in the needed quantities to anybody who is prepared to pay for them. Unless this condition is fulfilled, production with the help of specialized machines is too risky to be undertaken both from the point of view of the merchant who stakes his money and of the community as a whole which comes to depend upon continuous production for incomes, employment, and provisions.

Now, in an agricultural society such conditions would not naturally be given; they would have to be created. That they would be created gradually in no way affects the startling nature of the changes involved. The transformation implies a change in the motive of action on the part of the members of society: for the motive of subsistence that of gain must be substituted. All transactions are turned into money transactions, and these in turn require that a medium of exchange be introduced into every articulation of industrial life. All incomes must derive from the sale of something or other, and whatever the actual source of a person's income, it must be regarded as resulting from sale. No less is implied in the simple term "market system," by which we designate the institutional pattern described. But the most startling peculiarity of the system lies in the fact that, once it is established, it must be allowed to function without outside interference. Profits are not any more guaranteed, and the merchant must make his profits on the market. Prices must be allowed to regulate themselves. Such a self-regulating system of markets is what we mean by a market economy.

The transformation to this system from the earlier economy is so complete that it resembles more the metamorphosis of the caterpillar than any alteration that can be expressed in terms of continuous growth and development. Contrast, for example, the merchant-producer's selling activities with his buying activities; his sales concern only artifacts; whether he succeeds or not in finding purchasers, the fabric of society need not be affected. But what he *buys* is raw materials and labor—nature and man. Machine production in a commercial society involves, in effect, no less a transformation than that of the natural and human substance of society into commodities. The conclusion, though weird, is inevitable; nothing less will serve the purpose: obviously, the dislocation caused by such devices must disjoint man's relationships and threaten his natural habitat with annihilation.

Such a danger was, in fact, imminent. We shall perceive its true character if we examine the laws which govern the mechanism of a self-regulating market.

Chapter 4: Societies and Economic Systems

Before we can proceed to the discussion of the laws governing a market economy, such as the nineteenth century was trying to establish, we must first have a firm grip on the extraordinary assumptions underlying such a system.

Market economy implies a self-regulating system of markets; in slightly more technical terms, it is an economy directed by market prices and nothing but market prices. Such a system capable of organizing the whole of economic life without out-side help or interference would certainly deserve to be called self-regulating. These rough indications should suffice to show the entirely unprecedented nature of such a venture in the history of the race.

Let us make our meaning more precise. No society could, naturally, live for any length of time unless it possessed an economy of some sort; but previously to our time no economy has ever existed that, even in principle, was controlled by mar-kets. In spite of the chorus of academic incantations so persistent in the nineteenth century, gain and profit made on exchange never before played an important part in human economy. Though the institution of the market was fairly common since the later Stone Age, its role was no more than incidental to economic life.

We have good reason to insist on this point with all the emphasis at our command. No less a thinker than Adam Smith suggested that the division of labor in society was dependent upon the existence of markets, or, as he put it, upon man's "propensity to barter, truck and exchange one thing for another." This phrase was later to yield the concept of the Economic Man. In retrospect it can be said that no misreading of the past ever proved more prophetic of the future. For while up to Adam Smith's time that propensity had hardly shown up on a considerable scale in the life of any observed community, and had remained, at best, a subordinate feature of economic life, a hundred years later an industrial system was in full swing over the major part of the planet which, practically and theoretically, implied that the human race was swayed in all its economic activities, if not also in its political, intellectual, and spiri-tual pursuits, by that one particular propensity. Herbert Spencer, in the second half of the nineteenth century, could, without more than a cursory acquaintance with eco-nomics, equate the principle of the division of labor with barter and exchange, and another fifty years later, Ludwig von Mises and Walter Lippmann could repeat this same fallacy. By that time there was no need for argument. A host of writers on politi-cal economy, social history, political philosophy, and general sociology had followed in Smith's wake and established his paradigm of the bartering savage as an axiom of their respective sciences. In point of fact, Adam Smith's suggestions about the eco-nomic psychology of early man were as false as Rousseau's were on the political psy-chology of the savage. Division of labor, a phenomenon as old as society, springs from differences inherent in the facts of sex, geography, and individual endowment; and the alleged propensity of man to barter, truck, and exchange is almost entirely apoc-ryphal. While history and ethnography know of various kinds of economies, most of them comprising the institution of markets, they know of no economy prior to our own, even approximately controlled and regulated by markets. This will become abundantly clear from a bird's-eye view of the history of economic systems and of markets, presented separately. The role played by markets in the internal economy of the various countries, it will appear, was insignificant up to recent times, and the change-over to an economy dominated by the market pattern will stand out all the more clearly.

To start with, we must discard some nineteenth century prejudices that underlay Adam Smith's hypothesis about primitive man's alleged predilection for gainful occu-pations. Since his axiom was much more relevant to the immediate future than to the dim past, it induced in his followers a strange attitude toward man's early history. On the face of it, the evidence seemed to indicate that primitive man, far from having a capitalistic psychology, had, in effect, a communistic one (later this also proved to be mistaken). Consequently, economic historians tended to confine their interest to that comparatively recent period of history in which truck and exchange were found on any considerable scale, and primitive economics was relegated to prehistory. Unconsciously, this led to a weighting of the scales in favor of a marketing psychology, for within the relatively short period of the last few centuries everything might be taken to tend towards the establishment of that which was eventually established, *i.e.*, a market system, irrespective of other tendencies which were temporarily submerged. The corrective of such a "short-run" perspective would obviously have been the linking up of economic history with social anthropology, a course which was consistently avoided.

We cannot continue today on these lines. The habit of looking at the last ten thousand years as well as at the array of early societies as a mere prelude to the true history of our civilization which started approximately with the publication of the *Wealth of Nations* in 1776, is, to say the least, out of date. It is this episode which has come to a close in our days, and in trying to gauge the alternatives of the future, we should subdue our natural proneness to follow the proclivities of our fathers. But the same bias which made Adam Smith's generation view primeval man as bent on barter and truck induced their successors to disavow all interest in early man, as he was now known *not* to have indulged in those laudable passions. The tradition of the classical economists, who attempted to base the law of the market on the alleged propensities of man in the state of nature, was replaced by an abandonment of all interest in the cultures of "uncivilized" man as irrelevant to an understanding of the problems of our age.

Such an attitude of subjectivism in regard to earlier civilizations should make no appeal to the scientific mind. The differences existing between civilized and "uncivilized" peoples have been vastly exaggerated, especially in the economic sphere. According to the historians, the forms of industrial life in agricultural Europe were, until recently, not much different from what they had been several thousand years earlier. Ever since the introduction of the plow—essentially a large hoe drawn by animals—the methods of agriculture remained substantially unaltered over the major part of Western and Central Europe until the beginning of the modern age. Indeed, the progress of civilization was, in these regions, mainly political, intellectual, and spiritual; in respect to material conditions, the Western Europe of 1100 A.D. had hardly caught up with the Roman world of a thousand years before. Even later, change flowed more easily in the channels of statecraft, literature, and the arts, but particularly in those of religion and learning, than in those of industry. In its economics, medieval Europe was largely on a level with ancient Persia, India, or China, and certainly could not rival in riches and culture the New Kingdom of Egypt, two thousand years before. Max Weber was the first among modern economic historians to protest against the brushing aside of primitive economics as irrelevant to the question of the motives and mechanisms of civilized societies. The subsequent work of social anthropology proved him emphatically right. For, if one conclusion stands out more clearly than another from the recent study of early societies it is the changelessness of man as a social being. His natural endowments reappear with a remarkable constancy in societies of all times and places; and the necessary preconditions of the survival of human society appear to be immutably the same.

The outstanding discovery of recent historical and anthropological research is that man's economy, as a rule, is submerged in his social relationships. He does not act so as to safeguard his individual interest in the possession of material goods; he acts so as to safeguard his social standing, his social claims, his social assets. He values material goods only in so far as they serve this end. Neither the process of production nor that of distribution is linked to specific economic interests attached to the possession of goods; but every single step in that process is geared to a number of social interests which eventually ensure that the required step be taken. These interests will be very different in a small hunting or fishing community from those in a vast despotic society, but in either case the economic system will be run on non-economic motives.

The explanation, in terms of survival, is simple. Take the case of a tribal society. The individual's economic interest is rarely paramount, for the community keeps all its members from starving unless it is itself borne down by catastrophe, in which case interests are again threatened collectively, not individually. The maintenance of social ties, on the other hand, is crucial. First, because by disregarding the accepted code of honor, or generosity, the individual cuts himself off from the community and becomes an outcast; second, because, in the long run, all social obligations are reciprocal, and their fulfillment serves also the individual's give-and-take interests best. Such a situation must exert a continuous pressure on the individual to eliminate economic self-interest from his consciousness to the point of making him unable, in many cases (but by no means in all), even to comprehend the implications of his own actions in terms of such an interest. This attitude is reinforced by the frequency of communal activities such as partaking of food from the common catch or sharing in the results of some far-flung and dangerous tribal expedition. The premium set on generosity is so great when measured in terms of social prestige as to make any other behavior than that of utter self-forgetfulness simply not pay. Personal character has little to do with the matter. Man can be as good or evil, as social or asocial, jealous or generous, in respect to one set of values as in respect to another. Not to allow anybody reason for jealousy is, indeed, an accepted principle of ceremonial distribution, just as publicly bestowed praise is the due of the industrious, skillful, or otherwise successful gardener (unless he be *too* successful, in which case he may deservedly be allowed to wither away under the delusion of being the victim of black magic). The human passions, good or bad, are merely directed towards noneconomic ends. Ceremonial display serves to spur emulation to the utmost and the custom of communal labor tends to screw up both quantitative and qualitative standards to the highest pitch. The performance of all acts of exchange as free gifts that are expected to be reciprocated though not necessarily by the same individuals—a procedure minutely articulated and perfectly safeguarded by elaborate methods of publicity, by magic rites, and by the establishment of "dualities" in which groups are linked in mutual obligations—should in itself explain the absence of the notion of gain or even of wealth other than that consisting of objects traditionally enhancing social prestige.

In this sketch of the general traits characteristic of a Western Melanesian community we took no account of its sexual and territorial organization, in reference to which custom, law, magic, and religion exert their influence, as we only intended to show the manner in which so-called economic motives spring from the context of social life. For it is on this one negative point that modern ethnographers agree: the absence of the motive of gain; the absence of the principle of laboring for remuneration; the absence of the principle of least effort; and, especially, the absence of any separate and distinct institution based on economic motives. But how, then, is order in production and distribution ensured?

The answer is provided in the main by two principles of behavior not primarily associated with economics: *reciprocity* and *redistribution*.[7] With the Trobriand Islanders of Western Melanesia, who serve as an illustration of this type of economy, reciprocity works mainly in regard to the sexual organization of society, that is, family and kinship; redistribution is mainly effective in respect to all those who are under a common chief and is, therefore, of a territorial character. Let us take these principles separately.

The sustenance of the family—the female and the children—is the obligation of their matrilineal relatives. The male, who provides for his sister and her family by delivering the finest specimens of his crop, will mainly earn the credit due to his good behavior, but will reap little immediate material benefit in exchange; if he is slack, it is first and foremost his reputation that will suffer. It is for the benefit of his wife and her children that the principle of reciprocity will work, and thus compensate him economically for his acts of civic virtue. Ceremonial display of food both in his own garden and before the recipient's storehouse will ensure that the high quality of his gardening be known to all. It is apparent that the economy of garden and household here forms part of the social relations connected with good husbandry and fine citizenship. The broad principle of reciprocity helps to safeguard both production and family sustenance.

The principle of redistribution is no less effective. A substantial part of all the produce of the island is delivered by the village headmen to the chief who keeps it in storage. But as all communal activity centers around the feasts, dances, and other occasions when the islanders entertain one another as well as their neighbors from other islands (at which the results of long distance trading are handed out, gifts are given and reciprocated according to the rules of etiquette, and the chief distributes the customary presents to all), the overwhelming importance of the storage system becomes apparent. Economically, it is an essential part of the existing system of division of labor, of foreign trading, of taxation for public purposes, of defense provisions. But these functions of an economic system proper are completely absorbed by the intensely vivid experiences which offer superabundant noneconomic motivation for every act performed in the frame of the social system as a whole.

However, principles of behavior such as these cannot become effective unless existing institutional patterns lend themselves to their application. Reciprocity and redistribution are able to ensure the working of an economic system without the help of written records and elaborate administration only because the organization of the societies in question meets the requirements of such a solution with the help of patterns such as *symmetry* and *centricity*.

Reciprocity is enormously facilitated by the institutional pattern of symmetry, a frequent feature of social organization among nonliterate peoples. The striking "duality" which we find in tribal subdivisions lends itself to the pairing out of individual relations and thereby assists the give-and-take of goods and services in the absence of permanent records. The moieties of savage society which tend to create a "pendant" to each subdivision, turned out to result from, as well as help to perform, the acts of reciprocity on which the system rests. Little is known of the origin of "duality"; but each coastal village on the Trobriand Islands appears to have its counterpart in an inland village, so that the important exchange of breadfruits and fish, though disguised as a reciprocal distribution of gifts, and actually disjoint in time, can be organized smoothly. In the Kula trade, too, each individual has his partner on another isle, thus personalizing to a remarkable extent the relationship of reciprocity. But for the frequency of the symmetrical pattern in the subdivisions of the tribe, in the location of settlements, as well as in intertribal relations, a broad reciprocity relying on the long-run working of separated acts of give-and-take would be impracticable.

The institutional pattern of centricity, again, which is present to some extent in all human groups, provides a track for the collection, storage, and redistribution of goods and services. The members of a hunting tribe usually deliver the game to the headman for redistribution. It is in the nature of hunting that the output of game is irregular, besides being the result of a collective input. Under conditions such as these no other method of sharing is practicable if the group is not to break up after every hunt. Yet in all economies of kind a similar need exists, be the group ever so numerous. And the larger the territory and the more varied the produce, the more will redistribution result in an effective division of labor, since it must help to link up geographically differentiated groups of producers.

Symmetry and centricity will meet halfway the needs of reciprocity and redistribution; institutional patterns and principles of behavior are mutually adjusted. As long as social organization runs in its ruts, no individual economic motives need come into play; no shirking of personal effort need be feared; division of labor will automatically be ensured; economic obligations will be duly discharged; and, above all, the material means for an exuberant display of abundance at all public festivals will be provided. In such a community the idea of profit is barred; higgling and haggling is decried; giving freely is acclaimed as a virtue; the supposed propensity to barter, truck, and exchange does not appear. The economic system is, in effect, a mere function of social organization.

It should by no means be inferred that socioeconomic principles of this type are restricted to primitive procedures or small communities; that a gainless and marketless economy must necessarily be simple. The Kula ring, in western Melanesia, based on the principle of reciprocity, is one of the most elaborate trading transactions known to man; and redistribution was present on a gigantic scale in the civilization of the pyramids.

The Trobriand Islands belong to an archipelago forming roughly a circle, and an important part of the population of this archipelago spends a considerable proportion of its time in activities of the Kula trade. We describe it as trade though no profit is involved, either in money or in kind; no goods are hoarded or even possessed permanently; the goods received are enjoyed by giving them away; no higgling and haggling, no truck, barter, or exchange enters; and the whole proceedings are entirely regulated by etiquette and magic. Still, it is trade, and large expeditions are undertaken periodically by natives of this approximately ring-shaped archipelago in order to carry one kind of valuable object to peoples living on distant islands situated clockwise, while other expeditions are arranged carrying another kind of valuable object to the islands of the archipelago lying counterclockwise. In the long run, both sets of objects—white-shell armbands and red-shell necklaces of traditional make—will move round the archipelago, a traject which may take them up to ten years to complete. Moreover, there are, as a rule, individual partners in Kula who reciprocate one another's Kula gift with equally valuable armbands and necklaces, preferably such that have previously belonged to distinguished persons. Now, a systematic and organized give-and-take of valuable objects transported over long distances is justly described as trade. Yet this complex whole is exclusively run on the lines of reciprocity. An intricate time-space-person system covering hundreds of miles and several decades, linking many hundreds of people in respect to thousands of strictly individual objects, is being handled here without any records or administration, but also without any motive of gain or truck. Not the propensity to barter, but reciprocity in social behavior dominates. Nevertheless, the result is a stupendous organizational achievement in the economic field. Indeed, it would be interesting to consider whether even the most advanced modern market organization, based on exact accountancy, would be able to cope with such a task, should it care to undertake it. It is to be feared that the unfortunate dealers, faced with innumerable monopolists buying and selling individual objects with extravagant restrictions attached to each transaction, would fail to make a standard profit and might prefer to go out of business.

Redistribution also has its long and variegated history which leads up almost to modern times. The Bergdama returning from his hunting excursion, the woman coming back from her search for roots, fruit, or leaves are expected to offer the greater part of their spoil for the benefit of the community. In practice, this means that the produce of their activity is shared with the other persons who happen to be living with them. Up to this point the idea of reciprocity prevails: today's giving will be recompensed by tomorrow's taking. Among some tribes, however, there is an intermediary in the person of the headman or other prominent member of the group; it is he who receives and distributes the supplies, especially if they need to be stored. This is redistribution proper. Obviously, the social consequences of such a method of distribution may be far reaching, since not all societies are as democratic as the primitive hunters. Whether the redistributing is performed by an influential family or an outstanding individual, a ruling aristocracy or a group of bureaucrats, they will often attempt to increase their political power by the manner in which they redistribute the goods. In the *potlatch* of the Kwakiutl it is a point of honor with the chief to display his wealth of hides and to distribute them; but he does this also in order to place the recipients under an obligation, to make them his debtors, and ultimately, his retainers.

All large-scale economies in kind were run with the help of the principle of redistribution. The kingdom of Hammurabi in Babylonia and, in particular, the New Kingdom of Egypt were centralized despotisms of a bureaucratic type founded on such an economy. The household of the patriarchal family was reproduced here on an enormously enlarged scale, while its "communistic" distribution was graded, involving sharply differentiated rations. A vast number of storehouses was ready to receive the produce of the peasant's activity, whether he was cattle breeder, hunter, baker, brewer, potter, weaver, or whatever else. The produce was minutely registered and, in so far as it was not consumed locally, transferred from smaller to larger storehouses until it reached the central administration situated at the court of the Pharaoh. There were separate treasure houses for cloth, works of art, ornamental objects, cosmetics, silverware, the royal wardrobe; there were huge grain stores, arsenals, and wine cellars.

But redistribution on the scale practiced by the pyramid builders was not restricted to economies which knew not money. Indeed, all archaic kingdoms made use of metal currencies for the payment of taxes and salaries, but relied for the rest on payments in kind from granaries and warehouses of every description, from which they distributed the most varied goods for use and consumption mainly to the nonproducing part of the population, that is, to the officials, the military, and the leisure class. This was the system practiced in ancient China, in the empire of the Incas, in the kingdoms of India, and also in Babylonia. In these, and many other civilizations of vast economic achievement, an elaborate division of labor was worked by the mechanism of redistribution.

Under feudal conditions also this principle held. In the ethnically stratified societies of Africa it sometimes happens that the superior strata consist of herdsmen settled among agriculturalists who are still using the digging stick or the hoe. The gifts collected by the herdsmen are mainly agricultural—such as cereals and beer—while the gifts distributed by them may be animals, especially sheep or goats. In these cases there is division of labor, though usually an unequal one, between the various strata of society: distribution may often cover up a measure of exploitation, while at the same time the symbiosis benefits the standards of both strata owing to the advantages of an improved division of labor. Politically, such societies live under a regime of feudalism, whether cattle or land be the privileged value. There are "regular cattle fiefs in East Africa." Thurnwald, whom we follow closely on the subject of redistribution, could therefore say that feudalism implied everywhere a system of redistribution. Only under very advanced conditions and exceptional circumstances does this system become predominantly political as happened in Western Europe, where the change arose out of the vassal's need for protection, and gifts were converted into feudal tributes.

These instances show that redistribution also tends to enmesh the economic system proper in social relationships. We find, as a rule, the process of redistribution forming part of the prevailing political regime, whether it be that of tribe, city-state, despotism, or feudalism of cattle or land. The production and distribution of goods is organized in the main through collection, storage, and redistribution, the pattern being focused on the chief, the temple, the despot, or the lord. Since the relations of the leading group to the led are different according to the foundation on which political power rests, the principle of redistribution will involve individual motives as different as the voluntary sharing of the game by hunters and the dread of punishment which urges the *fellaheen* to deliver his taxes in kind.

We deliberately disregarded in this presentation the vital distinction between homogeneous and stratified societies, *i.e.*, societies which are on the whole socially unified, and such as are split into rulers and ruled. Though the relative status of slaves and masters may be worlds apart from that of the free and equal members of some hunting tribes, and, consequently, motives in the two societies will differ widely, the organization of the economic system may still be based on the same principles, though accompanied by very different culture traits, according to the very different human relations with which the economic system is intertwined.

The third principle, which was destined to play a big role in history and which we will call the principle of *householding,* consists in production for one's own use. The Greeks called it *oeconomia,* the etymon of the word "economy." As far as ethnographical records are concerned, we should not assume that production for a person's or group's own sake is more ancient than reciprocity or redistribution. On the contrary, orthodox tradition as well as some more recent theories on the subject have been emphatically disproved. The individualistic savage collecting food and hunting on his own or for his family has never existed. Indeed, the practice of catering for the needs of one's household becomes a feature of economic life only on a more advanced level of agriculture; however, even then it has nothing in common either with the motive of gain or with the institution of markets. Its pattern is the closed group. Whether the very different entities of the family or the settlement or the manor formed the self-sufficient unit, the principle was invariably the same, namely, that of producing and storing for the satisfaction of the wants of the members of the group. The principle is as broad in its application as either reciprocity or redistribution. The nature of the institutional nucleus is indifferent: it may be sex as with the patriarchal family, locality as with the village settlement, or political power as with the seigneurial manor. Nor does the internal organization of the group matter. It may be as despotic as the Roman *familia* or as democratic as the South Slav *zadruga;* as large as the great domains of the Carolingian magnates or as small as the average peasant holding of Western Europe. The need for trade or markets is no greater than in the case of reciprocity or redistribution.

It is such a condition of affairs which Aristotle tried to establish as a norm more than two thousand years ago. Looking back from the rapidly declining heights of a world-wide market economy we must concede that his famous distinction of householding proper and money-making, in the introductory chapter of his *Politics,* was probably the most prophetic pointer ever made in the realm of the social sciences; it is certainly still the best analysis of the subject we possess. Aristotle insists on production for use as against production for gain as the essence of householding proper; yet accessory production for the market need not, he argues, destroy the self-sufficiency of the household as long as the cash crop would also otherwise be raised on the farm for sustenance, as cattle or grain; the sale of the surpluses need not destroy the basis of householding. Only a genius of common sense could have maintained, as he did, that gain was a motive peculiar to production for the market, and that the money factor introduced a new element into the situation, yet nevertheless, as long as markets and money were mere accessories to an otherwise self-sufficient household, the principle of production for use could operate. Undoubtedly, in this he was right, though he failed to see how impracticable it was to ignore the existence of markets at a time when Greek economy had made itself dependent upon wholesale trading and loaned capital. For this was the century when Delos and Rhodes were developing into emporia of freight insurance, sea-loans, and giro-banking, compared with which the Western Europe of a thousand years later was the very picture of primitivity. Yet Jowett, Master of Balliol, was grievously mistaken when he took it for granted that his Victorian England had a fairer grasp than Aristotle of the nature of the difference between householding and money-making. He excused Aristotle by conceding that the "subjects of knowledge that are concerned with man run into one another; and in the age of Aristotle were not easily distinguished." Aristotle, it is true, did not recognize clearly the implications of the division of labor and its connection with markets and money; nor did he realize the uses of money as credit and capital. So far Jowett's strictures were justified. But it was the Master of Balliol, not Aristotle, who was impervious to the human implications of money-making. He failed to see that the distinction between the principle of use and that of gain was the key to the utterly different civilization the outlines of which Aristotle accurately forecast two thousand years before its advent out of the bare rudiments of a market economy available to him, while Jowett, with the full-blown specimen before him, overlooked its existence. In denouncing the principle of production for gain "as not natural to man," as boundless and limitless, Aristotle was, in effect, aiming at the crucial point, namely the divorcedness of a separate economic motive from the social relations in which these limitations inhered.

Broadly, the proposition holds that all economic systems known to us up to the end of feudalism in Western Europe were organized either on the principles of reciprocity or redistribution, or householding, or some combination of the three. These principles were institutionalized with the help of a social organization which, *inter alia*, made use of the patterns of symmetry, centricity, and autarchy. In this framework, the orderly production and distribution of goods was secured through a great variety of individual motives disciplined by general principles of behavior. Among these motives gain was not prominent. Custom and law, magic and religion co-operated in inducing the individual to comply with rules of behavior which, eventually, ensured his functioning in the economic system.

The Greco-Roman period, in spite of its highly developed trade, represented no break in this respect; it was characterized by the grand scale on which redistribution of grain was practiced by the Roman administration in an otherwise householding economy, and it formed no exception to the rule that up to the end of the Middle Ages, markets played no important part in the economic system; other institutional patterns prevailed.

From the sixteenth century onwards markets were both numerous and important. Under the mercantile system they became, in effect, a main concern of government; yet there was still no sign of the coming control of markets over human society. On the contrary. Regulation and regimentation were stricter than ever; the very idea of a self-regulating market was absent. To comprehend the sudden change-over to an utterly new type of economy in the nineteenth century, we must now turn to the history of the market, an institution we were able practically to neglect in our review of the economic systems of the past.

Chapter 5: Evolution of the Market Pattern

The dominating part played by markets in capitalist economy together with the basic significance of the principle of barter or exchange in this economy calls for a careful inquiry into the nature and origin of markets, if the economic superstitions of the nineteenth century are to be discarded.[8]

Barter, truck, and exchange is a principle of economic behavior dependent for its effectiveness upon the market pattern. A market is a meeting place for the purpose of barter or buying and selling. Unless such a pattern is present, at least in patches, the propensity to barter will find but insufficient scope: it cannot produce prices.[9] For just as reciprocity is aided by a symmetrical pattern of organization, as redistribution is made easier by some measure of centralization, and householding must be based on autarchy, so also the principle of barter depends for its effectiveness on the market pattern. But in the same manner in which either reciprocity, redistribution, or householding may occur in a society without being prevalent in it, the principle of barter also may take a subordinate place in a society in which other principles are in the ascendant.

However, in some other respects the principle of barter is not on a strict parity with the three other principles. The market pattern, with which it is associated, is more specific than either symmetry, centricity, or autarchy—which, in contrast to the market pattern, are mere "traits," and do not create institutions designed for one function only. Symmetry is no more than a sociological arrangement, which gives rise to no separate institutions, but merely patterns out existing ones (whether a tribe or a village is symmetrically patterned or not involves no distinctive institution). Centricity, though frequently creating distinctive institutions, implies no motive that would single out the resulting institution for a single specific function (the headman of a village or another central official might assume, for instance, a variety of political, military, religious, or economic functions, indiscriminately). Economic autarchy, finally, is only an accessory trait of an existing closed group.

The market pattern, on the other hand, being related to a peculiar motive of its own, the motive of truck or barter, is capable of creating a specific institution, namely, the market. Ultimately, that is why the control of the economic system by the market is of overwhelming consequence to the whole organization of society: it means no less than the running of society as an adjunct to the market. Instead of economy being embedded in social relations, social relations are embedded in the economic system. The vital importance of the economic factor to the existence of society precludes any other result. For once the economic system is organized in separate institutions, based on specific motives and conferring a special status, society must be shaped in such a manner as to allow that system to function according to its own laws. This is the meaning of the familiar assertion that a market economy can function only in a market society.

The step which makes isolated markets into a market economy, regulated markets into a self-regulating market, is indeed crucial. The nineteenth century—whether hailing the fact as the apex of civilization or deploring it as a cancerous growth—naïvely imagined that such a development was the natural outcome of the spreading of markets. It was not realized that the gearing of markets into a self-regulating system of tremendous power was not the result of any inherent tendency of markets towards excrescence, but rather the effect of highly artificial stimulants administered to the body social in order to meet a situation which was created by the no less artificial phenomenon of the machine. The limited and unexpansive nature of the market pattern, as such, was not recognized; and yet it is this fact which emerges with convincing clarity from modern research.

"Markets are not found everywhere; their absence, while indicating a certain isolation and a tendency to seclusion, is not associated with any particular development any more than can be inferred from their presence." This colorless sentence from Thurnwald's *Economics in Primitive Communities* sums up the significant results of modern research on the subject. Another author repeats in respect to money what Thurnwald says of markets: "The mere fact, that a tribe used money differentiated it very little economically from other tribes on the same cultural level, who did not." We need hardly do more than point to some of the more startling implications of these statements.

The presence or absence of markets or money does not necessarily affect the economic system of a primitive society—this refutes the nineteenth century myth that money was an invention the appearance of which inevitably transformed a society by creating markets, forcing the pace of the division of labor, and releasing man's natural propensity to barter, truck, and exchange. Orthodox economic history, in effect, was based on an immensely exaggerated view of the significance of markets as such. A "certain isolation," or, perhaps, a "tendency to seclusion" is the only economic trait that can be correctly inferred from their absence; in respect to the internal organization of an economy, their presence or absence need make no difference.

The reasons are simple. Markets are not institutions functioning mainly within an economy, but without. They are meeting places of long-distance trade. Local markets proper are of little consequence. Moreover, neither long-distance nor local markets are essentially competitive, and consequently there is, in either case, but little pressure to create territorial trade, a so-called internal or national market. Every one of these assertions strikes at some axiomatically held assumption of the classical economists, yet they follow closely from the facts as they appear in the light of modern research.

The logic of the case is, indeed, almost the opposite of that underlying the classical doctrine. The orthodox teaching started from the individual's propensity to barter; deduced from it the necessity of local markets, as well as of division of labor; and inferred, finally, the necessity of trade, eventually of foreign trade, including even long-distance trade. In the light of our present knowledge we should almost reverse the sequence of the argument: the true starting point is long distance trade, a result of the geographical location of goods, and of the "division of labor" given by location. Long-distance trade often engenders markets, an institution which involves acts of barter, and, if money is used, of buying and selling, thus, eventually, but by no means necessarily, offering to some individuals an occasion to indulge in their alleged propensity for bargaining and haggling.

The dominating feature of this doctrine is the origin of trade in an external sphere unrelated to the internal organization of economy: "The application of the principles observed in hunting to the obtaining of goods found *outside the limits of the district,* led to certain forms of exchange which appear to us later as trade."[10] In looking for the origins of trade, our starting point should be the obtaining of goods from a distance, as in a hunt. "The Central Australian Dieri every year, in July or August, make an expedition to the south to obtain the red ochre used by them for painting their bodies. ... Their neighbors, the Yantruwunta, organize similar enterprises for fetching red ochre and sandstone slabs, for crushing grass seed, from the Flinders Hills, 800 kilometers distant. In both cases it might be necessary to fight for the articles wanted, if the local people offer resistance to their removal." This kind of requisitioning or treasure hunting is clearly as much akin to robbery and piracy as to what we are used to regard as trade; basically, it is a one-sided affair. It becomes two-sided, *i.e.*, "a certain form of exchange" often only through blackmail practiced by the powers on the site; or through reciprocity arrangements, as in the Kula ring, as with visiting parties of the Pengwe of West Africa, or with the Kpelle, where the chief monopolizes foreign trade by insisting on entertaining all the guests. True, such visits are not accidental, but—in our terms, not theirs—genuine trading journeys; the exchange of goods, however, is always conducted under the guise of reciprocal presents and usually by way of return visits.

We reach the conclusion that while human communities never seem to have foregone external trade entirely, such trade did not necessarily involve markets. External trade is, originally, more in the nature of adventure, exploration, hunting, piracy and war than of barter. It may as little imply peace as two-sidedness, and even when it implies both it is usually organized on the principle of reciprocity, not on that of barter.

The transition to peaceful barter can be traced in two directions, *viz.*, in that of barter and in that of peace. A tribal expedition may have to comply, as indicated above, with the conditions set by the powers on the spot, who may exact some kind of counterpart from the strangers; this type of relationship, though not entirely peaceful, may give rise to barter—one-sided carrying will be transformed into two-sided carrying. The other line of development is that of "silent trading" as in the African bush, where the risk of combat is avoided through an organized truce, and the element of peace, trust, and confidence is, with due circumspection, introduced into trade.

At a later stage, as we all know, markets become predominant in the organization of external trade. But from the economic point of view external markets are an entirely different matter from either local markets or internal markets. They differ not only in size; they are institutions of different function and origin. External trade is carrying; the point is the absence of some types of goods in that region; the exchange of English woolens against Portuguese wine was an instance. Local trade is limited to the goods of that region, which do *not* bear carrying because they are too heavy, bulky, or perishable. Thus both external trade and local trade are relative to geographical distance, the one being confined to the goods which cannot overcome it, the other to such only as can. Trade of this type is rightly described as complementary. Local exchange between town and countryside, foreign trade between different climatic zones are based on this principle. Such trade need not imply competition, and if competition would tend to disorganize trade, there is no contradiction in eliminating it. In contrast to both external and local trade, internal trade, on the other hand essentially competitive; apart from complementary exchanges it includes a very much larger number of exchanges in which similar goods from different sources are offered in competition with one another. Accordingly, only with the emergence of internal or national trade does competition tend to be accepted as a general principle of trading.

These three types of trade which differ sharply in their economic function are also distinct in their origin. We have dealt with the beginnings of external trade.

Markets developed naturally out of it where the carriers had to halt as at fords, seaports, riverheads, or where the routes of two land expeditions met. "Ports" developed at the places of transshipment.[11] The short flowering of the famous fairs of Europe was another instance where long-distance trade produced a definite type of market; England's staples were another example. But while fairs and staples disappeared again with an abruptness disconcerting to the dogmatic evolutionist, the *portus* was destined to play an enormous role in the settling of Western Europe with towns. Yet even where the towns were founded on the sites of external markets, the local markets often remained separate in respect not only to function but also to organization. Neither the port, nor the fair, nor the staple was the parent of internal or national markets. Where, then, should we seek for their origin?

It might seem natural to assume that, given individual acts of barter, these would in the course of time lead to the development of local markets, and that such markets, once in existence, would just as naturally lead to the establishment of internal or national markets. However, neither the one nor the other is the case. Individual acts of barter for exchange—this is the bare fact—do not, as a rule, lead to the establishment of markets in societies where other principles of economic behavior prevail. Such acts are common in almost all types of primitive society, but they are considered as incidental since they do not provide for the necessaries of life. In the vast ancient systems of redistribution, acts of barter as well as local markets were a usual, but no more than a subordinate trait. The same is true where reciprocity rules: acts of barter are here usually embedded in long-range relations implying trust and confidence, a situation which tends to obliterate the bilateral character of the transaction. The limiting factors arise from all points of the sociological compass: custom and law, religion and magic equally contribute to the result, which is to restrict acts of exchange in respect to persons and objects, time and occasion. As a rule, he who barters merely enters into a ready-made type of transaction in which both the objects and their equivalent amounts are given. *Utu* in the language of the Tikopia[12] denotes such a traditional equivalent as part of reciprocal exchange. That which appeared as the essential feature of exchange to eighteenth century thought, the voluntaristic element of bargain, and the higgling so expressive of the assumed motive of truck, finds but little scope in the actual transaction; in so far as this motive underlies the procedure, it is seldom allowed to rise to the surface.

The customary way to behave is, rather, to give vent to the opposite motivation. The giver may simply drop the object on the ground and the receiver will pretend to pick it up accidentally, or even leave it to one of his hangers-on to do so for him. Nothing could be more contrary to accepted behavior than to have a good look at the counterpart received. As we have every reason to believe that this sophisticated attitude is not the outcome of a genuine lack of interest in the material side of the transaction, we might describe the etiquette of barter as a counteracting development designed to limit the scope of the trait.

Indeed, on the evidence available it would be rash to assert that local markets ever developed from individual acts of barter. Obscure as the beginnings of local markets are, this much can be asserted: that from the start this institution was surrounded by a number of safeguards designed to protect the prevailing economic organization of society from interference on the part of market practices. The peace of the market was secured at the price of rituals and ceremonies which restricted its scope while ensuring its ability to function within the given narrow limits. The most significant result of markets—the birth of towns and urban civilization—was, in effect, the outcome of a paradoxical development. Because the towns, the offspring of the markets, were not only their protectors, but also the means of preventing them from expanding into the countryside and thus encroaching on the prevailing economic organization of society. The two meanings of the word "contain" express perhaps best this double function of the towns, in respect to the markets which they both enveloped and prevented from developing.

If barter was surrounded by taboos devised to keep this type of human relationship from abusing the functions of the economic organization proper, the discipline of the market was even stricter. Here is an example from the Chaga country: "The market must be regularly visited on market days. If any occurrence should prevent the holding of the market on one or more days, business cannot be resumed until the market-place has been purified. ... Every injury occurring on the market-place and involving the shedding of blood necessitated immediate expiation. From that moment no woman was allowed to leave the market-place and no goods might be touched; they had to be cleansed before they could be carried away and used for food. At the very least a goat had to be sacrificed at once. A more expensive and more serious expiation was necessary if a woman bore a child or had a miscarriage on the market-place. In that case a milch animal was necessary. In addition to this, the homestead of the chief had to be purified by means of sacrificial blood of a milch-cow. All the women in the country were thus sprinkled, district by district."[13] Rules such as these would not make the spreading of markets easier.

The typical local market at which housewives procure some of their daily needs, and growers of grain or vegetables as well as local craftsmen offer their wares for sale, shows an amazing indifference to time and place. Gatherings of this kind are not only fairly general in primitive societies, but remain almost unchanged right up to the middle of the eighteenth century in the most advanced countries of Western Europe. They are an adjunct of local existence and differ but little whether they form part of Central African tribal life, or a *cité* of Merovingian France, or a Scottish village of Adam Smith's time. But what is true of the village is also true of the town. Local markets are, essentially, neighborhood markets, and, though important to the life of the community, they nowhere showed any sign of reducing the prevailing economic system to their pattern. They were not starting points of internal or national trade.

Internal trade in Western Europe was actually created by the intervention of the state. Right up to the time of the Commercial Revolution what may appear to us as national trade was not national, but municipal. The Hanse were not German merchants; they were a corporation of trading oligarchs, hailing from a number of North Sea and Baltic towns. Far from "nationalizing" German economic life, the Hanse deliberately cut off the hinterland from trade. The trade of Antwerp or Hamburg, Venice or Lyons, was in no way Dutch or German, Italian or French. London was no exception: it was as little "English" as Luebeck was "German." The trade map of Europe in this period should rightly show only towns, and leave blank the countryside—it might as well have not existed as far as organized trade was concerned. So-called nations were merely political units, and very loose ones at that, consisting economically of innumerable smaller and bigger self-sufficing households and insignificant local markets in the villages. Trade was limited to organized townships which carried it on either locally as neighborhood trade or as long-distance trade—the two were strictly separated, and neither was allowed to infiltrate the countryside indiscriminately.

Such a permanent severance of local trade and long-distance trade within the organization of the town must come as another shock to the evolutionist, with whom things always seem so easily to grow into one another. And yet this peculiar fact forms the key to the social history of urban life in Western Europe. It strongly tends to support our assertion in respect to the origin of markets which we inferred from conditions in primitive economies. The sharp distinction drawn between local and long-distance trade might have seemed too rigid, especially as it led us to the somewhat surprising conclusion that neither long-distance trade nor local trade was the parent of the internal trade of modern times—thus apparently leaving no alternative but to turn for an explanation to the *deus ex machina* of state intervention. We will see presently that in this respect also recent investigations bear out our conclusions. But let us first give a bare outline of the history of urban civilization as it was shaped by the peculiar severance of local and long-distance trade within the confines of the medieval town.

This severance was, indeed, at the heart of the institution of medieval urban centers.[14] The town was an organization of the burgesses. They alone had right of citizenship and on the distinction between the burgess and the non-burgess the system rested. Neither the peasants of the countryside nor the merchants from other towns were, naturally, burgesses. But while the military and political influence of the town made it possible to deal with the peasants of the surroundings, in respect to the foreign merchant such authority could not be exerted. Consequently, the burgesses found themselves in an entirely different position in respect to local trade and long-distance trade.

As to food supplies, regulation involved the application of such methods as enforced publicity of transactions and exclusion of middlemen, in order to control trade and provide against high prices. But such regulation was effective only in respect to trade carried on between the town and its immediate surroundings. In respect to long-distance trade the position was entirely different. Spices, salted fish, or wine had to be transported from a long distance and were thus the domain of the foreign merchant and his capitalistic wholesale trade methods. This type of trade escaped local regulation and all that could be done was to exclude it as far as possible from the local market. The complete prohibition of retail sale by foreign merchants was designed to achieve this end. The more the volume of capitalistic wholesale trade grew, the more strictly was its exclusion from the local markets enforced as far as imports were concerned.

In respect to industrial wares, the separation of local and long-distance trade cut even deeper, as in this case the whole organization of production for export was affected. The reason for this lay in the very nature of craft gilds, in which industrial production was organized. On the local market, production was regulated according to the needs of the producers, thus restricting production to a remunerative level. This principle would naturally not apply to exports, where the interests of the producers set no limits to production. Consequently, while local trade was strictly regulated, production for export was only formally controlled by corporations of crafts.

The dominating export industry of the age, the cloth trade, was actually organized on the capitalistic basis of wage labor.

An increasingly strict separation of local trade from export trade was the reaction of urban life to the threat of mobile capital to disintegrate the institutions of the town. The typical medieval town did not try to avoid the danger by bridging the gap between the controllable local market and the vagaries of an uncontrollable long-distance trade, but, on the contrary, met the peril squarely by enforcing with the utmost rigor that policy of exclusion and protection which was the *rationale* of its existence.

In practice this meant that the towns raised every possible obstacle to the formation of that national or internal market for which the capitalist wholesaler was pressing. By maintaining the principle of a non-competitive local trade and an equally noncompetitive long-distance trade carried on from town to town, the burgesses hampered by all means at their disposal the inclusion of the countryside into the compass of trade and the opening up of indiscriminate trade between the towns of the country. It was this development which forced the territorial state to the fore as the instrument of the "nationalization" of the market and the creator of internal commerce.

Deliberate action of the state in the fifteenth and sixteenth centuries foisted the mercantile system on the fiercely protectionist towns and principalities. Mercantilism destroyed the outworn particularism of local and intermunicipal trading by breaking down the barriers separating these two types of noncompetitive commerce and thus clearing the way for a national market which increasingly ignored the distinction between town and countryside as well as that between the various towns and provinces.

The mercantile system was, in effect, a response to many challenges. Politically, the centralized state was a new creation called forth by the Commercial Revolution which had shifted the center of gravity of the Western world from the Mediterranean to the Atlantic seaboard and thus compelled the backward peoples of larger agrarian countries to organize for commerce and trade. In external politics, the setting up of sovereign power was the need of the day; accordingly, mercantilist statecraft involved the marshaling of the resources of the whole national territory to the purposes of power in foreign affairs. In internal politics, unification of the countries fragmented by feudal and municipal particularism was the necessary by-product of such an endeavor. Economically, the instrument of unification was capital, *i.e.*, private resources available in form of money hoards and thus peculiarly suitable for the development of commerce. Finally the administrative technique underlying the economic policy of the central government was supplied by the extension of the traditional municipal system to the larger territory of the state. In France, where the craft gilds tended to become state organs, the gild system was simply extended over the whole territory of the country; in England, where the decay of the walled towns had weakened that system fatally, the countryside was industrialized without the supervision of the gilds, while in both countries trade and commerce spread over the whole territory of the nation and became the dominating form of economic activity. In this situation lie the origins of the internal trade policy of mercantilism.

State intervention, which had freed trade from the confines of the privileged town, was now called to deal with two closely connected dangers which the town had successfully met, namely, monopoly and competition. That competition must ultimately lead to monopoly was a truth well understood at the time, while monopoly was feared even more than later as it often concerned the necessaries of life and thus easily waxed into a peril to the community. All-round regulation of economic life, only this time on a national, no more on a merely municipal, scale was the given remedy. What to the modern mind may easily appear as a shortsighted exclusion of competition was in reality the means of safeguarding the functioning of markets under the given conditions. For any temporary intrusion of buyers or sellers in the market must destroy the balance and disappoint regular buyers or sellers, with the result that the market will cease to function. The former purveyors will cease to offer their goods as they cannot be sure that their goods will fetch a price, and the market left without sufficient supply will become a prey to the monopolist. To a lesser degree, the same dangers were present on the demand side, where a rapid falling off might be followed by a monopoly of demand. With every step that the state took to rid the market of particularist restrictions, of tolls and prohibitions, it imperiled the organized system of production and distribution which was now threatened by unregulated competition and the intrusion of the interloper who "scooped" the market but offered no guarantee of permanency. Thus it came that although the new national markets were, inevitably, to some degree competitive, it was the traditional feature of regulation, not the new element of competition, which prevailed.[15] The self-sufficing household of the peasant laboring for his subsistence remained the broad basis of the economic system, which was being integrated into large national units through the formation of the internal market. This national market now took its place alongside, and partly overlapping, the local and foreign markets. Agriculture was now being supplemented by internal commerce—a system of relatively isolated markets, which was entirely compatible with the principle of householding still dominant in the countryside.

This concludes our synopsis of the history of the market up to the time of the Industrial Revolution. The next stage in mankind's history brought, as we know, an attempt to set up one big self-regulating market. There was nothing in mercantilism, this distinctive policy of the Western nation-state, to presage such a unique development. The "freeing" of trade performed by mercantilism merely liberated trade from particularism, but at the same time extended the scope of regulation. The economic system was submerged in general social relations; markets were merely an accessory feature of an institutional setting controlled and regulated more than ever by social authority.

Chapter 6: The Self-Regulating Market and the Fictitious Commodities: Labor, Land, and Money

This cursory outline of the economic system and markets, taken separately, shows that never before our own time were markets more than accessories of economic life. As a rule, the economic system was absorbed in the social system, and whatever principle of behavior predominated in the economy, the presence of the market pattern was found to be compatible with it. The principle of barter or exchange, which underlies this pattern, revealed no tendency to expand at the expense of the rest. Where markets were most highly developed, as under the mercantile system, they throve under the control of a centralized administration which fostered autarchy both in the households of the peasantry and in respect to national life. Regulation and markets, in effect, grew up together. The self-regulating market was unknown; indeed the emergence of the idea of self-regulation was a complete reversal of the trend of development. It is in the light of these facts that the extraordinary assumptions underlying a market economy can alone be fully comprehended.

A market economy is an economic system controlled, regulated, and directed by markets alone; order in the production and distribution of goods is entrusted to this self-regulating mechanism. An economy of this kind derives from the expectation that human beings behave in such a way as to achieve maximum money gains. It assumes markets in which the supply of goods (including services) available at a definite price will equal the demand at that price. It assumes the presence of money, which functions as purchasing power in the hands of its owners. Production will then be controlled by prices, for the profits of those who direct production will depend upon them; the distribution of the goods also will depend upon prices, for prices form incomes, and it is with the help of these incomes that the goods produced are distributed amongst the members of society. Under these assumptions order in the production and distribution of goods is ensured by prices alone.

Self-regulation implies that all production is for sale on the market and that all incomes derive from such sales. Accordingly, there are markets for all elements of industry, not only for goods (always including services) but also for labor, land, and money their prices being called respectively commodity prices, wages, rent, and interest. The very terms indicate that prices form incomes: interest is the price for the use of money and forms the income of those who are in the position to provide it; rent is the price for the use of land and forms the income of those who supply it; wages are the price for the use of labor power, and form the income of those who sell it; commodity prices, finally, contribute to the incomes of those who sell their entrepreneurial services, the income called profit being actually the difference between two sets of prices, the price of the goods produced and their costs, *i.e.,* the price of the goods necessary to produce them. If these conditions are fulfilled, all incomes will derive from sales on the market, and incomes will be just sufficient to buy all the goods produced.

A further group of assumptions follows in respect to the state and its policy. Nothing must be allowed to inhibit the formation of markets, nor must incomes be permitted to be formed otherwise than through sales. Neither must there be any interference with the adjustment of prices to changed market conditions—whether the prices are those of goods, labor, land, or money. Hence there must not only be markets for all elements of industry,[16] but no measure or policy must be countenanced that would influence the action of these markets. Neither price, nor supply, nor demand must be fixed or regulated; only such policies and measures are in order which help to ensure the self-regulation of the market by creating conditions which make the market the only organizing power in the economic sphere.

To realize fully what this means, let us return for a moment to the mercantile system and the national markets which it did so much to develop. Under feudalism and the gild system land and labor formed part of the social organization itself (money had yet hardly developed into a major element of industry). Land, the pivotal element in the feudal order, was the basis of the military, judicial, administrative, and political system; its status and function were determined by legal and customary rules. Whether its possession was transferable or not, and if so, to whom and under what restrictions; what the rights of property entailed; to what uses some types of land might be put—all these questions were removed from the organization of buying and selling, and subjected to an entirely different set of institutional regulations.

The same was true of the organization of labor. Under the gild system, as under every other economic system in previous history, the motives and circumstances of productive activities were embedded in the general organization of society. The relations of master, journeyman, and apprentice; the terms of the craft; the number of apprentices; the wages of the workers were all regulated by the custom and rule of the gild and the town. What the mercantile system did was merely to unify these conditions either through statute as in England, or through the "nationalization" of the gilds as in France. As to land, its feudal status was abolished only in so far as it was linked with provincial privileges; for the rest, land remained *extra commercium,* in England as in France. Up to the time of the Great Revolution of 1789, landed estate remained the source of social privilege in France, and even after that time in England Common Law on land was essentially medieval. Mercantilism, with all its tendency towards commercialization, never attacked the safeguards which protected these two basic elements of production—labor and land—from becoming the objects of commerce. In England the "nationalization" of labor legislation through the Statute of Artificers (1563) and the Poor Law (1601), removed labor from the danger zone, and the anti-enclosure policy of the Tudors and early Stuarts was one consistent protest against the principle of the gainful use of landed property.

That mercantilism, however emphatically it insisted on commercialization as a national policy, thought of markets in a way exactly contrary to market economy, is best shown by its vast extension of state intervention in industry. On this point there was no difference between mercantilists and feudalists, between crowned planners and vested interests, between centralizing bureaucrats and conservative particularists. They disagreed only on the methods of regulation: gilds, towns, and provinces appealed to the force of custom and tradition, while the new state authority favored statute and ordinance. But they were all equally averse to the idea of commercializing labor and land—the precondition of market economy. Craft gilds and feudal privileges were abolished in France only in 1790; in England the Statute of Artificers was repealed only in 1813–14, the Elizabethan Poor Law in 1834. Not before the last decade of the eighteenth century was, in either country, the establishment of a free labor market even discussed; and the idea of the self-regulation of economic life was utterly beyond the horizon of the age. The mercantilist was concerned with, the development of the resources of the country, including full employment, through trade and commerce; the traditional organization of land and labor he took for granted. He was in this respect as far removed from modem concepts as he was in the realm of politics, where his belief in the absolute powers of an enlightened despot was tempered by no intimations of democracy. And just as the transition to a democratic system and representative politics involved a complete reversal of the trend of the age, the change from regulated to self-regulating markets at the end of the eighteenth century represented a complete transformation in the structure of society.

A self-regulating market demands nothing less than the institutional separation of society into an economic and political sphere. Such a dichotomy is, in effect, merely the restatement, from the point of view of society as a whole, of the existence of a self-regulating market. It might be argued that the separateness of the two spheres obtains in every type of society at all times. Such an inference, however, would be based on a fallacy. True, no society can exist without a system of some kind which ensures order in the production and distribution of goods. But that does not imply the existence of separate economic institutions; normally, the economic order is merely a function of the social, in which it is contained. Neither under tribal, nor feudal, nor mercantile conditions was there, as we have shown, a separate economic system in society. Nineteenth century society, in which economic activity was isolated and imputed to a distinctive economic motive, was, indeed, a singular departure.

Such an institutional pattern could not function unless society was somehow subordinated to its requirements. A market economy can exist only in a market society. We reached this conclusion on general grounds in our analysis of the market pattern. We can now specify the reasons for this assertion. A market economy must comprise all elements of industry, including labor, land, and money. (In a market economy the last also is an essential element of industrial life and its inclusion in the market mechanism has, as we will see, far-reaching institutional consequences.) But labor and land are no other than the human beings themselves of which every society consists and the natural surroundings in which it exists. To include them in the market mechanism means to subordinate the substance of society itself to the laws of the market.

We are now in the position to develop in a more concrete form the institutional nature of a market economy, and the perils to society which it involves. We will, first, describe the methods by which the market mechanism is enabled to control and direct the actual elements of industrial life; second, we will try to gauge the nature of the effects of such a mechanism on the society which is subjected to its action.

It is with the help of the commodity concept that the mechanism of the market is geared to the various elements of industrial life. Commodities are here empirically defined as objects produced for sale on the market; markets, again, are empirically defined as actual contacts between buyers and sellers. Accordingly, every element of industry is regarded as having been produced for sale, as then and then only will it be subject to the supply-and-demand mechanism interacting with price. In practice this means that there must be markets for every element of industry; that in these markets each of these elements is organized into a supply and a demand group; and that each element has a price which interacts with demand and supply. These markets—and they are numberless—are interconnected and form One Big Market.[17]

The crucial point is this: labor, land, and money are essential elements of industry; they also must be organized in markets; in fact, these markets form an absolutely vital part of the economic system. But labor, land, and money are obviously *not* commodities; the postulate that anything that is bought and sold must have been produced for sale is emphatically untrue in regard to them. In other words, according to the empirical definition of a commodity they are not commodities. Labor is only another name for a human activity which goes with life itself, which in its turn is not produced for sale but for entirely different reasons, nor can that activity be detached from the rest of life, be stored or mobilized; land is only another name for nature, which is not produced by man; actual money, finally, is merely a token of purchasing power which, as a rule, is not produced at all, but comes into being through the mechanism of banking or state finance. None of them is produced for sale. The commodity description of labor, land, and money is entirely fictitious.

Nevertheless, it is with the help of this fiction that the actual markets for labor, land, and money are organized;[18] they are being actually bought and sold on the market; their demand and supply are real magnitudes; and any measures or policies that would inhibit the formation of such markets would *ipso facto* endanger the self-regulation of the system. The commodity fiction, therefore, supplies a vital organizing principle in regard to the whole of society affecting almost all its institutions in the most varied way, namely, the principle according to which no arrangement or behavior should be allowed to exist that might prevent the actual functioning of the market mechanism on the lines of the commodity fiction.

Now, in regard to labor, land, and money such a postulate cannot be upheld. To allow the market mechanism to be sole director of the fate of human beings and their natural environment, indeed, even of the amount and use of purchasing power, would result in the demolition of society. For the alleged commodity "labor power" cannot be shoved about, used indiscriminately, or even left unused, without affecting also the human individual who happens to be the bearer of this peculiar commodity. In disposing of a man's labor power the system would, incidentally, dispose of the physical, psychological, and moral entity "man" attached to that tag. Robbed of the protective covering of cultural institutions, human beings would perish from the effects of social exposure; they would die as the victims of acute social dislocation through vice, perversion, crime, and starvation. Nature would be reduced to its elements, neighborhoods and landscapes defiled, rivers polluted, military safety jeopardized, the power to produce food and raw materials destroyed. Finally, the market administration of purchasing power would periodically liquidate business enterprise, for shortages and surfeits of money would prove as disastrous to business as floods and droughts in primitive society. Undoubtedly, labor, land, and money markets *are* essential to a market economy. But no society could stand the effects of such a system of crude fictions even for the shortest stretch of time unless its human and natural substance as well as its business organization was protected against the ravages of this satanic mill.

The extreme artificiality of market economy is rooted in the fact that the process of production itself is here organized in the form of buying and selling.[19] No other way of organizing production for the market is possible in a commercial society. During the late Middle Ages industrial production for export was organized by wealthy burgesses, and carried on under their direct supervision in the home town. Later, in the mercantile society, production was organized by merchants and was not restricted any more to the towns; this was the age of "putting out" when domestic industry was provided with raw materials by the merchant capitalist, who controlled the process of production as a purely commercial enterprise. It was then that industrial production was definitely and on a large scale put under the organizing leadership of the merchant. He knew the market, the volume as well as the quality of the demand; and he could vouch also for the supplies which, incidentally, consisted merely of wool, woad, and, sometimes, the looms or the knitting frames used by the cottage industry. If supplies failed it was the cottager who was worst hit, for his employment was gone for the time; but no expensive plant was involved and the merchant incurred no serious risk in shouldering the responsibility for production. For centuries this system grew in power and scope until in a country like England the wool industry, the national staple, covered large sectors of the country where production was organized by the clothier. He who bought and sold, incidentally, provided for production—no separate motive was required. The creation of goods involved neither the reciprocating attitudes of mutual aid; nor the concern of the householder for those whose needs are left to his care; nor the craftsman's pride in the exercise of his trade; nor the satisfaction of public praise—nothing but the plain motive of gain so familiar to the man whose profession is buying and selling. Up to the end of the eighteenth century, industrial production in Western Europe was a mere accessory to commerce.

As long as the machine was an inexpensive and unspecific tool there was no change in this position. The mere fact that the cottager could produce larger amounts than before within the same time might induce him to use machines to increase earnings, but this fact in itself did not necessarily affect the organization of production. Whether the cheap machinery was owned by the worker or by the merchant made some difference in the social position of the parties and almost certainly made a difference in the earnings of the worker, who was better off as long as he owned his tools; but it did not force the merchant to become an industrial capitalist, or to restrict himself to lending his money to such persons as were. The vent of goods rarely gave out; the greater difficulty continued to be on the side of supply of raw materials, which was sometimes unavoidably interrupted. But, even in such cases, the loss to the merchant who owned the machines was not substantial. It was not the coming of the machine as such but the invention of elaborate and therefore specific machinery and plant which completely changed the relationship of the merchant to production. Although the new productive organization was introduced by the merchant—a fact which determined the whole course of the transformation—the use of elaborate machinery and plant involved the development of the factory system and therewith a decisive shift in the relative importance of commerce and industry in favor of the latter. Industrial production ceased to be an accessory of commerce organized by the merchant as a buying and selling proposition; it now involved long-term investment with corresponding risks. Unless the continuance of production was reasonably assured, such a risk was not bearable.

But the more complicated industrial production became, the more numerous were the elements of industry the supply of which had to be safeguarded. Three of these, of course, were of outstanding importance: labor, land, and money. In a commercial society their supply could be organized in one way only: by being made available for purchase. Hence, they would have to be organized for sale on the market—in other words, as commodities. The extension of the market mechanism to the elements of industry—labor, land, and money—was the inevitable consequence of the introduction of the factory system in a commercial society. The elements of industry had to be on sale.

This was synonymous with the demand for a market system. We know that profits are ensured under such a system only if self-regulation is safeguarded through interdependent competitive markets. As the development of the factory system had been organized as part of a process of buying and selling, therefore labor, land, and money had to be transformed into commodities in order to keep production going. They could, of course, not be really transformed into commodities, as actually they were not produced for sale on the market. But the fiction of their being so produced became the organizing principle of society. Of the three, one stands out: labor is the technical term used for human beings, in so far as they are not employers but employed; it follows that henceforth the organization of labor would change concurrently with the organization of the market system. But as the organization of labor is only another word for the forms of life of the common people, this means that the development of the market system would be accompanied by a change in the organization of society itself. All along the line, human society had become an accessory of the economic system.

We recall our parallel between the ravages of the enclosures in English history and the social catastrophe which followed the Industrial Revolution. Improvements, we said, are, as a rule, bought at the price of social dislocation. If the rate of dislocation is too great, the community must succumb in the process. The Tudors and early Stuarts saved England from the fate of Spain by regulating the course of change so that it became bearable and its effects could be canalized into less destructive avenues. But nothing saved the common people of England from the impact of the Industrial Revolution. A blind faith in spontaneous progress had taken hold of people's minds, and with the fanaticism of sectarians the most enlightened pressed forward for boundless and unregulated change in society. The effects on the lives of the people were awful beyond description. Indeed, human society would have been annihilated but for protective, countermoves which blunted the action of this self-destructive mechanism.

Social history in the nineteenth century was thus the result of a double movement: the extension of the market organization in respect to genuine commodities was accompanied by its restriction in respect to fictitious ones. While on the one hand markets spread all over the face of the globe and the amount of goods involved grew to unbelievable proportions, on the other hand a network of measures and policies was integrated into powerful institutions designed to check the action of the market relative to labor land, and money. While the organization of world commodity markets, world capital markets, and world currency markets under the aegis of the gold standard gave an unparalleled momentum to the mechanism of markets, a deep-seated movement sprang into being to resist the pernicious effects of a market controlled economy. Society protected itself against the perils inherent in a self-regulating market system—this was the one comprehensive feature in the history of the age.

Notes

1. Tawney, R.H., *The Agrarian Problem in the 16th Century*, 1912.
2. Gibbins, H. de B., *The Industrial History of England*, 1895.
3. Innes, A.D., *England under the Tudors*, 1932.
4. Gairdner, J., "Henry VIII," *Cambridge Modern History*, Vol. II, 1918.
5. Heckscher, E.F., *Mercantilism*, 1935, p. 104.
6. Clapham, J.H., *Economic History of Modern Britain*, Vol. III.

7. See Karl Polanyi, *The Great Transformation*, Beacon Press, 2001 ed.: pp. 276–280, "Notes on Sources: 6. Selected References to "Societies and Economic Systems."

8. See Karl Polanyi, *The Great Transformation*, Beacon Press, 2001 ed.: pp. 280–285, "Notes on Sources: 7. Selected References to "Evolution of the Market Pattern."

9. Hawtrey, G.R., *The Economic Problem*, 1925, p. 13. "The practical application of the principle of individualism is entirely dependent on the practice of exchange." Hawtrey, however, was mistaken in assuming that the existence of markets simply followed from the practice of exchange.

10. Thurnwald, R.C, *Economics in Primitive Communities*, 1932, p. 147.

11. Pirenne, H., *Medieval Cities*, 1925, p. 148 (footnote 12).

12. Firth, R., *Primitive Polynesian Economics*, 1939, p. 347.

13. Thurnwald, R.C., *op. cit.*, p. 162–164.

14. Our presentation follows H. Pirenne's well-known works.

15. Montesquieu, *L'Esprit del lois*, 1748. "The English constrain the merchant, but it is in favor of commerce."

16. Henderson, H.D., *Supply and Demand*, 1922. The practice of the market is twofold: the apportionment of factors between different uses, and the organizing of the forces influencing aggregate supplies of factors.

17. Hawtrey, G.R., *op. cit.* Its function is seen by Hawtrey in making "the relative market values of all commodities mutually consistent."

18. Marx's assertion of the fetish character of the value of commodities refers to the exchange value of genuine commodities and has nothing in common with the fictitious commodities mentioned in the text.

19. Cunningham, W., "Economic Change," *Cambridge Modern History*, Vol. I.

Neil Fligstein,
The Architecture of Markets (2001)*

2: Markets as Institutions

The modern nation-state is linked to the development of market society in myriad ways. The historical problem of producing stable capital, labor, and product markets eventually required governments and the representatives of capital and labor to produce general institutional arrangements (both laws and informal rules) around property rights, governance structures, and rules of exchange for all markets in capitalist societies. Within markets, cultural and historically specific rules and practices came to govern the relations among suppliers, customers, and workers (what I call conceptions of control).

Why do rules matter? Complex patterns of interaction that are stable require actors who share cognitive assumptions and expectations. To get such stability, people need either long experiences with one another, such that they settle into habitual patterns, or more formal rules to govern novel interactions. Rules based on experience or tradition or formally agreed to through negotiation then frequently become habitual in interaction (what in "institutional theory" is called "taken for grantedness" [DiMaggio and Powell 1991, chap. 1]). It is the instability produced by interactions in which actors do not share meanings that pushes actors to seek out more stable social conditions under which to interact (for example, see Haveman and Rao 1997; Dobbin and Sutton 1998).

There are two kinds of situations in which to study rules. In normal times rules are well known and taken for granted, and interactions are predictable as a result. There is conflict and contention between actors, but those conflicts are fought out under established rules, meanings, and practices. Analysts can identify who the players are, whether they are dominant or challengers, what their interests are, and what their actions mean.

In moments of the formation or transformation of political or market fields, actors become self-aware and engage in new forms of interaction to produce new arrangements. Because they try to forge new understandings, their interests and identities are in flux. They try to figure out what they want, how to get it, and how to get along with others who might want other things. The source of rules for new fields is often understandings brought from other fields. Actors modify these understandings in

* *The Architecture of Markets: An Economic Sociology of Twenty-First-Century Capitalist Societies.* © 2001 Princeton University Press. (pp. 27–44). Reprinted by permission of Princeton University Press.

the practice of interacting with other groups and create new practices. But these new practices are often laid down along lines set by existing understandings.

Why the state? As the possibility for complex patterns of interaction in the sphere of economic exchange has expanded, actors have proven incapable of providing rules for themselves. Actors have two sorts of problems. First, in the case of markets, actors have to worry about keeping their firms alive. It is difficult to devote resources to making rules and simultaneously to do business. Second, in the face of uncertainty and difficult competition, firms find it impossible to solve their collective problems of competition. Sometimes firms find a way to eliminate or co-opt their principal competitors. But often this does not happen. These conditions cause firms to seek out help by approaching the government to legislate to promote "fair" competition.[1]

What about power? Rules are not created innocently or without taking into account "interests." If the largest firms are able to work under a set of rules that allows them to dominate the main markets of a society and keep workers disorganized, those rules enforce a system of power. In order to get analytic leverage on real systems of rules and power, it is necessary to think systematically about how government capacity and the relative power of government officials, capitalists, and workers figure into the construction of new market rules to define the forms of economic activity that exist in a given society.

The political-cultural perspective can provide generic analytic tools to understand what a particular set of market arrangements implies about the power structure of a society. Once these arrangements are understood, it is possible to predict how existing institutions will be used by powerful actors to frame subsequent crises. This gives leverage on understanding many of the most important political-economic dynamics within societies.

There are three parts to my exposition. First, it is necessary to define markets and the institutions necessary for them to function. The key insight is that markets are a kind of field, one that depends not just on the power of incumbents, but on more general rules in society in order to stabilize the power of incumbents. Then, it is important to consider how governments in modern capitalist societies have been constructed to deal with problems of market regulation. I argue that governments develop different kinds of capacities to intervene in their economies that are characterized by three dimensions: their ability to intervene, the form of intervention, and whose interests dominate the intervention. I then generate some general propositions about how rules produced by firms and governments produce stability in market economies.

Market Institutions: Basic Definitions

One of the core ideas that differentiates modern society from the societies that preceded it is the idea that social organization is a human product. This implies that people can make choices and attempt to construct social-organizational vehicles to attain their ends. This does not mean that people are all successful or have the same opportunities to be actors. It does mean that the entire apparatus of modern economies is, at least partially, an outcome of these social technologies of organization. These have been invented and, upon reflection by the actors who use them, intentionally refined.

The organizations and institutions that existed before modernity were obviously social constructions as well. But they were not generally conceived that way. They established who was an actor and what actors could do. As people have become more self-aware in the past 350 years, they have examined existing social organizations, learned what seems to be successful, and used this knowledge to create new social arrangements. Over time, people have found ways to systematically produce new social technologies to attain ends (for example, legal incorporation to organize firms).

Modern governments, social movements, democratic politics, firms, and markets were invented by people collectively attempting to find ways to attain their ends (Fligstein 1997a). Often these "inventions" were accidental or reflected compromises between groups. The relations between the people who produced these social-organizational vehicles was, and continues to be, murky. But once these inventions were in place, other persons became aware of the various ways to organize and self-consciously built on them. The theory of fields is a generic theory of social organization in modernity. Our ability to recover that theory is itself an act of historical self-awareness. By abstracting away from the common experiences of social actors vying for control over their social arenas, social analysts have begun to appreciate that generic social processes underlie the construction of fields across states, markets, and the private nonprofit sector.

The theory of fields assumes that actors try to produce a "local" stable world where the dominant actors produce meanings that allow them to reproduce their advantage. These actors create status hierarchies that define the positions of incumbents and challengers. Actors face two related problems when constructing these fields: attaining a stable system of power and, once it is in place, maintaining it. The social organization of fields broadly refers to three features: the set of principles that organize thought and are used by actors to make sense of their situations (what might be called cognitive frames or worldviews), the routines or practices that actors perform in their day-to-day social relations, and the social relations that constitute fields that may or may not be consciously understood by actors (Bourdieu 1977).

The cognitive maps individuals possess offer them conceptual tools to understand or interpret the moves of others (White 1992; Emirbayer and Goodwin 1994). They also provide actors with tools to create new fields. Typically, the cognitive models that actors use are not included in conceptualizations of social organization. This is because human agency is typically undertheorized. Sociologists usually think that a person's position in a social structure dictates what the person does, while rational choice theories use interests as the main explanatory variable. Actors' common understandings are not assumed to be consequential to explaining their actions. But in the theory of fields, the skill of actors in interpreting their situations, constructing courses of action, and innovating on existing routines helps construct fields and maintain them once in place (Bourdieu and Wacquant 1992). While one can separate cognitive elements from social relations, social organization depends on both (Giddens 1981).

Social organization is the totality of what produces stable conditions for the privileged and not-so-privileged groups in society. It constitutes them as groups, defines their relations to one another, and maintains a certain order in existing fields. This discussion of the basic building blocks of fields is necessarily abstract. These building blocks contain no substance or, more precisely, "culture" (i.e., practices and local knowledge) (Geertz 1983). They do not tell us much about how a given field is going to be constructed and reproduced in reality because they do not specify what kind of field is being built (state, market, organization) nor the precise principles that structure the relations between the "players."

To apply the theory of fields to market society, it is necessary to define what kind of fields markets are, and what types of social organization are necessary for stable "markets as fields" to exist. Economic exchange ranges from infrequent and unstructured to frequent and structured. Markets are social arenas that exist for the production and sale of some good or service, and they are characterized by structured exchange. Structured exchange implies that actors expect repeated exchanges for their products and that, therefore, they need rules and social structures to guide and organize exchange. While the identities of their customers and suppliers may change over time, producers expect that they will continue to seek out customers and will need suppliers.

Actors in unstructured or haphazard exchange have little invested in the exchange, and participants may or may not interact again (either as buyers or sellers). While they may benefit from the exchange, the sellers' organizational survival does not depend on haphazard exchange. It is when the agents in exchange begin to view their own stability (i.e., reproduction) as contingent on stabilizing trade, that they turn to social-organizational vehicles. Exchange throughout human history has often been unstructured, but markets in the sense I use the term here preexisted modern capitalism. Markets (and this includes almost all modern production markets) are mainly structured by sellers looking for buyers.[2] A given market becomes a "stable market" (i.e., a field) when the product being exchanged has legitimacy with customers, and the suppliers of the good or service are able to produce a status hierarchy in which the largest suppliers dominate the market and are able to reproduce themselves on a period-to-period basis.

These actors produce organizations to make the good and create social relations between competitors to govern competition. Stable markets can be described as "self reproducing role structures" in which incumbent and challenger firms reproduce their positions on a period-of-period basis (White 1981).[3] The sellers generally produce the social structure in the market because their firms' existence is at stake if a stable market does not appear.[4] The particular problems of finding a stable market are the same for all sellers: they are looking to secure suppliers and customers and thereby find a way to reproduce themselves. The social relations between sellers in a stable market are such that one set of firms produces the dominant cultural meanings for the market and the other firms fall in line. This does not imply that the partners to any given exchange between buyers and sellers have to be the same actors. Sellers vie for customers, and customers may switch suppliers. The stability of the sellers, in the sense of their organizational survival, is what is important to the stability of the market. My operational definition of a market is the situation in which the status hierarchy and, by implication, the existence of the leading sellers are reproduced on a period-by-period basis.

For example, the steel industry in the United States, for much of the twentieth century, was a stable market in which firms had persistent identities and defined products.

The largest firms reproduced themselves by being vertically integrated and focused on stabilizing prices even as demand shifted radically (Fligstein 1990). Since the mid-1960s, the identities of the suppliers of steel products have been transformed. Many of the largest producers disappeared, and new firms began to dominate the market. The market itself became differentiated between products that were basic commodities and higher-end, higher-value-added products. The newer firms were able to take advantage of these changes to form a new market. The field that once existed has disappeared, and two new market fields have taken its place (Hogan 1984).

I do not mean to obliterate the distinction between a market and an industry. A market is a social arena where sellers and buyers meet. But for sellers and buyers to exist, a product has to exist and someone has to produce it. A market depends on the buyers continuing to "show up" in a particular social space to purchase the product. But the sellers' firms and their status relations define what stability means in the market. They define what the market is about, and their relations define the local culture by which money is to be made and stability produced. While there is obviously an interdependency between buyers and sellers, the sellers' stake in the arena is one of survival.

In spite of elaborate social mechanisms and rules to guide market interaction, markets are inherently unstable from the point of view of sellers. One of the deep insights of economics is that market society makes it very profitable to create new markets. At the beginning of markets, first movers can often reap huge rewards. But as other economic actors realize the opportunity, they enter into the market and prices drop. Moreover, as markets slow down in growth (as they inevitably do), firms have incentives to go after more market share and to cut prices. These forces intensify competition. Products can be delegitimated, most often by being superseded by other products. It is these opportunities and problems that create unstable conditions for producers.

Even where seller relations have been stabilized, they can be upset. The "game" for the incumbent firms is to find a way to produce a market as a stable field. These stable markets contain social structures that characterize the relations between dominant and challenger seller firms. The social relations are oriented toward maintaining the advantaged positions of the largest seller firms in the face of their challengers. They define how the market works and how competition is structured. For example, two main firms dominate the soft drink industry in the United States: Pepsi-Cola and Coca-Cola. These firms compete over market share and use advertising, diversification of products, and price discounts to do so. Although the firms compete, they have produced an equilibrium whereby both survive by following the accepted tactics of competition.

As forms of social organization, market structures involve both cognitive understandings and concrete social relations. The cognitive understandings are of two sorts: general societal understandings about how to organize firms and markets and find stable ways to compete, and specific understandings about the way a particular market works. These specific understandings structure the interactions between competitors but also allow actors to make sense of their competitors' actions. The concrete social relations in a given market reflect its unique history and its dependency on other markets. The links to suppliers and customers play a role in creating stable markets. The constitution of these relations determines which firms are dominant and why, and their relations to challenger firms. The ultimate success of firms in producing stable fields (i.e., social structures to stabilize their relationships with one another) is dependent on the general principles of making markets in their society, and the ability to find a way to do this within a particular market.

The first problem for a sociology of markets is to propose theoretically what kinds of rules and understandings are necessary to make structured exchange (i.e., markets as fields) possible in the first place. There are four types of rules relevant to producing social structures in markets—what can be called property rights, governance structures, rules of exchange, and conceptions of control. These categories are necessarily abstract. They refer to general types of rules that can appear as laws, understandings, or practices. They define issues about which actors who want to generate markets must create general understandings in order for stable markets to emerge. They need these rules whether they are aware of them or not. Failure, for example, to have property rights makes it difficult to have markets. If we do not know who owns what and who has the right to dispose of it, we are in the world of illegal trade and not the world of stable markets.

These four types of social structures have emerged historically as firms and governments have recognized certain generic problems in making markets work and then reflected on general solutions. Through understandings around these institutions actors produce social structures to organize themselves, to compete and cooperate, and to exchange with one another in a regular and reproducible fashion. Each of these types of social structure is directed at different problems of instability. Some are related to the general problem of creating a market in the first place, and others have to do with ensuring the stability of firms in a particular market.

Property rights are rules that define who has claims on the profits of firms (akin to what agency theorists call "residual claims" on the free cash flow of firms (Jensen and Meckling 1976; Fama 1980). This general statement leaves open the issues of the different legal forms of property rights (e.g., corporations vs. partnerships); the relationship between shareholders and employees, local communities, suppliers, and customers; and the role of the state in directing investment, owning firms, and preventing owners from harming workers. The holders of property rights are entitled to dispose of property or earn income from it. Patents and credentials are forms of property rights that entitle their holder to earn profits. The constitution of property rights is a continuous and contestable political process, not the outcome of an efficient process (for a similar argument, see Roe 1994). Organized groups from business, labor, government agencies, and political parties try to affect the constitution of property rights.

The division of property rights is at the core of market society. Property rights define who is in control of the capitalist enterprise and who has rights to claim the surplus. Property rights do not always favor the privileged groups in society. If, for instance, governments own firms and control investment decisions, their decisions can take into account different divisions of profits. Cooperative businesses or partnerships can allow for equal distribution of profits. Workers can receive part of their pay in profit-sharing schemes.

Property rights are necessary to markets because they define the social relationships between owners and everyone else in society. This stabilizes markets by making it clear who is risking what and who gets the reward in a particular market situation. A given firm's suppliers know who is the responsible entity. Property rights thus function to produce two forms of stability: defining the power relationships between constituencies in and around firms, and signaling to other firms who firms are.[5]

Governance structures refer to the general rules in a society that define relations of competition and cooperation and define how firms should be organized.[6] These rules define the legal and illegal forms of controlling competition. They take two forms: (1) laws and (2) informal institutional practices. Laws, called antitrust, competition, or anticartel laws, exist in most advanced industrial societies. The passage, enforcement, and judicial interpretation of these laws is contested (Fligstein 1990), and the content of such laws varies widely across societies. Some societies allow extensive cooperation between competitors, particularly when foreign trade is involved, while others try to reduce the effects of barriers to entry and promote competition. Competition is not just regulated within societies, but across societies. Countries have tariffs and trade barriers to help national industry to compete with foreign competitors. These laws often benefit particular sectors of the economy.

Firms' internal organization is also a response to legal and illegal forms of competition. Firms that vertically integrate often do so to ensure themselves supplies and deny those supplies to competitors. Firms also may horizontally integrate by buying up market share in order to produce stable order in a market. Firms may diversify products in order to protect themselves from the vagaries of particular products. They may also form long-term relationships with suppliers, customers, or financial organizations in order to respond to competition.

Market societies develop more informal institutional practices that are embedded in existing organizations as routines and are available to actors in other organizations. Mechanisms of transmission include professional associations, management consultants, and the exchange of professional managers (DiMaggio and Powell 1983; Meyer and Rowan 1977). Among these informal practices are how to arrange a work organization (such as the multidivisional form), how to write labor and management contracts, and where to draw the boundaries of the firm. So, for instance, firms can compete on price, but if they infringe on one another's patents or trade secrets, they are likely to run afoul of the law. They also include current views of what behavior of firms is legal or illegal. Governance structures help define the legal and normative rules by which firms structure themselves and their relations to competitors. In this way, they generally function to stabilize those relations.

Rules of exchange define who can transact with whom and the conditions under which transactions are carried out. Rules must be established regarding weights, common standards, shipping, billing, insurance, the exchange of money (i.e., banks), and the enforcement of contracts. Rules of exchange regulate health and safety standards of products and the standardization of products more generally. For example, many pharmaceutical products undergo extensive testing procedures. Health and safety standards help both buyers and sellers and facilitate exchange between parties who may have only fleeting interactions.

Product standardization has become increasingly important in the context of rules of exchange, particularly in the telecommunications and computer industries. National and international bodies meet to agree on standards for products across many industries. Standard setting produces shared rules that guarantee that products will be compatible. This process facilitates exchange by making it more certain that products will work the way they are intended.

Rules of exchange help stabilize markets by ensuring that exchanges occur under conditions that apply to everyone. If firms that ship their goods across a particular society do not have rules of exchange, such exchanges will be haphazard at best. Making these rules has become even more important for trade across societies. Many of the newest international trade agreements, including the European Union's Single Market Program and the last round of GATT (General Agreement on Tariffs and Trade), focus on producing and harmonizing practices around rules of exchange.

Conceptions of control reflect market-specific agreements between actors in firms on principles of internal organization (i.e., forms of hierarchy), tactics for competition or cooperation (i.e., strategies), and the hierarchy or status ordering of firms in a given market. A conception of control is a form of "local knowledge" (Geertz 1983).[7] Conceptions of control are historical and cultural products. They are historically specific to a certain industry in a certain society. They are cultural in that they form a set of understandings and practices about how things work in a particular market setting. A stable market is a social field in which a conception of control defines the social relations between incumbent and challenger seller firms such that the incumbent firms reproduce those relations on a period-to-period basis.

The purpose of action in a given market is to create and maintain stable worlds within and across firms that allow dominant seller firms to survive. Conceptions of control are social organizational vehicles for particular markets that refer to the cognitive understandings that structure perceptions of how a particular market works, as well as a description of the real social relations of domination that exist in a particular market. A conception of control is simultaneously a worldview that allows actors to interpret the actions of others and a reflection of how the market is structured.

State Building and Market Building

Creating a general set of rules whereby stable markets can be produced helps to structure exchange in particular product fields in a particular society. To move from unstructured to structured exchange in a market implies that actors became aware of systematic problems they had in stabilizing exchange. Their awareness stimulated them to search for social-organizational solutions to their problems. But this awareness did not come quickly or all at once. The emergence of the general social technologies that help actors to produce and maintain modern markets depended on discovering the problems presented by property rights (i.e., who owned what), governance structures (i.e., ways to organize, including fair and unfair forms of competition), rules of exchange (i.e., making exchanges), and conceptions of control (i.e., producing local status hierarchies within markets to stabilize the situation of dominant players).

Proposition 2.1. The entry of countries into capitalism pushes states to develop rules about property rights, governance structures, rules of exchange, and conceptions of control in order to stabilize markets.

The timing of entry of countries into capitalism has had huge effects on societal trajectories (Westney 1987; Chandler 1990; Fligstein 1990; Dobbin 1994). The
alliances made at this historical moment between workers, state officials, and capitalists structure the way in which states build policy domains and the policy styles that
develop in those domains. Once such styles are established, subsequent political and
economic crises are interpreted from these perspectives.

This does not mean that societies are forever locked into a set of institutions. But it
does mean that any new crisis is interpreted from the current dominant perspective.
This works in two ways. First, a system of rules is also a system of power. Incumbent
actors try to use the current rules for their benefit. But the current set of institutions
also provides actors with a way to figure out how to apply the old rules to new situations. For these reasons, we tend to observe incremental change, barring massive
societal failure due to war or depression. Then, crisis open up the possibility for new
political alliances and new rules.

For countries just establishing modern capitalist markets, creating stable conceptions of control is more difficult precisely because property rights, governance
structures, and rules of exchange are not well specified. Firms are exposed to cut-
throat competition and often demand that the state establish rules about property
rights, governance structures, and rules of exchange. Creating these new institutions
requires the interaction of firms, political parties, states, and newly invented (or borrowed) conceptions of regulation.[8]

People did not realize historically that they had to resolve these issues to make
structured exchange possible (see North 1990, chap. 1, on this point). Indeed, many
practices evolved in informal ways and stayed informal. Actors in markets found
ways of making themselves stable for relatively long periods of time in the absence
of formal institutions. But, as time went on, social technologies to solve problems
emerged in industrial societies. Large-scale social disruptions such as wars, depressions, or social movements caused political actors to craft general tools with which
to respond.

Once actors became aware of more general solutions, the solutions were used in
new circumstances. But novel situations often forced the modification of organizing
technology. So, for example, the modern American conception of the corporation (a
limited-liability joint stock corporation) started out as a state-directed conception
that emphasized limits on the exercise of property rights. This gave state legislators
a tool to use in development projects whereby they could delegate transportation
and communications projects to private firms and still maintain control over the
firm. People began to recognize two advantages to the corporate form: it allowed the
bringing together of more capital, and it restricted the liability of parties to the agreement to the assets they had invested in the corporation. These advantages pushed
entrepreneurs to demand more and more acts of incorporation. Finally, this led to a
broad conception of incorporation that made the form widely available (Friedman
1973; Roy 1997).

One way to partially understand governments is to view them as organized entities that produce and enforce market (and other) rules. However, this rule is not a historical necessity. It is theoretically possible for firms to routinize exchange with one
another without the benefit of rules or governments. After all, most trade before the

eighteenth century was done in the absence of strong states and legal systems (Greif 1989; Spruyt 1994). Before modernity, the problems posed by unstable exchange were solved by private parties to those exchanges.

There was a very practical reason for developing more general rules for markets. North and Thomas (1973) noted long ago that social institutions have made entrepreneurs richer, their firms bigger and more stable. For that reason, they argued, self-interested actors had an interest in producing rules. However, though we know rules encouraged markets as fields, entrepreneurs, managers, and governments did not comprehend that creating governmental capacity to make rules would help create wealth. So, for example, Carruthers (1996) shows that the first modern capital market in England was very much organized along political party lines. People would only trade with those with whom they agreed on politics. One of the purposes of the markets was to reward people in the party, by giving them access to friendly pools of capital.

North, in his later work (1990), realized that modern economic history cannot be read as the gradual reduction of transaction costs for markets by the production of rules that facilitate trade. He saw that entrepreneurs and government officials were unaware that their actions produced positive consequences. Their actions were not framed in these terms; indeed, their actions were often framed to benefit the friends of the rulers and cut out their enemies. Moreover, the rulers of premodern European states had time horizons far too short to understand what produced long-term economic growth. Most market institutions were the outcome of political struggles whereby one group of capitalists captured government and created rules to favor themselves over their political opponents. North's central insight is at the basis of the theory of market governance theory presented here.

The general rules that did eventually emerge reflected years of interactions with various forms of structured exchange and increasing awareness of the difficulty of managing large, complex production without rules. As one problem was solved and one set of markets stabilized, another set of problems emerged. The increasing scale of production, the growth of markets, and the growing awareness of entrepreneurs and managers of their common problems pushed the search for new common understandings.

It is still possible, of course, for structured exchange to occur without shared market institutions. But we now exist in a world where those institutions are ubiquitous and social actors are aware of them. It is this increasing self-awareness that leads modern actors in governments and firms to seek out general rules and forms of enforcement from the outset. As social organizational vehicles become more sophisticated and ways of managing sources of instability become better known, entrepreneurs and managers realize that common understandings over property rights, governance structures, rules of exchange, and conceptions of control are useful for dominant firms.

There were two historical problems that militated against entrepreneurs and managers producing common rules to stabilize exchanges. If governments were formed by a small number of capitalists to intervene in market processes, the group was likely to make rules to favor themselves and cut out others, thereby capturing the state for their narrow interests. This, of course, frequently happened. But such rent seeking was met by open political conflict.

Capitalists often faced collective action problems when it came to making market rules. How could entrepreneurs who focused on existing conceptions of control in a given market simultaneously develop more general rules about competition, cooperation, property rights, and rules of exchange with actors in other markets? The basic problem is that owners have to worry about organizational survival in the context of scarce organizational resources. Why would they want to produce general rules for all firms in a society?

Systemic economic crises produced economic depressions as a result of unstable systems of exchange. These became more severe and involved more and more people in societies across Europe and North America in the nineteenth century. Those with the largest investments in plants and other facilities found themselves in difficult situations. Managers and entrepreneurs responded to these crises caused by over competition by trying to control their main competitors. They used cartels or attempted to form monopolies. Firms also faced workers' organizations that resisted their attempt to lower wages and control labor markets. Class struggle led to bitter disputes between the large groups of workers who were located in the largest factories and the owners and managers (Edwards 1979). But frequently, firms and workers could not construct stable solutions, and they certainly could not construct "general" solutions. This conflict led both sides to go to governments to get them to produce stable outcomes (Fligstein 1990; Chandler 1990).

The organizations, groups, and institutions that comprise the fields of the state in modern capitalist society claim sovereignty, that is, the right to make and enforce the rules governing all interactions in a given geographic area (Krasner 1988).[9] Firms and workers' organizations came into conflict and turmoil, and they both tried to use governments to solve their problems of instability (Fligstein 1990). While most modern discussions of state building have focused on welfare and warfare, modern capitalist states have been constructed in interaction with the development of their economies, and the governance of their economies is part of the core of state building (Fligstein 1990; Hooks 1990; Campbell, Hollingsworth, and Lindberg 1991; Dobbin 1994; Evans 1995).[10]

As was stated in chapter 1, I conceive of the modern state as a set of fields that can be defined as policy domains. Policy domains are arenas of political action where bureaucratic agencies and representatives of firms and workers meet to form and implement policy.[11] The purpose of this policymaking is to make rules and governance mechanisms to produce stable patterns of interaction in nonstate fields. Modern states also typically develop legal systems with courts that adjudicate and interpret current laws and understandings. These legal fields are domains as well that contain judges, courts, lawyers, and law schools. One way to understand the legal system is to realize that legal systems are alternative ways for challenger groups to engage in political action. By using laws against incumbents, challengers can contest the rights and privileges of dominant groups (Shapiro 1980; Stone Sweet 2000).

The building of these domains, what others have called "state capacity" (Evans, Skocpol, and Rueschmeyer 1985), occurs under a set of interactions governed by rules that were usually put into place by a revolutionary social movement or a series of such movements or were imposed by outside invaders (or a succession of such forces). Once a government is formed in capitalist societies, the political processes in a society are about dominant groups building government capacity to ensure their dominant position and challenger groups trying to reorient existing domains or creating new ones to include them. The purpose of this confrontation within domains is to provide stabilizing rules that tend to benefit the most powerful groups.

State building can be defined as the development of domains set up by and for state officials, firms, and workers. The domains, once constructed, reflect the relative power of workers, capitalists, politicians, and state bureaucrats, inscribed in the law and the forms of regulation or intervention at the time they are formed. Domains are often focused on particular industries (for example, bank regulation) but can also be concerned with more general issues that apply across industries (for example, antitrust law or patents that define property rights). The way in which states are capable of intervening in their economies is inscribed by the power relations as constituted in particular domains when they are founded.

Proposition 2.2. Initial formation of policy domains and the rules they create affecting property rights, governance structures, and rules of exchange shape the development of new markets because they produce cultural templates that determine how to organize in a given society. The initial configuration of institutions and the balance of power between government officials, capitalists, and workers at that moment account for the persistence of, and differences between, national capitalisms.

The shape of initial regulatory institutions has a profound effect on subsequent capitalist development. They define the current state of rules and what is permissible. They also provide guidelines for how states can be subsequently organized to intervene in economies as new issues arise. Indeed, any new markets that come into existence do so under a given set of institutions. This is one of the most remarkable features of institutions: they enable newly organized actors to act. They do not just support the status quo, but allow entrepreneurs to come into existence without having to invent new ways to organize.

One can observe that, as countries industrialize, the demand for laws or enforceable understandings is high, and that once such understandings are produced, demand decreases. As new industries emerge or old ones are transformed, new rules are made in the context of the old rules. Dobbin (1994) has argued that societies create "regulatory styles." These styles are embedded in regulatory organizations and in the statutes that support them. States are often the focus of market crises, but actors continue to use an existing set of laws and practices to resolve crises. These general tactics are used to construct arguments about why and how governments should directly intervene in or mediate disputes between firms and workers and intervene in or regulate markets. Property rights, governance structures, conceptions of control, and rules of exchange are institutional issues about which modern states establish rules for economic actors. There can be specific state agencies oriented toward producing and enforcing institutions, such as patent offices for the registration of property rights. More common, however, are multiple domains where institutional issues enter in different ways.

A good example is modern states' extensive policy domains organized around the problems of agriculture. Most advanced industrial societies have programs oriented toward solving problems of competition (for instance, price support programs and subsidized foreign trade) and rules of exchange (for instance, health and safety standards and standard weights and measures). In many advanced industrial societies, these policies are buttressed with concerns for the property rights of "family" farmers. In the United States, special tax laws make it easier for family farmers to pass on their farms to their children.

Proposition 2.3. State actors are constantly attending to one market crisis or another. This is so because markets are always being organized or destabilized, and firms and workers are lobbying for state intervention.

In normal times, change in markets is incremental and dependent upon the construction of interests of actors in and around the state.[12] Having stable rules is often more important than the content of the rules. However, rules do embody the interests of dominant groups, and state actors do not intentionally transform rules unless dominant, groups are in crisis. Because of their central place in the creation and enforcement of market institutions, states become the focus of crisis in any important market. Given the turmoil inherent in markets, the state is constantly attending to some form of market crisis.

Pressure on states can come from two sources: other states (and by implication, their firms) and existing markets that can be constructed either locally (within the geography of the state) or globally (across states). As economic interdependence across societies has increased, there has been an explosion of cross-state agreements, particularly about rules of exchange. States provide stable and reliable conditions under which firms organize, compete, cooperate, and exchange. They also privilege some firms over others and often national large firms over small firms and firms from foreign countries. The enforcement of these rules affects what conceptions of control can produce stable markets. There are political contests over the content of laws, their applicability to given firms and markets, and the extent and direction of state intervention in the economy.

Power in Policy Domains and Market Institutions

States are important to the formation and ongoing stability of markets. How they are important and to what degree is a matter of historical process (Evans 1995; Ziegler 1997). Some states have greater capacities for intervention than others, and the likelihood of intervention depends on the nature of the crisis and the institutional history of the state (Dobbin 1994; Evans, Skocpol, and Rueschmeyer 1985; Ziegler 1997; Laumann and Knoke 1987).[13] Current organized interests use current rules to try to reproduce their positions. This explains why there appear to be so many forms of market arrangements across and within developed and developing societies (Evans 1995; Fligstein and Freeland 1995).

Proposition 2.4. Policy domains contain governmental organizations and representatives of firms, workers, and other organized groups. They are structured in two ways: (1) around the state's capacity to intervene, regulate, and mediate, and (2) around the relative power of societal groups to dictate the terms of intervention.

There are two important ways in which to characterize the political structure of policy domains of the state that focus on the relations between government officials, their organizations, capitalist firms, and workers. One important dimension is captured by the distinctions among direct intervention, regulation, and mediation. Domains are interventionist to the degree that government officials can directly make substantive decisions for markets. Governments may own firms, control the financial sector, direct investment, and heavily regulate firms' entries, exits, and competition in markets. Government officials have strong control over firms and workers in these domains. An example of an interventionist state is France, where historically officials in ministries were able to direct investment and control firms by virtue of government ownership.

In contrast, states dominated by regulatory regimes create agencies to enforce general rules in markets but do not decide who can own what or make what investment. Regulatory states put organizations in place in policy domains to play "traffic cop." Theoretically, regulatory bodies do not reflect the interest of any one group but use rules impartially to police the interactions of firms and workers who are represented in the domain. Often, regulatory bodies become captured by the dominant firms in an industry. Examples of regulatory agencies are the Securities and Exchange Commission in the United States and the Monopolies Board in the United Kingdom.

Both regulatory and interventionist states occasionally use mediation in policy arenas to help make policy or settle disputes. Interactions between industry representatives and state officials around an issue of common concern may result in the formation of a policy for a sector of the economy. If there is conflict between the organizations of firms or between firms and workers, state officials can act as mediators. It is clear that the Ministry of International Trade and Industry (MITI) played this role in Japanese development (Johnson 1982; Evans 1995).[14]

The second dimension that structures domains concerns whether or not they have undergone "capture." Economists argue that one problem of government intervention in markets is the temptation by government officials to "rent-seek" (Buchanan, Tellison, and Tulloch 1980). Rent seeking implies that government officials seek out payments from either firms or workers in a sector that involve bribes or taxes. In this case, the sector can be captured by the state. Evans (1995) has described as predatory states in some parts of the Third World that have this capacity.

Capture can occur as well if either a set of firms or an organized group of workers gets control over a policy domain (this is in fact the point of Buchanan, Tellison, and Tulloch's book [1980]). Regulatory agencies or even interventionist parts of ministries often rely on industry guidance for information and personnel. If workers or firms capture domains, they can attempt to use the domain to narrowly defend their privilege against other claims. To the degree that the industry is organized, it is possible for a set of firms to capture the regulatory agency and get government officials to accept their view of the industry and what should be done.

Workers can capture domains as well. Groups of workers may, for example, win the right to certify new workers, which, in essence, gives them the right to decide who has a "property right," that is, who owns a certificate that entitles them to make a profit from their skill. The government may directly intervene in this process or allow certification boards to be selected from members of workers' communities.

Professions, such as physicians in the United States, have used this tactic successfully for long periods of time to control the supply of doctors (Starr 1982).

I would like to reconceptualize the language of rent seeking to capture in a more neutral way who, among government officials or representatives of capitalist or worker interests, has the upper hand in making policy in a given domain. Rent seeking occurs in the sense that all groups are oriented toward using their power in policy domains for their own ends. But rent seeking can be more or less venal. When individual firms or government officials use their positions to advantage themselves and disadvantage of others in their fields, extreme predatory behavior can result.

Usually, rent seeking only occurs where there is little countervailing power. If a set of capitalist firms is not opposed by government officials or workers, the firms are more likely to set in place governance structures that allow collusion and rules of exchange that prevent other firms from competing. But it is also the case that the interests of a small set of firms and organized workers may produce the same effect. By such means textile manufacturers in the United States have been able to protect their markets by allying themselves with workers under the guise of saving jobs.

Notes

1. Incumbent firms that capture markets will try to obtain regulatory capture of states to buttress their position in markets. In societies with more interventionist traditions, governments can try to organize the market and control competition from the outset.

2. The idea of a market as a field does not assume that all market actors are in physical proximity, only social proximity. In modern society, trade shows, stock exchanges, commodity exchanges, shopping malls, shops in general are locales for physical markets. But markets do not have to be located in physical space. Many sales are made directly between buyer and seller, often through salespeople. But in these situations, buyers often compare prices of sellers by talking to multiple suppliers.

3. This model, with a little modification, can also be applied to labor markets, where some workers are organized and others are not.

4. Sellers can greatly affect the stability of market structures. If sellers stop buying a certain good, then the social organization of the market will do the producers no good. If markets are totally dependent on a single seller, then that seller can dictate market structure as well. But generally, even in these situations, sellers will frame their actions vis-à-vis one another in order to promote the survival of their firm (White 1981).

5. Institutional economics has recognized the importance of property rights for market stability (Jensen and Meckling 1976; Fama and Jensen 1983a, 1983b; Williamson 1985; North 1990). The division of property rights makes the firm possible in the first place, allows investment to occur, and constrains and enables managers and workers. In places where firm property rights do not exist, investment is haphazard and the economy is operated at the point of the barrel of a gun.

6. The term "governance" structure has been used to refer to both property rights questions (Jensen and Meckling 1976) and issues about how to draw the boundaries of firms (Williamson 1985). I have chosen to separate the question of who owns firms from the question of how markets and firms are actually organized in terms of how firms

compete, how they are to be internally organized, and if competitors can cooperate to control competition. Legitimate and illegitimate ways to compete and organize are not considered governance in economics.

7. I discuss the dynamics of particular markets and the formation of conceptions of control in chapter 14.

8. Late developers have the advantage of being able to borrow institutions from other societies. Japan, for example, self-consciously examined organizational practices of many societies to aid its late development project (Westney 1987).

9. My purpose is not to propose a theory of the state. Instead, I want to focus on how the theory of fields helps make sense of the organization of modern states and consider the links between the markets as fields and the states as fields.

10. Much of this discussion is inspired by the recent literature in political science that defines itself as historical institutionalism (March and Olsen 1989; Hall 1989; Steinmo, Thelen, and Longstreth 1992).

11. I am using *domain* in a very abstract fashion. I want to include pluralist, corporatist, and even totalitarian regimes under this rubric. I have in mind the general idea that governmental capacity includes relations that organize people who run governments, firms, and workers. But these relations can be hierarchical, voluntary, or democratic. They can be inscribed in constitutions or can evolve from preexisting social institutions.

12. The purpose here is not to develop a theory of the forms of states, but only to note their potential influence on market formation through their power to make the rules that govern all forms of social activity in a given geographic area.

13. This perspective does not imply that the state is pivotal for every economic process. Even in societies where states have a history of intervention, state involvement is variable and its effects are variable as well. The state's role depends on which market is being discussed and the current conditions in that or related markets.

14. In practice, the distinction between intervention and mediation may be difficult to make. Johnson described MTTI's actions more as direct interventions into markets, while Evans stresses the mediator role. As the Japanese economy has become more developed, firms have developed their own capacity for having policy preferences. This makes MTTI more a shaper of consensus.

References

Bourdieu, P. 1977. *Outline of a Theory of Practice*. Cambridge: Cambridge University Press.

Bourdieu, P., and L. Wacquant. 1992. *An Invitation to Reflexive Sociology*. Chicago: University of Chicago Press.

Buchanan, J., R. Tellison, and G. Tulloch. 1980. *Toward a Theory of the Rent-Seeking Society*. College Station: Texas A&M Press.

Campbell, J., J. R. Hollingsworth, and L. Lindberg. 1991. *Governance of the American Economy*. Cambridge: Cambridge University Press.

Carruthers, B. 1996. *City of Capital: Politics and Markets in the English Financial Revolution*. Princeton, N.J.: Princeton University Press.

Chandler, A. 1990. *Scale and Scope: The Dynamics of Industrial Capitalism*. Cambridge: Belknap Press of Harvard University Press.

DiMaggio, P. and W. Powell. 1983. "The Iron Cage Revisited: Institutional Isomorphism and Collective Rationality in Organizational Fields." *American Sociological Review* 48(2): 147–60.

_____, eds. 1991. *The New Institutionalism in Organizational Analysis*. Chicago: University of Chicago Press.

Dobbin, F. 1994. *Forging Industrial Policy: The U.S., Britain, and France in the Railway Age*. New York: Cambridge University Press.

Dobbin, F. and J. Sutton. 1998. "The Strength of a Weak State: The Rights Revolution and the Rise of Human Resource Management Divisions." *American Journal of Sociology* 104(2): 441–76.

Edwards, R. 1979. *Contested Terrain: The Transformation of the Workplace in the Twentieth Century*. New York: Basic Books.

Emirbayer, M., and J. Goodwin. 1994. "Network Analysis, Culture and the Problem of Agency." *American Journal of Sociology* 103:271–307.

Evans, P. 1995. *Embedded Autonomy: States and Industrial Transformation*. Princeton, N.J.: Princeton University Press.

Evans, P., T. Skocpol, and D. Rueschemeyer. 1985. "On the Road toward a More Adequate Understanding of the State." In P. Evans, T. Skocpol, and D. Ruechemeyer, eds., *Bringing the State Back In*. New York: Cambridge University Press.

Fama, E. 1980. "Agency Problems and the Theory of the Firm." *Journal of Political Economy* 88(2):288–307.

Fama, E., and M. Jensen. 1983a. "Separation of Ownership and Control." *Journal of Law and Economics* 26(2):301–25.

_____. 1983b. "Agency Problems and Residual Claims." *Journal of Law and Economics* 26(2):327–49.

Fligstein, N. 1990. *The Transformation of Corporate Control*. Cambridge: Harvard University Press.

_____. 1997. "Fields, Power, and Social Skill: A Critical Analysis of the 'New Institutionalisms.'" Working paper, Center for Culture, Organizations, and Politics, University of California, Berkeley.

Friedman, L. 1973. *A History of American Law*. New York: Simon and Schuster.

Geertz, C. 1983. *Local Knowledge: Further Essays in Interpretive Sociology*. New York: Basic Books.

Giddens, A. 1981. *A Contemporary Critique of Historical Materialism*. London: Macmillan.

Greif, A. 1989. "Reputations and Coalitions in Medieval Trade: Evidence on the Magrebhi Traders." *Journal of Economic History* 49:857–82.

Hall, P., ed. 1989. *The Political Power of Economic Ideas: Keynesianism across Nations*. Princeton, N.J.: Princeton University Press.

Haveman, H., and H. Rao. 1997. "Structuring a Theory of Moral Sentiments: Institutional and Organizational Coevolution in the Early Thrift Industry." *American Journal of Sociology* 102(6): 1606–51.

Hogan, W. T. 1984. *Steel in the United States: Restructuring to Compete*. Lexington, Mass.: Lexington.

Hooks, G. 1990. "The Rise of the Pentagon and the U.S. State Building: The Defense Program as Industrial Policy." *American Journal of Sociology* 96(2): 358–404.

Jensen, M. and W. Meckling. 1976. "Theory of the Firm: Managerial Behavior, Agency Costs, and Ownership Structure." *Journal of Financial Economics* 3(4):305–60.

Johnson, C. 1982. *MITI and the Japanese Miracle: The Growth of Industrial Policy*. Stanford, Calif.: Stanford University Press.

Krasner, S. 1988. "Sovereignty: An Institutional Perspective." *Comparative Political Studies* 21(1):66–94.

Laumann, E., and D. Knoke. 1987. *The Organizational State: Social Change in National Policy Domains*. Madison: University of Wisconsin Press.

March, J., and J. Olsen. 1989. *Rediscovering Institutions: The Organizational Basis of Politics*. New York: Free Press.

Meyer, J., and B. Rowan. 1977. "Institutionalized Organizations: Formal Structure as Myth and Ceremony." *American Journal of Sociology* 82(2):340–63.

North, D. 1990. *Institutions, Institutional Change, and Economic Performance*. Cambridge: Cambridge University Press.

North, D., and R. Thomas. 1973. *The Rise of the Western World: A New Economic History*. Cambridge: Cambridge University Press.

Roe, M. 1994. *Strong Managers, Weak Owners: The Political Roots of American Corporate Finance*. Princeton: Princeton University Press.

Roy, W. 1997. *Socializing Capital*. Princeton: Princeton University Press.

Shapiro, M. 1980. *Courts: A Comparative and Political Analysis*. Chicago: University of Chicago Press.

Spruyt, H. 1994. *The Sovereign State and Its Competitors: An Analysis of Systems Change*. Princeton, N.J.: Princeton University Press.

Starr, P. 1982. *The Social Transformation of American Medicine*. New York: Basic Books.

Steinmo, S., K. Thelen, and F. Longstreth. 1992. *Structuring Politics: Historical Institutionalism in Comparative Analysis*. Cambridge: Cambridge University Press.

Stone Sweet, A. 2000. *Governing with Judges: Constitutional Politics in Europe*. Oxford: Oxford University Press.

Westney, E. 1987. *Imitation and Innovation: The Transfer of Western Organizational Patterns to Meiji Japan*. Cambridge: Harvard University Press.

White, H. 1981. "Where Do Markets Come From?" *American Journal of Sociology* 87(3):517–47.

_____. 1992. *Identity and Control: A Structural Theory of Social Action*. Princeton, N.J.: Princeton University Press.

Williamson, O. 1985. *The Economic Institutions of Capitalism: Firms, Markets, Relational Contracting*. New York: Free Press.

Ziegler, N. 1997. *Governing Ideas: Strategies for Innovation in France and Germany*. Ithaca, N.Y.: Cornell University Press.

4

The New Institutional Economics

The New Institutional Economics (NIE) paradigm shares the rationalist and utility maximization foundations of neoclassical economics, yet NIE theorists criticize neoclassical economics for ignoring the role of institutions and transaction costs in political economy. NIE analyses thus focus on market institutions, such as property rights regimes, and their role in facilitating economic activity, and they are interested in explaining processes of institutional change. Many NIE theorists, such as Douglass North, explicitly focus on the role of the state in creating laws and enforcing the contracts necessary to reduce transaction costs. Like **Adam Smith,** they see the state as indispensable in providing the basic infrastructure in which markets function but move closer to the market-institutional perspective advocated in this reader by focusing analytical attention on other central institutions that underpin economic interaction.

The NIE builds on the Nobel Prize–winning work of Ronald Coase, who introduced a theory of transaction cost economics in a landmark article titled "The Nature of the Firm."[1] Asking why we have firms instead of just a series of people contracting with one another, Coase observed that there are a multitude of transaction costs involved in market exchange. These transaction costs—particularly information and enforcement costs—add to the price of procuring something from the market. Coase concluded that firms arise to reduce these transaction costs by producing internally and expand to the point where the returns from production disappear; at that point, the market takes over. New institutional economists have since built on Coase's logic to examine other economic institutions.

Douglass North has been a central scholar in the paradigm, both in terms of theory development and its application to empirical economic and institutional phenomena. His broad concern in his body of work has been to develop an analytical framework that explains the relationships among institutions, institutional change, and economic history and performance. North's definition of institutions has come to be a standard in the field and reveals the broad scope of NIE concerns and research. In his view, institutions are the rules of the game in society, the humanly devised constraints that shape human interaction and structure incentives in political, social, and economic exchange.[2] Institutions can be formal—that is, laws and rules—or informal—such as codes of conduct and implicit understandings informed by culture. In the piece presented here, he describes the phenomenon of market exchange, pointing out that even the simplest market transaction is underpinned by a complex legal structure of property rights and their enforcement that reduce the information and monitoring costs of transaction. He also reviews Coase's and other theorists' explanations for the existence of hierarchical organizations such as the firm.

North develops a general transaction cost framework to explain all forms of economic organization or systems of exchange. Compliance costs in any form of organized economic activity consist of measurement (information) and monitoring (enforcement) costs, and organizations develop to minimize those transaction costs. Transaction costs are essentially anything that impedes seamless exchange, or the perfect functioning of markets, and property rights are the solution to this problem, as they reduce transaction costs. A system of perfectly specified and costlessly enforced property rights would drive transaction costs to zero. These conditions do not obtain in reality, but lowering transaction costs through property rights leads to a more efficient economy. (See **Hernando de Soto's** article in this volume for a discussion of the importance of property rights in developing countries.) In North's view, the state is an essential coercive third party to exchange that can monitor and enforce property rights. He thus recognizes that the state is paramount in developing an institutional regime that sustains and supports markets.

A central tenet of the NIE, mentioned briefly in the North piece, is the view—often criticized as overly functionalist—that more efficient organizational forms and institutions continually replace less efficient ones, in a rational process. North is less insistent on this point in his later work, where he focuses more on institutional change and allows that institutional outcomes may not always be efficient. But the functionalist logic is common to the NIE, as it generally assumes that institutions develop as needed in efficient forms. This does not mean that only one set of institutional solutions is appropriate to facilitate market exchange. On the contrary, different societies approach institutional design in different ways, and NIE theorists believe that emphasizing institutions can help to explain variation and divergence across national political–economic systems. For example, the **Peter Hall and David Soskice** "varieties of capitalism" framework, which we encounter later in the reader, builds on the NIE logic in specifying two different sets of political–economic institutions that fit together in efficient, transaction cost-reducing ways.

Oliver Williamson builds even more directly than North on the tradition of transaction cost economics in studying the economic institutions of capitalism. He is especially interested in Coase's original question about the boundary between firms (or what he calls "hierarchy") and market and in how firms make decisions about whether to vertically integrate to produce in-house or to buy parts on the market. In this analysis, he considers a full spectrum of other possibilities between firms and markets, such as long-term relational contracting and modes of private enforcement. One of Williamson's key concepts is that of "asset specificity." This gauges the degree of transferability of an asset intended for a specific use and a specific partner to other uses and partners. Assets with low specificity, Williamson argues, should be procured through the market. Highly specific assets, on the other hand, have little value beyond their use in a particular transaction. For these assets, companies are vulnerable to the threat of opportunism on the part of their suppliers. Production of highly specific assets should thus be vertically integrated into the firm or safeguarded through other institutions developed to limit opportunism—such as strong contracts, cross-holding shares to align incentives between buyer and supplier, or a cultivated norm of reciprocity. In Williamson's more general view, as expressed in the larger book, the economic institutions of capitalism have the main purpose and effect of reducing transaction costs, although he concedes that it is not their only purpose. In his analysis, the potential scope of transaction cost economics is much broader than it might appear at first glance, as the transaction is the basic unit of analysis in understanding capitalism.

Notes

1. Ronald Coase, "The Nature of the Firm," *Economica* 4 (1937): 386–405.
2. Douglass C. North, *Institutions, Institutional Change and Economic Performance* (Cambridge: Cambridge University Press, 1990).

Douglass C. North,
Structure and Change in Economic History (1981)*

Chapter 4: A Framework for Analyzing Economic Organization in History

I

Throughout history economic activity has occurred by means of an immense variety of organizational forms. From the so-called re-distributive societies of the Egyptian dynasties, to the patron-client relationship in Republican Rome, to the feudal manor, these organizational forms have been the subject of historical investigation; but most of the research has been devoid of analytical content.[1] Much the same criticism can be made of economists' work dealing with modern-day economic organization. In fact, as recently as 1968, the *International Encyclopedia of the Social Sciences* included no essay on the market, the most fundamental institution of modern Western economies and central to the performance of economies of the past, as well.

To account analytically for economic organization we must use a theory of transaction costs together with a theory of the state. A theory of transaction costs is necessary because under the ubiquitous condition of scarcity and therefore competition, more efficient forms of economic organization will replace less efficient forms under *ceteris paribus* conditions. The state, however—as I have argued in the previous chapter—will encourage and specify efficient property rights only to the extent that they are consistent with the wealth-maximizing objectives of those who run the state. Hence the need for a model that incorporates both. I shall begin here by developing a transaction-cost approach to economic organization and then I shall combine it with the analysis of the state developed in the previous chapter.

Any form of economic organization must have provisions for the specifying and enforcing of the terms of exchange. Abstracting from the role of the state, the choice of organizational form will be dictated by the relative amount of resources required for a given amount of output. A market-price system is costly because it is costly first to measure the dimensions of the good or service transacted and then to enforce the terms of exchange. And there is really a third cost involved as well: that associated with the external effects that arise because measurement was imperfect. In contrast,

* From: *Structure and Change in Economic History* by Douglass C. North. Copyright © 1981 by W. W. Norton & Company, Inc. (pp. 33–44) Used by permission of W. W. Norton & Company, Inc.

hierarchical forms of organization substitute the directives of a central authority: a contractual arrangement restricts the options of the parties to exchange wherein one party gives up control of decisions to the other party.[2] The costs of this organizational form are the costs of measuring the performance of agents; the inefficiencies associated with imperfect measurement; and the costs of enforcement. Because the resource costs of compliance are different from those involved in the market-price system, they lead to different results. Let me illustrate market exchange, then explore the reasons for the existence of the firm (or other hierarchical organization), and then attempt to explain economic organization in history.

II

I begin by simply describing a transaction I make every week in my local public market. It is the purchase of a quantity of oranges (fourteen oranges for one dollar in 1980). I purchase oranges for orange juice and therefore I want the oranges to contain a great deal of juice (rather than pulp) and to have a tart flavor. What I really would like to specify in the exchange is a certain quantity of orange juice with a combination of organic ingredients that produces the flavor I want. Why aren't oranges sold in a way that I can get precisely what I want? In part, they are. Valencia oranges are juice oranges and are sold separately from Navel or other eating oranges. But the amount of juice and the flavor that I will get from the oranges cannot be specified at low cost. If the measurement of these ingredients were possible at no or little cost, then I could obtain the precise combination I want. Instead, purchases are made by number, weight, volume, length; and resources are devoted to seeing that these objective measurement characteristics are met.

The seller of the oranges bought them from a wholesaler; within the crates he received were some oranges not in good condition. He stands to lose money on those oranges, since if he tries to give them to me for my dollar I will go to another stall at the public market to buy my oranges. In short, the competition of a large number of sellers constrains his behavior. Does he slip a few of the rotten oranges in the bottom of the sack where I won't notice them until I get home? He might if he never expects to see me again since it is the only way he can get rid of the oranges that otherwise would be a loss to him. But that is why I go to the same dealer, Morris, each week. He knows I will not return if he slips such oranges into my sack. I am valuable as a repeat customer; opportunism, then, is constrained by repetitive dealings. Morris, on his part, accepts my check for one dollar without inquiring whether I have sufficient funds in the bank to cover the check, or whether the dollar he gets when he cashes my check will be accepted unquestionably by his wholesaler or by anyone else from whom he wishes to purchase goods or services.

It should be readily apparent not only that this simple exercise was really complex in terms of its fundamental characteristics, but also that we have examined only its superficial manifestations. Underlying the transaction—making it possible—was a complex structure of law and its enforcement. Both Morris and I accept that we each have property rights over the oranges and the dollar—and that these rights are enforceable in a court of law. Morris accepts a piece of paper as a legitimate surrogate for a command over a certain amount of other resources and knows that he can use it for that purpose. In brief, uncertainty is reduced or completely eliminated by an accepted structure of property rights and their enforcement.

Let me summarize the implications of the foregoing illustration. One must be able to measure the quantity of a good in order for it to be exclusive property and to have value in exchange. Where measurement costs are very high, the good will be a common property resource. The technology of measurement and the history of weights and measures is a crucial part of economic history since as measurement costs were reduced the cost of transacting was reduced. The fourteen oranges in the illustration above are an imperfect surrogate for the quantity desired, which is a given quantity of juice with a certain flavor. The separation of oranges by type or the grading of oranges is a step in the right direction; but so long as *some* characteristic of a good that has economic value is not measured, then there is divergence between private and social cost.[3]

Information costs are reduced by the existence of large numbers of buyers and sellers. Under these conditions, prices embody the same information that would require large search costs by individual buyers and sellers in the absence of an organized market.[4]

Opportunism is constrained by the competition of large numbers (and by personalized exchange). We can think loosely of opportunism, at this point, as the ability of one party to an exchange to benefit at the expense of the other party by violating the agreement in his or her post-contractual behavior.

The transfer of property rights amongst individual owners through contracting in the market place requires that the rights be exclusive.[5] Not only must the rights be measurable; they must also be enforceable. Note that there are two stages to the transfer process. The first stage involves the costs of defining and policing exclusivity in the absence of exchange; the second, the costs associated with negotiating and enforcing the contracts for the exchange and transfer of rights.

A third party, the state, can lower the costs of transacting through the development of an impersonal body of law and enforcement. Since the development of law is a public good there are important scale economies associated with it. If a body of law exists, negotiation and enforcement costs are substantially reduced since the basic rules of exchange are already spelled out.

Finally before leaving this illustration, let me note one additional point. Even if Morris had known he would never see me again, he probably would not have slipped some rotten oranges in the bottom of the sack; and I know, on my part, that while Morris's back was turned, filling up the sack, I would not have slipped a couple of oranges into my pocket even though there was no chance of being detected. The reason is that both of us viewed the exchange as fair or legitimate, and we were constrained in our behavior by that conviction.

III

Why does the firm replace the market? That was the question Ronald Coase asked in his essay "The Nature of the Firm" (1937). He characterized the firm as that range of exchanges over which the market system was suppressed and resource allocation was accomplished instead by authority and direction. Alchian and Demsetz, confronting the same question (1972), emphasized the importance of monitoring the inputs where the gains of joint team production (resulting from specialization and division of labor) make it difficult to measure inputs; Jensen and Meckling (1976) extended the monitoring argument to the effort of principals (owners of a set of property rights) to control the behavior of agents (persons engaged by the principals to perform services in their behalf) so that they will act in the principal's interests. The difference between Coase and Alchian and Demsetz requires some elaboration.

According to Coase, the advantage of the firm over transacting in the market is a gain as a result of a reduction in transaction costs. (In effect, a firm has reduced one set of transactions—those in the product market—and increased another set—those in the factor market. Therefore, the efficient size of the firm is determined as that at which the gains and costs at the margin are equal.) Alchian and Demsetz stress the productivity gains from team production, which Coase ignores; but they then emphasize that a byproduct of team production will be shirking or cheating and that therefore a monitor is needed to reduce these transaction costs.[6]

Both Williamson (1975) and Klein, Crawford, and Alchian (1979) stress the role of opportunism in inducing the vertical integration of economic activity. Where there are appropriable quasi rents (defined as the excess of an asset's value over its next best use) as assets become more specific, the costs of contracting will increase more than the costs of vertical integration; we will observe vertical integration to prevent a firm's being held up by another contracting party in the position of being able to cause the firm large losses by altering the terms of the agreement at a strategic moment.

Alchian and Demsetz (and Jensen and Meckling) emphasize that the firm is simply a legal fiction and a nexus of contracting relationships, whereas Coase emphasizes that the firm is governed by authority. Coase's position is in some respects close to that of New Left critics such as Marglin, who has argued (1974) that the productivity gains from the celebrated Smithian specialization and division of labor do not require the hierarchical organization of the firm, and that the reason for the existence of the firm is that it is an exploitative vehicle by which bosses exploit workers. The difference is that Coase emphasizes the real transaction cost gains from the firm (presumably at least partly in consequence of the authority), whereas Marglin and other New Left critics argue that there are no savings in real cost as a consequence of the hierarchy imposed by the firm. Marglin's argument, however, will not survive critical scrutiny. If there were no real costs savings from the disciplined hierarchical firm structure, then we surely would observe non-authoritative organizational forms effectively competing with firms. Since there have been literally thousands of utopian, cooperative, and other experimental organizational forms in American economic history, we would expect that many should survive in competition with the traditional firm. They haven't; and even a casual examination of the sources of their failure suggests that there were fundamental transaction cost problems impeding the survival of such non-authoritarian forms of organization. If that evidence were not sufficient, we could equally turn to look at the many experiments in socialist countries. Clearly there are both production-cost (from economies of scale) and transaction cost advantages to hierarchical organization.[7]

IV

Let us see if we can fit the pieces from the two previous sections into a general transaction cost framework of economic organization, before adding the state to the analysis.[8]

The resource costs devoted to compliance differ with alternative forms of organized economic activity. These compliance costs consist of the costs of measurement in alternative organizational forms and the costs of enforcing an agreement. Clearly, measurement costs in markets contrast to those of hierarchical organizations.

Markets dominate the sale of goods to consumers, and there will be both a subjective measurement element (such as the freshness of produce or the flavor of the orange juice) and the less costly but less accurate objective measurement costs (such as the weight, number, color, or grade of the good—the observable surrogates used by consumers). When we shift from orange juice to more complex goods or services such as a television set, the quality of repair work on an automobile or the quality of a physician's service, the costs of measurement are increased immensely and we tend to rely on various surrogates such as brand names, trade marks, warranties, reputation; but the key element is the degree of competition which constrains the principals.

When we turn to intermediate goods and services, such as a machine tool which is used in making an automobile, the exchange may be a market exchange or one internalized inside a firm, but the measurement costs will be different. When the exchange consists of purchases in the market, competition constrains the seller to meet the measurement specifications of the contract or lose out to a competitor. The pecuniary income of the seller therefore is directly tied to performance. When machine tool making is consolidated inside a firm, measurement is still necessary to see that the machine tool meets quality specifications and that the firm uses a variety of monitoring devices, such as quality-control inspectors and accounting methods, to measure performance. However, the income of the worker, now a part of team production in making the machine tool (and an agent rather than a principal), is no longer directly tied to his or her productive activity. The market no longer serves as a direct constraint on performance. If it were costless to measure the output (quantity and quality) of the individual worker, then the market would indeed be an equally effective constraint, the worker's income would be tied directly to performance, and the worker would be paid by his or her output (piece rate) rather than by input (hourly rate). But because it is costly to measure individual performance (and perfect measurement is frequently impossible), shirking, cheating, and so forth are common, workers are paid by input, and various costly but imperfect monitoring devices are employed to reduce shirking.

There are also costs in enforcing a contract: those of measuring the damages or injury to a party to the contract, of enacting penalties, and of compensating the injured party.

In order to measure damages one must first be able to measure performance; contracts therefore include detailed specifications, designed to spell out the characteristics of the exchange that indicate performance.

The enactment of penalties and compensation for damages not only entails a body of law, judicial process, and enforcement, but is heavily influenced by moral and ethical codes of behavior (that is, by the perceived legitimacy of the law and the contractual relationship). Personalized exchange in simple, unspecialized societies depends for enforcement upon such behavioral codes, and the perceived legitimacy of the contractual relationship significantly influences judges and juries. If measurement were perfect and the judicial process precisely awarded the "correct" amount of damages to injured parties in a contract violation, then opportunism would not play the part that it does in influencing economic organization. But the judicial process is implemented by rulers' agents who cannot themselves be perfectly constrained and who are guided by their own interests as well as their subjective evaluation of the justice of the contract.

Therefore enforcement is imperfect, particularly concerning such agreements as long lived contracts where future prices and risks cannot be specified.[9] It is equally imperfect where specialized physical or human capital, which can make hold-up or opportunism profitable, is employed.

With home production there are no transaction costs: therefore no proxy for subjective measurement is required, since individuals tailor their home production to their own utility function. There is complete vertical integration, but at the cost of specialization.

The greater the specialization and division of labor, the more steps in the production process from initial producer to final consumer and the greater the total costs of measurement (since measurement must occur at each step). The choice of organizational form will be influenced by the characteristics of the good or service and by the technology of measurement of the attributes.

Hierarchical organization replaces the market first of all because economies of scale arise from team production; but the scale economies come at the price of higher measurement costs of the performance of individual members of the team (agents). "A firm internalizes external effects [that is, realizes scale economies] by making an individual's productive activity external or independent of his pecuniary income from production" (McManus, 1975: 346). Hence the firm hires monitors to constrain the behavior of agents and reduce shirking and cheating.

Hierarchical organization will also replace market transactions where specialized human or physical capital investment makes the principals vulnerable to post-contractual opportunism because of imperfect enforcement. Vertical integration can reduce the likelihood of hold-up where substantial quasi-rents are appropriable; there will, however, be the same monitoring costs as above.

All of the modern neoclassical literature discusses the firm as a substitute for the market. For the economic historian this perspective is useful; its usefulness is limited, however, because it ignores a crucial fact of history: hierarchical organization forms and contractual arrangements in exchange predate the price-making market (like that for oranges). The first known price-making market was in the Athenian agora in the sixth century B.C., but exchange had been going on for millennia before that. We now possess the clue to account for such early forms of organization.

In order to do so we must clarify a confusion that has been propagated by Karl Polanyi and many subsequent writers.[10] Polanyi made a *market* synonymous with a *price-making market*. It should be readily apparent, however, that any form of voluntary contractual exchange involves a market and that its form will be dictated by the considerations advanced above. Polanyi made a basic error in thinking that any deviation from the Agora-type market implied non-economizing behavior: even the era which, in *The Great Transformation* (1957), he regarded as the epitome of the market mentality was characterized by an enormous variety of contractual arrangements that were not price-making markets.[11] Two considerations militated against the existence of price-making markets before the 6th century B.C. One was the transaction costs considerations that have been the subject of this chapter; the second was the wealth-maximizing objectives of the rulers of the state.

Price-making markets require well-defined and enforced property rights. It must be possible to measure the dimensions of a good or service; moreover, the consequent rights must be exclusive and there must be an enforcement mechanism to police the exchange of goods. Small numbers involved in exchange, the possibility of opportunism, and uncertainty as a result of a lack of well-defined property rights or an inability to forecast changes in conditions over the life of an exchange agreement all result in alternative contractual arrangements designed to reduce the attendant transactions or production costs.

V

The foregoing analysis has assumed that under the ubiquitous conditions of scarcity and competition, more efficient organizational forms will replace less efficient and that it would be possible to predict the forms that would exist. Even in the presence of a state that operated in the way that a contract theory would imply, modifications of the organizational forms would result since any form of taxation would alter the relevant measurement costs and the consequent organization; but the theory of the state elaborated in the preceding chapter implies much greater modification.

The state will specify rules to maximize the income of the ruler and his group and then, subject to that constraint, will devise rules that would lower transaction costs. Nonvoluntary forms of organization will exist if profitable to the ruler (nonvoluntary slavery, for example); relatively inefficient forms of organization will survive if more efficient forms threaten the survival of the ruler from within or without (the collective farm in the Soviet Union today, or the organization of the Athenian grain trade in the classical world, for example);[12] and forms of organization that have low measurement costs to the rulers for tax collecting will persist even though they are relatively inefficient (monopoly grants as in Colbert's France, for example).

Given this initial constraint, however, the ruler will provide the public good of a set of rules and their enforcement designed to lower transaction costs. Included will be the specification of uniform weights and measures,[13] a set of property rights to encourage production and trade, a judicial system to settle differences, and enforcement procedures to enforce contracts.

VI

The foregoing neoclassical approach to economic organization is deficient in at least two respects.

First, the more diffuse the distribution of political control as a result of the ability of groups of constituents to capture an interest in the state, the more difficult it becomes to predict or explain the ensuing forms of property rights which will develop. It is not too difficult to account for economic organization of the redistributive societies of the ancient dynasties in Egypt; it is much more difficult to explain the complex economic organization in modern democratic societies where many interests compete with each other in controlling the state and modifying property rights and, hence, economic organizations.[14]

A more serious problem is that the theory is incomplete, as even a casual inspection of the literature on industrial organization will attest. This literature is full of references to simple self-interest versus self-interest with guile (in opportunistic behavior); sometimes individuals will take advantage of each other and sometimes they won't; sometimes individuals are hard working and sometimes not. Honesty, integrity, and gentlemen's agreements are important in contractual arrangements; equally important are the ubiquitous loafing on the job, cheating, white collar crime, and sabotage.

To put it succinctly, the measurement costs of constraining behavior are so high that in the absence of ideological convictions to constrain individual maximizing, the viability of economic organization is threatened. Investment in legitimacy is as much a cost of economic organization as are the measurement and enforcement costs detailed in the preceding sections of this chapter. Indeed, as briefly discussed above, a major issue in enforcement is the perceived legitimacy of the contractual relations.

Notes

1. An exception is the work of Karl Polanyi. For a review of his contribution see North (1977).
2. In this context, authority is simply a contract in which this delegation of decision making is implied and a structure of decision making specified. In the absence of coercion by the state, which can impose nonvoluntaristic forms of organization, the neoclassical definition will serve. However, I examine the issue further in examining the literature on the firm and in considering ideology.
3. See Barzel (1974) and Cheung (1974).
4. The original contributions were those of Hayek (1937 and 1945). See also Stigler (1961).
5. The rights that are transferred must be exclusive, but we should note that the sale of a good or service does not imply unrestricted rights. When I sell my house the new owner is as constrained by zoning laws in his use of the house as I was. What I am transferring is a specific bundle of rights.
6. However, as McManus (1975) points out, Alchian and Demsetz are incorrect in asserting that team production per se is the cause of the problem. It is the costliness of measuring inputs and outputs that generates monitoring costs.
7. For psychological experiments demonstrating and measuring shirking in groups as compared to individual performance, see Latane, Silliams, and Harkinds (1979).
8. For an elaboration of the argument presented here see McManus (1975) and Barzel (unpublished 1980).
9. Goldberg (1976) has termed such contractual relations "relational exchange."
10. While Polanyi has had little influence on economists, he has had a much larger impact on the other social sciences and amongst historians.
11. See North (1977).

12. See the account of the Athenian grain trade in Polanyi (1977).

13. However, it should be noted that the way weights and measures will be devised will be with the objective of maximizing the ruler's income. The history of weights and measures makes sense only if we recognize the priority of the ruler's interest.

14. The burgeoning literature in such specialized journals as the *Bell Journal* and the *Journal of Law and Economics* provides ample evidence of this difficulty.

References

Alchian, A. and Demsetz, H. 1972. "Production, Information Costs and Economic Organization." *American Economic Review* (December).

Barzel, Y. 1974. "A Theory of Rationing by Waiting." *Journal of Law and Economics* (April).

Barzel, Y. 1980. "Measurement Cost and the Organization of Markets." Unpublished Manuscript.

Cheung, S. N. S. 1974. "A Theory of Price Control." *Journal of Law and Economics* (April).

Coase, Ronald 1937. "The Nature of the Firm." *Economica* (November).

Goldberg, Victor 1976. "Regulation and Administered Contracts." *The Bell Journal* (Autumn).

Hayek, F. A. 1937. "Economics and Knowledge." *Economica* (February).

Hayek, F. A. 1945. "The Use of Knowledge in Society." *American Economic Review* (September).

Jensen, M. and Meckling, W. 1976. "Theory of the Firm: Managerial Behavior, Agency Costs and Ownership Structure." *Journal of Financial Economics* (October).

Klein, B. Crawford, R. C., and Alchian, A. 1978. "Vertical Integration, Appropriable Rents, and the Competitive Contracting Process." *Journal of Law and Economics* (October).

Latane, Bibb; Sialliams, Kipling; and Harkinds, Stephen 1979. "Social Loafing." *Psychology Today* (October).

Marglin, Stephen 1974. "What Do Bosses Do?" *Review of Radical Political Economy* (Summer).

McManus, John 1975. "The Costs of Alternative Economic Organization." *Canadian Journal of Economics* (August).

North, Douglass C. 1977. "Non-Market Forms of Economic Organization: The Challenge of Karl Polanyi." Journal *of European Economic History* (Fall).

Polanyi, Karl 1957. *The Great Transformation*. New York: Rinehold.

Polanyi, Karl 1977. *The Livelyhood of Man*. New York: Academic Press.

Stigler, George 1961, "The Economics of Information." *Journal of Political Economy* (June).

Williamson, Oliver 1975. *Markets and Hierarchy*. New York: Free Press.

Oliver E. Williamson,
The Economic Institutions of Capitalism (1985)*

Chapter 1: Transaction Cost Economics

Firms, markets, and relational contracting are important economic institutions. They are also the evolutionary product of a fascinating series of organizational innovations. The study of the economic institutions of capitalism has not, however, occupied a position of importance on the social science research agenda.

Partly this neglect is explained by the inherent complexity of those institutions. But complexity can and often does serve as an inducement rather than a deterrent. The primitive state of our knowledge is at least equally explained by a reluctance to admit that the details of organization matter. The widespread conception of the modern corporation as a "black box" is the epitome of the noninstitutional (or pre-microanalytic) research tradition.

Merely to acknowledge that the microanalytic details of organization matter does not, however, suffice. The salient structural features of market, hierarchical, and quasi-market forms of organization need to be identified and linked to economic consequences in a systematic way. Lack of agreement on (or misconceptions regarding) the main purposes served by economic organization has also been an impediment to research progress.

A chapter in some yet unwritten history of economic thought will be needed to sort those matters out. Whatever the eventual explanation, the fact is that the study of economic institutions has witnessed a renaissance. Thus, whereas the study of institutional economics reached a nadir in the immediate postwar period, a renewal of interest in institutions and a reaffirmation of their economic importance can, with the benefit of hindsight, be traced to the early 1960s.[1] Operational content began to appear in the early 1970s.[2] A common characteristic of the new line of research is that the concept of firm as production function is supplanted (or augmented) by the concept of firm as governance structure. Research of the New Institutional Economics kind had reached a critical mass by 1975.[3] The ensuing decade has witnessed exponential growth.

Transaction cost economics is part of the New Institutional Economics research tradition. Although transaction cost economics (and, more generally, the New Institutional Economics) applies to the study of economic organization of all kinds, this

---

book focuses primarily on the economic institutions of capitalism, with special reference to firms, markets, and relational contracting. That focus runs the gamut from discrete market exchange at the one extreme to centralized hierarchical organization at the other, with myriad mixed or intermediate modes filling the range in between. The changing character of economic organization over time—within and between markets and hierarchies—is of particular interest.

Although the remarkable properties of neoclassical markets, where prices serve as sufficient statistics, are widely conceded—as Friedrich Hayek put it, the market is a "marvel" (1945, p. 525)—opinions differ in assessing transactions that are organized within quasi-market and nonmarket modes of organization. At best the administrative apparatus and private ordering supports that attend these transactions are messy. Some scholars decline even to deal with them. Others regard the deviations as evidence of a pervasive condition of "market failure." Until very recently the primary economic explanation for nonstandard or unfamiliar business practices was monopoly:[4] "[I]f an economist finds something—a business practice of one sort or another—that he does not understand, he looks for a monopoly explanation" (Coase, 1972, p. 67). That other social scientists should regard these same institutions as antisocial is unsurprising. The enforcement of antitrust from 1945 through 1970 reflected that orientation.

To be sure, a net negative social assessment is sometimes warranted. A more subtle and discriminating understanding of the economic institutions of capitalism has nevertheless been evolving. Many puzzling or anomalous practices have been cast into different relief in the process. This book advances the proposition that the economic institutions of capitalism have the main purpose and effect of economizing on transaction costs.

Main purpose is not, however, to be confused with sole purpose. Complex institutions commonly serve a variety of objectives. This is no less true here. The inordinate weight that I assign to transaction cost economizing is a device by which to redress a condition of previous neglect and undervaluation. An accurate assessment of the economic institutions of capitalism cannot, in my judgment, be reached if the central importance of transaction cost economizing is denied.[5] Greater respect for *organizational* (as against technological) features and for *efficiency* (as against monopoly) purposes is needed. This theme is repeated, with variation, throughout this book.

I submit that the full range of organizational innovations that mark the development of the economic institutions of capitalism over the past 150 years warrant reassessment in transaction cost terms. The proposed approach adopts a contracting orientation and maintains that any issue that can be formulated as a contracting problem can be investigated to advantage in transaction cost economizing terms. Every exchange relation qualifies. Many other issues which at the outset appear to lack a contracting aspect turn out, upon scrutiny, to have an implicit contracting quality. (The cartel problem is an example.) The upshot is that the actual and potential scope of transaction cost economics is very broad.

As compared with other approaches to the study of economic organization, transaction cost economics (1) is more microanalytic, (2) is more self-conscious about its behavioral assumptions, (3) introduces and develops the economic importance of asset specificity, (4) relies more on comparative institutional analysis, (5) regards the business firm as a governance structure rather than a production function, and (6) place greater weight on the *ex post* institutions of contract, with special emphasis on private ordering (as compared with court ordering). A large number of additional implications arise upon addressing problems of economic organization in this way. The study of the economic institutions of capitalism, as herein proposed, maintains that the transaction is the basic unit of analysis and insists that organization form matters. The underlying viewpoint that informs the comparative study of issues of economic organization is this: Transaction costs are economized by assigning transactions (which differ in their attributes) to governance structures (the adaptive capacities and associated costs of which differ) in a discriminating way.[6]

Given the complexity of the phenomena under review, transaction cost economics should often be used in addition to, rather than to the exclusion of, alternative approaches. Not every approach is equally instructive, however, and they are sometimes rival rather than complementary.

The nature of transaction costs is developed in section 1. A cognitive map of contract, in which alternative approaches to economic organization are described and with respect to which transaction cost economics is located, is set out in section 2. The relation between behavioral assumptions and alternative conceptions of contract is presented in section 3. A rudimentary contracting schema on which the argument in the book repeatedly relies is developed in section 4. Contractual issues that arise in organizing the company town are examined in section 5. Other applications are sketched in section 6. Concluding remarks follow.

1. Transaction Costs

1.1 Frictionlessness

Kenneth Arrow has defined transaction costs as the "costs of running the economic system" (1969, p. 48). Such costs are to be distinguished from production costs, which is the cost category with which neoclassical analysis has been preoccupied. Transaction costs are the economic equivalent of friction in physical systems. The manifold successes of physics in ascertaining the attributes of complex systems by assuming the absence of friction scarcely require recounting here. Such a strategy has had obvious appeal to the social sciences. Unsurprisingly, the absence of friction in physical systems is cited to illustrate the analytic power associated with "unrealistic" assumptions (Friedman, 1953, pp. 16–19).

But whereas physicists were quickly reminded by their laboratory instruments and the world around them that friction was pervasive and often needed to be taken expressly into account, economists did not have a corresponding appreciation for the costs of running the economic system. There is, for example, no reference whatsoever to transaction costs, much less to transaction costs as the economic counterpart of friction, in Milton Friedman's famous methodological essay (1953) or in other postwar treatments of positive economics.[7] Thus although positive economics admitted that frictions were important in principle, it had no language to describe frictions in fact.[8]

The neglect of transaction costs had numerous ramifications, not the least of which was the way in which nonstandard modes of economic organization were interpreted. Until express provision for transaction costs was made, the possibility that nonstandard modes of organization—customer and territorial restrictions, tie-ins, block booking, franchising, vertical integration, and the like—operate in the service of transaction cost economizing was little appreciated. Instead, most economists invoked monopoly explanations—be it of the leverage, price discrimination, or entry barriers kinds—when confronted with nonstandard contracting practices (Coase, 1972, p. 67). Donald Turner's views are representative: "I approach customer and territorial restrictions not hospitably in the common law tradition, but inhospitably in the tradition of antitrust."[9] As discussed below, the research agenda and public policy toward business were massively influenced by that monopoly predisposition. The prevailing view of the firm as production function was centrally implicated in that situation.

1.2 Explication

Transaction cost economics poses the problem of economic organization as a problem of contracting. A particular task is to be accomplished. It can be organized in any of several alternative ways. Explicit or implicit contract and support apparatus are associated with each. What are the costs?

Transaction costs of *ex ante* and *ex post* types are usefully distinguished. The first are the costs of drafting, negotiating, and safeguarding an agreement. This can be done with a great deal of care, in which case a complex document is drafted in which numerous contingencies are recognized, and appropriate adaptations by the parties are stipulated and agreed to in advance. Or the document can be very incomplete, the gaps to be filled in by the parties as the contingencies arise. Rather, therefore, than contemplate all conceivable bridge crossings in advance, which is a very ambitious undertaking, only actual bridge-crossing choices are addressed as events unfold.

Safeguards can take several forms, the most obvious of which is common ownership. Faced with the prospect that autonomous traders will experience contracting difficulties, the parties may substitute internal organization for the market. This is not, to be sure, without problems of its own. Moreover, *ex ante* interfirm safeguards can sometimes be fashioned to signal credible commitments and restore integrity to transactions. The study of "nonstandard" contracting is centrally concerned with such matters.

Most studies of exchange assume that efficacious rules of law regarding contract disputes are in place and are applied by the courts in an informed, sophisticated, and low-cost way. Those assumptions are convenient, in that lawyers and economists are relieved of the need to examine the variety of ways by which individual parties to an exchange "contract out of or away from" the governance structures of the state by devising private orderings. Thus arises a division of effort whereby economists are preoccupied with the economic benefits that accrue to specialization and exchange, while legal specialists focus on the technicalities of contract law.

The "legal centralism" tradition reflects the latter orientation. It maintains that "disputes require 'access' to a forum external to the original social setting of the dispute [and that] remedies will be provided as prescribed in some body of authoritative learning and dispensed by experts who operate under the auspices of the state" (Galanter, 1981, p. 1). The facts, however, disclose otherwise. Most disputes, including many that under current rules could be brought to a court, are resolved by avoidance, self-help, and the like (Galanter, 1981, p. 2).

The unreality of the assumptions of legal centralism can be defended by reference to the fruitfulness of the pure exchange model. That is not disputed here. My concern is that the law and economics of private ordering have been pushed into the background as a consequence. That is unfortunate, since in "many instances the participants can devise more satisfactory solutions to their disputes than can professionals constrained to apply general rules on the basis of limited knowledge of the dispute" (Galanter, 1981, p. 4).[10]

The issues here are akin to those that were of concern to Karl Llewellyn in his discussion of contract in 1931 but have been systematically evaded since.[11] But for the limitations of legal centralism, the *ex post* side of contract can be disregarded. Given the very real limitations, however, with which court ordering is beset, the *ex post* costs of contract unavoidably intrude. Transaction cost economics insists that contracting costs of all kinds be accorded parity.

Ex post costs of contracting take several forms. These include (1) the maladaption costs incurred when transactions drift out of alignment in relation to what Masahiko Aoki refers to as the "shifting contract curve" (1983),[12] (2) the haggling costs incurred if bilateral efforts are made to correct *ex post* misalignments, (3) the setup and running costs associated with the governance structures (often not the courts) to which disputes are referred, and (4) the bonding costs of effecting secure commitments.

Thus suppose that the contract stipulates x but, with the benefit of hindsight (or in the fullness of knowledge), the parties discern that they should have done y. Getting from x to y, however, may not be easy. The manner in which the associated benefits are divided is apt to give rise to intensive, self-interested bargaining. Complex, strategic behavior may be elicited. Referring the dispute to another forum may help, but that will vary with the circumstances. An incomplete adaptation will be realized if, as a consequence of efforts of both kinds, the parties move not to y but to y'.

A complicating factor in all of this is that the *ex ante* and *ex post* costs of contract are interdependent. Put differently, they must be addressed simultaneously rather than sequentially. Also, costs of both types are often difficult to quantify. The difficulty, however, is mitigated by the fact that transaction costs are always assessed in a comparative institutional way, in which one mode of contracting is compared with another. Accordingly, it is the difference between rather than the absolute magnitude of transaction costs that matters. As Herbert Simon has observed, the comparison of discrete structural alternatives can employ rather primitive apparatus—"such analyses can often be carried out without elaborate mathematical apparatus or marginal calculation. In general, much cruder and simpler arguments will suffice to demonstrate an inequality between two quantities than are required to show the conditions under which these quantities are equated at the margin" (1978, p. 6). Empirical research on transaction cost matters almost never attempts to measure such costs directly. Instead, the question is whether organizational relations (contracting practices; governance structures) line up with the attributes of transactions as predicted by transaction cost reasoning or not.

1.3 The Larger Context

This book concentrates on transaction cost economizing, but the costs need to be located in the larger context of which they are a part. Among the relevant factors—to which I sometimes (but not continuously) refer—are the following:

1. Holding the nature of the good or service to be delivered constant, economizing takes place with reference to the sum of production and transaction costs, whence tradeoffs in this respect must be recognized.
2. More generally, the design of the good or service to be delivered is a decision variable that influences demand as well as costs of both kinds, whence design is appropriately made a part of the calculus.
3. The social context in which transactions are embedded—the customs, mores, habits, and so on—have a bearing, and therefore need to be taken into account, when moving from one culture to another.[13]
4. The argument relies in a general, background way on the efficacy of competition to perform a sort between more and less efficient modes and to shift resources in favor of the former. This seems plausible, especially if the relevant outcomes are those which appear over intervals of five and ten years rather than in the very near term.[14] This intuition would nevertheless benefit from a more fully developed theory of the selection process. Transaction cost arguments are thus open to some of the same objections that evolutionary economists have made of orthodoxy (Nelson and Winter, 1982, pp. 356–70), though in other respects there are strong complementarities (pp. 34–38).
5. Whenever private and social benefits and costs differ, the social cost calculus should govern if prescriptive treatments are attempted.

---

7. Concluding Remarks

Transaction cost economics relies on and develops the following propositions:

1. The transaction is the basic unit of analysis.
2. Any problem that can be posed directly or indirectly as a contracting problem is usefully investigated in transaction cost economizing terms.
3. Transaction cost economies are realized by assigning transactions (which differ in their attributes) to governance structures (which are the organizational frameworks within which the integrity of a contractual relation is decided) in a discriminating way. Accordingly:
   a. The defining attributes of transactions need to be identified.
   b. The incentive and adaptive attributes of alternative governance structures need to be described.
4. Although marginal analysis is sometimes employed, implementing transaction cost economics mainly involves a comparative institutional assessment of discrete institutional alternatives—of which classical market contracting is located at one

extreme; centralized, hierarchical organization is located at the other; and mixed modes of firm and market organization are located in between.

5. Any attempt to deal seriously with the study of economic organization must come to terms with the *combined* ramifications of bounded rationality and opportunism in conjunction with a condition of asset specificity.

Note, with respect to this last, that the main differences in the four concepts of contract that are discussed in the text can be traced to variations in one or more of these three conditions. Thus contract as comprehensive *ex ante* planning and contract as promise both make heroic assumptions about human nature—the absence of bounded rationality being featured by the one (planning); the absence of opportunism being presumed by the other (promise). By contrast, concepts of contract as competition and contract as governance make less severe demands in behavioral respects. Both accommodate and/or make express provision for bounds on rationality and the hazards of opportunism.

Thus it is the condition of asset specificity that distinguishes the competitive and governance contracting models. Contract as competition works well where asset specificity is negligible. This being a widespread condition, application of the competitive model is correspondingly broad. Not all investments, however, are highly redeployable. Use of the competitive model outside of the circumstances to which it is well-suited can be and sometimes is misleading.

Whereas the competitive model of markets has been developed to a refined degree, the formidable difficulties that attend contracting in the context of nonredeployable investments have only recently come under scrutiny. This is largely because the sources and economic importance of asset specificity had previously been undervalued. Extending the theory of economic organization to deal with asset specificity has been a central preoccupation of the New Institutional Economics research agenda.

Notes

1. The early contributions include Ronald Coase's reconceptualization of social costs (1960), Armen Alchian's pioneering treatment of properly rights (1961), Kenneth Arrow's work on the troublesome economic properties of information (1962, 1963), and Alfred Chandler, Jr.'s contribution to business history (1962).

2. These include my first efforts to recast the vertical integration problem in transaction cost terms (Williamson, 1971) and efforts to generalize that approach in the context of markets and hierarchies (Williamson, 1973); the treatments by Armen Alchian and Harold Demsetz of the "classical capitalist firm" in terms of team organization (1972) and their related work on property rights (1973); the proposed reformulation of economic history by Lance Davis and Douglass North (1971); the important work by Peter Doeringer and Michael Piore (1971) on labor markets; and Janos Kornai's provocative treatment of disequilibrium economics (1971).

3. Some of this is described in the first chapter of *Markets and Hierarchies* (1975), which is titled "Toward a New Institutional Economics." The conference on "The Economics of Internal Organization" held at the University of Pennsylvania in 1974 (the papers from which were published in 1975 and 1976 in the *Bell Journal of Economics*) helped to

redefine the research agenda. Many of the articles in the *Journal of Economic Behavior and Organization,* which first began publication in 1980, are in the New Institutionalist spirit. For recent commentary and contributions to this literature, see the March 1984 issue of the *Journal of Institutional and Theoretical Economics* and the forthcoming book of readings edited by Louis Putterman and Victor Goldberg.

4. Important exceptions to this tradition—which, however, were widely ignored—are Lester Telser's (1965) and Lee Preston's (1965) treatments of restrictive trade practices.

5. A balanced view of the economic institutions of capitalism will await more concerted attention to the sociology of economic organization, which, happily, is in progress. For recent work of this kind, see Harrison White (1981), Martha Feldman and James March (1981), Arthur Stinchcombe (1983), Mark Granovetter (forthcoming), and James Coleman (1982).

6. Indeed, transaction cost economizing is central to the study of economic organization quite generally—in capitalist and non capitalist economies alike.

7. Herbert Simon's treatments of decision-making in economics focus mainly on individual rather than institutional features of economic organization (1959; 1962).

8. To be sure, the market failure literature was concerned with many of the relevant issues. But it rarely posed the issues in transaction cost terms. Arrow's remarks are thus prescient: "I contend that market failure is a more general category than externality. ... [Moreover], market failure is not absolute; it is better to consider a broader category, that of transaction costs, which in general impede and in particular cases completely block the formation of markets" (1969, p. 48).

9. The quotation is attributed to Turner by Stanley Robinson, 1968, N.Y. Staar Association, Antitrust Symposium, p. 29.

10. Marc Galanter elaborates as follows: "The variability of preferences and of situations, compared to the small number of things that can be taken into account by formal rules ... and the loss of meaning in transforming the dispute into professional categories suggest limits on the desirability of conforming outcomes to authoritative rules" (1981, p. 4).

11. See "Prologue," Section 1.2.

12. The *ex post* transaction costs are related to, but plainly differ from, what Michael Jensen and William Meckling refer to as agency costs, which they define as the sum of "(1) the monitoring expenditures of the principal, (2) the bonding expenditures by the agent, and (3) the residual loss" (1976, p. 308)—this last being a very expansive category.

13. See Mark Granovetter (1983) for a discussion of the importance of embeddedness. Also see Douglass North (1981).

14. This intuition is akin to that expressed by Michael Spence in his conjecture that entry barrier arguments give way to contestable markets in the long run (1983, p. 988). Although the long run for Spence probably exceeds five or ten years, some of the evolutionary phenomena of interest to me also span half a century. One way of putting it is that I subscribe to weak-form rather than strong-form selection, the distinction being that "in a relative sense, the *fitter* survive, but there is no reason to suppose that they are *fittest* in any absolute sense" (Simon's 1983, p. 69; emphasis in original).

References

Alchian, Armen. 1961. *Some Economics of Property.* RAND D–2316. Santa Monica, Calif.: RAND Corporation.

Alchian, Armen, and H. Demsetz. 1972. "Production, information costs, and economic organization," *American Economic Review*, 62 (December): 777–95.

_____. 1973. "The property rights paradigm," *Journal of Economic History*, 33(March): 16–27.

Aoki, Masahiko. 1983. "Managerialism revisited in the light of bargaining–game theory," *International Journal of Industrial Organization*, 1:1–21.

Arrow, Kenneth J. 1962. "Economic welfare and the allocation of resources of invention." In National Bureau of Economic Research, ed., *The Rate and Direction of Inventive Activity: Economic and Social Factors*. Princeton, N.J.: Princeton University Press, pp. 609–25.

_____. 1969. "The organization of economic activity: Issues pertinent to the choice of market versus nonmarket allocation." In *The Analysis and Evaluation of Public Expenditure: The PPB System*. Vol. 1. U.S. Joint Economic Committee, 91st Congress, 1st Session. Washington, D.C.: U.S. Government Printing Office, pp. 59–73.

Chandler, A. D., Jr. 1962. *Strategy and Structure*. Cambridge, Mass.: MIT Press. Subsequently published in New York: Doubleday & Co., 1996.

Coase, Ronald H. 1960. "The Problem of social cost," *Journal of Law and Economics*, 3(October): 1–44.

_____. 1972. "Industrial organization: A proposal for research." In V. R. Fuchs, ed., *Policy Issues and Research Opportunities in Industrial Organization*. New York: National Bureau of Economic Research, pp. 59–73.

Coleman, James. 1982. *The Asymmetric Society*. Syracuse, N.Y.: Syracuse University Press.

Davis, Lance E., and Douglass C. North. 1971. *Institutional Change and American Economic Growth*. Cambridge, Eng.: Cambridge University Press.

Doeringer, P., and M. Piore. 1971. *Internal Labor Markets and Manpower Analysis*. Lexington, Mass.: D.C. Health.

Feldman, Martha S., and James G. March. 1981. "Information in organizations as signal and symbol," *Administrative Science Quarterly*, 26(April): 171–86.

Friedman, Milton. 1953. *Essays in Positive Economics*. Chicago: University of Chicago Press.

Galanter, Marc. 1981. "Justice in many rooms: Courts, private ordering, and indigenous law," *Journal of Legal Pluralism*, no. 19, pp. 1–47.

Granovetter, Mark. 1985. "Economic action and social structure: A theory of embeddedness," *American Journal of Sociology*.

Hayek, F. 1945. "The use of knowledge in society," *American Economic Review*, 35(September): pp. 519–30.

Jensen, Michael, and William Mechling. 1976. "Theory of the firm: Managerial behavior, agency costs, and capital structure," *Journal of Financial Economics*, 3(October): 305–60.

Kornai, J. 1971. *Anti-equilibrium*. Amsterdam: North-Holland Publishing Company.

Nelson, Richard R., and S. G. Winter. 1982. *An Evolutionary Theory of Economic Change*. Cambridge, Mass.: Harvard University Press.

North, Douglass. 1981. *Structure and Change in Economic History*. New York: W.W. Norton.

Preston, Lee. 1965, "Restrictive distribution arrangements: Economic analysis and public policy standards," *Law and Contemporary Problems*, 30:506–34.

Simon, Herbert A. 1959. "Theories of decision making in economics and behavioral science," *American Economic Review*, 49(June): 253–58.

_____. 1962. "The architecture of complexity," *Proceedings of the American Philosophical Society*, 106(December): 467–82.

_____. 1978. "Rationality as process and as product of thought," *American Economic Review*, 68(May): 1–16.

_____. 1983. *Reason in Human Affairs.* Stanford: Stanford University Press.

Spence, A. M. 1983. "Contestable markets and the theory of industry structure: A review article," *Journal of Economic Literature,* 21(September): 981–90.

Stinchcombe, Arthur L. 1983. "Contracts as hierarchical documents." Unpublished manuscript, Stanford Graduate School of Business.

Telser, Lester. 1965. "Abusive trade practices: An economic analysis," *Law and Contemporary Problems,* 20(Summer): 488–510.

White, Harrison. 1981. "Where do markets come from?" *American Journal of Sociology,* 87(November): 517–47.

Williamson, O. E. 1971. "The vertical integration of production: Market failure considerations," *American Economic Review,* 61(May): 112–23.

_____. 1973. "Markets and hierarchies: Some elementary considerations," *American Economic Review,* 63(May): 316–25.

_____. 1975. *Markets and Hierarchies: Analysis and Antitrust Implications.* New York: Free Press.

5

Historical Perspectives

Historians tend to reject monocausal or simplistic explanations that rely on specific variables, and their explanations of events and outcomes are usually more richly descriptive than economic, sociological, or political science approaches. Moreover, historians tend to look further back in time for contributing patterns and events in explaining phenomena, tying together different sets of explanatory variables in a narrative that builds over time. For these reasons, historical perspectives on industrialization richly interweave the various explanations that other paradigms elaborate. The trade-offs to this approach are that historical explanations as a group can seem eclectic, and some may seem too particular to one specific instance of a more generalizable phenomenon.

Economic historians often examine advanced country industrialization to generate theories of economic development. As we shall see in this section, however, different historians come to varied conclusions on the relationships among markets, government, and society based on their analyses of the historical record of industrialization. We have already encountered a major economic historian in **Karl Marx,** who used his analysis of the history of British industrialization to lay out a sequence of stages that all political economies would pass through. The British Industrial Revolution was a phenomenon of economic, technological, and social transformation that took place in and through a capitalist political–economic system. It occurred gradually from about 1760 to 1830, over a longer period of time in comparison to later industrializers, and built on two centuries of preceding economic development. It was rooted in light industries, such as textiles and rural craft. Capital accumulation for industrial investment came from Britain's extensive trade ties, a benefit of its colonial empire and also of its standing as the premier trading nation of the era. Britain is really the only pure case of early industrialization, the nation that industrialized first with no blueprint or technology to copy from another nation, and no technology gap to overcome. Industrial development in later industrializers, unlike Britain, relied on advanced technology, focused on heavy industry, and was much more eruptive, or burstlike, in nature.

Walt Whitman Rostow elaborates a "stages-of-growth" perspective on modernization and industrialization that builds on his interpretation of economic history. Like many of the foremost social scientists of his generation, Rostow began his career as a Marxist but reversed his analytical viewpoint in light of the successes of industrial America and the postwar political climate. His modernization theory approach was a liberal, "anticommunist," manifesto in the context of the Cold War. It was self-consciously intended as an alternative to Marxist theory, both in terms of the predicted end point that political economies reach and also in terms of the relationship between economics and sociopolitical phenomena. Marx's material analysis, as we have seen, viewed economics and the mode of production as the driving force of history and changes in the social and political superstructure that would lead to communism as the final stage. Modernization theory, on the other hand, a popular social science approach in the 1950s and 1960s, viewed all the aspects of modernization—social mobilization, economic development, and political participation—as interacting and changing together on the road to modernity as the final stage.[1] Many have criticized modernization theory for failing to make clear causal arguments about political and economic development.

Rostow's *Stages of Economic Growth* builds on the experiences of the advanced industrialized countries—including Britain, the United States, other European countries, and Japan—to lay out a specific path composed of five serial steps that all countries, including late developers, will go through as they modernize and industrialize. A hallmark of classical modernization theory, as represented in the Rostow selection, was this unilinear and teleological quality, a result of the belief that the Western European and American advanced country model of modernization and economic development could be applied as a template to all newly modernizing countries. This elevation of the idealized historical experience of Western industrialized societies to a single framework for the development path of all nations was also the drawback of the classical modernization paradigm: the empirical reality of cross-national industrialization since the 1950s does not support the theory.

Alexander Gerschenkron's historical analysis of industrialization is a comparative explanation of differences in the industrialization experiences of late industrializers, and thus poses a counterpoint to Rostow's linear trajectory. Gerschenkron points out that it was Marx who established the generalization in which the history of advanced industrial countries maps out the trajectory for less developed countries. Yet Gerschenkron argues that history also demonstrates that this generalization is only half true, so that the development of a backward country can, as a result of its backwardness, differ fundamentally from that of a more advanced country. He demonstrates that countries experience different paths of growth depending on timing and the environment, thereby building a framework that can account for key differences among political–economic systems today.

Gerschenkron emphasizes the centrality of the process of capital accumulation in overcoming the technological gap necessary for industrialization. He argues specifically that the manner and timing of capital accumulation in different countries lay out varied paths to industrialization. Thus, although industrialization broadly looks the same everywhere, its institutional characteristics vary across countries, a central tenet of the market-institutional perspective. Gerschenkron provides both a historical analysis of industrialization in the original late industrializers—France, Germany, and Russia—and a manual for future industrializers. Captured in his famous phrase "the magnitude of the challenge changes the *quality* of the response"[2] is the idea that countries accumulate the capital necessary for industrialization through different sets of institutional and ideological solutions with varying degrees of state involvement.

Gerschenkron's argument is institutionalist at its core and also functionalist, because institutions emerge to fulfill the need (for capital accumulation) that arises. He does not unpack the politics of why these institutional solutions come about. Yet, unlike the classical theorists, such as Smith and Marx, Gerschenkron provides well-defined conceptions of the role of institutions and government in industrialization. Countries are able to imitate earlier industrializers to accumulate capital and furthermore improve on the necessary institutional innovation given their own circumstances. Late industrializers can self-consciously emulate or innovate on institutional design to pass through the capital accumulation phase necessary for industrial development and enter into industrialization through more technologically advanced and capital-intensive sectors. In this viewpoint, economic backwardness is actually an unexpected advantage that offers leapfrogging potential. Although capital accumulation in Britain had been gradual and held by merchants and private firms, the *crédit mobilier* or industrial bank system evolved in France to mobilize capital. German banks then became the paradigmatic universal bank for capital accumulation, adapting the best of the French industrial banking and British commercial banking systems. Finally, in Russia, where the scarcity of capital was even more extreme, an even stronger institutional innovation was necessary, so the state played a role in accumulating capital through militarization and a centralized bureaucracy. The Russian case illustrates the potentially troubling message, since revisited by even later developers such as the East Asian newly industrializing countries, that rapid industrial transformation may require limits on democracy.

Furthermore, these initial institutional substitutions were not neutral but "sticky" and persisted through time, even though they evolved. Differences in the history of industrialization shape political–economic trajectories and have a lasting subsequent impact on the varieties of political–economic systems in the world today. In the German case, for example, funds for the universal banks came from firms, and the banks were able to exert a great deal of leverage over industrial enterprises, in an interdependent relationship. The German political economy today continues to exhibit this close interdependence between the financial system and private firms, although it is now a more coequal relationship (see **Peter Hall and David Soskice,** this volume).

Gerschenkron views institutional substitution and the social ideologies of industrialization as interlinked in the pursuit of economic development. He points out that socialist ideas cloaked decidedly capitalist practices in France, and he mentions the nationalist sentiment of **Friedrich List** as an example of the ideology of industrialization in Germany. Finally, the extreme backwardness of Russia required the much more powerful ideology of orthodox Marxism during the course of industrialization. Contemporary political–economic ideology continues to vary across states, as it evolved as the rationale for the institutional responses necessary to overcome economic backwardness. Gerschenkron anticipated that his historical analysis could be used as a justification of countries' varying institutional and ideological approaches to industrialization, replacing dogmatic notions of right and wrong practice when it comes to markets or industrialization. This is an insight that today's developing countries have since used in making the case for straying from the path of neoliberal economic orthodoxy, particularly in terms of justifying state intervention in the economy.

David Landes argues that contemporary international empirical evidence is against neoclassical economic theory and its belief that all nations will eventually industrialize and converge. He thus disagrees with Rostow's unilinear perspective. But in his analysis of why convergence has not occurred, he moves even further away from neoclassical economics than did Gerschenkron's institutional perspective. Landes agrees that government can have a very important role to play (both empirically and normatively) in late development and points to historical evidence of the necessity of state intervention in development. In addition, he emphasizes culture as a factor in the pursuit of national wealth but admits that culture is as unsatisfying a monocausal answer as economics. Put simply, the two interact—in the language of this reader, economics and culture are tied together in the history of development.

Notes

1. Many of the fundamental tenets of the classical modernization paradigm are found in Seymour Martin Lipset's classic work on the social bases of economic growth. Seymour Martin Lipset, *Political Man: The Social Bases of Politics* (New York: Doubleday, 1959).
2. Alexander Gerschenkron, this volume, p. 220.

W.W. Rostow,
The Stages of Economic Growth (1960)*

Chapter 1: Introduction

This book presents an economic historian's way of generalizing the sweep of modern history. The form of this generalization is a set of stages-of-growth.

I have gradually come to the view that it is possible and, for certain limited purposes, it is useful to break down the story of each national economy—and sometimes the story of regions—according to this set of stages. They constitute, in the end, both a theory about economic growth and a more general, if still highly partial, theory about modern history as a whole.

But any way of looking at things that pretends to bring within its orbit, let us say, significant aspects of late eighteenth-century Britain and Khrushchev's Russia; Meiji Japan and Canada of the pre-1914 railway boom; Alexander Hamilton's United States and Mao's China; Bismarck's Germany and Nasser's Egypt—any such scheme is bound, to put it mildly, to have certain limitations.

I cannot emphasize too strongly at the outset, that the stages-of-growth are an arbitrary and limited way of looking at the sequence of modern history: and they are, in no absolute sense, a correct way. They are designed, in fact, to dramatize not merely the uniformities in the sequence of modernization but also—and equally— the uniqueness of each nation's experience.

As Croce said in discussing the limits of historical materialism: '... whilst it is possible to reduce to general concepts the particular factors of reality which appear in history ... it is not possible to work up into general concepts the single complex whole formed by these factors'.[1] We shall be concerned here, then, with certain 'particular factors of reality' which appear to run through the story of the modern world since about 1700.

Having accepted and emphasized the limited nature of the enterprise, it should be noted that the stages-of-growth are designed to grapple with a quite substantial range of issues. Under what impulses did traditional, agricultural societies begin the process of their modernization? When and how did regular growth come to be a built-in feature of each society? What forces drove the process of sustained growth along and determined its contours? What common social and political features of the growth process may be discerned at each stage? And in which directions did the

---

* From: *The Stages of Economic Growth: A Non-Communist Manifesto.* Copyright © Cambridge University Press 1960, 1971, 1990. (pp. 1–16) Reprinted with the permission of Cambridge University Press.

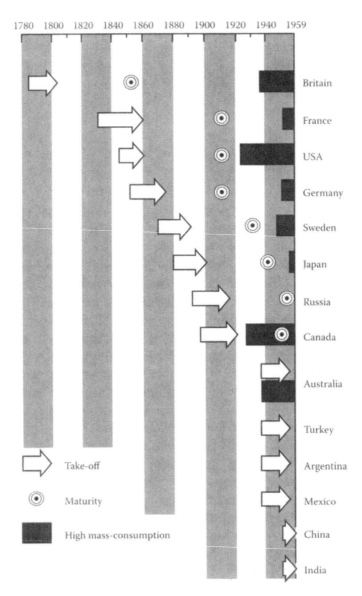

FIGURE 5.1.1 Chart of the stages of economic growth in selected countries. Note that Canada and Australia have entered the stage of high mass-consumption before reaching maturity. [By courtesy of the *Economist*.]

uniqueness of each society express itself at each stage? What forces have determined the relations between the more developed and less developed areas; and what relation, if any, did the relative sequence of growth bear to the outbreak of war? And, finally, where is compound interest[2] taking us? Is it taking us to Communism; or to the affluent suburbs, nicely rounded out with social overhead capital; to destruction; to the moon; or where?

The stages-of-growth are designed to get at these matters; and, since they constitute an alternative to Karl Marx's theory of modern history, I have given over the final chapter to a comparison between his way of looking at things and mine.

But this should be clear: although the stages-of-growth are an economic way of looking at whole societies, they in no sense imply that the worlds of politics, social organization, and of culture are a mere superstructure built upon and derived uniquely from the economy. On the contrary, we accept from the beginning the perception on which Marx, in the end, turned his back and which Engels was only willing to acknowledge whole-heartedly as a very old man; namely, that societies are interacting organisms. While it is true that economic change has political and social consequence, economic change is, itself, viewed here as the consequence of political and social as well as narrowly economic forces. And in terms of human motivation, many of the most profound economic changes are viewed as the consequence of non-economic human motives and aspirations. The student of economic growth concerned with its foundation in human motivation should never forget Keynes's dictum: 'If human nature felt no temptation to take a chance no satisfaction (profit apart) in constructing a factory, a railway, a mine or a farm, there might not be much investment merely as a result of cold calculation'.[3]

The exposition begins with an impressionistic definition of the five major stages-of-growth and a brief statement of the dynamic theory of production which is their bone-structure.

Now, then, what are these stages-of-growth?

Chapter 2: The Five Stages-of-Growth—A Summary

It is possible to identify all societies, in their economic dimensions, as lying within one of five categories: the traditional society, the preconditions for take-off, the take-off, the drive to maturity, and the age of high mass-consumption.

The Traditional Society

First, the traditional society. A traditional society is one whose structure is developed within limited production functions, based on pre-Newtonian science and technology, and on pre-Newtonian attitudes towards the physical world. Newton is here used as a symbol for that watershed in history when men came widely to believe that the external world was subject to a few knowable laws, and was systematically capable of productive manipulation.

The conception of the traditional society is, however, in no sense static; and it would not exclude increases in output. Acreage could be expanded; some *ad hoc* technical innovations, often highly productive innovations, could be introduced in trade, industry and agriculture; productivity could rise with, for example, the improvement of irrigation works or the discovery and diffusion of a new crop. But the central fact about the traditional society was that a ceiling existed on the level of attainable output per head. This ceiling resulted from the fact that the potentialities which flow from modern science and technology were either not available or not regularly and systematically applied.

Both in the longer past and in recent times the story of traditional societies was thus a story of endless change. The area and volume of trade within them and between them fluctuated, for example, with the degree of political and social turbulence, the efficiency of central rule, the upkeep of the roads. Population—and, within limits, the level of life—rose and fell not only with the sequence of the harvests, but with the incidence of war and of plague. Varying degrees of manufacture developed; but, as in agriculture, the level of productivity was limited by the inaccessibility of modern science, its applications, and its frame of mind.

Generally speaking, these societies, because of the limitation on productivity, had to devote a very high proportion of their resources to agriculture; and flowing from the agricultural system there was an hierarchical social structure, with relatively narrow scope—but some scope—for vertical mobility. Family and clan connexions played a large role in social organization. The value system of these societies was generally geared to what might be called a long-run fatalism; that is, the assumption that the range of possibilities open to one's grandchildren would be just about what it had been for one's grandparents. But this long-run fatalism by no means excluded the short-run option that, within a considerable range, it was possible and legitimate for the individual to strive to improve his lot, within his lifetime. In Chinese villages, for example, there was an endless struggle to acquire or to avoid losing land, yielding a situation where land rarely remained within the same family for a century.

Although central political rule—in one form or another—often existed in traditional societies, transcending the relatively self-sufficient regions, the centre of gravity of political power generally lay in the regions, in the hands of those who owned or controlled the land. The landowner maintained fluctuating but usually profound influence over such central political power as existed, backed by its entourage of civil servants and soldiers, imbued with attitudes and controlled by interests transcending the regions.

In terms of history then, with the phrase 'traditional society' we are grouping the whole pre-Newtonian world: the dynasties in China; the civilization of the Middle East and the Mediterranean; the world of medieval Europe. And to them we add the post-Newtonian societies which, for a time, remained untouched or unmoved by man's new capability for regularly manipulating his environment to his economic advantage.

To place these infinitely various, changing societies in a single category, on the ground that they all shared a ceiling on the productivity of their economic techniques, is to say very little indeed. But we are, after all, merely clearing the way in order to get at the subject of this book; that is, the post-traditional societies, in which each of the major characteristics of the traditional society was altered in such ways as to permit regular growth: its politics, social structure, and (to a degree) its values, as well as its economy.

The Preconditions for Take-Off

The second stage of growth embraces societies in the process of transition; that is, the period when the preconditions for take-off are developed; for it takes time to transform a traditional society in the ways necessary for it to exploit the fruits of modern science, to fend off diminishing returns, and thus to enjoy the blessings and choices opened up by the march of compound interest.

The preconditions for take-off were initially developed, in a clearly marked way, in Western Europe of the late seventeenth and early eighteenth centuries as the insights of modern science began to be translated into new production functions in both agriculture and industry, in a setting given dynamism by the lateral expansion of world markets and the international competition for them. But all that lies behind the break-up of the Middle Ages is relevant to the creation of the preconditions for take-off in Western Europe. Among the Western European states, Britain, favoured by geography, natural resources, trading possibilities, social and political structure, was the first to develop fully the preconditions for take-off.

The more general case in modern history, however, saw the stage of preconditions arise not endogenously but from some external intrusion by more advanced societies. These invasions—literal or figurative—shocked the traditional society and began or hastened its undoing; but they also set in motion ideas and sentiments which initiated the process by which a modern alternative to the traditional society was constructed out of the old culture.

The idea spreads not merely that economic progress is possible, but that economic progress is a necessary condition for some other purpose, judged to be good: be it national dignity, private profit, the general welfare, or a better life for the children. Education, for some at least, broadens and changes to suit the needs of modern economic activity. New types of enterprising men come forward—in the private economy, in government, or both—willing to mobilize savings and to take risks in pursuit of profit or modernization. Banks and other institutions for mobilizing capital appear. Investment increases, notably in transport, communications, and in raw materials in which other nations may have an economic interest. The scope of commerce, internal and external, widens. And, here and there, modern manufacturing enterprise appears, using the new methods. But all this activity proceeds at a limited pace within an economy and a society still mainly characterized by traditional low-productivity methods, by the old social structure and values, and by the regionally based political institutions that developed in conjunction with them.

In many recent cases, for example, the traditional society persisted side by side with modern economic activities, conducted for limited economic purposes by a colonial or quasi-colonial power.

Although the period of transition—between the traditional society and the take-off—saw major changes in both the economy itself and in the balance of social values, a decisive feature was often political. Politically, the building of an effective centralized national state—on the basis of coalitions touched with a new nationalism, in opposition to the traditional landed regional interests, the colonial power, or both, was a decisive aspect of the preconditions period; and it was, almost universally, a necessary condition for take-off.

The Take-Off

We come now to the great watershed in the life of modern societies: the third stage in this sequence, the take-off. The take-off is the interval when the old blocks and resistances to steady growth are finally overcome. The forces making for economic progress, which yielded limited bursts and enclaves of modern activity, expand and come to dominate the society. Growth becomes its normal condition. Compound interest becomes built, as it were, into its habits and institutional structure.

In Britain and the well-endowed parts of the world populated substantially from Britain (the United States, Canada, etc.) the proximate stimulus for take-off was mainly (but not wholly) technological. In the more general case, the take-off awaited not only the build-up of social overhead capital and a surge of technological development in industry and agriculture, but also the emergence to political power of a group prepared to regard the modernization of the economy as serious, high-order political business.

During the take-off, the rate of effective investment and savings may rise from, say, 5% of the national income to 10% or more; although where heavy social overhead capital investment was required to create the technical preconditions for take-off the investment rate in the preconditions period could be higher than 5%, as, for example, in Canada before the 1890s and Argentina before 1914. In such cases capital imports usually formed a high proportion of total investment in the preconditions period and sometimes even during the take-off itself, as in Russia and Canada during their pre-1914 railway booms.

During the take–off new industries expand rapidly, yielding profits a large proportion of which are reinvested in new plant; and these new industries, in turn, stimulate, through their rapidly expanding requirement for factory workers, the services to support them, and for other manufactured goods, a further expansion in urban areas and in other modern industrial plants. The whole process of expansion in the modern sector yields an increase of income in the hands of those who not only save at high rates but place their saying at the disposal of those engaged in modern sector activities. The new class of entrepreneurs expands; and it directs the enlarging flows of investment in the private sector. The economy exploits hitherto unused natural resources and methods of production.

New techniques spread in agriculture as well as industry, as agriculture is commercialized, and increasing numbers of farmers are prepared to accept the new methods and the deep changes they bring to ways of life. The revolutionary changes in agricultural productivity are an essential condition for successful take-off; for modernization of a society increases radically its bill for agricultural products. In a decade or two both the basic structure of the economy and the social and political structure of the society are transformed in such a way that a steady rate of growth can be, thereafter, regularly sustained.

One can approximately allocate the take-off of Britain to the two decades after 1783; France and the United States to the several decades preceding 1860; Germany, the third quarter of the nineteenth century; Japan, the fourth quarter of the nineteenth century; Russia and Canada the quarter-century or so preceding 1914; while during the 1950's India and China have, in quite different ways, launched their respective take-offs.

The Drive to Maturity

After take-off there follows a long interval of sustained if fluctuating progress, as the now regularly growing economy drives to extend modern technology over the whole front of its economic activity. Some 10–20% of the national income is steadily invested, permitting output regularly to outstrip the increase in population. The make-up of the economy changes unceasingly as technique improves, new industries accelerate, older industries level off. The economy finds its place in the international economy: goods formerly imported are produced at home; new import requirements develop, and new export commodities to match them. The society makes such terms as it will with the requirements of modern efficient production, balancing off the new against the older values and institutions, or revising the latter in such ways as to support rather than to retard the growth process.

Some sixty years after take-off begins (say, forty years after the end of take-off) what may be called maturity is generally attained. The economy, focused during the take-off around a relatively narrow complex of industry and technology, has extended its range into more refined and technologically often more complex processes; for example, there may be a shift in focus from the coal, iron, and heavy engineering industries of the railway phase to machine-tools, chemicals, and electrical equipment. This, for example, was the transition through which Germany, Britain, France, and the United States had passed by the end of the nineteenth century or shortly thereafter. But there are other sectoral patterns which have been followed in the sequence from take-off to maturity.

Formally, we can define maturity as the stage in which an economy demonstrates the capacity to move beyond the original industries which powered its take-off and to absorb and to apply efficiently over a very wide range of its resources—if not the whole range—the most advanced fruits of (then) modern technology. This is the stage in which an economy demonstrates that it has the technological and entrepreneurial skills to produce not everything, but anything that it chooses to produce. It may lack (like contemporary Sweden and Switzerland, for example) the raw materials or other supply conditions required to produce a given type of output economically; but its dependence is a matter of economic choice or political priority rather than a technological or institutional necessity.

Historically, it would appear that something like sixty years was required to move a society from the beginning of take-off to maturity. Analytically the explanation for some such interval may lie in the powerful arithmetic of compound interest applied to the capital stock, combined with the broader consequences for a society's ability to absorb modern technology of three successive generations living under a regime where growth is the normal condition. But, clearly, no dogmatism is justified about the exact length of the interval from take-off to maturity.

The Age of High Mass-Consumption

We come now to the age of high mass-consumption, where, in time, the leading sectors shift towards durable consumers' goods and services: a phase from which Americans are beginning to emerge; whose not unequivocal joys Western Europe and Japan are beginning energetically to probe; and with which Soviet society is engaged in an uneasy flirtation.

As societies achieved maturity in the twentieth century two things happened: real income per head rose to a point where a large number of persons gained a command over consumption which transcended basic food, shelter, and clothing; and the structure of the working force changed in ways which increased not only the proportion of urban to total population, but also the proportion of the population working in offices or in skilled factory jobs—aware of and anxious to acquire the consumption fruits of a mature economy.

In addition to these economic changes, the society ceased to accept the further extension of modern technology as an overriding objective. It is in this post-maturity stage, for example, that, through the political process, Western societies have chosen to allocate increased resources to social welfare and security. The emergence of the welfare state is one manifestation of a society's moving beyond technical maturity; but it is also at this stage that resources tend increasingly to be directed to the production of consumers' durables and to the diffusion of services on a mass basis, if consumers' sovereignty reigns. The sewing-machine, the bicycle, and then the various electric-powered household gadgets were gradually diffused. Historically, however, the decisive element has been the cheap mass automobile with its quite revolutionary effects—social as well as economic—on the life and expectations of society.

For the United States, the turning point was, perhaps, Henry Ford's moving assembly line of 1913–14; but it was in the 1920s, and again in the post-war decade, 1946–56, that this stage of growth was pressed to, virtually, its logical conclusion. In the 1950s Western Europe and Japan appear to have fully entered this phase, accounting substantially for a momentum in their economies quite unexpected in the immediate post-war years. The Soviet Union is technically ready for this stage, and, by every sign, its citizens hunger for it; but Communist leaders face difficult political and social problems of adjustment if this stage is launched.

Beyond Consumption

Beyond, it is impossible to predict, except perhaps to observe that Americans, at least, have behaved in the past decade as if diminishing relative marginal utility sets in, after a point, for durable consumers' goods; and they have chosen, at the margin, larger families—behaviour in the pattern of Buddenbrooks dynamics.[4] Americans have behaved as if, having been born into a system that provided economic security and high mass-consumption, they placed a lower valuation on acquiring additional increments of real income in the conventional form as opposed to the advantages and values of an enlarged family. But even in this adventure in generalization it is a shade too soon to create—on the basis of one case—a new stage-of-growth, based on babies, in succession to the age of consumers' durables: as economists might say, the income-elasticity of demand for babies may well vary from society to society. But it is true that the implications of the baby boom along with the not wholly unrelated deficit in social overhead capital are likely to dominate the American economy over the next decade rather than the further diffusion of consumers' durables.

Here then, in an impressionistic rather than an analytic way, are the stages-of-growth which can be distinguished once a traditional society begins its modernization: the transitional period when the preconditions for take-off are created generally in response to the intrusion of a foreign power, converging with certain domestic forces making for modernization; the take-off itself; the sweep into maturity generally taking up the life of about two further generations; and then, finally, if the rise of income has matched the spread of technological virtuosity (which, as we shall see, it need not immediately do) the diversion of the fully mature economy to the provision of durable consumers' goods and services (as well as the welfare state) for its increasingly urban—and then suburban—population. Beyond lies the question of whether or not secular spiritual stagnation will arise, and, if it does, how man might fend it off.

In the four chapters that follow we shall take a harder, and more rigorous look at the preconditions, the take-off, the drive to maturity, and the processes which have led to the age of high mass-consumption. But even in this introductory chapter one characteristic of this system should be made clear.

A Dynamic Theory of Production

These stages are not merely descriptive. They are not merely a way of generalizing certain factual observations about the sequence of development of modern societies. They have an inner logic and continuity. They have an analytic bone-structure, rooted in a dynamic theory of production.

The classical theory of production is formulated under essentially static assumptions which freeze—or permit only once-over change—in the variables most relevant to the process of economic growth. As modern economists have sought to merge classical production theory with Keynesian income analysis they have introduced the dynamic variables: population, technology, entrepreneurship etc. But they have tended to do so in forms so rigid and general that their models cannot grip the essential phenomena of growth, as they appear to an economic historian. We require a dynamic theory of production which isolates not only the distribution of income between consumption, saving, and investment (and the balance of production between consumers and capital goods) but which focuses directly and in some detail on the composition of investment and on developments within particular sectors of the economy. The argument that follows is based on such a flexible, disaggregated theory of production.

When the conventional limits on the theory of production are widened, it is possible to define theoretical equilibrium positions not only for output, investment, and consumption as a whole, but for each sector of the economy.[5]

Within the framework set by forces determining the total level of output, sectoral optimum positions are determined on the side of demand, by the levels of income and of population, and by the character of tastes; on the side of supply, by the state of technology and the quality of entrepreneurship, as the latter determines the proportion of technically available and potentially profitable innovations actually incorporated in the capital stock.[6]

In addition, one must introduce an extremely significant empirical hypothesis: namely, that deceleration is the normal optimum path of a sector, due to a variety of factors operating on it, from the side of both supply and demand.[7]

The equilibria which emerge from the application of these criteria are a set of sectoral paths, from which flows, as first derivatives, a sequence of optimum patterns of investment.

Historical patterns of investment did not, of course, exactly follow these optimum patterns. They were distorted by imperfections in the private investment process, by the policies of governments, and by the impact of wars. Wars temporarily altered the profitable directions of investment by setting up arbitrary demands and by changing the conditions of supply; they destroyed capital; and, occasionally, they accelerated the development of new technology relevant to the peacetime economy and shifted the political and social framework in ways conducive to peacetime growth.[8] The historical sequence of business-cycles and trend-periods results from these deviations of actual from optimal patterns; and such fluctuations, along with the impact of wars, yield historical paths of growth which differ from those which the optima, calculated before the event, would have yielded.

Nevertheless, the economic history of growing societies takes a part of its rude shape from the effort of societies to approximate the optimum sectoral paths.

At any period of time, the rate of growth in the sectors will vary greatly; and it is possible to isolate empirically certain leading sectors, at early stages of their evolution, whose rapid rate of expansion plays an essential direct and indirect role in maintaining the overall momentum of the economy.[9] For some purposes it is useful to characterize an economy in terms of its leading sectors; and a part of the technical basis for the stages of growth lies in the changing sequence of leading sectors. In essence it is the fact that sectors tend to have a rapid growth-phase, early in their life, that makes it possible and useful to regard economic history as a sequence of stages rather than merely as a continuum, within which nature never makes a jump.

The stages-of-growth also require, however, that elasticities of demand be taken into account, and that this familiar concept be widened; for these rapid growth phases in the sectors derive not merely from the discontinuity of production functions but also from high price- or income-elasticities of demand. Leading sectors are determined not merely by the changing flow of technology and the changing willingness of entrepreneurs to accept available innovations: they are also partially determined by those types of demand which have exhibited high elasticity with respect to price, income, or both.

The demand for resources has resulted, however, not merely from demands set up by private taste and choice, but also from social decisions and from the policies of governments—whether democratically responsive or not. It is necessary, therefore, to look at the choices made by societies in the disposition of their resources in terms which transcend conventional market processes. It is necessary to look at their welfare functions, in the widest sense, including the non-economic processes which determined them.

The course of birth-rates, for example, represents one form of welfare choice made by societies, as income has changed; and population curves reflect (in addition to changing death-rates) how the calculus about family size was made in the various stages; from the usual (but not universal) decline in birth-rates, during or soon after the take-off, as urbanization took hold and progress became a palpable possibility, to the recent rise, as Americans (and others in societies marked by high mass-consumption) have appeared to seek in larger families values beyond those afforded by economic security and by an ample supply of durable consumers' goods and services.

And there are other decisions as well that societies have made as the choices open to them have been altered by the unfolding process of economic growth; and these broad collective decisions, determined by many factors—deep in history, culture, and the active political process—outside the market-place, have interplayed with the dynamics of market demand, risk-taking, technology and entrepreneurship, to determine the specific content of the stages of growth for each society.

How, for example, should the traditional society react to the intrusion of a more advanced power: with cohesion, promptness, and vigour, like the Japanese; by making a virtue of fecklessness, like the oppressed Irish of the eighteenth century; by slowly and reluctantly altering the traditional society, like the Chinese?

When independent modern nationhood is achieved, how should the national energies be disposed: in external aggression, to right old wrongs or to exploit newly created or perceived possibilities for enlarged national power; in completing and refining the political victory of the new national government over old regional interests; or in modernizing the economy?

Once growth is under way, with the take-off, to what extent should the requirements of diffusing modern technology and maximizing the rate of growth be moderated by the desire to increase consumption *per capita* and to increase welfare?

When technological maturity is reached, and the nation has at its command a modernized and differentiated industrial machine, to what ends should it be put, and in what proportions: to increase social security, through the welfare state; to expand mass-consumption into the range of durable consumers' goods and services; to increase the nation's stature and power on the world scene; or to increase leisure?

And then the question beyond, where history offers us only fragments: what to do when the increase in real income itself loses its charm? Babies, boredom, three-day week-ends, the moon, or the creation of new inner, human frontiers in substitution for the imperatives of scarcity?

In surveying now the broad contours of each stage-of-growth, we are examining, then, not merely the sectoral structure of economies, as they transformed themselves for growth, and grew; we are also examining a succession of strategic choices made by various societies concerning the disposition of their resources, which include but transcend the income- and price-elasticities of demand.

Notes

1. B. Croce, *Historical Materialism and the Economics of Karl Marx*, tr. C. M. Meredith (London), pp. 3–4.
2. This phrase is used as a shorthand way of suggesting that growth normally proceeds by geometric progression, much as a savings account if interest is left to compound with principal.
3. John Maynard Keynes, *The General Theory of Employment, Interest and Money*, (Macmillan Cambridge University Press, 1936), p. 150.

4. In Thomas Mann's novel of three generations, the first sought money; the second, born to money, sought social and civic position; the third, born to comfort and family prestige, looked to the life of music. The phrase is designed to suggest, then, the changing aspirations of generations, as they place a low value on what they take for granted and seek new forms of satisfaction.

5. W.W. Rostow, *The Process of Economic Growth* (Oxford, 1953), especially chapter IV. Also 'Trends in the Allocation of Resources in Secular Growth', chapter 15 of *Economic Progress*, ed. Leon H. Dupriez, with the assistance of Douglas C. Hague (Louvain, 1955).

6. In a closed model, a dynamic theory of production must account for changing stocks of basic and applied science, as sectoral aspects of investment, which is done in *The Process of Economic Growth*, especially pp. 22–5.

7. *Process of Economic Growth*, pp. 96–103.

8. *Process of Economic Growth*, chapter VII, especially pp. 164–7.

9. For a discussion of the leading sectors, their direct and indirect consequences; and the diverse routes of their impact, see 'Trends in the Allocation of Resources in Secular Growth', *loc. cit.*

Alexander Gerschenkron,
Economic Backwardness in Historical Perspective (1962)*

I: Economic Backwardness in Historical Perspective

A historical approach to current problems calls perhaps for a word of explanation. Unlike so many of their predecessors, modern historians no longer announce to the world what inevitably will, or at least what ideally should, happen. We have grown modest. The prophetic fervor was bound to vanish together with the childlike faith in a perfectly comprehensible past whose flow was determined by some exceedingly simple and general historical law. Between Seneca's assertion of the absolute certainty of our knowledge of the past and Goethe's description of history as a book eternally kept under seven seals, between the *omnia certa sunt* of the one and the *ignorabimus* of the other, modern historical relativism moves gingerly. Modern historians realize full well that comprehension of the past—and that perforce means the past itself—changes perpetually with the historian's emphasis, interest, and point of view. The search is no longer for a determination of the course of human events as ubiquitous and invariant as that of the course of the planets. The iron necessity of historical processes has been discarded. But along with what John Stuart Mill once called "the slavery of antecedent circumstances" have been demolished the great bridges between the past and the future upon which the nineteenth-century mind used to travel so safely and so confidently.

Does this mean that history cannot contribute anything to the understanding of current problems? Historical research consists essentially in application to empirical material of various sets of empirically derived hypothetical generalizations and in testing the closeness of the resulting fit, in the hope that in this way certain uniformities, certain typical situations, and certain typical relationships among individual factors in these situations can be ascertained. None of these lends itself to easy extrapolations. All that can be achieved is an extraction from the vast storehouse of the past of sets of intelligent questions that may be addressed to current materials. The importance of this contribution should not be exaggerated. But it should not be underrated either. For the quality of our understanding of current problems depends largely on the broadness of our frame of reference. Insularity is a limitation on comprehension. But insularity in thinking is not peculiar to any special geographic area.

---

* "Economic Backwardness in Historical Perspective" in *The Progress of Underdeveloped Areas*, B. F. Hoselitz, ed. Copyright © 1962 The University of Chicago. (pp. 5–30) Reproduced by permission of The University of Chicago Press.

Furthermore, it is not only a spatial but also a temporal problem. All decisions in the field of economic policies are essentially decisions with regard to combinations of a number of relevant factors. And the historian's contribution consists in pointing at *potentially* relevant factors and at *potentially* significant combinations among them which could not be easily perceived within a more limited sphere of experience. These are the questions. The answers themselves, however, are a different matter. No past experience, however rich, and no historical research, however thorough, can save the living generation the creative task of finding their own answers and shaping their own future. The following remarks, therefore, purport to do no more than to point at some relationships which existed in the past and the consideration of which in current discussions might prove useful.

The Elements of Backwardness

A good deal of our thinking about industrialization of backward countries is dominated—consciously or unconsciously—by the grand Marxian generalization according to which it is the history of advanced or established industrial countries which traces out the road of development for the more backward countries. "The industrially more developed country presents to the less developed country a picture of the latter's future."[1] There is little doubt that in some broad sense this generalization has validity. It is meaningful to say that Germany, between the middle and the end of the last century, followed the road which England began to tread at an earlier time. But one should beware of accepting such a generalization too whole-heartedly. For the half-truth that it contains is likely to conceal the existence of the other half—that is to say, in several very important respects the development of a backward country may, by the very virtue of its backwardness, tend to differ fundamentally from that of an advanced country.

It is the main proposition of this essay that in a number of important historical instances industrialization processes, when launched at length in a backward country, showed considerable differences, as compared with more advanced countries, not only with regard to the speed of the development (the rate of industrial growth) but also with regard to the productive and organizational structures of industry which emerged from those processes. Furthermore, these differences in the speed and character of industrial development were to a considerable extent the result of application of institutional instruments for which there was little or no counterpart in an established industrial country. In addition, the intellectual climate within which industrialization proceeded, its "spirit" or "ideology," differed considerably among advanced and backward countries. Finally, the extent to which these attributes of backwardness occurred in individual instances appears to have varied directly with the degree of backwardness and the natural industrial potentialities of the countries concerned.

Let us first describe in general terms a few basic elements in the industrialization processes of backward countries as synthesized from the available historical information on economic development of European countries[2] in the nineteenth century and up until the beginning of the First World War. Thereupon, on the basis of concrete examples, more will be said on the effects of what may be called "relative backwardness" upon the course of industrial development in individual countries.

The typical situation in a backward country prior to the initiation of considerable industrialization processes may be described as characterized by the tension between the actual state of economic activities in the country and the existing obstacles to industrial development, on the one hand, and the great promise inherent in such a development, on the other. The extent of opportunities that industrialization presents varied, of course, with the individual country's endowment of natural resources. Furthermore, no industrialization seemed possible, and hence no "tension" existed, as long as certain formidable institutional obstacles (such as the serfdom of the peasantry or the far-reaching absence of political unification) remained. Assuming an adequate endowment of usable resources, and assuming that the great blocks to industrialization had been removed, the opportunities inherent in industrialization may be said to vary directly with the backwardness of the country. Industrialization always seemed the more promising the greater the backlog of technological innovations which the backward country could take over from the more advanced country. Borrowed technology, so much and so rightly stressed by Veblen, was one of the primary factors assuring a high speed of development in a backward country entering the stage of industrialization. There always has been the inevitable tendency to deride the backward country because of its lack of originality. German mining engineers of the sixteenth century accused the English of being but slavish imitators of German methods, and the English fully reciprocated these charges in the fifties and sixties of the past century. In our own day, Soviet Russia has been said to have been altogether imitative in its industrial development, and the Russians have retorted by making extraordinary and extravagant claims. But all these superficialities tend to blur the basic fact that the contingency of large imports of foreign machinery and of foreign know-how, and the concomitant opportunities for rapid industrialization with the passage of time, increasingly widened the gulf between economic potentialities and economic actualities in backward countries.

The industrialization prospects of an underdeveloped country are frequently judged, and judged adversely, in terms of cheapness of labor as against capital goods and of the resulting difficulty in substituting scarce capital for abundant labor. Sometimes, on the contrary, the cheapness of labor in a backward country is said to aid greatly in the processes of industrialization. The actual situation, however, is more complex than would appear on the basis of simple models. In reality, conditions will vary from industry to industry and from country to country. But the overriding fact to consider is that industrial labor, in the sense of a stable, reliable, and disciplined group that has cut the umbilical cord connecting it with the land and has become suitable for utilization in factories, is not abundant but extremely scarce in a backward country. Creation of an industrial labor force that really deserves its name is a most difficult and protracted process. The history of Russian industry provides some striking illustrations in this respect. Many a German industrial laborer of the nineteenth century had been raised in the strict discipline of a Junker estate which presumably made him more amenable to accept the rigors of factory rules. And yet the difficulties were great, and one may recall the admiring and envious glances which, toward the very end of the century, German writers like Schulze-Gaevernitz kept casting across the Channel at the English industrial worker, "the man of the future ... born and educated for the machine ... [who] does not find his equal in the past." In our time, reports from industries in India repeat in a still more exaggerated form the past predicaments of European industrializations in the field of labor supply.

Under these conditions the statement may be hazarded that, to the extent that industrialization took place, it was largely by application of the most modern and efficient techniques that backward countries could hope to achieve success, particularly if their industrialization proceeded in the face of competition from the advanced country. The advantages inherent in the use of technologically superior equipment were not counteracted but reinforced by its labor-saving effect. This seems to explain the tendency on the part of backward countries to concentrate at a relatively early point of their industrialization on promotion of those branches of industrial activities in which recent technological progress had been particularly rapid; while the more advanced countries, either from inertia or from unwillingness to require or impose sacrifices implicit in a large investment program, were more hesitant to carry out continual modernizations of their plant. Clearly, there are limits to such a policy, one of them being the inability of a backward country to extend it to lines of output where very special technological skills are required. Backward countries (although not the United States) were slow to assimilate production of modern machine tools. But a branch like iron and steel production does provide a good example of the tendency to introduce most modern innovations, and it is instructive to see, for example, how German blast furnaces so very soon become superior to the English ones, while in the early years of this century blast furnaces in still more backward southern Russia were in the process of outstripping in equipment their German counterparts. Conversely, in the nineteenth century, England's superiority in cotton textile output was challenged neither by Germany nor by any other country.

To a considerable extent (as in the case of blast furnaces just cited), utilization of modern techniques required, in nineteenth-century conditions, increases in the average size of plant. Stress on bigness in this sense can be found in the history of most countries on the European continent. But industrialization of backward countries in Europe reveals a tendency toward bigness in another sense. The use of the term "industrial revolution" has been exposed to a good many justifiable strictures. But, if industrial revolution is conceived as denoting no more than cases of sudden considerable increases in the rate of industrial growth, there is little doubt that in several important instances industrial development began in such a sudden, eruptive, that is, "revolutionary," way.

The discontinuity was not accidental. As likely as not the period of stagnation (in the "physiocratic" sense of a period of low rate of growth) can be terminated and industrialization processes begun only if the industrialization movement can proceed, as it were, along a broad front, starting simultaneously along many lines of economic activities. This is partly the result of the existence of complementarity and indivisibilities in economic processes. Railroads cannot be built unless coal mines are opened up at the same time; building half a railroad will not do if an inland center is to be connected with a port city. Fruits of industrial progress in certain lines are received as external economies by other branches of industry whose progress in turn accords benefits to the former. In viewing the economic history of Europe in the nineteenth century, the impression is very strong that only when industrial development could commence on a large scale did the tension between the preindustrialization conditions and the benefits expected from industrialization become sufficiently strong to overcome the existing obstacles and to liberate the forces that made for industrial progress.

This aspect of the development may be conceived in terms of Toynbee's relation between challenge and response. His general observation that very frequently small challenges do not produce any responses and that the volume of response begins to grow very rapidly (at least up to a point) as the volume of the challenge increases seems to be quite applicable here. The challenge, that is to say, the "tension," must be considerable before a response in terms of industrial development will materialize.

The foregoing sketch purported to list a number of basic factors which historically were peculiar to economic situations in backward countries and made for higher speed of growth and different productive structure of industries. The effect of these basic factors was, however, greatly reinforced by the use in backward countries of certain institutional instruments and the acceptance of specific industrialization ideologies. Some of these specific factors and their mode of operation on various levels of backwardness are discussed in the following sections.

The Banks

The history of the Second Empire in France provides rather striking illustrations of these processes. The advent of Napoleon III terminated a long period of relative economic stagnation which had begun with the restoration of the Bourbons and which in some sense and to some extent was the result of the industrial policies pursued by Napoleon I. Through a policy of reduction of tariff duties and elimination of import prohibitions, culminating in the Cobden-Chevalier treaty of 1860, the French government destroyed the hothouse in which French industry had been kept for decades and exposed it to the stimulating atmosphere of international competition. By abolishing monopoly profits in the stagnating coal and iron production, French industry at length received profitable access to basic industrial raw materials.

To a not inconsiderable extent, the industrial development of France under Napoleon III must be attributed to that determined effort to untie the strait jacket in which weak governments and strong vested interests had inclosed the French economy. But along with these essentially, though not exclusively, negative policies of the government, French industry received a powerful positive impetus from a different quarter. The reference is to the development of industrial banking under Napoleon III.

The importance of that development has seldom been fully appreciated. Nor has it been properly understood as emanating from the specific conditions of a relatively backward economy. In particular, the story of the Crédit Mobilier of the brothers Pereire is often regarded as a dramatic but, on the whole, rather insignificant episode. All too often, as, for instance, in the powerful novels of Éimile Zola, the actual significance of the developments is almost completely submerged in the description of speculative fever, corruption, and immorality which accompanied them. It seems to be much better in accord with the facts to speak of a truly momentous role of investment banking of the period for the economic history of France and of large portions of the Continent.

In saying that, one has in mind, of course, the immediate effects of creating financial organizations designed to build thousands of miles of railroads, drill mines, erect factories, pierce canals, construct ports, and modernize cities. The ventures of the Pereires and of a few others did all that in France and beyond the boundaries of France over vast areas stretching from Spain to Russia. This tremendous change in economic scenery took place only a few years after a great statesman and a great historian of the July monarchy assured the country that there was no need to reduce the duties on iron because the sheltered French iron production was quite able to cope with the iron needs of the railroads on the basis of his estimate of a prospective annual increase in construction by some fifteen to twenty miles.

But no less important than the actual economic accomplishments of a few men of great entrepreneurial vigor was their effect on their environment. The Crédit Mobilier was from the beginning engaged in a most violent conflict with the representatives of "old wealth" in French banking, most notably with the Rothschilds. It was this conflict that had sapped the force of the institution and was primarily responsible for its eventual collapse in 1867. But what is so seldom realized is that in the course of this conflict the "new wealth" succeeded in forcing the old wealth to adopt the policies of its opponents. The limitation of old wealth in banking policies to flotations of government loans and foreign-exchange transactions could not be maintained in the face of the new competition. When the Rothschilds prevented the Pereires from establishing the Austrian Credit-Anstalt, they succeeded only because they became willing to establish the bank themselves and to conduct it not as an old-fashioned banking enterprise but as a crédit mobilier, that is, as a bank devoted to railroadization and industrialization of the country.

This conversion of the old wealth to the creed of the new wealth points out the direction of the most far-reaching effects of the Crédit Mobilier. Occasional ventures of that sort had been in existence in Belgium, Germany, and France herself. But it was the great eruptive effect of the Pereires that profoundly influenced the history of Continental banking in Europe from the second half of the past century onward. The number of banks in various countries shaped upon the image of the Pereire bank was considerable. But more important than their slavish imitations was the creative adaptation of the basic idea of the Pereires and its incorporation in the new type of bank, the universal bank, which in Germany, along with most other countries on the Continent, became the dominant form of banking. The difference between banks of the crédit-mobilier type and commercial banks in the advanced industrial country of the time (England) was absolute. Between the English bank essentially designed to serve as a source of short-term capital and a bank designed to finance the long-run investment needs of the economy there was a complete gulf. The German banks, which may be taken as a paragon of the type of the universal bank, successfully combined the basic idea of the crédit mobilier with the short-term activities of commercial banks.

They were as a result infinitely sounder financial institutions than the Crédit Mobilier, with its enormously swollen industrial portfolio, which greatly exceeded its capital, and its dependence on favorable developments on the stock exchange for continuation of its activities. But the German banks, and with them the Austrian and Italian banks, established the closest possible relations with industrial enterprises. A German bank, as the saying went, accompanied an industrial enterprise from the cradle to the grave, from establishment to liquidation throughout all the vicissitudes of its existence. Through the device of formally short-term but in reality long-term current account credits and through development of the institution of the supervisory boards to the position of most powerful organs within corporate organizations, the banks acquired a formidable degree of ascendancy over industrial enterprises, which extended far beyond the sphere of financial control into that of entrepreneurial and managerial decisions.

It cannot be the purpose of this presentation to go into the details of this development. All that is necessary is to relate its origins and effects to the subject under discussion. The industrialization of England had proceeded without any substantial utilization of banking for long-term investment purposes. The more gradual character of the industrialization process and the more considerable accumulation of capital, first from earnings in trade and modernized agriculture and later from industry itself, obviated the pressure for developing any special institutional devices for provision of long-term capital to industry. By contrast, in a relatively backward country capital is scarce and diffused, the distrust of industrial activities is considerable, and, finally, there is greater pressure for bigness because of the scope of the industrialization movement, the larger average size of plant, and the concentration of industrialization processes on branches of relatively high ratios of capital to output. To these should be added the scarcity of entrepreneurial talent in the backward country.

It is the pressure of these circumstances which essentially gave rise to the divergent development in banking over large portions of the Continent as against England. The continental practices in the field of industrial investment banking must be conceived as specific instruments of industrialization in a backward country. It is here essentially that lies the historical and geographic locus of theories of economic development that assign a central role to processes of forced saving by the money-creating activities of banks. As will be shown presently, however, use of such instruments must be regarded as specific, not to backward countries in general, but rather to countries whose backwardness does not exceed certain limits. And even within the latter for a rather long time it was mere collection and distribution of available funds in which the banks were primarily engaged. This circumstance, of course, did not detract from the paramount importance of such activities on the part of the banks during the earlier industrialization periods with their desperate shortages of capital for industrial ventures.

The effects of these policies were far-reaching. All the basic tendencies inherent in industrial development in backward countries were greatly emphasized and magnified by deliberate attitudes on the part of the banks. From the outset of this evolution the banks were primarily attracted to certain lines of production to the neglect, if not virtual exclusion, of others. To consider Germany until the outbreak of World War I, it was essentially coal mining, iron- and steelmaking, electrical and general engineering, and heavy chemical output which became the primary sphere of activities of German banks. The textile industry, the leather industry, and the foodstuff-producing industries remained on the fringes of the banks' interest. To use modern terminology, it was heavy rather than light industry to which the attention was devoted.

Furthermore, the effects were not confined to the productive structure of industry. They extended to its organizational structure. The last three decades of the nineteenth century were marked by a rapid concentration movement in banking. This process indeed went on in very much the same way on the other side of the English Channel. But in Britain, because of the different nature of relations between banks and industry, the process was not paralleled by a similar development in industry.

It was different in Germany. The momentum shown by the cartelization movement of German industry cannot be fully explained, except as the natural result of the amalgamation of German banks. It was the mergers in the field of banking that kept placing banks in the positions of controlling competing enterprises. The banks refused to tolerate fratricidal struggles among their children. From the vantage point of centralized control, they were at all times quick to perceive profitable opportunities of cartelization and amalgamation of industrial enterprises. In the process, the average size of plant kept growing, and at the same time the interests of the banks and their assistance were even more than before devoted to those branches of industry where cartelization opportunities were rife.

Germany thus had derived full advantages from being a relatively late arrival in the field of industrial development, that is to say, from having been preceded by England. But, as a result, German industrial economy, because of specific methods used in the catching-up process, developed along lines not insignificantly different from those in England.

The State

The German experience can be generalized. Similar developments took place in Austria, or rather in the western sections of the Austrian-Hungarian Empire, in Italy, in Switzerland, in France, in Belgium, and in other countries, even though there were differences among the individual countries. But it certainly cannot be generalized for the European continent as a whole, and this for two reasons: (1) because of the existence of certain backward countries where no comparable features of industrial development can be discovered and (2) because of the existence of countries where the basic elements of backwardness appear in such an accentuated form as to lead to the use of essentially different institutional instruments of industrialization.

Little need be said with reference to the first type of country. The industrial development of Denmark may serve as an appropriate illustration. Surely, that country was still very backward as the nineteenth century entered upon its second half. Yet no comparable sudden spurts of industrialization and no peculiar emphasis on heavy industries could be observed. The reasons must be sought, on the one hand, in the paucity of the country's natural resources and, on the other hand, in the great opportunities for agricultural improvement that were inherent in the proximity of the English market. The peculiar response did not materialize because of the absence of the challenge.

Russia may be considered as the clearest instance of the second type of country. The characteristic feature of economic conditions in Russia was not only that the great spurt of modern industrialization came in the middle of the 1880s, that is to say, more than three decades after the beginning of rapid industrialization in Germany; even more important was the fact that at the starting point the level of economic development in Russia had been incomparably lower than that of countries such as Germany and Austria.

The main reason for the abysmal economic backwardness of Russia was the preservation of serfdom until the emancipation of 1861. In a certain sense, this very fact may be attributed to the play of a curious mechanism of economic backwardness, and a few words of explanation may be in order. In the course of its process of territorial expansion, which over a few centuries transferred the small duchy of Moscow into the huge land mass of modern Russia, the country became increasingly involved in military conflicts with the West. This involvement revealed a curious internal conflict between the tasks of the Russian government that were "modern" in the contemporaneous sense of the word and the hopelessly backward economy of the country on which the military policies had to be based. As a result, the economic development in Russia at several important junctures assumed the form of a peculiar series of sequences: (1) Basic was the fact that the state, moved by its military interest, assumed the role of the primary agent propelling the economic progress in the country. (2) The fact that economic development thus became a function of military exigencies imparted a peculiarly jerky character to the course of that development; it proceeded fast whenever military necessities were pressing and subsided as the military pressures relaxed. (3) This mode of economic progress by fits and starts implied that, whenever a considerable upsurge of economic activities was required, a very formidable burden was placed on the shoulders of the generations whose lifespan happened to coincide with the period of intensified development. (4) In order to exact effectively the great sacrifices it required, the government had to subject the reluctant population to a number of severe measures of oppression lest the burdens imposed be evaded by escape to the frontier regions in the southeast and east. (5) Precisely because of the magnitude of the governmental exactions, a period of rapid development was very likely to give way to prolonged stagnation, because the great effort had been pushed beyond the limits of physical endurance of the population and long periods of economic stagnation were the inevitable consequences. The sequences just mentioned present in a schematic way a pattern of Russian economic development in past centuries which fits best the period of the reforms under Peter the Great, but its applicability is by no means confined to that period.

What must strike the observer of this development is its curiously paradoxical course. While trying, as Russia did under Peter the Great, to adopt Western techniques, to raise output and the skills of the population to levels more closely approaching those of the West, Russia by virtue of this very effort was in some other respects thrown further away from the West. Broadly speaking, placing the trammels of serfdom upon the Russian peasantry must be understood as the obverse side of the processes of Westernization. Peter the Great did not institute serfdom in Russia, but perhaps more than anyone else he did succeed in making it effective. When in subsequent periods, partly because of point 2 and partly because of point 5 above, the state withdrew from active promotion of economic development and the nobility emancipated itself from its service obligations to the government, peasant serfdom was divested of its connection with economic development. What once was an indirect obligation to the state became a pure obligation toward the nobility and as such became by far the most important retarding factor in Russia's economic development.

Readers of Toynbee's may wish to regard this process, ending as it did with the emancipation of the peasantry, as an expression of the "withdrawal and return" sequence. Alternatively they may justifiably prefer to place it under the heading of "arrested civilizations." At any rate, the challenge-response mechanism is certainly useful in thinking about sequences of that nature. It should be noted, however, that the problem is not simply one of quantitative relationship between the volume of the challenge and that of the response. The crucial point is that the magnitude of the challenge changes the *quality* of the response and, by so doing, not only injects powerful retarding factors into the economic process but also more likely leads to a number of undesirable noneconomic consequences. To this aspect, which is most relevant to the current problem of industrialization of backward countries, we shall advert again in the concluding remarks of this essay.

To return to Russian industrialization in the eighties and the nineties of the past century, it may be said that in one sense it can be viewed as a recurrence of a previous pattern of economic development in the country. The role of the state distinguishes rather clearly the type of Russian industrialization from its German or Austrian counterpart.

Emancipation of the peasants, despite its manifold deficiencies, was an absolute prerequisite for industrialization. As such it was a negative action of the state designed to remove obstacles that had been earlier created by the state itself and in this sense was fully comparable to acts such as the agrarian reforms in Germany or the policies of Napoleon III which have been mentioned earlier. Similarly, the great judicial and administrative reforms of the sixties were in the nature of creating a suitable framework for industrial development rather than promoting it directly.

The main point of interest here that, unlike the case of Western Europe, actions of this sort did not per se lead to an upsurge of individual activities in the country; and for almost a quarter of a century after the emancipation the rate of industrial growth remained relatively low. The great industrial upswing came when, from the middle of the eighties on, the railroad building of the state assumed unprecedented proportions and became the main lever of a rapid industrialization policy. Through multifarious devices such as preferential orders to domestic producers of railroad materials, high prices, subsidies, credits, and profit guarantees to new industrial enterprises, the government succeeded in maintaining a high and, in fact, increasing rate of growth until the end of the century. Concomitantly, the Russian taxation system was reorganized, and the financing of industrialization policies was thus provided for, while the stabilization of the ruble and the introduction of the gold standard assured foreign participation in the development of Russian industry.

The basic elements of a backward economy were, on the whole, the same in Russia of the nineties and in Germany of the fifties. But quantitatively the differences were formidable. The scarcity of capital in Russia was such that no banking system could conceivably succeed in attracting sufficient funds to finance a large-scale industrialization; the standards of honesty in business were so disastrously low, the general distrust of the public so great, that no bank could have hoped to attract even such small capital funds as were available, and no bank could have successfully engaged in long-term credit policies in an economy where fraudulent bankruptcy had been almost elevated to the rank of a general business practice. Supply of capital for the needs of industrialization required the compulsory machinery of the government, which, through its taxation policies, succeeded in directing incomes from consumption to investment. There is no doubt that the government as an *agens movens* of industrialization discharged its role in a far less than perfectly efficient manner. Incompetence and corruption of bureaucracy were great. The amount of waste that accompanied the process was formidable. But, when all is said and done, the great success of the policies pursued under Vyshnegradski and Witte is undeniable. Not only in their origins but also in their effects, the policies pursued by the Russian government in the nineties resembled closely those of the banks in Central Europe. The Russian state did not evince any interest in "light industry." Its whole attention was centered on output of basic industrial materials and on machinery production; like the banks in Germany, the Russian bureaucracy was primarily interested in large-scale enterprises and in amalgamations and coordinated policies among the industrial enterprises which it favored or had helped to create. Clearly, a good deal of the government's interest in industrialization was predicated upon its military policies. But these policies only reinforced and accentuated the basic tendencies of industrialization in conditions of economic backwardness.

Perhaps nothing serves to emphasize more these basic uniformities in the situation and the dependence of actual institutional instruments used on the degree of backwardness of the country than a comparison of policies pursued within the two halves of the Austrian-Hungarian monarchy, that is to say, within one and the same political body. The Austrian part of the monarchy was backward in relation to, say, Germany, but it was at all times much more advanced than its Hungarian counterpart. Accordingly, in Austria proper the banks could successfully devote themselves to the promotion of industrial activities. But across the Leitha Mountains, in Hungary, the activities of the banks proved altogether inadequate, and around the turn of the century the Hungarian government embarked upon vigorous policies of industrialization. Originally, the government showed a considerable interest in developing the textile industry of the region. And it is instructive to watch how, under the pressure of what the French like to call the "logic of things," the basic uniformities asserted themselves and how the generous government subsidies were more and more deflected from textile industries to promotion of heavy industries.

The Gradations of Backwardness

To return to the basic German-Russian paradigm: what has been said in the foregoing does not exhaust the pattern of parallels. The question remains as to the effects of successful industrializations, that is to say, of the gradual diminution of backwardness.

At the turn of the century, if not somewhat earlier, changes became apparent in the relationship between German banks and German industry. As the former industrial infants had grown to strong manhood, the original undisputed ascendancy of the banks over industrial enterprises could no longer be maintained. This process of liberation of industry from the decades of tutelage expressed itself in a variety of ways. Increasingly, industrial enterprises transformed connection with a single bank into cooperation with several banks. As the former industrial protectorates became economically sovereign, they embarked upon the policy of changing alliances with regard to the banks. Many an industrial giant, such as the electrical engineering industry, which could not have developed without the aid and entrepreneurial daring of the banks, began to establish its own banks. The conditions of capital scarcity to which the German banks owed their historical position were no longer present. Germany had become a developed industrial country. But the specific features engendered by a process of industrialization in conditions of backwardness were to remain, and so was the close relation between banks and industry, even though the master-servant relation gave way to cooperation among equals and sometimes was even reversed.

In Russia the magnificent period of industrial development of the nineties was cut short by the 1900 depression and the following years of war and civil strife. But, when Russia emerged from the revolutionary years 1905–1906 and again achieved a high rate of industrial growth in the years 1907–1914, the character of the industrialization processes had changed greatly. Railroad construction by the government continued but on a much smaller scale both absolutely and even more so relatively to the increased industrial output. Certain increases in military expenditures that took place could not begin to compensate for the reduced significance of railroad-building. The conclusion is inescapable that, in that last period of industrialization under a prerevolutionary government, the significance of the state was very greatly reduced.

At the same time, the traditional pattern of Russian economic development happily failed to work itself out. The retrenchment of government activities led not to stagnation but to a continuation of industrial growth. Russian industry had reached a stage where it could throw away the crutches of government support and begin to walk independently—and, yet, very much less independently than industry in contemporaneous Germany, for at least to some extent the role of the retreating government was taken over by the banks.

A great transformation had taken place with regard to the banks during the fifty years that had elapsed since the emancipation. Commercial banks had been founded. Since it was the government that had fulfilled the function of industrial banks, the Russian banks, precisely because of the backwardness of the country, were organized as "deposit banks," thus resembling very much the type of banking in England. But, as industrial development proceeded apace and as capital accumulation increased, the standards of business behavior were growingly Westernized. The paralyzing atmosphere of distrust began to vanish, and the foundation was laid for the emergence of a different type of bank. Gradually, the Moscow deposit banks were overshadowed by the development of the St. Petersburg banks that were conducted upon principles that were characteristic not of English but of German banking. In short, after the economic backwardness of Russia had been reduced by state-sponsored industrialization processes, use of a different instrument of industrialization, suitable to the new "stage of backwardness," became applicable.

Ideologies of Delayed Industrializations

Before drawing some general conclusions, a last differential aspect of industrialization in circumstances of economic backwardness should be mentioned. So far, important differences with regard to the character of industrial developments and its institutional vehicles were related to conditions and degrees of backwardness. A few words remain to be said on the ideological climate within which such industrialization proceeded.

Again we may revert to the instructive story of French industrialization under Napoleon III. A large proportion of the men who reached positions of economic and financial influence upon Napoleon's advent to power were not isolated individuals. They belonged to a rather well-defined group. They were not Bonapartists but Saint-Simonian socialists. The fact that a man like Isaac Pereire, who contributed so much, perhaps more than any other single person, to the spread of the modern capitalist system in France should have been—and should have remained to the end of his days—an ardent admirer of Saint-Simonian doctrines is on the face of it surprising. It becomes much less so if a few pertinent relationships are considered.

It could be argued that Saint-Simon was in reality far removed from being a socialist; that in his vision of an industrial society he hardly distinguished between laborers and employers; and that he considered the appropriate political form for his society of the future some kind of corporate state in which the "leaders of industry" would exercise major political functions. Yet arguments of that sort would hardly explain much. Saint-Simon had a profound interest in what he used to call the "most numerous and most suffering classes"; more importantly, Saint-Simonian doctrines, as expanded and redefined by the followers of the master (particularly by Bazard), incorporated into the system a good many socialist ideas, including abolition of inheritance and establishment of a system of planned economy designed to direct and to develop the economy of the country. And it was this interpretation of the doctrines which the Pereires accepted.

It is more relevant to point to the stress laid by Saint-Simon and his followers upon industrialization and the great task they had assigned to banks as an instrument of organization and development of the economy. This, no doubt, greatly appealed to the creators of the Crédit Mobilier, who liked to think of their institution as of a "bank to a higher power" and of themselves as "missionaries" rather than bankers. That Saint-Simon's stress upon the role to be played by the banks in economic development revealed a truly amazing—and altogether "unutopian"—insight into the problems of that development is as true as the fact that Saint-Simonian ideas most decisively influenced the course of economic events inside and outside France. But the question remains: why was the socialist garment draped around an essentially capitalist idea? And why was it the socialist form that was so readily accepted by the greatest capitalist entrepreneurs France ever possessed?

It would seem that the answer must again be given in terms of basic conditions of backwardness. Saint-Simon, the friend of J.B. Say, was never averse to ideas of laissez-faire policies. Chevalier, the coauthor of the Franco-English treaty of commerce of 1860 that ushered in the great period of European free trade, had been an ardent Saint-Simonian. And yet under French conditions a laissez-faire ideology was altogether inadequate as a spiritual vehicle of an industrialization program.

To break through the barriers of stagnation in a backward country, to ignite the imaginations of men, and to place their energies in the service of economic development, a stronger medicine is needed than the promise of better allocation of resources or even of the lower price of bread. Under such conditions even the businessman, even the classical daring and innovating entrepreneur, needs a more powerful stimulus than the prospect of high profits. What is needed to remove the mountains of routine and prejudice is faith—faith, in the words of Saint-Simon, that the golden age lies not behind but ahead of mankind. It was not for nothing that Saint-Simon devoted his last years to the formulation of a new creed, the New Christianity, and suffered Auguste Comte to break with him over this "betrayal of true science." What sufficed in England did not suffice in France.

Shortly before his death, Saint-Simon urged Rouget de Lisle, the aged author of the "Marseillaise," to compose a new anthem, an "Industrial Marseillaise." Rouget de Lisle complied. In the new hymn the man who once had called upon "enfants de la patrie" to wage ruthless war upon the tyrants and their mercenary cohorts addresses himself to "enfants de l'industrie"—the "true nobles"—who would assure the "happiness of all" by spreading industrial arts and by submitting the world to the peaceful "laws of industry."

Ricardo is not known to have inspired anyone to change "God Save the King" into "God Save Industry." No one would want to detract from the force of John Bright's passionate eloquence, but in an advanced country rational arguments in favor of industrialization policies need not be supplemented by a quasi-religious fervor. Buckle was not far wrong when in a famous passage of his *History* he presented the conversion of public opinion in England to free trade as achieved by the force of incontrovertible logic. In a backward country the great and sudden industrialization effort calls for a New Deal in emotions. Those carrying out the great transformation as well as those on whom it imposes burdens must feel, in the words of Matthew Arnold, that

> ... Clearing a stage
> Scattering the past about
> Comes the new age.

Capitalist industrialization under the auspices of socialist ideologies may be, after all, less surprising a phenomenon than would appear at first sight.

Similarly, Friedrich List's industrialization theories may be largely conceived as an attempt, by a man whose personal ties to Saint-Simonians had been very strong, to translate the inspirational message of Saint-Simonism into a language that would be accepted in the German environment, where the lack of both a preceding political revolution and an early national unification rendered nationalist sentiment a much more suitable ideology of industrialization.

After what has been just said it will perhaps not seem astonishing that, in the Russian industrialization of the 1890s, orthodox Marxism can be said to have performed a very similar function. Nothing reconciled the Russian intelligentsia more to the advent of capitalism in the country and to the destruction of its old faith in the mir and the artel than a system of ideas which presented the capitalist industrialization of the country as the result of an iron law of historical development. It is this connection which largely explains the power wielded by Marxist thought in Russia when it extended to men like Struve and in some sense even Milyukov, whose Weltanschauung was altogether alien to the ideas of Marxian socialism. In conditions of Russian "absolute" backwardness, again, a much more powerful ideology was required to grease the intellectual and emotional wheels of industrialization than either in France or in Germany. The institutional gradations of backwardness seem to find their counterpart in men's thinking about backwardness and the way in which it can be abolished.

Conclusions

The story of European industrialization in the nineteenth century would seem to yield a few points of view which may be helpful for appreciation of present-day problems.

1. If the spurtlike character of the past century's industrialization on the European continent is conceived of as the result of the specific preindustrial situations in backward countries and if it is understood that pressures for high-speed industrializations are inherent in those situations, it should become easier to appreciate the oft-expressed desires in this direction by the governments of those countries. Slogans like "Factories quick!" which played such a large part in the discussions of the pertinent portions of the International Trade Organization charter, may then appear less unreasonable.

2. Similarly, the tendencies in backward countries to concentrate much of their efforts on introduction of the most modern and expensive technology, their stress on large-scale plant, and their interest in developing investment-goods industries need not necessarily be regarded as flowing mainly from a quest for prestige and from economic megalomania.

3. What makes it so difficult for an advanced country to appraise properly the industrialization policies of its less fortunate brethren is the fact that, in every instance of industrialization, imitation of the evolution in advanced countries appears in combination with different, indigenously determined elements. If it is not always easy for advanced countries to accept the former, it is even more difficult for them to acquiesce in the latter. This is particularly true of the institutional instruments used in carrying out industrial developments and even more so of ideologies which accompany it. What can be derived from a historical review is a strong sense for the significance of the native elements in the industrialization of backward countries.

A journey through the last century may, by destroying what Bertrand Russell once called the "dogmatism of the untravelled," help in formulating a broader and more enlightened view of the pertinent problems and in replacing the absolute notions of what is "right" and what is "wrong" by a more flexible and relativistic approach.

It is, of course, not suggested here that current policies vis-à-vis backward areas should be formulated on the basis of the general experience of the past century without taking into account, in each individual instance, the degree of endowment with natural resources, the climatic disabilities, the strength of institutional obstacles to industrialization, the pattern of foreign trade, and other pertinent factors. But what is even more important is the fact that, useful as the "lessons" of the nineteenth century may be, they cannot properly be applied without understanding the climate of the present century, which in so many ways has added new and momentous aspects to the problems concerned.

Since the present problem of industrialization of backward areas largely concerns non-European countries, there is the question of the effects of their specific preindustrial cultural development upon their industrialization potentialities. Anthropological research of such cultural patterns has tended to come to rather pessimistic conclusions in this respect. But perhaps such conclusions are unduly lacking in dynamic perspective. At any rate, they do not deal with the individual factors involved in terms of their specific changeabilities. At the same time, past Russian experience does show how quickly in the last decades of the past century a pattern of life that had been so strongly opposed to industrial values, that tended to consider any nonagricultural economic activity as unnatural and sinful, began to give way to very different attitudes. In particular, the rapid emergence of native entrepreneurs with peasant-serf backgrounds should give pause to those who stress so greatly the disabling lack of entrepreneurial qualities in backward civilizations. Yet there are other problems.

In certain extensive backward areas the very fact that industrial development has been so long delayed has created, along with unprecedented opportunities for technological progress, great obstacles to industrialization. Industrial progress is arduous and expensive; medical progress is cheaper and easier of accomplishment. To the extent that the latter has preceded the former by a considerable span of time and has resulted in formidable overpopulation, industrial revolutions may be defeated by Malthusian counterrevolutions.

Closely related to the preceding but enormously more momentous in its effects is the fact that great delays in industrialization tend to allow time for social tensions to develop and to assume sinister proportions. As a mild example, the case of Mexico may be cited, where the established banks have been reluctant to cooperate in industrialization activities that are sponsored by a government whose radical hue they distrust. But the real case in point overshadowing everything else in scope and importance is, of course, that of Soviet Russia.

If what has been said in the preceding pages has validity, Soviet industrialization undoubtedly contains all the basic elements that were common to the industrializations of backward countries in the nineteenth century. The stress on heavy industry and oversized plant is, as such, by no means peculiar to Soviet Russia. But what is true is that in Soviet Russia those common features of industrialization processes have been magnified and distorted out of all proportion.

The problem is as much a political as it is an economic one. The Soviet government can be properly described as a product of the country's economic backwardness. Had serfdom been abolished by Catherine the Great or at the time of the Decembrist uprising in 1825, the peasant discontent, the driving force and the earnest of success of the Russian Revolution, would never have assumed disastrous proportions, while the economic development of the country would have proceeded in a much more gradual fashion. If anything is a "grounded historical assumption," this would seem to be one: the delayed industrial revolution was responsible for a political revolution in the course of which the power fell into the hands of a dictatorial government to which in the long run the vast majority of the population was opposed. It is one thing for such a government to gain power in a moment of great crisis; it is another to maintain this power for a long period. Whatever the strength of the army and the ubiquitousness of the secret police which such a government may have at its disposal, it would be naive to believe that those instruments of physical oppression can suffice. Such a government can maintain itself in power only if it succeeds in making people believe that it performs an important social function which could not be discharged in its absence.

Industrialization provided such a function for the Soviet government. All the basic factors in the situation of the country pressed in that direction. By reverting to a pattern of economic development that should have remained confined to a long-bygone age, by substituting collectivization for serfdom, and by pushing up the rate of investment to the maximum point within the limits of endurance of the population, the Soviet government did what no government relying on the consent of the governed could have done. That these policies, after having led through a period of violent struggles, have resulted in permanent day-to-day friction between the government and the population is undeniable. But, paradoxical as it may sound, these policies at the same time have secured some broad acquiescence on the part of the people. If all the forces of the population can be kept engaged in the processes of industrialization and if this industrialization can be justified by the promise of happiness and abundance for future generations and—much more importantly—by the menace of military aggression from beyond the borders, the dictatorial government will find its power broadly unchallenged. And the vindication of a threatening war is easily produced, as is shown by the history of the cold-war years. Economic backwardness, rapid industrialization, ruthless exercise of dictatorial power, and the danger of war have become inextricably intertwined in Soviet Russia.

This is not the place to elaborate this point further with regard to Soviet Russia. The problem at hand is not Soviet Russia but the problem of attitudes toward industrialization of backward countries. If the Soviet experience teaches anything, it is that it demonstrates *ad oculos* the formidable dangers inherent in our time in the existence of economic backwardness. There are no four-lane highways through the parks of industrial progress. The road may lead from backwardness to dictatorship and from dictatorship to war. In conditions of a "bipolar world" this sinister sequence is modified and aggrandized by deliberate imitation of Soviet policies by other backward countries and by their voluntary or involuntary incorporation in the Soviet orbit.

Thus, conclusions can be drawn from the historical experience of both centuries. The paramount lesson of the twentieth century is that the problems of backward nations are not exclusively their own. They are just as much problems of the advanced countries. It is not only Russia but the whole world that pays the price for the failure to emancipate the Russian peasants and to embark upon industrialization policies at an early time. Advanced countries cannot afford to ignore economic backwardness. But the lesson of the nineteenth century is that the policies toward the backward countries are unlikely to be successful if they ignore the basic peculiarities of economic backwardness. Only by frankly recognizing their existence and strength, and by attempting to develop fully rather than to stifle what Keynes once called the "possibilities of things," can the experience of the nineteenth century be used to avert the threat presented by its successor.

Notes

1. Karl Marx, *Das Kapital* (1st ed.), preface.
2. It would have been extremely desirable to transcend the European experience at least by including some references to the industrialization of Japan. Unfortunately, the writer's ignorance of Japanese economic history has effectively barred him from thus broadening the scope of his observations. The reader must be referred, however, to the excellent study by Henry Rosovsky, *Capital Formation in Japan, 1868–1940* (Glencoe, 1961), in which the validity of this writer's approach for Japanese industrial history is explicitly discussed.

David S. Landes,
The Wealth and Poverty of Nations (1998)*

Chapter 29: How Did We Get Here?
Where Are We Going?

Historians like to look back, not ahead. They try to understand and explain the record. Economists also want to know the past, but believe what they know about it only insofar as it accords with theory and logic; and since they have the assurance of basic principles, they are less averse to telling a future shaped by rationality. To be sure, economists recognize the possibility of accident and unreason, but these can in the long run only delay the logically inevitable. Reason will triumph because reason pays. More is better, and in choosing goals, material achievement is the best argument.

So, whereas historians are agnostics about the future, hence virtual pessimists, economists and business people tend to be optimists.[1] Optimism has to do, above all, with increase of wealth, what Adam Smith called "the natural progress of opulence." Even for the poor: "In almost any way you care to measure, life is getting better for people in developing nations."[2] Also longer; and these data on life expectancy should settle the issue. In the same way, poor people are *on average* better off. Not fewer; but better off. Economists now opine that the world will continue to get richer, that the poor will catch up with the rich, that islands of growth will become continents, that knowledge can solve problems and overcome material and social difficulties along the way.[3] So it was, and so shall be.

Economists have not always felt this way.[4] Adam Smith's successors anticipated stagnation: Malthus, with his inexorable press of people on food supply; Ricardo, with his "stationary state" as land and rent soaked up the surplus; Jevons, with his bogey of fuel exhaustion. In those times, economics wore the sobriquet of "the dismal science." Subsequent progress has allayed these fears, although some see the Malthusian doom as only postponed.[5]

Meanwhile a new rider joins the horsemen of the apocalypse: ecological disaster. We no longer have to worry about the exhaustion of this or that resource; technology will find substitutes.[6] But we do have to attend to the serious, progressive, and possibly irremediable damage we are inflicting on the environment. This threat to well-being ties directly to economic development, for waste, pollution, and environmental damage grow with wealth and output. *Other things equal, it is the rich who poison the earth.*

229

To be sure, the rich see the peril—at least some do—and their wealth permits them to spend on clean-up and dump their waste elsewhere.[7] They also abound in good ecological advice to the new industrializers. These in turn are quick to point to the pollution perpetrated by today's rich countries in their growth period. Why should today's latecomers have to be careful? Besides, most developing countries are ready to pay the environmental price: wages and riches now; disease and death down the road. To be sure, no one has taken a poll, but this preference seems plausible. Young people—and developing countries are full of young people—think they'll live forever. Meanwhile who can confine pollution and disease? The rich are frightened, even if the poor are not. The rich have much more to lose.

If we learn anything from the history of economic development, it is that culture makes all the difference. (Here Max Weber was right on.) Witness the enterprise of expatriate minorities—the Chinese in East and Southeast Asia, Indians in East Africa, Lebanese in West Africa, Jews and Calvinists throughout much of Europe, and on and on. Yet culture, in the sense of the inner values and attitudes that guide a population, frightens scholars. It has a sulfuric odor of race and inheritance, an air of immutability. In thoughtful moments, economists and social scientists recognize that this is not true, and indeed salute examples of cultural change for the better while deploring changes for the worse. But applauding or deploring implies the passivity of the viewer—an inability to use knowledge to shape people and things. The technicians would rather do: change interest and exchange rates, free up trade, alter political institutions, manage. Besides, criticisms of culture cut close to the ego, injure identity and self-esteem. Coming from outsiders, such animadversions, however tactful and indirect, stink of condescension. Benevolent improvers have learned to steer clear.

Besides, if culture does so much, why does it not work consistently? Economists are not alone in asking why some people—the Chinese, say—have long been so unproductive at home and yet so enterprising away. If culture matters, why didn't it change China? (It is doing so, now.) An economist friend, master of political-economic therapies, solves this paradox by denying any connection. Culture, he says, does not enable him to predict outcomes. I disagree. One could have foreseen the postwar economic success of Japan and Germany by taking account of culture. The same with South Korea vs. Turkey, Indonesia vs. Nigeria.

On the other hand, culture does not stand alone. Economic analysis cherishes the illusion that one good reason should be enough, but the determinants of complex processes are invariably plural and interrelated. Monocausal explanations will not work. The same values thwarted by "bad government" at home can find opportunity elsewhere. Hence the special success of emigrant enterprise. The ancient Greeks, as usual, had a word for it: these *metics*, alien residents, were the leaven of societies that sneered at crafts (hence the pejorative sense of "banausic") and at money. So strangers found and sold the goods and made the money.

Meanwhile, because culture and economic performance are linked, changes in one will work back on the other. In Thailand, all good young men used to spend years undergoing a religious apprenticeship in Buddhist monasteries. This period of ripening was good for the spirit and soul; it also suited the somnolent pace of traditional economic activity and employment. That was then. Today, Thailand moves faster; commerce thrives; business calls. As a result, young men spiritualize for a few weeks—time enough to learn some prayers and rituals and get back to the real, material world. Time, which everyone knows is money, has changed in relative value. One could not have imposed this change, short of revolution. The Thais have voluntarily adjusted their priorities.

The Thai story illustrates culture's response to economic growth and opportunity. The reverse is also possible—culture may shift against enterprise. We have the Russian case, where seventy-five years of anti-market, antiprofit schooling and insider privilege have planted and frozen anti-entrepreneurial attitudes. Even after the regime has fallen—people fear the uncertainties of the market and yearn for the safe tedium of state employment. Or for equality in poverty. As the Russian joke has it, peasant Ivan is jealous of neighbor Boris, because Boris has a goat. A fairy comes along and offers Ivan a single wish. What does he wish for? That Boris's goat should drop dead.

Fortunately, not all Russians think that way. The collapse of Marxist prohibitions and inhibitions has led to a rush of business activity, the best of it linked to inside deals, some of it criminal, much of it the work of non-Russian minorities (Armenians, Georgians, *et al.*). The leaven is there, and often that suffices: the initiative of an enterprising, different few. In the meantime, old habits remain, corruption and crime are rampant, culture war rages, elections hang on these issues, and the outcome is not certain.[8]

Convergence is the watchword of the day, the promise of eventual equality, of the generalization of prosperity, health, and happiness. That, at any rate, is what economic theory tells us, assuming mobility of the factors of production.

Experience is another matter. The numbers for the small set of advanced industrial countries seem to confirm convergence, but individual countries do not always stay with the pack. Will Japan continue to pull ahead? Will the United Kingdom continue to fall behind, or is this decade's good news the promise of tomorrow? Will this be the East Asian century? And what about the United States? Americans should remember the refusal of the British to face up to their troubles before they too let themselves be soothed by optimistic prognoses. That's the weakness of futurism: the soothsayers do not hang around to take responsibility for their errors. Even if they do, no one notices them any more; and they themselves remember only the good guesses. (Besides, remember the basic law: I was right when I said it.)

Meanwhile advanced and backward, rich and poor do not seem to be growing closer. Optimistic number-crunchers point to overall mini-convergence, but they put Asia with the poor, and only the special success of East Asia yields this optical illusion. Africa and the Middle East are still going nowhere. Latin America is doing a mixed job, mixed over time and space. The former Socialist bloc is in transition: some countries are doing well; others, particularly the former Soviet Union, swing in high uncertainty.

And what about contingency and mess? So many things to go wrong—war, revolution, natural disaster, bad government, crime, antiproductive ideology. Many success stories seem brittle, dependent on the political status quo. Every day's newspaper brings messages of hope: India is changing and beginning to encourage foreign investment; peace and order "take root" in Sierra Leone; after years of internecine strife, Argentina is coming back; Russia bubbles with new enterprise as Pepsi-Cola plans new investments. Can one take these happy turns as definite? Every other day, the same newspaper brings its warnings of trouble and reversal.

The British colony of Hong Kong is perhaps the best example of wobbling uncertainty. It went back to China on 1 July 1997. The returns are not yet in. China may choose to cherish it; or it may decide to force it into line with the mainland economy. To be sure, it seems improbable that China would kill the goose that lays so many golden eggs. But how important are Hong Kong's eggs in the larger Chinese picture? Besides, history has known similar irrationalities, and China has a history of sacrificing trade to imperial principle. Meanwhile Hong Kong business families have taken their precautions, both ways—to stay or to go. They have taken up citizenship in safer havens (some 600,000 of them hold foreign passports).[9] They are also learning to speak Mandarin as well as their native Cantonese and replacing Western executives with Chinese.[10] A rational "minimax" strategy: minimize maximum potential loss.

Do globalization and convergence signal the end of national striving? Does the very idea of international economic competitiveness no longer make sense? The economist Paul Krugman would say so: the "views [of those who call for a national economics] are based on a failure to understand even the simplest economic facts and concepts."[11]

Peremptory and dismissive, and yet the proponents of state intervention have not surrendered. We are talking here of two goals, power and wealth; and two ideals, distributive justice and impersonal efficiency. All of these hang together. Each has its own appeal, constituency, and justification.

Even within the economics profession, opinions differ. The neo-classicists say no: for them, no signals more reliable than market signals. They follow here in the steps of the great master: "Great nations are never impoverished by private, though they sometimes are by public prodigality and misconduct. The whole, or almost the whole public revenue, is in most countries employed in maintaining unproductive hands."[12] Adam Smith worried that these place servers might consume the produce needed to sustain the productive members of the society. (There are countries like that.)

Yet Adam Smith also understood that the state can (will) do some things—defense, police—better than private enterprise. In Ottoman Turkey, firefighting was in the hand of private companies, who came running when the alarm sounded. They competed with one another and negotiated price with house owners on the spot. As the negotiation proceeded, the fire burned higher and the stakes diminished. Or spread. Neighbors had an interest in contributing to the pot. 'Twixt meanness and greed, many a house fire turned into mass conflagration.

The issue presses in those countries where enterprise is wanting. In a world of rapid change and international competition, can society afford to wait for private initiative? Look at the role of the state in such exemplary countries as Korea, Taiwan, and even Japan: triggering, sheltering, and guiding nominally free market enterprise. To which the free marketeers make reply by recalling Pearl Harbor.

The record, then, is clearly mixed. State intervention is like the little girl who had a little curl right in the middle of her forehead: when she was good, she was very, very good; and when she was bad, she was horrid.

Besides, the state can be very useful as the servant of business. Officials have always been liable to temptation (bribes); that's human nature. But the growth of private salaries and bonuses in expanding economies has inflated and accelerated this venal-ization of government and administration. Men of money can buy men of power. Presidents and prime ministers act as traveling salesmen and judge their success by deals closed and contracts signed. The British are talking of replacing the royal yacht with an even bigger vessel, the equivalent of a cruise ship for two, plus guests. This liner would cost hundreds of millions of pounds, and if experience be a guide, would eventually take more to run than to build—the more so as the very existence of such an expensive toy compels its use. (Royalty has no notion of the doctrine of sunk costs.) No matter. The ship's proponents assure the British taxpayer that it will bring in trade. Meanwhile ideals yield to interest. China is behaving badly? The best way to straighten it out is to say nothing and do business. That may seem cynical; but it may be as good a cure as any for despotic irrationality.

The selection process goes on. Today's search for cheap labor has moved jobs from rich countries to poor, or more precisely, to some poor countries.[13] Happiness to some, deprivation to others. This mix of good news and bad is what economic change is all about. Economists and moralists applaud such transfers as rational, reflecting comparative advantage, hence reasonable and desirable. Why should employment for Malaysians and Mexicans be any less desirable than for Americans and Germans? Krugman again: "One might have expected everyone to welcome this change in the global landscape, to see the rapid improvement in the living standards of hundreds of millions of people, many of whom had previously been desperately poor, as prog-ress—and as an unprecedented business opportunity."[14]

No reason, except that job losers are unhappy and angry, and in advanced indus-trial nations, job losers vote. They also demonstrate and riot. The same observers who worry about the mistakes of "strategic" trade policy might focus instead on the risks and costs of conflict. A cool economist may argue that nations do not compete as corporations do; or that loss of export markets and jobs does not make that much difference to a rich country like the United States;[15] or that bars to imports will not promote productivity or raise the standard of living at home; or that loss of jobs in branches that are no longer "advantageous" will be compensated by the creation of other jobs in other areas. These reasonings and clevernesses will not help workers and unions intimidated by the threat of job emigration. Nor will they console someone who loses a place and must take something less satisfying and less well paid, or who is of that twilight age that makes the very idea of starting over impractical.[16]

How much more vexing are the sassy dismissals that tell the public to rejoice at the prospect of cheaper cars and TV sets, which they can no longer afford, and advise them to seek jobs growing soy beans or servicing bank accounts. This, remember, is a replay of the advice John Bowring gave the member states of the German Zollver-ein in 1840: grow wheat, and sell it to buy British manufactures. This was a sublime example of economic good sense; but Germany would have been the poorer for it. Today's comparative advantage, we have seen, may not be tomorrow's. Is protection legitimate only for infant industries? Are rich countries morally obliged to eschew the devices routinely adopted by developing countries? Proponents of dependency theory have long stressed the injustice of allegedly unequal trade between strong and weak, rich and poor. But asymmetry goes both ways.

These questions do not have simple, unambiguous answers. It is one thing to advocate an active government policy; quite another to take the right measures and carry them out. One thing seems clear to me, however. The present tendency to global industrial diffusion will entail, for the richer countries, a leveling down of wages, increased inequality of incomes, and/or high levels of (transitional?) unemployment. No one has abrogated the law of supply and demand. Many, if not most, economists will disagree. They rely here on the sacred certainty of gains from trade for all. International competition, they tell us, is a positive-sum game: everyone benefits.

In the long run. This is not the place to attempt, in a few pages, a survey of the differences of opinion on this issue, which continues to generate a library of material.[17] I would simply argue here, from the historical record, that

- The gains from trade are unequal. As history has shown, some countries will do much better than others. The primary reason is that comparative advantage is not the same for all, and that some activities are more lucrative and productive than others. (A dollar is not a dollar is not a dollar.) They require and yield greater gains in knowledge and know-how, within and without.
- The export and import of jobs is not the same as trade in commodities. The two may be fungible in theory, but the human impact is very different.
- Comparative advantage is not fixed, and it can move for or against.
- It always helps to attend and respond to the market. But just because markets give signals does not mean that people will respond timely or well. Some people do this better than others, and culture can make all the difference.
- Some people find it easier and more agreeable to take than to make. This temptation marks all societies, and only moral training and vigilance can hold it in check.

Withal, I do not want to advocate any particular national policy, the less so as activist intervention can as easily make things worse as better. Each case must be judged on the merits, and governments are capable of as many mistakes, and bigger, than the businessmen who try to shape and play the market. (And vice versa. Much depends on what one is trying to maximize—wealth, equality, security, salvation, or what have you.)[18] I just want to say that the current pattern of technological diffusion and catch-up development will press hard on the haves, especially the individual victims of economic regrouping, while bringing "goodies" and hope to some of the have-nots, and despair, disappointment, and anger to many of the others.

To be sure, the rich, industrial countries can defend themselves (ease but not eliminate the pain) by remaining on the cutting edge of research, by moving into new and growing branches (creating new jobs), by learning from others, by finding the right niches, by cultivating and using ability and knowledge. They can go a long way on cruise control and safety nets, helping the losers to learn new skills, get new jobs, or just retire. Much will depend on their spirit of enterprise, their sense of identity and commitment to the common weal, their self-esteem, their ability to transmit these assets across the generations.

Meanwhile what about the poor, the backward, and the disadvantaged? After all, the rich industrial countries, however much pressed by the new competition, are so much better off that it is hard to work up concern and sympathy. With all their troubles, they have a continuing obligation, moral even more than prudential, to those less fortunate. Should they give for the sake of giving? Give only when it makes sense (pays) to give? Give, as bankers do, preferably to those who do not need help? Hard love, soft? Both? I ask these questions not because I know the answers (only true believers claim to know), but because one must be aware of the inextricable tangle of conflicting motive and contradictory effects. Navigation through these rapids demands constant adjustment and correction, the more difficult because policy is constrained by domestic politics.

And what of the poor themselves? History tells us that the most successful cures for poverty come from within. Foreign aid can help, but like windfall wealth, can also hurt. It can discourage effort and plant a crippling sense of incapacity. As the African saying has it, "The hand that receives is always under the one that gives."[19] No, what counts is work, thrift, honesty, patience, tenacity. To people haunted by misery and hunger, that may add up to selfish indifference. But at bottom, no empowerment is so effective as self-empowerment.

Some of this may sound like a collection of clichés—the sort of lessons one used to learn at home and in school when parents and teachers thought they had a mission to rear and elevate their children. Today, we condescend to such verities, dismiss them as platitudes. But why should wisdom be obsolete? To be sure, we are living in a dessert age. We want things to be sweet; too many of us work to live and live to be happy. Nothing wrong with that; it just does not promote high productivity. You want high productivity? Then you should live to work and get happiness as a by-product.

Not easy. The people who live to work are a small and fortunate elite. But it is an elite open to newcomers, self-selected, the kind of people who accentuate the positive. In this world, the optimists have it, not because they are always right, but because they are positive. Even when wrong, they are positive, and that is the way of achievement, correction, improvement, and success. Educated, eyes-open optimism pays; pessimism can only offer the empty consolation of being right.

The one lesson that emerges is the need to keep trying. No miracles. No perfection. No millennium. No apocalypse. We must cultivate a skeptical faith, avoid dogma, listen and watch well, try to clarify and define ends, the better to choose means.

... I have set before thee life and death, the blessing and the curse; therefore choose life.

—Deuteronomy 30:19

Notes

1. On the proliferation of what Ferdinand Mount calls "Endist" books, see his review "No End in Sight," *TLS*, 3 May 1996, p. 30. He writes: "One thing is common to this grand cacophony of prophecy and prescription: the refusal to pause and consider, with even the appearance of care, any arguments of their opponents or any weaknesses in their own."
2. B. Biggs, chairman, Morgan Stanley Asset Management, cited in Robert D. Kaplan, *The Ends of the Earth: A Journey at the Dawn of the 21st Century* (New York: Random House, 1996), p. 297.

3. Islands of growth: not everyone is enthralled. Paul Kennedy asks in *Preparing for the Twenty-First Century* (New York: Random House, 1993): "How comfortable would it be to have islands of prosperity in a sea of poverty?" Jeremy Rifkin, *The End of Work: The End of the Global Labor Force and the Dawn of the Post-Market Era* (New York: Putnam, 1995), is comparably scandalized by the contrasts of rich and poor. If that's the way it's going to be, we should move on to a "post-market society," whatever that is. Cf. Mount, "No End in Sight." What with the proliferating succession of post-this and post-that, we may soon see post-post and post-post-post.

4. Smith does give some credence to limits, for he speaks of a country "which had acquired that full complement of riches which the nature of its soil and climate, and its situation with respect to other countries, allowed it to acquire; which could, therefore, advance no further"—Adam Smith, *Inquiry into the Nature and Causes of the Wealth of Nations* (1776), Book I, ch. 9: "Of the Profits of Stock." But he treats this as a distant prospect, "perhaps" not as yet experienced, and adverts to the opportunities for transcending these limits with better "laws and institutions."

5. Thanks to botanical research and the invention of "miracle rice," the world rice harvest nearly doubled from 1967 to 1992. India had its "Green Revolution." Now population is once again pressing on supply, and the International Rice Research Institute promises a "super rice" that will yield 20 to 25 percent more—Seth Mydans, "Scientists Developing 'Super Rice' to Feed Asia," *New York Times*, 6 April 1997, p. A-9. Will that be enough? And what about Africa?

6. Cf. Partha S. Dasgupta "Natural Resources in an Age of Substitutability," in A. V. Kneese and J. L. Sweeny, eds., *Handbook of Natural Resources and Energy Economics.* Amsterdam: Elsevier (1993), III, 111–30. This speaks of a third stage, the "Age of Substitutability": "In this final Age, economic activities will be based almost exclusively on materials that are virtually inexhaustible, with relatively little loss in living standards" (p. 128).

7. But not always, because nobody wants that stuff. On 7 May 1996 rioters in Germany protested the return of radioactive wastes, German in origin, sent to France for processing and then brought back to Germany for presumably safe storage. The Germans spent millions of dollars to contain the angry crowds. That is why one economist recently proposed that rich nations dump unwanted wastes in such poor places as Africa—all that sand, and the Africans need the money. The very idea is symbolically unacceptable.

8. Russia is not a safe place to do business. Cf. David Remnick, *Lenin's Tomb: The Last Days of the Soviet Empire* (New York: Random House, 1993) and *Resurrection: The Struggle for a New Russia* (New York: Random House, 1997). Ukraine may well be worse. Cf. R. Bonner, "Ukraine Staggers on Path to the Free Market," *New York Times*, 9 April 1997, p. A-3.

9. Cf. Edward A. Gargan, "A Year from Chinese Rule, Dread Grows in Hong Kong," *New York Times*, 1 July 1996, p. A-1; and Peter Stein, "China Is Slow to Handle Issues on Hong Kong," *Wall St. Journal*, p. B7D.

10. Compare the precautions of Russian firms, setting up headquarters in Cyprus to get away from the crime and potential chaos at home. Mark M. Nelson, "Economic Fugitives," *Wall St. Journal*, 9 May 1996, p. 1.

11. Paul Krugman, *Pop Internationalism* (Cambridge, MA: MIT Press, 1996), p. 70.

12. Smith, *Wealth of Nations*, Book II, ch. 3.

13. *New York Times*, 19 June 1996, p. D-5: "Moulinex [French maker of household appliances] Is Shifting Production to Mexico." Not all: four of eleven plants, 2,600 of 11,300 jobs. The firm had suffered a loss of 702 m. francs for the year ended 3/31, after a loss of 213 m. a year earlier.

14. Krugman, *Pop Internationalism*, p. 50.

15. Cf. *ibid.*, pp. 112–13, which says that even a successful "strategic trade policy" would add no more than 1/15 of 1 percent to American national income. This puts such policy "as an issue in the same league as pricing policies for ranchers and miners operating on federal land." I disagree. Insofar as government can promote competitiveness, it should, on the principle that more knowledge and better performance are contagious. And insofar as the government is leading federal land for less than market value, it should stop, on the principle that successful rent seeking is a bad habit and also contagious. The only real argument against government intervention is that it often botches the job. And that's also contagious.

16. Cf. Louis Uchitelle, "Like Oil and Water: A Tale of Two Economists," *New York Times*, 16 February 1997, p. 3, 1. This article is a comparison of the economics—content and tone—of Lester Thurow and Paul Krugman.

17. Among the more recent contributions are the essays in Krugman, *Pop Internationalism*, which denounce protectionism and other efforts to manage trade. Krugman is especially severe toward his intellectual adversaries, defining "pop internationalism" as "glib rhetoric that appeals to those who want to sound sophisticated without engaging in hard thinking." Cited in review by Charles Wolf, Jr., in the *Wall St. Journal*, 1 June 1996, p. A-12.

18. For a skeptical view of market efficiency and a defense of the advantage of government intervention, see Robert Kuttner, *Everything for Sale: The Virtues and Limits of Markets* (New York: Knopf, 1997).

19. See Hughes le Masson, *Faut-il encore aider les pays en développement? Histoire d'un cas exemplaire* (Paris: Editions du Félin, 1992), p. 145.

6

Political Science and
Political Economy

The lenses employed by political scientists in the study of political economy range from the macrolevel, encompassing national political systems and their relationships to the global economy (see **Robert Gilpin** and **Susan Strange,** this volume), to the microlevel, focusing on how innovation on the factory shop floor is intertwined with broader political–economic processes.[1] As a group, however, political scientists are interested in relationships of power among economic actors, society, and government, and they devote significant analytical attention to the role of the state and other political–economic institutions in examining how those relationships come to be embedded in markets. The perspectives presented in this section all examine the politics of the phenomenon of markets as institutions by contrasting different types of political economy. **Charles Lindblom** focuses on differing conceptions of the government's role vis-à-vis market activity. **Chalmers Johnson** lays out two different governmental approaches to industrialization, focusing on specific policies and institutional mechanisms. **Peter Hall** and **David Soskice** develop an analytical framework that compares the linkages among macroinstitutions and microinstitutions in different political–economic systems.

Charles Lindblom moves away from a simplistic dichotomy of whether governments intervene in markets. He builds on theories we have already examined, taking from **Adam Smith** and the liberals the notion that markets are efficient coordination mechanisms and from **Karl Marx** critiques of authority and class capture of the state. In particular, Lindblom argues that business interests occupy a privileged role in relation to government, exercising a great degree of discretion in economic production. Government relies heavily on business for good economic performance, giving corporate interests disproportionate influence in society. Lindblom also introduced the concept of "circularity" in markets and politics in contrast to traditional linear models of economics and politics that emphasize the power of individual choices over outcomes. As a result of circularity, he argued, businesses influence the demands of consumers (through advertising and marketing) and governments influence the demands of citizens (through agenda setting).[2]

In the selection presented here, Lindblom provides a clear introduction to what the perspective of markets as institutions means in concrete terms, viewing the market system as a set of activities in a distinctive pattern for which the state provides the foundation. He argues that there are a series of practical, rather than dogmatic, reasons for why people may decide not to leave everything to markets. Lindblom emphasizes that the state is a major participant in market systems; in addition to being the biggest single purchaser in an economy, government is a possible alternative to markets in coordinating economic activity. He also points out that the market is an administrative instrument through which the state can achieve various social objectives as laid out by citizens or rulers. These controls make the market system "livable," although governments have varying capacities to use market controls. All societies have choices on how government should be involved in market activity, and different sets of choices and government capacities lead to different types of market systems.

Chalmers Johnson contributes to the study of comparative political economy with his analysis of the ingredients of Japan's incredible postwar economic growth. Japan is an important case in the study of contemporary capitalism because, as Johnson argues, it is an excellent example of a state-guided market system. Johnson terms Japan a "developmental state" in contrast to the American "regulatory state" and provides a contrast of the two types of market system and the state's role within them. In analyzing the Japanese political economy, Johnson discusses the inadequacy of various noninstitutional explanations for Japanese economic success—including those based on national culture, on the tenets of economic liberalism, or on the particularities of Japanese microinstitutions. Foreshadowing the "varieties of capitalism" approach that will be discussed next, Johnson emphasizes that Japanese institutions constitute a system that was favorable for economic growth. Yet the crucial ingredient was the role of the state in planning and guiding economic activity, through what came to be known as industrial policy.

Johnson focuses on the Ministry of International Trade and Industry as the most important state actor in the economy. He builds on **Alexander Gerschenkron's** work in arguing that the state led Japan's late industrialization drive—the Japanese developmental state partners with the private sector to channel investment into favored industrial sectors. He also echoes **Friedrich List** in stressing that the developmental state's objectives are politically derived and based on the importance of nationalism in economic affairs. Johnson and later theorists elaborated on the Japanese experience to derive a developmental state model of industrialization that applied to the newly industrializing economies of East Asia, such as South Korea and Taiwan. The prescriptive implication that emerges from this line of work is that if a country develops the right institutions, it can achieve the type of explosive growth experienced in East Asia.

Peter Hall and David Soskice state that their objective is to elaborate a new framework for understanding the variation in the political economies of developed countries. The selection presented here is the introductory chapter of a volume that attempts to make more explicit a framework that had been evolving in the study of comparative political economy. They trace their intellectual lineage to three major approaches to comparative capitalism that fall within the rubric of political economy:[3] (1) a perspective oriented around the strategic use of "national champions" in core industrial sectors[4] and state strength in leveraging key institutional structures such as economic plans and the financial system;[5] (2) neocorporatist analyses that focused on the interaction of trade unions, employers, and the state;[6] and (3) a series of broader viewpoints that engage sociology in studying "social systems of production," such as collective institutions at the sectoral level,[7] national systems of innovation, and flexible production regimes on the factory shop floor.[8]

The "varieties of capitalism" approach elaborated by Hall and Soskice argues that the role and capacity of government should not be overstated. In their view, firms are the key actors in a capitalist economy, whose activities aggregate into national economic performance. Although they take a national-level comparative perspective that recognizes that market-institutional structures are dependent on national regulatory regimes, they develop a comparative framework centered on firms and their relationships. They concentrate on four spheres of market institutions in which firms develop relationships to carry out economic activities: industrial relations between companies and employees, vocational training and education, corporate governance relations between firms and investors, and interfirm relations. In examining the importance of institutions in a market system, they emphasize the manner and extent to which those institutions condition strategic interaction among firms and other political–economic actors. They build on the New Institutional Economics tradition, which emphasizes, as we have seen, the development of contractual relationships to overcome transaction costs in economic collaboration. They also recognize the political factors at play and build on the economic sociology approach by recognizing that the firm is embedded in a web of interdependent social relationships and shared cultural meanings.

The centerpiece of the varieties of capitalism framework is the dichotomous representation of liberal market economies (LMEs) and coordinated market economies (CMEs) and the comparison of their characteristics in terms of both relationships and outcomes. In broad strokes, the differences between these two types of capitalist economies are explained in terms of how firms coordinate their relationships and production activities through different sets of solutions. In LMEs—such as the United States and Great Britain—firms primarily coordinate internally through hierarchical arrangements and externally through competitive market relationships. In CMEs—such as Germany and Japan—firms are more reliant on nonmarket relationships such as relational contracting and collaborative networking. Even though LMEs function through the price signals and formal contracts emphasized by neoclassical economics and New Institutional Economics and CMEs seem to be more embedded in social relations in the manner emphasized by economic sociology, both systems are embedded in different ways in society and politics. One of the major utilities of the varieties of capitalism approach is that it prevents us from falling into the analytical trap of assuming that one type of system is the default and the other the deviation to be explained.

Hall and Soskice point out that markets are institutions that support this variety of firm-centered relationships. Systematic variation in corporate practice between

LMEs and CMEs is generated by their different market-institutional makeup. More-over, "institutional complementarities" buttress these firm-centered relationships and the differences between LMEs and CMEs. This concept suggests that if political economies have developed one type of interaction (price-based versus relational) in one sphere of economic practice, they tend to develop—through the actions of all actors, including the state—complementary practices in other spheres, reinforcing the type of system and its outcomes. A related concept is that of "comparative insti-tutional advantage," the notion that different types of market-institutional systems structure differing advantages for the firms functioning within them. Firms will be able to perform some types of economic activities more effectively because of the types of market institutions they are embedded within.

Notes

1. See, for example, Michael Piore and Charles Sabel, *The Second Industrial Divide* (New York: Basic Books, 1984).
2. Charles E. Lindblom, *Politics and Markets: The World's Political Economic Systems* (New York: Basic Books, 1977); see especially pp. 170–88 on the privileged position of busi-ness and pp. 201–21 on circularity in markets and politics.
3. Peter A. Hall and David Soskice, this volume pp. 290–291.
4. Shonfield (1965) is widely considered the paradigm of this approach. Andrew Shon-field, *Modern Capitalism: The Changing Balance of Public and Private Power* (New York: Oxford University Press, 1965).
5. See, for example, **Chalmers Johnson** in this volume; John Zysman, *Governments, Mar-kets and Growth: Financial Systems and the Politics of Industrial Change* (Ithaca: Cor-nell University Press, 1983); and Peter J. Katzenstein, ed., *Between Power and Plenty: Foreign Economic Policies of Advanced Industrial States* (Madison: University of Wis-consin Press, 1978).
6. See, for example, Philippe Schmitter and Gerhard Lehmbruch, eds., *Trends toward Corporatist Intermediation* (Beverly Hills: Sage, 1979); Suzanne Berger, ed., *Organizing Interests in Western Europe: Pluralism, Corporatism, and the Transformation of Politics* (Cambridge: Cambridge University Press, 1981); and Peter J. Katzenstein, *Corporatism and Change* (Ithaca: Cornell University Press, 1985).
7. Gary Herrigel, *Industrial Constructions: The Sources of German Industrial Power* (Cam-bridge: Cambridge University Press, 1996).
8. Piore and Sabel, *The Second Industrial Divide*.

Charles E. Lindblom,
The Market System (2001)*

Chapter 4: Bones Beneath Flesh

The market system is not a place or a thing or even a collection of things. It is a set of activities of distinctive pattern. Certain customs and rules are required to make a market system, and to the degree that they are observed, a market system exists. Think of them as constituting the skeleton of the market system.

To identify these customs and rules is to throw various lights on the market system. They illuminate, for example, how it could have come into being and why participants play the roles they do. The lights also reveal the tight connections of the market system with liberty and property, and they place money and entrepreneurship in the system.

Let's start from scratch, building the skeleton one bone at a time.

1. Custom and law grant broad (but not equal) control to participants over the disposition of their own time and energy—in others words, legal *liberty*—in the pursuit of aspirations or claims of any kinds. *You are free, for example, to put your energies into building a house.*

In that statement there is hardly a hint of cooperation, only of possible mutual injury and the consequent need for peacekeeping. Nor is there yet a hint of market interactions. Nevertheless, broad personal freedom (of scope and limits to be discussed later) is a building bone or building block. Without it—peasants under feudal obligations were without it—a market system is impossible.

2. To broad rights to control one's own time and energy we add a parallel set of broad rights to control useful things. They are ordinarily known as *property* rights—customs and laws that enforce distribution of rights to make use of, offer, or deny to others such objects, including land, that people find useful in pursuing any aspirations. *To build a house, you possess—specifically, exercise control over—a piece of land, some building materials, a hammer and saw.*

The required rights do not have to be precisely the bundle of rights that in existing market systems goes by the name of private property. In particular, these rights may diverge from the great inequality of existing property rights. "Private property" is a term that raises people's temperatures when they move, as they often do, to the defense or the attack. Whether, however, existing property rights are applauded or

* From: *The Market System: What It Is, How It Works, and What To Make of It*, Charles E. Lindblom, Copyright © 2001 by Yale University. (pp. 52–60, 97–107, 253-64) Reprinted by permission of Yale University Press.

deplored, some broad set of rights to control useful things is a necessity. Together with liberty it will set mutual adjustment into motion as people use their freedom and assets to pursue their aspirations.

These two rights, liberty and property, seem like perverse foundations for a system of broad social coordination, for they guarantee that, except for specific prohibitions, people can do as they wish. Yet coordination would seem to require that people do not simply do as they wish but instead bend to the requirements of cooperation and peacekeeping. All the more interesting, then, are the ways in which the two rights support cooperation and peacekeeping.

3. The third custom and rule necessary to a market system: quid pro quo. Aside from persuasion, the only permissible way to obtain desired performances or objects from another person, unless they are given as gifts, is through contingent offers of benefit to the other. This rule immediately displays the possibilities of cooperation, and peaceful cooperation at that. One can neither threaten nor steal nor ask the state to use its powers to take or to compel another's cooperation. Interchange takes the form of a quid pro quo. *You can obtain your neighbors' help on your house or induce them to build it for you by offering them contingent benefits.*

The three customs and rules create a widespread process of mutual adjustment in which each participant explores innumerable possibilities of benefit for both self and other, thus innumerable opportunities for cooperating and reducing conflict. You can offer objects or your help—a performance—to induce others to teach your children or provide you with food or entertainment. You can cast about to obtain a variety of benefits offered in response to your offers. There is no prescribed list of options, no prescribed channel. You can search in any direction in pursuit of any aspirations with as much energy as you care to throw into the search.

There remains, however, a constraint on your opportunities to pursue your aspirations or claims. So far as our rules provide, you are limited to bartering. You have to find someone who can provide what you want. You want a massage—can you find someone who has the skill? That requires a *coincidence*. And if you find such a person, you are still blocked unless the masseur wants what you can offer. Will the masseur accept some vegetables from your garden? That requires a *second coincidence*.

Even so, barter is an advance over a kind of loose coordination common in many earlier societies, like the Kwakiutl, in which gifts obligate the recipient to make a reciprocal gift. Since the receiver decides how and when to reciprocate and can delay, such a custom of reciprocal gift-giving—unlike barter—offers little opportunity to use an offer of benefits to obtain a specified benefit in exchange.

The first step in solving the double-coincidence obstruction to coordination is a fourth rule or custom.

4. Some object of value that everyone is pleased to have enters into exchanges. Whether seashells, gold, or paper certificates, it is *money*. With money, the need for coincidence drops from two to only one—the second coincidence is no longer necessary. Although you still have to find someone who can offer you what you want, you do not now have to find one who wants a particular service or object that you can offer, for you offer not a particular service or object but the universally desired object. *To induce a carpenter or metalworker to help with your house, you do not have to find*

those who want your performance or objects. Any carpenter or hardware supplier will accept money as a sufficient inducement to give you the help you want.

5. With the use of money comes a shift of participants' activities from household use to performances and objects for *sale*. Instead of persisting in traditional household efforts together with peripheral barter or sales of surpluses, participants now let sales opportunities determine what they do. *You decide not to build a house but instead look for a line of activity that will increase or maximize your money income. Then you use the money income for various purposes, including buying a house.*

The shift to production for sale now eliminates the need for the first coincidence, which is that each person finds others who have what he or she is willing to buy. Can one find such others? With activity now aimed at sales, the society is full of people motivated to anticipate and satisfy my desires by offering whatever I stand ready to buy.

The market would be a pitifully poor social coordinator if it were, as it is sometimes naively conceived to be, a set of interactions in which people exchange surpluses of things they happen to find themselves able to offer. The market system is not a gigantic continuing flea market; indeed, it is not fairly characterized as an exchange system. Market relations do not begin with exchanges of performances and objects somehow "there" to be exchanged. Market relations determine what is to be made or done—and brought to exchange.

6. The search for sales opportunities gives rise to *intermediaries*. Would-be sellers find opportunities to sell objects and performances not only to people who directly want their goods, but to others who are also engaged in selling. They find it possible to sell trucks to persons selling kitchen appliances. Or they sell parts to the manufacturers of the appliances. Or parts to the manufacturers of other parts. Or electric power to any and all manufacturers. Or financial and accounting services to them. It is thanks to chains and webs of these intermediaries that the cafe operator and the coffee grower can cooperate to provide a cup of coffee to a customer. The intermediates provide the shipping, warehousing, processing, and other performances that forge the links between grower and cafe. Separated from and ignorant of each other as grower and cafe are, they could not otherwise be linked together. Thus *the house you buy drew for its construction on innumerable performances and objects coordinated through transactions to which you were not party.*

7. Some participants become specialized in intermediary roles, specifically in creating new intermediate links and in organizing combinations of labor, land, and capital either for an intermediate link or for end objects and performances. To say the same thing less precisely but in a more familiar way, some participants create enterprises, and they are called entrepreneurs.

Entrepreneurs take advantage of the possibilities of round-aboutness. They offer not just hardware to users but create factories and office buildings, machines, equipment, parts, and other inputs for making hardware. In so doing they create enormous productive capital that accounts for much of the great increase in output that has accompanied the rise of market systems. To Marx this cumulation of capital was the core process of the market system, warranting the name capitalism.

When the entrepreneur who makes hardware counts on other entrepreneurs to build a factory and on still others for necessary machinery, each of these entrepreneurs counts on other entrepreneurs in turn. Long chains or large webs are thus constructed, and coordination of them becomes intricate and enormously far ranging.

Not ordinary people but entrepreneurs are the most frequent participants in market systems. They make careers of activities that move and transform labor and other inputs into called-for objects and performances. They are the moving spirits in the market system, the participants who make not only the most frequent but the most consequential decisions.

8. Many entrepreneurs operate on a scale that transforms their roles. They create collectives that can do what individual entrepreneurs cannot. They do this through the common practice of assembling spending power—that is, by borrowing through offers of interest or dividends. That enables them to organize larger feats of coordination than are otherwise possible. *Thus, the construction of your house made use of electric power and materials that could have been provided only by a collective like Morgan Building Materials with capacities beyond those of an individual market participant.* The familiar dominant legal form of these collectives in our time is the corporation, odd as it may seem to call the corporation a collective.

These, then, are the bones of the market system: liberty, property, the quid pro quo, money, activity for sale, intermediaries, entrepreneurs, and collectives. Again the market dance waits for the state to provide the floor and the orchestra. Even the ordinary market participant counts on the state for safety on the way to the supermarket, but the dependence of entrepreneurs on state aid might be called desperate. Their initiatives put them at high risk of great loss; hence, as noted, they will move only timidly or not at all without a variety of state aids.

The "Chaos" of the Market?

When we reflect on the millions of people who cooperate to deliver a cup of coffee from Colombia to Milan or on the claim that no institution, not even the state, matches the market in capacity to organize cooperation, we might wonder why we still hear from time to time the phrase "the chaos of the market." Chaos it is not. What might people mean by such a charge? To some people it means only that markets often look chaotic. An early morning wholesale produce market looks messy. Trading in many stock exchanges—a turbulence of gestures and cries—sometimes looks more like a street demonstration than an organized interchange. I grant the superficial appearance of disorder in some markets. Despite this appearance, all the noise and movement are part of a precise, fast-moving coordination. To supply a city with fresh produce constitutes an impressive feat of coordination, yet the accomplishment is a daily one in early morning fruit and vegetable markets all over the world.

Others see more than a superficial appearance of disorder. Through recorded history and folk memories, we are repeatedly reminded of the depression of the 1930s in which many millions of people all over the world were exiled from the system by losing their jobs—a descent toward chaos for them. In some nations that descent engulfed a third of the population, even if most people in every society continued to find orderly life, work, and social interchange. One might fear that it could happen again. Perhaps. But more than a half century has gone by without a repetition of such a catastrophe. Societies have greatly improved their knowledge of how to stabilize the market system through, among other possibilities, governmental expenditure and management of the supply of money and credit.

Still, like all social institutions large and small, the market system in its normal operations fails us—falters in its coordination—on some counts. Every few years it falls into that abnormality called recession—small depressions dwarfed by that of the 1930s, yet still damaging. So frequently does it fall into recession that we might as well call those abnormalities normal. They impose hardship on millions of people. But neither recessions nor any of the other defects of the market system warrant the careless assertion that the market system produces chaos. In our time the greatest threat of worldwide disorganization of the market system may lie in reckless banking and incompetent governmental regulation of financial markets. Feeding on itself and growing, disorder might spread from one country to another, as it did from Indonesia in 1997 to other Asian economies, Brazil, and Russia. Even for that, however, "chaos" is hyperbole.

Chapter 7: Chosen Domain

Wisely or foolishly, societies—more specifically those masses or elites that make policy—choose not to use the market system as fully as they might. They turn instead to other methods of coordination, or they mix the market system with the others. Public education in most societies is not organized by market demand, although teachers are recruited through the market system. Many societies also try to keep child labor—or narcotics or judicial decisions—out of the market system. Why do societies curb the use of the market system? It is not hard to find good reasons, and some poor reasons as well.

One reason is ideological or philosophical hostility, such as Lenin and his associates brought to the new Soviet Union and Mao to China. Lying behind ideology are, however, a set of specific objections to the market system. Almost everyone acknowledges the validity of most of them. I shall not, however, evaluate them. I want simply to display the variety of objections to the market system that account for its less than maximum scope.

Many people believe that, regardless of output, the market *process* itself is sometimes undesirable—even unethical or immoral. Blood donors, many people believe, should give their blood, not sell it. Many people shrink from engaging in financial transactions with friends or family members. Some people fear that social solidarity is undercut by the very process of buying and selling. At least a few eccentrics will not protect themselves by buying insurance, fearing that doing so would reveal to God their lack of faith in divine care. And if many people enjoy shopping, some detest it so much that they will make do without some of the services and goods that the market offers. Some people—perhaps most of us—enjoy some performances and objects only if they are given to us; the pleasure is spoiled if we have to buy them. We love to get something for "free." And research studies report that some people find no pleasure in voluntary work when they are paid for it. A great historical example of society turning against the very process of buying and selling is the Council of Trent's prohibition in 1562 of the selling of indulgences; societies still struggle with whether prostitution and drugs should be legalized. Most people now find the idea of a market in slaves abhorrent. For similar reasons, some societies long ago decided to curb the hiring of children to labor in mines and factories.

Many people doubt the competence or motives of individual choice and want to establish a deliberating collective authority over some decisions. They are now engaged in debating, for example, whether the body parts of deceased human beings can be marketed or should instead be allocated by a collective authority. Many societies prefer collective decisions on environmental protection to individual or corporate market decisions—they want the state, not the corporation, to control emissions of industrial wastes. For good reason, people do not trust sellers to be wholly truthful about their products and therefore favor governmental regulation of food and drugs.

To many, market inequality is unacceptable. Most societies want at least an early elementary education for children, regardless of parental ability to buy it: hence taxes and compulsory education rather than a market. Some medical services, especially those that reduce epidemics, are distributed freely rather than sold, for fear that market distribution would not be wide enough. To deal with wartime scarcity, many societies rationed essential commodities rather than let low-income families be frozen out.

For many people, the market is too harsh. They want employers to be restricted in their rights to discharge employees, or they may want the state to bail out an enterprise on point of failing. Saving jobs in enterprises that can no longer survive without government subsidies is a worldwide phenomenon, prominent in Italy, India, and China.

In perhaps most societies, "upper classes" think that both philanthropy and government subsidies are necessary to raise the provision of the fine arts above what the "lower classes" would otherwise be willing to pay for in the market. Were the arts left wholly to the market system, orchestral and operatic classical music might vanish from concert halls.

All societies forbid some of the market interactions through which a person might construct inadmissible control, outside the market system, over others. For example, they do not permit individuals to use the market, except under great restriction, to recruit, equip, and organize private armies. Exceptions are small private armed forces that enterprises use for security of their premises, neighborhood security services, and the private "armies" that enterprises have sometimes used to break strikes. Some societies prohibit market purchase of firearms.

Many societies also restrict some market interactions that concentrate control of communications in private hands or in too few private hands. They also want to keep government officials at a distance from market forces. If litigants could buy favorable decisions from a judge, as they can in what we call corrupt judicial systems, one of the purposes for which societies establish a judiciary—dispassionate adjudication—is undercut.

Societies sometimes reduce the domain of the market system not because compulsion is necessary but because it is cheaper. Although we can imagine each of millions of householders paying neighbors to remove their unsightly and unsanitary trash, it would be cheaper simply to use municipal ordinances to compel their removal.

Similarly, wealthy people can buy a good deal of privacy—building secure living quarters and fences, hiring their own guards—but they will often find it cheaper simply to use the law to lay down and enforce rights to privacy. For all its rhetorical celebration of liberty, a society may draft rather than hire its army simply because it is cheaper to do so.

A large category of circumstances in which societies want to prohibit or constrain market coordination—one that includes some of the reasons already listed—consists of transactions that produce significant spillover effects, that is, consequences for persons not party to the transaction (see Chapter II). If, for example, the market transactions of business enterprises pollute air or water—or if I create nuisances for my neighbors—the state will often step in to overrule or modify market coordination.

A strikingly different objection to the market system is harbored by political elites in authoritarian systems. They fear a connection between the market system and the political power of citizens, for they see that market systems disperse power or control over the society. They would rather exercise the controls themselves, as indicated in persistent Soviet party and governmental refusals to disperse control through markets following announced intentions to do so. In democracies, rulers sometimes, for reasons that may include their own enrichment, prefer to maintain some control of the volume and allocation of new industrial investment rather than give it wholly to entrepreneurs.

Finally, however loud their commitment to the market system, entrepreneurs are highly motivated to seek—and win—a great variety of state protections for their own markets, protections that sometimes strengthen the market system but often restrict it. Italy, for example, has been operating under a complex licensing and regulatory system that has protected small, especially family, businesses from market rigors. Permits are required in order to establish a business and for each of various categories of products to be sold. Hours of work and scheduling of midday closings and vacations have also been governmentally controlled. More conspicuous protective dikes in any market system are tariffs and other curbs on imports, as well as outright subsidies to the petroleum, mining, and agriculture industries—for that matter, to many dozens of industries. They all have the effect of weakening the ordinary market direction of production, justified or not by their contribution to strengthening entrepreneurial initiatives. Taken together, they often represent a widespread slapdash introduction of central planning, a shunting aside of the conventional market system less by central direction than by central misdirection. And they narrow the range of market choice for both sellers and buyers.

Almost all these reasons for curbing the market are in principle good reasons. But they do not specify a correct choice between market system and alternatives; they only alert us to circumstances in which the choice is worth thinking about. Whether, for example, blood or body parts should be bought and sold is a question that has no right answer. The appropriate answer depends on such factors as what people value, their attitudes toward risk, and their confidence in what they believe they know. It also depends on the suitability of alternative coordinating processes.

Alternatives

I take note once more that the state is the greatest participant in market systems. It is a buyer of such things as public buildings, bridges, and armaments—a very long list.

Among its many purchases, it hires soldiers, astronauts, nurses, police officers, gardeners, and people in every other occupation one might think of. And of course both the corporation and the family or household participate in the market system.

Obvious as the market participation of these three institutions is, each is also an alternative to the market system. The state can hire an army or, not making use of the labor market, simply command its young people to enlist. A corporation can buy its electric power or produce its own. A household can patronize a barber or, setting aside the market system, do its haircutting at home. To the three I add a less familiar fourth alternative—civil society, amorphous as the concept is. The society's choice of domain for the market system depends on its estimate of the capacities of each of these four alternatives.

The state tends to overshadow the other alternatives. Because the market system cannot administer the compulsion necessary for social order, it is the state, foremost, that does so. And because the market system cannot establish itself, it is of course the state that does so, through, inter alia, laws on liberty and property. To be sure, custom also often serves this purpose, but never sufficiently.

The household is a nonmarket coordinator surrounded by market coordination. Within a nuclear family, members ordinarily do not sell and buy each other's performances or objects, although I have known husbands to tip their wives for a good dinner, very likely more demeaning than rewarding. Parents only peripherally pay children to do chores; in some societies they rent out their children. On the whole, children are coordinated by parental authority rather than market system. Between spouses too, the allocation of responsibilities is decided less by a market transaction than by various forms of inegalitarian mutual adjustment within a framework of moral rules.

Not infrequently, observers of the market system minimize the household as a social coordinator. True, the household cannot achieve the nationwide or global coordination that the market achieves. Yet in many societies in which women have chosen not to make their labor available to the market or have not been permitted to do so, nonmarket family labor of women and children, together with the part-time work in the home of the male spouse, add up to more than the total of labor coordinated through the market system. Even with two wage earners, contemporary families still coordinate a great amount of family labor—the family remains a prodigious social coordinator. Despite long-voiced speculation on possible societies without families, and despite some exploratory moves in that direction, as in the Israeli kibbutzim, the family's role in social coordination remains, for the time being, well established and a very great restriction on the scope of the market system.

Indeed, the market system is better described as a coordinator of collectivities called households than as a coordinator of individuals. It is as an agent of such a collectivity that a wage earner enters into the market to earn an income to be distributed within the household. And it is as an agent of it that some members of the household purchase goods and services to be distributed among its members.

The collective enterprise, especially the big corporation, is the third alternative to the market system. While enterprises extend the market system's domain in several dimensions, they restrict it in others. For enterprises constitute, as we have said, islands of nonmarket or managerial coordination in a market milieu. Where once a dozen smaller enterprises may have constituted, through their market interchanges with suppliers and customers, an important part of the steel industry, many of their market activities may have been brought under the authoritative direction of the single corporation that displaced those market interchanges.

Although the state is the principal instrument of systematic compulsion required to achieve social coordination, both enterprise and family are also instruments of compulsion. Enterprises are, among other things, systems for inducing people, in return for wages, to accept the compulsions of their employers. Enterprise compulsions are limited; obviously an employee can leave an enterprise more easily than a citizen or taxpayer can emigrate. Family compulsions are notorious.

A substantial and perhaps increasing share of the task of social coordination is borne by the fourth alternative: civil society. For some people who use the term, it denotes coordinating collectivities other than enterprises and governmental organizations. These collectivities, remarkably diverse in structure and objective, seem to resist efforts to be categorized as nonprofits. Among them are political parties, lobbying organizations, charities, clubs, research laboratories, and museums.

These entities may operate largely outside the market system—for example, a reading club whose members meet monthly for discussion. On the other hand, they, especially the larger ones, may make substantial use of the market to recruit staff and to assemble other inputs necessary for their activities—for example, a political party. Many make use of the market system for labor and other inputs. They may not sell anything; or, if they do, they may not maximize the quid for the quo they offer. At an extreme are some conventional business enterprises selling in the market but disguised as nonprofit enterprises to escape taxes on their income or to create an image of benevolence rather than profit seeking. Some motor clubs offering maps, travel information, insurance, and other products appear to be of this type.

For some people, civil society means more than organizations. Its activities also include acts of friendship or compassion, favors and return of favors, and other forms of personal cooperation neither compelled by the state nor organized by buying and selling. These are enormously important and ubiquitous forms of social cooperation and sociability. Some interpreters of civil society attach the greatest importance to those interchanges, believing that through them each of us forms and endlessly reconsiders our values, life purposes, and, for the shorter term perhaps, our recreation and politics. We are each a creation of these interchanges, beginning with parental influences over us.

In a variety of informal small-group interactions, as in family life, people curb mutual injury and help one another, whether out of affection or helpful impulse or habit. They look after other people's children, come to the aid of friends, enter into interchanges pleasant in themselves. People often seek in small-group interchanges an area of social interchange in which the market rule of quid pro quo can be forbidden.

In these personal relationships, peace and cooperation require neither the heavy hand of compulsion nor the kind of explicit quid pro quo benefits that people offer each other in the market. Although in these interchanges people pursue many of the same aspirations as in their market activity, here markets are unnecessary and in some cases would obstruct aspirations. If I want a genuine friendship, for example, the friendship relation would be destroyed if I paid for it. In these relationships there are often rewards on both sides but no specific contingent quid pro quo. From the activities of civil society, including play and adventure, people draw immediate satisfaction from experience. This differs from the means-end pattern of using resources to achieve satisfaction that characterizes life in market systems. Of course, we often use the market system to obtain necessary equipment or to bring us to a location where we will enjoy play or adventure. But once equipped and located, we can for a time stop our buying and selling.

Two final comments on scope or domain of the market system. The first is that social interchange and institutions cannot be partitioned into mutually exclusive domains. If we observe a group of people engaged in building a church with paid labor and bought materials, we can quickly identify the activity as within the market domain. But their purpose is to facilitate worship, thus the activity falls within the domain of religion. We might also look at the project, depending on the architecture, as an artistic effort or accomplishment, thus no less within the domain of the arts than in the market domain. We cannot partition social life into mutually exclusive territories.

The second comment: The idea of a society in which the market system alone is society's coordinator is obviously nonsense and is fortunately only rarely espoused. Most of us well understand the need for state, family, enterprise, and the various arrangements of civil society. There exists in some societies, however, conspicuously in the United States, a related idea—that government is best that governs least, a proposition usually attached to an unspoken corollary: that market system is best that coordinates most. Yet a market system of maximum domain would by most people be considered inhumane. And a "least" government would not only leave debris to gather in the streets but would allow the spread of deadly epidemics. Determining the domain for market, state, family, enterprise, and civil society—for each of them—is a serious task for every society, not to be disposed of by all-too-common dogma.

Chapter 18: Alternative Market Systems

In France, market and government elites cooperate more intimately than in the United States, where they more often look on each other as adversaries. Or contrast Japan's long inattention to environmental pollution—it was once the "most polluted nation in the world"—with Britain's government-business cooperation to curb it. From multiple causes, new forms of market system emerge, sometimes hardly winning the attention of policy makers, sometimes their deliberate creation.

In the twentieth century, while policy makers were concerned with other choices on their agendas, the place of the market system in our lives was changed in deeply consequential ways by a massive movement of women into the workforce. Their tasks would now in large part be set by market demands rather than by the authority of husband or family tradition. With their new money income, women now buy in the market many of the services—and some goods—earlier produced in the home. Equally weighty unplanned changes may in the twenty-first century emerge from the Internet and new technologies of multilateral communication. Internet auctions, for just one example, greatly widen the range of choice open to market participants and probably increase the volume of market activity.

In this chapter I look at some of the choices open within a market system. What I shall say will sometimes make a persuasive case for certain alternatives over others, but that is not my purpose. I discuss alternatives because they illuminate the market system on some attributes so far ignored or passed over too lightly.

Drawing on earlier chapters, we can deal with a number of specific alternatives quickly. Hypothetically, at least, every market society can choose a market system with very little, more, or a great deal more state control of

- spillovers
- monopoly in its many forms
- corporate powers other than monopoly, including political powers
- managerial authority within the enterprise
- entrepreneurial motivation
- investment
- distribution of income and wealth

The alternatives are not limited to small differences. They range from the intimacy between state and corporation in Japan in the 1960s to the continuing turbulent state-corporate relations of the United States. And within any one national system, on each of these variables wide choice is open and consequential. How large nations like China, India, Russia, and the United States choose to deal with spillovers may be pivotal for the whole world.

Hypothetically, I said, a society can choose. Whether in actual fact it can depends on how well the state, which is the main lever for working on the market system, can be harnessed either by a ruling elite or, in a democracy, by citizens. The odds are not encouraging, for the state itself is deeply flawed. Among other obstructions stands the corporation. In its role in government it is itself a major barrier to a better market system.

Among the aspects of the market system that have given rise to choices on degree and character of state control, today's most intense debates are on redistributions of income and wealth that depart from the rule of quid pro quo. The redistributions range from free public education through those of the welfare state, such as unemployment compensation and family allowances.

A colleague flatly declares to me that "the welfare state has proved it doesn't work." Clearly, the programs of the welfare state are often in trouble. Medical care is an especially telling example. Unwilling to consign lowest-income citizens to inadequate medical care, many market societies offer them subsidized or free care. But then how are demands for care to be held down to a feasible level, the price of care to the consumer no longer high enough to impose the necessary constraint? The welfare state is also plagued by government disposition to spend more than planned or anticipated. Welfare expenditures add to historically frequent excesses of spending, for example, on celebratory public works, on the military, on luxury for rulers, or on corporate welfare. But even taken by themselves welfare programs are the subject of increasingly severe questions when, with the aging of the population in many societies, the number of earners available to support beneficiaries continues to decline.

Nonetheless, these distributions appear to be here to stay. Market societies can choose among various designs of the welfare state, from stingy redistributions to careless excesses. A United Nations estimate rates the United States as the world's richest nation (per capita income), yet its welfare programs leave poverty at its highest level among industrialized nations. But abandoning the welfare state is not a choice. That welfare is judged necessary is a product of something called "civilization." It is also a strategy through which elites placate a potentially radical mass.

The welfare state has not yet had to cope with the prospect of permanent exile from the market system of able-bodied workers neither aged nor injured nor temporarily displaced but insufficiently productive. It is a frightening possibility: the rise of a new underclass consisting of millions of people with insufficient skill or capital to offer the required quid to win the necessary quo. If it forms, it needs not only income but jobs, together with the status that goes with jobs. Those not in the underclass are not likely to tolerate and support it in its idleness. Those in it are not likely to accept their idle exile quietly. Difficult choices may have to be made. Two legal scholars have recently presented a proposal to provide to every young adult American a once-in-a-lifetime $80,000 share in the capital wealth of that society, thus creating a society of stakeholders. One would expect significant national differences to emerge if the industrialized nations have to face a future of able-bodied market exiles.

Two Visions

Your choices—mine too, or a society's—on each of the listed and other aspects of the market system are probably guided by a theory or model—not precise but roughly sketched in the mind—of a preferred relation between state and market system.

A common model or vision places the market system front and center, leaving the state with two subsidiary roles. The first role is to establish the legal foundations without which the market system cannot operate. In this model, that first state role raises few questions and is for the most part dismissed. The second role is captured in such words as "interference" and "intervention," or words less critical yet still negative in coloration, like "regulation." The model conceives of the state as a discordant element, at best a partly successful tinkerer, at worst a disrupter. Market participants consist of individual persons. The state is not a participant but a regulator, thus an influence from "out-side" the market system and on that account to be regarded with suspicion. Insofar as the state tries to satisfy collective needs neglected by market purchases, it is inefficient. For it pursues such purposes as social amenities and environmental protection, which are of less value than marketed goods and services. It also often compels citizens who, the model postulates, should be free.

Among models alternative to this one, I choose a particular one not to advocate it—though its superiority to the first model will strike most readers as obvious—but to illuminate by contrast. In this second model, the state, a deeply imperfect institution, establishes, as in the first model, the legal foundations of the market system. But its support of the market system goes much further. That support—not interference or regulation but support—is constant and wide ranging. It includes the management of money and credit, subsidies and tax concessions, research and development, and opening up and protecting overseas markets, among many other aids. The state also plays a regulatory role, as in the first model; but that role is no more frequent or strong than the supportive role. The state is also a redistributor of income and wealth.

On top of these state roles in the second model are two other roles overlooked in the first model. The state is a market participant as buyer and seller. What is more, it is the largest buyer and seller in the system, buying the services of teachers, researchers, and highway contractors, as well as farm products, computers, and trucks. The state is also a price setter for many goods and services. It sets minimum prices on some farm products in order to bolster farm income. It sets maximum prices on electric power in order to curb monopoly. It uses tariffs to set high enough prices on an import to protect domestic producers of it. Price setting is sometimes part of the state's regulatory role, sometimes part of its supportive role, and sometimes a part of its redistributive role. As a multipurpose price setter, the state becomes a constant participant in markets, just as it does in its role as buyer and seller. Both roles make the state an insider rather than a force from outside the market system.

In this second model, the collective purposes pursued by the state are no less valuable than those pursued by individual participants in the market system. In fact, they are usually the same purposes. One of the reasons people who can afford to do so buy houses in the suburbs is that they want some of the amenities that more congested urban life does not give them. Or they want an immediate environment of green rather than of buildings and paved surfaces. Or they want quiet rather than noise. These purposes are also the purposes of collective choice in the hands of the state: amenities and environment, among others. Because in some circumstances they can be pursued effectively only through compulsion—public education requiring, for example, the compulsion of taxes—state compulsion is an accepted element in the model.

I prefer the second model and also find it more realistic. Whether you do or do not, there is an implication in it that greatly helps clarify our choices.

Market System as State Administrative Instrument

By implication in the second model—and in reality too—the market system is the major administrative instrument of the state. It is by no means its only instrument, for often the state proceeds through outright commands and prohibitions. But it is the nearest thing to an all-purpose instrument. The state's use of it is routine and commonplace. Does the state intend to increase the provision of medical care? Then lower its price. Stimulate research? Then provide funds for it. Clean the air? Then put a charge on industrial-waste emissions. Reduce ethnic conflict? Then curb ethnic discrimination in hiring. In short, the common rule for state administration is: use the market system.

Many of us have been on the wrong track in identifying the market system with individualism, as though it could not serve collective purposes or could do so only exceptionally and badly. Clearly the state pursues a great variety of collective purposes. It does so—usually, typically—with controls made possible by the existence of a market system. The future of the market system is not bound up exclusively with individualism but with collective ventures as well. Understanding that is a prerequisite to making a clearheaded choice.

I think it worth while to walk through an explanation of exactly why and how the market system becomes the major administrative instrument of the state because, although everyone knows, most of us do not know that we know.

How might a government induce its citizens to do as they or their rulers believe is necessary? One answer is that it prohibits by command, forbidding undesired behavior, like excessive highway speed or arson. But how does it obtain positive performances from its citizens—how, for example, to get laborers to build highways? For positive performance, command is used only in limited circumstances, as in military conscription. Even authoritarian governments cannot effectively command more than a few of the positive performances they want from millions of citizens. There are better alternatives.

In one, the state buys the performances it wants just as you and I do when we pay a hairdresser to cut our hair. Directly or through contracting enterprises, it buys the varied performances necessary for new highways, medical care and production of food for the poor. And it buys or hires the tools and equipment people need in order to do what they are paid to do.

Thus the *purchase,* simple as it is, is a powerfully and precisely effective governmental administrative tool. As an administrative device, it is in most cases superior to command—more precise, more widely usable, less frequently escaped, and far simpler in use.

Two other common methods by which governments induce positive performances operate through altering the prices that shape the behavior of citizens. One way to do so is subsidize: subsidies to apartment construction, health care, shipping, farming, or any other industry producing services or goods for which markets and prices are already established. The subsidy supplements the purchase as a fundamental administrative instrument.

If subsidies can induce desired performances, an easy inference is that specific or targeted taxes can discourage performances not desired. Taxes on goods and services can, for example, curb polluting industrial emissions or specific kinds of international financial transactions. The tax then supplements the purchase and the subsidy as administrative instrument.

For whatever collective purposes the government might intend, ranging from national defense to beautifying the landscape, the administrative trio—purchase, subsidy, and tax—is at hand. Thus state purchases of recreational areas or physicians' services, common in market societies. Or Holland's remarkable subsidies to artists, Italy's subsidies to heavy industry, and Norway's regional subsidies to keep northern Norway economically alive. And in many societies, taxes to protect consumers from their own incompetence. Although that requires some outright prohibitions as well, as in food and drug regulation, it might call for a tobacco tax or, as has been proposed, even a heavy tax on aggregate family spending in order to curb the excesses of keeping up with the Joneses. Taxes and subsidies are sometimes disguised. Subsidies to middle-class housing, for example, are obscured in tax deductions for home-ownership expenses or for interest on mortgages, although in magnitude they may dwarf conspicuous outright subsidies to low-cost housing.

To supplement the trio, governments also use other devices that make use of prices rather than administrative commands. For example, by issuing to enterprises tradable or marketable limited permissions to pollute, government can raise the income and outputs of nonpolluting enterprises (they can sell their permits) and lower the incomes and outputs of polluting enterprises (they must buy additional permits). Or through a treaty, a group of nations can assign marketable pollution permits to each nation, thus encouraging each nation to curb emissions in order to be able to sell its permits and escape the necessity of buying any.

Purchase, subsidy, tax, and related devices can be used wherever citizens or their rulers want the state to intervene. And they can be used to make precise choices, as in subsidizing the production of a specific pharmaceutical product; or broader choices, as in subsidizing child care; or still broader ones, as in subsidizing savings rather than consumer spending. They can be used to transfer responsibility for choice from person to state, as when a tax is imposed to reduce tobacco consumption, or to transfer it from state to person, as through the use of vouchers that permit parents to choose a school for their child.

They can be brought to bear anywhere in the chain of production, as in subsidies to or taxes on a specific input—say, subsidized employment of partially disabled workers—rather than on an end-of-the-line consumer service or good. The state may choose, say, to reduce auto production by taxing each auto, or reduce production of large autos by taxing according to their weight or length, or reduce the steel used by the auto industry by taxing the metal rather than the car. Or it can use subsidies to schools or students to raise the level of education generally, or to increase the numbers of students in mathematics and science, or to open up opportunities for disadvantaged students.

In the world's market systems, taxes to raise or lower the production of a good or service are not so common as subsidies yet nevertheless frequent: for example, in the form of tariffs or other import charges to curb imports as part of an economic development strategy. Subsidies are more widespread less for good reasons than for lamentable. They are distributed largely at the initiative of recipients, usually enterprises, who mobilize political influence and then join to it an at least superficially plausible reason for a grant.

No line separates a defensible subsidy from a political handout. Using tariffs and other import restrictions, Japan subsidized a number of industries as part of what might be called planning for a new role in world markets. But it then went on in the 1970s to subsidize industries largely irrelevant to such an aspiration: cement, glass, steel, and petroleum refining. Subsidies to the logging industry have the unfortunate effect of speeding deforestation, but they are supported both by political influence and some genuine concerns for the welfare of communities that would transitionally suffer if logging declined. Indefensible or hard to defend subsidies are tucked away here or there in more industries than not, gifts to influential industries and enterprises, occupational groups, and communities.

State purchases, taxes, subsidies, and other devices for dealing with spillovers increasingly present societies with major choices. A society troubled with urban congestion and blight, at least occasional threat of epidemics, falling soil fertility, declining forests, exhaustion of mineral resources, and uneasy about global warming might be expected to step up its efforts to control spillovers. That describes almost every contemporary society. The growing magnitude and threat of spillovers has already stimulated a round of environmental legislation from North to South America through Europe and Africa to Asia. The market systems of the world are heavy users of taxes and subsidies, as well as outright prohibitions, to cope with them. The Dutch government, for example, now subsidizes antipollution devices in enterprises in Poland and the Czech Republic in order to reduce the air pollution that reaches Holland from them.

I do not intend here to enter into the contemporary debate on when to use market controls and when to use outright commands and prohibitions to cope, say, with environmental problems. My point is simply that all governments in fact use the described market controls broadly for collective purposes and that every society has choices to make on how to use them. Obviously nonmarket mandatory controls have their place.

If we contemplate not only the use of state purchases, subsidies, and taxes to cope with spillover and other problems but also for programs for reducing poverty, dampening the greatest inequalities in wealth and income, and softening the hardships of the quid pro quo, the market system alone is in some respects like an unfinished apartment building in which people can live if they must, but not well. It is not habitable until internal partitions, heat, light, and other amenities are installed. Without them, most people find it too dark, cold, and insecure.

With purchases, taxes, and subsidies, societies make the market system livable. But just as the apartment's heating system may turn out to be a contractor's rip-off or the internal partitions too flimsy, what the state attaches to the market system may range from inconvenience to disaster. If the market system is a structure to which the state can attach many improvements, nations differ greatly in what they attach and with what success. In this respect, every market society has always had and continues to have great choices.

It is no small point, however, that such improvements (the governmental programs) need the structure (the market system) to which they are attached.

Chalmers Johnson,
MITI and the Japanese Miracle (1982)*

One: The Japanese "Miracle"

By common agreement among the Japanese, the "miracle" first appeared to them during 1962. In its issues of September 1 and 8, 1962, the *Economist* of London published a long two-part essay entitled "Consider Japan," which it later brought out as a book that was promptly translated and published in Tokyo as *Odorokubeki Nihon* (Amazing Japan). Up to this time most Japanese simply did not believe the rate of economic growth they were achieving—a rate unprecedented in Japanese history—and their pundits and economists were writing cautionary articles about how the boom would fail, about the crises to come, and about the irrationality of government policy.[1] Yet where the Japanese had been seeing irresponsible budgets, "over-loans," and tremendous domestic needs, the *Economist* saw expansion of demand, high productivity, comparatively serene labor relations, and a very high rate of savings. Thus began the praise, domestic and foreign, of the postwar Japanese economy—and the search for the cause of the "miracle."

First, some details on the miracle itself. Table 6.2.1 presents indices of industrial production for the entire period of this study, 1925 to 1975, with 1975 as 100. It reveals several interesting things. The miracle was actually only beginning in 1962, when production was just a third of what it would be by 1975. Fully half of Japan's amazing economic strength was to be manifested after 1966. The table also shows clearly the "recessions" of 1954, 1965, and 1974 that spurred the government to new and even more creative economic initiatives; and it demonstrates the ability of the Japanese economy to come back even more strongly from these periods of adversity. Intersectoral shifts are also recorded: the decline of mining as coal gave way to oil and the movement from textiles to machinery and finished metal products, a movement the Japanese call heavy and chemical industrialization (*jūkagaku kōgyōka*).

If we use a slightly different base line—for example, if we take 1951–53 to be 100—then the index of gross national product for 1934–36 is 90; for 1961–63, 248; and for 1971–73, 664; and the index of manufacturing production for 1934–36 is 87; for 1961–63, 400; and for 1971–73, 1,350. Over the whole postwar era, 1946 to 1976, the Japanese economy increased 55-fold.[2] By the end of our period Japan accounted for about 10 percent of the world's economic activity though occupying only 0.3 percent of the

---

TABLE 6.2.1. Indices of Japanese Mining and Manufacturing Production, 1926–1978 (1975 = 100)

Year	All Industry	Public Utilities	Mining and Manufacturing	Mining	All Manufacturing	Manufacturing Industries										
						Iron and Steel	Non-ferrous Metals	Metal Finished Goods	Machinery	Ceramics and Cement	Chemicals	Petroleum and Coal Products	Pulp and Paper	Textiles	Wood and Wood Products	Food
1926		2.5		54.5		1.5	4.0				1.5	0.7	4.9	17.4		
1927		2.8		59.7		1.7	4.1				1.7	0.8	5.3	18.8		
1928		3.3		62.0		2.0	4.6				1.8	1.0	5.8	18.1		
1929		3.6		63.2		2.2	4.6				2.2	1.0	6.4	18.9		
1930	5.5	3.9	5.8	62.0	5.3	2.1	4.8		1.4	8.4	2.5	1.0	5.5	21.8	15.8	21.0
1931	5.0	4.0	5.2	58.8	4.7	1.8	4.4		1.1	8.5	2.6	1.1	5.3	23.0	15.2	19.0
1932	5.3	4.3	5.5	60.0	5.0	2.3	4.9		1.0	9.2	3.2	1.2	5.3	24.9	16.0	20.8
1933	6.4	4.9	6.7	68.6	6.1	3.1	5.7		1.4	10.3	3.7	1.4	5.8	28.6	18.8	22.3
1934	6.9	5.3	7.2	75.1	6.5	3.7	5.6		1.4	10.0	4.3	1.7	5.4	31.5	24.0	22.5
1935	7.3	6.0	7.6	81.0	6.9	4.4	6.7		1.4	11.6	5.2	1.8	5.9	33.4	26.4	22.5
1936	8.2	6.5	8.6	89.6	7.8	4.9	7.4		1.7	12.0	6.2	2.1	7.0	35.8	27.6	23.0
1937	9.6	7.1	10.0	97.5	9.2	5.7	8.7		2.3	12.7	7.1	2.5	8.0	40.8	27.9	25.2
1938	9.9	7.7	10.3	103.8	9.4	6.5	9.1		2.5	13.5	8.1	2.7	7.2	33.6	27.5	25.5
1939	10.9	8.1	11.4	108.8	10.5	7.2	10.3		3.1	14.2	8.6	3.2	8.3	33.6	32.2	26.1
1940	11.4	8.3	12.0	116.7	11.0	7.3	10.1		3.8	14.7	8.5	3.4	8.3	30.4	26.8	22.7
1941	11.8	9.1	12.4	117.1	11.3	7.5	9.6		4.4	13.1	8.5	4.0	8.5	24.6	33.5	19.7
1942	11.5	9.1	12.0	114.4	11.0	7.9	10.9		4.5	10.8	7.1	4.0	6.7	19.5	31.7	17.5
1943	11.7	9.2	12.1	115.5	11.1	8.9	13.3		5.0	9.6	6.1	4.0	5.7	12.7	28.0	14.5
1944	11.9	9.0	12.4	105.1	11.4	8.3	14.7		5.8	7.5	5.7	3.2	3.3	6.8	24.8	11.9
1945	5.2	5.4	5.3	55.5	4.8	2.9	5.5		2.5	2.9	2.3	0.9	1.6	2.6	14.8	7.9
1946	2.3	6.9	2.2	40.9	1.8	1.0	2.9		0.8	3.1	1.4	0.4	1.7	4.3	22.7	7.0
1947	2.9	7.8	2.7	54.0	2.3	1.3	4.0		0.9	3.8	1.9	0.5	2.4	5.8	29.9	6.3
1948	3.8	8.5	3.6	66.2	3.0	2.1	5.5		1.4	5.8	2.5	0.8	3.5	6.6	34.7	7.7
1949	4.8	9.6	4.6	75.7	4.0	3.7	6.3		1.7	7.6	3.5	0.9	4.9	8.9	34.8	11.7
1950	5.9	10.3	5.7	80.0	5.1	5.1	7.3		1.8	9.0	4.7	1.7	6.7	12.6	36.5	13.1
1951	8.0	11.0	7.8	91.4	7.1	6.9	8.8		2.9	12.5	6.3	2.8	9.1	17.9	54.7	16.8
1952	8.6	11.9	8.4	94.4	7.7	7.1	9.3		3.0	13.0	6.9	3.6	10.4	20.3	58.2	17.2
1953	10.4	12.7	10.2	101.2	9.5	8.4	9.9		3.8	15.4	8.6	4.6	13.3	24.4	55.7	26.3
1954	11.2	13.5	11.1	97.5	10.4	8.8	11.5		4.3	17.5	9.8	5.4	14.5	26.5	54.6	28.5
1955	12.1	14.5	11.9	98.0	11.3	9.8	12.2		4.3	17.7	11.3	6.2	16.6	29.6	54.4	30.3

1956	14.9	16.7	14.6	108.3	13.9	12.0	14.7		6.2	21.5	13.6	8.0	19.2	35.2	60.8	32.0
1957	17.3	18.6	17.3	119.3	16.5	13.6	16.4		8.7	25.3	16.0	9.6	21.7	38.9	64.1	30.7
1958	17.4	19.7	17.3	115.7	16.6	12.8	16.0	15.6	9.3	23.9	16.0	10.0	21.3	34.8	61.8	35.6
1959	20.9	22.6	20.8	114.6	20.1	17.0	21.0	19.2	12.0	28.3	18.5	12.4	27.9	40.6	65.9	37.7
1960	26.0	26.5	25.9	125.2	25.3	22.4	27.8	24.4	16.5	25.7	22.3	15.8	33.6	47.9	73.2	39.9
1961	31.0	30.8	31.0	134.0	30.4	28.3	33.3	28.8	21.4	41.5	25.5	19.0	40.5	51.7	77.5	43.1
1962	33.5	32.9	33.6	137.0	32.9	28.3	32.5	30.3	24.0	45.3	29.2	21.4	43.4	54.5	79.3	46.6
1963	37.3	36.0	37.4	135.9	36.7	31.9	37.2	34.0	26.5	48.1	32.2	25.6	48.0	58.6	83.8	57.8
1964	43.2	40.6	43.3	137.1	42.6	39.7	45.6	39.6	32.3	55.5	36.6	30.3	54.5	64.8	88.9	62.7
1965	44.9	43.3	44.9	135.2	44.3	40.8	45.3	40.5	32.8	57.1	40.1	34.8	55.7	69.4	90.0	66.7
1966	50.7	47.6	50.8	143.1	50.2	47.2	51.0	48.0	38.1	62.2	45.3	40.0	62.5	76.4	95.4	73.1
1967	60.5	54.0	60.7	141.0	60.2	61.1	61.6	58.6	49.6	72.8	53.0	48.1	69.6	83.3	102.5	76.8
1968	69.7	59.6	70.1	142.1	69.6	68.4	74.3	71.0	61.5	81.4	62.6	56.9	76.9	88.4	107.0	78.7
1969	80.7	67.0	81.3	142.9	80.9	82.6	86.6	84.0	74.8	90.3	73.7	67.9	86.6	97.0	113.9	83.6
1970	91.8	75.9	92.5	139.2	92.2	94.2	93.8	96.9	87.7	101.0	86.8	79.8	98.2	105.2	118.7	89.9
1971	94.3	80.6	94.9	131.6	94.6	91.2	95.7	100.1	89.8	102.6	91.6	87.4	100.6	109.4	117.1	92.6
1972	101.1	87.4	101.8	121.9	101.6	98.7	108.4	111.0	87.3	109.5	97.2	91.5	106.7	110.8	120.7	97.8
1973	116.2	97.4	117.0	112.8	117.0	118.8	128.6	133.4	117.4	126.5	110.2	106.6	119.3	118.5	122.1	98.6
1974	111.7	97.3	112.3	105.8	112.4	116.9	112.6	123.0	116.2	117.0	109.9	104.4	113.7	106.1	109.1	97.5
1975	100.0	100.0	100.0	100.0	100.0	100.0	100.0	100.0	100.0	100.0	100.0	100.0	100.0	100.0	100.0	100.0
1976	111.0	108.5	111.1	100.0	111.2	109.5	119.3	116.8	113.7	110.4	111.5	102.7	113.3	108.4	106.8	101.1
1977	115.6	113.7	115.7	103.1	115.7	108.1	125.0	124.9	121.3	115.2	117.2	104.7	115.3	106.7	104.4	104.6
1978	122.7	119.9	122.8	105.9	123.0	110.1	135.0	134.9	131.5	121.0	131.0	104.0	120.8	107.7	107.0	106.1

Source: Mainichi Shimbun Sha, ed., *Shōwa shi jiten* (Dictionary of Shōwa History), Tokyo, 1980, p. 457.

world's surface and supporting about 3 percent of the world's population. Regardless of whether or not one wants to call this achievement a "miracle," it is certainly a development worth exploring.

Many voyagers have navigated these waters before me, and a survey of their soundings is a necessary introduction to this study and to my particular point of view. The task of explaining Japanese economic growth—and its repeated renewals after one or another set of temporary advantages had been exhausted or removed—is not easy, as the frequent use of the term "miracle" suggests; and the term cannot be isolated and applied only to the high-speed growth that began in 1955. As early as 1937 a much younger Prof. Arisawa Hiromi (b. 1896), one of the people who must be included on any list of the two or three dozen leading formulators of postwar industrial policy, used the phrase "Japanese miracle" to describe the increase of 81.5 percent in Japanese industrial output from 1931 to 1934.[3] Today we know why that particular miracle occurred: it resulted from the reflationary deficit financing of Finance Minister Takahashi Korekiyo, who at 81 was assassinated by young military officers on the morning of February 26, 1936, for trying to apply the brakes to the process he had started.

This earlier miracle is nonetheless problematic for scholars because of what Charles Kindleberger refers to as "the riddle" of how Japan "produced Keynesian policies as early as 1932 without a Keynes."[4] Some Japanese have not been overly exercised by this riddle; they have simply settled for calling Takahashi the "Keynes of Japan."[5] As I hope to make clear in this book, this kind of sleight of hand will not do; there was more to state intervention in the thirties than Keynesianism, and Arisawa and his colleagues in the government learned lessons in their formative years that are quite different from those that make up what has come to be known in the West as mainstream governmental fiscal policy.

Kindleberger's "riddle" does serve to draw attention to the projectionists, one major category among modern explorers of the Japanese economic miracle. These are writers who project onto the Japanese case Western—chiefly Anglo-American—concepts, problems, and norms of economic behavior. Whatever the value of such studies for the countries in which they were written, they need not detain us long here. This type of work is not so much aimed at explaining the Japanese case (although it may abstract a few principles of Japanese political economy) as it is at revealing home-country failings in light of Japan's achievements, or at issuing warnings about the possible effects of Japan's growth on other parts of the world. Even the *Economist's* brilliant little tract of 1962 might better have been called *Consider Britain in Light of What the Japanese Are Doing*, which was in any case its true purpose. Successors to the *Economist* include Ralph Hewins, *The Japanese Miracle Men* (1967), P. B. Stone, *Japan Surges Ahead: The Story of an Economic Miracle* (1969), Robert Guillain, *The Japanese Challenge* (1970), Herman Kahn, *The Emerging Japanese Superstate* (1970), and Hakan Hedberg, *Japan's Revenge* (1972). Perhaps the most prominent work in this genre, because it is so clearly hortatory about what Americans might learn from Japan rather than analytical about what has caused the phenomenal Japanese growth, is Ezra Vogel's *Japan as Number One: Lessons for Americans* (1979). My study does not follow these earlier works in advocating the adoption of Japanese institutions outside of Japan. It does, however, try to lay out in their full complexity some of the main Japanese institutions in the economic field so that those who are interested in adopting them will have an idea of what they are buying in terms of the Japanese system's consequences—intended, unintended, and even unwanted.

A second and entirely different set of explanations of the Japanese miracle belongs to the socioeconomic school, or what I have sometimes called the "anything-but-politics" approach to "miracle" research. This broad school includes four major types of analysis that often overlap with each other but that are clearly isolable for purposes of identification, although they rarely appear in pure form. These are the "national character–basic values–consensus" analysis favored by humanists in general and the anthropologically oriented in particular; the "no-miracle-occurred" analysis, chiefly the work of economists; the "unique-structural-features" analysis promoted by students of labor relations, the savings ratio, corporate management, the banking system, the welfare system, general trading corporations, and other institutions of modern Japan; and the various forms of the "free-ride" analysis, that is, the approach that stresses Japan's real but transitory advantages in launching high-speed growth in the postwar world. Before proceeding to sketch the qualities of these types of analysis, let me say that to a certain extent I can agree with all of them. My interest is not in disputing the facts that they have revealed nor in questioning their relevance to the miracle. However, I believe it can be shown that many of them should be reduced to more basic categories of analysis, particularly to the effects of state policy, and that they need to be weighed according to standards different from those used in the past, thereby giving greater weight to the state and its industrial policy.

The national-character explanation argues that the economic miracle occurred because the Japanese possess a unique, culturally derived capacity to cooperate with each other. This capacity to cooperate reveals itself in many ways—lower crime rates than in other, less homogeneous societies; subordination of the individual to the group; intense group loyalties and patriotism; and, last but not least, economic performance. The most important contribution of the culture to economic life is said to be Japan's famous "consensus," meaning virtual agreement among government, ruling political party, leaders of industry, and people on the primacy of economic objectives for the society as a whole—and on the means to obtain those objectives. Some of the terms invented to refer to this cultural capability of the Japanese are "rolling consensus,"[6] "private collectivism,"[7] "inbred collectivism,"[8] "spiderless cobweb,"[9] and "Japan, Inc."[10]

My reservations about the value of this explanation are basically that it is overgeneralized and tends to cut off rather than advance serious research. Consensus and group solidarity have been important in Japan's economic growth, but they are less likely to derive from the basic values of the Japanese than from what Ruth Benedict once called Japan's "situational" motivations: late development, lack of resources, the need to trade, balance of payments constraints, and so forth.[11] Positing some "special capacity to cooperate" as an irreducible Japanese cultural trait leads inquiry away from the question of *why* Japanese cooperate when they do (they did not cooperate during almost half of the period under study here), and away from the probability that this cooperation can be, and on occasion has been, quite deliberately engineered by the government and others. David Titus's research into the use of the Imperial institution in prewar Japan to "privatize" rather than to "socialize" societal conflict is one creative way to look at this problem of consensus.[12]

Many instances to be discussed later in this study illustrate how the government has consciously induced cooperation among its clients—with much better results than during the Pacific War, when it sought to control them. In the final analysis it is indeed probable that Japanese basic values are different from those of the Western world, but this needs to be studied, not posited; and explanations of social behavior in terms of basic values should be reserved for the final analysis, that is, for the residue of behavior that cannot be explained in other more economical ways. Actually, the explanation of the Japanese economic miracle in terms of culture was more prevalent a few years ago, when the miracle had occurred only in Japan. Now that it is being duplicated or matched in the Republic of Korea, Taiwan, Hong Kong, and Singapore—and perhaps even in some non–East Asian nations—the cultural explanation has lost much of its original interest.[13]

Exemplars of the "no-miracle-occurred" school of analysis do not literally assert that nothing happened to Japan's economy, but they imply that what did happen was not miraculous but a normal outgrowth of market forces. They come from the realm of professional economic analyses of Japanese growth, and therefore in their own terms are generally impeccable, but they also regularly present extended conclusions that incorporate related matters that their authors have not studied but desperately want to exclude from their equations. Hugh Patrick argues, "I am of the school which interprets Japanese economic performance as due primarily to the actions and efforts of private individuals and enterprises responding to the opportunities provided in quite free markets for commodities and labor. While the government has been supportive and indeed has done much to create the environment for growth, its role has often been exaggerated."[14] But there is a problem, he concedes. "It is disturbing that the macro explanations of Japanese postwar economic performance—in terms of increases in aggregate labor and capital inputs and in their more productive allocation—leave 40 percent plus of output growth and half of labor productivity growth unexplained."[15] If it can be shown that the government's industrial policy made the difference in the rate of investment in certain economically strategic industries (for instance, in developing the production and successful marketing of petrochemicals or automobiles), then perhaps we may say that its role has not been exaggerated. I believe this can be demonstrated and I shall attempt to do so later in this study.

Many Japanese would certainly dispute Patrick's conclusion that the government provided nothing more than the environment for economic growth. Sahashi Shigeru, former vice-minister of MITI (the Ministry of International Trade and Industry), asserts that the government is responsible for the economy as a whole and concludes, "It is an utterly self-centered [businessman's] point of view to think that the government should be concerned with providing only a favorable environment for industries without telling them what to do."[16] There have been occasions when industries or enterprises revolted against what the government told them to do—incidents that are among the most sensational in postwar politics—but they did not, and do not, happen often enough to be routine.

Discussions of the Japanese economy in purely economic terms seem to founder on their assumptions rather than on their analyses. It is assumed, for example, that the Japanese developmental state is the same thing as the American regulatory state. Philip Trezise argues, "In essentials, Japanese politics do not differ from politics in other democracies."[17] But one way they differ is in a budgetary process where appropriations *precede* authorizations and where, "with the single exception of 1972, when a combination of government mishandling and opposition unity led to small reductions in defense spending, the budget has not been amended in the Diet since 1955"; before that there was no pretense that the Diet did anything more than rubber-stamp the bureaucracy's budget.[18]

Another difference between Japan and the United States is to be found in the banking system. Before the war the rate of owned capital of all corporations in Japan was around 66 percent—a rate comparable to the current U.S. rate of 52 percent—but as late as 1972 the Japanese rate of owned capital was around 16 percent, a pattern that has persisted throughout the postwar period. Large enterprises obtain their capital through loans from the city banks, which are in turn over-loaned and therefore utterly dependent on the guarantees of the Bank of Japan, which is itself—after a fierce struggle in the 1950s that the bank lost—essentially an operating arm of the Ministry of Finance. The government therefore has a direct and intimate involvement in the fortunes of the "strategic industries" (the term is standard and widely used, but not in the military sense) that is much greater than a formal or legal comparison between the Japanese and other market systems would indicate. MITI was not just writing advertising copy for itself when in 1974 it publicly introduced the concept of a "plan-oriented market economy system," an attempt to name and analyze what it had been doing for the previous twenty years (the twenty years before that it had spent perfecting the system by trial and error).[19] The plan-oriented market economy system most decidedly includes some differences from "politics in other democracies," one of them being the care and feeding of the economic miracle itself.

The "no-miracle-occurred" school of miracle researchers agrees that Japanese economic growth took place but insists that this was because of the availability of capital, labor, resources, and markets all interacting freely with each other and unconstrained in any meaningful ways. It rejects as contrary to economic logic, and therefore as spurious, all the concepts that the Japanese have invented and employed continuously in discussing and managing their economy—such concepts as "industrial structure," "excessive competition," "coordination of investment," and "public-private cooperation." Most seriously, from a historical point of view, this explanation short-circuits attempts to analyze what difference the government's intervention has actually made by declaring in advance and as a matter of principle that it made no difference. The result is, as John Roberts has put it, that Japan's "'miraculous' emergence as a first-rate economic power in the 1960s has been described exhaustively by Japanese and foreign writers, and yet very little of the literature provides credible explanations of how it was done, or by whom."[20] This study is an attempt to answer these questions.

The third prevalent type of analysis of the Japanese miracle—stressing the influence of unusual Japanese institutions—is by far the most important of the four I have isolated, and the one that has been most thoroughly discussed in Japan and abroad. In its simplest form it asserts that Japan obtained a special economic advantage because of what postwar Japanese employers habitually call their "three sacred treasures"—the "lifetime" employment system, the seniority (*nenkō*) wage system, and enterprise unionism.[21] Amaya Naohiro of MITI, for example, cites these three institutions as the essence of what he terms Japan's *uchiwa* (all in the family) economic system; and in reporting to the Organization for Economic Cooperation and Development's Industry Committee during 1970, the former MITI vice-minister Ōjimi Yoshihisa referred to various "typically Japanese phenomena" that had helped Japan to obtain its high-speed growth—the phenomena again being the three sacred treasures.[22] Because of these institutions, the argument goes, Japan obtains greater labor commitment, loses fewer days to strikes, can innovate more easily, has better quality control, and in general produces more of the right things sooner than its international competitors.

This argument is undoubtedly true, but it has never been clearly formulated and is, at best, simplistic. There are several points to be made. First, the three sacred treasures are not the only "special institutions," and they are certainly not the most sacred. Others include the personal savings system; the distribution system; the "descent from heaven" (*amakudari*) of retired bureaucrats from the ministries into senior management positions in private enterprises; the structure of industrial groupings (*keiretsu,* or the oligopolistic organization of each industry by conglomerates); the "dual economy" (what Clark usefully terms the system of "industrial gradation")[23] together with the elaborate structure of subcontracting it generates; the tax system; the extremely low degree of influence exercised over companies by shareholders; the hundred-odd "public policy companies" (public corporations of several different forms); and, perhaps most important of all, the government-controlled financial institutions, particularly the Japan Development Bank and the "second," or investment, budget (the Fiscal Investment and Loan Plan).[24]

It is unnecessary here to describe each of these institutions. Most of them are quite familiar even to novice Japan watchers, and others will be analyzed in detail later in this book since they constitute some of the primary tools of the government for influencing and guiding the economy. What needs to be stressed is that they constitute a system—one that no individual or agency ever planned and one that has developed over time as ad hoc responses to, or unintended consequences of, Japan's late development and the progrowth policies of the government. Taken together as a system, they constitute a formidable set of institutions for promoting economic growth (a "GNP machine," in Amaya's metaphor), but taken separately, as they most commonly are, they do not make much sense at all.[25] And this is the primary reservation that one must make about the unique-institutions explanation: it never goes far enough and therefore fails as anything more than a partial explanation.

Let us take one example. As a result of the recognition of the Japanese miracle around the world, some American professors of business administration have begun to recommend to American entrepreneurs that they experiment with one or all of the three sacred treasures. Sometimes Japanese practices, suitably modified, travel well.[26] However, an American businessman who really attempted to institute "lifetime" employment without the backing of the other institutions of the Japanese system would soon find himself bankrupt. Among other things, lifetime employment in Japan is not for life but until the middle or late fifties; and although wage raises are tied to seniority, job security is not: it is those with most seniority who are the first fired during business downturns because they are the most expensive. Lifetime employment also does not apply to the "temporaries," who may spend their entire working lives in that status, and temporaries constitute a much larger proportion of a firm's work force than any American union would tolerate (42 percent of the Toyota Motor Company's work force during the 1960s, for example).[27]

Even if these problems could be taken care of, the American employer still would not have below him the extensive enterprise sector of medium and smaller subcontractors that his Japanese counterpart can squeeze in difficult times. Tomioka calls the subcontractors the "shock absorbers" of the Japanese business cycle—the smaller firms on the receiving end when large firms find they can no longer carry the fixed costs of their labor force and must "shift the strain" (*shiwayose*).[28] On the other hand, the American employee would not have Japan's extensive if redundant distribution system to fall back on in case he did get laid off. The distribution system in Japan serves as a vast sponge for the unemployed or underemployed when economic conditions require it. As testimony to the layers of middlemen in Japan, the volume of transactions among Japanese wholesalers in 1968 exceeded the total of retail sales by a ratio of 4.8 to 1, whereas the United States figure was 1.3 to 1.[29] It is not surprising that many knowledgeable Japanese do not want to change the distribution system, despite protests from foreign salesmen who have trouble breaking into it, because it performs other functions for the society than distribution, not the least of which is reducing the tax burden necessary to provide adequate unemployment insurance.

Lifetime employment, Japanese style, offers many advantages from the point of view of economic growth: it provides a strong incentive to the employer to operate at full or close to full capacity; it inhibits a horizontally structured trade union movement; and, in the words of Ohkawa and Rosovsky, it gives the Japanese entrepreneur "a labor force without incentives to oppose technological and organizational progress even of the labor-saving type."[30] But it does not exist in isolation and would not work without the rest of the system of "unique institutions."

The second main point about these special institutions concerns the date of their origins and how they are maintained. It is here that this school of explanations of the miracle sometimes blends imperceptibly with the first school, which says that Japanese culture and the Japanese national character support the economy. Amaya, for example, traces the three sacred treasures to the traditional world of family (*ie*), village (*mura*); and province (*kuni*); which he believes have all been homogenized and reincarnated today within the industrial enterprise.[31] It has to be stated that assertions of this type are a form of propaganda to defend these special institutions from hostile (often foreign) critics. Extensive research by scholars in Japan and abroad has demonstrated that virtually all of the so-called special institutions date from the twentieth century and usually from no earlier than the World War I era.

Lifetime employment, for example, has been traced to several influences, including the efforts during World War I to inhibit the growth of a left-wing social reform movement; the introduction of large numbers of Korean and Taiwanese laborers during the 1920s, which caused Japanese workers to seek job security at all costs; and the wartime munitions companies, which had to guarantee the jobs of their best employees in order to keep them. R.P. Dore, one of the leading authorities on Japanese industrialism, summarizes the state of research on this subject as follows: "Japan's employment system in 1900 was pretty much as market-oriented as Britain's: It was conscious institutional innovation which began to shape the Japanese system in the first two decades of this century, perfected the system of enterprise familism (or what one might call corporate paternalism) in the 1930s, and revamped the system to accommodate the new strength of unions in the late 1940s to produce what is called [by Dore] the 'welfare corporatism' of today."[32]

Nakamura Takafusa finds the roots of a whole range of important institutions in the wartime control era—including the bank-centered keiretsu (industrial groups based on the Designated Financial Organs System of the time) and the subcontracting system, which though it existed before the war was greatly strengthened by the forced mergers of medium and small enterprises with big machinery manufacturers (the so-called *kigyō seibi,* or "enterprise readjustment," movement.[33]

There are several ways in which the government has influenced the structure of Japan's special institutions. Many of these institutions it created directly in the course of its "industrial rationalization" campaigns of the 1930s or in the prosecution of the Pacific War. When the government did not create them directly, it nonetheless recognized their usefulness for its own purposes and moved to reinforce them. The savings system is an example. It is possible, as many commentators have urged, that the savings of private Japanese households—the highest rate of savings as a share of GNP ever recorded by any market economy in peacetime—is due to the natural frugality of the Japanese. But there are some strong external pressures that encourage the Japanese to save: a comparatively poor social security system; a wage system that includes large lump-sum bonus payments twice a year; a retirement system that cuts a worker's income substantially before he reaches the age of 60; a shortage of new housing and housing land, as well as a premium on university education for one's children, both of which require large outlays; an underdeveloped consumer credit system; a government-run postal savings system with guaranteed competitive interest rates; the lack of a well-developed capital market or other alternatives to personal saving; and a substantial exemption from income taxes for interest earned on savings accounts. The government is quite aware of these incentives to save and of the fact that money placed in the postal savings system goes directly into Ministry of Finance accounts, where it can be reinvested in accordance with government plans. Innate frugality may indeed play a role in this system, but the government has worked hard at engineering that frugality.

The theory of the "free ride," our fourth category of explanations, argues that Japan is the beneficiary of its postwar alliance with the United States, and that this alliance accounts at least for the miraculous part of Japan's rapid economic growth, if not for all of it. There are three ways in which Japan is said to have enjoyed a free ride: a lack of defense expenditures, ready access to its major export market, and relatively cheap transfers of technology.

Although it is true that Japan has not had to devote much of its national income to armaments, this factor cannot have influenced its growth rate significantly. If Japan's overall rate of investment had been very low—as low, for example, as it was in China—then the demands of defense could have had a retarding effect. But in Japan, where capital formation exceeded 30 percent of GNP during high-speed growth, the effect of low defense expenditures was negligible. The cases of South Korea and Taiwan, which have been pursuing the high investment strategy of the Japanese with equal or even more spectacular results, illustrate this point: their very high defense expenditures have had little or no impact on their economic performance.

The case of exports is more important. Japan profited enormously from the open trading system that developed throughout the world after World War II, and Japanese government leaders have repeatedly acknowledged the favorable effects for them of such institutions as the General Agreement on Tariffs and Trade, the International Monetary Fund, and, until 1971, stable exchange rates—all institutions that they had no role in creating. In fact, in their more pessimistic moods MITI leaders have speculated on the historical observation that Japan's great economic achievements came in the relatively open periods of world commerce—from the Meiji Restoration to World War I and from 1945 to 1970—and they have expressed concern that the post-1970s era could look like 1920–45 when seen in historical perspective.[34]

Nonetheless, the important point for our discussion is that Japan's growth did not depend nearly so much on exports as it did on the development of the domestic market (a market half the size of the United States' in terms of population). Eleanor Hadley notes that although Japan's economy in the early sixties was roughly three times the size of the 1934–36 economy, exports as a proportion of GNP were only about two-thirds what they had been in the mid-1930s.[35] By the late 1960s Japan's exports were only 9.6 percent of GNP, compared for example with Canada's 19.8 percent.[36] From 1953 to 1972 Japan had a consistently lower dependency on exports and imports as a percentage of GNP at constant prices than France, Germany, Italy, Britain, or OECD Europe as a whole. Japan's exports ran at about 11.3 percent of GNP, and its imports at 10.2 percent, whereas the OECD European figures were 21.2 percent and 20.9 percent respectively.[37] There is no question that Japan, as a heavily populated resource-deficient country, has to export in order to pay for its vital imports, but foreign sales were not the main factor driving its economic activity during high-speed growth.

Home demand led Japan's growth for the twenty years after 1955. The demand was there, of course, before 1955, but with the coming to power of the Ishibashi government in December 1956 and Ikeda Hayato's return to the post of minister of finance, Ishibashi and Ikeda launched the policy of "positive finance." Under the slogan "a hundred billion yen tax cut is a hundred billion yen of aid" as the basis for the fiscal 1957 budget, Ikeda opened up domestic demand as it had never been opened before.[38] Balance of payments problems slowed positive finance during the "bottom-of-the-pot" recession (with its trough in June 1958), but the economy responded quickly to government discipline and rebounded in the Iwato Boom (July 1958–December 1961), during which Ikeda became prime minister and launched the Income-doubling Plan. The propelling force of the economy in this and later periods was private corporate investment nurtured by favorable expectations for the longer term that were created by the government; it was not export sales.

Technology transfers—the third alleged "free ride"—were not exactly free, but there can be no question that they were crucial to Japanese economic growth and that the prices paid were slight compared with what such technology would cost today, if it could be bought at any price. Japan imported virtually all of the technology for its basic and high-growth industries, and it imported the greater proportion of this technology from the United States. But it is trivial and misleading to refer to this movement of patent rights, technology, and know-how across the Pacific and from Europe as a "free ride." It was, in fact, the heart of the matter.

The importation of technology was one of the central components of postwar Japanese industrial policy, and to raise the subject is to turn the discussion to MITI and the Japanese government's role. Before the capital liberalization of the late 1960s and 1970s, no technology entered the country without MITI's approval; no joint venture was ever agreed to without MITI's scrutiny and frequent alteration of the terms; no patent rights were ever bought without MITI's pressuring the seller to lower the royalties or to make other changes advantageous to Japanese industry as a whole; and no program for the importation of foreign technology was ever approved until MITI and its various advisory committees had agreed that the time was right and that the industry involved was scheduled for "nurturing" (*ikusei*).

From the enactment of the Foreign Capital Law in 1950 (it remained on the books for the next thirty years), the government was in charge of technology transfers. What it did and how it did it was not a matter of a "free ride" but of an extremely complex process of public-private interaction that has come to be known as "industrial policy." MITI is the primary Japanese government agency charged with the formulation and execution of industrial policy.

Thus I come to the final school, in which I place myself, the school that stresses the role of the developmental state in the economic miracle. Although the rest of this book is devoted to this subject—and to some of the nonmiracles produced by the developmental state in its quest for the miracle—several further points are needed by way of introduction. What do I mean by the developmental state? This is not really a hard question, but it always seems to raise difficulties in the Anglo-American countries, where the existence of the developmental state in any form other than the communist state has largely been forgotten or ignored as a result of the years of disputation with Marxist-Leninists. Japan's political economy can be located precisely in the line of descent from the German Historical School—sometimes labeled "economic nationalism," *Handelspolitik,* or neomercantilism; but this school is not exactly in the mainstream of economic thought in the English-speaking countries. Japan is therefore always being studied as a "variant" of something other than what it is, and so a necessary prelude to any discussion of the developmental state must be the clarification of what it is not.

The issue is not one of state intervention in the economy. All states intervene in their economies for various reasons, among which are protecting national security (the "military-industrial complex"), insuring industrial safety, providing consumer protection, aiding the weak, promoting fairness in market transactions, preventing monopolization and private control in free enterprise systems, securing the public's interest in natural monopolies, achieving economies of scale, preventing excessive competition, protecting and rearing industries, distributing vital resources, protecting the environment, guaranteeing employment, and so forth. The question is how the government intervenes and for what purposes. This is one of the critical issues in twentieth-century politics, and one that has become more acute as the century has progressed. As Louis Mulkern, an old hand in the Japanese banking world, has said, "I would suggest that there could be no more devastating weakness for any major nation in the 1980s than the inability to define the role of government in the economy."[39] The particular Japanese definition of this role and the relationship between that role and the economic miracle are at once major components and primary causes of the resurgent interest in "political economy" in the late twentieth century.

Nowhere is the prevalent and peculiarly Western preference for binary modes of thought more apparent than in the field of political economy. In modern times Weber began the practice with his distinction between a "market economy" (*Verkehrwirtschaft*) and a "planned economy" (*Planwirtschaft*). Some recent analogues are Dahrendorf's distinction between "market rationality" and "plan rationality," Dore's distinction between "market-oriented systems" and "organization-oriented systems," and Kelly's distinction between a "rule-governed state" (*nomocratic*) and a "purpose-governed state" (*telocratic*).[40] I shall make use of several of these distinctions later, but first I must stress that for purposes of the present discussion the right-hand component of these pairs is *not* the Soviet-type command economy. Economies of the Soviet type are not *plan rational* but *plan ideological*. In the Soviet Union and its dependencies and emulators, state ownership of the means of production, state planning, and bureaucratic goal-setting are not rational means to a developmental goal (even if they may once have been); they are fundamental values in themselves, not to be challenged by evidence of either inefficiency or ineffectiveness. In the sense I am using the term here, Japan is plan rational, and the command economies are not; in fact, the history of Japan since 1925 offers numerous illustrations of why the command economy is not plan rational, a lesson the Japanese learned well.

At the most basic level the distinction between market and plan refers to differing conceptions of the functions of the state in economic affairs. The state as an institution is as old as organized human society. Until approximately the nineteenth century, states everywhere performed more or less the same functions that make large-scale social organization possible but that individuals or families or villages cannot perform for themselves. These functions included defense, road building, water conservancy, the minting of coins, and the administration of justice. Following the industrial revolution, the state began to take on new functions. In those states that were the first to industrialize, the state itself had little to do with the new forms of economic activity but towards the end of the nineteenth century the state took on *regulatory* functions in the interest of maintaining competition, consumer protection, and so forth. As Henry Jacoby puts it, "Once capitalism transformed the traditional way of life, factors such as the effectiveness of competition, freedom of movement, and the absence of any system of social security compelled the state to assume responsibility for the protection and welfare of the individual. Because each man was responsible for himself, and because that individualism became a social principle, the state remained as almost the only regulatory authority."[41]

In states that were late to industrialize, the state itself led the industrialization drive, that is, it took on *developmental* functions. These two differing orientations toward private economic activities, the regulatory orientation and the developmental orientation, produced two different kinds of government-business relationships. The United States is a good example of a state in which the regulatory orientation predominates, whereas Japan is a good example of a state in which the developmental orientation predominates. A regulatory, or market-rational, state concerns itself with the forms and procedures—the rules, if you will—of economic competition, but it does not concern itself with substantive matters. For example, the United States government has many regulations concerning the antitrust implications of the size of firms, but it does not concern itself with what industries ought to exist and what industries are no longer needed. The developmental, or plan-rational, state, by contrast, has as its dominant feature precisely the setting of such substantive social and economic goals.

Another way to make this distinction is to consider a state's priorities in economic policy. In the plan-rational state, the government will give greatest precedence to industrial policy, that is, to a concern with the structure of domestic industry and with promoting the structure that enhances the nation's international competitiveness. The very existence of an industrial policy implies a strategic, or goal-oriented, approach to the economy. On the other hand, the market-rational state usually will not even have an industrial policy (or, at any rate, will not recognize it as such). Instead, both its domestic and foreign economic policy, including its trade policy, will stress rules and reciprocal concessions (although perhaps influenced by some goals that are not industrially specific, goals such as price stability or full employment). Its trade policy will normally be subordinate to general foreign policy, being used more often to cement political relationships than to obtain strictly economic advantages.

These various distinctions are useful because they draw our attention to Japan's emergence, following the Meiji Restoration of 1868, as a developmental, plan-rational state whose economic orientation was keyed to industrial policy. By contrast, the United States from about the same period took the regulatory, market-rational path keyed to foreign policy. In modern times Japan has always put emphasis on an overarching, nationally supported goal for its economy rather than on the particular procedures that are to govern economic activity. The Meiji-era goal was the famous *fukoku-kyōhei* (rich country, strong military) of the late nineteenth and early twentieth centuries. This was followed during the 1930s and 1940s by the goals of depression recovery, war preparation, war production, and postwar recovery. From about 1955, and explicitly since the Income-doubling Plan of 1960, the goal has been high-speed growth, sometimes expressed as "overtake Europe and America" (*Ōbei ni oikose*). Amaya lists the goals of the past century in detail: *shokusan kōgyō* (increase industrial production), *fukoku-kyōhei* (rich country, strong military), *seisanryoku kakujū* (expand productive capacity), *yushutsu shinkō* (promote exports), *kanzen koyō* (full employment), and *kōdo seichō* (promote exports), *kanzen koyō* (full employment), and *kōdo seichō* (high-speed growth).[42] Only during the 1970s did Japan begin to shift to a somewhat regulatory, foreign-policy orientation, just as America began to show early signs of a new developmental, industrial-policy orientation. But the Japanese system remains plan rational, and the American system is still basically market rational.[43]

This can be seen most clearly by looking at the differences between the two systems in terms of economic and political decision-making. In Japan the developmental, strategic quality of economic policy is reflected within the government in the high position of the so-called economic bureaucrats, that is, the officials of the ministries of Finance, International Trade and Industry, Agriculture and Forestry, Construction, and Transportation, plus the Economic Planning Agency. These official agencies attract the most talented graduates of the best universities in the country, and the positions of higher-level officials in these ministries have been and still are the most prestigious in the society. Although it is influenced by pressure groups and political claimants, the elite bureaucracy of Japan makes most major decisions, drafts virtually all legislation, controls the national budget, and is the source of all major policy innovations in the system. Equally important, upon their retirement, which is usually between the ages of 50 and 55 in Japan, these bureaucrats move from government to powerful positions in private enterprise, banking, the political world, and the numerous public corporations—a direction of elite mobility that is directly opposite to that which prevails in the United States.[44] The existence of a powerful, talented, and prestige-laden economic bureaucracy in a natural corollary of plan rationality.

In market-rational systems such as the United States, public service does not normally attract the most capable talent, and national decision-making is dominated by elected members of the professional class, who are usually lawyers, rather than by the bureaucracy. The movement of elites is not from government to the private sector but vice versa, usually through political appointment, which is much more extensive than in Japan. The real equivalent of the Japanese Ministry of International Trade and Industry in the United States is not the Department of commerce but the Department of Defense, which by its very nature and functions shares MITI's strategic, goal-oriented outlook. In fact, the pejorative connotations in the United States of terms such as "Japan, Inc." are similar to those surrounding the domestic expression "military-industrial complex" referring to a close working relationship between government and business to solve problems of national defense. (Not to be outdone, some Japanese have taken to calling the Japanese government-business relationship a "bureaucratic-industrial complex.")[45] American economic decisions are made most often in Congress, which also controls the budget, and these decisions reflect the market-rational emphasis on procedures rather than outcomes. During the 1970s Americans began to experiment with industrial policy bureaucracies such as the Department of Energy, but they are still rather wary of such organizations, whose prestige remains low.

Another way to highlight the differences between plan rationality and market rationality is to look at some of the trade-offs involved in each approach. First, the most important evaluative standard in market rationality is "efficiency." But in plan rationality this takes lower precedence than "effectiveness." Both Americans and Japanese tend to get the meanings of efficiency and effectiveness mixed up. Americans often and understandably criticize their official bureaucracy for its inefficiency, failing to note that efficiency is not a good evaluative standard for bureaucracy. Effectiveness is the proper standard of evaluation of goal-oriented strategic activities.[46] On the other hand, Japanese continue to tolerate their wildly inefficient and even inappropriate agricultural structure at least in part because it is mildly effective: it provides food that does not have to be imported.

Second, both types of systems are concerned with "externalities," or what Milton Friedman has called "neighborhood effects"—an example would be the unpriced social costs of production such as pollution. In this instance, however, the plan-rational system has much greater difficulty than the market-rational system in identifying and shifting its sights to respond to effects external to the national goal. The position of the plan-rational system is like that of a military organization: a general is judged by whether he wins or loses. It would be good if he would also employ an economy of violence (be efficient), but that is not as important as results. Accordingly, Japan persisted with high-speed industrial growth long after the evidence of very serious environmental damage had become common knowledge. On the other hand, when the plan-rational system finally shifts its goals to give priority to a problem such as industrial pollution, it will commonly be more effective than the market-rational system, as can be seen in the comparison between the Japanese and American handling of pollution in the 1970s.

Third, the plan-rational system depends upon the existence of a widely agreed upon set of overarching goals for the society, such as high-speed growth. When such a consensus exists, the plan-rational system will outperform the market-rational system on the same benchmark, such as growth of GNP, as long as growth of GNP is the goal of the plan-rational system. But when a consensus does not exist, when there is confusion or conflict over the overarching goal in a plan-rational economy, it will appear to be quite adrift, incapable of coming to grips with basic problems and unable to place responsibility for failures. Japan has experienced this kind of drift when unexpected developments suddenly upset its consensus, such as during the "Nixon shocks" of 1971, or after the oil shock of 1973. Generally speaking, the great strength of the plan-rational system lies in its effectiveness in dealing with routine problems, whereas the great strength of the market-rational system lies in its effectiveness in dealing with critical problems. In the latter case, the emphasis on rules, procedures, and executive responsibility helps to promote action when problems of an unfamiliar or unknown magnitude arise.

Fourth, since decision-making is centered in different bodies in the two systems— in an elite bureaucracy in one and in a parliamentary assembly in the other—the process of policy change will be manifested in quite different ways. In the plan-rational system, change will be marked by internal bureaucratic disputes, factional infighting, and conflict among ministries. In the market-rational system, change will be marked by strenuous parliamentary contests over new legislation and by election battles. For example, the shift in Japan during the late 1960s and throughout the 1970s from protectionism to liberalization was most clearly signaled by factional infighting within MITI between the "domestic faction" and the "international faction." The surest sign that the Japanese government was moving in a more open, free-trade direction was precisely the fact that the key ministry in this sector came to be dominated by internationalistic bureaucrats. Americans are sometimes confused by Japanese economic policy because they pay too much attention to what politicians say and because they do not know much about the bureaucracy, whereas Japanese have on occasion given too much weight to the statements of American bureaucrats and have not paid enough attention to Congressmen and their extensive staffs.

Looked at historically, modern Japan began in 1868 to be plan rational and developmental. After about a decade and a half of experimentation with direct state operation of economic enterprises, it discovered the most obvious pitfalls of plan rationality: corruption, bureaucratism, and ineffective monopolies. Japan was and remained plan rational, but it had no ideological commitment to state ownership of the economy. Its main criterion was the rational one of effectiveness in meeting the goals of development. Thus, Meiji Japan began to shift away from state entrepreneurship to collaboration with privately owned enterprises, favoring those enterprises that were capable of rapidly adopting new technologies and that were committed to the national goals of economic development and military strength. From this shift developed the collaborative relationship between the government and big business in Japan. In the prewar era this collaboration took the form of close governmental ties to the *zaibatsu* (privately owned industrial empires). The government induced the *zaibatsu* to go into areas where it felt development was needed. For their part the *zaibatsu* pioneered the commercialization of modern technologies in Japan, and they achieved economies of scale in manufacturing and banking that were on a par with those of the rest of the industrial world. There were many important results of this collaboration, including the development of a marked dualism between large advanced enterprises and small backward enterprises. But perhaps the most important result was the introduction of a needed measure of competition into the plan-rational system.

In the postwar world, the reforms of the occupation era helped modernize the zaibatsu enterprises, freeing them of their earlier family domination. The reforms also increased the number of enterprises, promoted the development of the labor movement, and rectified the grievances of the farmers under the old order, but the system remained plan rational: given the need for economic recovery from the war and independence from foreign aid, it could not very well have been otherwise. Most of the ideas for economic growth came from the bureaucracy, and the business community reacted with an attitude of what one scholar has called "responsive dependence."[47] The government did not normally give direct orders to businesses, but those businesses that listened to the signals coming from the government and then responded were favored with easy access to capital, tax breaks, and approval of their plans to import foreign technology or establish joint ventures. But a firm did not have to respond to the government. The business literature of Japan is filled with descriptions of the very interesting cases of big firms that succeeded without strong governmental ties (for example, Sony and Honda), but there are not many to describe.

Observers coming from market-rational systems often misunderstand the plan-rational system because they fail to appreciate that it has a political and not an economic basis. During the 1960s, for example, when it became fashionable to call the Japanese "economic animals," the most knowledgeable foreign analysts avoided the term because, in Henderson's words, there was "no doubt that Japan's center of gravity is in the polity not the economy—a source of puzzlement for Japan's numerous economic determinists of various Marxist stripe in academia and opposition politics."[48] One did not have to be an economic determinist or a Marxist to make this error; it was ubiquitous in English-language writing on Japan.

J.P. Nettl's comment on Marx is relevant to this point: "The notion that 'the modern state power is merely a committee which manages the common business of the bourgeoisie' is one of the historically least adequate generalizations that Marx ever made."[49] It is not merely historically inadequate; it obscures the fact that in the developmental state economic interests are explicitly subordinated to political objectives. The very idea of the developmental state originated in the situational nationalism of the late industrializers, and the goals of the developmental state were invariably derived from comparisons with external reference economies. The political motives of the developmental state are highlighted by Daniel Bell's observation—based on Adam Smith—that there would be little stimulus to increase production above necessities or needs if people were ruled by economic motives alone.[50] "The need for economic growth in a developing country has few if any economic springs. It arises from a desire to assume full human status by taking part in an industrial civilization, participation in which *alone* enables a nation or an individual to compel others to treat it as an equal. Inability to take part in it makes a nation militarily powerless against its neighbors, administratively unable to control its own citizens, and culturally incapable of speaking the international language."[51]

All of these motives influenced Meiji Japan, and there were others that were peculiar to Japan. Among these was one deriving from the treaties Japan was forced to conclude after its first contacts with Western imperialism in the nineteenth century: Japan did not obtain tariff autonomy until 1911. This meant that Japan was not able to aid its developing industries by the protective duties and other practices recommended by the market-oriented theories of the time, and the Meiji government consequently concluded that it had to take a direct hand in economic development if Japan was ever to achieve economic independence.[52]

A second special problem for Japan lasted until the late 1960s, when it temporarily disappeared only to return after the oil crisis of the 1970s; this was a shortage in its international balance of payments and the resultant need for the government to manage this most implacable of ceilings in a country with extremely few natural resources. As early as the 1880s, Tiedemann writes that in order to keep foreign payments in balance with customs receipts, "all agencies were required to prepare a foreign exchange budget as well as their normal yen budget."[53] Such a foreign exchange budget came into being again in 1937 and lasted in one form or another until 1964, when trade liberalization was carried out. In the era of high-speed growth, control of the foreign exchange budget meant control of the entire economy. It was MITI that exercised this controlling power, and foreign currency allocations were to become its decisive tool for implementing industrial policy.

The political nature of plan rationality can be highlighted in still other ways. MITI may be an economic bureaucracy, but it is not a bureaucracy of economists. Until the 1970s there were only two Ph.D.s in economics among the higher career officials of the ministry; the rest had undergraduate degrees in economics or, much more commonly, in public and administrative law. Not until Ueno Kōshichi became vice-minister in June 1957 was modern economic theory even introduced into the ministry's planning processes (Ueno studied economics during a long convalescence from tuberculosis before assuming the vice-ministership). Amaya Naohiro reflects this orientation of the ministry when he contrasts the views of the scholar and of the practitioner and notes that many things that are illogical to the theorist are vital to the practitioner—for instance, the reality of nationalism as an active element in economic affairs. Amaya calls for a "science of the Japanese economy," as distinct from "economics generally," and pleads that some things, perhaps not physics but certainly economics, have national grammars.[54] One further difference between the market-rational state and the plan-rational state is thus that economists dominate economic policy-making in the former while nationalistic political officials dominate it in the latter.

Within the developmental state there is contention for power among many bureaucratic centers, including finance, economic planning, foreign affairs, and so forth. However, the center that exerts the greatest *positive* influence is the one that creates and executes industrial policy. MITI's dominance in this area has led one Japanese commentator to characterize it as the "pilot agency," and a journalist of the *Asahi* who has often been highly critical of MITI nonetheless concedes that MITI is "without doubt the greatest concentration of brain power in Japan."[55] MITI's jurisdiction ranges from the control of bicycle racing to the setting of electric power rates, but its true defining power is its control of industrial policy (*sangyō seisaku*). Although the making and executing of industrial policy is what the developmental state does, industrial policy itself—what it is and how it is done—remains highly controversial.

Industrial policy, according to Robert Ozaki, "is an indigenous Japanese term not to be found in the lexicon of Western economic terminology. A reading through the literature suggests a definition, however: it refers to a complex of those policies concerning protection of domestic industries, development of strategic industries, and adjustment of the economic structure in response to or in anticipation of internal and external changes which are formulated and pursued by MITI in the cause of the national interest, as the term 'national interest' is understood by MITI officials."[56] Although this definition is somewhat circular—industrial policy is what MITI says it is—Ozaki makes one important point clear: industrial policy is a reflection of economic nationalism, with nationalism understood to mean giving priority to the interests of one's own nation but not necessarily involving protectionism, trade controls, or economic warfare. Nationalism *may* mean those things, but it is equally possible that free trade will be in the national economic interest during particular periods, as was true of Japan during the 1970s. Industrial policy is, however, a recognition that the global economic system is *never* to be understood in terms of the free competitive model: labor never moves freely between countries, and technology is only slightly more free.

There are two basic components to industrial policy, corresponding to the micro and macro aspects of the economy: the first the Japanese call "industrial rationalization policy" (*sangyō gōrika seisaku*), and the second, "industrial structure policy" (*sangyō kōzō seisaku*). The first has a long history in Japan, starting from the late 1920s, when it was quite imperfectly understood, as we shall see later in this book. MITI's *Industrial Rationalization Whitepaper* (1957) says that industrial rationalization subsumes a theory of economic development in which Japan's "international backwardness" is recognized and in which "contradictions" in the areas of technology, facilities, management, industrial location, and industrial organization are confronted and resolved.

Concretely, according to the *Whitepaper*, industrial rationalization means: (1) the rationalization of enterprises, that is, the adoption of new techniques of production, investment in new equipment and facilities, quality control, cost reduction, adoption of new management techniques, and the perfection of managerial control; (2) the rationalization of the environment of enterprises, including land and water transportation and industrial location; (3) the rationalization of whole industries, meaning the creation of a framework for all enterprises in an industry in which each can compete fairly or in which they can cooperate in a cartellike arrangement of mutual assistance; and (4) the rationalization of the industrial structure itself in order to meet international competitive standards.[57] (The last element of the definition was included before the concept of "industrial structure" had been invented by MITI. After about 1960 it was no longer included in the concept of industrial rationalization.)

The short definition is that industrial rationalization means state policy at the micro level, state intrusion into the detailed operations of individual enterprises with measures intended to improve those operations (or, on occasion, to abolish the enterprise). Nawa Tarō says that in its simplest terms industrial rationalization is the attempt by the state to discover what it is individual enterprises are already doing to produce the greatest benefits for the least cost, and then, in the interest of the nation as a whole, to cause all the enterprises of an industry to adopt these preferred procedures and techniques.[58]

Industrial rationalization in one form or another is an old and familiar movement going back to Frederick W. Taylor's system of "scientific management" of the progressive era in the United States (1890–1920); it exists or has appeared in every industrialized country, although it probably lasted longer and was carried further in Japan than in any other country.[59] Industrial structure policy, on the other hand, is more radical and more controversial. It concerns the proportions of agriculture, mining, manufacturing, and services in the nation's total production; and within manufacturing it concerns the percentages of light and heavy and of labor-intensive and knowledge-intensive industries. The application of the policy comes in the government's attempts to change these proportions in ways it deems advantageous to the nation. Industrial structure policy is based on such standards as income elasticity of demand, comparative costs of production, labor absorptive power, environmental concerns, investment effects on related industries, and export prospects. The heart of the policy is the selection of the strategic industries to be developed or converted to other lines of work.

Robert Gilpin offers a theoretical defense of industrial structure policy in terms of a posited common structural rigidity of the corporate form of organization:

> The propensity of corporations is to invest in particular industrial sectors or product lines even though these areas may be declining. That is to say, the sectors are declining as theaters of innovation; they are no longer the leading sectors of industrial society. In response to rising foreign competition and relative decline, the tendency of corporations is to seek protection of their home market or new markets abroad for old products. Behind this structural rigidity is the fact that for any firm, its experience, existing real assets, and know-how dictate a relatively limited range of investment opportunities. Its instinctive reaction, therefore, is to protect what it has. As a result, there may be no powerful interests in the economy favoring a major shift of energy and resources into new industries and economic activities.[60]

Whether this is true or not, MITI certainly thinks it is true and considers that one of its primary duties is precisely the creation of those powerful interests in the economy that favor shifts of energy and resources into new industries and economic activities. Like Gilpin, MITI is convinced that market forces alone will never produce the desired shifts, and despite its undoubted commitment in the postwar era to free enterprise, private ownership of property, and the market, it has never been reticent about saying so publicly (sometimes much too publicly for its own good).

Although some may question whether industrial policy should exist at all in an open capitalist system, the real controversy surrounding it concerns not whether it should exist but how it is applied. This book is in part devoted to studying the controversy over means that has gone on in Japan since industrial policy first appeared on the scene. The tools of implementation themselves are quite familiar. In Japan during high-speed growth they included, on the protective side, discriminatory tariffs, preferential commodity taxes on national products, import restrictions based on foreign currency allocations, and foreign currency controls. On the developmental (or what the Japanese call the "nurturing") side, they included the supply of low-interest funds to targeted industries through governmental financial organs, subsidies, special amortization benefits, exclusion from import duties of designated critical equipment, licensing of imported foreign technology, providing industrial parks and transportation facilities for private businesses through public investments, and "administrative guidance" by MITI (this last and most famous of MITI's powers will be analyzed in Chapter 7).[61] These tools can be further categorized in terms of the types and forms of the government's authoritative intervention powers (its *kyoninkaken,* or licensing and approval authority) and in terms of its various indirect means of guidance—for example, its "coordination of plant and equipment investment" for each strategic industry, a critically important form of administrative guidance.

The particular mix of tools changes from one era to the next because of changes in what the economy needs and because of shifts in MITI's power position in the government. The truly controversial aspect of these mixes of tools—one that greatly influences their effectiveness—is the nature of the relationship between the government and the private sector. In one sense the history of MITI is the history of its search for (or of its being compelled to accept) what Assar Lindbeck has called "market-conforming methods of intervention."[62] MITI's record of success in finding such methods—from the founding of the Ministry of Commerce and Industry (MCI) in 1925 to the mid-1970s—is distinctly checkered, and everyone in Japan even remotely connected with the economy knows about this and worries about MITI's going too far. MITI took a long time to find a government-business relationship that both enabled the government to achieve genuine industrial policy and also preserved competition and private enterprise in the business world. However, from approximately 1935 to 1955 the hard hand of state control rested heavily on the Japanese economy. The fact that MITI refers to this period as its "golden era" is understandable, if deeply imprudent.

Takashima Setsuo, writing as deputy director of MITI's Enterprises Bureau, the old control center of industrial policy, argues that there are three basic ways to implement industrial policy: bureaucratic control (*kanryō tōsei*), civilian self-coordination (*jishu chōsei*), and administration through inducement (*yūdō gyōsei*).[63] Between 1925 and 1975 Japan tried all three, with spectacularly varied results. However, at no time did the Japanese cease arguing about which was preferable or about the proper mix of the three needed for particular national situations or particular industries. The history of this debate and its consequences for policy-making is the history of MITI, and tracing its course should give pause to those who think that Japanese industrial policy might be easily installed in a different society.

What difference does industrial policy make? This, too, is part of the controversy surrounding MITI. Ueno Hiroya acknowledges that it is very difficult to do cost-benefit analyses of the effects of industrial policy, not least because some of the unintended effects may include bureaucratic red tape, oligopoly, a politically dangerous blurring of what is public and what is private, and corruption.[64] Professional quantitative economists seem to avoid the concept on grounds that they do not need it to explain economic events. For example, Ohkawa and Rosovsky cite as one of their "behavioral assumptions ... based on standard economic theory and observed history ... that the private investment decision is mainly determined by profit expectations, based among other things on the experience of the recent past as affected by the capital-output ratio and labor-cost conditions."[65]

I cannot prove that a particular Japanese industry would not or could not have grown and developed at all without the government's industrial policy (although I can easily think of the likely candidates for this category). What I believe can be shown are the differences between the course of development of a particular industry without governmental policies (its imaginary or "policy-off" trajectory) and its course of development with the aid of governmental policies (its real or "policy-on" trajectory). It is possible to calculate quantitatively, if only retrospectively, how, for example, foreign currency quotas and controlled trade suppress potential domestic demand to the level of the supply capacity of an infant domestic industry; how high tariffs suppress the price competitiveness of a foreign industry to the level of a domestic industry; how low purchasing power of consumers is raised through targeted tax measures and consumer-credit schemes, thereby allowing them to buy the products of new industries; how an industry borrows capital in excess of its borrowing capacity from governmental and government-guaranteed banks in order to expand production and bring down unit costs; how efficiency is raised through the accelerated depreciation of specified new machinery investments; and how tax incentives for exports function to enlarge external markets at the point of domestic sales saturation. Kodama Fumio has calculated mathematically the gaps between the real trajectory and the policy-off trajectory of the Japanese automobile industry during its infant, growing, and stable phases (the data are of course not yet available for a future declining phase).[66] His measures are also tools for analyzing the appropriateness and effectiveness of the various governmental policies for the automobile industry during these phases.

The controversy over industrial policy will not soon end, nor is it my intention to resolve it here. The important point is that virtually all Japanese analysts, including those deeply hostile to MITI, believe that the government was the inspiration and the cause of the movement to heavy and chemical industries that took place during the 1950s, regardless of how one measures the costs and benefits of this movement. A measurement of what MITI believes and others consider to be its main achievement is provided by Ohkawa and Rosovsky: "In the first half of the 1950s, approximately 30 percent of exports still consisted of fibres and textiles, and another 20 percent was classified as sundries. Only 14 percent was in the category of machinery. By the first half of the 1960s, after the great investment spurt, major changes in composition had taken place. Fibres and textiles were down to 8 percent and sundries to 14 percent, and machinery with 39 percent had assumed its position of leading component, followed by metals and metal products (26 percent)."[67]

This shift of "industrial structure" was the operative mechanism of the economic miracle. Did the government in general, or MITI in particular, cause it to occur? Or, to put it more carefully, did they accelerate it and give it the direction it took? Perhaps the best answer currently available is Boltho's comparative appraisal: "Three of the countries with which Japan can most profitably be compared (France, Germany, and Italy) shared some or all of Japan's initial advantages—e.g., flexible labor supplies, a very favorable (in fact even more favorable) international environment, the possibility of rebuilding an industrial structure using the most advanced techniques. Yet other conditions were very dissimilar. The most crucial difference was perhaps in the field of economic policies. Japan's government exercised a much greater degree of both intervention and protection than did any of its Western European counterparts; and this brings Japan closer to the experience of another set of countries—the centrally planned economies."[68]

If a prima facie case exists that MITI's role in the economic miracle was significant and is in need of detailed study, then the question still remains why this book adopts the particular time frame of 1925–75. Why look at the prewar and wartime eras when the miracle occurred only in postwar Japan? There are several reasons. First, although industrial policy and MITI's "national system" for administering it are the subjects of primary interest in this study, the leaders of MITI and other Japanese realized only very late in the game that what they were doing added up to an implicit theory of the developmental state. That is to say, MITI produced no theory or model of industrial policy until the 1960s at the earliest, and not until the creation of the Industrial Structure Council (Sangyō Kōzō Shingikai) in 1964 was analytical work on industrial policy begun on a sustained basis. All participants are agreed on this. Amaya quotes Hegel about the owl of Minerva spreading her wings at dusk. He also thinks that maybe it would have been just as well if the owl had never awakened at all, for he concludes with hindsight that the fatal flaw of MITIs prized but doomed Special Measures Law for the Promotion of Designated Industries of 1962–63 (a major topic of Chapter 7) was that it made explicit what had long been accepted as implicit in MITI's industrial policy.[69]

As late as 1973 MITI was writing that Japan's industrial policy just grew, and that only during the 1970s did the government finally try to rationalize and systematize it.[70] Therefore, an individual interested in the Japanese system has no set of theoretical works, no locus classicus such as Adam Smith or V.I. Lenin, with which to start. This lack of theorizing has meant that historical research is necessary in order to understand how MITI and industrial policy "just grew." Certain things about MITI are indisputable: no one ever planned the ministry's course from its creation as the Ministry of Commerce and Industry (MCI) in 1925, to its transformation into the Ministry of Munitions (MM) in 1943, to its reemergence as the MCI in 1945, down to its reorganization as MITI in 1949. Many of MITI's most vital powers, including their concentration in one ministry and the ministry's broad jurisdiction, are all unintended consequences of fierce intergovernmental bureaucratic struggles in which MITI sometimes "won" by losing. This history is well known to ministerial insiders— it constitutes part of their tradition and is a source of their high esprit de corps—but it is not well known to the Japanese public and is virtually unknown to foreigners.

Another reason for going back into history is that all the insiders cite the prewar and wartime eras as the time when they learned *how* industrial policy worked. As will become clear in subsequent chapters, there is direct continuity between prewar and postwar officials in this particular branch of the Japanese state bureaucracy; the postwar purge touched it hardly at all. The last vice-minister during the period of this study, Komatsu Yūgorō, who held the office from November 1974 to July 1976, entered the ministry in the class of 1944. All postwar vice-ministers previous to him came from earlier classes, going back to the first postwar vice-minister, Shiina Etsusaburō of the class of 1923. Wada Toshinobu, who became vice-minister in 1976, was the first without any experience of the Ministry of Munitions era.

Nakamura Takafusa locates the "roots" of both industrial policy and administrative guidance in the controlled economy of the 1930s, and he calls MITI the "reincarnation" of the wartime MCI and MM.[71] Arisawa Hiromi says that the prosperity of the 1970s was a product of the "control era," and no less a figure than Shiina Etsusaburō, former vice-minister, twice MITI minister, and vice-president of the Liberal Democratic Party, credits the experiences of old trade-and-industry bureaucrats in Manchuria in the 1930s, his own and Kishi Nobusuke's included.[72] Tanaka Shin'ichi—who was one of the leading officials of the Cabinet Planning Board (Kikaku-in) before it was merged with MCI to form the MM, and who became a postwar MITI official—argues that wartime planning was the basis for the work of the postwar Economic Stabilization Board (Keizai Antei Honbu) and MCI.[73] And Maeda Yasuyuki, one of Japan's leading scholars of MITI, writes that "the heritage of the wartime economy is that it was the first attempt at heavy and chemical industrialization; more important, the war provided the 'how' for the 'what' in the sense of innumerable 'policy tools' and accumulated 'know-how.' "[74]

Even more arresting than these comments from participants and analysts is the fact that the Japanese economy began to change in quite decisive ways around 1930. It is true that industrial policy in one form or another goes back to the Meiji era, but it is also true that after the turn of the century the government moved progressively away from its former policies of interference in the domestic economy (if not in those of the colonies or dependencies), and that for about thirty years an approximation of laissez faire was in vogue. Rodney Clark's observation is startling but true: "The organization of Japanese and Western industry was probably more similar in 1910 than in 1970."[75]

MITI and modern Japanese industrial policy are genuine children of the Shōwa era (1926–), and the present study is for that reason virtually coterminous with the reign of Emperor Hirohito. To carry the story back any further is to lose focus on the postwar economic miracle, but to fail to incorporate the history of the prewar MCI is to ignore MITI's traditions and collective consciousness. MITI men learned their trade in MCI, MM, and the Economic Stabilization Board. These were once such fearsome agencies that it was said the mere mention of their names would stop a child from crying. Admirers of the Japanese miracle such as I have a duty to show how the disastrous national experiences of the 1940s gave birth to the achievements of the 1950s and 1960s.

Notes

1. One of the most prominent Japanese economists, Shinohara Miyohei, subsequently acknowledged that he had not always understood or approved of government policy but that with hindsight he had changed his mind. See Shinohara. For the influence of the London *Economist's* book, see Arisawa, 1976, p. 371.

2. William W. Lockwood, "Economic Developments and Issues," in Passin, p. 89; Uchino Tatsurō *Japan's Postwar Economic Policies* (Tokyo: Ministry of Foreign Affairs, 1976), p. 6.

3. Arisawa, 1937, p. 4.

4. Kindleberger, p. 17.

5. See Gotō.

6. Richard Halloran, *Japan: Images and Realities* (New York: Knopf. 1970), p. 72.

7. Hadley, p. 87.

8. *Consider Japan*, p. 16.

9. Haitani, p. 181.

10. Kaplan, p. 14.

11. Ruth Benedict, *The Chrysanthemum and the Sword* (Boston: Houghton Mifflin, 1946), p. 316.

12. Titus, p. 312.

13. See Chen.

14. Hugh Patrick, "The Future of the Japanese Economy: Output and Labor Productivity," *The Journal of Japanese Studies,* 3 (Summer 1977): 239.

15. *Ibid.*, p. 225.

16. Sahashi, 1972, p. 190.

17. Philip H. Trezise, "Politics, Government, and Economic Growth in Japan," in Patrick and Rosovsky, p. 782.

18. Campbell, pp. 2, 200. Slight Diet alterations of the budget also occurred in 1977 and 1978, during the period of thin majorities for the LDP.

19. Industrial Structure Council, *Japan's Industrial Structure: A Long Range Vision* (Tokyo: JETRO, 1975), p. 9.

20. Roberts, p. 439.

21. On the Three Sacred Treasures, see Shimada Haruo, "The Japanese Employment System," *Japanese Industrial Relations,* Series 6 (Tokyo: Japan Institute of Labor, 1980), p. 8. For background and bibliography, see Organization for Economic Cooperation and Development, 1977a.

22. Amaya, p. 18; Organization for Economic Cooperation end Development, 1972, p. 14.

23. Clark, p. 64.

24. On public corporations and the Fiscal Investment and Loan Plan, see Johnson, 1978.

25. Amaya, p. 20.

26. See, e.g., Richard Tanner Johnson and William G. Ouchi, "Made in America (Under Japanese Management)," *Harvard Business Review,* Sept.–Oct. 1974, pp. 61–69; and William McDonald Wallace, "The Secret Weapon of Japanese Business," *Columbia Journal of World Business,* Nov.–Dec. 1972, pp. 43–52.

27. Allinson, p. 178.

28. Tomioka, pp. 15–16.

29. M.Y. Yoshino, p. 17.

30. Ohkawa and Rosovsky, p. 220.

31. Amaya, pp. 9–69.

32. R.P. Dore, "Industrial Relations in Japan and Elsewhere," in Craig, p. 327.

33. Nakamura, 1974, pp. 165–67.

34. See Toda.

35. Hadley, p. 393.

36. Kaplan, p. 3.

37. Boltho, p. 140.

38. Yasuhara, pp. 200–201.

39. Louis Mulkern, "U.S.-Japan Trade' Relations: Economic and Strategic Implications," in Abegglen et al., pp. 26–27.

40. Wolfgang J. Mommsen, *The Age of Bureaucracy: Perspectives on the Political Sociology of Max Weber* (New York: Harper Torchbooks, 1977), p. 64; Dahrendorf, 1968, p. 219; Dore, in Craig, p. 326; George Armstrong Kelly, "Who Needs a Theory of Citizenship?" *Daedalus,* Fall 1979, p. 25.

41. *The Bureaucratization of the World* (Berkeley: University of California Press, 1973), p. 147.

42. Amaya, p. 51.

43. For the signs of an incipient American industrial policy, see David Vogel. "The Inadequacy of Contemporary Opposition to Business," *Daedalus,* Summer 1980, pp. 47–58.

44. See Johnson, 1974; Johnson, 1975.

45. Shibagaki Kazuo, "Sangyō kōzō no henkaku" (Change of industrial structure), in Tokyo University, 1975, 8: 89.

46. See Drucker.

47. Allinson, pp. 34–35.

48. Henderson, p. 40.

49. Netll, pp. 571–72.

50. Bell, p. 22, n. 23.

51. Ernest Gellner, "Scale and Nation," *Philosophy of the Social Sciences,* 3 (1973): 15–16.

52. Black, p. 171.

53. Tiedemann, p. 138.

54. Amaya, p. 1.

55. Kakuma, 1979a, p. 58; Nawa, 1975, p. 88.

56. Ozaki, 1970, p. 879.

57. MITI, 1957, pp. 3–4.

58. Nawa, 1974, p. 22.

59. On Taylorism, see Samuel Haber, *Efficiency and Uplift: Scientific Management in the Progressive Era* (Chicago, Ill.: University of Chicago Press, 1964). Denis Healey describes "a new approach to improving our industrial performance," which he established in Great Britain in 1974 after he became Chancellor of the Exchequer. It actually boiled down to an attempt at industrial rationalization. See Denis Healey, *Managing the Economy.* The Russell C. Leffingwell Lectures (New York: Council on Foreign Relations, 1980), p. 29.

60. Gilpin, pp. 70–71.

61. See Ueno, p. 27.

62. *Can Pluralism Survive?* The William K. McInally Lecture (Ann Arbor: Graduate School of Business Administration, University of Michigan, 1977), p. 24.

63. Takashima Setsuo, p. 30.

64. Ueno, p. 14.

65. Ohkawa and Rosovsky, p. 200.

66. See Kodama.

67. Ohkawa and Rosovsky, p. 182.

68. Boltho, pp. 168–89.

69. Amaya, p. 78.

70. MITI, *Industrial Policy and MITI's Role* (Tokyo: MITI, 1973), p. 1.

71. In Arisawa, 1976, p. 133; and Nakamura, 1974, p. 164.

72. Arisawa, quoted in Obayashi, p. 69; Shiina, 1976, pp. 106–14.

73. Tanaka, pp. 655–56.
74. Maeda, 1975, p. 9.
75. Clark, p. 258.

References

Abegglen, James C., et al. *U.S.–Japan Economic Relations*. Brekeley: University of California Institute of East Asian Studies, 1980.

Allinson, Gary D. *Japanese Urbanism: Industry and Politics in Kariya, 1872–1972*. Berkeley: University of California Press, 1975.

Amaya Naohiro, *Hyōryū-suru Nihon keizai, shin sangyō seisaku no bijon* (The Japanese economy adrift: a vision of the new industrial policy). Tokyo: Mainichi Shimbun Sha, 1975.

Arisawa Hiromi. *Nihon kōgyō tōsei ron* (The control of Japanese industry). Tokyo: Yūhikaku, 1937.

_____, ed. *Shōwa keizai shi* (Economic history of the Shōwa era). Tokyo: Nihon Keizai Shimbun Sha, 1976.

Bell, Daniel. *The Cultural Contradictions of Capitalism*. New York: Basic Books, 1976.

Black, Cyril E., et al. *The Modernization of Japan and Russia*. New York: Free Press, 1975.

Boltho, Andrea. Japan: *An Economic Survey, 1953–1973*. London: Oxford University Press, 1975.

Campbell, John Creighton. *Contemporary Japanese Budget Politics*. Berkeley: University of California Press, 1977.

Chen, Edward K. Y. *Hyper-growth in Asian Economies: A Comparative Study of Hong Kong, Japan, Korea, Singapore, and Taiwan*. London: Macmillan, 1979.

Consider Japan. Comp. by the staff of the *Economist*. London: Duckworth, 1963.

Craig, Albert M., ed. *Japan: A Comparative View*. Princeton, N.J.: Princeton University Press, 1979.

Dahrendorf, Ralf. *Essays in the Theory of Society*. Stanford, Calif.: Stanford University Press, 1968.

Drucker, Peter F. "Managing the Public Service Institution." *The Public Interest*, 33(Fall, 1973): 43–60.

Gilpin, Robert. *U.S. Power and the Multinational Corporation*. New York: Basic Books, 1975.

Gotō Shin'ichi. *Takahashi Korekiyo, Nihon no "Keinzu"* (Takahashi Korekiyo: the "Keynes" of Japan). Tokyo: Nihon Keizai Shimbun Sha, 1977.

Hadley, Eleanor M. *Antitrust in Japan*. Princeton, N.J.: Princeton University Press, 1970.

Haitani Kanji. *The Japanese Economic System: An Institutional Overview*. Lexington, Mass.: D.C. Heath, 1976.

Henderson, Dan Fenno. *Foreign Enterprise in Japan: Laws and Policies*. Tokyo: Tuttle, 1975.

Johnson, Chalmers. "The Reemployment of Retired Government Bureaucrats in Japanese Big Business." *Asian Survey, 14* (Nov. 1974): 953–65.

_____. "Japan: Who Governs? An Essay on Official Bureaucracy." *Journal of Japanese Studies*, 2(Autumn 1975): 1–28.

_____. *Japan's Public Policy Companies*. Washington, D.C.: American Enterprise Institute, 1978.

Kakuma Takashi. *Dokyumento Tsūsan-shō, I, "shinkanryō" no jidai* (Documentary on MITI, I: the era of the "new bureaucrats"). Kyoto: P.H.P. Kenkyū-jo, 1979a.

Kaplan, Eugene J. *Japan: The Government–Business Relationship*. Washington, D.C.: U.S. Department of Commerce, 1972.

Kindleberger, Charles P. *The World in Depression, 1929-1939*. Berkeley: University of California Press, 1973.

Kodama Fumio. "A Framework of Retrospective Analysis of Industrial Policy." Institute for Policy Science Research Report No. 78-2. Saitama University, Graduate School of Policy Science. July 1978.

Maeda Yasuyuki. "Tsūshō sangyō seisaku no rekishi-teki tenkai" (The historical development of trade and industrial policy). *Tsūsan jyānaru (rinji zōkan)*, May 24, 1975, pp. 8–18.

Ministry of International Trade and Industry (MITI) (Tsūshō Sangyō-shō). *Sangyō gōrika hakusho* (Industrial rationalization whitepaper). Tokyo: Nikkan Kōgyō Shimbun Sha, 1957.

Nakamura Takafusa. *Nihon no keizai tōsei, senji sengo no keiken to kyōkun* (Japan's economic controls: experiences and lessons from wartime and postwar periods). Tokyo: Nihon Keizai Shimbun Sha, 1974.

Nawa Taro. *Tsūsan-shō* (MITI). Tokyo: Kyoiku Sha, 1974.

_____. "Kankai jinmyaku chiri" (Geography of bureaucratic personnel relations). *Kankai*, 1(Nov. 1975): 80–88.

Nettl, J. P. "The State as a Conceptual Variable." *World Politics*, 20(July 1968): 559–92.

Obayashi Kenji, "'Nihon Kabushiki Kaisha' no shukuzu, Sankōshin no kanmin kyōchō-buri" (The epitome of "Japan, Inc.": official–civilian cooperation in the Industrial Structure Council). *Nikkei bijinesu*, July 26, 1971, pp. 68–70.

Ohkawa Kaushi and Rosovsky, Henry. *Japanese Economic Growth: Trend Acceleration in the Twentieth Century*. Stanford, Calif.: Stanford University Press, 1973.

Organization for Economic Cooperation and Development. *The Industrial Policy of Japan*. Paris: OECD, 1972.

_____. *The Development of Industrial Relations Systems: Some Implications of Japanese Experience*. Paris: OECD, 1977.

Ozaki, Robert S. "Japanese Views on Industrial Organization." *Asian Survey*, 10(Oct. 1970): 872–89.

Passin, Herbert, ed. *The United States and Japan*. 2nd. Rev. ed. Washington D.C.: Columbia Books, 1975.

Patrick, Hugh, and Rosovsky, Henry, eds. *Asia's New Giant: How the Japanese Economy Works*. Washington, D.C.: Brookings Institution, 1976.

Roberts, John G. *Mitsui*. Tokyo: Weatherhill, 1973.

Sahashi Shigeru. *Nihon e no chokugen* (Straight talk to Japan). Tokyo: Mainichi Shimbun Sha, 1972.

Shiina Etsusaburo. "Nihon sangyō no daijikkenjō, Manshū" (Manchuria: the great proving ground for Japanese industry). *Bungei shunjū* (Feb. 1976): 106–14.

Takashima Setsuo. "Nihon no sangyō gyōsei to kyōchō hōshiki" (Japan's industrial administration and the cooperation formula). *Keizai hyōron*, 12(May 1963): 26–33.

Tanaka Shin'ichi. *Nihon senji keizai hishi* (Secret history of Japan's wartime economy). Tokyo: Computer Age, 1974.

Tiedemann, Arthur E. "Japan's Economic Foreign Policies, 1868–1893." In James W. Morely, ed., *Japan's Foreign Policy 1868-1941*. New York: Columbia University Press, 1974.

Titus, David Anson. *Palace and Politics in Prewar Japan*. New York: Columbia University Press, 1974.

Toda Eisuke. "Mokuhyō o miushinatta Tsūsan kanryō" (MITI bureaucrats who have lost their objective). *Ekonomisuto*, May 31, 1977, pp. 24–29.

Tokyo University, Social Science Research Institute (Tokyo Daigaku Shakai Kagaku Kenkyū-jo), ed. *Sengo kaikaku* (Postwar reform). Vols. 3, 8. Tokyo: Tokyo Daigaku Shuppankai, 1974, 1975.

Tomioka Tadao. *Chūshō Kigyō-chō* (The Medium and Smaller Enterprises Agency). Tokyo: Kyōiku Sha, 1974.

Ueno Hiroya. *Nihon no keizai seido* (The economic system of Japan). Toyko: Nihon Keizai Shimbun Sha, 1978.

Yasuhara Kazuo. *Ōkura-shō* (The Ministry of Finance). Tokyo: Kyōiku Sha, 1974.

Yoshino, M. Y. *The Japanese Marketing System*. Cambridge: Massachusetts Institute of Technology Press, 1971.

Peter A. Hall and David Soskice,
Varieties of Capitalism (2001)*

1: An Introduction to Varieties of Capitalism

1.1 Introduction

Political economists have always been interested in the differences in economic and political institutions that occur across countries. Some regard these differences as deviations from 'best practice' that will dissolve as nations catch up to a technological or organizational leader. Others see them as the distillation of more durable historical choices for a specific kind of society, since economic institutions condition levels of social protection, the distribution of income, and the availability of collective goods—features of the social solidarity of a nation. In each case, comparative political economy revolves around the conceptual frameworks used to understand institutional variation across nations.

On such frameworks depend the answers to a range of important questions. Some are policy-related. What kind of economic policies will improve the performance of the economy? What will governments do in the face of economic challenges? What defines a state's capacities to meet such challenges? Other questions are firm-related. Do companies located in different nations display systematic differences in their structure and strategies? If so, what inspires such differences? How can national differences in the pace or character of innovation be explained? Some are issues about economic performance. Do some sets of institutions provide lower rates of inflation and unemployment or higher rates of growth than others? What are the trade-offs in terms of economic performance to developing one type of political economy rather than another? Finally, second-order questions about institutional change and stability are of special significance today. Can we expect technological progress and the competitive pressures of globalization to inspire institutional convergence? What factors condition the adjustment paths a political economy takes in the face of such challenges?

The object of this book is to elaborate a new framework for understanding the institutional similarities and differences among the developed economies, one that offers a new and intriguing set of answers to such questions.[1] We outline the basic approach in this Introduction. Subsequent chapters extend and apply it to a wide range of issues. In many respects, this approach is still a work-in-progress. We see

* From: "An Introduction to Varieties of Capitalism" in *Varieties of Capitalism: The Institutions of Comparative Advantage*, Peter A. Hall and David Soskice, eds., Oxford, New York: Oxford University Press, 2001. (pp. 1–36, 54–60) By permission of Oxford University Press.

it as a set of contentions that open up new research agendas rather than settled wisdom to be accepted uncritically, but, as the contributions to this volume indicate, it provides new perspectives on an unusually broad set of topics, ranging from issues in innovation, vocational training, and corporate strategy to those associated with legal systems, the development of social policy, and the stance nations take in international negotiations.

As any work on this topic must be, ours is deeply indebted to prior scholarship in the field. The 'varieties of capitalism' approach developed here can be seen as an effort to go beyond three perspectives on institutional variation that have dominated the study of comparative capitalism in the preceding thirty years.[2] In important respects, like ours, each of these perspectives was a response to the economic problems of its time.

The first of these perspectives offers a *modernization approach* to comparative capitalism nicely elucidated in Shonfield's magisterial treatise of 1965. Devised in the post-war decades, this approach saw the principal challenge confronting the developed economies as one of modernizing industries still dominated by pre-war practices in order to secure high rates of national growth. Analysts tried to identify a set of actors with the strategic capacity to devise plans for industry and to impress them on specific sectors. Occasionally, this capacity was said to reside in the banks but more often in public officials. Accordingly, those taking this approach focused on the institutional structures that gave states leverage over the private sector, such as planning systems and public influence over the flows of funds in the financial system (Cohen 1977; Estrin and Holmes 1983; Zysman 1983; Cox 1986). Countries were often categorized, according to the structure of their state, into those with 'strong' and 'weak' states (Katzenstein 1978*b*; Sacks 1980; Nordlinger 1981; Skocpol and Amenta 1985). France and Japan emerged from this perspective as models of economic success, while Britain was generally seen as a laggard (Shonfield 1965; Johnson 1982).

During the 1970s, when inflation became the preeminent problem facing the developed economies, a number of analysts developed a second approach to comparative capitalism based on the concept of *neo-corporatism* (Schmitter and Lehmbruch 1979; Berger 1981; Goldthorpe 1984; Alvarez et al. 1991). Although defined in various ways, neo-corporatism was generally associated with the capacity of a state to negotiate durable bargains with employers and the trade union movement regarding wages, working conditions, and social or economic policy.[3] Accordingly, a nation's capacity for neo-corporatism was generally said to depend on the centralization or concentration of the trade union movement, following an Olsonian logic of collective action which specifies that more encompassing unions can better internalize the economic effects of their wage settlements (Olson 1965; Cameron 1984; Calmfors and Driffill 1988; Golden 1993). Those who saw neo-corporatist bargains as a 'political exchange' emphasized the ability of states to offer inducements as well as the capacity of unions to discipline their members (Pizzorno 1978; Regini 1984; Scharpf 1987, 1991; cf. Przeworski and Wallerstein 1982). Those working from this perspective categorized countries largely by reference to the organization of their trade union movement; and the success stories of this literature were the small, open economies of northern Europe.

During the 1980s and 1990s, a new approach to comparative capitalism that we will term a *social systems of production* approach gained currency. Under this rubric, we group analyses of sectoral governance, national innovation systems, and flexible production regimes that are diverse in some respects but united by several key analytic features. Responding to the reorganization of production in response to technological change, these works devote more attention to the behavior of firms. Influenced by the French regulation school, they emphasize the movement of firms away from mass production toward new production regimes that depend on collective institutions at the regional, sectoral, or national level (Piore and Sabel 1984; Dore 1986; Streeck and Schmitter 1986; Dosi et al. 1988; Boyer 1990; Lazonick 1991; Campbell et al. 1991; Nelson 1993; Hollingsworth et al. 1994; Herrigel 1996; Hollingsworth and Boyer 1997; Edquist 1997; Whitley 1999). These works bring a wider range of institutions into the analysis and adopt a more sociological approach to their operation, stressing the ways in which institutions generate trust or enhance learning within economic communities. As a result, some of these works resist national categories in favor of an emphasis on regional success of the sort found in Baden-Württemberg and the Third Italy.

Each of these bodies of work explains important aspects of the economic world. However, we seek to go beyond them in several respects. Although those who wrote within it characterized national differences in the early post-war era well, for instance, some versions of the modernization approach tend to overstate what governments can accomplish, especially in contexts of economic openness where adjustment is firm-led. We will argue that features of states once seen as attributes of strength actually make the implementation of many economic policies more difficult; and we seek a basis for comparison more deeply rooted in the organization of the private sector.

Neo-corporatist analysis directs our attention to the organization of society, but its emphasis on the trade union movement underplays the role that firms and employer organizations play in the coordination of the economy (cf. Soskice 1990a; Swenson 1991). We want to bring firms back into the center of the analysis of comparative capitalism and, without neglecting trade unions, highlight the role that business associations and other types of relationships among firms play in the political economy.

The literature on social systems of production accords firms a central role and links the organization of production to the support provided by external institutions at many levels of the political economy. However, without denying that regional or sectoral institutions matter to firm behavior, we focus on variation among national political economies. Our premise is that many of the most important institutional structures—notably systems of labor market regulation, of education and training, and of corporate governance—depend on the presence of regulatory regimes that are the preserve of the nation-state. Accordingly, we look for national-level differences and terms in which to characterize them that are more general or parsimonious than this literature has generated.[4]

Where we break most fundamentally from these approaches, however, is in our conception of how behavior is affected by the institutions of the political economy. Three frameworks for understanding this relationship dominate the analysis of comparative capitalism. One sees institutions as *socializing agencies* that instill a particular set of norms or attitudes in those who operate within them. French civil servants, for instance, are said to acquire a particular concern for the public interest by virtue of their training or the ethos of their agencies. A second suggests that the effects of an institution follow from the *power* it confers on particular actors through the formal sanctions that hierarchy supplies or the resources an institution provides for mobilization. Industrial policy-makers and trade union leaders are often said to have such forms of power. A third framework construes the institutions of the political economy as a *matrix of sanctions and incentives* to which the relevant actors respond such that behavior can be predicted more or less automatically from the presence of specific institutions, as, for instance, when individuals refuse to provide public goods in the absence of selective incentives. This kind of logic is often cited to explain the willingness of encompassing trade unions to moderate wages in order to reduce inflation.

Each of these formulations captures important ways in which the institutions of the political economy affect economic behavior and we make use of them. However, we think these approaches tend to miss or model too incompletely the *strategic interactions* central to the behavior of economic actors. The importance of strategic interaction is increasingly appreciated by economists but still neglected in studies of comparative capitalism.[5] If interaction of this sort is central to economic and political outcomes, the most important institutions distinguishing one political economy from another will be those conditioning such interaction, and it is these that we seek to capture in this analysis. For this purpose, we construe the key relationships in the political economy in game-theoretic terms and focus on the kinds of institutions that alter the outcomes of strategic interaction. This approach generates an analysis that focuses on some of the same institutions others have identified as important but construes the impact of those institutions differently as well as one that highlights other institutions not yet given enough attention in studies of comparative capitalism.

By locating the firm at the center of the analysis, we hope to build bridges between business studies and comparative political economy, two disciplines that are all too often disconnected. By integrating game-theoretical perspectives on the firm of the sort that are now central to microeconomics into an analysis of the macroeconomy, we attempt to connect the new microeconomics to important issues in macroeconomics. Ours is a framework that should be of interest to economists, scholars of business, and political scientists alike. We turn now to an elucidation of its basic elements.

1.2 The Basic Elements of the Approach

This *varieties of capitalism* approach to the political economy is actor-centered, which is to say we see the political economy as a terrain populated by multiple actors, each of whom seeks to advance his interests in a rational way in strategic interaction with others (Scharpf 1997a). The relevant actors may be individuals, firms, producer groups, or governments. However, this is a firm-centered political economy that regards companies as the crucial actors in a capitalist economy. They are the key agents of adjustment in the face of technological change or international competition whose activities aggregate into overall levels of economic performance.

1.2.1 A Relational View of the Firm

Our conception of the firm is relational. Following recent work in economics, we see firms as actors seeking to develop and exploit *core competencies* or *dynamic capa-*

bilities understood as capacities for developing, producing, and distributing goods and services profitably (Teece and Pisano 1998). We take the view that critical to these is the quality of the relationships the firm is able to establish, both internally, with its own employees, and externally, with a range of other actors that include suppliers, clients, collaborators, stakeholders, trade unions, business associations, and governments. As the work on transactions costs and principal-agent relationships in the economics of organization has underlined, these are problematic relationships (Milgrom and Roberts 1992). Even where hierarchies can be used to secure the cooperation of actors, firms encounter problems of moral hazard, adverse selection, and shirking. In many cases, effective operation even within a hierarchical environment may entail the formation of implicit contracts among the actors; and many of a firm's relationships with outside actors involve incomplete contracting (cf. Williamson 1985). In short, because its capabilities are ultimately relational, a firm encounters many coordination problems. Its success depends substantially on its ability to coordinate effectively with a wide range of actors.

For the purposes of this inquiry, we focus on five spheres in which firms must develop relationships to resolve coordination problems central to their core competencies. The first is the sphere of *industrial relations* where the problem facing companies is how to coordinate bargaining over wages and working conditions with their labor force, the organizations that represent labor, and other employers. At stake here are wage and productivity levels that condition the success of the firm and rates of unemployment or inflation in the economy as a whole. In the sphere of *vocational training and education*, firms face the problem of securing a workforce with suitable skills, while workers face the problem of deciding how much to invest in what skills. On the outcomes of this coordination problem turn not only the fortunes of individual companies and workers but the skill levels and competitiveness of the overall economy.

Issues of coordination also arise in the sphere of *corporate governance*, to which firms turn for access to finance and in which investors seek assurances of returns on their investments. The solutions devised to these problems affect both the availability of finance for particular types of projects and the terms on which firms can secure funds. The fourth sphere in which coordination problems crucial to the core competencies of an enterprise appear is the broad one of *inter-firm relations*, a term we use to cover the relationships a company forms with other enterprises, and notably its suppliers or clients, with a view to securing a stable demand for its products, appropriate supplies of inputs, and access to technology. These are endeavors that may entail standard-setting, technology transfer, and collaborative research and development. Here, coordination problems stem from the sharing of proprietary information and the risk of exploitation in joint ventures. On the development of appropriate relationships in this sphere, however, depend the capacities of firms to remain competitive and technological progress in the economy as a whole.

Finally, firms face a set of coordination problems vis-à-vis their own *employees*. Their central problem is to ensure that employees have the requisite competencies and cooperate well with others to advance the objectives of the firm. In this context, familiar problems of adverse selection and moral hazard arise, and issues of information-sharing become important (see Milgrom and Roberts 1992). Workers develop reservoirs of specialized information about the firm's operations that can be of value to management, but they also have the capacity to withhold information or effort. The relationships firms develop to resolve these problems condition their own competencies and the character of an economy's production regimes.

1.2.2 Liberal Market Economies and Coordinated Market Economies

From this perspective, it follows that national political economies can be compared by reference to the way in which firms resolve the coordination problems they face in these five spheres. The core distinction we draw is between two types of political economies, liberal market economies and coordinated market economies, which constitute ideal types at the poles of a spectrum along which many nations can be arrayed.[6]

In *liberal market economies,* firms coordinate their activities primarily via hierarchies and competitive market arrangements. These forms of coordination are well described by a classic literature (Williamson 1985). Market relationships are characterized by the arm's-length exchange of goods or services in a context of competition and formal contracting. In response to the price signals generated by such markets, the actors adjust their willingness to supply and demand goods or services, often on the basis of the marginal calculations stressed by neoclassical economics.[7] In many respects, market institutions provide a highly effective means for coordinating the endeavors of economic actors.

In *coordinated market economies,* firms depend more heavily on non-market relationships to coordinate their endeavors with other actors and to construct their core competencies. These non-market modes of coordination generally entail more extensive relational or incomplete contracting, network monitoring based on the exchange of private information inside networks, and more reliance on collaborative, as opposed to competitive, relationships to build the competencies of the firm. In contrast to liberal market economies (LMEs), where the equilibrium outcomes of firm behavior are usually given by demand and supply conditions in competitive markets, the equilibria on which firms coordinate in coordinated market economies (CMEs) are more often the result of strategic interaction among firms and other actors.

Market relations and hierarchies are important to firms in all capitalist economies, of course, and, even in liberal market economies, firms enter into some relationships that are not fully mediated by market forces.[8] But this typology is based on the contention that the incidence of different types of firm relationships varies systematically across nations. In some nations, for instance, firms rely primarily on formal contracts and highly competitive markets to organize relationships with their employees and suppliers of finance, while, in others, firms coordinate these endeavors differently. In any national economy, firms will gravitate toward the mode of coordination for which there is institutional support.

1.2.3 The Role of Institutions and Organizations

Institutions, organizations, and culture enter this analysis because of the support they provide for the relationships firms develop to resolve coordination problems. Following North (1990: 3), we define institutions as a set of rules, formal or informal, that actors generally follow, whether for normative, cognitive, or material reasons, and organizations as durable entities with formally recognized members, whose rules also contribute to the institutions of the political economy.[9]

From this perspective, markets are institutions that support relationships of particular types, marked by arm's-length relations and high levels of competition. Their concomitant is a legal system that supports formal contracting and encourages relatively complete contracts, as the chapters by Teubner and Casper indicate. All capitalist economies also contain the hierarchies that firms construct to resolve the problems that cannot be addressed by markets (Williamson 1985). In liberal market economies, these are the principal institutions on which firms rely to coordinate their endeavors.

Although markets and hierarchies are also important elements of coordinated market economies, firms in this type of economy draw on a further set of organizations and institutions for support in coordinating their endeavors. What types of organizations and institutions support the distinctive strategies of economic actors in such economies? Because the latter rely more heavily on forms of coordination secured through strategic interaction to resolve the problems they face, the relevant institutions will be those that allow them to coordinate on equilibrium strategies that offer higher returns to all concerned. In general, these will be institutions that reduce the uncertainty actors have about the behavior of others and allow them to make credible commitments to each other. A standard literature suggests that these are institutions providing capacities for (i) the *exchange of information* among the actors, (ii) the *monitoring* of behavior, and (iii) the *sanctioning* of defection from cooperative endeavor (see Ostrom 1990). Typically, these institutions include powerful business or employer associations, strong trade unions, extensive networks of cross-shareholding, and legal or regulatory systems designed to facilitate information-sharing and collaboration. Where these are present, firms can coordinate on strategies to which they would not have been led by market relations alone.

The problem of operating collaborative vocational training schemes provides a classic example. Here, the willingness of firms to participate depends on the security of their beliefs that workers will learn useful skills and that firms not investing in training will not poach extensively from those who do, while the participation of workers depends on assurances that training will lead to remunerative employment. As Culpepper's chapter in this volume indicates, it is easier for actors to secure these assurances where there are institutions providing reliable flows of information about appropriate skill levels, the incidence of training, and the employment prospects of apprentices (Finegold and Soskice 1988; Culpepper and Finegold 1999).

Similarly, the terms on which finance is provided to firms will depend on the monitoring capacities present in the economy. Where potential investors have little access to inside information about the progress of the firms they fund, access to capital is likely to depend on highly public criteria about the assets of a firm of the sort commonly found on balance sheets. Where investors are linked to the firms they fund through networks that allow for the development of reputations based on extensive access to information about the internal operations of the firm, however, investors will be more willing to supply capital to firms on terms that do not depend entirely on their balance sheets. The presence of institutions providing network reputational monitoring can have substantial effects on the terms on which firms can secure finance.

In short, this approach to comparative capitalism emphasizes the presence of institutions providing capacities for the exchange of information, monitoring, and the sanctioning of defections relevant to cooperative behavior among firms and other actors; and it is for the presence of such institutions that we look when comparing nations.

In addition, examination of coordinated market economies leads us to emphasize the importance of another kind of institution that is not normally on the list of those crucial to the formation of credible commitments, namely institutions that provide actors potentially able to cooperate with one another with a capacity for *deliberation*. By this, we simply mean institutions that encourage the relevant actors to engage in collective discussion and to reach agreements with each other.[10] Deliberative institutions are important for several reasons.

Deliberative proceedings in which the participants engage in extensive sharing of information about their interests and beliefs can improve the confidence of each in the strategies likely to be taken by the others. Many game-theoretic analyses assume a level of common knowledge that is relatively thin, barely stretching past a shared language and familiarity with the relevant payoffs. When multiple equilibria are available, however, coordination on one (especially one that exchanges higher payoffs for higher risks) can be greatly facilitated by the presence of a thicker common knowledge, one that extends beyond the basic situation to a knowledge of the other players sufficiently intimate to provide confidence that each will coordinate on a specific equilibrium (Eichengreen 1997). Deliberation can substantially thicken the common knowledge of the group.

As Scharpf (1987: ch. 4) has pointed out, although many think only of a 'prisoner's dilemma' game when they consider problems of cooperation, in the political economy many such problems take quite different forms, including 'battle of the sexes' games in which joint gains are available from more than one strategy but are distributed differently depending on the equilibrium chosen. Distributive dilemmas of this sort are endemic to political economies, and agreement on the distribution of the relevant gains is often the prerequisite to effective cooperation (Knight 1992). In some cases, such as those of collaborative research and development, the problem is not simply to distribute the gains but also the risks attendant on the enterprise. Deliberation provides the actors with an opportunity to establish the risks and gains attendant on cooperation and to resolve the distributive issues associated with them. In some cases, the actors may simply be negotiating from positions of relative power, but extensive deliberation over time may build up specific conceptions of distributive justice that can be used to facilitate agreement in subsequent exchanges.

Finally, deliberative institutions can enhance the capacity of actors in the political economy for strategic action when faced with new or unfamiliar challenges. This is far from irrelevant since economies are frequently subject to exogenous shocks that force the actors within them to respond to situations to which they are unaccustomed. The history of wage negotiations in Europe is replete with examples. In such instances, developments may outrun common knowledge, and deliberation can be instrumental to devising an effective and coordinated response, allowing the actors to develop a common diagnosis of the situation and an agreed response.

In short, deliberative institutions can provide the actors in a political economy with strategic capacities they would not otherwise enjoy; and we think cross-national comparison should be attentive to the presence of facilities for deliberation as well as institutions that provide for the exchange of information in other forms, monitoring, and the enforcement of agreements.

1.2.4 The Role of Culture, Informal Rules, and History

Our approach departs from previous works on comparative capitalism in another respect.[11] Many analyses take the view that the relevant outcomes in economic performance or policy follow more or less directly from differences in the formal organization of the political economy. Particular types of wage settlements or rates of inflation and unemployment are often said to follow, for instance, from the organizational structure of the union movement. Because we believe such outcomes are the products of efforts to coordinate in contexts of strategic interaction, however, we reject the contention that they follow from the presence of a particular set of institutions alone, at least if the latter are defined entirely in terms of formal rules or organizations.

As we have noted, the presence of a set of formal institutions is often a necessary precondition for attaining the relevant equilibrium in contexts of coordination. But formal institutions are rarely sufficient to guarantee that equilibrium. In multi-player games with multiple iterations of the sort that characterize most of the cases in which we are interested, it is well known that there exist multiple equilibria, any one of which could be chosen by the actors even in the presence of institutions conducive to the formation of credible commitments (Fudenberg and Maskin 1986). Something else is needed to lead the actors to coordinate on a specific equilibrium and, notably, on equilibria offering high returns in a non-cooperative context.[12] In many instances, what leads the actors to a specific equilibrium is a set of shared understandings about what other actors are likely to do, often rooted in a sense of what it is appropriate to do in such circumstances (March and Olsen 1989).

Accordingly, taking a step beyond many accounts, we emphasize the importance of informal rules and understandings to securing the equilibria in the many strategic interactions of the political economy. These shared understandings are important elements of the 'common knowledge' that lead participants to coordinate on one outcome, rather than another, when both are feasible in the presence of a specific set of formal institutions. By considering them a component of the institutions making up the political economy, we expand the concept of institutions beyond the purely formal connotations given to it in some analyses.

This is an entry point in the analysis for history and culture. Many actors learn to follow a set of informal rules by virtue of experience with a familiar set of actors and the shared understandings that accumulate from this experience constitute something like a common culture. This concept of culture as a set of shared understandings or available 'strategies for action' developed from experience of operating in a particular environment is analogous to those developed in the 'cognitive turn' taken by sociology (Swidler 1986; DiMaggio and Powell 1991). Our view of the role that culture can play in the strategic interactions of the political economy is similar to the one Kreps (1990) accords it in organizations faced with problems of incomplete contracting.

The implication is that the institutions of a nation's political economy are inextricably bound up with its history in two respects. On the one hand, they are created by actions, statutory or otherwise, that establish formal institutions and their operating procedures. On the other, repeated historical experience builds up a set of common expectations that allows the actors to coordinate effectively with each other. Among other things, this implies that the institutions central to the operation of the political economy should not be seen as entities that are created at one point in time and can then be assumed to operate effectively afterwards. To remain viable, the shared understandings associated with them must be reaffirmed periodically by appropriate historical experience. As Thelen emphasizes in this volume, the operative force of many institutions cannot be taken for granted but must be reinforced by the active endeavors of the participants.

1.2.5 Institutional Infrastructure and Corporate Strategy

This varieties of capitalism approach draws its basic conceptions of how institutions operate from the new economics of organization. We apply a set of concepts commonly used to explain behavior at the micro level of the economy to problems of understanding the macroeconomy (Milgrom and Roberts 1992). One of the advantages is an analysis with robust and consistent postulates about what kind of institutions matter and how they affect behavior. Another is the capacity of the approach to integrate analysis of firm behavior with analysis of the political economy as a whole.

However, there are at least two respects in which our account deviates from mainstream views in the new economics of organization. First, although we make use of the influential dichotomy between 'markets' and 'hierarchies' that Williamson (1975) has impressed on the field, we do not think this exhausts the relevant variation. Markets and hierarchies are features of LMEs and CMEs but we stress the systematic variation found in the character of corporate structure (or hierarchies) across different types of economies and the presence of coordination problems even within hierarchical settings (Milgrom and Roberts 1992). Even more important, we do not see these two institutional forms as the only ones firms can employ to resolve the challenges they confront. In coordinated market economies in particular, many firms develop relationships with other firms, outside actors, and their employees that are not well described as either market-based or hierarchical relations but better seen as efforts to secure cooperative outcomes among the actors using a range of institutional devices that underpin credible commitments. Variation in the incidence and character of this 'third' type of relationship is central to the distinctions we draw between various types of political economies.[13]

Second, it is conventional in much of the new economics of organization to assume that the core institutional structures of the economy, whether markets, hierarchies, or networks, are erected by firms seeking the most efficient institutions for performing certain tasks. The postulate is that (institutional) structure follows (firm) strategy (cf. Chandler 1974; Williamson 1975, 1985; Chandler and Daems 1980). In a restricted sense, this is certainly true: firms can choose whether to contract out an endeavor or perform it in-house, for instance, and they enjoy some control over their own corporate form.

However, we think it unrealistic to regard the overarching institutional structures of the political economy, and especially those coordinating the endeavors of many actors (such as markets, institutional networks, and the organizations supporting collaborative endeavor), as constructs created or controlled by a particular firm. Because they are collective institutions, a single firm cannot create them; and, because they have multifarious effects, it may be difficult for a group of firms to agree on them.[14] Instead, as Calvert (1995) observes, the construction of coordinating institutions should be seen as a second-order coordination problem of considerable magnitude. Even when firms can agree, the project may entail regulatory action by the government and the formation of coalitions among political parties and labor organizations motivated by considerations going well beyond efficiency (Swenson 1991, 1997).

As a result, the firms located within any political economy face a set of coordinating institutions whose character is not fully under their control. These institutions offer firms a particular set of opportunities; and companies can be expected to gravitate toward strategies that take advantage of these opportunities. In short, there are important respects in which strategy follows structure. For this reason, our approach predicts systematic differences in corporate strategy across nations, and differences that parallel the overarching institutional structures of the political economy. This is one of the most important implications of the analysis.

Let us stress that we refer here to broad differences. Of course, there will be additional variation in corporate strategies inside all economies in keeping with differences in the resource endowments and market settings of individual firms. The capabilities of management also matter, since firms are actors with considerable autonomy. Our point is that (institutional) structure conditions (corporate) strategy, not that it fully determines it. We also agree that differences in corporate strategy can be conditioned by the institutional support available to firms at the regional or sectoral levels (Campbell et al. 1991; Hollingsworth et al. 1994; Herrigel 1996). Many of the works making this point are congruent with our own in that they stress the importance of the institutional environment to firm strategy, even though there has been fruitful disagreement about which features of that environment matter most (cf. Streeck 1992b).[15]

However, we emphasize variations in corporate strategy evident at the national level. We think this justified by the fact that so many of the institutional factors conditioning the behavior of firms remain nation-specific. There are good reasons why that should be the case. Some of the relevant institutions were deeply conditioned by nationally specific processes of development, as are most trade unions and employers' associations. In others, the relevant institutions depend heavily on statutes or regulations promulgated by national states, as do many institutions in the financial arena and labor market, not to mention the sphere of contract law.

In sum, we contend that differences in the institutional framework of the political economy generate systematic differences in corporate strategy across LMEs and CMEs. There is already some evidence for this. For instance, the data that Knetter (1989) has gathered are especially interesting. He finds that the firms of Britain, a typical LME, and those of Germany, a CME, respond very differently to a similar shock, in this case an appreciation of the exchange rate that renders the nation's goods more expensive in foreign markets. British firms tend to pass the price increase along to customers in order to maintain their profitability, while German firms maintain their prices and accept lower returns in order to preserve market share.

Our approach predicts differences of precisely this sort. We would argue that British firms must sustain their profitability because the structure of financial markets in a liberal market economy links the firm's access to capital and ability to resist takeover to its current profitability; and they can sustain the loss of market share because fluid labor markets allow them to lay off workers readily. By contrast, German firms can sustain a decline in returns because the financial system of a coordinated market economy provides firms with access to capital independent of current profitability; and they attempt to retain market share because the labor institutions in such an economy militate in favor of long-term employment strategies and render layoffs difficult.

These are only some of the ways in which the institutional arrangements of a nation's political economy tend to push its firms toward particular kinds of corporate strategies. We explore more of these below with special emphasis on innovation.

To put the point in the most general terms, however, firms and other actors in coordinated market economies should be more willing to invest in *specific* and *co-specific assets* (i.e. assets that cannot readily be turned to another purpose and assets whose returns depend heavily on the active cooperation of others), while those in liberal market economies should invest more extensively in *switchable assets* (i.e. assets whose value can be realized if diverted to other purposes). This follows from the fact that CMEs provide more institutional support for the strategic interactions required to realize the value of co-specific assets, whether in the form of industry-specific training, collaborative research and development, or the like, while the more fluid markets of LMEs provide economic actors with greater opportunities to move their resources around in search of higher returns, encouraging them to acquire switchable assets, such as general skills or multi-purpose technologies.[16]

1.2.6 Institutional Complementarities

The presence of *institutional complementarities* reinforces the differences between liberal and coordinated market economies. The concept of 'complementary goods' is a familiar one: two goods, such as bread and butter, are described as complementary if an increase in the price of one depresses demand for the other. However, complementarities may also exist among the operations of a firm: marketing arrangements that offer customized products, for instance, may offer higher returns when coupled to the use of flexible machine tools on the shop floor (Jaikumar 1986; Milgrom and Roberts 1990, 1995).

Following Aoki (1994), we extend this line of reasoning to the institutions of the political economy. Here, two institutions can be said to be complementary if the presence (or efficiency) of one increases the returns from (or efficiency of) the other.[17] The returns from a stock market trading in corporate securities, for instance, may be increased by regulations mandating a fuller exchange of information about companies.

Of particular interest are complementarities between institutions located in different spheres of the political economy. Aoki (1994) has argued that long-term employment is more feasible where the financial system provides capital on terms that are not sensitive to current profitability. Conversely, fluid labor markets may be more effective at sustaining employment in the presence of financial markets that transfer resources readily among endeavors thereby maintaining a demand for labor (cf. Caballero and Hamour 1998; Fehn 1998). Casper explores complementarities between national systems of contract law and modes of inter-firm collaboration, and we identify others in the sections that follow.

This point about institutional complementarities has special relevance for the study of comparative capitalism. It suggests that nations with a particular type of coordination in one sphere of the economy should tend to develop complementary practices in other spheres as well.[18] Several logics may be operative here. In some cases, the institutions sustaining coordination in one sphere can be used to support analogous forms of coordination in others. Where dense networks of business associations support collaborative systems of vocational training, for instance, those same networks may be used to operate collective standard-setting. Similarly, firms may pressure governments to foster the development of institutions complementary to those already present in the economy in order to secure the efficiency gains they provide.

If this is correct, institutional practices of various types should not be distributed randomly across nations. Instead, we should see some clustering along the dimensions that divide liberal from coordinated market economies, as nations converge on complementary practices across different spheres. Figure 6.3.1 presents some support

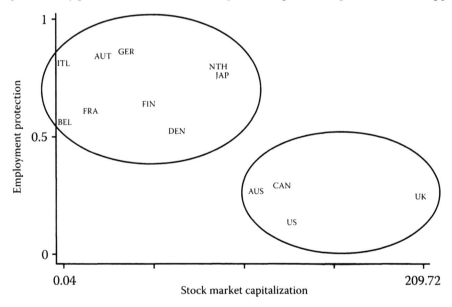

FIGURE 6.3.1 Institutions across sub-spheres of the political economy. (Note. Employment protection refers to the index of employment protection developed by Estevez-Abe, Iversen, and Soskice in this volume. Stock market capitalization is the market value of listed domestic companies as a percentage of GDP.) (Source: International Federation of Stock Exchanges, *Annual Report*.)

TABLE 6.3.1 The Economic Performance of Liberal and Coordinated Market Economies

Liberal Market Economies

	Growth Rate of GDP			GDP per Capita		Unemployment Rate		
	61–73	74–84	85–98	74–84	85–97	60–73	74–84	85–98
Australia	5.2	2.8	3.3	7932	16701	1.9	6.2	8.5
Canada	5.3	3.0	2.3	9160	18835	5.1	8.4	9.5
Ireland	4.4	3.9	6.5	4751	12830	5.0	9.1	14.1
New Zealand	4.0	1.8	1.7	7378	14172	0.2	2.2	6.9
UK	3.1	1.3	2.4	7359	15942	2.0	6.7	8.7
United States	4.0	2.2	2.9	11055	22862	4.9	7.5	6.0
LME average	4.3	2.5	3.2	7939	16890	3.2	6.7	8.9

Coordinated Market Economies

	Growth Rate of GDP			GDP per Capita		Unemployment Rate		
	61–73	74–84	85–98	74–84	85–97	60–73	74–84	85–98
Austria[a]	4.9	2.3	2.5	7852	17414	1.6	2.2	5.3
Belgium	4.9	2.0	2.2	8007	17576	2.2	8.2	11.3
Denmark	4.4	1.8	2.2	8354	18618	1.4	7.1	9.3
Finland	5.0	2.7	2.2	7219	15619	2.0	4.8	9.4
Iceland	5.7	4.1	2.7	8319	18285	0.6	0.6	2.5
Germany	4.3	1.8	2.2	7542	16933	0.8	4.6	8.5
Japan	9.7	3.3	2.6	7437	18475	1.3	2.1	2.8
Netherlands[b]	4.9	1.9	2.8	7872	16579	1.5	5.6	6.8
Norway	4.3	4.0	2.9	8181	19325	1.6	2.1	4.3
Sweden	4.2	1.8	1.5	8450	16710	1.9	2.3	4.8
Switzerland	4.4	.58	1.3	10680	21398	.01	0.4	2.5
CME average	5.1	2.4	2.3	8174	17902	1.3	3.6	6.1

Notes: Growth rate of GDP: average annual growth in GDP, averaged for the time-periods indicated. GDP per capita: per capita GDP at purchasing power parity, averaged for the time-periods indicated. Unemployment rate: annual unemployment rate.

[a] *Unemployment series begins in 1964.*

[b] *Unemployment series begins in 1969.*

Sources. Growth rate of GDP: World Bank, *World Development Indicators CD-ROM* (2000); except for Germany, for which data were taken from OECD, *Historical Statistics* (1997), for 1960–91, and *WDI* for years thereafter. GDP per capita: OECD, *OECD Statistical Compendium CD-ROM* (2000). Unemployment rate: OECD, *OECD Statistical Compendium CD-ROM* (2000).

for these propositions. It locates OECD nations on two axes that provide indicators for the character of institutions in the spheres of corporate finance and labor markets respectively. A highly developed stock market indicates greater reliance on market modes of coordination in the financial sphere, and high levels of employment protection tend to reflect higher levels of non-market coordination in the sphere of industrial relations.[19] Although there is some variation within each group, a pronounced clustering is evident. Nations with liberal market economies tend to rely on markets to coordinate endeavors in both the financial and industrial relations systems, while those with coordinated market economies have institutions in both spheres that reflect higher levels of non-market coordination.

Among the large OECD nations, six can be classified as liberal market economies (the USA, Britain, Australia, Canada, New Zealand, Ireland) and another ten as coordinated market economies (Germany, Japan, Switzerland, the Netherlands, Belgium, Sweden, Norway, Denmark, Finland, and Austria) leaving six in more ambiguous positions (France, Italy, Spain, Portugal, Greece, and Turkey).[20] However, the latter show some signs of institutional clustering as well, indicating that they may constitute another type of capitalism, sometimes described as 'Mediterranean', marked by a large agrarian sector and recent histories of extensive state intervention that have left them with specific kinds of capacities for non-market coordination in the sphere of corporate finance but more liberal arrangements in the sphere of labor relations (see Rhodes 1997).

Although each type of capitalism has its partisans, we are not arguing here that one is superior to another. Despite some variation over specific periods, both liberal and coordinated market economies seem capable of providing satisfactory levels of long-run economic performance, as the major indicators of national well-being displayed in Table 6.3.1 indicate. Where there is systematic variation between these types of political economies, it is on other dimensions of performance. We argue below that the two types of economies have quite different capacities for innovation. In addition, they tend to distribute income and employment differently. As Figure 6.3.2 indicates, in liberal market economies, the adult population tends to be engaged more extensively in paid employment and levels of income inequality are high.[21] In coordinated market economies, working hours tend to be shorter for more of the population and incomes more equal. With regard to the distribution of well-being, of course, these differences are important.

To make this analytical framework more concrete, we now look more closely at coordination in the principal spheres of firm endeavor in coordinated and liberal market economies, drawing on the cases of Germany and the United States for examples and emphasizing the institutional complementarities present in each political economy.

1.3 Coordinated Market Economies: The German Case

As we have noted, we regard capitalist economies as systems in which companies and individuals invest, not only in machines and material technologies, but in competencies based on relations with others that entail coordination problems. In coordinated market economies, firms resolve many of these problems through strategic interaction. The resulting equilibria depend, in part, on the presence of supportive institutions. Here, we use the case of Germany to illustrate how non-market coordination is achieved in each of the principal spheres of firm endeavor. Of course, the institutions used to secure coordination in other CMEs may differ to some extent from those of Germany.

(i) The *financial system* or *market for corporate governance* in coordinated market economies typically provides companies with access to finance that is not entirely dependent on publicly available financial data or current returns. Access to this kind of 'patient capital' makes it possible for firms to retain a skilled workforce through

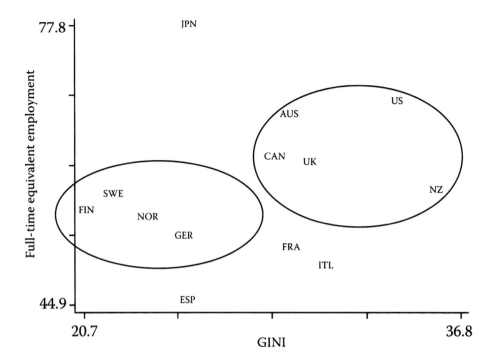

FIGURE 6.3.2 Distributional outcomes across political economies. (Note: Full-time equivalent employment is defined as the total number of hours worked per year divided by full-time equivalent hours per year per person times working age population. GINI refers to the gini coefficient measuring post-tax, post-transfer income inequality.) (Sources: For full-time equivalent unemployment: OECD (1996*a*). For GINI index: Spain, Japan, New Zealand are from Deiniger and Squire (1996); the remaining countries are from OECD (1996*a*).)

economic downturns and to invest in projects generating returns only in the long run. The core problem here is that, if finance is not to be dependent on balance-sheet criteria, investors must have other ways of monitoring the performance of companies in order to ensure the value of their investments. In general, that means they must have access to what would normally be considered 'private' or 'inside' information about the operation of the company.

This problem is generally resolved in CMEs by the presence of dense networks linking the managers and technical personnel inside a company to their counterparts in other firms on terms that provide for the sharing of reliable information about the progress of the firm. Reliability is secured in a number of ways. Firms may share information with third parties in a position to monitor the firm and sanction it for misleading them, such as business associations whose officials have an intimate knowledge of the industry. Reputation is also a key factor: where membership in a network is of continuing value, the participants will be deterred from providing false information lest their reputation in the network and access to it suffer. CMEs usually have extensive systems for what might be termed 'network reputational monitoring' (Vitols et al. 1997).

In Germany, information about the reputation and operation of a company is available to investors by virtue of (*a*) the close relationships that companies cultivate with major suppliers and clients, (*b*) the knowledge secured from extensive networks of cross-shareholding, and (*c*) joint membership in active industry associations that gather information about companies in the course of coordinating standard-setting, technology transfer, and vocational training. Other companies are not only represented on the supervisory boards of firms but typically engaged closely with them in joint research, product development, and the like. In short, firms sit inside dense business networks from which potential hinders can gain a considerable amount of inside information about the track record and projects of a firm.[22]

The overall structure of the market for corporate governance is equally important. Since firms often fund their activities from retained earnings, they are not always sensitive to the terms on which external finance is supplied. But they can be forced to focus on profitability and shareholder value if faced with the prospect of hostile takeover by others claiming to be able to extract more value from the company. Thus, the corporate strategies found in many CMEs also depend on tax provisions, securities regulations, and networks of cross-shareholding that discourage hostile mergers and acquisitions, which were very rare until recently, for instance, in Germany.

(ii) The *internal structure* of the firm reinforces these systems of network monitoring in many CMEs. Unlike their counterparts in LMEs, for instance, top managers in Germany rarely have a capacity for unilateral action. Instead, they must secure agreement for major decisions from supervisory boards, which include employee representatives as well as major shareholders, and from other managers with entrenched positions as well as major suppliers and customers. This structural bias toward consensus decision-making encourages the sharing of information and the development of reputations for providing reliable information, thereby facilitating network monitoring.

In the perspective we present, the incentives facing individuals, whether managers or workers, are as important as those facing firms. In CMEs, managerial incentives tend to reinforce the operation of business networks. Long-term employment contracts and the premium that firm-structure places on a manager's ability to secure consensus for his projects lead managers to focus heavily on the maintenance of their reputations, while the smaller weight given to stock-option schemes in managerial compensation in CMEs relative to LMEs inclines them to focus less on profitability than their counterparts in LMEs. The incentives for managers are broadly aligned with those of firms.

(iii) Many firms in coordinated market economies employ production strategies that rely on a highly skilled labor force given substantial work autonomy and encouraged to share the information it acquires in order to generate continuous improvements in product lines and production processes (Sorge and Warner 1986; Dore 1986). However, companies that adopt such strategies are vulnerable to 'hold up' by their employees and the 'poaching' of skilled workers by other firms, while employees who share the information they gain at work with management are open to exploitation.[23] Thus, CMEs need *industrial relations* institutions capable of resolving such problems.

The German industrial relations system addresses these problems by setting wages through industry-level bargains between trade unions and employer associations that generally follow a leading settlement, normally reached in engineering where the union is powerful enough to assure the labor movement that it has received a good deal. Although union density is only moderately high, encompassing employers' associations bind their members to these agreements. By equalizing wages at equivalent skill levels across an industry, this system makes it difficult for firms to poach workers and assures the latter that they are receiving the highest feasible rates of pay in return for the deep commitments they are making to firms. By coordinating bargaining across the economy, these arrangements also limit the inflationary effects of wage settlements (Streeck 1994; Hall and Franzese 1998).

The complement to these institutions at the company level is a system of works councils composed of elected employee representatives endowed with considerable authority over layoffs and working conditions. By providing employees with security against arbitrary layoffs or changes to their working conditions, these works councils encourage employees to invest in company-specific skills and extra effort. Their effectiveness is underpinned by the capacity of either side to appeal a disputed decision to the trade unions and employers' associations, who act as external guarantors that the councils function as intended (Thelen 1991).

(iv) Because coordinated market economies typically make extensive use of labor with high industry-specific or firm-specific skills, they depend on *education and training systems* capable of providing workers with such skills.[24] As Culpepper notes in his chapter, the coordination problems here are acute, as workers must be assured that an apprenticeship will result in lucrative employment, while firms investing in training need to know that their workers will acquire usable skills and will not be poached by companies that do not make equivalent investments in training. CMEs resolve these problems in a variety of ways.

Germany relies on industry-wide employer associations and trade unions to supervise a publicly subsidized training system. By pressuring major firms to take on apprentices and monitoring their participation in such schemes, these associations limit free-riding on the training efforts of others; and, by negotiating industry-wide skill categories and training protocols with the firms in each sector, they ensure both that the training fits the firms' needs and that there will be an external demand for any graduates not employed by the firms at which they apprenticed. Because German employer associations are encompassing organizations that provide many benefits to their members and to which most firms in a sector belong, they are well placed to supply the monitoring and suasion that the operation of such a system demands as well as the deliberative forums in which skill categories, training quotas, and protocols can be negotiated. Workers emerge from their training with both company-specific skills and the skills to secure employment elsewhere.

(v) Since many firms in coordinated market economies make extensive use of long-term labor contracts, they cannot rely as heavily on the movement of scientific or engineering personnel across companies, to effect technology transfer, as liberal market economies do. Instead, they tend to cultivate *inter-company relations* of the sort that facilitate the diffusion of technology across the economy. In Germany, these relationships are supported by a number of institutions. Business associations promote the diffusion of new technologies by working with public officials to determine where firm competencies can be improved and orchestrating publicly subsidized programs to do so. The access to private information about the sector that these associations enjoy helps them ensure that the design of the programs is effective for these purposes. A considerable amount of research is also financed jointly by companies, often in collaboration with quasi-public research institutes. The common technical standards fostered by industry associations help to diffuse new technologies, and they contribute to a common knowledge-base that facilitates collaboration among personnel from multiple firms, as do the industry-specific skills fostered by German training schemes (Lütz 1993; Soskice 1997b; Ziegler 1997).

Casper's chapter in this volume shows that Germany has also developed a system of contract law complementary to the presence of strong industry associations that encourages relational contracting among companies and promotes this sort of technology transfer. Because of the many contingencies that can arise in close inter-firm relationships involving joint research or product development, tightly written, formal contracts are often inadequate to sustain such relationships. However, the German courts permit unusually open-ended clauses in inter-firm contracts on the explicit condition that these be grounded in the prevailing standards of the relevant industry association. Thus, the presence of strong industry associations capable of promulgating standards and resolving disputes among firms is the precondition for a system of contract law that encourages relational contracting (cf. Casper 1997; Teubner in this volume).

In these respects, German institutions support forms of relational contracting and technology transfer that are more difficult to achieve in liberal market economies. One of the effects is to encourage corporate strategies that focus on product differentiation and niche production, rather than direct product competition with other firms in the industry, since close inter-firm collaboration is harder to sustain in the presence of the intense product competition that tends to characterize LMEs. The chapter by Estevez-Abe, Iversen, and Soskice examines the linkages between these product market strategies, skill systems, and social-policy regimes.

The complementarities present in the German political economy should be apparent from this account. Many firms pursue production strategies that depend on workers with specific skills and high levels of corporate commitment that are secured by offering them long employment tenures, industry-based wages, and protective works councils. But these practices are feasible only because a corporate governance system replete with mechanisms for network monitoring provides firms with access to capital on terms that are relatively independent of fluctuations in profitability. Effective vocational training schemes, supported by an industrial-relations system that discourages poaching, provide high levels of industry-specific skills. In turn, this encourages collective standard-setting and inter-firm collaboration of the sort that promotes technology transfer. The arrows in Figure 6.3.3 summarize some of these complementarities. Since many of these institutional practices enhance the effectiveness with which others operate, the economic returns to the system as a whole are greater than its component parts alone would generate.

1.4 Liberal Market Economies: The American Case

Liberal market economies can secure levels of overall economic performance as high as those of coordinated market economies, but they do so quite differently. In LMEs, firms rely more heavily on market relations to resolve the coordination problems that

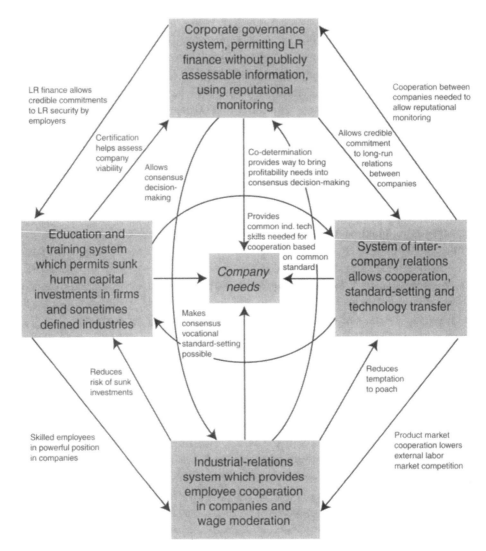

FIGURE 6.3.3 Complementarities across subsystems in the German coordinated market economy

firms in CMEs address more often via forms of non-market coordination that entail collaboration and strategic interaction. In each of the major spheres of firm endeavor, competitive markets are more robust and there is less institutional support for non-market forms of coordination.

(i) Several features of the *financial systems* or *markets for corporate governance* of liberal market economies encourage firms to be attentive to current earnings and the price of their shares on equity markets. Regulatory regimes are tolerant of mergers and acquisitions, including the hostile takeovers that become a prospect when the market valuation of a firm declines. The terms on which large firms can secure finance are heavily dependent on their valuation in equity markets, where dispersed investors depend on publicly available information to value the company. This applies to both bonds, share issues, and bank lending.[25] Compensation systems that reward top management for increases in net earnings or share price are common in such economies. Liberal market economies usually lack the close-knit corporate networks capable of providing investors with inside information about the progress of companies that allows them to supply finance less dependent on quarterly balance sheets and publicly available information. The relevant contrast is with CMEs, where firms need not be as attentive to share price or current profitability in order to ensure access to finance or deter hostile takeovers.

Of course, there are some qualifications to these generalizations. Companies with readily assessable assets associated with forward income streams, such as pharmaceutical firms with a 'pipeline' of drugs, consumer-goods companies with strong reputations for successful product development, and firms well positioned in high-growth markets, need not be as concerned about current profitability. New firms in high-technology fields can often secure funds from venture-capital companies that develop the resources and technical expertise to monitor their performance directly and trade ownership stakes in these firms for the high risks they take.[26] On the whole, however, the markets for corporate governance in LMEs encourage firms to focus on the publicly assessable dimensions of their performance that affect share price, such as current profitability.

(ii) In the *industrial relations arena,* firms in liberal market economies generally rely heavily on the market relationship between individual worker and employer to organize relations with their labor force. Top management normally has unilateral control over the firm, including substantial freedom to hire and fire.[27] Firms are under no obligation to establish representative bodies for employees such as works councils; and trade unions are generally less powerful than in CMEs, although they may have significant strength in some sectors. Because trade unions and employer associations in LMEs are less cohesive and encompassing, economy-wide wage coordination is generally difficult to secure. Therefore, these economies depend more heavily on macroeconomic policy and market competition to control wages and inflation (see Franzese in this volume; Hall and Franzese 1998).

The presence of highly fluid labor markets influences the strategies pursued by both firms and individuals in liberal market economies. These markets make it relatively easy for firms to release or hire labor in order to take advantage of new opportunities but less attractive for them to pursue production strategies based on promises of long-term employment. They encourage individuals to invest in general skills, transferable across firms, rather than company-specific skills and in career trajectories that include a substantial amount of movement among firms.

(iii) The *education and training systems* of liberal market economies are generally complementary to these highly fluid labor markets. Vocational training is normally provided by institutions offering formal education that focuses on general skills because companies are loath to invest in apprenticeship schemes imparting industry-specific skills where they have no guarantees that other firms will not simply poach their apprentices without investing in training themselves. From the perspective of workers facing short job tenures and fluid labor markets, career success also depends on acquiring the general skills that can be used in many different firms; and most educational programs from secondary through university levels, even in business and engineering, stress 'certification' in general skills rather than the acquisition of more specialized competencies.

High levels of general education, however, lower the cost of additional training. Therefore, the companies in these economies do a substantial amount of in-house training, although rarely in the form of the intensive apprenticeships used to develop company-specific or industry-specific skills in CMEs. More often, they provide further training in the marketable skills that employees have incentives to learn. The result is a labor force well equipped with general skills, especially suited to job growth in the service sector where such skills assume importance, but one that leaves some firms short of employees with highly specialized or company-specific skills.

(iv) *Inter-company relations* in liberal market economies are based, for the most part, on standard market relationships and enforceable formal contracts. In the United States, these relations are also mediated by rigorous antitrust regulations designed to prevent companies from colluding to control prices or markets and doctrines of contract laws that rely heavily on the strict interpretation of written contracts, nicely summarized by MacNeil's dictum: 'sharp in by clear agreement, sharp out by clear performance' (Williamson 1985). Therefore, companies wishing to engage in relational contracts with other firms get little assistance from the American legal system, as Casper observes.

In some fields of endeavor, such as after-sales service, companies can engage successfully in incomplete contracting by building up reputations on which other parties rely. But extensive reputation-building is more difficult in economies lacking the dense business networks or associations that circulate reputations for reliability or sharp practice quickly and widely. Because the market for corporate governance renders firms sensitive to fluctuations in current profitability, it is also more difficult for them to make credible commitments to relational contracts that extend over substantial periods of time.

How then does technology transfer take place in liberal market economies? In large measure, it is secured through the movement of scientists and engineers from one company to another (or from research institutions to the private sector) that fluid labor markets facilitate. These scientific personnel bring their technical knowledge with them. LMEs also rely heavily on the licensing or sale of innovations to effect technology transfer, techniques that are most feasible in sectors of the economy where effective patenting is possible, such as biotechnology, micro-electronics, and semiconductors. In the United States, the character of standard-setting reinforces the importance of licensing. Since few sectors have business associations capable of securing consensus on new standards, collective standard-setting is rarely feasible. Instead, standards are often set by market races, whose winners then profit by licensing their technology to many users (see also Tate in this volume). The prominence of this practice helps to explain the presence of venture-capital firms in liberal market economies: one success at standard-setting can pay for many failed investments (Borrus and Zysman 1997).

In LMEs, research consortia and inter-firm collaboration, therefore, play less important roles in the process of technology transfer than in CMEs where the institutional environment is more conducive to them. Until the National Cooperative

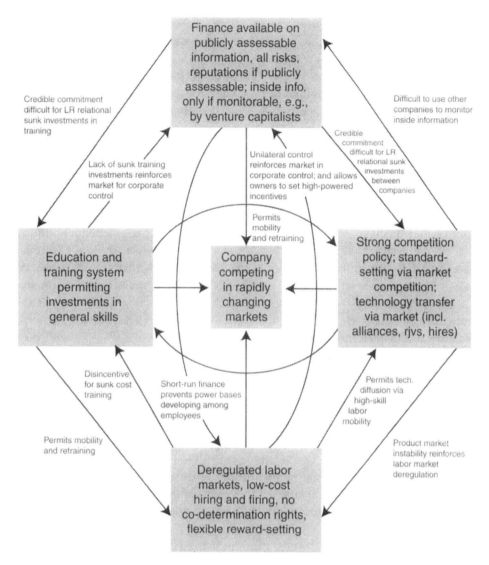

FIGURE 6.3.4 Complementarities across subsystems in the American liberal market economy.

Research Act of 1984, American firms engaging in close collaboration with other firms actually ran the risk of being sued for triple damages under antitrust law; and it is still estimated that barely 1 to 7 per cent of the funds spent on research and development in the American private sector are devoted to collaborative research.

It should be apparent that there are many institutional complementarities across the sub-spheres of a liberal market economy (see Figure 6.3.4). Labor market arrangements that allow companies to cut costs in a downturn by shedding labor are complementary to financial markets that render a firm's access to funds dependent on current profitability. Educational arrangements that privilege general, rather than firm-specific, skills are complementary to highly fluid labor markets; and the latter render forms of technology transfer that rely on labor mobility more feasible. In the context of a legal system that militates against relational contracting, licensing agreements are also more effective than inter-firm collaboration on research and development for effecting technology transfer.

Special note should be taken of the complementarities between the internal structure of firms and their external institutional environment in liberal and coordinated market economies. In LMEs, corporate structures that concentrate authority in top management make it easier for firms to release labor when facing pressure from financial markets and to impose a new strategy on the firm to take advantage of the shifting market opportunities that often present themselves in economies characterized by highly mobile assets. By contrast, in CMEs, where access to finance and technology often depends on a firm's attractiveness as a collaborator and hence on its reputation, corporate structures that impose more consensual forms of decision-making allow firms to develop reputations that are not entirely dependent on those of its top management. By reducing the capacity of top management to act arbitrarily, these structures also enhance the firm's capacity to enter credibly into relational contracts with employees and others in economies where a firm's access to many kinds of assets, ranging from technology to skills, may depend on its capacity for relational contracting. Lehrer's chapter explores some of these linkages between corporate structure and the external environment in more detail.

1.5 Comparing Coordination

Although many of the developed nations can be classified as liberal or coordinated market economies, the point of this analysis is not simply to identify these two types but to outline an approach that can be used to compare many kinds of economies. In particular, we are suggesting that it can be fruitful to consider how firms coordinate their endeavors and to analyze the institutions of the political economy from a perspective that asks what kind of support they provide for different kinds of coordination, even when the political economies at hand do not correspond to the ideal types we have just outlined.

It is important to note that, even within these two types, significant variations can be found. Broadly speaking, liberal market economies are distinguishable from coordinated market economies by the extent to which firms rely on market mechanisms to coordinate their endeavors as opposed to forms of strategic interaction supported by non-market institutions. Because market institutions are better known, we will not explore the differences among liberal market economies here. But a few words about variation in coordinated market economies may be appropriate, if only to show that variation in the institutional structures under-pinning strategic coordination can have significant effects on corporate strategy and economic outcomes.

One important axis of difference among CMEs runs between those that rely primarily on *industry-based coordination,* as do many of the northern European nations, and those with institutional structures that foster *group-based coordination* of the sort found in Japan and South Korea. As we have seen, in Germany, coordination depends on business associations and trade unions that are organized primarily along sectoral lines, giving rise to vocational training schemes that cultivate industry-specific skills, a system of wage coordination that negotiates wages by sector, and corporate collaboration that is often industry-specific. By contrast, the business networks of most importance in Japan are built on *keiretsu,* families of companies with dense interconnections cutting across sectors, the most important of which is nowadays the *vertical keiretsu* with one major company at its center.

These differences in the character of business networks have major implications. In Germany, companies within the same sector often cooperate in the sensitive areas of training and technology transfer. But the structure of the Japanese economy encourages sharp competition between companies in the same industry. Cooperation on sensitive matters is more likely to take place within the *keiretsu,* i.e. among firms operating in different sectors but within one 'family' of companies. The sectoral cooperation that takes place usually concerns less sensitive matters, including recession cartels, licensing requirements, and entry barriers as well as the annual wage round (Soskice 1990a). Partly for this reason, the attempts of MTTI to develop cooperative research projects within sectors have had very limited success; serious research and development remains the preserve of the laboratories of the major companies.

This pattern of *keiretsu*-led coordination also has significant implications for patterns of skill acquisition and technology transfer. Serious training, technology transfer and a good deal of standard-setting take place primarily within the vertical *keiretsu.* Workers are encouraged to acquire firm- or group-specific skills, and notably strong relational skills appropriate for use within the family of companies within which they have been trained. In order to persuade workers to invest in skills of this specificity, the large firms have customarily offered many of them life-time employment. And, in order to sustain such commitments, many Japanese firms have cultivated the capacity to move rapidly into new products and product areas in response to changes in world markets and technologies. This kind of corporate strategy takes advantage of the high levels of workforce cooperation that lifetime employment encourages. To reinforce it, Japanese firms have also developed company unions providing the workforce with a voice in the affairs of the firm.

Japanese firms tend to lack the capacities for radical innovation that American firms enjoy by virtue of fluid market settings or for sector-centered technology transfer of the sort found in Germany. Instead, the group-based organization of the Japanese political economy has encouraged firms there to develop distinctive corporate strategies that take advantage of the capacities for cross-sector technology transfer and rapid organizational redeployment provided by the *keiretsu* system. These translate into comparative institutional advantages in the large-scale production of consumer goods, machinery, and electronics that exploit existing technologies and capacities for organizational change. Although Japan is clearly a coordinated market economy, the institutional structures that support group-based coordination there have been conducive to corporate strategies and comparative advantages somewhat different from those in economies with industry-based systems of coordination.

The varieties of capitalism approach can also be useful for understanding political economies that do not correspond to the ideal type of a liberal or coordinated market economy. From our perspective, each economy displays specific capacities for coordination that will condition what its firms and government do.

France is a case in point, and the chapters in this volume by Lehrer, Culpepper, and Hancké explore some of the implications of this approach for it. Collaboration across French companies is based on career patterns that led many of the managers of leading firms through a few elite schools and the public service before taking up their positions in the private sector. Lehrer observes that the top managers of many French firms, therefore, have close ties to the state and weak ties to the rest of the enterprise. As a result, he argues, they are less likely to pursue the corporate strategies found in Britain or Germany and more likely to look to the state for assistance than their counterparts in other nations. Using the case of vocational training, however, Culpepper shows that there are clear limits to what states can do in the absence of strong business associations capable of monitoring their members. Hancké examines how large French firms are adapting to these limits, suggesting that many are taking industrial reorganization upon themselves, sometimes devising new networks to coordinate their activities.

In sum, although the contrast between coordinated and liberal market economies is important, we are not suggesting that all economies conform to these two types. Our object is to advance comparative analysis of the political economy more generally by drawing attention to the ways in which firms coordinate their endeavors, elucidating the connections between firm strategies and the institutional support available for them, and linking these factors to patterns of policy and performance. These are matters relevant to any kind of political economy.

1.8 The Dynamics of Economic Adjustment

Although we have emphasized differences among political economies that have been relatively durable, ours is not a static conception of the political economy. On the contrary, we expect the corporate strategies, policies, and institutions of each nation to evolve in response to the challenges they face, and our approach contains a number of conceptual tools for understanding both the nature of contemporary challenges and the shape this evolution is likely to take. In this section, we discuss some of the dynamic elements of the analysis.

1.8.1 The Challenge of Globalization

The developed economies are currently experiencing profound changes. A technological revolution is creating entirely new sectors, based on biotechnology, microprocessors, and telecommunications, whose products are transforming business practices across the economy. A wave of managerial innovations has seen companies around the world adopt new forms of supplier–client relations, just-in-time inventory systems, quality control, and team production. Economic activity is shifting from the industrial sector into the service sector. Capitalism seems to be in the midst of one of those 'cycles of creative destruction' that Schumpeter (1950) identified.

If technology provided the spark for this revolution, the accelerant has been liberalization in the international economy. With declining transport and communication costs, more liberal trade and financial regimes have inspired vast new flows of goods and capital across national borders, including a large increase in foreign direct investment. All the developed economies are more open than they were twenty years ago, and intense international competition is enforcing innovation of many firms. The watchword for these developments has become *globalization*—a term summing up the hopes of some for global prosperity and the fears of many that their way of life will be lost to international forces beyond the control even of their government (Berger and Dore 1996; Keohane and Milner 1996; Friedman 1999).[28]

For political economy, the principal issue raised by globalization concerns the stability of regulatory regimes and national institutions in the face of heightened competitive pressure (Boyer and Drache 1996; Rodrik 1997). Will institutional differences among nations of the sort we have identified remain significant or will the processes of competitive deregulation unleashed by international integration drive all economies toward a common market model?

To these questions, the conventional view of globalization prominent in the press and much of the literature gives an ominous answer. It is built on three pillars. First, it sees firms as essentially similar across nations at least in terms of basic structure and strategy. Second, it associates the competitiveness of firms with their unit labor costs, from which it follows that many will move production abroad if they can find cheaper labor there. And, third, these propositions generate a particular model of the political dynamic inspired by globalization, of the following type.

In the face of threats from firms to exit the economy, governments are said to come under increasing pressure from business to alter their regulatory frameworks so as to lower domestic labor costs, reduce rates of taxation, and expand internal markets via deregulation. What resistance there is to such steps will come from trade unions, seeking to protect the wages of their members, and social democratic parties, seeking to preserve social programs. The precise effects that each nation suffers in the face of globalization will thus be determined by the amount of political resistance that labor and the left can mount to proposals for change. But, because international interdependence provides capital with more exit opportunities than it does for labor, the balance of power is said to have shifted dramatically toward capital. In short, this is a model that predicts substantial deregulation and a convergence in economic institutions across nations. Conventional views of globalization contain a 'convergence hypothesis' analogous in force, but considerably less sanguine in implications, to an earlier one based on theories of industrialism (Kerr et al. 1960; Graubard 1964).

To date, the principal challenges to this view have come in two forms. Some scholars argue that the internationalism of trade and finance has not been as extensive or unprecedented as is often believed. Others argue that national governments are not as defenseless in the face of these developments as they appear, because governments have simply used international institutions or the excuse of global pressure to pursue reforms they wanted in any case (Wade 1996; Boyer 1996; Cohen 1996). There is some validity to both arguments. However, the analysis developed in this volume provides another basis for reevaluating the effects of globalization.

1.8.2 Reconsidering Globalization

The varieties of capitalism approach calls into question each of the assumptions underpinning the conventional view of globalization. First, it suggests that firms are not essentially similar across nations. On the contrary, firms in LMEs and CMEs develop distinctive strategies and structures to capitalize on the institutions available for market or non-market coordination in the economy. There is substantial evidence that firms in different types of economies react differently to similar challenges (Knetter 1989). Thus, we should not expect identical responses from them to globalization.

Second, our perspective suggests that firms will not automatically move their activities off-shore when offered low-cost labor abroad. Cheaper labor that comes with commensurate skill and productivity levels is always attractive, but firms also derive competitive advantages from the institutions in their home country that support specific types of inter- and intra-firm relationships. Many firms will be reluctant to give these up simply to reduce wage costs. Comparative institutional advantages tend to render companies less mobile than theories that do not acknowledge them imply.

Of course, with international liberalization, there will be some movement of corporate activities across national borders, as firms seek access to new markets and new sources of supply, but our approach suggests dimensions to this movement that conventional views do not anticipate. It implies, for instance, that firms based in LMEs may be more inclined to move their activities abroad to secure cheaper labor than companies based in CMEs, because the former already coordinate their endeavors using the market structures that less developed nations usually provide, while the latter often pursue corporate strategies that rely on high skills and institutional infrastructure difficult to secure elsewhere.

Our concept of comparative institutional advantage also suggests that firms may exploit new opportunities for movement to engage in a form of *institutional arbitrage*. By this, we mean that companies may shift particular activities to other nations in order to secure the advantages that the institutional frameworks of their political economies offer for pursuing those activities. Thus, companies may move some of their activities to liberal market economies, not simply to lower labor costs, but to secure access to institutional support for radical innovation. This helps to explain why Nissan locates design facilities in California, Deutsche Bank acquires subsidiaries in Chicago and London, and German pharmaceutical firms open research labs in the United States. Conversely, companies may locate other activities in coordinated market economies in order to secure access to the quality control, skill levels, and capacities for incremental innovation that their institutional frameworks offer: General Motors locates its engine plant in Düsseldorf rather than in Spain. Over time, corporate movements of this sort should reinforce differences in national institutional frameworks, as firms that have shifted their operations to benefit from particular institutions seek to retain them.

Finally, our perspective calls into question the monolithic political dynamic conventionally associated with globalization. It predicts one dynamic in liberal markets economies and a different one in coordinated market economies. In the face of more intense international competition, business interests in LMEs are likely to pressure governments for deregulation, since firms that coordinate their endeavors primarily through the market can improve their competencies by sharpening its edges. The government is likely to be sympathetic because the comparative advantage of the economy as a whole rests on the effectiveness of market mechanisms. Organized labor will put up some resistance, resulting in mild forms of class conflict. But, because international liberalization enhances the exit options of firms in LMEs, as

TABLE 6.3.2 Changes in Trade Union Density and the Level of Collective Bargaining, 1950–1992

Liberal Market Economies

	Trade Union Density			Bargaining Level[a]		
	1950–73	1974–84	1985–92	1950–73	1974–84	1985–92
Australia[b]	54	52	49	3.0	3.1	3.0
Canada	30	33	32	1.0	1.8	1.0
UK	45	51	41	1.7	2.1	1.0
United States	29	23	15	1.3	1.0	1.0
LME average	39	4.	34	1.7	2.0	1.5

Coordinate Market Economies

	Trade Union Density			Bargaining Level[a]		
	1950–73	1974–84	1985–92	1950–73	1974–84	1985–92
Austria	63	58	55	2.2	2.0	2.0
Belgium	48	68	69	2.0	2.9	2.5
Denmark	59	77	81	4.0	3.3	2.8
Finland	41	78	88	3.2	2.8	2.8
Germany	38	40	37	2.0	2.0	2.0
Japan	34	31	25	1.4	2.0	2.0
The Netherlands	40	36	28	3.7	3.4	2.1
Norway	58	61	63	3.8	3.6	3.6
Sweden	71	86	95	3.7	3.7	2.9
Switzerland	37	35	29	2.0	2.0	2.0
CME average	49	57	57	2.8	2.8	2.5

[a] *1 = Plant-level wage-setting; 2 = industry-level; 3 = central wage-setting without sanctions; 4 = central wage-setting with sanctions. Value recorded is the average for the period indicated.*
[b] *Trade union series ends in 1989.*
Source: Visser (1996). Compiled in Golden et al. (1997)

noted above, the balance of power is likely to tilt toward business. The result should be some weakening of organized labor and a substantial amount of deregulation, much as conventional views predict.

In coordinated market economies, however, the political dynamic inspired by globalization should be quite different. Here, governments should be less sympathetic to deregulation because it threatens the nation's comparative institutional advantages.[29] Although there will be some calls for deregulation even in such settings, the business community is likely to provide less support for it, because many firms draw competitive advantages from systems of relational contracting that depend on the presence of supportive regulatory regimes. In these economies, firms and workers have common interests to defend because they have invested in many co-specific assets, such as industry-specific skills. Thus, the political dynamic inspired by globalization in these countries is likely to entail less class conflict and to center around the formation of cross-class coalitions, as firms and workers with intense interests in particular regulatory regimes align against those with interests in others (cf. Swenson 1991, 1997).[30]

The analysis explains several outcomes in the spheres of policy and politics that are otherwise puzzling. Globalization was expected to weaken trade unions across the industrialized world. But comparative data show that trade union membership and the locus of collective bargaining has dropped far more substantially in some nations than in others (Lange et al. 1995; Ebbinghaus and Visser 2000). Our analysis predicts most of the patterns observed (see Table 6.3.2). Trade unions have been weakened by business initiative and deregulation in LMEs but remain strong in CMEs where cross-class coalitions help to preserve them and some degree of wage coordination.

Instead of the monolithic movement toward deregulation that many expect from globalization, our analysis predicts a bifurcated response marked by widespread deregulation in liberal market economies and limited movement in coordinated market economies.[31] This is precisely the pattern of policy across the OECD in recent decades. Deregulation has been far-reaching in the liberal market economies of Britain, the united States, New Zealand, Canada, and Australia but much less extensive in the Coordinated market economies of northern Europe and east Asia (Vogel 1996; Ellis 1998; Story and Walter 1997; Wood 1997; King and Wood 1999).[32] Moreover, Wood and Thelen report finding just the sort of politics this approach would lead one to expect in both liberal and coordinated market economies in recent year (Wood 1997; Thelen 2000).

Ultimately, it is not surprising that increasing flows of trade have not erased the institutional differences across nations. After all, world trade has been increasing for fifty years without enforcing convergence. Because of comparative institutional advantage, nations often prosper, not by becoming more similar, but by building on their institutional differences.[33]

Notes

1. We concentrate here on economies at relatively high levels of development because we know them best and think the framework applies well to many problems there. However, the basic approach should also have relevance for understanding developing economies as well (cf. Bates 1997).

2. Of necessity, this summary is brief and slightly stylized. As a result, it does not do full justice to the variety of analyses found within these literatures and neglects some discussions that fall outside them. Note that some of our own prior work can be said to fall within them. For more extensive reviews, see Hall (1999, 2001).

3. An alternative approach to neo-corporatism, closer to our own, which puts less emphasis on the trade union movement and more on the organization of business was also developed by Katzenstein (1985a, 1985b) among others (Offe 1981).

4. One of the pioneering works that some will want to compare is Albert (1993), who develops a contrast between the models of the Rhine and America that parallels ours in some respects. Other valuable efforts to identify varieties of capitalism that have influenced us include Hollingsworth and Boyer (1997), Crouch and Streeck (1997b), and Whitley (1999).

5. There are a few notable exceptions that influence our analysis, including the work of Scharpf (1987, 1997a) and Przeworski and Wallerstein (1982).

6. In other works by the contributors to this volume, 'organized market economy' is some times used as a term synonymous with 'coordinated market economy'. Although all of the economies we discuss are 'coordinated' in the general sense of the term, by markets if not by other institutions, the term reflects the prominence of strategic interaction and hence of coordination in the game-theoretic sense in CMEs.

7. Although we do not emphasize it here, this is not meant to deny the observation of Granovetter (1985) and others that market relations are usually underpinned by per-sonal relationships of familiarity and trust.

8. This point applies with particular force to market relationships in which one or more of the participants has substantially more market power than the others, as in cases of oligopoly, oligopsony, and the relations found in some supplier chains. We are not argu-ing that all markets in LMEs are perfectly competitive.

9. Note that, from time to time, we refer loosely to the 'institutions' or 'organization' of the political economy to refer to both the organizations and institutions found within it.

10. One political economist who has consistently drawn attention to the importance of deliberation is Sabel (1992, 1994) and the issue is now the subject of a growing game-theoretic literature (see Elster 1998).

11. Here we depart from some of our own previous formulations as well (cf. Hall 1986; Soskice 1990b).

12. Culpepper documents this problem and explores some solutions to it in this volume and Culpepper (1998).

13. Williamson (1985) himself acknowledges the presence of institutionalized relationships extending beyond markets or hierarchies, albeit without characterizing them precisely as we do here.

14. At the sectoral or regional level, of course, large firms may be able to exercise substantial influence over the development of these institutions, as Hancké shows in this volume (see also Hancké forthcoming).

15. It is possible to apply the general analytical framework of this volume to variations at the regional or sectoral level, as the chapter by Hancké does in some respects. From the per-spective of this volume, institutional variation at the regional or sectoral level provides an additional layer of support for particular types of coordination and one that enhances a nation's capacity to support a range of corporate strategies and production regimes.

16. For examples in one sphere, see the essay by Estevez-Abe, Iversen, and Soskice in this volume.

17. Conversely, two institutions can be said to be 'substitutable' if the absence or ineffi-ciency of one increases the returns to using the other. Note that we refer to total returns, leaving aside the question of to whom they accrue, which is a matter of property rights, and we define efficiency as the net returns to the use of an institution given its costs.

18. Of course, there are limits to the institutional isomorphism that can be expected across spheres of the economy. Although efficiency considerations may press in this direc-tion, the presence of functional equivalents for particular arrangements will limit the institutional homology even across similar types of political economies, and the impor-tance to institutional development of historical processes driven by considerations other than efficiency will limit the number of complementarities found in any economy.

19. The employment protection index developed by Estevez-Abe, Iversen, and Sockice in their chapter for this volume is a composite measure of the relative stringency of leg-islation or collective agreements dealing with hiring and firing, the level of restraint

embedded in collective dismissal rules, and the extent of firm-level employment protection. Stock market capitalization is the market value of listed domestic companies as a percentage of GDP.

20. Luxembourg and Iceland have been omitted from this list because of their small size and Mexico because it is still a developing nation.

21. The Gini Index used in Fig. 6.3.2 is a standard measure for income inequality, measured here as post-tax, post-transfer income, reported in the Luxembourg Income Study for the mid- to late 1980s. Full-time equivalent employment is reported as a percentage of potential employment and measured as the total number of hours worked per year divided by full-time equivalent hours per person (37.5 hours at 50 weeks) times the working-age population. It is reported for the latest available of 1993 or 1994.

22. In previous decades, the German banks were also important contributors to such networks by virtue of their control over large numbers of shares in industrial firms (Hall 1986: ch. 9). In recent years, the role of the large commercial banks has declined, as they divest themselves of many holdings (Griffin 2000).

23. 'Hold up' is Williamson's (1985) term for the withdrawal of active cooperation to back up demands.

24. Compared to general skills that can be used in many settings, industry-specific skills normally have value only when used within a single industry and firm-specific skills only in employment within that firm.

25. Firms in LMEs tend to rely on bond and equity markets for external finance more heavily than those in CMEs. However, bank lending in such economies also privileges publicly accessible, balance-sheet criteria, since banks find it difficult to monitor the less-obvious dimensions of corporate progress in an environment that lacks the close-knit corporate networks conveying such information in CMEs. Intense monitoring by a loan officer is feasible only when small sums are involved, since it exposes the bank to problems of moral hazard that are especially acute in countries where officers can take advantage of fluid labor markets to move elsewhere.

26. Note that we avoid a distinction often drawn between countries in which firms can raise 'long-term' capital versus those in which only 'short-term' capital is available because this distinction is rarely meaningful. Many companies in LMEs with established market reputations can raise capital for projects promising revenues only in the medium to long term, and firms often finance the bulk of their activities from retained earnings. Of more relevance are the rules governing hostile takeovers, whose prospect can induce firms to pay more attention to corporate earnings and the price of their shares.

27. Partly for this reason, the market valuation of firms in LMEs often depends more heavily on the reputation of its CEO than it does in CMEs.

28. We use the term 'globalization' in this chapter to refer to the developments that have made it easier for companies to locate operations abroad, including the liberalization of trade, the deregulation and expansion of international financial markets, the new accessibility and expansion of markets in what was the communist world, and declining transportation or communication costs.

29. Note that we are not claiming all types of non-market institutions contribute to the efficiency of the economy. We have identified some specific types of inter- and intra-firm relations and supporting institutions that we associate with effective firm performance. There are other 'non-market' institutions in many economies that simply generate economic rents or detract from economic efficiency. The point is to distinguish among them and not to label all 'non-market' institutions efficient or inefficient.

30. Note that this observation corresponds to the predictions of Frieden and Rogowski (1996) that class conflict is more likely in economies where switchable assets predominate and sectoral conflict characterized by cross-class coalitions more likely in economies where asset specificity is high. However, because firms and workers share some interests in all economies, we do not exclude the possibility that some cross-class coalitions will also be formed in liberal market economies, as Swenson (1997) suggests.

31. We use 'deregulation' as a convenient shorthand to refer to policies that remove regulations limiting competition, expand the role of markets in the allocation of resources, or Sharpen market incentives in the economy. Of course, we recognize that all deregulation is implicitly a form of reregulation (Vogel 1996).

32. We predict some, if more limited, deregulation in CMEs because, alongside non-market institutions, they also use market mechanisms whose operation can be improved by a measured amount of deregulation.

33. The effects of trade integration seem to have fallen, less substantially on the differences between CMEs and LMEs, and more heavily on practices of state intervention of that sort once prominent in France and the developing world, as governments found that *dirigiste* policies cannot ensure competitiveness on international markets (cf. Hall 1990; Ziegler 1997; McArthur and Scott 1969).

References

Albert, Michel. 1993. *Capitalism against Capitalism*. London: Whurr.

Alvarez, R. Michael, Geoffrey Garret, and Peter Lange. 1991. "Government Partisanship, Labor Organization, and Macroeconomic Performance." *American Political Science Review* 85 (June): 539–56.

Aoki, Masahiko. 1994. "The Japanese Firm as a System of Attributes: A Survey and Research Agenda." In *The Japanese Firm: Sources of Competitive Strength*, ed. Masahiko Aoki and Ronald Dore. Oxford: Clarendon Press: 11–40.

Bates, Robert. 1997. *Open-Economy Politics: The Political Economy of the World Coffee Trade*. Princeton: Princeton University Press.

Berger, Suzanne, ed. 1981. *Organizing Interests in Western Europe: Pluralism, Corporatism, and the Transformation of Politics*. Cambridge: Cambridge University Press.

_____ and Ronald Dore, eds. 1996. *National Diversity and Global Capitalism*. Ithaca, NY: Cornell University Press.

Borrus, Michael and John Zysman. 1997. "Wintelism and the Changing Terms of Global Competition: Prototype of the Future?" BRIE Working Paper 96B (February). Berkeley, Calif.: BRIE.

Boyer, Robert. 1990. *The Regulation School: A Critical Introduction*. New York: Columbia University Press.

_____. 1996. "The Convergence Hypothesis Revisited: Globalization but Still the Century of Nations?" In *National Diversity and Global Capitalism*, ed. Suzanne Berger and Ronald Dore. Ithaca, NY: Cornell University Press: 29–59.

_____ and Daniel Drache, eds. 1996. *States against Markets*. New York: Routledge.

Caballero, R. and M. Hamour. 1998. "The Macroeconomics of Specificity." *Journal of Political Economy* 106 (August): 724–67.

Calmfors, Lars, and John Driffill. 1988. "Centralisation of Wage Bargaining and Macroeconomic Performance." *Economic Policy* 6 (April): 13–61.

Calvert, R. 1995. "The Rational Choice Theory of Social Institutions: Cooperation, Coordination, and Communication." In *Modern Political Economy*, ed. J. Banks and E. Hanushek. New York: Cambridge University Press: 216–67.

Cameron, David R. 1984. "Social Democracy, Corporatism, Labor Quiescence and the Representation of Economic Interest in Advanced Capitalist Society." In *Order and Conflict in Contemporary Capitalism: Studies in the Political Economy of Western European Nations*, ed. John H. Goldthorpe. New York: Oxford University Press: 143–78.

Campbell, John L., Rogers Hollingsworth, and Leon Lindberg. 1991. *Governance of the American Economy*. New York: Cambridge University Press.

Casper, Steven. 1997. "Reconfiguring Institutions: The Political Economy of Legal Development in Germany and the United States." Ph.D. dissertation, Cornell University, Ithaca, NY.

Chandler, Alfred. 1974. *The Visible Hand*. Cambridge, Mass.: Harvard University Press.

_____ and Harold Daems, eds. 1980. *Managerial Hierarchies: Comparative Perspectives on the Rise of the Modern Corporation*. Cambridge, Mass.: Harvard University Press.

Cohen, Elie. 1996. *La Tentation hexagonale*. Paris: Fayard.

Cohen, Stephen. 1997. *Modern Capitalist Planning*. Berkeley and Los Angeles: University of California Press.

Cox, Andrew. 1986. *The State, Finance and Industry*. Brighton: Wheatsheaf.

Crouch, Colin, and Wolfgang Streeck, eds. 1997. *Political Economy of Modern Capitalism: Mapping Convergence and Diversity*. London: Sage.

Culpepper, Pepper D. 1998. "Rethinking Reform: The Politics of Decentralized Cooperation in France and Germany." Ph.D. dissertation, Harvard University.

_____ and David Finegold, eds. 1999. *The German Skills Machine*. Oxford: Berghahn.

Deiniger, Klaus, and Lyn Squire. 1996. "Measuring Income Inequality: A New DataBase." Development Discussion Paper No. 537, Harvard Institute for International Development.

DiMaggio, Paul, and Walter Powell. 1991. "Introduction." In *The New Institutionalism in Organizational Analysis*. Chicago: University of Chicago Press: 1–40.

Dore, Ronald. 1986. *Flexible Rigidities*. Stanford, Calif.: Stanford University Press.

Dosi, Giovanni, C. Freeman, R. Nelson, G. Silverberg, and L. Soete. 1988. *Technical Change and Economic Theory*. London: Pinter.

Ebbinghaus, Bernhard, and Jelle Visser. 2000. *Trade Unions in Western Europe since 1945*. London: Macmillan.

Edquist, Charles. 1997. *Systems of Innovation*. London: Pinter.

Eichengreen, Barry. 1997. "Institutions and Economic Growth after World War II." In *Economic Growth in Europe since 1945*, ed. Nicholas Crafts and Gianni Toniolo. Cambridge: Cambridge University Press: 38–72.

Ellis, James W. 1998. "Voting for Markets or Marketing for Votes: The Politics of Neo-Liberal Economic Reform." Ph.D. dissertation, Department of Government, Harvard University.

Elster, Jon, ed. 1998. *Deliberative Democracy*. New York: Cambridge University Press.

Estrin, Saul, and Peter Holmes. 1983. *French Planning in Theory and Practice*. London: Allen & Unwin.

Fehn, Rainer. 1998. "Capital Market Imperfections, Greater Volatilities and Rising Unemployment: Does Venture Capital Help?" Working Paper, Baerische Julius-Maximillians-Universität Wurtzbürg.

Finegold, David, and David Soskice. 1988. "The Failure of Training in Britain: Analysis and Prescription." *Oxford Review of Economic Policy* 4(3): 21–53.

Frieden, Jeffry, and Ronald Rogowski. 1996. "The Impact of the International Economy on National Policies: An Analytical Overview." In *Internationalization and Domestic Politics*, ed. Robert Keohane and Helen Milner. New York: Cambridge University Press: 25–47.

Friedman, Thomas. 1999. *The Lexus and the Olive Tree*. New York: Farrar, Strauss, and Giroux.

Fudenberg, Drew, and Eric Maskin. 1986. "The Folk Theorem in Repeated Games with Discounting and Incomplete Information." *Econometrica* 54(May): 533–54.

Golden, Miriam. 1993. "The Dynamics of Trade Unionism and National Economic Performance." *American Political Science Review* 87(June): 439–54.

_____, Lange, Peter, and Wallerstein, Michael. 1997. "Union Centralization among Advanced Industrial Societies: An Empirical Study." Dataset available at http://www.shelley.sscnet.ucla.edu/data.

Goldthorpe, John H., ed. 1984. *Order and Conflict in Contemporary Capitalism*. New York: Oxford University Press.

Granovetter, Mark. 1985. "Economic Action and Social Structures: The Problem of Embeddedness." *American Journal of Sociology* 91(3): 482–510.

Graubard, Stephen. 1964. *A New Europe?* Boston: Beacon Press.

Griffin, John. 2000. "Making Money Talk: A New Bank–Firm Relationship in German Banking?" Paper presented to the Annual Conference of the Society for the Advancement of Socio-economics, London, July.

Hall, Peter A. 1986. *Governing the Economy: The Politics of State Intervention in Britain and France*. New York: Oxford University Press.

_____. 1990. "The State and the Market." In *Developments in French Politics*, ed. Peter A. Hall, Jack Hayward, and Howard Machin. London: Macmillan: 171–87.

_____. 1999. "The Political Economy of Europe in an Era of Interdependence." In *Continuity and Change in Contemporary Capitalism*, ed. Herbert Kitschelt et al. Cambridge: Cambridge University Press: 135–63.

_____. 2001. "The Evolution of Economic Policy in the European Union." In *From Nation-State to European Union*, ed. Anand Menon and Vinvent Wright. Oxford: Oxford University Press: 214–45.

_____ and Robert Franzese, Jr. 1998. "Mixed Signals: Central Bank Independence, Coordinated Wage Bargaining, and European Monetary Union." *International Organization* 52(Summer): 502–36.

Herrigel, Gary. 1996. *Industrial Constructions: The Sources of German Industrial Power*. Cambridge: Cambridge University Press.

Hollingsworth, J. Rogers, Philippe C. Schmitter, and Wolfgang Streeck, eds. 1994. *Governing Capitalist Economies*. New York: Oxford University Press.

Hollingsworth, J. Rogers, and Robert Boyer, eds. 1997. *Contemporary Capitalism: The Embeddedness of Institutions*. Cambridge: Cambridge University Press.

Jaikumar, R. 1986. "Postindustrial Manufacturing." *Harvard Business Review* (November–December): 69–76.

Johnson, Chalmers. 1982. *MITI and the Japanese Miracle: The Growth of Industrial Policy 1925–1975*. Stanford, Calif.: Stanford University Press.

Katzenstein, Peter J. 1978. "Conclusion: Domestic Sources and Strategies of Foreign Economic Policy." In *Between Power and Plenty: Foreign Economic Policies of Advanced Industrial States*, ed. Peter J. Katzenstein. Madison: University of Wisconsin Press: 295–336.

_____. 1985a. *Corporatism and Change*. Ithaca, NY: Cornell University Press.

_____. 1985b. *Small States in World Markets*. Ithaca, NY: Cornell University Press.

Keohane, Robert and Helen V. Milner, eds. 1996. *Internationalization and Domestic Politics*. New York: Cambridge University Press.

Kerr, Clark, John Dunlop, Frederick Harbison, and Charles Myers. 1960. *Industrialism and Industrial Man*. Cambridge, Mass: Harvard University Press.

King, Desmond and Stewart Wood. 1999. "The Political Economy of Neoliberalism: Britain and the United States in the 1980s." In *Continuity and Change in Contemporary Capitalism*, ed. Herbert Kitschelt, Peter Lange, Gary Marks, and John D. Stephens. Cambridge: Cambridge University Press: 371–97.

Knetter, M. 1989. "Price Discrimination by US and German Exporters." *American Economic Review* 79(1): 198–210.

Knight, Jack. 1992. *Institutions and Social Conflict*. New York: Cambridge University Press.

Kreps, David. 1990. "Corporate Culture and Economic Theory." In *Perspectives on Positive Political Economy*, ed. James E. Alt and Kenneth A. Shepsle. New York: Cambridge University Press: 90–143.

Lange, Peter, Michael Wallerstein, and Miriam Golden. 1995. "The End of Corporatism? Wage Setting in the Nordic and Germanic Countries." In *Workers of Nations: Industrial Relations in a Global Economy*, ed. Sanford M. Jacoby. Oxford: Oxford University Press: 101–26.

Lazonick, William. 1991. *Business Organization and the Myth of the Market Economy*. Cambridge: Cambridge University Press.

McArthur, John, and Bruce Scott. 1969. *Industrial Planning in France*. Boston: Harvard Business School.

March, James G. and Johan P. Olsen. 1989. *Rediscovering Institutions: The Organizational Basis of Politics*. New York: Free Press.

Milgrom, Paul, and John Roberts. 1990. "The Economics of Modern Manufacturing: Technology, Strategy and Organization." *American Economic Review* 80: 511–28.

_____. 1992. *Economics, Organization and Management*. Englewood Cliffs, NJ: Prentice Hall.

_____. 1995. "Complementarities, Industrial Strategy, Structure and Change in Manufacturing." *Journal of Accounting and Economics* 19: 179–208.

Nelson, Richard R., ed. 1993. *National Innovation Systems*. New York: Oxford University Press.

Nordlinger, Eric. 1981. *On the Autonomy of the Democratic State*. Cambridge, Mass.: Harvard University Press.

North, Douglass C. 1990. *Institutions, Institutional Change and Economic Performance*. New York: Cambridge University Press.

OECD. 1996. *OECD Economies at a Glance: Structural Indicators*. Paris: OECD.

Offe, Claus. 1981. "The Attribution of Public Status to Interest Groups: Observations on the West German Case." In *Organizing Interests in Western Europe*, ed. Suzanne Berger. Cambridge: Cambridge University Press.

Olson, Mancur. 1965. *The Logic of Collective Action: Public Goods and the Theory of Groups*. Cambridge, Mass.: Harvard University Press.

Ostrom, Elior, 1990. *Governing the Commons: The Evolution of Institutions for Collective Action*. New York: Cambridge University Press.

Piore, Michael, and Charles Sabel. 1984. *The Second Industrial Divide*. New York: Basic Books.

Pizzorno, Alessandro. 1978. "Political Exchange and Collective Identity in Industrial Conflict.' In *The Resurgence of Class Conflict in Western Europe*, vol. i, ed. Colin Crouch and Alessandro Pizzorno. London: Macmillan: 177–98.

Przeworski, Adam, and Michael Wallerstein. 1982. "The Structure of Class Conflict in Democratic Capitalist Societies." *American Political Science Review* 76(2): 215–38.

Regini, Marino. 1984. "The Conditions for Political Exchange: How Concertation Emerged and Collapsed in Britain and Italy." In *Order and Conflict in Contemporary Capitalism: Studies in the Political Economy of Western European Nations*, ed. J. H. Goldthorpe. New York: Oxford University Press: 124–42.

Rhodes, Martin. 1997. "Globalisation, Labour Markets and Welfare States: A Future of 'Competitive Corporatism'?" In *The Future of European Welfare*, ed. Martin Rhodes and Yves Meny. London: Macmillan.

Rodrik, Dani. 1997. *Has Globalization Gone too Far?* Washington: Institute for International Economics.

Sabel, Charles F. 1992. "Studied Trust: Building New Forms of Cooperation in a Volatile Economy." In *Industrial Districts and Local Economic Reorganization*, ed. Frank Pyke and Werner Sengenberger. Geneva: International Institute for Labor Studies: 215–50.

_____. 1994. "Learning by Monitoring: The Institutions of Economic Development." In *The Handbook of Economic Sociology*, ed. Neil Smelser and Richard Swedberg. Princeton: Princeton University Press.

Sacks, Paul M. 1980. "State Structure and the Asymmetrical Society." *Comparative Politics* (April): 349–76.

Scharpf, Fritz W. 1987. "Game-Theoretical Interpretations of Inflation and Unemployment in Western Europe." *Journal of Public Policy* 7(3): 227–57.

_____. 1991. *Crisis and Choice in European Social Democracy*. Ithaca, NY: Cornell University Press.

_____. 1997. *Games Real Actors Play: Actor-Centered Institutionalism in Policy Research.* Boulder, Colo.: Westview Press.

Schmitter, Philippe, and Gerhard Lehmbruch, eds. 1979. *Trends toward Corporatist Intermediation*. Beverly Hills, Calif.: Sage.

Schumpeter, Joseph. 1950. *Capitalism, Socialism and Democracy*. 3rd edn. New York: Harper.

Shonfield, Andrew. 1965. *Modern Capitalism*. New York: Oxford University Press.

Skocpol, Theda, and Edwin Amenta. 1985. "Did Capitalists Shape Social Security?" *American Sociological Review* 50(4): 572–5.

Sorge, Arndt, and Michael Warner. 1986. *Comparative Factory Organization*. Aldershot: Gower.

Soskice, David. 1990a. "Wage Determination: The Changing Role of Institutions in Advanced Industrialized Countries." *Oxford Review of Economic Policy* 6(4): 36–61.

_____.1990b. "Reinterpreting Corporatism and Explaining Unemployment: Coordinated and Non-coordinated Market Economies." In *Labour Relations and Economic Performance*, ed. Renato Brunetta and Carlo Dell'Aringa. Proceedings of a conference held by the International Economics Association in Venice, Italy. Vol. 95. London: Macmillan: 170–214.

_____. 1997. "German Technology Policy, Innovation, and National Institutional Frameworks." *Industry and Innovation* 4(1): 75–96.

Story, Jonathan, and Ingo Walter. 1997. *Political Economy of Financial Integration in Europe*. Manchester: Manchester University Press.

Streeck, Wolfgang. 1992. *Social Institutions and Economic Performance: Studies on Industrial Relations in Advanced European Capitalist Countries*. London: Sage.

_____. 1994. "Pay Restraint without Incomes Policy: Institutionalized Monetarism and Industrial Unionism in Germany?" In *The Return of Incomes Policy*, ed. Ronald Dore, Robert Boyer, and Zoë Mars. London: Pinter: 118–40.

_____ and Philip Schmitter, eds. 1986. *Private Interest Government: Beyond Market and State*. Beverly Hills, Calif.: Sage.

Swenson, Peter. 1991. "Bringing Capital Back in, or Social Democracy Reconsidered: Employer Power, Cross-class Alliances, and Centralization of Industrial Relations in Denmark and Sweden." *World Politics* 43(July): 513–44.

_____. 1997. "Arranged Alliance: Business Interests in the New Deal." *Politics and Society* 25(March): 66–116.

Swidler, Ann. 1986. "Culture in Action: Symbols and Strategies." *American Sociological Review* 51(2): 273–86.

Teece, David, and Gary Pisano. 1998. "The Dynamic Capabilities of Firms." In *Technology, Organization and Competitiveness*, ed. Giovanni Dosi, David J. Teece, and Josef Chytry. Oxford: Oxford University Press: 193–212.

Thelen, Kathleen. 1991. *Union of Parts: Labor Politics in Postwar Germany*. Ithaca, NY: Cornell University Press.

_____. 2000. "Why German Employers Cannot Bring Themselves to Abandon the German Mode." In *Unions, Employers and Central Banks*, ed. Torben Iversen, Jonas Pontusson, and David Soskice. New York: Cambridge University Press.

Visser, Jelle. 1996. "Unionization Trends Revisited." Unpublished paper, University of Amsterdam.

Vitols, Sigurt, Steven Casper, David Soskice, and Stephen Woolcock. 1997. *Corporate Governance in Large British and German Companies: Comparative Institutional Advantage or Competing for Best Practice*. London: Anglo German Foundation.

Vogel, Steven. 1996. *Freer Markets, More Rules*. Ithaca, NY: Cornell University Press.

Wade, Robert. 1996. "Globalization and its Limits: Reports of the Death of the National Economy are Greatly Exaggerated." In *National Diversity and Global Capitalism*, ed. Suzanne Berger and Ronald Dore. Ithaca, NY: Cornell University Press: 60–88.

Whitley, Richard. 1999. *Divergent Capitalisms: The Social Structuring and Change of Business Systems*. Oxford: Oxford University Press.

Williamson, Oliver. 1975. *Markets and Hierarchies*. New York: Free Press.

_____. 1985. The Economic Institutions of Capitalism: Firms, Markets, Relational Contracting. New York: Free Press.

Wood, Stewart. 1997. "Capitalist Constitutions: Supply-Side Reforms in Britain and West-Germany 1960–1990." Ph. D. dissertation, Department of Government, Harvard University.

Ziegler, J. Nicholas. 1997. *Governing Ideas: Strategies for Innovation in France and Germany*. Ithaca, NY: Cornell University Press.

Zysman, John. 1983. *Governments, Markets, and Growth: Financial systems and the Politics of Industrial Change*. Ithaca, NY: Cornell University Press.

Part II

Contemporary Debates:
Three Types of Market Reform

1

Market Reform in Advanced Industrial Countries

Thus far we have come through a series of contending perspectives or paradigms that differ on how precisely markets are institutions and how individuals, societies, and governments interact in the forming and functioning of markets. Now we turn to a series of contemporary issues to further illustrate how some of these theoretical debates can be applied to the practice of political economy. Even in rich democracies, where the market tradition is well established, thickly institutionalized, and underpinned by the rule of law, debate persists on how exactly markets should be structured to achieve efficient and desired outcomes. In advanced countries, the public policy discourse has tended to focus on the degree of government involvement in economic activity, and policy battles have centered on reforms to reduce or enlarge the extent and nature of that role.

For about twenty years after the Second World War, the advanced industrialized countries enjoyed a period—often called the "golden age of capitalism"—in which the Keynesian consensus succeeded in generating a period of rapid growth with high employment and low inflation.[1] Many of these countries moved at the same time to adopt a welfare state model of state social service provision.[2] The postwar period through the mid-1970s thus tended, for the most part, to be an era of big government in the rich democracies of the United States and Europe, where the state played numerous roles in the economy, ranging from regulator to actual producer. But, as discussed earlier with respect to the liberal paradigm, free market liberalism made a comeback, both intellectually and in terms of policy impact, in the late 1970s and on through the remainder of the twentieth century. The Reagan–Thatcher revolution of the 1980s, in particular, was animated by a commitment to reducing and limiting the roles of government in the economy as much as possible. This free market reform agenda of the 1980s was driven philosophically by the liberal mantra of the superiority of individualism to collectivism. This conservative revolution was in many ways a reaction to the social democratic welfare states that had developed in Europe since the end of the Second World War, matched to some extent by Lyndon B. Johnson's "Great Society" in the United States.

Arthur Seldon was one of the leading thinkers behind the reversing of the tide from what he (following his mentor Friedrich Hayek) called collectivism to capitalism. Seldon was a cofounding president of the Institute of Economic Affairs, a conservative think tank based in London that was central to Margaret Thatcher's program of deregulation, liberalization, and privatization in the United Kingdom. His ideas hew closely to the economic liberal views of **Friedrich Hayek** and **Milton Friedman,** presented earlier in this volume. All three of them understand that markets are complex institutions, and all of them agree that the government must play a role in facilitating economic activity, particularly in ensuring the rule of law. Yet free market liberals see market reform essentially as a negative exercise: the process of shrinking government and limiting its role in markets and economic activity. Thus Thatcherism in the United Kingdom, matched by Reaganomics in the United States, emphasized scaling back the size of the public sector; freeing markets as much as possible through deregulation; privatizing industries, removing the state as a producer; opposing trade unions by use of executive privilege; lowering direct (income) tax, often matched by higher indirect taxation (e.g., sales tax or the infamous poll tax); and leveling general animosity toward welfare state programs such as nationalized health care and other elements of collective social insurance.

In the short selection presented here, Seldon covers much of this ground. He criticizes, in particular, the welfare state and the mentality that "free services" should be offered to the poor. He advocates a pruning of the public sector so that things are marketized where they can be; that is, even though the line between private and public goods is not always sharp, if prices can be charged they should be, and taxes should be levied for government-provided public goods only where pricing is impractical. Seldon also extols the virtues of private enterprise; he makes the case that competition in the private sector should always be allowed to flourish and that specific enterprises must not be protected against competition. He echoes Milton Friedman on the point that government failure in a statist or mixed economy is more a reality than market failure in a capitalist economy.

Steven Vogel articulates the market-institutional counterpoint to the liberal perspective on the relationship between the state and markets. He argues that "marketizing" reforms in advanced industrialized countries should be seen as a positive, creative process that entails the development and transformation of market institutions rather than perceived as a negative process of stripping away government regulation. Vogel builds on **Karl Polanyi's** work in tackling the notion that markets are free or perfect and hence challenges the prevailing liberal discourse on the relationship between markets and governments. The central element of Vogel's argument is the step away from the conventional regulation–competition dichotomy that dominates most debates about market reforms. He points out that liberalization of markets to increase competition actually requires reregulation rather than deregulation: in a phrase, freer markets require more rules.[3] Indeed, some of the boldest deregulation programs, including those of the Thatcher era, have been accompanied by a proliferation of rules and regulatory agencies.

The **Peter Hall and David Soskice** framework presented in the preceding section sheds more light on deregulation in a comparative context. They explicitly discuss movements toward regulatory reform in the context of globalization. They anticipate one dynamic response to globalization in liberal market economies (LMEs)—where firms will pressure governments for more deregulation to enhance their flexibility in coordinating through markets—and another in coordinated market economies (CMEs)—where firms and governments should be more resistant to deregulatory pressures because they challenge their comparative institutional advantage. Their framework predicts a bifurcated response to globalization—widespread deregulation in LMEs and limited change in CMEs—and they marshal evidence to claim that this does in fact represent the reality of deregulation efforts in advanced industrial countries.[4]

Notes

1. See p. 89, fn. 3 for a description of Keynesianism.
2. Although it is not covered explicitly in this volume, aside from a brief mention in the **Peter Hall and David Soskice** selection, the literature on the welfare state is distinguished and varied. For further reference on contemporary scholarship on the varieties of political economy of the welfare state, see in particular Gosta Esping-Andersen, *The Three Worlds of Welfare Capitalism* (Princeton: Princeton University Press, 1990); Torben Iversen, *Capitalism, Democracy, and Welfare* (Cambridge: Cambridge University Press, 2005); Isabela Mares, *The Politics of Social Risk: Business and Welfare State Development* (Cambridge: Cambridge University Press, 2001); Paul Pierson, ed., *The New Politics of the Welfare State* (Oxford: Oxford University Press, 2001); and Harold Wilensky, *Rich Democracies: Political Economy, Public Policy, and Performance* (Berkeley: University of California Press, 2002).
3. See also Steven Vogel, *Freer Markets, More Rules: Regulatory Reform in Advanced Industrial Countries* (Ithaca: Cornell University Press, 1996).
4. Peter A. Hall and David Soskice, this volume, pp. 314–318.

Arthur Seldon,
The Virtues of Capitalism (1980)*

Chapter 5: Reversing the Tide

Some years ago, until the middle 1960s, it would have been possible to speak of the tide of collectivisation as almost irresistible. Since then, sobering experience of the Great Society in the USA, which its advocates thought would solve social problems by increasing welfare bureaucracies armed with tax money, police powers and government authority; further evidence in Britain of the ineffectiveness of government in social engineering; the results in the industrial countries of Europe of liberating human energies by reducing barriers to exchange; the prodigious success of the market oases of Asia: all these developments have gradually but fundamentally changed the attitudes of thinkers in diverse schools and of politicians in all parties to the long repeated but never demonstrated claims for state collectivism. The move of intellectuals from the state to the market, visionary or belated, is historically remarkable. Not least there has been increasing rebellion in all social classes in almost all countries against governments that claim more taxes but fail to provide acceptable benefits in return.

Intellectual Reaction

The intellectual reaction against the state has been strongest in the USA. In Britain, the home of much that has gone wrong since the war and now of the hope that it may go right, there has been an unprecedented intellectual conversion among the leaders of the Conservative Party. But many Conservatives, some senior and influential, remain paternalists or collectivists and look nostalgically to the state to preserve a "sense of community." The senior Liberal politician has re-affirmed the classical liberal place of the market in economic policy,[1] though the official party leader remains a Beveridge type paternalist. Not least, a former Labour Chancellor of the Exchequer has also put a return to the market as the centre-piece of his economic policy for a new alignment of non-socialist politicians.[2]

Several more junior Labour thinkers have been vividly sensing that the ordinary people are reacting against the state. Although, not unnaturally, reaffirming their "socialist" principles, they are using a new language—or a language they had not

* From: *The Virtues of Capitalism*. Copyright © 1980 Institute of Economic Affairs. (pp. 40–49) Reprinted by permission of the Institute of Economic Affairs.

used before their party polled a smaller percentage of votes (28 per cent) than at any time since 1931. A former Minister of Education said:

> modern democratic socialism must oppose concentrations of economic and political power whether in private or State hands. It must seek to disperse power. ...[3]

A former Minister of Transport has said:

> What is wrong with choice and diversity? Why should enterprise and opportunity be dirty words? Many people see social progress as a higher net income and more money to spend on themselves.[4]

All three Party groups are, in effect, revealing the conviction that experience has at last taught them that state economy has failed and that the hope of the future lies with a large element of private enterprise despite its known defects. All three parties are thus experiencing agonising intellectual reappraisal. The post-war all-party consensus on state compassion and beneficence is increasingly contested by a classical liberal reaction against over centralised government.

This intellectual/philosophic conversion may both reflect and confirm the public's rejection of the state, of which it has had 30 post-war years' experience. It has become disillusioned with big government, antipathetic to bureaucracy, resentful of high taxation, suspicious of monopoly whether "public" or private, in industry or among trade unions.

The Two Nations: Private Affluence, Public Squalor

All this is to be expected. It could hardly have been supposed that people accustomed to rising standards, personal service and choice in everyday personal purchases or household budgeting would have continued much longer to tolerate deteriorating standards, impersonal service and denial of choice in government-supplied monopoly transport, fuel, education, medicine, housing and a host of smaller services.

The intellectual tide has turned. Public opinion is not far behind. But the politicians lag behind both. Many seem to wait until their followers are out in front. What is now required to restore in the public mind support for the principles of competitive private enterprise sufficiently to give it the prospect of showing what it can do? There are five main requirements:

1. education—public, academic, political, industrial;
2. the removal of poverty;
3. pruning the public sector;
4. competition in the private sector;
5. new entrepreneurs.

1. Education

(a) The general public in the post-war Western world has been misled about social democracy, the welfare state, the alleged beneficence of government. It is still told by a former Labour Prime Minister that it is essential for government to supply welfare, otherwise the social fabric and family life will fail.

The two massive errors in this conventional view hardly require much emphasis. First, most people, even with middling and lower incomes, are paying in taxes, direct or indirect, more or less what they receive in social benefits. They do not therefore have to buy education, medical care (apart from public health), housing or other "social" benefits from the state.

The notion that state welfare services maintain the family is, moreover, the opposite of the truth. Family life has been weakened because the state has usurped the role of parents as providers. Children sense that their parents have little influence in their education, their health care, their homes, their national insurance when unemployed or sick and so on. Little wonder the bonds of the family have weakened.

Neither do transport, fuel, postal services, libraries, sports amenities, abattoirs, car-parking, home helps, employment agencies or many other goods and services have to be supplied by government, central or local. Public complaints about deteriorating standards could be shown to be based largely on a lack of consumer control because of the absence of choice between competing suppliers.

The costs of supplying services now supplied by government would often be lower in private enterprise, as they are in countries overseas. Office staff in Britain are being trained by private colleges at one-third to one-half the cost of government Further Education Colleges.

(b) Academics and teachers now in their 40s and 50s were taught 20–30 years ago by early post-war graduates who absorbed the ruling Beveridge–Bevan–Keynes consensus. They find it difficult to adapt their thinking to the adverse experience of post-war state economy, to the more recent developments among younger academics such as the "economics of politics" school who examine "government failure" as well as "market failure," or to the change in aspirations of the new generations with higher real incomes who want better services than the state aims (but fails) to supply equally out of taxes.

It seems doubtful whether most teachers or preachers in their 40s and 50s will change. They are now increasingly lagging behind events, new teaching and public sentiment and the younger generation whose world confounds their faith in the state.

(c) Many politicians of all parties, Conservative and Liberal as well as Labour, are inclined to think there is little wrong with state economy as long as *they* run it. Many Conservatives in Britain resist their Government's effort to "roll back the state." They have yet to acknowledge the massive failure of government to disentangle itself from, not least, rent control and the housing market as rising incomes make the state an increasingly embarrassing encumbrance.

(d) Industrialists accustomed or tempted to seek assistance from government naturally see the advantages but overlook the risks of gradually increasing political influence. Protected industrialists are often critical of "market forces" (that is, the men and women who are their customers). The more adventurous entrepreneurs recognize that their safety, as well as their long-term prosperity, lies in their ability to adapt themselves to changing markets. Change is uncomfortable, but political influence can be death to the independence of private enterprise. It can now rise from its knees before its detractors but must drop its crutches of political protection to regain its moral stature with public opinion. Industrial organizations could alert entrepreneurs to these dangers.

2. Removal of Poverty

The most stubborn objection to the restoration of private enterprise in services and industries now dominated by government is that some people could not pay market prices. The remedy is not "free" services but to top up low incomes so that all can pay. This task has not yet been faced or solved, even by governments that value private enterprise.

The ultimate solution lies in a form of reverse (or negative) income tax and a structure of vouchers.

3. Pruning the Public Sector

When poverty has been removed it will be easier to prune the public sector of the services that could be farmed out or returned to private enterprise. They include parts of the transport and fuel industries, much of education, medical care, all of housing, many welfare services and a wide range of local authority activities misdescribed as "public services." Where such services are supplied or controlled by government, their claim to be competently managed and sensitive to consumer preferences would be securely based only where they are not protected from competing private enterprise in a free market. Even where very large economies of scale limit enterprises to a few, possibly to two or three in small countries, general government surveillance combined with private commercially-motivated management may give better results than direct government administration of day-to-day activities. Government is better confined to *government*—laying down the framework of general law, but not detailed rules—for private enterprise; it is rarely better than private enterprise in running competitive business, especially in international markets. Even if it were as efficient as private enterprise, its Achilles' Heel is its political inability to disengage itself from involvement when technical or social change renders it superfluous. Private enterprise in a market has to change gear, accelerate, decelerate and reverse. Government is not designed for flexibility, loss-cutting, reversibility. Its engine is used too long, its gears tend to jam, its brakes fade, and it has no reverse gear.

Government should largely confine itself to "public goods"—defence, law and order, environmental protection and other activities that require finance by taxation because their benefits cannot be refused to people who refuse to pay in prices. The remainder is better left to private enterprise to finance by charging. The dividing line between public and private goods is not always sharply defined; a practical working rule-of-thumb is: tax where you must (because pricing is impracticable); charge where you can. This rule yields approximate results, a kind of rough justice. But contrasted with the deficiencies, inefficiencies, inflexibility and corruption of government in state economy it scores very high. Of that, the history of the West since the Industrial Revolution, and especially since the 1939–45 war, leaves no doubt.

There is thus a large field for the expansion of private enterprise. Unless it is envisaged that the Western countries will huddle behind their home markets artificially protected by tariff walls, more of the activities of private firms will be subject to competition from imports. Expansion into formerly "public" services should be welcomed by private enterprise as new markets with a measure of natural "protection" from overseas competition. This new scope for private enterprise has been neglected because of outdated political and sociological arguments for state (or municipal) supply.

4. Competition in the Private Sector

Private enterprise entails risks—of changing consumer preferences, technical innovation, new firms, new ideas. Enterprise is vindicated only if it faces these risks and earns the rewards of success. It must therefore not expect to be protected from competition, internal or external, when market conditions change. There is no lasting safety in resisting change. The search for "security" ends in suppressing progress. Economic systems that cannot cope with uncertainty do not survive.

The best hope for private enterprise lies rather in international accord to remove the plausible reasons for complaint—selling below cost to gain temporary advantage, etc., rather than in sheltering behind tariffs that encourage sluggish reactions to change in overseas markets. There is no lasting refuge, especially by small countries, in excluding imports, except possibly to bargain for *reduction* of trade barriers. Protection of high-cost industries against imports is, in any event, a crude instrument: it may preserve jobs at the expense of shrivelling living standards. Protective devices should be used, *if at all* (and that is a strong reservation, since it cannot be assumed that government will so use them), for the very opposite from their conventional purpose—to remove rather than erect trade barriers.

5. New Entrepreneurs

In post-war Britain and other Western countries too many university graduates have gone into teaching, "public" services and social work, and not enough into private enterprise. No doubt this is in part the result of the 20th-century version of the 18th-century aversion to "trade," but intensified by the sociologists' condemnation of private enterprise, profit-making, advertising and commerce in general. Living standards can be maintained and raised only by using human and natural resources to produce goods and services wanted by the world. National self-sufficiency has retarded or destroyed economic growth and reduced living standards. The market inducement of profit and capital gains would encourage individuals to make a more than proportionate contribution to prosperity and rising living standards for all.

Chapter 6: Finale: Summary and Policy

1. Private enterprise is the source of economic growth and rising living standards because it works with the grain of human nature expressed through voluntary exchange in the market.

2. For over a century private enterprise has been the object of intellectual assault based on contempt for public preferences and unfounded faith in the power of government. In all Western countries the people have been misled by a small number of intellectuals who taught the erroneous contrast between the "*market* failure" of capitalism and the theoretical but nowhere realised achievement of state economy. Their power over public opinion has now been undermined in all Western countries by experience of the "*government* failure" of state economy. Experience has caught up with ideas thought wildly premature ten—even five—years ago. Economists ignored by knowing "practical men" are being heard—belatedly.

3. The lessons of this experience can now be reinforced by education of employees, men and women in public life, the bureaucracy, the press and broadcasting, not least the general public.

4. Government is necessary only for the supply of public goods, but it is a necessary evil since its authority is easily abused even by well-meaning men and asserted by increasing coercion. On the side of demand it tends to neglect or over-ride public preferences. On the side of supply it tends either to retard technological advance by creating monopoly and protecting established industries or to inflate technological possibilities beyond their economic optimum at grievous hidden costs borne by the public—as in the Anglo-French Concorde, the British National Health Service's extravagant use of resources in spectacular surgery, the Russian and American investment in space research and the expenditure of poor, developing countries on prestigious but uneconomic industry and airlines.

5. Private enterprise is a more invigorating avocation than administering others from a government office. It engages the most stimulating faculties in a battle of wits with the consumer—not to outwit but to anticipate and serve him. It can be made to appeal to young people anxious for adventure. And their sympathies can be engaged by showing that it alone produces the wealth from which to help the developing countries establish their own market economies to raise their living standards.

6. The choice for private enterprise is to be indebted to the politician, and fall under his influence, or to serve the consumer, and retain independence from eventual political subservience. Government protection tends to make private enterprise neither private nor enterprising. It would produce the corporate state by sliding into government "power-sharing" with "representatives" of industry and trade unions.

7. Private enterprise requires to encourage and facilitate labour mobility. Maintaining high employment independently of market conditions requires inflationary budget deficits and debilitating balance-of-payments deficits and retards the long-run rise in living standards.

8. The effort of government to organise society from the centre has had a long trial and has failed. It has ended by concealing and trying to escape from the reality of supply and demand—technological change and public preferences. The only policy that can satisfy the aspirations of the people of free societies is to work with the market by nurturing private enterprise.

9. Government failure is incorrigible; market failure is corrigible.

10. To strengthen private enterprise in a market economy we have to

(a) remove poverty once for all by reverse income taxes and voucher systems as the means to eventual reduction in taxes;

(b) replace benefits in kind by benefits in cash;

(c) charge for "public" services and let private enterprise try to replace them at lower cost;

(d) confine government to its unique function of providing public goods;

(e) remove protective devices from private enterprise, especially where it serves a large internal market, such as transport, because they discourage efficiency, expansion and growth by tolerating second-rate technology, management, financing and marketing;

(f) enable private enterprise to progress from manufacturing to services where manpower is deployed more effectively to satisfy demand at home or from overseas;

(g) encourage the opportunities for profits to indicate, in competitive conditions, where earnings are high so that more capital could be used productively;

(h) as industry is made competitive, remove legal privileges that enable trade unions to drive wage costs beyond output, reduce employment, discourage investment and retard improvements in living standards;

(i) use emigration as an index and a danger-signal that living standards have been depressed below those obtainable in culturally comparable countries;

(j) as industry adapts itself to changing technology and markets, ease labour mobility by insurance, loans for removal to new jobs and areas and by restoring a free market in housing;

(k) agree with like-minded nations to remove subsidies to exports and the remaining barriers that obstruct mutually beneficial international exchange.

Notes

1. Jo Grimond, *The Common Welfare,* Maurice Temple Smith, 1978.
2. Roy Jenkins, *Home from Abroad* (the 1979 Richard Dimbleby Lecture, first reprinted in *The Listener,* 29 November 1979), BBC Publications, December 1979.
3. Shirley Williams, "Why we lost—how to win," *Observer,* 13 May 1979.
4. William Rodger, "A good time to learn and listen," *Guardian,* 14 May 1979.

Steven K. Vogel,
"Why Freer Markets Need More Rules" (2007)*

Scholars of political economy increasingly stress that modern market systems are not natural phenomena that spontaneously arise, but complex institutions that must be created and sustained by the visible hand of the government.[1] They have applied this logic more to transitional economies and developing countries that are trying to create market institutions than to developed economies that are trying to reform them. If markets are institutions, however, then market reform should be more a process of building institutions than one of removing constraints, and this should be no less true for more developed market systems than for less developed ones.

I contend here that this simple recognition has profound implications for market reform in the advanced industrial countries, both in theory and in practice. I use the term "market reform" to refer to a wide range of measures that enhance the role of markets in society. I shall propose a simple typology of market reform measures below, but I begin by outlining some of the ramifications of a "market-institutional" perspective, and then review concrete examples from particular countries (Japan) and sectors (telecommunications and finance) to illustrate the argument.

Markets as Institutions: Some Implications

1. **There are no "free" markets.** Economists commonly assume perfect markets for analytical purposes, but these frictionless markets do not really exist. In the most basic case of two people exchanging goods, then the rules that govern their transactions may be very simple. Real-life market systems in advanced industrial countries, however, are embedded in highly complex networks of laws, practices, and norms. This first point may not be particularly controversial in itself, but it leads us logically to propositions (below) that challenge the prevailing discourse on the relationship of governments and markets.

2. **There is no such thing as a disembedded or even a less embedded market system.** Scholars have developed various typologies for the varieties of national market systems, such as liberal market economies versus coordinated market economies.[2] They often employ language that implies that liberal market systems are less embedded in politics and society than other systems.[3] Yet an American-style liberal mar-

* "Why Freer Markets Need More Rules" An earlier version of this chapter appeared in *Creating Competitive Markets: The Politics of Regulatory Reform*, Marc K. Landy, Martin A. Levin, and Martin Shapiro, eds., Brookings Institution Press, 2007. Reprinted by permission of Steven K. Vogel and Brookings Institution Press. The author is grateful to Roselyn Hsueh and participants in the Creating Competitive Market Projects for valuable feedback.

ket economy is not disembedded from society, nor is it even less embedded than a Japanese-style coordinated market economy. An American-style external labor market, for example, is not any less embedded than a Japanese-style internal labor market; an American equity-based financial system is not any less embedded than a Japanese credit-based system; and an American antitrust regime is not any less embedded than a Japanese corporate network (*keiretsu*). That is, an American-style liberal market economy is embedded in its own specific matrix of policies, practices, and norms. The Japanese labor market, for example, may be embedded in a broader political–economic system in which government policies discourage labor mobility, large firms favor new graduates over mid-career hires, employees are reluctant to defect from large firms to their competitors, and social norms place a premium on employment stability and employee loyalty. But the American labor market is equally embedded in a system in which government policies encourage labor mobility, firms embrace mid-career hires, employees commonly defect to competitors, and prevailing norms encourage firms to lay off workers and employees to offer their services to the highest bidders.

3. **Market reform involves changes at every level of a political-economic system: government policies, private sector practices, and social norms.** Most scholars focus on government policy as the primary locus of the market reform process. This is natural, for government policy is the component of a market system that is most amenable to conscious reform. But we must keep in mind that government policy only affects market outcomes in *interaction* with private sector behavior. The government may liberalize a particular sector, for example, but it does not automatically follow that new entrants will emerge or that firms will begin to compete on price.

Economists differ on whether they view competition as fragile or robust, and this in turn affects their views on how far government must go to generate competition. As Adam Smith himself attests, most businessmen would prefer the comfort of collusion over the challenge of competition.[4] In many cases, businesses must not only be allowed to compete, but also be forced to do so. Even if we accept that individuals and businesses do have some natural propensity to engage in market activity (without the government forcing them to do so), social relations and prevalent norms still shape *how* they do so. For example, policymakers may give employers greater flexibility to dismiss workers, but this policy change may not result in more competitive labor markets if managers refrain from dismissals due to their relations with workers or broader societal norms.

4. **The regulation-versus-competition dichotomy that animates most debates about market reform is fundamentally misleading.** The very language of deregulation belies this misperception. In conventional discourse, the term *deregulation* refers to less regulation and more competition, as if these two developments were naturally associated. In fact, generating more competition usually requires more regulation, not less. Thus the dominant trend in advanced industrial countries has not been one of deregulation (less regulation), but rather liberalization (more competition) combined with reregulation (more regulation)—or "freer markets and more rules."

In sum, popular discourse presupposes a negative relationship between regulation and competition, yet the relationship is actually more positive than negative. We can refine this point by noting that the actual relationship varies across time and across sectors and subsectors. That is, it may be more positive at an early stage, when government has to create the basic infrastructure to support market competition, and more negative at a later stage, when an incremental increase in the government's role would be more likely to impede than to enhance competition. Or it may be more positive in sectors that are particularly conducive to monopoly (network industries) and more negative in sectors where competition is more likely to evolve naturally (retail). In reality, of course, the relationship is even more complex than this. Some regulations enhance competition, while others impede it. The process of liberalization is one of increasing regulations that enhance competition, such as antitrust rules, and removing regulations that impede it, such as price and entry restrictions. Yet the story does not end there: policies that enhance competition are almost always accompanied by corollary regulations that facilitate this competition, such as financial disclosure requirements; that protect society from negative side effects, such as environmental regulations; and/or compensate potential losers from these policies, such as welfare policies.

5. **The government-versus-market dichotomy that animates most debates about economic policy is also misleading.** The basic logic of the relationship between regulation and competition also holds true for the broader relationship between government and market. The assumption that there is a negative relationship between government and market obscures a more sophisticated understanding of this relationship. As we move from a thin definition of market institutions (the minimal rules of the game) to a thicker one (a broad range of laws, practices, and norms), the relationship between government and market becomes more positive and less negative. This is not simply because competition requires regulation (point 4, above), but because market competition is not incompatible with a substantial government role in the marketplace beyond that of a referee. The government is the largest consumer, employer, lender, borrower, insurer, and property owner in market economies.[5] Moreover, the government can still manipulate the terms of competition to favor certain marketplace outcomes even if it allows and/or promotes competition.

To push this argument further, we would need to refine language to differentiate the government's role in creating and sustaining markets from its role in impeding or crowding out markets. The more common analytical distinctions in the literature—such as the government as a referee versus the government as a player, passive regulation versus active intervention, or setting the rules versus shaping outcomes—provide a useful start, but they do not settle the issue. For all governments are by definition market players as well as referees; all passive regulation entails some active intervention; and all rule setting has some ramifications for outcomes.

6. **Market reform is primarily a creative process, not a destructive one.** Given points 4 and 5 above, market reform implies not the dismantling of institutions that impede competition so much as the creation of institutions that sustain it. We cannot simply get the government out of the way and expect greater competition to arise naturally. As noted above, scholars have gone further in fleshing out the implications of this for transitional economies and developing countries than for advanced industrial countries. If we view market reform as a negative process, then shifting from a command economy to a market system should be easy: just dismantle the command system and let markets flourish. Fostering markets in developing countries should be equally straightforward: just get interventionist governments to back

off and then markets will take over. If we view market development as a constructive project, however, then the transition would entail a complex process of building new market institutions. In the following section, I apply this basic logic to the more subtle transition involved in market reform in advanced countries via an extended example from Japan.

How to Make a Market: Evidence from Japan

The debates over market reform in post-communist and developing countries boil down to a simple question at the core: How do you make a market? These cases are especially illuminating because these countries are attempting a wholesale transition from plan to market or from primitive markets to a functioning national market system. Yet the same insights apply to advanced industrial countries that already have market systems, but are attempting more modest transitions toward a system in which the role of markets is significantly enhanced.

The United States and other advanced industrial economies are governed by a market infrastructure—a complex web of government policies, corporate practices, and social norms—that continuously evolves over time. Current-day Japan provides an especially vivid example to illustrate this point, however, because reformers have been striving to fundamentally shift the Japanese economic system from a coordinated market architecture to a more liberal one.[6] They have not simply been striving to liberalize specific industrial sectors ("deregulation"—the topic to be addressed in the next section), but to enhance competition by altering the overall governance of the economic system, including labor and capital markets.

Japan already has a well developed legal system that defines and enforces property rights, a modern financial system, and a regulatory bureaucracy, yet its labor and capital markets nevertheless differ fundamentally from those of the United States. For example, Japan lacks a "real" labor market in the sense of an active labor market for the core employees of large corporations. Scholars in the field contrast Japanese "internal" labor markets with American "external" labor markets. They mean by this that Japanese companies rotate their core employees across functions, divisions, and locations within the firm and/or corporate group, but they do not poach employees from competitors and employees do not defect to competitors. Thus companies do not compete for workers on the basis of wages, and workers compete with each other for internal promotions but not for outside offers.[7]

Likewise, Japan lacks a "real" capital market in the sense of an active market for corporate control.[8] Industrial corporations and banks maintain a substantial proportion of their shares in friendly hands via cross-holdings of shares within business groups, thus insulating them from the threat of hostile takeover. The Japanese government has gradually eased regulations that impede corporate takeovers and introduced policies to facilitate them, yet the mergers and acquisitions market has only recently begun to emerge—and that from a very low base compared to the United States.

So what would it take for Japan to develop a "real" labor market or a "real" capital market? Here is where the logic of post-communist transition and the creation of market institutions in developing countries can be applied to an advanced industrial economy. If we adopt a classical liberal perspective, this should be a relatively simple process that is primarily negative in the sense of removing constraints rather than building institutions. Regulating markets requires hard work, but liberating them should be easy. Since Japan already has a basic system of property rights, then just get the government out of the way and more active labor and capital markets should spontaneously emerge. If we adopt a market-institutional perspective, however, this should be an exceedingly complex process and it should be primarily constructive in the sense of creating new market institutions and transforming old ones.

To develop a "real" labor market, the Japanese government would have to begin by removing constraints on employers and nurturing the infrastructure for a more active labor market (see Table 1.2.1). For example, it would have to give employers more flexibility in setting wages, benefits, hours, and working conditions and ease restrictions on hiring non-regular workers, but also strengthen organizations to match employers with workers and disseminate more information to both employers and workers. It would have to address areas outside of labor policy itself, including revisions to financial regulations, accounting standards, and commercial laws that would encourage firms to be more responsive to shareholders and less beholden to their workers. And it would have to promote portable pension plans, such as 401(k) plans in the United States, so that employees who switch employers would not sacrifice their retirement benefits.

TABLE 1.2.1 What Would It Take to Turn Japan into a Liberal Market Economy?

Labor	
Government Policy	**Corporate Behavior**
Laws	Practices
• Labor market reform	• Lay off workers when necessary
• Changes in case law doctrine	• Do not favor new graduates over mid-career hires
• Corporate governance reform	
• Pension reform	• Shift from seniority to merit-based pay
• Financial reform	• Introduce stock options
Norms	Norms
• The government should not use regulation to preserve employment.	• Companies should not preserve employment at the expense of profits.
Net Result: An Active External Labor Market	

Finance	
Government Policy	**Corporate Behavior**
Laws	Practices
• Financial reform	• Sell off cross-held shares
• Banking crisis resolution	• Banks make lending decisions and price loans on the basis of risk
• Corporate governance reform	
• Pension reform	• Corporations choose banks on the basis of price
• Tax reform	
Norms	• Banks stop lending to insolvent firms
• The government should not protect banks or manipulate financial markets.	Norms
	• Companies should maximize shareholder value
Net Result: A Market for Corporate Control	

Source: Vogel, *Japan Remodeled*, p. 6.

Over the past decade, the Japanese government has made considerable progress on a package of reforms that might promote a more active labor market, but it has watered down some measures and failed to complete others. In any case, government policy alone is not sufficient to transform corporate practices. For a true labor market for managers to emerge, companies would have to renegotiate their compacts with their workers and redesign their systems of employee representation. They would have to become less loyal to their workers, and the workers would have to become less loyal to them. And there would need to be sufficient numbers of employers looking for workers and workers looking for new employers to provide ample liquidity in the market.

Likewise, to cultivate a "real" capital market, the government would have to enact substantial reforms in financial regulation and corporate governance, but also in areas less directly related to capital markets, such as pensions, antitrust, and taxation. Here again, the Japanese government has made substantial progress on this agenda, but it has not completed the full slate of reforms that would be required. To create a market for corporate control, it would have to abandon its propensity to protect domestic financial institutions and corporations and to manipulate financial markets. Corporations would have to go even further in unwinding cross-shareholdings, become less loyal to members of their corporate group, and embrace a philosophy of maximizing shareholder value. Shareholders would have to become more assertive in pressing managers to maximize returns. And banks would have to stop protecting their main bank clients from takeover bids.

Deregulation and Variations across Sectors

Now let us turn from market reform in the broadest sense—the enhancement of the basic market infrastructure of an economy as a whole, to market reform in a narrower sense, as it is more commonly studied in advanced industrial countries—that is, regulatory reform to promote competition in specific sectors. Both of these types of reform require "more rules," but they do so in a slightly different sense. In one case, the government and the private sector enhance the basic institutions that govern markets, whereas in the other, the government intervenes more actively to create or sustain competition in sectoral markets in which private actors are prone to collude or competition is not likely to emerge on its own. Analyzing the latter type of reform demands greater attention to cross-sectoral variation.

Given the argument presented thus far, we must be wary of an overly simplistic dichotomy between "regulated" and "unregulated" sectors. All sectors are governed in the sense that they rely on a common market infrastructure; all sectors are subject to social regulations such as health, safety and environmental codes; and all sectors are subject to economic regulations in that unregulated sectors are inevitably linked to regulated sectors. In fact, some of the most heavily regulated sectors constitute the core infrastructure for the rest of the economy, including finance, energy, transport, telecommunications, and retail. There is nonetheless a qualitative difference between sectors that are directly subject to economic (price and entry) regulation, such as the infrastructure sectors listed above, and those that are not, such as most manufacturing sectors.

The "deregulation" movement that began in the United States in the mid 1970s and spread to all advanced industrial countries addressed both economic and social regulation, but the core agenda was curtailing economic regulation.[9] Economists increasingly challenged the public interest rationale for regulation, arguing that market failures do not constitute sufficient justification for regulation. That is, policymakers should not assume that any market failure requires government regulation as a response, but should carefully weigh the costs and the benefits of regulation. Furthermore, they contended that technological change and market dynamics had undermined the original rationale for regulation in many of these sectors. In the United States, an unusual bipartisan coalition including academics, business and consumer groups pressed for broad-based regulatory reform in the late 1970s. Britain and Japan followed in the early 1980s, and most Western European countries followed suit after that.

Yet as noted above, the deregulation movement comprised little true deregulation, but rather a combination of liberalization with reregulation. The U.S. government came closest to true deregulation (freer markets and *fewer* rules) in the airline industry, where it eliminated an entire regulatory agency (the Civil Aeronautics Board) and abandoned economic regulation. Even in this case, it coupled deregulation with a substantial strengthening of safety regulation.

Other deregulation programs, however, have been accompanied by an explosive proliferation of rules. The Thatcher reforms, for example, led to the creation of no less than twelve new regulatory agencies. Britain's "Big Bang" financial liberalization of 1986 coincided with the passage of the Financial Services Act, which ushered in a far more extensive, intrusive, and legalistic regulatory regime. In the one country with hard data on the actual numbers of regulations—Japan—government officials made the reduction of this number an explicit goal of their regulatory reform program, and yet they confronted utter frustration as the number increased instead. For every regulation they eliminated, another would somehow emerge.[10]

The logic by which liberalization drives reregulation varies according to the nature of the pre-existing regime and the character of the transition toward greater competition. A shift from monopoly to competition, for example, typically requires pro-competitive regulation to jump-start competition (see the discussion of telecommunications below). A transition from public to private provision of services often requires new regulation to mandate public service requirements (such as universal access or interoperability) that were previously met directly by the public corporation. An increase in the number and diversity of market players generally demands a more codified regulatory regime ("more rules" in the literal sense). And an intensification of competition may spur companies to behave worse (to produce greater externalities), therefore requiring an increase in social, environmental, or other types of protective regulation.

When British authorities launched a bold telecommunications reform program in the early 1980s, advocates recognized that they would need to increase regulation in order to generate competition, but they believed that this would be a temporary phenomenon. As competition took hold, they could allow regulation to wither away.[11] Yet regulation of telecommunications has turned out not to be a temporary measure to jump-start competition but rather an ongoing necessity to sustain and govern competition. In every case of telecommunications reform, the government initially had to confront the monopoly power of the incumbent service provider. The incumbents held an overwhelming advantage because they owned and operated the national infrastructure; possessed access to all existing customers; dictated technical standards; and commanded the relevant technical knowledge and expertise in the sector.

So the government could not simply allow competition—it had to *create* it. It usually did this with some form of "asymmetric" regulation: imposing restraints on the incumbent and giving advantages to the competitors. It could break up the incumbent into multiple companies (divided along functional and/or regional lines); force the incumbent to reduce charges in non-competitive areas (such as local service); prohibit the incumbent from lowering charges in competitive areas (such as long distance); restrain the incumbent from introducing new services; and/or require the incumbent to lease its lines at reduced rates. This last measure is critical, because the incumbent carrier controlled the phone lines, so creating competition meant forcing the incumbent to lease lines to its competitors. The regulatory battle then hinged on the rate of the interconnection charge the incumbent would levy on its competitors.

In many cases, the incumbent and the competitors devised complex rationales to justify their own positions (incumbents favor "historic" cost calculations whereas challengers prefer "incremental" costs), yet these debates essentially boiled down to political judgments about how far to favor the incumbent versus the challengers. The process never ends because the incumbent never completely loses its structural advantage, and technological and market changes require constant recalibration of the regulatory balance.

Given the growing complexity of the telecommunications sector and the interrelationships between many different lines of business (land-based telephony, mobile communications, satellite communications, cable television, Internet services, etc.), the overall level of regulation is more likely to increase than to decrease. Mobile technology has altered the dynamics by allowing new carriers to challenge incumbents without relying as heavily on the incumbents' land-based network. Yet to the extent that mobile customers call other customers on the incumbent's land-based network, the mobile carriers still confront the issue of interconnection charges. Ongoing market developments are bound to change this further, but regulators are not likely to reach a point in the foreseeable future where they can simply withdraw and let free and fair competition take over.

Other network industries share common features with telecommunications. They are natural monopolies in that the network infrastructure is so costly that duplication would be inefficient, so liberalization takes the form of fabricating competition over a common infrastructure. Governments can strive to achieve this through franchising, whereby they grant monopoly franchises to operators for a limited period via competitive bidding. They can adopt a highway model in which the government runs the infrastructure and allows operators (such as trucking companies) to compete freely using that infrastructure, but this is more difficult in other sectors (railways, telecommunications, energy). The British government tried this approach for railways, creating a single public railtrack authority and auctioning franchises to service providers, with problematic results.[12] In energy sectors, governments have generally separated generation from distribution, allowing competition in generation while restricting it for distribution. They have also distinguished between large corporate users and household consumers, allowing more competition in the industrial sector.

In many cases, decreases in economic regulation are accompanied by increases in social regulation. Regulators typically fear that companies that face greater competition will be more likely to compromise health, safety, or environmental standards. Trucking companies may push their drivers to work too hard; airlines may take shortcuts on safety codes; or utility companies may lower standards for pollution emissions. So governments strengthen regulations in these areas to compensate. Furthermore, many of the old licensing regimes fused economic and social regulations. That is, the same licensing system served to limit entry and to maintain standards of conduct. So regulatory reform means separating out economic regulation from social regulation, and reducing the former while increasing the latter.

In finance, the connection between liberalization and reregulation is particularly striking. In order for capital markets to operate properly, for example, investors must have accurate information about the financial circumstances of publicly listed firms. Insiders must be prohibited from taking advantage of their information advantage vis-à-vis the broader public, and managers and large investors must be prohibited from manipulating share prices for short-term gain. Moreover, corporate boards must be required to serve the interests of the shareholders as a whole.

In recent years, governments have responded to various scandals by substantially strengthening regulations on securities transactions and corporate governance. If we look at financial regulation more broadly, we find a general trend of greater competition coupled with a massive expansion of regulation. Governments have eliminated many forms of price regulation, such as regulations on deposit interest rates and stock commissions and lowered barriers between business lines within finance (banking versus securities, for example). Meanwhile, they have substantially augmented and codified other types of regulation, such as prudential supervision and disclosure requirements. There is a logical connection between these two facets of reform, because intensified competition begets greater incentives for risky behavior, which requires tougher regulation, and brings in new players who are less likely to play by informal rules, which spurs further codification.

Ultimately, as noted above, we need to develop language to move beyond the presumption of a negative relationship between regulation and competition. In an earlier work, I proposed four categories of regulatory reform that entail more regulation, not less.[13] Government authorities introduce *pro-competitive reregulation* in order to create competition, by offering regulatory advantages to competitors or imposing disadvantages on incumbents, in a market such as basic telephone service where competition is not likely to arise naturally. They employ *juridical reregulation* by adding more detail to existing regulations, by putting tacit rules into written form or by putting administrative rules into legal form. They implement *strategic reregulation* when they favor particular firms, often national champions, within a newly opened market. And they engage in *expansionary reregulation* when they create new regulations to prevent the loss of bureaucratic authority that can accompany the liberalization process, or when they simply take advantage of the process to expand their powers.

Alternatively, we might devise analytical categories that would stress the varieties of market reform rather than the (related) varieties of reregulation. For example, we might begin by breaking down market reform into two broad categories—primary and corollary measures—and then subdivide these further. Primary measures would include: (1) enhancing the basic infrastructure of a market economy, such as the financial and legal systems; (2) strengthening related policies that sustain competition, such as disclosure requirements and corporate governance codes; (3) tightening antitrust policy and pro-competitive regulation; (4) removing or relaxing anti-competitive regulations, such as price and entry controls; and (5) reducing the government's role in functions that could be performed by private actors.

Corollary measures would include those policies that tend to accompany the market reform process, and facilitate it for functional and/or political reasons. For example, governments typically couple reductions in economic regulation with increases in health, safety, and environmental regulations for the functional reasons outlined above. They also couple liberalization with politically motivated adjustments, including compensation for social groups for the costs of increased competition via subsidies, insurance, or welfare policies.

The Market Reform Process

I have argued here that a sophisticated understanding of the relationship between regulation and competition, and between governments and markets, is a prerequisite for understanding market reform in advanced industrial countries. While I have introduced various examples to illustrate this point, let me conclude by recapitulating the argument with special attention to implications for the market reform *process*.

1. **Market reform is a highly complex process precisely because it requires building new institutions and not simply removing barriers**. The standard government-versus-markets rhetoric is particularly misleading on this point because it makes it seem as though market reform should be easy: just get the government out of the way and markets will flourish. In this view, the only reason things do not work out this way is because of political opposition: vested interests that benefit from protection and regulation block liberalization. But this misses a critical part of the story: it is not easy to enhance market systems or to make them more competitive. In other words, the challenge of market reform is functional as well as political, and the political difficulty is compounded by the functional complexity. This implies that market reform requires considerable attention to the specifics of market design.

2. **Market reform often requires not just one policy change but a wide range of inter-related steps**. We might think of this in terms of policy linkages, or macro-macro links. The example of Japanese labor and capital markets demonstrated how reform in one area might only have its intended effect if combined with related steps in other areas. In addition to functional linkages across policy areas, there are also political linkages. For example, many argue that Japan cannot fully liberalize service sectors because it lacks a sufficient social safety net in the form of a well developed unemployment insurance system. That is, policymakers recognize that more competition would mean greater labor dislocation and unemployment, and they judge that this would be politically unacceptable because they do not have sufficient policies in place to cope with this dislocation.[14]

I would put this slightly differently: in the Japanese context, anti-competitive regulation *is* a critical component of the social safety net. Regulations that buffer businesses from failure also buffer their workers from unemployment. Once we grasp this connection, the Japanese government's response to economic stagnation in the 1990s makes more sense. The government was slow to liberalize service sectors because this would generate labor dislocation, and it was slow to develop a more standard social safety net because this would justify greater liberalization of service sectors.[15]

These policy linkages also help us to understand why governments have been plagued by problems of partial reform. They have found that reforms do not achieve the expected results because they have enacted one part of a policy package but not another. Or even worse, they have generated or exacerbated major crises via incompatible combinations of policies or poor sequencing. Some blame financial liberalization for the U.S. savings and loan (S&L) crisis while others blame too little liberalization, yet in fact the particular combination of policies produced the crisis. The government deregulated deposit interest rates; liberalized the S&Ls' use of funds, and maintained deposit insurance—giving the S&Ls both the freedom and the incentive to take greater risks. And the government did not combine this package with an increase in prudential regulation. The Japanese government followed suit a decade later, producing a full-fledged banking crisis by combining poor macroeconomic management, financial liberalization, and a tacit guarantee to bail out failing banks with lax banking supervision.[16]

3. **Market reform is not simply a process of policy change, but a combination of policy change and societal response**. We might think of this in terms of public–private linkages, or macro–micro links. We miss the essence of what is happening if we focus on one piece of the story—policy change, for example, without the other—the private sector response. Market reform often means replacing existing market institutions with alternatives. This includes not only switching from one type of government regulation to another, but also switching modes of governance, replacing government regulation with private sector regulation and vice versa. Market reform often requires a broader transformation of social norms as well.

This interaction can take many different forms. In Japan, government policies to liberalize markets have often been accompanied by private sector responses to preserve some form of insulation from the full force of competition. In the 1960s, for example, the government removed capital controls, and corporations responded by substantially increasing their cross-shareholdings to protect themselves from foreign takeovers. In the 1970s, the government moved forward with trade liberalization, and some industries replaced tariffs and quotas with private-sector substitutes, including preferential procurement practices, exclusive dealerships, and cartels. Kodak argued this point in its WTO case against Fuji Film, contending that the Ministry of International Trade and Industry worked with Fuji to establish exclusive dealer networks that effectively shut out foreign suppliers. Then in the 1980s, the government implemented sector-specific liberalization ("deregulation"), yet the removal of government regulation sometimes failed to spur competition or was replaced with outright collusion among producers. The liberalization of deposit interest rates, for example, led to very little actual competition for deposits based on price.[17] More recently, Prime

Minister Junichiro Koizumi pledged in 2003 to double foreign investment into Japan by 2008, and government measures to facilitate foreign mergers with and acquisitions of Japanese companies (discussed above) were the centerpieces of this effort. Yet at the same time, the government enacted reforms of laws on corporate takeover defenses and issued guidelines to clarify what defense strategies would be legal and appropriate, and companies rushed to prepare defenses to insulate themselves from foreign takeovers.

For a different kind of example, let us turn to labor market trends in the United States, Germany, and Japan. I cannot capture the full complexity of this story here, but let me offer a stylized interpretation that should illustrate the general point that government reforms and private sector developments do not necessarily move in tandem. I would characterize the broad trends as liberalization without policy change in the United States, policy change without liberalization in Japan, and partial liberalization via policy change in Germany. The U.S. government has not made major changes to labor law over the past two decades, but adjustments in policy implementation and corporate practices have combined to produce more competitive labor markets. The Japanese government has enacted considerable policy reforms, as discussed above, yet corporate practices have not fundamentally transformed. In Germany, the government stalled for years but moved forward with substantial reforms beginning in 2003. Policy reforms have more impact in Germany than in Japan because the legal framework plays a greater role in structuring labor markets.

4. **There is no single equilibrium for optimal market reform**. We know that perfect markets do not exist, but they serve as a useful fiction for analytical purposes. Many experts also assume that they provide an optimal target against which we can assess reform progress. But the positive relationship between regulation and competition complicates this picture. Market reform advocates themselves divide among those who favor a *laissez faire* variant of liberalism and those who prefer a more pro-competitive approach. The former are more skeptical of the benefit of government action to generate or enforce competition, while the latter are more favorable toward aggressive antitrust policy and pro-competitive regulation. This philosophical difference takes a very concrete form in many policy debates, such as the public controversy over the Microsoft antitrust case or rulings by the Federal Communications Commission.

5. **Market reform is inherently a political process**. This final point may be the most obvious of all, but points 1 through 4 above help us to fill out *how* and *why* this is so. It is not simply that government regulation generates winners and losers, so regulatory decisions involve political battles. The market reform process is inherently so complex that it involves linkages across policy arenas and combinations of government policy and private sector response, and this makes the process of reform even more political than it would be if it were only a matter of repealing a specific regulation. Likewise, because there is no agreed-upon target for market reform, even among its advocates, the political process inevitably involves a contest of ideas as well as a clash of interests.

Notes

1. Douglass C. North, *Structure and Change in Economic History* (New York: W.W. Norton & Company, 1981); Kiren Chaudhry, "The Myths of the Market and the Common History of Late Developers," *Politics and Society* 21 (1993): 245–274; Neil Fligstein, *The Architecture of Markets: An Economic Sociology of Twenty-First Century Capitalist Societies* (Princeton University Press, 2001); World Bank, *World Development Report 2002: Building Institutions for Markets* (Oxford University Press, 2002).
2. Peter Hall and David Soskice, eds., *Varieties of Capitalism: The Institutional Foundations of Comparative Advantage* (Oxford University Press, 2001).
3. Colin Crouch and Wolfgang Streeck, eds., *Political Economy of Modern Capitalism* (London: Sage, 1997).
4. Adam Smith, *The Wealth of Nations* (University of Chicago Press, 1976), Vol. 1, 278.
5. Charles E. Lindblom, *Politics and Markets: The World's Political-Economic Systems* (New York: Basic Books, 1977), 107–114.
6. This section builds on Steven K. Vogel, *Japan Remodeled: How Government and Industry Are Transforming Japanese Capitalism* (Cornell University Press, 2006).
7. Japan's "lifetime" employment system for core employees at large companies is complemented by more flexible employment relations for non-core employees. "Permanent" employees, mostly men, enjoy higher status, salary, benefits, and job security than "temporary" workers, mostly women.
8. On this point, the United States is more the outlier than Japan. While some European countries have more active mergers and acquisition markets than Japan, none has a market for corporate control comparable to that of the United States. For that matter, the United States only developed an active market for corporate control in the 1980s.
9. This section builds on Steven K. Vogel, *Freer Markets, More Rules: Regulatory Reform in Advanced Industrial Countries* (Cornell University Press, 1996).
10. The number of regulations increased from 10,054 in 1985 to 12,376 in 2005 (Ministry of Internal Affairs and Communications data).
11. Stephen Littlechild, *Regulation of British Telecommunications Profitability* (London: Department of Industry, 1983).
12. Vogel, *Freer Markets*, 124–125.
13. Vogel, *Freer Markets*, 17.
14. Jonah Levy, Mari Miura, and Gene Park, "Exiting *Étatisme*? New Directions in State Policy in France and Japan," in *The State after Statism: New State Activities in the Age of Liberalization*, edited by Jonah Levy (Cambridge: Harvard University Press, 2006), 93–136.
15. In other words, the government does not have an easy way to move from one political equilibrium (employment maintenance, or anti-competitive regulation as social protection) to another (employment adjustment, or more competition coupled with unemployment insurance as social protection).
16. Ryoichi Mikitani and Adam S. Posen, eds., *Japan's Financial Crisis and Its Parallels to U.S. Experience* (Washington: Institute for International Economics, 2000).
17. On the trend toward private sector governance in Japan since the 1980s, see Ulrike Schaede, *Cooperative Capitalism: Self-Regulation, Trade Associations, and the Antimonopoly Law in Japan* (Oxford University Press, 2000). Richard Vietor argues that U.S. incumbents responded to deregulation not by outright collusion but by devising market

strategies to impede new entry, including market segmentation and manipulation of distribution channels: Vietor, *Contrived Competition: Regulation and Deregulation in America* (Cambridge: Belknap Press, 1994), 320–321.

2

Market Transition in Eastern Europe and China

Market transitions in Eastern Europe and China have provided live laboratories for theories of markets and political economy to play out in practice and be tested against each other. In the transition from plan to market, observers witnessed in real time what the notion of markets as institutions means, including practical considerations of how to build market institutions. Transition experiences allow scholars and practitioners to debate whether all components of economic reform must proceed together and whether economic and political liberalization go together. This set of issues came to be framed as a contest between shock therapy and gradualism. Yet market transition comprises different dimensions: liberalization, or moving to markets and the price mechanism; privatization, that is, transferring state ownership of assets to private ownership; and stabilization of the macroeconomy, including inflation and exchange rates. In reality, different countries pursued transition in various sequences and at different speeds, so assessing the merits of shock therapy versus gradualism is not as simple as it may appear.

Poland is often invoked as an example of the success of shock therapy, or the "big bang" approach. There, **Jeffrey Sachs** argues, reformers took advantage of a window of opportunity for dramatic change and implemented a far-reaching set of reforms that have proved to be extremely successful. Sachs is an economist who is widely known for his role as policy advisor to governments all over the world: he began his policy career advising the Bolivian government in ending extreme hyperinflation in the mid-1980s and has more recently turned his attention to poverty reduction efforts such as the United Nations Millennium Development Goals. He was a central figure in developing Poland's economic transition strategy and, more broadly, in the policy debates about Eastern European transition. The shock therapy logic, as expressed by Sachs, is that transformation from a planned system to a market economy requires "a leap across the institutional chasm."[1] The prescription is a comprehensive reform package, where price controls are eliminated and market forces are introduced completely and wholesale, and stabilization, liberalization, and privatization are pursued together. Shock therapy in terms of liberalizing price controls had almost immediate salutary effects in Poland, with markets, prices, consumers, and entrepreneurs adjusting in a matter of weeks. But privatization efforts created serious dislocation in the nation's state-owned enterprises and tremendous pain for many of their employees. In the end, however, Poland emerged with the most successful growth record of any postcommunist country.

Yet even a major proponent of shock therapy such as Sachs cannot conclude it works everywhere. He advocated the initial big bang shock of market liberalization and quick moves toward privatization in Russia but concluded later that transition there was staggeringly different from that in Poland, a much larger-scale and more entrenched problem. **Joseph Stiglitz** weighs in on market transition in Russia as part of a larger criticism of what he terms the "market fundamentalism" of Western advisers, including the International Monetary Fund (IMF). Stiglitz won the Nobel Prize for his incisive analysis of the role of information asymmetries in economic activity. In the 1990s, a decade of enormous change and turmoil in the global political economy, he served as chair of President Clinton's Council of Economic Advisors and then as chief economist and vice president of the World Bank. Toward the end of his tenure at the World Bank, he attracted a great deal of attention for his criticisms of the IMF. He charged that the IMF relentlessly pursued neoliberal economic dogma in both the Eastern European transition of the 1990s and the East Asian financial crisis of 1997–98, against mounting evidence that its assumptions were faulty, and compounded the damage in its client economies through its errors. Turning to Russia in particular, Stiglitz argues that reformers failed to recognize the centrality of social and political transformation as a necessary complement to economic transition and that they must take some of the blame for the failures of transition.

In the language of this reader, in other words, economic reformers failed to grasp the import of markets as institutions and gave short shrift to the necessity of building an institutional infrastructure to support markets and capitalism. Stiglitz advocates a gradualist paradigm of market transition, in which reforms should proceed at a reasonable speed and in the right sequence. Perfect market institutions cannot be created overnight, and certain institutional prerequisites must be put in place before other reforms can be successfully enacted. Gradualists argue that market transition is not a leap across a chasm but rather a careful process of building a bridge across the chasm that can support both the old and the new sets of institutions. Stiglitz emphasizes the extent to which market transactions are embedded in social relationships and also pays a great deal of attention to the relationship between political and economic liberalization. He claims these are two central things that shock therapy proponents in Russia ignored in their insistence that neoclassical economics held all the answers.

China and Russia are often compared in terms of the political dimension of transition, because they have managed the relationship between political and economic liberalization in very different ways. **Doug Guthrie** emphasizes the social and political embeddedness of China's economic reforms in making the case that state-controlled gradualism is a superior policy to shock therapy. He argues, contrary to shock therapists, that China proves that privatization is not a necessary part of market transition. Contrary to neoclassical and new institutional economics, by extension, the Chinese experience demonstrates that private property is not a necessary ingredient for a market economy to function. Many Eastern European countries emphasized speed in privatizing property, extricating the state from the economy, and constructing new market institutions. China, on the contrary, has implemented institutional change much more slowly: the state has controlled the transition to capitalism through incremental institutional experiments while it has continued to be involved in the economy.

Guthrie takes a sociological approach to the study of markets and economic reform, based on the understanding that economic systems are inherently social and cultural systems where economic activity is embedded in rules and norms. Economic transition thus goes hand in hand with social, cultural, and political change that requires the gradual construction of new market institutions while ensuring ongoing institutional stability in the existing system. Guthrie lays out how the Chinese state has implemented this type of institutional change through a series of controlled experiments, including dual-track, or plan and market, state enterprise reform; the complex transformation of property rights; firm-level organizational change and new corporate forms; piecemeal price reform; and new taxation and legal systems. Deng Xiaoping, the architect of China's reforms, summed up the gradualist and experimental nature of Chinese transition in the famous phrase "groping for stones to cross the river."

Note

1. Jeffrey D. Sachs, this volume, p. 359.

Jeffrey D. Sachs,
The End of Poverty (2005)*

A Plan to Establish a Market Economy

We arrived at midnight in the newsroom, recently converted from a kindergarten classroom. I sat at the keyboard, and Lipton and I began to write a plan for the transformation of Poland from a socialist economy in the Soviet orbit to a market economy within the European Community. We worked through the night until dawn, at which point we printed out a fifteen-page paper with key concepts and a planned chronology of reforms. It was the first time, I believe, that anyone had written down a comprehensive plan for the transformation of a socialist economy to a market economy. It briefly touched on the questions of trade, exchange rates, price liberalization, convertibility of the currency, stabilization, industrial policy, debt cancellation, and a bit on privatization, which was the area of greatest uncertainty.

Our proposal was for a dramatic, quick transformation to a market economy—a leap across the institutional chasm—with market forces to be introduced even before widespread privatization could be achieved. Our hypothesis, which proved to be correct, was that the state-owned enterprises would function somewhat like regular businesses if they were allowed to operate according to market forces, despite the fact that they were bureaucratic entities without owners other than the state. We stressed that sooner rather than later the state would have to find real owners for these enterprises, through various methods of privatization.

In an economic shorthand that was to be repeated many times in the coming years, our program, in essence, was described as resting on five pillars:

- Stabilization—ending the high inflation and establishing a stable, convertible currency
- Liberalization—allowing markets to function by legalizing private economic activity, ending price controls, and establishing the necessary commercial law
- Privatization—identifying private owners for assets currently held by the states. These assets might be privatized in the form of entire enterprises, or piecemeal (machinery, buildings, land), depending on the circumstances
- Social Safety Net—pensions, health care, and other benefits for the elderly and the poor, especially to help cushion the transition

- Institutional Harmonization—adopting, step by step, the economic laws, procedures, and institutions of Western Europe in order to be a successful candidate for
the European Union (still the European Community as of 1989)

Poland's challenges had some similarities to the problems in Latin America, but also
some profound differences. The similarities were mainly macroeconomic. Like Latin
America, Poland had high inflation, a large budget deficit, and a large overhang of
foreign debt. As in parts of Latin America, Poland's currency was unstable and not
freely convertible at the official exchange rate, so there was a huge gap between the
official exchange rate and the black market rate. That gap, in turn, led to massive
smuggling and tax evasion.

The differences were perhaps even more important. Poland was a literate and ethnically homogeneous society. The ethnic and class tensions that divided Bolivia were,
mercifully, not present. Poland was also not impoverished. Yes, its infrastructure was
in a dilapidated state and needed a massive overhaul; its air and water were polluted
after decades of energy-intensive industrialization and lack of environmental control;
and its Soviet-era factories were uncompetitive in Western markets. But still, Poland
was largely urban, literate, and equipped with basic infrastructure (roads, electricity, piped water and sewerage, seaports and airports). Geography was also favorable.
Poland's proximity to Germany, for once in its modern history, would be a big plus
because it would ease the two-way trade between Poland and the largest economy in
Western Europe. (In the past, the same proximity had meant repeated invasions and
conquest by outside forces.)

The biggest difference with Latin America, by far, was that Polish society knew
where to head: toward Western Europe. Before 1945, Poland had been a market
economy, and part of the reforms would be to dust off the commercial codes of the
1930s. Another part would be to adopt the more modern commercial laws that were
the shared legal base of the European Community. In its quest to return to Europe,
Poland also had a worthy role model, at least in part: Spain, after the death of the
dictator Francisco Franco.

In important ways, Spain and Poland shared a similar position in Europe. Both are
Catholic countries of around forty million people. Both are in the periphery of the
continental European economy, roughly equidistant from the heartland of the Rhine
industrial region, with Spain to the south and Poland to the east. As such, both were
late industrializers in Europe.

In 1955, the per capita GDPs of the two economies were roughly of equal size: Spain
was at $516 per capita; Poland at $755. Both countries had been damaged by war (civil
war in Spain's case); Poland was newly under the political control of the Soviet Union.
Spain gradually liberalized, even while Franco was still alive, and then accelerated its
integration with Europe after Franco's death in 1975. It finally became a member of
the European Community in 1986. Spain's return to Europe had done wonders for
its economic growth. Spain attracted Western European tourists and investments,
and enjoyed an export boom to its neighboring countries, thereby becoming one of
Europe's fastest growing economies. By 1989 Spain's per capita GDP was roughly four
times that of Poland.

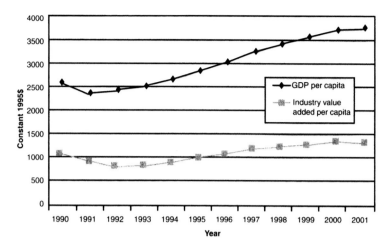

FIGURE 2.1.1 GDP and Industrial Production in Poland. (Source: Calculated using data from World Bank (2004).)

My explicit hope and belief was that Poland could enjoy a Spanish type of boom to start making up for nearly forty years of lost time. As we wrote the plan, there was one big uncertainty, however. What would happen to the old heavy industry built in Poland on the basis of trade and energy links with the Soviet Union? We were soon to find out. The start of the transition involved a large reduction in production by the old industry. The first changes, therefore, saw a dramatic decline in industrial production as a shakeout of the old Soviet-era enterprises occurred. It was two years into the reform, in 1991, when a recovery in GNP began to occur. Fortunately, that recovery would soon gain momentum and carry Poland above its 1989 GDP and industrial production levels, as is evident in Figure 2.1.1.

Launching the Plan

We took the document to Jacek Kuron the next morning. "Good, this is good," said Kuron. "Go see Michnik." Adam Michnik, the *Gazeta* editor, was the third member of Solidarity's intellectual triumvirate. Brave and visionary, Michnik was as clear thinking as anyone I met in the democratic upheavals of Eastern Europe and the former Soviet Union.

I laid out the plan to him. We talked a bit. He kept saying, "I'm not an economist. I don't understand these things." At the end of our conversation he asked, "Will this work? That's what I want to know. Will this work?" I said, 'Yes, this is going to work." He said, "Are you really confident that it's going to work?" I said, "This is good. This will work." Michnik said, "Okay, then you have filled in the last piece of my puzzle. I've known what to do politically. Now you tell me that there is an economic strategy as well. In that case, we're going to go for government."

Within a few days, Michnik wrote a lead editorial in the *Gazeta Wyborcza* that defined Poland's political transformation: "Wasza Prezydentura, Nasz Premier" ("Your Presidency, Our Prime Minister"). Power would be shared. Solidarity would form the government; the communists would keep the presidency and the "power ministries" (defense, interior, intelligence, police). It was a brilliant gambit, building confidence across an embittered half-century political divide. Michnik's compromise proposal was based not only on political realism, but also on the fundamental insight that the leaders of Solidarity and of Poland's Communist Party were all Polish patriots, with much more uniting them than dividing them. With the power ministries in communist hands, the Soviets were much more likely to assent to Solidarity's leadership in the civilian ministries.

At this point, Michnik, Kuron, and Geremek all advised Lipton and me that it was time for us to brief Lech Walesa. We got on a little plane a few days later to fly from Warsaw to Gdansk. Upon landing, we took a taxi to a nearly empty, cavernous building across the street from the famed Gdansk Shipyard, the place where Lech Walesa had jumped the wall in 1980 to start the revolution of freedom in Eastern Europe.

We were led into Walesa's office. The walls were covered with pictures of Martin Luther King, Jr., and John and Robert Kennedy, and various proclamations and awards. Out of the window we could see the great anchor at the shipyard entrance. Walesa came in and we greeted him. He began abruptly. "What are you doing here? What do you want?" I said, "Mr. Walesa, we're here to talk to you about the fact that Poland is slipping into hyperinflation. We have a plan for economic stabilization and reforms that we'd like to present." He immediately interrupted me. "I didn't come here for an abstract discussion; I want to know how we get banks into Gdansk."

I was nonplussed, but I pushed back firmly. "Mr. Walesa, hyperinflation is not an abstract issue. The current economic crisis could really destroy Polish society." I began to try to describe what I thought was happening. He listened, asked a question or two, and then said, "I want to know how we get foreign banks to come here. We've got good buildings here. We need banks. I want you to help me get a bank to Gdansk." I said, "Well, I'll certainly be working to try to help you with that." We discussed a little bit more, and he thanked us for coming, and we were led out. I was bewildered.

A few years later I was at the Belgian embassy in Moscow, speaking to a number of ambassadors. The Belgian ambassador pulled me aside, and said, "You'll be a little bit surprised to know that I was the next visitor to see Lech Walesa after you met him in the summer of 1989. I was Belgium's ambassador to Poland at the time." I expressed my amazement. He continued, "Well, Mr. Walesa said to me, 'I don't know what that fellow was talking about, but it sure sounded interesting.'"

As it turned out, I had many subsequent meetings with Lech Walesa. My admiration for Walesa was, and remains, sky-high. He was surely the inspiration that had brought me to Poland in the first place. Having been an electrician who jumped a shipyard wall and brought freedom to his country, Walesa had not had much time to learn macroeconomics. He clearly understood human nature and politics, however, and I learned a lot from him on both counts, as did the entire world. Walesa was a great president of Poland in the early 1990s and is one of the world's heroic freedom fighters.

Lipton and I flew back to the United States. About a week later, in mid-July, I talked with Michnik by phone. "So, what's going to happen?" Michnik responded, "It's okay; it's going to work." "What do you mean?" I asked. He said, "Gorbachev called us, and he's agreed with the proposed change." The Soviet Union was going to accept a Solidarity prime minister and a communist president. This decision was yet another of Gorbachev's extraordinary contributions to world peace and the end of the Cold War.

Gorbachev had actively helped to broker the arrival of Solidarity to power in Poland. Solidarity's rise to power was not a fait accompli grudgingly accepted by the Soviet leader. It was something Gorbachev promoted in the interest of peace.

Lipton and I returned to Poland in early August, and we introduced the reform plan to the Solidarity members of the Polish parliament. *Gazeta Wyborcza* also ran several big stories promoting the "Sachs Plan" as the way out of Poland's economic crisis. On August twenty-fourth, the day that Prime Minister Mazowiecki came to power, I was invited to speak to the Solidarity members of parliament. This was Poland's first day of political freedom in almost half a century. The national and international media were there, and as it turned out, so too were Senate Majority Leader Bob Dole and his wife, Elizabeth Dole.

Senator Dole spoke first. He brought the good wishes of the president of the United States and the American people. Dole wanted the Polish people to know that the American people stood with them in this moment of freedom. The United States would help to ensure that Poland was successful on its path to democracy and freedom. He sat down after prolonged applause. I was called to the podium next.

I started by saying that Poland's economic crisis was very deep, that a hyperinflation was brewing and the socialist system was collapsing. Poland was going to have to move with boldness and urgency to the market system. Then I said that there was one huge issue that was on everyone's mind: the crushing $40 billion of foreign debt that Poland owed to the world. Many people feared that this debt would become the real barrier separating Poland from Europe and from prosperity.

"I want to remind you of what Senator Dole just said. Senator Dole said that the American people are with you. I have no doubt that that's true. We Americans understand that after forty-five years of domination, Poland today marks one of the most important and positive events in modern history. Americans will be with you; Europe will be with you. So I'm sure Senator Dole agrees that Poland's debt should just be canceled. There's no way that the Soviet-era debt should in any way risk the freedom of the Polish people."

I then used the line that was often repeated afterward. I said, "Your debt crisis is over. All you have to do is send a postcard to your creditors: 'Thank you very much, but now we're in the age of freedom and democracy, and we can't pay you the Soviet-era debts.'" And I said, "Don't think about it again; it's done." A huge, thunderous applause erupted, not surprisingly, along with some shock.

After that evening there were a lot of people in Washington who tried to tell the new Polish leaders that I was dangerous. At least one well-placed Pole in Washington advised the prime minister to get me out of the country before I did real damage to Poland's economic reforms. I was worried, of course. Even though I felt that my concepts were right, my toehold as adviser was tenuous. Poland needed a decisive transformation to a market economy, combined with stabilization, currency convertibility, and debt cancellation. It was an attractive package of reforms that had a good chance of working despite the deepening crisis.

The next evening Lipton and I met the new prime minister, Tadeusz Mazowiecki. We were led in late at night to the Stalinesque Council of Ministers building. The prime minister greeted us wearily; his burden was evident. He was an older man, and the difficult months ahead were going to be exhausting. I didn't know what to expect of his approach to the economic crisis. In one sentence he dispelled my concerns and got it exactly right. He said to me, "I'm looking for Poland's Ludwig Erhard."

Ludwig Erhard had been the minister of economic affairs of postwar West Germany who decisively put the country on the path of market reform. He was a famously successful and bold economic manager who went on to become a somewhat less successful chancellor in the early 1960s. Erhard was especially famous for having ended price controls overnight in West Germany, a move that allowed goods to come back into the stores from the black markets. I had been recommending this kind of dramatic step, what would later be called shock therapy. Erhard had also been a major inspiration for Gonzalo Sánchez de Lozada in Bolivia.

We talked further. I described the ideas that I had, and he replied that the plans sounded very much like what he wanted to do. He needed to find someone who could really lead such a dramatic effort. He named a fellow whom I did not know, Leszek Balcerowicz. Balcerowicz ultimately headed the economic effort, and he was the true Ludwig Erhard of Poland—a brave, brilliant, and decisive leader.

Lipton and I met Balcerowicz two weeks later. I spent a few minutes describing our plan, with which he was already familiar. He then took out a large flow diagram and unfolded it on the table. He said, "We're going to do this, and we're going to do this dramatically fast." Balcerowicz was a professor at the Warsaw School of Economics and Planning. He was a respected, politically independent scholar who had received a master's degree in business at St. John's University in New York City. He spoke perfect English, understood the market economy, and was a long-distance runner. He would need this endurance for what lay ahead.

We began to work with Balcerowicz and his team to turn concepts into policies. It was one thing to sketch out some ideas, another to elaborate a program, and still another to construct a legislative, budgetary, and financial agenda. The details are overwhelming and unavoidable. That is why reforms cannot be led from the sidelines of parliament. Reforms have to be led by an executive team, with a real executive leader. Balcerowicz's first presentation of his plans would be in Washington, in late September 1989, at the annual IMF meetings. We helped draft the plan that he circulated to financial leaders at that occasion. It was an important moment. The world was waiting to hear what Poland planned to do.

Early one morning during the IMF meetings, I called Balcerowicz and said, "Leszek, I have an idea. I want to get you a billion dollars today. I want to raise money for a stabilization fund for the Polish currency, the Zloty Stabilization Fund. If we're going to make the Polish zloty a convertible currency, I think we should try to peg the zloty at a stable value right from the start of the reforms. To do that, Poland will need foreign exchange reserves, which could be put in a highly visible stabilization fund." Balcerowicz replied, "Do you think you could raise that money? If you can get a billion dollars, great."

As we had become accustomed to doing, Lipton and I set up a computer on Lipton's dining room table, and typed out a one-page memo explaining the idea of the $1 billion Zloty Stabilization Fund. The memo explained the concept of currency convertibility and stability as a linchpin of Poland's return to Europe. We then went to see Senator Dole. We explained the idea and he liked it. He invited us to return to his office in an hour to meet with General Brent Scowcroft, the National Security

Adviser. We presented the concept to General Scowcroft, who also liked it. By the end of the day the plan had been accepted at the White House; and by the end of the week, the Bush administration had announced its support for the $1 billion Zloty Stabilization Fund, of which the United States would contribute $200 million and would seek $800 million in contributions from other governments. The fund was put together by the end of the year, and was in place at the start of Poland's reforms on January 1, 1990.

From Plan to Action

Poland's "big bang," or shock therapy as it came to be called, began on the first day of the new year. Virtually all price controls were eliminated. The currency was steeply devalued and then pegged at the new rate of 9,500 zlotys per dollar. The currency was backed by the Zloty Stabilization Fund, and the Central Bank of Poland announced that it was prepared to intervene in the foreign exchange market to keep the rate at 9,500 per dollar. A raft of new economic legislation went into effect, especially laws allowing private companies to open for business. Trade barriers with Western Europe were eliminated, and private traders were free to travel to and from Western European neighbors to buy and sell goods.

The first days were frightening. With the end of price controls, the pent-up excess demand of the socialist era caused a massive jump in prices, on the order of a fivefold increase. The price of a particular cut of meat, for example, might rise within days from 1,000 zlotys per kilo to 5,000 zlotys per kilo. In the prereform days, however, the 1,000-zloty price was mostly a fiction. Only those people who queued up early in the morning and were lucky to pick the right shops could get meat at that price, but most shoppers would find only empty store counters. If they really wanted to get meat, they would have to pay black market prices, which could be even higher than 5,000 zlotys per kilo. Thus what looked like a shocking fivefold jump in prices was, in many cases, an actual decline in prices if one compared the black market prices before January 1, 1990, with the free-market prices afterward. After the reforms, the goods were available in the shop counters, not the alleys of the black market. This change, too, lowered the cost of goods by lowering the time and effort that went into buying them.

Theory is one thing, and practice is quite another. Even though I was confident that the end of price controls on January 1, 1990, would put goods back into the shops, at affordable prices, the early days of 1990 were nerve-racking. I called Poland regularly from the United States. Larry Lindenberg was getting more and more nervous. "It's been a week, and we don't see any goods in the shops yet." And then, suddenly, the breakthrough came. "Jeff, there are goods in the stores! In fact, the department store down the block is having a sale, cutting the price that it was charging for some appliances. This is the first time in my adult life I've seen a sale. Something is starting to happen."

Indeed, within a few weeks the markets filled again. On our visits to Poland at the time, Lipton and I kept a reconnaissance on the availability of kielbasa in a shop around the corner from the Ministry of Finance. Throughout late 1989 there were no sausages available at all. By the middle of January, the sausages lasted until about eleven in the morning. A few weeks later, the sausages were amply available the entire day. An amazing shuttle trade also began between Germany and Poland. Poles would take their little cars and drive across the border to Germany to buy goods to sell in Poland. They would sell the goods out of the trunk of the car, convert the zlotys into deutsche marks (a conversion legal after the start of the year), and then use the deutsche marks for the next round of purchases. Others were selling Polish goods—such as processed meats—or Polish labor on construction sites in Western Europe, bolstering the flow of deutsche marks and other Western European currencies on the Polish market.

None of this trade made Poland rich overnight. The newly available goods were expensive, and incomes were low. Still, Poles stopped spending their daily lives searching for goods in the black market or queuing up for goods in front of empty shops. The freedom to trade would become an underpinning of economic growth during the coming years. There were, of course, some very sharp changes in consumption patterns, some highly desirable, others quite painful. One change for the better was in the composition of the Polish diet. Until 1990, the Polish diet had been overstuffed with fatty dairy products, the result of heavy subsidies for dairy farmers. At the start of 1990, the subsidies were eliminated, and the diet shifted toward fruit and vegetables and away from cholesterol-laden dairy products. Fruit that had simply been unavailable in Poland, such as bananas, was now available through the shuttle trade. The new diet led to a significant drop in heart disease within a few years.

The biggest dislocation, by far, came in Poland's large state-owned industrial enterprises. Many enterprises had survived only because of central planning. They were not manufacturing products that were marketable, especially when Western goods became readily available. Many were making products that had been sold to the Soviet Union, which was not much of a customer any longer. Most of heavy industry had relied for decades on the delivery of very cheap and plentiful Soviet energy to Poland. In the beginning of 1990, with the end of communist rule in Poland, the Soviet Union began selling oil and gas to Eastern Europe on a strictly market basis, leading to a huge drop in supplies. Poland's large heavy industrial firms were forced to scale back their workforce, and some closed their doors permanently. The greatest pain was endured by middle-aged workers in their forties and fifties who had been trained for a Soviet economy that no longer existed. Most of these laid-off workers ended up on the unemployment dole for a while, then on pensions after early retirement. History had cheated them of the training and knowledge for a full lifetime of productive employment.

Fortunately, foreign investment from Germany and other Western European countries began to pick up relatively early. In late 1989, I was asked to meet with a senior executive of Asea Brown Boveri in the Zurich airport as I was traveling back to Boston. She told me that the company was considering an investment in Poland: taking over a state-owned power turbine factory. She asked if I would meet with the board, and when I did, they were very surprised when I told them how optimistic I was about Poland. Fortunately, enough of the ABB leadership shared that optimism, and the proposed investment went ahead. It became very successful, and the company ended up selling power turbines all over the world through ABB's global production network. Its success was a clear example of how Poland's integration into the world economy could create jobs in Poland, raise the productivity of local industry, help integrate Poland into the European economy, and begin the long process of raising productivity and living standards.

In general, Western European firms began to invest in Eastern Europe after 1989, often setting up production facilities in order to export manufactured goods to Western European markets, taking advantage of the lower wages in the east. This same pattern fueled Spain's rapid economic progress once it had become integrated with the European Community in the 1970s and 1980s. Geography, as usual, showed its power to shape economic events in the east. The farther a postcommunist country was from Western European markets, the lower the foreign direct investment (FDI) per person that flowed into the country. This is illustrated in Figure 2.1.2. The distance of each postcommunist country's capital city from Stuttgart, in the heart of the European economy, is plotted on the horizontal axis, and the amount of foreign direct investment per person as of 1996 on the vertical axis. Though not a rigorous analysis, the downward sloping line shows a strong relationship: the closer to Western Europe, the higher the FDI.

Within two years, it was beginning to dawn on many people that Poland was out of disaster and, in fact, beginning to grow. That resurgence was the first case of postsocialist growth in all of the countries of Eastern Europe. A degree of optimism began to creep in, even in a milieu that was historically so riddled with pessimism. The real revival of optimism, however, awaited a solution to the foreign debt, which hung over Poland's future like a persistent storm cloud.

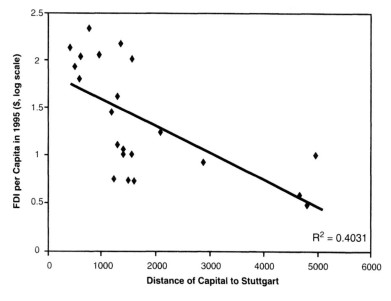

FIGURE 2.1.2 FDI and Location in Eastern Europe and former Soviet Union. (Note: Calculated using data from World Bank (2004).)

Ending the Strangle Hold of Soviet-Era Debt

Balcerowicz was not going to be able to manage the strife and dislocation of wrenching economic reforms if the benefits of the reforms were gobbled up by increased debt servicing. The gains from reform had to accrue to the Polish people, not to Poland's foreign creditors, a basic point of political economy that I had been stressing for many years about Latin America and Eastern Europe. Balcerowicz decided to draw the line, just as I had recommended. Poland would aim for a negotiated cancellation of a significant part of its external debts to ensure that its future was not held hostage to Soviet-era debts and that the Polish people themselves would be the beneficiaries of their brave plunge into democracy and a globally integrated market economy.

Alas, the negotiations would not be so simple. I heard repeatedly from senior finance officials of the United States, Europe, and Japan that the Western creditor nations would not forgive the debt of a European country. Bolivia was one thing, they argued, but Poland was quite another. Then the breakthrough came, when Balcerowicz went to see Helmut Kohl. Before he left, I suggested to Balcerowicz that it would be helpful for him to read the 1953 London Agreement, in which the allied victors of World War II had given the new Democratic Federal Republic of Germany a fresh start by reducing the burden of pre-World War II-era debts. In their meeting, as Chancellor Kohl started to object to debt cancellation for Poland, Balcerowicz told him that Germany had received the same treatment that he was asking for, and then he proceeded to summarize the 1953 settlement. Kohl ultimately agreed to do the same for Poland as had been done for Germany, calling it a historic time. That was the breakthrough. In the end, Poland received a cancellation of 50 percent of its debt, roughly $15 billion.

Countries are often told that if their debts are cancelled, they will no longer be creditworthy. This argument is backward. If a country has too much debt, it cannot be creditworthy. Rational investors will not make new loans. If debt cancellation is warranted by financial realities, is negotiated in good faith, and the country pursues sound economic policies afterward, then debt cancellation raises creditworthiness rather than reduces it. After all, a well-governed country with low debts can afford to take on new debts. Debt cancellation cannot be for a lark or whim. It must not be a game to avoid past obligations. Debt cancellation must reflect true social, economic, and political realities. Under those circumstances, a negotiated cancellation of debt can give new hope and new economic opportunities to the debtor country, and renewed creditworthiness. This is exactly what happened with Poland, which returned to the capital markets in the 1990s.

Alas, Yugoslavia was not so fortunate. At the time that I was advising Poland, I was also asked to help Yugoslavia escape from a similar spiral of hyperinflation, excessive foreign debt, and socialist collapse. The last prime minister of federal Yugoslavia, Ante Markovic, launched a stabilization plan in January 1990 that I had helped to devise. That plan got off to a wonderful start and could actually have worked, but for Slobodan Milosevic's deliberate and disastrously successful moves to undermine the federal government and its economic program. Markovic needed bolstering in his struggle with Milosevic, who was at that point head of Serbia. Markovic appealed to the Western powers to postpone—not to forgive—Yugoslavia's debts. A postpone-ment would have given financial breathing room and political prestige to Markovic, both of which would have strengthened the stabilization plan, whose success would have further strengthened him.

Yet while Milosevic gained strength in his battle to bring down Yugoslavia, the first Bush administration, the European Union, and the IMF refused even the modest request to reschedule Yugoslavia's debts. This refusal reflected, in my opinion, the stu-pidity of having foreign policy and international economic policy divorced from each other. Although Milosevic, not the West, must be blamed for the collapse of Yugosla-via, there was no effort of any sophistication to help hold the country together. The U.S. ambassador at the time, Warren Zimmerman, with whom I dealt briefly, wrote an account of the collapse of Yugoslavia, *Origins of a Catastrophe: Yugoslavia and Its Destroyers,* which arrived at the same conclusion.

Lessons from Poland's Reforms

By 2002, Poland was more than 50 percent richer in per capita terms than it had been in 1990, and it had logged the most successful growth record of any postcommu-nist country in Eastern Europe or the former Soviet Union. On May 1, 2004, fifteen years after the start of democracy, Poland became a member of the European Union. Poland has indeed returned to Europe. Its economic reforms have succeeded, even if the country faces many continuing challenges and decades more before it closes the income and wealth gaps with its richer neighbors in Western Europe.

I had first been invited to Poland because of my experience with Bolivia and its neighbors in South America. The lessons of Latin American stabilization and debt cancellation had indeed proved useful for Poland, as Krzysztof Krowacki hoped when he had first come to my office at Harvard in January 1989. I learned a vast amount after arriving in Poland, and the lessons were vital not only for understand-ing what was needed in Poland (and its neighbors) but also for understanding events and economic development strategies in Latin America and other parts of the world. Both the similarities and differences with Bolivia captivated me. I began to under-stand how a country's geography, history, and internal social dynamics shaped its economic performance. Clinical economics was beginning to evolve.

First, I realized more than ever how a country's fate is crucially determined by its specific linkages to the rest of the world. Bolivia's history, crises, and economic prospects all thoroughly reflected its situation as a mountainous, landlocked coun-try making its living by exporting natural resources. Poland's history, crises, and economic prospects, by contrast, all thoroughly reflected its situation as a mainly low-lying plain sandwiched between Germany to the west and Russia to the east. Throughout the two centuries from 1763 to 1989, the long, flat Pomeranian plain had been among the worst, if not the very worst, plots of real estate on the planet. German and Russian armies had invaded Poland many times. Poland had disappeared from the map—consumed by its more powerful neighbors in the second half of the eigh-teenth century—only to reappear in 1919 as part of the peace settlement after World War I. But independence was not true freedom. Poland was invaded in the same month by Germany and the Soviet Union, in September 1939, the launch of World War II, and then it fell under Soviet domination between 1945 and 1989.

I believed that although Poland's geography had been perhaps the most adverse in the world for two centuries, it would likely prove to be among the most fortunate after 1989. With peace in Europe, that broad flat plain between Germany and Russia would be perfect for trucks carrying merchandise and cars carrying tourists, instead of tanks carrying conquering armies. Indeed, geography did work to Poland's advantage after 1989, with a boom of trade and foreign investment. ABB, Volkswagen, and dozens of other Western European companies viewed Poland as an enormously convenient base of operations for production for the European market. Poland thereby took in billions of dollars of foreign investment in ways that Bolivia, up in the mountains, could only dream about.

Second, I learned once again about the importance of a basic guiding concept for broad-based economic transformation, a concept powerful enough to frame the great debates in a society and give guidance to millions of individuals about the changes ahead. In Bolivia, the guiding concepts were democracy, the end of hyperinflation, and the reinvention of the country, from a tin and coca producer to something new. In Poland, the guiding principle, above all others, was the return to Europe. Western Europe, and particularly the European Community (and later the European Union), provided the reference point, the organizing principles, even the specific tasks ahead for Poland's transformation. Hardship and uncertainty would be tolerated in Polish society if the end point seemed reachable. Indeed, the promise of membership in the European Union was fulfilled fourteen years after the start of the reforms.

Third, and crucially, I saw again the practical possibilities of large-scale conceptual thinking. Poland needed a fundamental transformation from a moribund socialist economy to a market economy. The end point was clear, but the path was not. Certain facts seemed to stand in the way. Poland needed to integrate with the neighboring market economies, especially Germany's. For that it needed a stable, convertible currency for market-based trade. But convertibility of the zloty seemed a long way off, unless confidence in the zloty could be restored quickly. Hence the idea of the Zloty Stabilization Fund. Poland needed to reestablish creditworthiness, but the overhang of Soviet-era debt seemed to stand in the way; hence the idea of a negotiated debt cancellation. By showing how these specific policy initiatives fit into a grander vision, and with practical historical precedents (like Germany's debt agreement in 1953), I was able to sell the pragmatic approaches needed to clear away the stumbling blocks on Poland's way back to Europe.

Fourth, I learned not to take no for an answer. For almost two years I had been told by senior finance officials of the seven richest countries, the G7, that Poland's debts would not be cancelled. In the end, they were. Logic prevailed, as indeed it often does. Sometimes, however, logic fails, as it did in Yugoslavia, and as it did in important ways in the Russian reforms as well. Still, the experience of hearing no, no, no, eventually followed by yes, has deeply affected my view of policy advocacy. I do not take as a given what is considered politically impossible, but rather I am prepared to argue incessantly, and annoyingly, for what needs to be done, even when it is claimed to be impossible. That leads to some striking successes as well as some deep disappointments, something I would experience in the case of Russia's reforms.

Russia: A World Apart

The differences between Russia and what we had seen elsewhere were staggering. Everything in Russia was vastly more complex than in Poland: the scale of the problems; the extent of the socialist straitjacket on the society; the thousand years of autocracy; the eleven time zones in Russia alone; a population almost four times as large as Poland's; and profound geographical, cultural, religious, and linguistic differences within Russia and between Russia and the West. Even the knowledge of what a market economy meant was vastly greater in Poland than in Russia. Poland's minister of finance, Leszek Balcerowicz, had studied in the United States for two years and received a master's degree. No one in the Russian leadership had anything like that experience. Gaidar had spent just a few weeks in the West, and he was by far the most worldly of all of the emerging Russian leaders at the time.

Russia was truly a world apart. I realized that although Russia could not organize its reforms around the concept of the return to Europe as Poland had done, it could follow Yeltsin's call for Russia to be a "normal" power—one not seeking empire but embracing democracy and adopting a market economy. In the shadow of Russian history, normalcy was a riveting and revolutionary concept, but who in Russia truly knew what it meant? Nobody in Russia had ever lived under normalcy. Russians had lived under Stalin, seventy-five years of central planning, a thousand years of Russian autocracy, and centuries of serfdom in which the overwhelming majority of the population lived as peasants without freedom. Normalcy would not be so easy to achieve. I never once claimed it would be easy, only that it could be possible.

This transformation would be the hardest in modern history because the gap between where Russia was and where it needed to be—for domestic peace, stability, and economic development—was as vast as imaginable. All of Russia's basic economic and political institutions would need an overhaul. Russia's economic structure—the interconnections of factories, people, natural resources, and technology—had already reached a dead end. People were literally in the wrong places. They were in Siberia, living in large secret cities that had been created for military purposes. They were working in heavy industries utterly dependent on the massive use of oil and gas reserves, as if there was no limit to those resources. In 1989, for example, the Soviet Union produced 557 kilograms of steel per person, compared with just 382 kilograms in the United States, despite Russia's per capita income being less than one third of the United States in purchasing-power terms. Yet during that same period, the late 1980s and early 1990s, its oil and gas production was plummeting. Existing reservoirs were being depleted, and the Soviets were not investing adequately in new reservoirs in difficult locations, often in the tundra. According to estimates by the U.S. Energy Information Administration, overall Soviet oil production fell from 12 million barrels per day in 1989 to 10.3 million barrels in 1991.

No economic policy could be massive enough to relocate people, factories, and assets in a matter of days or weeks or even a few years. The transformation that Russia needed would be complex and contentious. The phrase shock therapy, a journalistic concoction to describe radical reform, was all wrong. There would be no single jolt to end Russia's tribulations. The initial shocks of price decontrol, currency convertibility, and market liberalization could help, as such measures did in Poland, but they would not solve the problems of underlying structural disarray, falling energy supplies, and a myriad of other interconnected crises. The reform measures, at their very best, would help to steer Russia onto a path of massive, generation-long economic and social transformation. Nevertheless, Russia would need considerable international help to pull all of this off successfully, including the now-familiar components of financial reserves for stabilization of the Russian currency, the ruble, and cancellation of part of the Soviet-era debt.

Could it work? I thought so. I certainly thought it was worth a try. What, after all, were the alternatives? Civil war? A quick descent into a new tyranny? Anarchy? A new conflict with the West? I took on the assignment of adviser to Gaidar and his team not because I was sure, or even confident, that the reforms would work, but rather because I thought they needed to be tried. They offered the best chance for peace, democracy, and economic prosperity.

My essential advice to Russia was to move quickly on the key reforms that were possible—such as stabilization and market liberalization—and to move definitively, although not overnight, on privatization. Aim for normalcy rather than uniqueness, we kept repeating. We also urged them to get all the external financial help possible. Gaidar shared this vision. He appointed a group of advisers from abroad, and asked us to prepare a strategy paper that could be presented to President Yeltsin in December. I became the main drafter and spokesman of the group, and we met twice with Yeltsin in December 1991 at the Kremlin.

In the second of the meetings, the morning of December eleventh, Yeltsin came in beaming, arms outstretched, and sat down as happy and as radiant as he could be. "Gentlemen, I want to tell you, indeed I can be the first to tell you, the Soviet Union is finished." He continued, "I just met in the next room with the Soviet generals, and they've agreed to the dissolution of the Soviet Union." Our work took on an added urgency. The Soviet Union was finished; Russia would soon be independent, and economic reforms would be launched within weeks.

Russia launched the reforms on January 2, 1992, two years to the day after Poland had launched its reforms. Gaidar became acting prime minister during 1992, until he was replaced as prime minister by Viktor Chernomyrdin at the end of the year. By the end of the first week, the differences between Russia and Poland regarding social and political attitudes to reform had become clear. In Poland, the early days of reform were met with trepidation and grim acceptance. In Russia, the attacks on Gaidar and his team began immediately, including from within the cabinet and from his rival and eventual successor Chernomyrdin, but more forcefully from leaders in the Russian Duma (parliament) who almost immediately called for Gaidar's resignation. It would be like that for years, with the reformers barely holding on to office and, even more rarely, to power. Most reforms were implemented only as pale shadows of what had been planned.

Lessons from Russia

Even a dozen years after the start of reforms, it is too early to make a final judgment about Russia's prospects for democracy and market economy. One recalls Chinese Premier Chou En-lai's quip when asked whether the French Revolution had been a success or failure: "It's too soon to say." We do not know yet whether Russia will become a "normal" country, with a functioning democracy and market economy. We do know, however, that many opportunities have been squandered. Russia could have stabilized much more easily if it had had the benefit of a stabilization fund, a debt standstill, a partial cancellation of debts, and a real aid program. The reformers would have been able to keep their place at the table of power. Corruption would have been less, and the oligarchs might never have become household names. And with oil and gas revenues flowing into the Russian treasury rather than private pockets, the situation of pensioners, the unemployed, and others depending on public revenues could have been ameliorated, and the country could have made the public investments needed to resume economic growth.

Still, despite the turmoil, much went right even as much went wrong. The world was lucky. Despite the upheavals of the 1990s and the lack of consequential help from outside, Russia remained at peace and in cooperation with the rest of the world. In Chechnya, violence flared at huge cost, and continues to rage, but matters could have been much worse. There were predictions of civil war, nuclear proliferation, pogroms, and more, yet none of those scenarios has come to pass.

Russia became a market economy, albeit one that remains lopsided toward primary commodities, especially oil and gas. Stabilization was only achieved at the end of the 1990s, after years of high inflation followed by a very sharp balance of payments crisis in 1998. After that, however, the economy began to grow, quite rapidly in fact, on the basis of high international energy prices and a devalued currency that promoted exports.

The biggest question is whether Russia will become a democracy, beating the odds and a history of a thousand years of authoritarianism. The tendencies toward authoritarian rule remain strong. Though President Vladimir Putin rules with the trappings of constitutionalism and multiparty democracy, he has also successfully centralized power, tamed the media, and muzzled the independent opposition. As always throughout Russian history, much remains murky. Putin's attack on the oligarchs in 2003 and 2004 can be viewed as an utterly appropriate challenge to ill-gotten wealth. Alternatively, it can be viewed as an attack on the kind of independent wealth that could challenge the supremacy of the state. It is probably a bit of both. Time will tell.

Russia, like Bolivia and Poland, bears the powerful imprint of its physical conditions, and thus adds another piece to our puzzle of global economic geography. Russia has two overwhelming geographical features that shape its fate. First, it is a huge landmass, the largest of any country in the world. Russia's population lives in the interior of Eurasia, mostly far from ports, navigable rivers, and international trade. Thus, throughout Russian history, the country has had only relatively weak economic engagements with the rest of the world. Second, Russia is a high-latitude country, marked by short growing seasons and an often forbidding climate. Population densities throughout Russian history have been low because food production per hectare has also tended to be low. As a result, during most of Russian history, more than 90 percent of the population lived as farmers in sparsely populated villages, producing food with very low yields. Cities were few and far between. The division of labor that depends on urban life and international trade were never dominant features of social life.

Adam Smith made the point vividly 228 years ago when he noted in *The Wealth of Nations*,

> All that part of Asia which lies any considerable way north of the Euxine and Caspian seas, the antient Scythia, the modern Tartary and Siberia, seem in all ages of the world to have been in the same barbarous and uncivilized state in which we find them at present. The sea of Tartary is the frozen ocean which admits of no navigation, and though some of the greatest rivers in the world run through that country, they are at too great a distance from one another to carry commerce and communication through the greater part of it.

Looking back, would I have advised Russia differently knowing what I know today? I would have been less optimistic about getting large-scale U.S. aid—especially with Richard Cheney and Paul Wolfowitz in leadership positions, with their visions of Russia as a continuing threat rather than a future trade and foreign policy partner. Knowing that, I would have been less sanguine about the chances for success. But would the advice have been different? To a larger extent, the answer is no. I viewed external help as needed to cushion the reforms, but even without the foreign help, the reforms needed to be made. Without adequate aid, the political consensus around the reforms was deeply undermined, and the reform process was thereby compromised and put at increased risk of failure. But as for recommendations regarding budget balance, currency convertibility, international trade, and the like, these changes made sense with or without external aid. Most of the bad things that happened—such as the massive theft of state assets under the rubric of privatization—were directly contrary to the advice that I gave and to the principles of honesty and equity that I hold dear.

China had a much less tumultuous escape from its socialist economy, as I detail next, but China's meteoric economic rise is more the result of China's very different geography, geopolitics, and demography than a difference of policy choices.

Joseph E. Stiglitz,
Globalization and Its Discontents (2002)*

Chapter 5: Who Lost Russia?

With the fall of the Berlin Wall in late 1989, one of the most important economic transitions of all time began. It was the second bold economic and social experiment of the century.[1] The first was Russia's transition to communism seven decades earlier. Over the years, the failures of this first experiment became apparent. As a consequence of the 1917 Revolution and the Soviet hegemony over a large part of Europe after World War II, some 8 percent of the world's population that lived under the Soviet Communist system forfeited both political freedom and economic prosperity. The second transition in Russia as well as in Eastern and Southeastern Europe is far from over, but this much is clear: in Russia it has fallen far short of what the advocates of the market economy had promised, or hoped for. For the majority of those living in the former Soviet Union, economic life under capitalism has been even worse than the old Communist leaders had said it would be. Prospects for the future are bleak. The middle class has been devastated, system of crony and mafia capitalism has been created, and the one achievement, the creation of a democracy with meaningful freedoms, including a free press, appears fragile at best, particularly as formerly independent TV stations are shut down one by one. While those in Russia must bear much of the blame for what has happened, the Western advisers, especially from the United States and the IMF, who marched in so quickly to preach the gospel of the market economy, must also take some blame. At the very least, they provided support to those who led Russia and many of the other economies down the paths they followed, arguing for a new religion—market fundamentalism—as a substitute for the old one—Marxism—which had proved so deficient.

Russia is an ever-unfolding drama. Few anticipated the sudden dissolution of the Soviet Union and few anticipated the sudden resignation of Boris Yeltsin. Some see the oligarchy, the worst excesses of the Yeltsin years, as already curbed; others simply see that some of the oligarchs have fallen from grace. Some see in the increases in output that have occurred in the years since its 1998 crisis as the beginning of a renaissance, one which will lead to the recreation of a middle class; others see it as taking years just to repair the damage of the past decade. Incomes today are markedly lower than they were a decade ago, and poverty is much higher. The pessimists see the country as a nuclear power wavering with political and social instability. The optimists (!) see a semiauthoritarian leadership establishing stability, but at the price of the loss of some democratic freedoms.

Russia experienced a burst of growth after 1998, based on high oil prices and the benefits of the devaluation which the IMF so long opposed. But as oil prices have come down, and the benefits of the devaluation have been reaped, growth too has slowed. Today, the economic prognosis is somewhat less bleak than it was at the time of the 1998 crisis, but it is no less uncertain. The government barely made ends meet when oil prices—the country's main exports—were high. If oil prices fall, as they seem to be as this book goes to press, it could spell real trouble. The best that can be said is that the future remains cloudy.

It is not surprising that the debate over who lost Russia has had such resonance. At one level, the question is clearly misplaced. In the United States it evokes memories of the debate a half century ago about who lost China, when the Communists took over that country. But China was not America's to lose in 1949, nor was Russia America's to lose a half century later. In neither case did America and the Western European countries have control over the political and social evolution. At the same time, it is clear that something has clearly gone wrong, not only in Russia but also in most of the more than twenty countries that emerged from the Soviet empire.

The IMF and other Western leaders claim that matters would have been far worse were it not for their help and advice. We had then, and we have now, no crystal ball to tell us what would happen if alternative policies were pursued. We have no way of running a controlled experiment, going back in time to try an alternative strategy. We have no way of being *certain* of what might have been.

But we do know that certain political and economic judgment calls were made, and we know that the outcomes have been disastrous. In some cases, the link between the policies and the consequences is easy to see: The IMF worried that a devaluation of the ruble would set off a round of inflation. Its insistence on Russia maintaining an overvalued currency and its supporting that with billions of dollars of loans ultimately crushed the economy. (When the ruble was finally devalued in 1998, inflation did not soar as the IMF had feared, and the economy experienced its first significant growth.) In other cases, the links are more complicated. But the experiences of the few countries that followed different policies in managing their transitions help guide us through the maze. It is essential that the world make an informed judgment about the IMF policies in Russia, what drove them and why they were so misguided. Those, myself included, who have had an opportunity to see firsthand how decisions were made and what their consequences were have a special responsibility to provide their interpretations of relevant events.

There is a second reason for a reappraisal. Now, over ten years after the fall of the Berlin Wall, it is clear that the transition to a market economy will be a long struggle, and many, if not most, of the issues that seemed settled only a few years ago will need to be revisited. Only if we understand the mistakes of the past can we hope to design policies that are likely to be effective in the future.

The leaders of the 1917 Revolution recognized that what was at stake was more than a change in economics; it was a change in society in all of its dimensions. So, too, the transition from communism to a market economy was more than just an economic experiment: it was a transformation of societies and of social and political structures. Part of the reason for the dismal results of the economic transition was the failure to recognize the centrality of these other components.

The first Revolution recognized how difficult the task of transformation was, and the revolutionaries believed that it could not be accomplished by democratic means; it had to be led by the "dictatorship of the proletariat." Some of the leaders of the second revolution in the 1990s at first thought that, freed from the shackles of communism, the Russian people would quickly appreciate the benefits of the market. But some of the Russian market reformers (as well as their Western supporters and advisers) had very little faith or interest in democracy, fearing that if the Russian people were allowed to choose, they would not choose the "correct" (that is *their*) economic model. In Eastern Europe and the former Soviet Union, when these "market reform" benefits failed to materialize in country after country, democratic elections rejected the extremes of market reform, and put social democratic parties or even "reformed" Communist parties, many with former Communists at the helm, into power. It is not surprising that many of the market reformers showed a remarkable affinity to the old ways of doing business: in Russia, President Yeltsin, with enormously greater powers than his counterparts in any Western democracy, was encouraged to circumvent the democratically elected Duma (parliament) and to enact market reforms by decree.[2] It is as if the market Bolsheviks, native true believers, as well as the Western experts and evangelists of the new economic religion who flew into the post-Socialist countries, attempted to use a benign version of Lenin's methods to steer the post-communism, "democratic" transition.

The Challenges and Opportunities of Transition

As the transition began in the early 1990s, it presented both great challenges and opportunities. Seldom before had a country deliberately set out to go from a situation where government controlled virtually every aspect of the economy to one where decisions occurred through markets The People's Republic of China had begun its transition in the late 1970s, and was still far from a full-fledged market economy. One of the most successful transitions had been Taiwan, 100 miles off the shore of mainland China. It had been a Japanese colony since the end of the nineteenth century. With China's 1949 revolution, it became the refuge for the old Nationalist leadership, and from their base in Taiwan, they claimed sovereignty over the entire mainland, keeping the name—"the Republic of China." They had nationalized and redistributed the land, established and then partially privatized an array of major industries, and more broadly created a vibrant market economy. After 1945 many countries, including the United States, moved from wartime mobilization to a peacetime economy. At the time, many economists and other experts feared a major recession would follow wartime demobilization, which entailed not only a change in how decisions were made (ending versions of command economies in which wartime governments made the major decisions about production and returning to private sector management of production) but also an enormous reallocation of production of goods, for example, from tanks to ears. But by 1947, the second full postwar year, production in the United States was 9.6 percent higher than 1944, the last full war year. By the end of the war, 37 percent of GDP (1945) was devoted to defense. With peace, this number was brought down rapidly to 7.4 percent (1947).

There was one important difference between the transition from war to peace, and from communism to a market economy, as I will detail later: Before World War II, the United States had the basic market institutions in place, even though during the war many of these were suspended and superseded by a "command and control" approach. In contrast, Russia needed both resource redeployment *and* the wholesale creation of market institutions.

But Taiwan and China faced similar problems to the economies in transition. Both faced the challenge of a major transformation of their societies, including the establishment of the institutions that underlay a market economy. Both have had truly impressive successes. Rather than prolonged transition recession, they had close to double-digit growth. The radical economic reformers who sought to advise Russia and many of the other countries on transition paid scant attention to these experiences, and the lessons that could be learned. It was not because they believed that Russian history (or the history of the other countries making the transition) made these lessons inapplicable. They studiously ignored the advice of Russian scholars, whether they were experts in its history, economics, or society, for a simple reason: they believed that the *market revolution* which was about to occur made all of the knowledge available from these other disciplines irrelevant. What the market fundamentalists preached was textbook economics—an oversimplified version of market economics which paid scant attention to the dynamics of change.

Consider the problems facing Russia (or the other countries) in 1989. There were institutions in Russia that had names *similar* to those in the West, but they did not perform the same functions. There were banks in Russia, and the banks did garner savings; but they did not make decisions about who got loans, nor did they have the responsibility for monitoring and making sure that the loans were repaid. Rather, they simply provided the "funds," as dictated by the government's central planning agency. There were firms, enterprises producing goods in Russia, but the enterprises did not make decisions: they produced what they were told to produce, with inputs (raw material, labor, machines) that were allocated to them. The major scope for entrepreneurship lay in getting around problems posed by the government: the government would give enterprises quotas on output, without necessarily providing the inputs needed, but in some cases providing more than necessary. Entrepreneurial managers engaged in trades to enable themselves to fulfill their quotas, in the meanwhile getting a few more perks for themselves than they could have enjoyed on their official salaries. These activities—which had always been necessary to make the Soviet system merely function—led to the corruption that would only increase as Russia moved to a market economy.[3] Circumventing what laws were in force, if not breaking them outright, became part of the way of life, a precursor to the breakdown of the "rule of law" which was to mark the transition.

As in a market economy, under the Soviet system there were prices, but the prices were set by government fiat, not by the market. Some prices, such as those for basic necessities, were kept artificially low—enabling even those at the bottom of the income distribution to avoid poverty. Prices for energy and natural resources also were kept artificially low—which Russia could only afford because of its huge reservoirs of these resources.

Old-fashioned economics textbooks often talk about market economics as if it had three essential ingredients: prices, private property, and profits. Together with competition, these provide incentives, coordinate economic decision making, ensuring that firms produce what individuals want at the lowest possible cost. But there has also long been a recognition of the importance of *institutions*. Most important are legal and regulatory frameworks, to ensure that contracts are enforced, that there is an orderly way of resolving commercial disputes, that when borrowers cannot repay what is owed, there are orderly bankruptcy procedures, that competition is maintained, and that banks that take depositors are in a position to give the money back to depositors when they ask. This framework of laws and agencies helps ensure that securities markets operate in a fair manner, that managers do not take advantage of shareholders nor majority shareholders of minority shareholders. In the nations with mature market economies, the legal and regulatory frameworks had been built up over a century and a half, in response to problems encountered in unfettered market capitalism. Bank regulation came into place after massive bank failures; securities regulation after major episodes in which unwary shareholders were cheated. Countries seeking to create a market economy did not have to relive these disasters: they could learn from the experiences of others. But while the market reformers may have mentioned this institutional infrastructure, they gave it short shrift. They tried to take a shortcut to capitalism, creating a market economy without the underlying institutions, and institutions without the underlying institutional infrastructure. Before you set up a stock market, you have to make sure there are real regulations in place. New firms need to be able to raise new capital, and this requires banks that are real banks, not the kinds of banks that characterized the old regime, or banks that simply lend money to government. A real and effective banking system requires strong banking regulations. New firms need to be able to acquire land, and this requires a land market and land registration.

Similarly, in Soviet-era agriculture, farmers used to be given the seeds and fertilizer they needed. They did not have to worry about getting these and other inputs (such as tractors) or marketing their output. Under a market economy, markets for inputs and outputs had to be created, and this required new firms or enterprises. Social institutions are also important. Under the old system in the Soviet Union, there was no unemployment, and hence no need for unemployment insurance. Workers typically worked for the same state enterprise for their entire lives, and the firm provided housing and retirement benefits. In post-1989 Russia, however, if there were to be a labor market, individuals would have to be able to move from firm to firm. But if they could not obtain housing, such mobility would be almost impossible. Hence, a housing market was necessary. A minimal level of social sensitivity means that employers will be reluctant to fire workers if there is nothing for them to fall back on. Hence, there could not be much "restructuring" without a social safety net. Unfortunately, neither a housing market nor a real safety net existed in the new Russia of 1989.

The challenges facing the economies of the former Soviet Union and the other Communist bloc nations in transition were daunting: they had to move from one price system—the distorted price system that prevailed under communism—to a market price system; they had to create markets and the institutional infrastructure that underlies it; and they had to privatize all the property which previously had belonged to the state. They had to create a new kind of entrepreneurship—not just the kind that was good at circumventing government rules and laws—and new enterprises to help redeploy the resources that had previously been so inefficiently used.

No matter how one looked at it, these economies faced hard choices, and there were fierce debates about which choices to make. The most contentious centered on the speed of reform: some experts worried that if they did not privatize quickly, creating a large group of people with a vested interest in capitalism, there would be a reversion to communism. But others worried that if they moved too quickly, the reforms would be a disaster—economic failures compounded by political corruption—opening up the way to a backlash, either from the extreme left or right. The former school was called "shock therapy," the latter "gradualist."

The views of the shock therapists—strongly advocated by the U.S. Treasury and the IMF—prevailed in most of the countries. The gradualists, however, believed that the transition to a market economy would be better managed by moving at a reasonable speed, in good order ("sequencing"). One didn't need to have *perfect* institutions; but, to take one example, privatizing a monopoly before an effective competition or regulatory authority was in place might simply replace a government monopoly with a private monopoly, even more ruthless in exploiting the consumer. Ten years later, the wisdom of the gradualist approach is at last being recognized: the tortoises have overtaken the hares. The gradualist critics of shock therapy not only accurately predicted its failures but also outlined the reasons why it would not work. Their only failure was to underestimate the magnitude of the disaster.

If the challenges posed by transition were great, so were the opportunities. Russia was a rich country. While three quarters of a century of communism may have left its populace devoid of an understanding of market economics, it had left them with a high level of education, especially in technical areas so important for the New Economy. After all, Russia was the first country to send a man into space.

The economic theory explaining the failure of the communism was clear: Centralized planning was doomed to failure, simply because no government agency could glean and process all the relevant information required to make an economy function well. Without private property and the profit motive, incentives—especially managerial and entrepreneurial incentives—were lacking. The restricted trade regime, combined with huge subsidies and arbitrarily set prices, meant the system was rife with distortions.

It followed that replacing centralized planning with a decentralized market system, replacing public ownership with private property, and eliminating or at least reducing the distortions by liberalizing trade, would cause a burst of economic output. The cutback in military expenditures—which had absorbed a huge share of GDP when the USSR was still in existence, five times larger than in the post-Cold War era—provided even more room for increases in standards of living. Instead, however, the standard of living in Russia, and many of the other East European transition countries, fell.

The "Reform" Story

The first mistakes occurred almost immediately as the transition began. In the enthusiasm to get on with a market economy, most prices were freed overnight in 1992, setting in motion an inflation that wiped out savings, and moved the problem of macrostability to the top of the agenda. Everybody recognized that with hyperinflation (inflation at double-digit rates *per month*), it would be difficult to have a successful transition. Thus, the first round of shock therapy—instantaneous price liberalization—necessitated the second round: bringing inflation down. This entailed tightening monetary policy—raising interest rates.

While most of the prices were completely freed, some of the most important prices were kept low—those for natural resources. With the newly declared "market economy," this created an open invitation: If you can buy, say, oil and resell it in the West, you could make millions or even billions of dollars. So people did. Instead of making money by creating new enterprises, they got rich from a new form of the old entrepreneurship—exploiting mistaken government policies. And it was this "rent-seeking" behavior that would provide the basis of the claim by reformers that the problem was not that the reforms had been too quick, but that they had been too slow. If only *all* prices had been freed immediately! There is considerable validity in this argument, but as a defense of the radical reforms it is disingenuous. Political processes never give the technocrat free rein, and for good reason: as we have seen, technocrats often miss out on important economic, social, and political dimensions. Reform, even in well-functioning political and economic systems, is always "messy." Even if it made sense to push for instantaneous liberalization, the more relevant question is, how should one have proceeded with liberalization if one could not succeed in getting important sectors, like energy prices, liberalized quickly?

Liberalization and stabilization were two of the pillars of the radical reform strategy. Rapid privatization was the third. But the first two pillars put obstacles in the way of the third. The initial high inflation had wiped out the savings of most Russians so there were not enough people in the country who had the money to buy the enterprises being privatized. Even if they could afford to buy the enterprises, it would be difficult to revitalize them, given the high interest rates and lack of financial institutions to provide capital.

Privatization was supposed to be the first step in the process of restructuring the economy. Not only did ownership have to change but so did management; and production had to be reoriented, from producing what firms were told to produce to producing what consumers wanted. This restructuring would, of course, require new investment, and in many cases job cuts. Job cuts help overall efficiency, of course, only if they result in workers moving from low-productivity jobs to high-productivity employment. Unfortunately, too little of this positive restructuring occurred, partly because the strategy put almost insurmountable obstacles in the way.

The radical reform strategy did not work: gross domestic product in post-1989 Russia fell, year after year. What had been envisioned as a short transition recession turned into one of a decade or more. The bottom seemed never in sight. The devastation—the loss in GDP—was greater than Russia had suffered in World War II. In the period 1940–46 the Soviet Union industrial production fell 24 percent. In the period

1990–99, Russian industrial production fell by almost 60 percent—even greater than the fall in GDP (54%). Those familiar with the history of the earlier transition in the Russian Revolution, *into* communism, could draw some comparisons between that socioeconomic trauma and the post-1989 transition: farm livestock decreased by half, investment in manufacturing came almost to a stop. Russia was able to attract some foreign investment in natural resources; Africa had shown long ago that if you price natural resources low enough, it is easy to attract foreign investment in them.

The stabilization/liberalization/privatization program was, of course, not a growth program. It was intended to set the preconditions for growth. Instead, it set the preconditions for decline. Not only was investment halted, but capital was used up— savings vaporized by inflation, the proceeds of privatization or foreign loans largely misappropriated. Privatization, accompanied by the opening of the capital markets, led not to wealth creation but to asset stripping. It was perfectly logical. An oligarch who has just been able to use political influence to garner assets worth billions, after paying only a pittance, would naturally want to get his money out of the country. Keeping money in Russia meant investing it in a country in deep depression, and risking not only low returns but having the assets seized by the next government, which would inevitably complain, quite rightly, about the "illegitimacy" of the privatization process. Anyone smart enough to be a winner in the privatization sweepstakes would be smart enough to put their money in the booming U.S. stock market, or into the safe haven of secretive offshore bank accounts. It was not even a close call; and not surprisingly, billions poured out of the country.

The IMF kept promising that recovery was around the corner. By 1997, it had reason for this optimism. With output having already fallen 41 percent since 1990, how much further down could it go? Besides, the country was doing much of what the Fund had stressed. It had liberalized, if not completely; it had stabilized, if not completely (inflation rates were brought down dramatically); and it had privatized. But of course it is easy to privatize quickly, if one does not pay any attention to *how* one privatizes: essentially give away valuable state property to one's friends. Indeed, it can be highly profitable for governments to do so—whether the kickbacks come back in the form of cash payments or in campaign contributions (or both).

But the glimpses of recovery seen in 1997 were not to last long. Indeed, the mistakes the IMF made in a distant part of the world were pivotal. In 1998, the fallout from the East Asian crisis hit. The crisis had led to a general skittishness about investing in emerging markets, and investors demanded higher returns to compensate them for lending capital to these countries. Mirroring the weaknesses in GDP and investment were weaknesses in public finance: the Russian government had been borrowing heavily. Though it had difficulty making budget ends meet, the government, pressured by the United States, the World Bank, and the IMF to privatize rapidly, had turned over its state assets for a pittance, and done so before it had put in place an effective tax system. The government created a powerful class of oligarchs and businessmen who paid but a fraction of what they owed in taxes, much less what they would have paid in virtually any other country.

Thus, at the time of the East Asia crisis, Russia was in a peculiar position. It had an abundance of natural resources, but its government was poor. The government was virtually giving away its valuable state assets, yet it was unable to provide pensions for the elderly or welfare payments for the poor. The government was borrowing billions from the IMF, becoming increasingly indebted, while the oligarchs, who had received such largesse from the government, were taking billions out of the country. The IMF had encouraged the government to open up its capital accounts, allowing a free flow of capital. The policy was supposed to make the country more attractive for foreign investors; but it was virtually a one-way door that facilitated a rush of money out of the country.

The 1998 Crisis

The country was deeply in debt, and the higher interest rates that the East Asia crisis had provoked created an enormous additional strain. This rickety tower collapsed when oil prices fell. Due to recessions and depressions in Southeast Asia, which IMF policies had exacerbated, oil demand not only failed to expand as expected but actually contracted. The resulting imbalance between demand and supply of oil turned into a dramatic fall in crude oil prices (down over 40% in the first six months of 1998 compared to the average prices in 1997). Oil is both a major export commodity and a source of government tax revenue for Russia, and the drop in prices had a predictably devastating effect. At the World Bank, we became aware of the problem early in 1998, when prices looked ready to fall even below Russia's cost of extraction plus transportation. Given the exchange rate at the time, Russia's oil industry could cease being profitable. A devaluation would then be inevitable.

It was clear that the ruble was overvalued. Russia was flooded with imports, and domestic producers were having a hard time competing. The switch to a market economy and away from the military was supposed to allow a redeployment of resources to produce more consumer goods, or more machines to produce consumer goods. But investment had halted, and the country was not producing consumer goods. The overvalued exchange rate—combined with the other macroeconomic policies foisted on the country by the IMF—had crushed the economy, and while the official unemployment rate remained subdued, there was massive disguised unemployment. The managers of many firms were reluctant to fire workers, given the absence of an adequate safety net. Though unemployment was disguised, it was no less traumatic: while the workers only pretended to work, the firms only pretended to pay. Wage payments fell into massive arrears, and when workers were paid, it was often with bartered goods rather than rubles.

If for these people, and for the country as a whole, the overvalued exchange rate was a disaster, for the new class of businessmen the overvalued exchange rate was a boon. They needed fewer rubles to buy their Mercedes, their Chanel handbags, and imported Italian gourmet foods. For the oligarchs trying to get their money out of the country, too, the overvalued exchange rate was a boon—it meant that they could get more dollars for their rubles, as they squirreled away their profits in foreign bank accounts.

Despite this suffering on the part of the majority of Russians, the reformers and their advisers in the IMF feared a devaluation, believing that it would set off another round of hyperinflation. They strongly resisted any change in the exchange rate and were willing to pour billions of dollars into the country to avoid it. By May, and certainly by June of 1998, it was clear Russia would need outside assistance to maintain its exchange rate. Confidence in the currency had eroded. In the belief that a devaluation was inevitable, domestic interest rates soared and more money left the country as people converted their rubles for dollars. Because of this fear of holding rubles, and the lack of confidence in the government's ability to repay its debt, by June 1998 the government had to pay almost 60 percent interest rates on its ruble loans (GKOs, the Russian equivalent of U.S. Treasury bills). That figure soared to 150 percent in a matter of weeks. Even when the government promised to pay back in dollars, it faced high interest rates (yields on dollar-denominated debt issued by the Russian government rose from slightly over 10% to almost 50%, 45 percentage points higher than the interest rate the U.S. government had to pay on its Treasury bills at the time); the market thought there was a high probability of default, and the market was right. Even that rate was lower than it might otherwise have been because many investors believed that Russia was too big and too important to fail. As the New York investment banks pushed loans to Russia, they whispered about how big the IMF bailout would have to be.

The crisis mounted in the way that these crises so frequently do. Speculators could see how much in the way of reserves was left, and as reserves dwindled, betting on a devaluation became increasingly a one-way bet. They risked almost nothing betting on the ruble's crash. As expected, the IMF came to the rescue with $4.8 billion in July 1998.[4]

In the weeks preceding the crisis, the IMF pushed policies that made the crisis, when it occurred, even worse. The Fund pushed Russia into borrowing more in foreign currency and less in rubles. The argument was simple: The ruble interest rate was much higher than the dollar interest rate. By borrowing in dollars, the government could save money. But there was a fundamental flaw in this reasoning. Basic economic theory argues that the difference in the interest rate between dollar bonds and ruble bonds should reflect the expectation of a devaluation. Markets equilibrate so that the risk-adjusted cost of borrowing (or the return to lending) is the same. I have much less confidence in markets than does the IMF, so I have much less faith that in fact the risk-adjusted cost of borrowing is the same, regardless of currency. But I also have much less confidence than the Fund that the Fund's bureaucrats can predict exchange rate movements better than the market. In the case of Russia, the IMF bureaucrats believed that they were smarter than the market—they were willing to bet Russia's money that the market was wrong. This was a misjudgment that the Fund was to repeat, in varied forms, time and time again. Not only was the judgment flawed; it exposed the country to enormous risk: if the ruble did devalue, Russia would find it far more difficult to repay the dollar-denominated loans.[5] The IMF chose to ignore this risk. By inducing greater foreign borrowing, by making Russia's position once it devalued so much less tenable, the IMF was partly culpable for the eventual suspension of payments by Russia on its debts.

The Rescue

When the crisis hit, the IMF led the rescue efforts, but it wanted the World Bank to provide $6 billion of the rescue package. The total rescue package was for $22.6 billion. The IMF would provide $11.2 billion of this total, as I stated before; the World Bank would lend $6 billion, and the rest would be provided by the Japanese government.

This was hotly debated inside the World Bank. There were many of us who had been questioning lending to Russia all along. We questioned whether the benefits to possible future growth were large enough to justify loans that would leave a legacy of debt. Many thought that the IMF was making it easier for the government to put off meaningful reforms, such as collecting taxes from the oil companies. The evidence of corruption in Russia was clear. The Bank's own study of corruption had identified that region as among the most corrupt in the world. The West knew that much of those billions would be diverted from their intended purposes to the families and associates of corrupt officials and their oligarch friends. While the Bank and the IMF had seemingly taken a strong stance against lending to corrupt governments, it appeared that there were two standards. Small nonstrategic countries like Kenya were denied loans because of corruption while countries such as Russia where the corruption was on a far larger scale were continually lent money.

Apart from these moral issues, there were straightforward economic issues. The IMF's bailout money was supposed to be used to support the exchange rate. However, if a country's currency is overvalued and this causes the country's economy to suffer, maintaining the exchange rate makes little sense. If the exchange rate support works, the country suffers. But in the more likely case that the support does not work, the money is wasted, and the country is deeper in debt. Our calculations showed that Russia's exchange rate was overvalued, so providing money to maintain that exchange rate was simply bad economic policy. Moreover, calculations at the World Bank before the loan was made, based on estimates of government revenues and expenditures over time, strongly suggested that the July 1998 loan would not work. Unless a miracle brought interest rates down drastically, by the time autumn rolled around, Russia would be back in crisis.

There was another route by which I reached the conclusion that a further loan to Russia would be a great mistake. Russia was a naturally resource-rich country. If it got its act together, it didn't need money from the outside; and if it didn't get its act together, it wasn't clear that any money from the outside would make much difference. Under either scenario, the case against giving money seemed compelling.

In spite of strong opposition from its own staff, the Bank was under enormous political pressure from the Clinton administration to lend money to Russia. The Bank managed a compromise, publicly announcing a very large loan, but providing the loan in trenches—installments. A decision was taken to make $300 million available immediately, with the rest available only later, as we saw how Russia's reforms progressed. Most of us thought that the program would fail long before the additional money had to be forthcoming. Our predictions proved correct. Remarkably, the IMF seemed able to overlook the corruption, and the attendant risks with what would happen with the money. It actually thought that maintaining the exchange rate at an overvalued level was a good thing, and that the money would enable it to do this for more than a couple months. It provided billions to the country.

The Rescue Fails

Three weeks after the loan was made, Russia announced a unilateral suspension of payments and a devaluation of the ruble.[6] The ruble crashed. By January 1999, the ruble had declined in real effective terms by more than 45 percent from its July 1998 level.[7] The August 17 announcement precipitated a global financial crisis. Interest rates to emerging markets soared higher than they had been at the peak of the East Asian crisis. Even developing countries that had been pursuing sound economic policies found it impossible to raise funds. Brazil's recession deepened, and eventually it too faced a currency crisis. Argentina and other Latin American countries only gradually recovering from previous crises were again pushed nearer the brink. Ecuador and Colombia went over the brink and into crisis. Even the United States did not remain untouched. The New York Federal Reserve Bank engineered a private bailout of one of the nation's largest hedge funds, Long Term Capital Management, since the Fed feared its failure could precipitate a global financial crisis.

The surprise about the collapse was not the collapse itself, but the fact that it really did take some of the IMF officials—including some of the most senior ones—by surprise. They had genuinely believed that their program would work.

Our own forecasts proved only partially correct: we thought that the money might sustain the exchange rate for three months; it lasted three weeks. We felt that it would take days or even weeks for the oligarchs to bleed the money out of the country; it took merely hours and days. The Russian government even "allowed" the exchange rate to appreciate. As we have seen, this meant the oligarchs would need to spend fewer rubles to purchase their dollars. A smiling Viktor Gerashchenko, the chairman of the Central Bank of Russia, told the president of the World Bank and me that it was simply "market forces at work. "When the IMF was confronted with the facts—the billions of dollars that it had given (loaned) Russia was showing up in Cypriot and Swiss bank accounts just days after the loan was made—it claimed that these weren't *their* dollars. The argument demonstrated either a remarkable lack of understanding of economics or a level of disingenuousness that rivaled Gerashchenko's, or both. When money is sent to a country, it is not sent in the form of marked dollar bills. Thus, one cannot say it is "my" money that went anywhere. The IMF had lent Russia the dollars—funds that allowed Russia, in turn, to give its oligarchs the dollars to take out of the country. Some of us quipped that the IMF would have made life easier all around if it had simply sent the money directly into the Swiss and Cyprus bank accounts.

It was, of course, not just the oligarchs who benefited from the rescue. The Wall Street and other Western investment bankers, who had been among those pressing the hardest for a rescue package, knew it would not last: they too took the short respite provided by the rescue to rescue as much as they could, to flee the country with whatever they could salvage.

By lending Russia money for a doomed cause, IMF policies led Russia into deeper debt, with nothing to show for it. The cost of the mistake was not borne by the IMF officials who gave the loan, or America who had pushed for it, or the Western bankers and the oligarchs who benefited from the loan, but by the Russian taxpayer.

There was one positive aspect of the crisis: The devaluation spurred Russia's import competing sectors—goods actually produced in Russia finally took a growing share of the home market. This "unintended consequence" ultimately led to the long-awaited growth in Russia's real (as opposed to black) economy. There was a certain irony in this failure: macroeconomics was supposed to be the IMF's strength, and yet even here it had failed. These macroeconomic failures compounded the other failures, and contributed mightily to the enormity of the decline.

The Failed Transitions

Seldom has the gap between expectations and reality been greater than in the case of the transition from communism to the market. The combination of privatization, liberalization, and decentralization was supposed to lead quickly, after perhaps a short transition recession, to a vast increase in production. It was expected that the benefits from transition would be greater in the long run than in the short run, as old, inefficient machines were replaced, and a new generation of entrepreneurs was created. Full integration into the global economy, with all the benefits that that would bring, would also come quickly, if not immediately.

These expectations for economic growth were not realized, not only in Russia but in *most* of the economies in transition. Only a few of the former Communist countries—such as Poland, Hungary, Slovenia, and Slovakia—have a GDP equal to that of a decade ago. For the rest, the magnitudes of the declines in incomes are so large that they are hard to fathom. According to World Bank data, Russia today (2000) has a GDP that is less than two-thirds of what it was in 1989. Moldova's decline is the most dramatic, with output today less than a third of what it was a decade ago. Ukraine's 2000 GDP is just a third of what it was ten years ago.

Underlying the data were true symptoms of Russia's malady. Russia had quickly been transformed from an industrial giant—a country that had managed with Sputnik to put the first satellite into orbit—into a natural resource exporter; resources, and especially oil and gas, accounted for over half of all exports. While the Western reform advisers were writing books with titles like *The Coming Boom in Russia* or *How Russia Became a Market Economy*, the data itself was making it hard to take seriously the rosy pictures they were painting, and more dispassionate observers were writing books like *The Sale of the Century: Russia's Wild Ride from Communism to Capitalism*.[8]

The magnitude of GDP decline in Russia (not to mention other former Communist countries) is the subject of controversy, and some argue that because of the growing and critical informal sector—from street vendors to plumbers, painters, and other service providers, whose economic activities are typically hard to capture in national income statistics—the numbers represent an overestimate of the size of the decline. However, others argue that because so many of the transactions in Russia entail barter (over 50% of industrial sales),[9] and because the "market" prices are typically higher than these "barter" prices, the statistics actually underestimate the decline.

Taking all this into account, there is still a consensus that most individuals have experienced a marked deterioration in their basic standard of living, reflected in a host of social indicators. While in the rest of the world life spans were increasing markedly, in Russia they were over three years shorter, and in Ukraine almost three years shorter. Survey data of household consumption—what people eat, how much they spend on clothing, and what type of housing they live in—corroborates a marked decline in standards of living, on par with those suggested by the fall in GDP statistics. Given that the government was spending less on defense, standards of living should have increased even more than GDP. To put it another way, assume that somehow previous expenditures on consumption could have been preserved, and a third of the expenditures on military could have been shifted into new production of consumption goods, and that there had been no restructuring to increase efficiency or to take advantage of the new trade opportunities. Consumption—living standards—would then have increased by 4 percent, a small amount but far better than the actual decline.

Increased Poverty and Inequality

These statistics do not tell the whole story of the transition in Russia. They ignore one of the most important successes: How do you value the benefits of the new democracy, as imperfect as it might be? But they also ignore one of the most important failures: The increase in poverty and inequality.

While the size of the national economic pie was shrinking, it was being divided up more and more inequitably so the average Russian was getting a smaller and smaller slice. In 1989, only 2 percent of those living in Russia were in poverty. By late 1998, that number had soared to 23.8 percent, using the $2 a day standard. More than 40 percent of the country had less than $4 a day, according to a survey conducted by the World Bank. The statistics for children revealed an even deeper problem, with more than 50 percent living in families in poverty. Other post-Communist countries have seen comparable, if not worse, increases in poverty.[10]

Shortly after I arrived at the World Bank, I began taking a closer look at what was going on, and at the strategies that were being pursued. When I raised my concerns about these matters, an economist at the Bank who had played a key role in the privatizations responded heatedly. He cited the traffic jams of cars, many of them Mercedes, leaving Moscow on a summer weekend, and the stores filled with imported luxury goods. This was a far different picture from the empty and colorless retail establishments under the former regime. I did not disagree that a substantial number of people had been made wealthy enough to cause a traffic jam, or to create a demand for Gucci shoes and other imported luxury items sufficient for certain stores to prosper. At many European resorts, the wealthy Russian has replaced the wealthy Arab of two decades ago. In some, street signs are even given in Russian along with the native language. But a traffic jam of Mercedes in a country with a per capita income of $4,730 (as it was in 1997) is a sign of a sickness, not health. It is a clear sign of a society that concentrates its wealth among the few, rather than distributing it among the many.

While the transition has greatly increased the number of those in poverty, and led a few at the top to prosper, the middle class in Russia has perhaps been the hardest hit. The inflation first wiped out their meager savings, as we have seen. With wages not keeping up with inflation, their real incomes fell. Cutbacks in expenditures on education and health further eroded their standards of living. Those who could, emigrated. (Some countries, like Bulgaria, lost 10% or more of their population, and an even larger fraction of their educated workforce.) The bright students in Russia and other countries of the former Soviet Union that I've met work hard, with one ambition in mind: to migrate to the West. These losses are important not just for what they imply today for those living in Russia, but for what they portend for the future: historically, the middle class has been central to creating a society based on the rule of law and democratic values.

The magnitude of the increase in inequality, like the magnitude and duration of the economic decline, came as a surprise. Experts did expect some increase in inequality, or at least measured inequality. Under the old regime, incomes were kept similar by suppressing wage differences. The Communist system, while it did not make for an easy life, avoided the extremes of poverty, and kept living standards relatively equal, by providing a high common denominator of quality for education, housing, health care and child care services. With a switch to a market economy, those who worked hard and produced well would reap the rewards for their efforts, so some increase in inequality was inevitable. However, it was expected that Russia would be spared the inequality arising from inherited wealth. Without this legacy of inherited inequality, there was the promise of a more egalitarian market economy. How differently matters have turned out! Russia today has a level of inequality comparable with the worst in the world, those Latin American societies which were based on a semifeudal heritage.[11]

Russia has gotten the worst of all possible worlds—an enormous decline in output and an enormous increase in inequality. And the prognosis for the future is bleak: extremes of inequality impede growth, particularly when they lead to social and political instability.

How Misguided Policies Led to the Failures of Transition

We have already seen some of the ways that the Washington consensus policies contributed to the failures: privatization done the wrong way had not led to increased efficiency or growth but to asset stripping and decline. We have seen how the problems were compounded by interactions between reforms, as well as their pace and sequencing: capital market liberalization and privatization made it easier to take money out of the country; privatization before a legal infrastructure was in place enhanced the ability and incentive for asset stripping rather than reinvesting in the country's future. A full description of what went on, and a full analysis of the ways in which IMF programs contributed to the decline of the country, is a book in itself. Here, I want to sketch three examples. In each case, defenders of the IMF will say that things would have been worse, but for their programs. In some cases—such as the absence of competition policies—the IMF will insist that such policies were part of the program, but, alas, Russia did not implement them. Such a defense is ingenuous: with dozens of conditions, *everything* was in the IMF program. Russia knew, however, that when it came to the inevitable charade in which IMF would threaten to cut off aid, Russia would bargain hard, an agreement (not often fulfilled) would be reached, and the money spigot opened up again. What was important were the monetary targets, the budget deficits, and the pace of privatization—the number of firms that had been turned over to the private sector, never mind how. Almost everything else was secondary; much—like competition policy—was virtually window-dressing, a defense against critics who said they were leaving out important ingredients to a successful transition strategy. As I repeatedly pushed for stronger competition policies, those inside Russia who agreed with me, who were trying to establish a true market economy, who were trying to create an effective competition authority, repeatedly thanked me.

Deciding what to emphasize, establishing priorities, is not easy. Textbook economics often provides insufficient guidance. Economic theory says that for markets to work well, there must be both competition and private property. If reform was easy, one would wave a magic wand and have both. The IMF chose to emphasize privatization, giving short shrift to competition. The choice was perhaps not surprising: corporate and financial interests often oppose competition policies, for these policies restrict their ability to make profits. The consequences of IMF's mistake here were far more serious than just high prices: privatized firms sought to establish monopolies and cartels, to enhance their profits, undisciplined by effective antitrust policies. And as so often happens, the profits of monopoly prove especially alluring to those who are willing to resort to mafialike techniques either to obtain market dominance or to enforce collusion.

Inflation

Earlier we saw how the rapid liberalization at the beginning had led to the burst of inflation. The sad part of Russia's story was that each mistake was followed by another, which compounded the consequences.

Having set off the rapid inflation through abrupt price liberalization in 1992, it was necessary for the IMF and the Yeltsin regime to contain it. But balance has never been the strong suit of the IMF, and its excessive zeal led to excessively high interest rates. There is little evidence that lowering inflation below a moderate level increases growth. The most successful countries, like Poland, ignored the IMF's pressure and maintained inflation at around 20 percent through the critical years of adjustment. IMF's star pupils, like the Czech Republic, which pushed inflation down to 2 percent, saw their economy stagnate. There are some good reasons to believe that excessive zeal in fighting inflation can dampen real economic growth. The high interest rate clearly stifled new investment. Many of the new, privatized firms, even those who began without an eye to looting them, saw that they could not expand and switched to asset stripping. The IMF-driven high interest rates led to an overvaluation of the exchange rate, making imports cheap and exports difficult. No wonder then that any visitor to Moscow after 1992 could see the stores filled with imported clothing and other goods, but would be hard-pressed to find much with a "Made in Russia" label. And this was true even five years after the transition began.

The tight monetary policies also contributed to the use of barter. With a shortage of money, workers were paid in kind—with whatever it was that the factory produced or had available, from toilet paper to shoes. While the flea markets that were established everywhere throughout the country as workers tried to get cash to buy the bare necessities of life gave a semblance of entrepreneurial activity, they masked huge inefficiencies. High rates of inflation are costly to an economy because they interfere with the workings of the price system. But barter is every bit as destructive to the effective workings of the price system, and the excesses of monetary stringency simply substituted one set of inefficiencies for a possibly even worse set.

Privatization

The IMF told Russia to privatize as fast as possible; how privatization was done was viewed as secondary. Much of the failure of which I wrote earlier—both the decline in incomes and the increase in inequality—can be directly linked to this mistake. In a World Bank review of the ten-year history of transition economies, it became apparent that privatization, in the absence of the institutional infrastructure (like corporate governance), had no positive effect on growth.[12] The Washington Consensus had again just gotten it wrong. It is easy to see the links between the way privatization was done and the failures.

For instance, in Russia and other countries, the lack of laws ensuring good corporate governance meant that those who could get control of a corporation had an incentive to steal assets from the minority shareholders; and managers had similar incentives vis-à-vis shareholders. Why expend energy in creating wealth when it was so much easier to steal it? Other aspects of the privatization process, as we have seen, enhanced the incentives as well as opportunities for corporate theft. Privatization in Russia turned over large national enterprises, typically to their old managers. Those insiders knew how uncertain and difficult was the road ahead. Even if they were predisposed to do so, they dared not wait for the creation of capital markets and the hosts of other changes that would be required for them to reap the full value of any investments and restructuring. They focused on what they could get out of the firm in the next few years, and all too often, this was maximized by stripping assets.

Privatization was also supposed to eliminate the role of the state in the economy; but those who assumed that had a far too naive view of the role of the state in the modern economy. It exercises its influence in a myriad of ways at a myriad of levels. Privatization did reduce the power of the central government, but that devolution left the local and regional governments with far wider discretion. A city like, say, St. Petersburg, or an *oblast* (regional government) like Novgorod, could use a host of regulatory and tax measures to extort "rents" from firms that operated in their jurisdiction. In advanced industrial countries there is a rule of law which keeps local and state governments from abusing their potential powers; not so in Russia. In advanced industrial countries, competition among communities makes each try to make itself more attractive to investors. But in a world in which high interest rates and an overall depression make such investments unlikely in any case, local governments spent little time creating attractive "environments for investment" and focused instead on seeing how much they could extract from existing enterprises—just as the owners and managers of newly privatized firms themselves did. And when these privatized firms operated across many jurisdictions, authorities in one district reasoned that they had better take what they could grab before others took their own bites out of assets. And this only reinforced the incentive of managers to grab whatever they could as quickly as possible. After all, the firms would be left destitute in any case. It was a race to the bottom. There were incentives for asset stripping at every level.

Just as the radical "shock therapy" reformers claim that the problem with liberalization was not that it was too slow, but that it was not fast enough, so too with privatization. While the Czech Republic, for example, was praised by the IMF even as it faltered, it became clear that the country's rhetoric had outpaced its performance: it had left the banks in state hands. If a government privatizes corporations, but leaves banks in the state hands, or without effective regulation, that government does not create the hard budget constraints that lead to efficiency, but rather an alternative, less transparent way of subsidizing firms—and an open invitation to corruption. Critics of Czech privatization claim the problem was not that privatization was too rapid, but that it was too slow. But no country has succeeded in privatizing everything, overnight, well, and it is likely that were a government to try to do instantaneous privatization, there would be a mess. The task is too difficult, the incentives for malfeasance too high. The failures of the rapid privatization strategies were predictable—and predicted.

Not only did privatization, as it was imposed in Russia (as well as in far too many of its former Soviet bloc dependencies), not contribute to the economic success of the country; it undermined confidence in government, in democracy, and in reform. The result of giving away its rich natural resources before it had in place a system to collect natural resource taxes was that a few friends and associates of Yeltsin became billionaires, but the country was unable to pay pensioners their $15 a month pension.

The most egregious example of bad privatization was the loans-for-share program. In 1995, the government, instead of turning to the Central Bank for needed funds, turned to private banks. Many of these private banks belonged to friends of the government who had been given bank charters. In an environment with underregulated banks, the charters were effectively a license to print money, to make loans either to themselves or their friends or to the government. As a condition of the loan, the government put up shares of its own enterprises as collateral. Then—surprise!—the government defaulted on its loans; the private banks took over the companies in what might be viewed as a sham sale (though the government did go through a charade of having "auctions"); and a few oligarchs became instant billionaires. These privatizations had no political legitimacy. And, as noted previously, the fact that they had no legitimacy made it even more imperative that the oligarchs take their funds quickly out of the country—before a new government that might try to reverse the privatizations or undermine their position came to power.

Those who benefited from the largesse of the state, or more accurately from Yeltsin's largesse, worked hard to ensure Yeltsin's reelection. Ironically, while there was always a presumption that part of Yeltsin's giveaway went to finance his campaign, some critics think that the oligarchs were far too smart to use their money to pay for the election campaign; there was plenty of government slush funds that could be used. The oligarchs provided Yeltsin with something that was far more valuable—modern campaign management techniques and positive treatment by the TV networks they controlled.

The loans-for-share scheme constituted the final stage of the enrichment of the oligarchs, the small band of people (some of whom owed their origins, reportedly at least, partly to mafialike connections) who came to dominate not just the economic but the political life of the country. At one point, they claimed to control 50 percent of the country's wealth! Defenders of the oligarchs liken them to America's robber barons, the Harrimans and Rockefellers. But there is a big difference between the activities of such figures in nineteenth-century capitalism, even those carving out railway and mining baronies in America's Wild West, and the Russian oligarchy's exploitation of Russia, what has been called the Wild East. America's robber barons created wealth, even as they accumulated fortunes. They left a country much richer, even if they got a big slice of the larger pie. Russia's oligarchs stole assets, stripped them, leaving their country much poorer. The enterprises were left on the verge of bankruptcy, while the oligarch's bank accounts were enriched.

The Social Context

The officials who applied Washington Consensus policies failed to appreciate the social context of the transition economies. This was especially problematic, given what had happened during the years of communism.

Market economies entail a host of economic relationships—exchanges. Many of these exchanges involve matters of trust. An individual lends another money, trusting that he will be repaid. Backing up this trust is a legal system. If individuals do not live up to their contractual obligations, they can be forced to do so. If an individual steals property from another, he can be brought to court. But in countries with mature market economies and adequate institutional infrastructures, individuals and corporations resort only occasionally to litigation.

Economists often refer to the glue that holds society together as "social capital." Random violence and Mafia capitalism are often cited as reflections of the erosion of social capital, but in some of the countries of the former Soviet Union that I visited, one could see everywhere, in more subtle ways, direct manifestations of the erosion of social capital. It is not just a question of the misbehavior of a few managers; it is an almost anarchic theft by all from all. For instance, the landscape in Kazakhstan is dotted with greenhouses—missing their glass. Of course, without the glass, they fail to function. In the early days of the transition, there was so little confidence in the future that each individual took what he could: each believed that others would take the glass out of the greenhouse—in which case the greenhouse (and their livelihood) would be destroyed. But if the greenhouse was, in any case, fated to be destroyed, it made sense for each to take what he could—even if the value of the glass was small.

The way in which transition proceeded in Russia served to erode this social capital. One got wealthy not by working hard or by investing, but by using political connections to get state property on the cheap in privatizations. The social contract, which bound citizens together with their government was broken, as pensioners saw the government giving away valuable state assets, but claiming that it had no money to pay their pensions.

The IMF's focus on macroeconomics—and in particular on inflation—led it to shunt aside issues of poverty, inequality, and social capital. When confronted about this myopia of focus, it would say, "Inflation is especially hard on the poor." But its policy framework was not designed to minimize the impact on the poor. And by ignoring the impacts of its policies on the poor and on social capital, the IMF actually impeded *macroeconomic* success. The erosion of social capital created an environment that was not conducive to investment. The Russian government's (and the IMF's) lack of attention to a minimal safety net slowed down the process of restructuring, as even hardheaded plant managers often found it difficult to fire workers, knowing there was little standing between their fired workers and extreme hardship, if not starvation.

Shock Therapy

The great debate over reform strategy in Russia centered on the pace of reform. Who was right, in the end—the "shock therapists" or the "gradualists"? Economic theory, which focuses on equilibrium and idealized models, has less to say about dynamics, the order, timing, and pacing of reforms, than one would like—though IMF economists often tried to convince client countries otherwise. The debaters resorted to metaphors to convince others of the merits of their side. The rapid reformers said, "You can't cross a chasm in two leaps," while the gradualists argued that it took nine months to make a baby, and talked about crossing the river by feeling the stones. In some cases, what separated the two views was more a difference in perspective than reality. I was present at a seminar in Hungary where one participant said, "We must have rapid reform! It must be accomplished in five years." Another said, "We should have gradual reform. It will take us five years." Much of the debate was more about the manner of reform than the speed.

We have already encountered two of the essential critiques of the gradualists: "Haste makes waste"—it is hard to design good reforms well; and sequencing matters. There are, for instance, important prerequisites for a successful mass privatization, and creating these prerequisites takes time.[13] Russia's peculiar pattern of reforms demonstrates that incentives do matter, but that Russia's kind of ersatz capitalism did not provide the incentives for wealth creation and economic growth but rather for asset stripping. Instead of a smoothly working market economy, the quick transition led to a disorderly Wild East.

The Bolshevik Approach to Market Reform

Had the radical reformers looked beyond their narrow focus on economics, they would have found that history shows that most of the experiments in radical reform were beset by problems. This is true from the French Revolution in 1789, to the Paris Commune of 1871, to the Bolshevik Revolution in Russia in 1917, and to China's Cultural Revolution of the 1960s and 1970s. It is easy to understand the forces giving rise to each of these revolutions, but each produced its own Robespierre, its own political leaders who were either corrupted by the revolution or took it to extremes. By contrast, the successful American "Revolution" was not a true revolution in society; it was a *revolutionary* change in political structures, but it represented an *evolutionary* change in the structure of society. The radical reformers in Russia were trying simultaneously for a revolution in the economic regime and in the structure of society. The saddest commentary is that, in the end, they failed in both: a market economy in which many old party apparatchiks had simply been vested with enhanced powers to run and profit from the enterprises they formerly managed, in which former KGB officials still held the levers of power. There was one new dimension: a few new oligarchs, able and willing to exert immense political and economic power.

In effect, the radical reformers employed Bolshevik strategies—though they were reading from different texts. The Bolsheviks tried to impose communism on a reluctant country in the years following 1917. They argued that the way to build socialism was for an elite cadre to "lead" (often a euphemism for "force") the masses into the correct path, which was not necessarily the path the masses wanted or thought best. In the "new" post-Communist revolution in Russia, an elite, spearheaded by international bureaucrats, similarly attempted to force rapid change on a reluctant population.

Those who advocated the Bolshevik approach not only seemed to ignore the history of such radical reforms but also postulated that political processes would work in ways for which history provided no evidence. For instance, economists such as Andrei Shleifer, who recognized the importance of the institutional infrastructure for a market economy, believed that privatization, no matter how implemented, would lead to a political demand for the institutions that govern private property.

Shleifer's argument can be thought of as an (unwarranted) extension of Coase's theorem. The economist Ronald H. Coase, who was awarded a Nobel Prize for his work, argued that in order to achieve efficiency, well-defined property rights are essential. Even if one distributed assets to someone who did not know how to manage them well, in a society with well-defined property rights that person would have an incentive to sell to someone who could manage the assets efficiently. That is why, advocates of rapid privatization argued, one didn't really need to pay close attention to how privatization was accomplished. It is now recognized that the conditions under which Coase's conjecture is valid are highly restrictive[14]—and certainly weren't satisfied in Russia as it embarked on its transition.

Shleifer and company, however, took Coase's ideas further than Coase himself would have done. They believed that political processes were governed in the same way as economic processes. If a group with vested interests in property could be created, it would demand the establishment of an institutional infrastructure necessary to make a market economy work, and its demands would be reflected in the political process. Unfortunately, the long history of political reforms suggests that the distribution of income does matter. It has been the middle class that has demanded the reforms that are often referred to as "the rule of law." The very wealthy usually do far better for themselves behind closed doors, bargaining special favors and privileges. Certainly it has not been demands from the Rockefellers and the Bill Gates of the world that have led to strong competition policies. Today, in Russia, we do not see demands for strong competition policy forthcoming from the oligarchs, the new monopolists. Demands for the rule of law have come from these oligarchs, who obtained their wealth through behind-the-scenes special deals within the Kremlin, only as they have seen their special influence on Russia's rulers wane.

Demands for an open media, free from concentration in the hands of a few, came from the oligarchs, who sought to control the media in order to maintain their power—but only when the government sought to use its power to deprive them of theirs. In most democratic and developed countries such concentrations of economic power would not long be tolerated by a middle class forced to pay monopoly prices. Americans have long been concerned with the dangers of concentration of media power, and concentrations of power in the United States on a scale comparable to that in Russia today would be unacceptable. Yet U.S. and IMF officials paid little attention to the dangers posed by the concentration of media power; rather, they focused on the rapidity of privatization, a sign that the privatization process was proceeding apace. And they took comfort, indeed even pride, in the fact that the concentrated private media was being used, and used effectively, to keep their friends Boris Yeltsin and the so-called reformers in power.

One of the reasons that it is important to have an active and critical media is to ensure that the decisions that get made reflect not just the interests of a few but the general interest of society. It was essential for the continuation of the Communist system that there not be public scrutiny. One of the problems with the failure to create an effective, independent, and competitive media in Russia was that the policies—such as the loans-for-share scheme—were not subjected to the public critique that they deserved. Even in the West, however, the critical decisions about Russian policy, both at the international economic institutions and in the U.S. Treasury, went on largely behind closed doors. Neither the taxpayers in the West, to whom these institutions were supposed to be accountable, nor the Russian people, who paid the ultimate price, knew much about what was going on at the time. Only now are we wrestling with the question of "Who lost Russia?"—and why. The answers, as we are beginning to see, are not edifying.

Notes

1. Much of this and the next two chapters is based on work reported more extensively elsewhere. See the following papers: J.E. Stiglitz, "Whither Reform? Ten Years of the Transition" (Annual World Bank Conference on Development Economics, 1999), in Boris Pleskovic and Joseph E. Stiglitz, eds., *The World Bank* (Washington, DC, 2000), pp. 27–56; J.E. Stiglitz, "Quis Custodiet Ipsos Custodes? Corporate Governance Failures in the Transition," in Pierre-Alain Muet and J.E. Stiglitz, eds., *Governance, Equity and Global Markets, Proceedings from the Annual Bank Conference on Development Economics in Europe,* June 1999 (Paris: Conseil & Analyse economique, 2000), pp. 51–84. Also published in *Challenge* 42(6) (November/December 1999), pp. 26–67. Preuch version: "Quis custodiet ipsos custodes? Les defaillances du gouvernement d'entreprise dans la transition," *Revue d'Economie du Development* 0 (1–2) (June 2000), pp. 33–70. In addition, see D. Ellerman and J.E. Stiglitz, "New Bridges Across the Chasm: Macro- and Micro-Strategies for Russia and other Transitional Economies," *Zagreb International Review of Economics and Bussiness* 3(1) (2000), pp. 41–72, and A. Hussain, N. Stern, and J.E. Stiglitz, "Chinese Reforms from a Comparative Perspective," in Peter J. Hammond and Gareth D. Myles, eds., *Incentives, Organization, and Public Economics. Papers in Honour of Sir James Mirrlees* (Oxford and New York: Oxford University Press, 2000), pp. 243–77.

   For excellent journalistic accounts of the transition in Russia, see Chrystia Freeland, *Sale of the Century* (New York: Crown. 2000); P. Klebnikov, *Godfather of the Kremlin, Boris Berezovsky and the Looting of Russia* (New York: Harcourt, 2000); R. Brady, Kapitalizm, *Russia's Struggle to Free Its Economy* (New Haven: Yale University Press, 1999); and John Lloyd, "Who Lost Russia?," *New York Times Magazine,* August 15, 1999.

   A number of political scientists have offered analyses broadly agreeing with the interpretations provided here. See, in particular, A. Cohen, *Russia's Meltdown: Anatomy of the IMF Failure,* Heritage Foundation Backgrounders No. 1228, October 23, 1998; S.F. Cohen, *Failed Crusade* (New York: W. W. Norton, 2000): P. Reddaway, and D. Glinski, *The Tragedy of Russia's Reforms: Market Bolshevism Against Democracy* (Washington,

DC: United States Institute of Peace, 2001); Michael McFaul, *Russia's Unfinished Revolution: Political Change from Gorbachev to Putin* (Ithaca, N.Y.: Cornell University Press, 2001); Archie Brown and Liliia Fedorovna Shevtskova, eds., *Gorbachev, Yeltsin and Putin: Political Leadership in Russia's Transition* (Washington, DC: Carnegie Endowment for International Peace, 2000); and Jerry F. Hough and Michael H. Armacost, *The Logic of Economic Reform in Russia* (Washington, DC: Brookings Institution, 2001).

Not surprisingly, a number of reformers have provided accounts that differ markedly from those presented here, though such interpretations were more frequent in the earlier, more hopeful days of the transition, some with titles that seem to jar with subsequent events. See, e.g., Anders Aslund, *How Russia Became a Market Economy* (Washington, DC: Brookings Institution, 1995) or Richard Layard and John Parker, *The Coming Russian Boom: A Guide to New Markets and Politics* (New York: The Free Press, 1996). For more critical perspectives, see Lawrence R. Klein and Marshall Pomer, eds. (with a foreword by Joseph E. Stiglitz), *The New Russia: Transition Gone Awry* (Palo Alto, Calif.: Stanford University Press, 2001).

Data cited in this chapter come largely from the World Bank, *World Development Indicators and Global Development Finance* (various years).

2. Jamine R. Wedel, "Aid to Russia," *Foreign Policy in Focus* 3 (25), Inter-hemispheric Resource Center and Institute Policy Studies, September 1998, pp. 1–4.

3. For further reading, see P. Murrell, "Can Neo-Classical Economics Underpin the Economic Reform of the Centrally Planned Economies?" *Journal of Economic Perspectives* 5(4) (1991), pp. 59–76.

4. See International Monetary Fund, "IMF Approves Augmentation of Russia Extended Arrangement and Credit Under CCFF, Activates GAB," Press release no. 98/31, Washington DC, July 20, 1998.

5. There is an argument that the IMF really did not ignore this. In fact, some believe that the Fund was trying to close the devaluation option by making the cost of devaluation so high that the country would not do it. If this was indeed the argument, the IMF miscalculated badly.

6. There was, of course, more to the Russian government's announcement of August 17, but these were among the central features for our purposes. In addition, the Russian government established temporary controls of capital such as a prohibition on non-residents investing in short-term ruble assets and a ninety-day moratorium on foreign exchange credit and insurance payments. The Russian government also announced its support to a payment pool set up by the largest Russian banks in order to maintain the payment stability and sent legislation for timely payments to government employees and for the rehabilitation of banks. For details, see the Web site www.bismis.doc. gov/bisnis/country/980818ru.htm, which provides the original texts of the two public announcements on August 17, 1998.

7. See the Web site of the Institute for the Economy in Transition, at http://www.jet. ru/trend/12-99/3_e.htm.

8. See Chrystia Freeland, op. cit.; Richard Layard and John Parker, op. cit.; and Anders Aslund, op. cit.

9. For the implications and costs that barter imposes on the Russian economy, see C.G. Gaddy and B.W. Ickes, "Russia's Virtual Economy," *Foreign Affairs* 77 (September–October 1998).

10. The transition has not appeared to benefit the poor. For example, the lowest quintile of the population had a share of income equal to 8.6% in Russia (in 1998), 8.8% in Ukraine (in 1999), 6.7% in Kazakhstan (in 1996) (World Bank, *World Development Indicators 2001*).

11. Using a standard measure of inequality (the Gini coefficient), by 1998 Russia had achieved a level of inequality twice that of Japan, 50% greater than UK and other European countries, a level comparable to Venezuela and Panama. Meanwhile, those countries that had undertaken gradualist policies, Poland and Hungary, had been able to keep their level of inequality low—Hungary's was even lower than Japan's and Poland's lower than the UK's. See Angus Maddison, *The World Economy: A Millennial Perspective* (Paris: Organization for Economic Cooperation and Development, 2001).

12. See Stiglitz, "Quis Custodiet Ipsos Custodes?" op. cit.

13. For instance: If one liberalizes capital markets before an attractive investment climate is created at home—as the IMF recommended—one is inviting capital flight. If one privatizes firms before an efficient capital market is created at home, in a way that puts ownership and/or control in the hands of those who are nearing retirement, there is no incentive for long-term wealth creation; there are incentives for asset stripping. If one privatizes before creating a regulatory and legal structure for ensuring competition, there are incentives to create monopolies, and there are *political* incentives to prevent the creation of an effective competition regime. If one privatizes in a federal system, but leaves state and local authorities free to impose taxes and regulations at will, one has not eliminated the power, and incentives, of public authorities to extract rents; in a sense, one has not really privatized at all.

14. For the Coase theorem itself, see R.H. Coase, "The Problem of Social Cost," *Journal of Law and Economics* 3 (1960), pp. 1–44. This theorem holds only where there are no transactions costs, and no imperfections of information. Coase himself recognized the force of these limitations. Moreover, it is never possible fully to specify property rights, and this was especially true for the economies in transition. Even in advanced industrialized countries, property rights are circumscribed by concerns for the environment, worker rights, zoning, and so forth. Although the law may try to be as clear on these matters as possible, disputes frequently arise, and have to be settled through legal processes. Fortunately, given the "rule of law," there is general confidence that this is done in a fair and equitable manner. But not so in Russia. See A. Shleifer and R. Vishny, *The Grabbing Hand: Government Pathologies and Their Cures* (Boston: Harvard University Press, 1999) for an articulation of the view that once property rights are granted, there will be strong forces for the creation of the rule of law. For a more extended discussion of Coase's theorem and the role it played in reasoning about appropriate privatization strategies, see J.E. Stiglitz, *Whither Socialism* (Cambridge: MIT Press, 1994); J.E. Stiglitz, "Whither Reform? Ten Years of the Transition," op. cit; J.E. Stiglitz, *Quis Custodiet Pisos Custodes,* op. cit.; and J. Kornai, "Ten Years After 'The Road to a Free Economy.' The Author Self-Evaluation," in Boris Pleskovic and Nicholas Stern, eds., *Annual World Bank Conference on Development Economics 2000* (Washington, DC: World Bank, 2001), pp. 49–66.

Doug Guthrie,
China and Globalization (2006)*

The Politics of Market Reform

Beginning with Hungary in the 1960s, many communist countries have embarked on the path of transition from planned to market economic systems. Understanding the paths of transition from socialism to capitalism is a complex task, but it is also an important one, as this process opens up questions about the nature of markets, the nature of economic systems, and the extent to which markets and economic systems are embedded in political and social worlds. Research on transforming socialist economies has given rise to two basic views of economic change in these societies. On one side of the fence sit those who believe that markets operate primarily, if not solely, through private interests and individual incentives, and that market economies are built upon the foundation of private ownership and incentives. Given that communist-planned economies are basically organized around state ownership—an institutional arrangement that often leads to many distortions in terms of market relationships—those from the privatization school believe that rapid privatization is the only viable path of transition from planned to market economies. Rapid privatization, which can create an extreme "shock" to the society undergoing such a transition, has accordingly been given such labels as "shock therapy" and the "big bang approach" to economic reform. The approaches adopted in countries such as Bulgaria, the Czech Republic, and Russia fit this model of economic reform.

A second school of researchers—which includes scholars like Barry Naughton, Thomas Rawski, Andrew Walder, and Jean Oi—argues that markets are fundamentally political, social, and cultural systems, and a stable transition to a capitalist system must occur in a gradual fashion, with significant and constant support and guidance from the state. Market institutions and the economic practices that individuals and organizations adopt cannot be reduced to a simple equation of private interests and the individual pursuit of profits. The political, cultural, and social forces to which market institutions are subject are simply too powerful to ignore, so economic change must move forward in a slow, incremental fashion. The strategies of reform that arise from this view of economic systems see the state as a critical player in the transition to a market economic system. As practitioners, the architects of the Chinese reforms have embraced the gradualist view, and it has led to a gradual and

---

stable path through the economic reforms. Furthermore, the dramatic success of the first two-and-a-half decades of reform in China (compared with the turmoil caused by rapid reform programs in countries like Russia) raises serious doubts about the shock therapy approach and the economic assumptions that undergird that view. In many ways, by spurning the views of Western economic advisors and then gradually piecing together the most successful reform process of any transforming planned economy, China has served as the strongest indictment of the simpleminded nature of the market-driven economic logic of the rapid privatization school.

At the center of the tension between these two schools of economic reform is a debate over the role of the state in the construction and maintenance of new markets and the extent to which economic processes are fundamentally political processes. China's reform process serves as a perfect example of the extent to which economic development and transitions to capitalism are, indeed, political processes. In the case of China, we see that strong guidance from the state has led to a high level of stability in a process that inevitably leads to social upheaval. In the two-and-a-half decades of economic reform in China, the state has consistently and methodically guided the reform process, maintaining control over the majority of the industrial economy and tightening fiscal constraints for the inefficient state sector at only a gradual rate. More than this, the state has experimented with, and gradually introduced, the policies and laws through which the new markets that increasingly govern economic processes in China have been constructed. Even beyond methodical involvement of the state in shaping China's transition path, the political nature of economic change runs even deeper, as the legacies of the former institutions of the state-run economy shape the country's development path in important ways.

The critical point here is that China's successful path through two-and-a-half decades of economic reform has been gradual, experimental, and fundamentally political. Politics and economics have been so closely intertwined that we cannot understand one part without the other. Advocates of the rapid privatization approach claim that China's reforms have been successful despite the state's close relationship with the economy. For example, Sachs and Woo (1994, 1997) argue that the economic structure of China—largely peasant-based agricultural economy with a large supply of surplus labor and a tight monetary policy—explains China's success relative to Eastern Europe. They argue that, even with the dramatic growth in China's economy over the last two-and-a-half decades, the reform effort there would have been much more successful if a program of rapid privatization were adopted. It is difficult to see, at this point, how one could argue that gradualism was not a dramatic success in the China case.[1] But these claims ring hollow, especially when one compares the undeniable success of economic reform in China with the serious problems experienced in countries such as the Czech Republic and Russia. As we examine China's successful path and trajectory through the economic reforms, the heavy hand of the state lurks everywhere, and we must understand this reform process through this lens. Other authors have argued that because of the state's role as a continuing agent in the economy, corruption is endemic (e.g., Know 1997; Gong 1994) and the collapse of this national economy is inevitable (e.g., Chang 2001). This position is also not credible, as it is simply not supported by the empirical reality of what is occurring in China. A third position on China's progress is that the authoritarian government has held onto power and not allowed a democratic transition to occur there. However, here again, the reality is much different: although China remains an authoritarian political system, over the last two-and-a-half decades of reform, the government has gone a great distance in gradually making the transition to democracy. Though many in the West—particularly among U.S. politicians—do not want to acknowledge it, China is gradually but steadily building the institutions of a democratic society.

Culture and Capitalism

In the most general sense, *culture* refers to the norms, values, and systems that shape social action and behavior. It is that part of political, economic, and social systems that produces deeply ingrained understandings of the world. Many scholars have written on the nature of economic behavior in Asia and the ways that the economic decisions of Chinese people are shaped as much by culture as by the changing economic and political systems in which individuals are embedded (Hamilton 1996; Hamilton and Biggart 1988; Bian 1994; Yang 1994). They have argued that there is something distinctive about Asian and, specifically, Chinese business practices. Despite the fact that some of these writings border on essentialism in their understandings of Chinese culture, it is important to take some of the notions depicted in these scholarly works seriously.[2] There are two ways that culture plays an important role in China's transforming economy. First, Chinese society *is* different in undeniable ways. Its institutional and cultural history is unique, and this history has an impact on the type of capitalism that is emerging in China. This becomes important as China enters the global market because, in the global marketplace, negotiations often hinge on common understandings, expectations, and norms of behavior, all of which can be heavily influenced and shaped by different cultural traditions.

Second, and perhaps more important, contrary to the economic assumptions that link capitalism and human nature, I argue here that capitalism itself is a system that requires deeply ingrained practices that must be learned over time. I am interested in the extent to which economic systems are shaped by political institutions and norms of behavior. The process of building a new global economic system in China is not only about a clash of cultures in the marketplace. It is also about the ways that economic systems are themselves cultural systems, where learned practices and behaviors become embedded in the norms and rules by which individuals operate *over time*. As Chinese managers make the transition from the old economic system to the new, they must unlearn the practices, norms, rules, and meanings through which the old system operated and learn the practices, norms, rules, and meanings of the new system.

Moreover, markets themselves are social systems. Rather than the abstract mechanistic structures that are often portrayed in theoretical economic models, markets are embedded in complex social worlds, and they are shaped by the social institutions, norms, and customs that define a given society. The social embeddedness of markets is a basic feature of capitalist systems, but it is particularly important for understanding the emergence of markets in China in two ways. First, the transition from a command to market economic system requires the destruction (or, in the Chinese case, the gradual erosion) of existing institutions and the construction of new institutions. In the period of transition between systems, institutional instability pervades, and the reliance on social networks and social institutions becomes exaggerated. This is exactly what occurred in Chinese society in the 1980s during the first decade of economic reform. However, that is a situation that has eroded as the new institutions of China's emerging market economy have become more stable. Second, in the case of Chinese society, there is a long tradition of emphasizing the importance of personal networks, and the cultural prominence of social networks in Chinese society has important implications for the emergence of markets there.

The Quiet Revolution: The Era of Economic Reform in China

When Deng Xiaoping unveiled his vision of economic reform to the Third Plenum of the Eleventh Central Committee of the Chinese Community Party in December 1978, the Chinese economy was faltering.[3] Reeling from a decade of stagnation during the Cultural Revolution and already appearing to fall short of the projections set forth in the ten-year plan of 1976, it would take much more than a new plan and the Soviet-style economic vision of Deng's political rival, Hua Guofeng. At the time, Deng's plan was to lead the country down a road of gradual and incremental economic reform, leaving the state apparatus in tact while slowly unleashing market forces.

Since that time, the most common image is of an unbending authoritarian regime that has engineered a remarkable period of rapid economic growth but has seen little real substantive change politically. There is often a sense that China remains an entrenched and decaying authoritarian government run by corrupt party officials (extreme accounts depict it as an economy on the verge of collapse). However, this vision simply does not square with reality on a number of levels. While it is true that China remains an authoritarian one-party system, it is also the most successful case of economic reform of any communist-planned economy of the twentieth century. Today, as the sixth largest economy in the world, it is fast emerging as one of the world's most dynamic market economies. Understanding how this change has come about requires an examination of three broad changes that have come together to shape China's transition to capitalism: (1) the gradual receding of the state from control over the economy, a process that brought about a shift in economic control without privatization; (2) the steady growth of foreign investment; and (3) the gradual emergence of a rational-legal system to support these economic changes.

During the 1980s and '90s, economists and institutional advisors from the West advocated the rapid transition to market institutions as the necessary medicine for transforming communist societies. Scholars argued that private property provides the institutional foundation of a market economy, and, therefore, communist societies making the transition to a market economy must privatize industry and other public goods. The radical members of this school argued that *rapid* privatization— the so-called shock therapy or big bang approach to economic reforms—was the only way to avoid costly abuses in these transitional systems.[4] The Chinese path has been very different from the shock therapy approach. While countries like Russia have followed Western advice—constructing market institutions at a rapid pace, immediately removing the state from control over the economy, and rapidly privatizing property—China has taken its time in implementing institutional change. The state has gradually receded from control over the economy, taking the time to experiment with new institutions and to implement them slowly and incrementally within the context of existing institutional arrangements.

The success of gradual reform in China can be attributed to two factors. First, as Barry Naughton has argued, through gradual reform, the government retained its role as a stabilizing force in the midst of the turbulence that inevitably accompanies the transition from plan to market. Institutions such as the "dual-track" system kept large state-owned enterprises partially on the plan and, at the same time, gave them incentives to generate extra income through selling what they could produce above the plan in China's nascent markets. Over time, as market economic practice became more successful, the *plan* part of an enterprise's portfolio was reduced and the *market* part grew. Enterprises were thus given the stability of a continued but gradually diminishing planned economy system and the time to learn the practices of setting prices, competing for contracts, and producing efficiently (Naughton 1995; see also Rawski 1994, 1995, 1999). Second, the government has gradually pushed ownership-like control down the government administrative hierarchy to the localities. As a result, the central government was able to give economic control over to local administrators without privatization. But with economic control came accountability, and local administrators became very invested in the successful economic reform of the villages, townships, and municipalities under their jurisdictions. In a sense, as Andrew Walder has argued, pushing economic responsibilities onto local administrators created an incentive structure much like those experienced by managers of large industrial firms.[5]

Even as reform in China has proceeded at a gradual pace, the cumulative changes over two decades of economic reform have been nothing short of radical. These economic reforms have proceeded on four levels. First, the transformation of China's economy begins with institutional changes set in motion at the highest levels of government; second, they have been followed by firm-level institutions that reflect the rational-legal system emerging at the state level; third, these firm-level changes have been supported by a budding legal system that provides workers institutional support for grievance proceedings, a dynamic that is heavily influenced by relationships with foreign investors; and fourth, labor relations have been shaped by the emergence of new labor markets in China, which allow workers the freedom and mobility to find new employment when necessary. The result of these changes has been the emergence of a rational-legal regime of labor, where the economy increasingly rests upon an infrastructure of rational law, and workers hold the right to invoke these laws in the legal system when necessary.

The process began with a gradual introduction of economic autonomy to enterprise managers and local officials in industrial areas and decollectivization in the countryside. As of the early 1980s, individuals increasingly had the freedom to pursue their fortunes in the newly emerging markets of the Chinese economy, and many individuals chose to do so. Enterprise autonomy for managers and officials meant that the party and industrial bureaus were no longer standing over the shoulders of economic actors in the industrial economy. Thus, the gradual reforms hit squarely at the heart of the central institutions around which communist China was organized. Once Deng wrested power from the conservative factions of the party, his tasks included:

- transforming incentives in the agricultural economy;
- forcing the central government to give local bureaucrats some measure of economic control over the localities they govern;
- creating a system that kept in place the planned economy while at the same time giving autonomy over the local enterprises;
- beginning a process that would address the economic burden that the social security system posed for Chinese enterprises;
- facilitating the development of a private economy;
- attracting foreign direct investment.

Several of these goals began to emerge explicitly onto the agenda at the Third Plenum of the Eleventh Central Committee of the Chinese Communist Party in December 1978. For example, on December 15, the party announced that it would establish full diplomatic relations with the United States on January 1, 1979. During this time, the party also laid the groundwork for the passage (in 1979) of the Law of the PRC on Chinese-Foreign Equity Joint Ventures, which would allow foreign firms to enter the Chinese economy for the first time since the founding of the PRC. It would also signal a reversal of Mao's "revolutionary" governance structure with the passage (again in 1979) of the Resolution of the Standing Committee of the National People's Congress Authorizing Provinces Autonomous Regions, and Municipalities Directly under the Central Government to Change Revolutionary Committees to People's Governments.

Following his political breakthrough in 1978, Deng symbolically signaled these changes with a crucial visit to the United States in January 1979. During this trip, Deng officially normalized relations with the United States, which in turn officially ended formal U.S. diplomatic relations with Taiwan and explicitly conceded China's position on the "one-China" policy.[6] Many nations in the international community would follow by normalizing relations with China.[7] During that trip, Deng also visited Atlanta, Houston, and Seattle to see the facilities of the first two companies with which agreements would be signed—Coca-Cola and Boeing.

Developing an Independent Mindset in the Rural Economy

Initially, Deng's reform agenda aimed to loosen the central government's control over the economy, stimulating economic growth, controlling unemployment and inflation, and improving the Chinese citizens' living standards. It was not clear, in these early years of reform, that Deng had in mind the creation of a market economy; instead, he seemed to have in mind a one-step-at-a-time approach to creating a more robust economy in China. It was under these auspices that Deng became famous for the notion of "groping for stones to cross the river." In other words, "We don't know yet how we are crossing this river, but we will get there one step at a time."

One thing that was clear, even in the early years of the economic reforms, was that, if the central government was going to successfully break down the planned economy and allow the economy to be kick-started by the gradual emergence of markets, it would need to develop an economy of (semi-)independent market actors. One of the early keys to developing such an economy was to gradually allow individuals to harness individual-level incentives to participate in the market economy. With the breakup of the commune system and the establishment of the Household Responsibility System in the early 1980s, peasants in rural areas were allowed to lease land and produce agricultural goods on a household basis as if they were running a household business. They still had to deliver a minimum quota of grain to the government—usually to the collective from which the land was leased—but beyond that amount, they were free to sell the surplus in emerging rural markets. Rural markets were thus opened to a large portion of the Chinese populace (about 80 percent of the population at that time), the first step toward establishing a grassroots movement to a market economy. The "dual track" nature of this arrangement would also become a model for enterprise reform in the industrial economy.

This system had three immediate positive consequences. First, it allowed an infusion of cash to flow into individual households, which were still, by world standards, extremely poor. Annual per-capita net income in rural areas of China in 1978 was 133.6 yuan (about $16.25), or about $70 in total annual household income. Individuals were still reliant on the state for the provision of goods and services, so a low per-capita income overstated the poverty (because individuals had access to nonwage benefits), but the economy at this point was still extremely poor. As local governments began to withdraw the social support that was the hallmark of the "iron rice bowl," individuals would need new sources of income to cover those costs. The Household Responsibility System provided those sources of income. Second, although there were concerns that rural production of grain would suffer as a result of this semiprivatization effort, the system actually stimulated grain output significantly: from 1978 to 1984, grain production grew by over 100 million tons, from 305 to 407 million tons.[8] Third, by creating incentives for individuals to produce and then creating the autonomy for them to do so, Deng Xiaoping created a large constituency that supported the economic reforms from its early stages.

Local Governmental Autonomy

One of the interesting differences between China's planned economy and that of the Soviet Union was that China's was much more decentralized. This fact has played a crucial role in the success of China's economic reforms, as a number of scholars have argued.[9] Nevertheless, despite the relative decentralization in China, giving autonomy over to localities was still a key factor that guided the economic reforms forward. Economic decentralization ushered in two forces that have been key to the economic reforms: (1) local officials, who were much closer to the economic strengths, opportunities, and necessities of their localities, would be given the autonomy to pursue various development strategies, and (2) this measure would introduce a level of competition among local officials vying for different economic opportunities. Deng Xiaoping clearly recognized the importance of these potential forces by passing the elaborately titled Resolution of the Standing Committee of the National People's Congress Authorizing the People's Congresses of Guangdong and Fujian Provinces and Their Standing Committees to Formulate Separate Economic Regulations for Their Respective Special Economic Zones.[10] This resolution, one of the early resolutions passed in the era of Deng's economic reforms, clearly recognized the importance of political decentralization in the reform project. National development has proceeded along these lines throughout the era of the economic reforms. Individual provinces and municipalities have had the autonomy to make economic decisions and innovations in developmental strategies to gain advantages over neighboring regions and provinces. It is also the case that individual regions, provinces, and municipalities were given the power to create small-scale special economic zones for the localities within their jurisdictions.

New Autonomy and Incentives for Factory Managers

While creating a fledgling market economy mind-set among the peasantry and local officials was a crucial first step in the gradual creation of a market economy, tackling the industrial economy was an equally important, though exceptionally more complex, next step. Even before the Third Plenum, Sichuan Province had begun experimenting with giving autonomy to factory managers, a fact that would position Zhao Ziyang to emerge as one of Deng's early partners in the reform agenda. The basic strategy here was to turn autonomy over to economic organizations. There were a number of specific institutional reforms that pushed the development of enterprise reform in China forward. I will discuss a few of these reforms as examples here.

The Dual-Track System

One of the early enterprise reforms institutionalized by the Chinese government was the dual-track system, characterized by the coexistence of two coordination mechanisms (*plan* and *market*) within the state sector.[11] This economic policy maintained the elements of the planned economy while attempting, at the same time, to give state-owned organizations incentives to develop *market*-oriented strategies that would work above and beyond the *plan*. Continuing to govern each sector in the economy allowed the government to continue using direct controls over finance and investment and provided a degree of stability during the transition process. However, instituting the dual-track system also allowed the existence of a two-tiered pricing system for goods and allowed the state firms to sell the goods above plan quotas and keep extra profits. This two-tiered system greatly stimulated the incentives of the enterprises, as anything that firms produced above the plan could be sold within China's newly emerging markets at a market price. The system also provided valuable flexibility by allowing the state firms to transact and cooperate with non-state and foreign sectors.

Economic growth was thus concentrated in the market "track," and, over time, the "plan" became proportionately less and less important in the transition process.

Allowing new firms into the marketplace was crucial, and reformers could not have anticipated how rapidly the non-state sector would grow. But even more important, they had little sense of the profound political and economic impacts the growth of this sector—combined with enterprise autonomy—would bring about.[12] As the market replaced the plan, the state fiscal system eroded, putting further pressure on reformers to experiment with new paths toward marketization; the pressure of the market and the fiscal crisis pushed bureaucrats to seek ways to help firms become more productive. Thus, the economy "gradually grew out of the plan" as the plan itself and the state sector became less important parts of the economy. Some of this may have been unintentional: as Barry Naughton (1995) describes it, China's reform effort is characterized by an interaction between early governmental policies and the "unforeseen consequences of economic change." While economic reformers adopted early strategies to make the initial move away from a purely command economy, it was only in the later stages of the reform period that the goal of a market-based system emerged. In other words, early policy decisions began the process of reform, but soon the consequences of this early reform effort caused the system to unravel, pushing the reforms far beyond leaders' original intentions. However, the gradual nature of this process allowed the state sector to remain, at least in the early years, the anchor of the economy that it had been in the prereform era, creating some degree of stability throughout the process.

Property Rights

In the realm of enterprise autonomy, it is also useful to examine the institutional transformation of property rights in China. On one end of the spectrum, the view of property rights in market transitions has been unequivocal: the rapid privatization of property is necessary in the successful transition to a market economy. This view is partly ideological, but it is also grounded in theory and experience. For decades, the planned economies of the Soviet Union and China were rife with the inefficiencies that accompany state ownership. State-owned factories operated on the principles of a redistributive system, whereby revenues were turned over to the government and input costs were drawn from state coffers and "redistributed" to the factories owned by the state. This system of "soft budget constraints," in which factories could draw endlessly from state coffers regardless of revenues, led to problems of rent seeking, a lack of connection between input and output costs, and the absence of pressure within factories to operate efficiently. Thus, the privatization of property, which places fiscal responsibilities squarely within the firm, came to be viewed by many Western economists as a necessary step in reforming the inefficiencies of the planned system.

The Chinese experience belies this view. As China has marched through two decades of double-digit economic growth, the rapid and complete privatization of property has not been part of this story. Property rights have played a complex role in reform-era China, in fact. In an insightful essay on this topic, Andrew Walder and Jean Oi begin by rejecting the notion that property can be adequately understood in the crude categories of private or state owned. Drawing on earlier work in this area (esp. Demsetz 1967; Furubotn and Pejovich 1974), Walder and Oi argue that property should be conceived of as a "bundle of rights," where questions of managerial control, the ability to extract revenue, and the ability to transfer ownership must all be addressed in a full understanding of this institution. The view of property rights as dependent upon shifting politics and relations has a long history in legal scholarship (Singer 1982, 1988), dating perhaps as far back as Hohfeld's (1913) reconceptualization of rights nearly a century ago. Unfortunately, however, the field of economics has, until only recently, been blind to a more nuanced view of institutions such as property rights. The central point here is that while many firms in China are still officially state owned, individual parameters within these bundles of rights have been reformed to various degrees, so firms are often free to act independent of state control, despite the fact that they are still officially state owned. This perspective helps us resolve the puzzle of how it is that China has successfully reformed its planned economy—though this process is far from complete—without relying on the mandate of rapid privatization: the state has gradually allowed for the reform of some parts of these bundles of rights, while leaving others intact. To systematize this analysis, Walder and Oi also outline five ideal types of ownership arrangements that exist along a continuum, with state-owned enterprises occupying one end of this spectrum and fully private enterprises occupying the other. Between these ends of the continuum, we find firms that have incorporated innovative reforms including management incentive contracts, government-management partnerships, and leased public assets.

Local Governments as Industrial Firms

The central government kept control over policy making and shifted economic decision making down to local governments and to the management of the enterprises. One key effect of this policy is that it allowed local officials to aggressively pursue development strategies for the firms under their jurisdictions. The earliest sector of the Chinese economy to surge in growth and output in China's reform era was that of the township and village enterprises (TVEs). Indeed, the rapid growth of China's economy in the 1980s was largely due to the exceptional growth rates of the rural industrial economy, where the vast majority of TVEs are. As the primary segment contributing to China's high economic growth in the 1980s, the TVE sector expanded to 24,529 in 1993, almost fifteen times its size in 1978. By 1998, however, the number had dropped to 20,039 due to the informal privatization processes led by the local governments in the 1990s.[13] These organizations were essentially state owned. Though not controlled by the national or provincial governments, they were still controlled by the state, as township and village governments owned the property. Local governments were the residual claimants, and they controlled managerial decisions and the rights of transferring assets. However, after the economic reforms began, TVEs faced few of the institutional and organizational legacies of the planned economy that larger state-owned organizations controlled by higher levels of government faced.[14]

As the economic reforms progressed, managerial and ownership control were quickly decentralized to give local officials direct control over the firms under their jurisdictions. This strategy was partly borne out of necessity: as the central government sought to gradually dismantle the redistributive economy, firms in the rural economy were the first to be cut off from funds from state coffers. However, local officials were also given free reign to generate income as they could. Thus, local officials were given incentives to behave like managers and run their TVEs like local industrial firms (Walder 1995). From this frame of reference, TVEs rapidly came to resemble business organizations in crucial ways, yet the property rights still resided in the hands of the local state. As a result, decentralization has greatly stimulated the rural industrialization driven by the development of TVEs. These sectors have been pushed to respond more to the market forces and less to the governmental plan. With harder budgets, the non-state sectors (which also include the private and foreign sectors) have become the most competitive firms and today contribute to over 70 percent of China's gross domestic product.

Organizational Structure: Dismantling the Old and Creating the New

Chinese industrial firms have been transformed in dramatic ways over the course of China's economic reforms. Perhaps the most important change set in place over the course of the economic reforms in China came when the state handed economic decision making over to industrial managers (Naughton 1995; Guthrie 1999). While some of the organizational changes occurring in industrial firms are in direct response to the hundreds of new directives and economic laws being promulgated by the state, many of the changes occurring in Chinese industrial firms come from decisions made by autonomous managers who are transforming their firms by force of creativity, will, and, in some cases, pure desperation. In the uncertain environment of China's newly emerging markets, managers have been impelled to innovate, create, strategize, and improvise their way through the economic reforms. For many of these managers, they learned the ways of markets, competition, and economic survival through experimenting with and implementing the new organizational strategies and structures their firms were adopting in this period.

Innovative managers within the organizations carried out these firm-level changes as organizational strategies. The transformation of Chinese industrial firms is just as much a reflection of managerial decision making, then, as it is some abstract notion of organizational strategies, because it is largely the general managers (along with the local bureaucrats in some administrative jurisdictions) who are running the show in China today. These firm-level changes are very much about innovation, experimentation, and finding creative solutions to organizational problems; they are thus driven by entrepreneurial decisions of the general managers who run these firms. The first dramatic change that aggressive managers are implementing in their organizations is a clearing of the decks. Wiping out the old system has been an important step in aggressive enterprise reform in China, but it has not been an easy one. Inasmuch as industrial enterprises under the command economy served as the nation's social security system, dismantling this system of extensive benefit packages amounted to nothing less than a fundamental transformation of the labor relationship and the meaning of work in China. Although these changes are often not commonly acknowledged as such, they comprise a dramatic shift that is occurring in Chinese firms, leading to newly emerging organizational structures and forms. Since the late 1980s, we have witnessed the emergence of bureaucratic structures that look strikingly like the type of organizational structures we find in Western economies. The construction of these new "ultra-organizational" structures in Chinese firms over the last decade has required innovation, experimentation, and imagination from industrial managers.

Today, the evidence of these new institutions and structures abound in the Chinese economy, yet industrial managers have embraced these changes at varying rates. Three key factors have driven this transformation forward. First, the background of the general managers has a significant impact on the extent to which they are actively reshaping the organizations they are running. Firms that are run by managers with backgrounds in business and economics are more likely to adopt the economic structures that are associated with the economic reforms. General managers with backgrounds in business and economics are also more prone to act in an entrepreneurial fashion with respect to organizational restructuring than their counterparts with training in other areas or no formal training at all. Second, the social world and the economic models present in that social world play a significant role in the aggressive adoption of new organizational forms in China. Firms that have joint ventures with foreign companies are significantly more likely to adopt the economic structures associated with the reforms. Third, the institutional structure in which a firm is embedded also plays a significant role in the adoption of new organizational structures and forms. Firms that are positioned under the jurisdiction of municipal companies tend to be aggressive adopters of the new organizational forms.[15]

The Company Law: Adopting New Corporate Forms

A second area of aggressive development can be seen as general managers lead their firms to take advantage of the institutional opportunities created by the state. As the state inundates society and the market with a horde of new laws and institutional rules, the really interesting question becomes which of these institutional changes have meaning for society. Which of these institutional reforms managers have adopted and which they have ignored is a key question in the reform era. In the end, the institutional reforms that really have meaning for the economic reforms are those that are aggressively adopted by actors in the economy. And it is often entrepreneurial managers taking advantage of—or, in some cases, avoiding—the institutional changes that breathe life into these reforms.

A fascinating case in point is that of the Chinese Company Law. Adopted by the National People's Congress on December 29, 1993, the Company Law provides the first legal basis in the history of the PRC for private, collective, and state enterprises to exist as autonomous legal entities. It is an institutional change that continues the process of separating—both legally and operationally—enterprises from the state redistributive system of the former command economy. Yet, while the law now exists in China, there is still considerable variation as to whether or not organizations have chosen to incorporate this change into their daily operations. Managers must actively choose to transform their firms into companies if they want to take advantage of the Company Law—they must apply to the Economic Commission to take on company status—and aggressive managers have seen this as an opportunity to become part of the "modern enterprise system." They must act as entrepreneurs with respect to this new institution, applying for this change in status, figuring out what it means for their organization, and adopting the changes that come with this economic transformation. As one general manager described this process,

> In 1986, business in our factory really started picking up. Before [that] we were a planned economy. But after the economic opening, our factory was one of the earliest to integrate a market economic approach. That year was actually the year that our profits really started picking up. Then last year we applied to have our factory changed from an enterprise to a company. So now we are under the Company Law, and our scope of business is much wider. It's really a much better situation for us in terms of development now. (Personal interview, 1995)

What types of managers and firms are transforming their organizations in this way? First, managers whose organizations are embedded in formal relationships with foreign companies are more likely to adopt the Company Law. Firms that are engaged in relationships with—and therefore under the influence of—foreign partners are more likely to pursue economic strategies that the state has defined as "modern enterprise system." A general manager's decision to adopt the Company Law is not significantly related to the profit margins of the firm or the firm's overall organizational health—other variables that would presumably be proxies for economic success; in other words, this change itself has little to do with past economic success. I think the stronger interpretation of the joint-venture effect is that a foreign partner provides a Chinese firm with up-close examples of how foreign firms operate. The "modern enterprise system" is, in many ways, a rhetorical stand-in for Western-style management practices. Managers who are exposed to the concept of the "modern enterprise system" through contact with foreign companies and through setting up a joint-venture company are more likely to see the institutional advantages (real or perceived) of broadening the organization's scope of operation and becoming an independent legal entity. Entrepreneurial managers pursue this change as a way of helping to shepherd their firms into the modern economy.

Second, Chinese organizations that are at the highest level of the government administrative hierarchy are more likely than those under more local governmental offices to adopt the Company Law. Central- and provincial-level government offices, with jurisdiction over many enterprises, do not have the administrative resources to monitor and offer administrative advice or to help the firms in the large organizational fields under their jurisdictions (Guthrie 1997, 1998a). As a result, firms under these levels of government experience a greater sense of being set adrift in the economic transition. They are thus encouraged—or they feel the impetus—to pursue economic strategies on their own. Adopting the Company Law and thereby broadening the scope of action in China's growing markets is one such strategy that firms, especially those under bureaus, are taking. Firms under the jurisdiction of district companies, on the other hand, are much more closely monitored by their government organizations (relative to those under bureaus), and these firms are offered a significant amount of administrative help and attention in the economic reform. The result is that when the opportunity to apply to become a company and adopt the Company Law arose, managers under high-level governmental offices had the autonomy (and the impetus) to move their firms toward adopting this institutional change.

Price Setting: Flexibility and Competition in the Market

A crucial issue in the transition from a command to market economy pertains to the setting of prices. Under the command economy, all price setting in large industrial organizations was controlled by the state. Reforming price-setting practices would prove to be a central issue of the economic transition. Price reform has followed the course of gradual reform that is indicative of China's reform process, laden with politics, experimentation, and piecemeal implementation. Government control of pricing began to change officially with general reforms in 1979 and then, more specifically, with the October 1984 Reform Declaration. Implementing a market pricing system may not have been a central part of the financial rationalizing system that was being promoted by Zhao Ziyang, but it was an important issue that was on the table for many years of the reform and often advocated by Zhao himself. The "price reformers" certainly saw the issue as crucial to the success of the reforms, and even if the "enterprise reformers" were antagonistic to the idea, the liberalization of prices was an issue that was central to the debates that raged between these two reform-minded groups. But if the debates over price control and liberalization were central to the reforms, progress on the issue was slow. By the end of 1984, factor prices were still unreformed, and product prices had still not yet been realigned.[16] Managers, for their part, have responded to the price reforms in China in a variety of ways—some have simply remained passive, following the market but pursuing few strategies in the negotiating that can often allow prices to shift in a market, while others have viewed price reform as an opportunity to aggressively negotiate with customers in the market (Guthrie 1999, ch. 5).

Transforming the Social Security System: Ending the Institution of Lifetime Employment

Command economies were typically known for having small variation in wages while offering a range of living benefits that were tied to the workplace. In the prereform era, China sat on the extreme end of this spectrum, because wage differentials were extremely narrow, and virtually all social security was tied to the work unit. Further, in China, lifetime employment was the very essence of the labor relationship that existed between enterprises and workers.[17] Workers entered their work unit, and, from that moment on, the work unit was the social system that dispensed their salary, housing, medical insurance, and any other benefits the unit might offer. In different periods, especially in the late 1970s, a small fraction of the population was classified as "waiting for employment," but for the most part, the state still fulfilled its promise of finding employment for everyone. This relationship would extend through the worker's retirement. This system was colloquially referred to as the "iron rice bowl."

Although by 1980, state sector jobs had become more competitive than ever before (only 37 percent of workers were assigned jobs in state-owned enterprises), still 80 percent of workers were assigned jobs in either state enterprises or collectively owned enterprises in that year (Walder 1986a, 57, 68–74). Once jobs were assigned, the job assignment was for life, except in rare cases of disciplinary firing and even rarer cases of layoffs (which were often followed by reassignment to another enterprise). This is not to say that workers never changed jobs or resigned from a given enterprise, but once workers were assigned to a work unit, except in unusual circumstances, they had the option of staying at that organization for life. With tightening fiscal constraints in the reform era, the heavy burdens of social security coupled with lifetime employment have crippled enterprises, and redefining the social security commitments of enterprises has become a central issue for the industrial reformers. Even in the reform era, it is not uncommon to walk into a factory, department store, or bank and see far more employees than are necessary to accomplish the tasks of that workplace. Why? The reason is that, under the planned economy, workers are simply assigned to work within various work units, and these units are responsible for supplying social security benefits. In the reform era, these work units have been reluctant to simply fire workers or cut pensions for retired workers as a way to cut costs. As one manager explained,

> Many of these employees have been working for this factory for twenty or more years; they have spent most of their lives working for this factory, but they just haven't reached retirement age. yet. To suddenly cut these people off would be cruel. Suddenly they would have no retirement security; that would be very unfair to them. ... It's no way to treat people who have been working for you for so long. (Personal interview, 1995)

Another manager assessed the challenges that are associated with this mind-set:

> The biggest problem that our state-owned enterprises have is the retired workers. We are taking care of so many people in comparison to other private companies. We can't compete with them in terms of development. They take all of their profits and put them back into the company; we have to use all of our profits to take care of workers who are no longer working here. And many of these retired people are now working at other companies, but they still come here every month to get their pay. (Personal interview, 1995)

Nevertheless, many broad institutional changes have emerged to redefine the labor relationship, including the new pension system (which does not really function to cover the costs of retired workers), labor contracts, the Labor Law (PRC 1994), and the existence of Labor Arbitration Commissions, which give workers some recourse against the factories where they are employed (these issues will be dealt with in Chapter 6). The emergence of labor contracts in China marks an important turning point for the socialist system created under Mao, as it marks the effective end of lifetime employment in China. This fact relieves work units of a large future burden of lifetime commitment to the workers they employ while, at the same time, breaking the commitment of the iron rice bowl for individuals.

Developing a Private Economy

While many scholars have argued that privatization is a necessary step in the transition from plan to market, the case of China belies this claim in important ways. However, an important distinction is necessary here: despite the fact that China did not move quickly along the road of privatizing state-owned enterprises, the government did allow a private economy to emerge, and this private economy has played an important role in the reform era. As Barry Naughton (1995) has pointed out, the private economy in China played an important role in teaching the state sector how to compete. State-owned factories were not privatized, but they were subjected to market competition from below by the emerging private sector.

It is important to note here that the private sector in China actually consists of three components. First, there are the small-scale entrepreneurs of the household economy (the "household enterprises"), which occupy a legal category that demands that they do not grow beyond seven employees. These small-scale organizations were very important in the early years of the economic reforms, as they provided opportunities for the large numbers of individuals who were "waiting for employment," including those who had returned home to urban areas after being "sent down" to the countryside during the Cultural Revolution. Some scholars have also suggested that this sector of the population provided a much-needed outlet for innovation and political resistance in the early years of the reforms (Gold 1989a, 1989b, 1990, 1991; Wank 1999). Second, the private enterprises have also played a crucial role in the development of the private economy in China. Private enterprises are different from household enterprises because they are allowed to grow beyond seven employees. It is this group of enterprises that has grown to challenge the state sector across a number of sectors in the economy. Like their smaller-scale counterparts in the household economy, this sector of the economy has also been an important force in social change. Some scholars have argued, for example, that this sector played a crucial role in the evolution of the Tiananmen Movement of 1989, as they had the resources to help the students organize in significant ways (Guthrie 1995; Perry and Wasserstrom 1991). A third sector of the private economy has to do with the publicly listed companies on China's stock exchanges in Shanghai and Shenzhen. These companies are becoming "privatized" in some ways; as some 30 percent of shares enter the free-floating market, however, the ownership and control of these companies still largely rests in state hands, as it is typical for a firm listed on either of China's stock exchanges for the government to maintain control over 40–50 percent of the stock issued by the company.

Enticing Foreign Investment

By the early 1990s, it was still premature for China to claim that its economic system was an established market economy, but it had already made important strides away from the planned economic system. The long-term debate on whether China should focus on a plan-track policy or a market-driven policy between "hard-liners" (e.g., Li Peng) and "pragmatists" (e.g., Hu Yaobang and Zhao Ziyang) among Chinese leadership ended in the spring of 1992, when Deng Xiaoping took his "southern tour" to Shenzhen and officially declared the Chinese economic system as a market economy with socialist characteristics. One of the most important forces that pushed toward the building and maturation of market institutions came from the influence of foreign capital, driven by the opening-up policy in late 1979. The establishment of Special Economic Zones in the 1980s in coastal areas greatly contributed to the inflow of foreign capital into China. China has taken a much more aggressive view toward FDI than any other developing country in recent years. Not only is the magnitude of foreign investment in China greater, but foreign-invested firms in China are playing a role in the growth of exports that has no parallel elsewhere in East Asia. The magnitude of foreign investment in China dwarfs that of Japan in comparable development periods.[18] China's foreign investment regime is also far more liberal than that of South Korea. At the same time, the state-led project of building a rational-legal system is helping the Chinese market system to get on track with the international community, deal better with its foreign partners, and introduce advanced technology (Guthrie 1999).[19]

It is still too soon to give a definite picture of, or evaluate, how open China's markets are today, but it is very clear that China's market for goods has developed significantly, driven by the export-oriented development strategy and the rise of consumption within China. Clearly, labor markets have developed in significant ways, which has resulted mainly from the restructuring of the state sector, the booming of the non-state sectors, and state-led law building. The openness of China's economy is also evidenced by its liberal legal provisions facilitating exports based on processing or assembly activity. In addition, over the last two decades, China has become one of the major trading nations of the world. Despite claims that markets in China have been closed to foreign producers, for the first decade of the reforms, China ran a trade deficit with the world, which meant that more goods were being sold in China than the country was able to sell to the rest of the world. However, today China does enjoy a trade surplus with respect to the United States. The ratio of U.S. imports from China relative to U.S. exports is somewhere around 3.5 to 1. Nevertheless, the main point here is that even at their early stages of development, domestic equities markets in China are significantly more open than those in Japan, South Korea, and Taiwan at comparable stages.

Beyond the openness of the export economy, which has been a crucial factor in attracting foreign capital, the Chinese economy has also attracted investors of another type—those interested in capturing the internal market in China. The lure of the billion-person marketplace has been a key factor in attracting the likes of Coca-Cola, DuPont, General Motors, Kodak, Motorola, and many other blue-chip foreign firms that have been positioning themselves for years to capture the internal marketplace in China. These investors have also played an important role in China's economic reforms, because they have something to offer in return for access to China's internal markets: technology transfer is a central point of negotiation in the joint venture and licensing agreements they negotiate.

Taxation

Another significant change that has played a fundamental rule in the emergence of China's market economy lies in the area of taxation. One of the features that defined the redistributive economy was the fact that administrative offices collected the revenues and were therefore in a position to extract excess revenues from the factories under their jurisdictions; they would then redistribute these resources as they saw fit. In China today, however, this is largely a thing of the past. Three key changes have transformed this system. First, the extraction of revenues has been standardized in the taxation system (i.e., governing organizations are no longer permitted to simply extract all "excess" revenues), a change that officially came about with the Second Phase Profits Changed to Taxes Reform of 1985.[20] Second, today taxation is basically standardized—with value-added tax (17 percent of turnover) and income tax (33 percent of net income) as basic standards for firms and individuals. Third, most firms pay their taxes directly into the Government Tax Bureau, which has one bureau office for each district and each municipality, instead of to their governing organization.[21] Tax breaks and subsidized loan repayment make the concept of standardized taxation less meaningful, and it is often the case that implementing these internal policies is a problem (i.e., they exist on paper but not in practice). There are still ways for governing organizations to extract revenues from firms, such as negotiations over profits and "management" fees. But the main point here is that taxes are now being paid to a central office—rather than the administrative organization extracting revenues. Without the convenience of revenue extraction across a wide base of firms, the ability of governing organizations to skim or extract excess amounts of revenue is significantly reduced.

Constructing a Rational-Legal System

Under Deng Xiaoping, Zhao Ziyang brought about radical change in China by pushing the country toward constitutionality and the emergence of the rule of law to create "rational" economic processes in China. This project would be carried on by Zhu Rongji after Zhao's ouster in 1989. These changes, which were set forth ideologically as a package of reforms that were necessary for economic development, fundamentally altered the role of politics and the role of the party in Chinese society. The early years of reform not only gave a great deal of autonomy to enterprise managers and small-scale entrepreneurs but also emphasized the legal reforms that would undergird this process of change. However, creating a body of civil and economic law, such as the Labor Law (1994), the Company Law (1994), and the National Compensation Law (1995), upon which the transforming economy would be based, meant that the party elites themselves would be held to the standards of these legal changes. Thus, in a number of ways, the rationalization of the economy led to a decline in the party's ability to rule over the working population.

In recent years, the next step in this process has come from global integration and the adoption of the norms of the international community. By championing global integration and the rule of law, Zhu Rongji also brought about broader political and social change in China, just as Zhao Ziyang did in the first decade of economic reform in China. Zhu's strategy has been to ignore questions of political reform and concentrate instead on the need for China to adopt economic and legal systems and norms that will allow the country to integrate smoothly with the rest of the global economy. From rhetoric on "linking up with the international community" (a very popular phrase among Chinese managers today) to laws like the Patent Law (2000) and institutions such as the State Intellectual Property Office and the Chinese International Economic Trade and Arbitration Commission, this phase of reform has been oriented toward creating the standards of the international investment community. Thus, Zhu's objective is to deepen all of the reforms that have been discussed above, but at the same time to begin to hold these changes up to the standards of the global economy.

After two decades of transition, the architects of the reforms have set in place about seven hundred new national laws and more than two thousand new local laws; these legal changes and many more regulations, along with experiments with new economic institutions, have driven forward the process of reform. A number of laws and policies in the 1980s laid the groundwork for a new set of policies that would redefine labor relations in fundamental ways. Take, for example, the policies that set in motion the emergence of labor contracts in China, which were officially introduced in 1986. The labor contract was further institutionalized by the Enterprise Law (PRC 1988, chapter 3, article 31), which codifies workers' rights for fair treatment and the right of due process in the event of unfair treatment. There are economic incentives behind the embracing of labor contracts by Chinese firms (the most important being the end of lifetime employment), but this institution, nevertheless, places the rationalization of the labor relationship, a guarantee of due process in the event of unfair treatment, and, ultimately, workers' rights at the center of the labor relationship. Other policies and laws also push this process forward (Guthrie 1998a). For example, the Labor Law (1994), Prison Reform Law (1994), and National Compensation Law (1995) are all examples of laws tied to labor that place the protection of individual civil liberties front and center. And the Company Law (1994), which has its roots in American and German corporate law, places much more emphasis on employee welfare than does the American version, to be sure. These laws and many others provide the legal infrastructure that allows workers to file grievances against managers, and individual citizens to file for compensation for past wrongs committed by the government. Laws such as these are a crucial part of the changes occurring in the conception of individual rights in China.

The obvious and most common response to these changes might be that they are symbolic rather than substantive in nature, that a changing legal and policy framework has little meaning when an authoritarian government still sits at the helm, but the scholarship that has looked extensively at the impact of these legal changes largely belies this view. For example, the rationalization of labor relations in the workplace is directly tied to institutional changes, such as the Labor Law, and other legal institutions that emphasize the individual civil liberties of workers (Guthrie 1999). Workers and managers take these new institutions seriously, and they have had a dramatic impact on the structure of authority relations and the conception of rights within the workplace. Research has also shown that legal and policy changes that place an emphasis on individual civil liberties matter in significant ways in other arenas as well. The most systematic and exhaustive study of the prison system to date shows that changes in the treatment of prisoners have indeed emerged in the wake of the Prison Reform Law (Seymour and Anderson 1999). And, although no scholarship has been done on the National Compensation Law, it is noteworthy that under this law, 97,569 suits were filed against the government in 1999, including such recent high-profile cases as a suit against the government for its hand in producing cigarettes and a suit against the government for the deaths in the Tiananmen Square massacre. These rational-legal institutions guarantee that, for the first time in the history of the PRC, individuals can now receive their day in court, and it is under this system that lawsuits against the government specifically have risen over 12,000 percent since the beginning of the economic reforms.[22]

The Labor Law (PRC 1994) and the Labor Arbitration Commission (of which there are branches in every urban district) work hand in hand in guaranteeing workers their individual rights as laborers. Chapter 10 of the Labor Law, entitled "Labor Disputes," is specifically devoted to articulating due process, which laborers are legally guaranteed should a dispute arise in the workplace. The law explains in an explicit fashion the rights of the worker to take disputes to outside arbitration (the district's Labor Arbitration Commission, or LAC) should the resolution in the workplace be unsatisfactory to the worker. Further, many state-owned enterprises have placed all of their workers on fixed-term labor contracts, which significantly rationalize the labor relationship beyond the personalized labor relations of the past. This bundle of changes has fundamentally altered the nature of the labor relationship and the mechanisms through which authority can be challenged (both within and outside the factory). For more than a decade now, it has been possible for workers to file grievances against superiors and have their grievances heard at the LACs, and, in 1999, out of 120,191 labor disputes that were settled by arbitration or mediation, 63,030 (52 percent) were decided wholly in favor of the workers filing the suits. These are official statistics, and we should be skeptical of their veracity. However, even if the magnitude is off, these numbers illuminate an important trend toward legal activity regarding workers' rights.

Many of these changes in labor practices were not originally adopted with workers' rights in mind, but the unintended consequence of these changes has been the construction of a regime of labor relations that emphasizes the rights of workers. For instance, extending upon the example of labor contracts, which were being experimented with as early as 1983, these were originally intended as a form of economic protection for ailing enterprises, allowing enterprises a formal way of ending lifetime employment. However, as the terms of employment were codified in these contracts, workers began using them as a vehicle for filing grievances when contractual agreements were not honored. With the emergence of the LACs in the late 1980s and the further codification of these institutions in the Labor Law of 1994, the changes that were afoot became formalized in a set of institutions that ultimately benefited workers in the realm of rights. In a similar way, workers' representative committees began as an institution formed in the state's interest, but once in place became an institution that workers claimed as their own. These institutions, which many managers I have spoken with refer to as "our own little democracy," were adopted early in the reforms as a compromise, a way of heading off the growing agitation for the creation of independent labor unions. These committees do not have the same power or status as independent labor unions in the West, but workers have nonetheless made them their own, and they are much more significant in factories today than they were originally intended to be.

Conclusions: Gradual Reform and China's Quiet Revolution

Much like the advocates of rapid economic reform, those demanding immediate political and social reform often take for granted the learning that must take place in the face of new institutions. The assumption most often seems to be that, given certain institutional arrangements, individuals will naturally know how to carry out the practices of capitalism. Yet, these assumptions reflect a neoclassical view of human nature in which rational humankind will thrive in a natural environment—free markets. Completely absent from this view are the roles of history, culture, and preexisting institutions, and it is a vision that is far too simplistic to comprehend the challenge of making rational economic and legal systems work in the absence of stable institutions and a history to which they can be tied. The transition from a command to a market economy can be a wrenching experience not only at the institutional level but also at the level of individual practice. Individuals must learn the rules of the market, and new institutions must be set in place long enough to gain stability and legitimacy; these are processes that occur slowly and over time. The government's methodical experimentation with different institutional forms and the party's gradual receding from control over the economy has brought about a "quiet revolution" in the Chinese economy. Yet this is a slow and gradual process and must be placed in the context of China's recent institutional history: when there is no immediate history of a rational-legal economic system, it is impossible to create it in one dramatic moment of institutional change. Thus, the architects of China's transition to capitalism have had success in reforming the economy. They have recognized that the transition to a radically different type of economic system must occur gradually, allowing for the maximum possible institutional stability as economic actors slowly learn the rules capitalism. Capitalism has arrived in China, and it has done so under the guise of gradual institutional reform under the communist mantle.

Notes

1. Also implicit in Sachs and Woo's (1994, 1997) argument is the a priori assumption that private ownership will always outperform state ownership. This is a stance that is reflected in the privatization school in general. See especially Woo (1999) and Sachs (1992, 1993, 1995b).
2. Essentialism is the notion that a group of people are defined by a few key traits or some sort of essence.
3. A number of scholars have used the term *quiet revolution* to describe China's reforms. See, for example, Goodman and Hooper 1994; Walder 1995c; and Guthrie 2003.
4. Sachs 1995a; Sachs and Woo 1997.
5. For discussion of the "attenuation of property rights" and the local control over enterprises, see Walder 1994a and Walder 1995a.
6. The "One-China" policy actually dates back to the Shanghai Communiqué, which was signed by both Mao Zedong and U.S. president Richard M. Nixon on February 28, 1972. As the communiqué stated,

The Taiwan question is the crucial question obstructing the normalization of relations between China and the United States; the Government of the PRC is the sole legal government of China; Taiwan is a province of China which has long been returned to the motherland; the liberation of Taiwan is China's internal affair in which no other country has the right to interfere; and all U.S. forces and military installations must be withdrawn from Taiwan. The Chinese government firmly opposes any activities which aim at the creation of "one China, one Taiwan," "One China, two governments," "an independent Taiwan" or advocate that "the status of Taiwan remains to be determined."

As a result of this agreement, any country wanting to form diplomatic relations with China had to end its formal diplomatic relations with Taiwan.

7. As a result of the Carter-Deng Normalization Agreement, in April 1979 the U.S. Congress passed the Taiwan Relations Act, which reflected the worries of pro-Taiwan forces by reaffirming the U.S. commitment to Taiwan and especially by underlining that the United States intended to provide Taiwan with arms of a defensive character and pledged to resist any coercion that would jeopardize the security or the social or economic system of the people of Taiwan.

8. Debora Spar, "China (A): The Great Awakening." Harvard Business School Case 9-794-019.

9. See Wong 1991; see also Oi 1992; Wong 1992; Walder 1995a; and Guthrie 1999.

10. This was first discussed at a working conference of the Central Committee in April 1979; it was officially adopted on November 26, 1981.

11. Naughton (1995) puts forth a broad analysis of the institutions that defined China's command economy, the new institutions that emerged in the market reforms, and the process of transition between the systems. Naughton's explanation of this process is one of the most comprehensive and insightful accounts published to date. He limits his study to the industrial economy because, as industry is so closely tied to state investment and saving—and therefore to government fiscal policy—reforming the industrial economy becomes the central task of economic transitions from planned to market-based systems. Naughton's work is also important because of what it says about the economic reform debate. Observing the early years of transforming command economies in Europe, China's reform experience and, more recently, the aggressive reform programs in Czechoslovakia and Russia have given researchers the rare opportunity to comparatively assess various strategies of economic reform. The central debate that has emerged over the utility of different reform strategies pits the gradualist, incremental approach to reforms against an approach that emphasizes rapid privatization—the so-called big bang or shock therapy models of economic reform. Advocates of the former argue that there are clear benefits to a gradual approach to economic reforms, while proponents of shock therapy argue that rapid and complete destruction of the command system is the only possible approach to creating a market-based system. Naughton takes a strong and convincing position in this debate, arguing that the China case shows that gradual reform is not only feasible but also preferable to the radical transformation of shock therapy.

12. While many accounts focus on the performance of the non-state sector, Naughton's focus is on the fact that this sector was an essential link to the creation of a competitive marketplace, which changed the behavior of firms in the state and non-state sectors alike.

13. *Chinese Statistical Yearbook of Enterprises*, 1999. See also the discussions in Oi and Walder 1999.

14. For example, according to Li's (1997) study of state enterprises in the 1980s, those enterprises supervised by local governments were more likely to reduce workers' wages based on "poor performance" than those supervised by the central state. Li's study also indicates the enterprise's hardening budget constraints in local governments' supervision of state enterprises.

15. In many ways, firms at this level of the industrial hierarchy are proving to be much more successful in reform than those at other levels of the urban industrial economy. For example, previous research suggests that firms under municipal companies have not only adopted the most extensive changes in intra-organizational structure but have also been the most productive in Shanghai's urban industrial economy (Guthrie 1999, 2001).

16. For a discussion of the 1984 Reform Declaration, see Naughton 1995, 248; for a discussion of the "price reformers" and "enterprise reformers," see Naughton 1995, 188-96; for a discussion of a lack of reform by the end of 1984, see Naughton 1995, 136.

17. As a document from the State Council put it in 1983, "The current system of employment in China, under which the majority are permanent workers, in practice operates as a kind of unconditional system of life tenure" (People's Republic of China 1983; for a full translation, see Josephs 1989, Appendix A). The Great Leap Forward (1958-60) actually provides a caveat to this system, as approximately sixteen million workers were laid off and sent down to the countryside during that campaign. This is the only period, however, where layoffs were not accompanied by reassignment (Walder 1986a).

18. The main reason for the difference is that the Japanese law on foreign investment, which dates to 1950, was extremely restrictive.

19. The term rational-legal refers to Max Weber's notion of rational-legal authority, one of the three ideal types of authority that characterize modern states. According to Weber, rational-legal authority is characterized by bureaucracy and a reliance on the rule of law.

20. Officially, revenue extraction was replaced by taxation in the Decision of the Standing Committee of the National People's Congress on Authorizing the State Council to Reform the System of Industrial and Commercial Taxes and Issue Relevant Draft Tax Regulations for Trial Application, adopted September 18, 1984, at the Seventh Meeting of the Standing Committee of the Sixth National People's Congress and later codified in the State-Owned Enterprise Second Phase Profits to Taxes Reform of 1985 (Statistical Yearbook of China 1994, 226); for other discussions, see Institutional Economic Yearbook of Shanghai 1994. The first of these documents states that the Standing Committee and State Council recommend "introducing the practice according to which state enterprises pay taxes instead of turning over their profit to the state and in the course reforming the system of industrial and commercial taxes" (People's Republic of China 1984). However, in practice, revenue extraction (and management and oversight fees) lasted for many more years, declining gradually over time. See Naughton 1995 for a further discussion of tax reform.

21. See "The Practical Applications and Experimental Methods of 'The Separation of Taxes and Profits, Fees After Taxes, and Residuals After Taxes' for State-Owned Enterprises," pp. 64-66 in The Shanghai Institutional Economic Yearbook, 1989-93 (1994).

22. For other estimates of the number of cases brought before court, see New York Times, April 27, 1998. For discussion of the percentage rise in suits against the government, see Pei 1995 and 1997.

References

Bian, Yanjie. 1994. *Work and Inequality in Urban China*. Albany: State University of New York Press.

Chang, Gordon. 2001. *The Coming Collapse of China*. New York: Random House.

Demsetz, Harold. 1967. Toward a Theory of Property Rights." In *Ownership, Control, and the Firm: The Organization of Economic Activity*, Volume 1. Blackwell.

Furubotn, Eirik, and Svetozar Pejovich, eds. 1974. *The Economics of Property Rights*. Cambridge, MA: Ballinger.

Gold, Thomas B. 1989a. "Guerilla Interviews among the Getihu." In *Popular Culture and Thought in the People's Republic*, edited by Perry Link, Richard Madsen and Paul Pickowicz, 175–92. San Francisco: Westview Press.

_____. 1989b. "Urban Private Business in China." *Studies in Comparative Communism* 22(2–3): 187–201.

_____. 1990. "Urban Private Business and Social Change." In *Chinese Society on the Eve of Tianamen: The Impact of Reform*, edited by Deborah Davis and Ezra F. Vogel. 157–78. Cambridge, MA: Harvard University Press.

Gong, Ting. 1994. *The Politics of Corruption in Contemporary China: An Analysis of Policy Outcomes*. Westport, CT: Praeger.

Goodman, David, and Beverley Hooper, eds. 1994. *China's Quiet Revolution*. Melbourne: Longman Cheshire.

Guthrie, Doug. 1995. "Political Theater and Student Organizations in the 1989 Chinese Movement: A Multivariate Analysis of Tianamen." *Sociological Forum* 10: 419–54.

_____. 1997. "Between Markets and Politics: Organizational Responses to Reform in China." *American Journal of Sociology* 102: 1258–1303.

_____. 1998. "Organzational Uncertainty and the End of Lifetime Employment in China." *Sociological Forum* 13(3): 457–94.

_____. 1999. *Dragon in a Three-Piece Suit: The Emergence of Capitalism in China*. Princeton, NJ: Princeton University Press.

Hamilton, Gary, and Nicole Woolsey Biggart. 1988. "Market, Culture, and Authority: A Comparative Analysis of Management and Organization in the Far East." *American Journal of Sociology* 94: S52–S94.

Hamilton, Gary G. 1991. *Business Networks and Economic Development in East and Southeast Asia*. Centre for East Asian Studies. Hong Kong: University of Hong Kong Press.

Hohfeld, Wesley. 1913. "Some Fundamental Legal Conceptions as Applied to Judicial Reasoning." *Yale Law Journal* 23(1): 16–59.

Kwong, Julia. 1997. *The Political Economy of Corruption in China*. Armonk, NY: M.E. Sharpe.

Li, Linda Chelan. 1997. "Provincial Discretion and National Power: Investment Policy in Guangdong and Shanghai, 1978–93." *The China Quarterly* 152: 778–804.

Naughton, Barry. 1995. *Growing Out of the Plan: Chinese Economic Reform 1978–1993*. New York: Cambridge University Press.

Oi, Jean C., and Andrew Walder, eds. 1999. *Property Rights and Economic Reform in China*. Stanford, CA: Stanford University Press.

People's Republic of China [Zhonghua renmin gongheguo]. 1988. Law of the People's Republic of China on Chinese-Foreign Contractual Joint Ventures. Adopted at the First Session of the Seventh National People's Congress and Promulgated by Order No. 4 of the President of the People's Republic of China on April 13, 1988.

_____. 1994. The Labor Law of the People's Republic of China. Adopted at the Eighth Meeting of the Standing Committee of the National People's Congress on July 5, 1994; effective January 1, 1995.

Perry, Elizabeth, and Jeffery Wasserstrom. 1992. *Popular Protest and Political Culture in Modern China: Learning from 1989*. Boulder, CO: Westview.

Rawski, Thomas G. 1994. "Progress without Privatization: The Reform of China's State Industries." In *Changing Political Economies: Privatization in Post-Communist and Reforming Communist States*, edited by Vedat Milor, 27–52. Boulder, Co: Lynn Reinner.

_____. 1995. "Implications of China's Reform Experience." *China Quarterly* 144: 1150–73.

_____. 1999. "Reforming China's Economy: What Have We Learned?" *The China Journal* 41: 139–56.

Sachs, Jeffrey D. 1992. "Privatization in Russia: Some Lessons from Eastern Europe." *American Economic Review* 80: 43–48.

_____. 1993. *Poland's Jump to the Market Economy*. Cambridge: MIT Press.

_____. 1995a. Consolidating Capitalism. *Foreign Policy* 98: 50–64.

_____. 1995b. Reforms in Eastern Europe and the Former Soviet Union in Light of the East Asian Experience. *Journal of the Japanese and International Economies* 9: 454–85.

Sachs, Jeffrey D., and Wing Thye Woo. 1994. "Structural Factors in the Economic Reforms of China, Eastern Europe, and the Former Soviet Union." *Economic Policy* 9(18): 101–31.

_____. 1997. "Understanding China's Economic Performance." Working Paper #5935, National Bureau of Economic Research, Inc. Working Paper Series.

Seymour, James D., and Richard Anderson. 1998. *New Ghosts, Old Ghosts: Prisons and Labor Reform Camps in China*. New York: M. E. Sharpe.

Singer, Joseph. 1982. "The Legal Rights Debate in Analytical Jurisprudence from Bentham to Hohfeld." *Wisconsin Law Review*: 980–1059.

_____. 1988. "The Reliance Interest in Property." *Stanford Law Review* 40(3): 611–751.

Walder, Andrew. 1986. *Communist Neo-Traditionalism: Work and Authority in Chinese Industry*. Berkeley and Los Angeles: University of California Press.

_____. 1994. "Corporate Organization and Local Government Property Rights in China." In *Changing Political Economies: Privatization in Post-Communist and Reforming Communist States*, edited by Vedat Milor, 53–66. Boulder CO: Lynn Reinner.

_____. 1995a. "Local Governments as Industrial Firms: An Organizational Analysis of China's Transitional Economy." *American Journal of Sociology* 101: 263–301.

_____. 1995b. "The Quiet Revolution from Within: Economic Reform as a Source of Political Decline." In *The Waning of the Communist State*, edited by Andrew Walder, 1–24. Berkeley and Los Angeles: University of California Press.

Walder, Andrew, ed. 1995. *The Waning of the Communist State: Economic Origins of Political Decline in China and Hungary*. Berkeley and Los Angeles: University of California Press.

Wank, David. 1999. *Commodifying Communism: Business, Trust, and Politics in a Chinese City*. New York: Cambridge University Press.

Wong, Christine. 1992. "Fiscal Reform and Local Industrialization: The Problematic Sequencing of Reform in Post-Mao China." *Modern China* 18: 197–227.

Woo, Wing Thye. 1999. "The Real Reasons for China's Growth." *The China Journal* 41: 115–37.

Yang, Mayfair Mei-hui. 1994. Gifts, Favors, and Banquets: The Art of Social Relationships in China. Ithaca, NY: Cornell University Press.

3

Market Development in Developing Countries

The relationship between states and markets and the appropriate domains for each of them in economic activity have been hotly contested topics in developing countries. Discourse about the economics of development has risen to new prominence in the past two decades, propelled by such intellectuals as the Nobel Prize-winning economist Amartya Sen and the theorists-cum-practitioners **Joseph Stiglitz** and **Jeffrey Sachs** (whose views we encountered in the previous section on market transition), as well as by more popular figures such as the rock star Bono of U2. Debate permeates both theoretical and practical realms in a high-stakes battle to achieve economic growth, reduce poverty, and improve human welfare, and it covers microlevel grassroots aid programs all the way through to prescriptions for reforming the international political economy architecture. In this section, we focus on how the concept of markets as institutions informs discussions of economic development.

Deepak Lal lays out a theoretical defense of the principles of neoclassical economics, or what we have termed in this reader the liberal view on markets. He inveighs against the tenets of "development economics," which was an influential perspective on development among economists and policy makers in the 1950s and 1960s.[1] Development economists criticized the insistence of neoclassical economics on perfect markets and were also motivated by the pragmatic need to solve real-world policy problems rather than build theoretical models. Development economics thus treated development policy as a response to the market failures peculiar to underdevelopment and recommended large-scale government intervention, or dirigisme, as a solution to those inefficiencies. Lal argues that development economics wrongly propagated the "dirigiste dogma," or the view that governments must intervene in the economy to aid development.

Lal is not a dogmatic laissez-faire liberal who sees no role for government; he recognizes that government must provide the foundation on which markets rest. Yet he believes that development economics, through the dirigiste dogma, falsely maintains that government intervention to supplant the price mechanism in markets can improve welfare in developing countries. He makes the case that government policy instruments are necessarily distortional; thus, although markets might not get things exactly right, government intervention will only make things worse. In his view, the most serious distortions in developing economies come not from inevitable imperfections of the market but from government intervention. He echoes **Friedrich Hayek** in arguing that imperfect markets will perform better and lead to better outcomes than imperfect planning.

Kiren Chaudhry presents a counterpoint to Lal's liberal perspective, building on the work of **Karl Polanyi** and **Alexander Gerschenkron** in stressing the role of the state and political development in relation to markets, particularly in late developers. She argues that governments need to perform certain functions to provide the institutional environment in which markets can function. Indeed, as Polanyi argues, state building and market building are mutually dependent, and the government must actively create markets—which are conscious political constructs rather than the neutral and natural phenomena assumed in neoclassical economics. Yet developing country governments are often too weak to create the necessary institutional infrastructure of markets. It is as a result of this administrative crisis, the inability to adequately provide rules and regulate the market, that governments take the relatively easier route of intervening directly in markets to produce and distribute goods and services.

In Chaudhry's analysis, dirigisme is a consequence of administrative weakness, not a philosophy but a de facto second-best option for poor nations. The problem in developing countries is not too much government intervention per se but too little government capacity and hence too little market infrastructure. This administrative crisis is compounded by a political crisis in which the goals of national political integration and economic development are in tension with each other. Chaudhry argues that the liberal impulse to undo statist mechanisms for governing developing economies "without replacing them with effective alternatives encourages economic, administrative, and even political fragmentation."[2] Thus, in the worst-case scenario, state collapse could be the result of blindly following neoliberal economic orthodoxy and liberalizing without considering the consequences.

The argument that market development in poor countries requires a solid institutional infrastructure and state administrative capacity has become more prevalent since the early 1990s. The World Bank's *World Development Report* of 2002 essentially imported the concept into the conventional wisdom, declaring that greater attention must be devoted to building institutions to support markets.[3] The World Bank concluded that market-enhancing institutions are necessary to make markets more effective in delivering growth and poverty reduction in developing countries. The *World Development Report* is heavily prescriptive, showing that the view of markets as institutions has important pragmatic and theoretical implications and that theory does indeed permeate through to policy. In the 1980s, a more neoliberal view of markets and economic development that emphasized liberalization and getting the government out of the economy reigned; this philosophy was named the Washington consensus, after the location of its two big proponents, the World Bank and the International Monetary Fund. It is thus quite remarkable that the World Bank's perspective has shifted of late to emphasizing the institutional foundations of markets, the tailoring of institutions to different national environments, and even the role of government in building market institutions. Yet this line of thinking remains grounded in the framework of the New Institutional Economics (NIE) rather than taking the broader political and sociological viewpoint articulated by Chaudhry.

In much the same vein as the World Bank's prescriptions, **Hernando de Soto** builds on the theoretical insights of the NIE. He elaborates a practical recipe for market development in poor countries that hinges on the reduction of transaction costs to facilitate economic activity. De Soto argues that in the developing world there exists an enormous amount of assets that have not been converted into productive capital because of a lack of property rights. If basic property rights could be introduced, he says, the huge economic potential of those assets could be unleashed. And the key to creating the right form of property ownership is in a legal and regulatory framework that only the state can provide. In some ways, this is a fairly neoliberal point of view, as it hinges on marketization and the faith that the market is the most efficient allocation mechanism. Yet, in other ways, it is a practical prescription that recognizes the centrality of institutions such as property rights to the proper functioning of markets and economic activity. Without such market institutions, de Soto argues, macroeconomic reform intended to stimulate economic development in poor countries simply will not work.

Notes

1. See, for example, Albert O. Hirschman, *The Strategy of Economic Development* (New Haven: Yale University Press, 1958), and Albert O. Hirschman, "The Rise and Decline of Development Economics," in *Essays in Trespassing* (Cambridge: Cambridge University Press, 1981).
2. Kiren Aziz Chaudhry, this volume, p. 465.
3. The World Bank, *World Development Report 2002: Building Institutions for Markets* (Oxford: Oxford University Press, 2002).

Deepak Lal,
The Poverty of "Development Economics" (1983)*

I. The Dirigiste Dogma

Introduction

The essential elements of the *Dirigiste Dogma*, as I see them, can be briefly stated. The major one is the belief that the price mechanism, of the working of a market economy, needs to be supplanted (and not merely supplemented) by various forms of direct government control, both national and international, to promote economic development. A complementary element is the belief that the traditional concern of orthodox micro-economics with the allocation of given (though changing) resources is at best of minor importance in the design of public policies. The essential task of governments is seen as charting and implementing a 'strategy' for rapid and equitable growth which attaches prime importance to macro-economic accounting aggregate such as savings, the balance of payments, and the relative balance between broadly defined 'sectors' such as 'industry' and ' agriculture'.

The third element is the belief that the classical 19th-century liberal case for free trade is invalid for developing countries, and thus government restriction of international trade and payments is necessary for development. Finally, it is believed that, to alleviate poverty and improve domestic income distribution, massive and continuing government intervention is required to re-distribute assets and to manipulate the returns to different types of labour and capital through pervasive price and (if possible) wage controls—and through controls which influence the composition of commodities produced and imported—so that scarce resources are used to meet the so-called 'basic needs' of the poor rather than the luxurious 'wants' of the rich.[1]

In arguing against the *Dirigiste Dogma*, I do not want to question the objectives it ostensibly seeks to serve, namely, equitable and rapid growth to make an appreciable dent, as quickly as possible, in poverty in the Third World. My case is that the means proposed are of dubious merit. Nor, more importantly, am I arguing for *laissez-faire*. That doctrine, as Keynes noted in his famous book, *The End of Laissez-Faire*—better known, alas, for its title than its contents—has been under attack by orthodox economics since John Stuart Mill.[2]

Sadly, many *dirigistes* implicitly contrast their set of beliefs as an alternative to one based on *laissez-faire*. The real issue between them and orthodox economists, however, is the form and extent of government intervention, not its complete absence. Just as Keynes noted that it was not the economists but 'the popularisers and vulgarisers'[3] who spread the *laissez-faire* doctrine, so it cannot be assumed that many distinguished contemporary economists whose views have fed the modern-day *Dirigiste Dogma* thereby necessarily subscribe to it themselves. It has been argued that Marx was not a Marxist, nor Keynes a Keynesian, and many a thinker who has nourished the *dirigiste* stream is not a *dirigiste*. This book, therefore, is concerned with correctly interpreting not so much what particular economists meant as what they have been taken to mean by a wider lay public. For it is the latter which ultimately determines the climate of opinion in which alternative policies are judged and implemented.

1. The Alleged Irrelevance of Orthodox Economics

Before we enter the more important debates on some of the specific beliefs of the *dirigistes,* it remains to chart the major intellectual foundations of the broad claim that *dirigisme* is required to promote development. Fortunately, an important contributor to this set of beliefs has recently characterised the major underlying assumptions which distinguish what he labels 'development economics' from both orthodox economics and various Marxist and neo-Marxist schools of thought on the economics of developing countries. Albert Hirschman distinguishes the various schools in terms of what he calls the 'mono-economics' claim and the 'mutual-benefit' claim.[4] According to Hirschman, the mono-economics claim asserts that traditional economics is applicable to developing countries in the same way as it is to developed ones; the mutual-benefit claim asserts that 'economic relations between these two groups of countries could be shaped in such a way as to yield gains for both'.[5] Whilst orthodox economics accepts both claims and neo-Marxists are presumed to reject both, Hirschman argues that development economics rejects the mono-economics but accepts the mutual-benefit claim—unlike Marx himself who would have accepted the mono-economics but rejected the mutual-benefit claim!

It is chiefly the influence of Hirschman's 'development economies' that I wish to counter in this Paper—though, to the extent there are many neo-Marxist influences on policies for and towards the Third World, I shall be dealing briefly with these too. Despite Hirschman's categorisation, development economics is closer to the neo-Marxists than to orthodox economics in its view of the mutual-benefit claim. For development economics, mutual gains can be realised only after legitimate departures from the orthodox case for free trade which must be enforced by government action both nationally and internationally. In practice, therefore, whilst not going as far as the neo-Marxists in their desire to smash the whole world capitalist system based on 'unequal exchange',[6] development economists nevertheless accept that developing countries are 'unequal partners'[7] in the current world trading and payments system, and that the rules of the game of the liberal international economic order must be changed to serve their interests.

2. The Keynesian Heritage

The analytical and empirical bases of development economics were provided by the Keynesian 'revolution' in economic thought and the experience of the developing countries during the Great Depression of the 1930s. While the next Section will consider the lessons that were drawn from the latter, a few remarks are required here about the Keynesian lineage of development economics and the revolt against orthodox economics that it was supposed to represent.

The specific Keynesian remedy for curing mass unemployment during a depression was soon seen to be irrelevant to developing countries which, unlike developed ones, did not face unemployment of both men and machines. Rather, their problem was too few 'machines' adequately to employ the existing 'men'.[8] All the same, in contrast with the orthodox economics castigated by Keynes, Keynesian modes of thought were seen as relevant to the problems of development. Both the central theoretical concern of Keynesian economics—namely, the determinants of the level of economic activity rather than the relative prices of commodities and factors of production—and its distinctive method—namely, national income-expenditure analysis—were enthusiastically adopted by development economics. The allocation of given resources, a major concern of orthodox economics, was considered of minor importance compared with the problems of increasing material resources—subsumed in the portmanteau term 'capital'—and of ensuring their fullest utilisation.

These Keynesian modes of thought also led to an implicit or explicit rejection of the primary rôle assigned by orthodox economics to changes in relative prices in mediating imbalances in the supply and demand for different 'commodities'—including not merely such obvious commodities as carrots and clothes, but also hypothetical composite 'commodities' such as 'savings', 'investment' and 'foreign exchange'. Changes in income were substituted as the major adjustment- mechanism for bringing supply and demand into balance. This neglect of the rôle of the price mechanism was usually justified by assumptions based on casual empiricism: that there were limited possibilities for consumers in developing countries to substitute different commodities as their relative prices changed since their consumption consisted of bare essentials, for which no substitutes existed; and that producers could not substitute cheaper inputs for more expensive ones because, by assumption, their production techniques required inputs to be used in fixed proportions. The implicit or explicit assumption of what economists call 'limited substitutability' in both consumption and production meant the downgrading of a large part of the rôle played by relative price changes in adjusting the demand and supply of different commodities and factors of production to each other.

Moreover, the concentration on macro-economics, flowing from Keynesian modes of thought, required thinking in terms of aggregates of different 'commodities'. At its simplest, this conceptual aggregation necessitates an assumption that the relative prices of real-world commodities which constitute the aggregate composite 'commodity' remain unchanged during the period of analysis. As a result, the neglect of the price mechanism, except for the relative 'prices' of these composite 'commodities', is almost inbuilt into macro-economic thinking. Though undoubtedly useful for certain analytical and policy purposes, there is a consequent temptation—not often resisted in development economics—to ignore micro-economic problems altogether in the design of public policies.

The concentration on macro-economics was further aided by the spread of national income accounting and the establishment of statistical offices in most developing countries to provide the necessary data. Though the resulting information has considerably improved our quantitative knowledge of developing countries, it has also given a fillip to a particular type of applied economics research in both developed and developing countries which can be termed 'mathematical planning'. Building on the work of Tinbergen and his associates[9] in estimating statistical macro-economic relationships (from the 'time series' data supplied by the national income statisticians), and on the work of Leontief in refining 'input-output analysis' to describe the interrelationships in the production structure of an economy, development planning seemingly acquired a hard scientific and quantifiable character.

The Leontief input-output system,[10] building as it did on the Soviet practice of 'material balance planning', ignored relative price changes by assuming that the inputs for producing particular real-world commodities were required, for technological reasons, in fixed proportions. The typical development plan first laid down a desired rate of growth of aggregate consumption. Then the quantities of different commodities required in fixed proportions, either as inputs into production or outputs for consumption, were derived from an input-output table for the economy. Since such plans were presented in terms of desired quantities of production of various goods, their implementation most often entailed direct controls on production, including state provision of some goods considered either too important to be supplied by the private sector or unlikely to be produced by the private sector in the planned amounts.

3. The Neglect of Welfare Economics

The final intellectual strand in the making of development economics was a neglect of the one branch of economic theory which provides the logic to assess the desirability of alternative economic policies, namely, welfare economics. This was due partly to its rejection of much of micro-economics, and partly to what was seen as the inherently limited applicability of conventional welfare economics, whether of the classical sort as systematised by Pigou or the 'new welfare economics' of Hicks and Kaldor. Broadly two types of objections were raised against this branch of economics, and they continue to be echoed in contemporary development economics. The first concerned its ethical foundations, the second the real-world relevance of its assumptions about consumers' tastes and producers' technology.

It is important to assess these objections, and the current status and scope of welfare economics, for three reasons. First, because welfare economics provides 'the grammar of arguments about policy':[11] those seeking to argue the case for increased government intervention might have been expected to use it to bolster their claims. Secondly, the development of what is labelled 'second-best' welfare economics was stimulated in part by the problems and debates about developing countries.[12] Thirdly, and equally important, the analytical framework for assessing the claims of the *Dirigiste Dogma* (as of *laissez-faire*) is provided in large part by welfare economics, and it is therefore necessary to outline briefly the logic of this important branch of economics.

Welfare economics is concerned with two general classes of practical questions: (a) the measurement of real national income,[13] and (b) the efficiency and equity of particular economic outcomes, including the scope for improving them through various instruments of public policy. These are the very issues of assessing economic performance and designing policies to improve it which lie at the heart of the practical debates on development taken up in later sections of this Paper. I turn, therefore, to outlining the development of modern welfare economics, albeit very cursorily, to show how it lends *prima facie* support to the *Dirigiste Dogma*, but also to show why this support is deceptive.

One major strand of objections to welfare economics concerns its ethical foundations. For our purpose, it is sufficient to note that such objections are related to questions about the distribution of income—whether and how the distributional effects of economic change should be accounted for in measuring changes in aggregate economic welfare.[14] Not surprisingly, there is no consensus to date on these normative issues since the ethics of income distribution and other political aspects of the good society remain controversial. But does that invalidate the 'positive' welfarist conclusions about the so-called optimum conditions for production and exchange required for an efficient allocation of resources? There are some development economists who believe so.[15] This is to misunderstand the logic of modern welfare economics, however, and to derive illegitimate inferences from the legitimate criticism that it might be ethically blinkered. For, as we shall see, the most useful results of modern applied welfare economics do not depend upon accepting a particular ethical viewpoint. They are 'the logical conclusions of a set of consistent value axioms which are laid down for the welfare economist, by some priest, parliament or dictator',[16] whilst, as far as the *Dirigiste Dogma* is concerned, the policies *it* has engendered have aided neither efficiency nor equity nor liberty in the Third World.

4. The Theoretical Attack on *Laissez-Faire*

It remains to chart the second set of objections to welfare economics which have also led to its neglect in development economics. These concern its 'positive' aspects. The basic theorems of welfare economics—rigorously derived in the 1950s by Professors Arrow and Debreu—show that, in a perfectly-competitive economy with universal markets for all commodities distinguishable not only by their spatial and temporal characteristics but also by the various conceivable future 'states of nature' under which they could be traded (that is, there is a 'complete' set of futures markets for so-called 'contingent' commodities[17]), a *laissez-faire* equilibrium will be Pareto-efficient in the sense that, with given resources and available technology, no individual can be made better-off without someone else being made worse-off. Since, however, this competitive, Pareto-efficient equilibrium may not yield the distribution of income considered socially desirable according to the prevailing ethics, government intervention may be necessary to legislate the optimum income distribution even in a perfectly competitive economy with complete markets. If government can levy lump-sum taxes and disburse lump-sum subsidies, the perfectly-competitive economy can attain a full 'welfare optimum'.

It is, however, premature to cheer this rigorous establishment of the case for a *laissez-faire* economy in which the government's rôle (apart from providing a legal framework to enforce property rights and maintain law and order) is confined to *lump-sum* re-distributive measures (assuming the unmodified distribution conflicts with prevailing ethical norms). For, as many critics of the price mechanism have been only too ready to point out, the conditions (or assumptions) for establishing it are extremely unrealistic. Broadly, the assumptions fall into those required for (a) perfect competition and (b) universal markets.

Perfect competition depends on stringent assumptions about the tastes of consumers and the nature of producers' technology. First, there must be no interdependencies in either consumption or production not mediated through markets (that is, there must be no so-called 'external effects', such as keeping up with the Jones's or emitting smoke which damages the output of a nearby laundry). And, secondly, there must not be too many industries with decreasing costs of production (that is, 'increasing returns' in production must not be large relative to the size of the economy) since these are likely to lead to monopoly. Development economists have emphasised the importance of 'externalities' and 'increasing returns' in developing countries.[18] Though usually asserted rather than empirically demonstrated, it has led them to reject the argument for a market economy implicit in the notion of a perfectly-competitive Utopia.

These two assumptions are not nearly as unrealistic,[19] however, as the other major one required to show the Pareto-efficiency of a *laissez-faire* competitive economy, namely, the existence of universal markets. The lack of markets for all current and future 'contingent' commodities is likely to be the fundamental cause of so-called 'market failure'. Externalities pose problems essentially because of the difficulty (if not impossibility) of creating a market for them even though, conceptually, they can be readily identified as 'commodities' (factory smoke, for example, is a commodity, but also a 'bad' for which there is no market). The reason is that, to create a market in any commodity, non-buyers must be excluded from obtaining it. Exclusion may be technically impossible or prohibitively expensive, in terms of resource costs, for most 'externalities'. Where exclusion is possible, there may be so few buyers and sellers in the market for the externality that it cannot be perfectly competitive.[20]

The difficulty of establishing markets in these commodities reflects what are broadly termed the costs of making transactions attached to any market or indeed any mode of resource allocation. Transaction costs include the costs of exclusion as well as those of acquiring and transmitting information by and to market participants. They drive a wedge, in effect, between the buyer's and the seller's price. The market for a particular good will cease to exist if the wedge is so large as to push the lowest price at which anyone is willing to sell above the highest price anyone is willing to pay.

Apart from making it difficult to deal through an unfettered market with externalities, these transactions costs will also limit the development of futures markets for all commodities. Thus, far from being an apologia for the *laissez-faire* doctrine, as many suppose, modern welfare economics provides the precise reasons why, even in the absence of distributional considerations, a real-world *laissez-faire* economy is not likely to be Pareto-efficient—because (a) it is unlikely to be perfectly competitive, and (b) it will certainly lack universal markets.

5. The Limits of Rational *Dirigisme*

Thus, even if income distribution is disregarded, there would seem to be a *prima facie* case for government intervention. It would be absurd, however, to jump to the conclusion that, because *laissez-faire* may be inefficient and inequitable, any form of government intervention thereby entails a welfare improvement. For transactions costs are also incurred in acquiring, processing and transmitting the relevant information to design public policies, as well as in enforcing compliance. There may consequently be as many instances of 'bureaucratic failure' as of 'market failure', making it impossible to attain a Pareto-efficient outcome.

Let us consider the question of legislating for the optimal income distribution in an otherwise competitive, Pareto-efficient economy. If government could levy *lump-sum* taxes which were inescapable and could not be avoided by economic agents altering their otherwise efficient choices, it could achieve the full welfare optimum. If, for example, income differences were related to the inescapable abilities of individuals, and there was an unambiguous and readily available (at low cost) index of these abilities, a lump-sum tax/subsidy system based on differential abilities would allow the full welfare optimum to be achieved (in a perfectly-competitive economy with complete markets). Clearly, such a system is not feasible because of the costs of acquiring the necessary information.

By contrast, a tax/subsidy system based on *income* differences which aimed at legislating for a desired income distribution would not be lump-sum because it would affect the choices individuals make at the margin between work and leisure. By distorting the initial, *ex hypothesis* efficient allocation, the income-based tax/subsidy system, though improving the distribution of income, would impair the productive efficiency of the economy; The feasible instrument of government intervention would mean that the welfare gain from an improved distribution could only be obtained by inflicting a welfare loss in the form of lower productive efficiency. Because of the 'bureaucratic failure' inherent in the inability of government to introduce a lump-sum tax/subsidy system, a full welfare optimum is not attainable even with government intervention. All that can be achieved is a 'second-best' optimum where the *net* gain from the distributional gain and efficiency loss are at a maximum.

The same argument applies to government intervention to correct market failures in any real-world economy which is not perfectly competitive or which lacks complete futures markets. There are few, if any, instruments of government policy which are non-distortionary, in the sense of not inducing economic agents to behave less efficiently in some respects. Neither markets nor bureaucrats as they exist can therefore be expected to lead an economy to a full welfare optimum. The best that can be expected is a second-best.

Given that the optimum is unattainable, the relevant policy problem becomes that of assessing to what extent particular government interventions may raise welfare in an inherently and inescapably imperfect economy. The Utopian theoretical construct of perfect competition then becomes relevant as a reference point by which to judge the health of an economy, as well as the remedies suggested for its amelioration. Since improvements will not necessarily entail a movement towards the perfectly-competitive theoretical norm, evaluating the likely consequences of alternative policies in an imperfect economy becomes a subtle exercise in what is nowadays termed 'second-best welfare economics'.

An early theoretical contribution by Lipsey and Lancaster correctly argued that, in an imperfect economy, the restoration of some of the conditions which would exist under perfect competition would not necessarily result in an improvement in welfare.[1] This insight was unfortunately taken to mean that there was no way in which the effects on economic welfare of alternative piecemeal policies to improve the working of the price mechanism or to alter the distribution of income could be judged. Many took it to imply that, since every economy is imperfect, welfare economics (and by implication microeconomics) was irrelevant in the design of public policy. One of the major analytical advances of the last two decades, prompted by the problems of developing countries, has been to show that this is not so.[22]

The major point to note is that no general rule of second-best welfare economics permits the deduction that, in a necessarily imperfect market economy, particular *dirigiste* policies will increase welfare. They may not; and they may even be worse than *laissez-faire*. Moreover, any economic justification for a *dirigiste* policy not based on die logic of second-best welfare economics must be incoherent, and akin to the miracle cures peddled by quacks which are adopted because of faith rather than reason. The burden of the case against the *Dirigiste Dogma* in its application to developing countries is that, though in many instances some forms of *dirigisme* may have been beneficial had they been feasible, the *dirigiste* policies actually adopted (either because they were considered the only feasible ones, or else because the relative costs and benefits of alternative policies were never examined) have often led to outcomes which, by the canons of second-best welfare economics, may have been even worse than *laissez-faire*. The conclusion, therefore, of this theoretical tour is that the very analysis which seemingly establishes a *prima facie* intellectual justification for the *Dirigiste Dogma* provides, in its fullness, the antidote!

VI. Some General Conclusions

Underlying much of development economics is the quest for a new 'unorthodox' economics, of special application to the Third World, which surfaced in the early 1960s with a debate initiated by an influential article by the late Dudley Seers.[23] Those who sought a new economics claimed that the orthodox neo-classical model was (a) unrealistic because of its behavioural, technological and institutional assumptions, and (b) irrelevant because it was concerned primarily with the efficient allocation of given resources and hence could deal with neither so-called dynamic aspects of growth nor with various ethical aspects of the alleviation of poverty or the distribution of income. Yet, as Myint noted, most of the unorthodox economics then put on offer consisted of little more than 'selecting the "queer cases" in the Western models of analysis and in taking it for granted that these exceptions to the standard case must automatically apply to the under-developed countries because they are so different from the advanced countries in their social attitudes and institutional setting'.[24]

This book has charted the various twists and turns that the unorthodox theories have subsequently taken. Mostly, they have sought to justify massive government intervention through forms of direct control usually intended to supplant the price mechanism. The empirical assumptions on which this *dirigisme* was based have been belied by the experience of numerous countries in the post-war period. The most serious current distortions in many developing economies are not those flowing from the inevitable imperfections of a market economy but the policy-induced, and thus far from inevitable, distortions created by irrational *dirigisme*. This concluding Section sums up the reasons why the assumptions underlying the *dirigisme* promoted by development economics, however plausible they may have seemed in the 1950s or early 1960s, are no longer persuasive.

At its bluntest, behind at least of the *dirigiste* case is a paternalistic attitude born of a distrust of, if not contempt for, the ordinary, poor, uneducated masses of the Third World. This attitude is not confined entirely, nor even primarily, to Western outsiders; it is shared by many in the ruling élites of the Third World. As a leading development economist has observed about Gunnar Myrdal, one of the Western economists to have fuelled the *Dirigiste Dogma*:

'As a proud, somewhat un Swedish Swede ... he [Myrdal] finds it easier to identify with liberal Americans than with the English or French, and easier with Englishmen than with the Indian masses. It is partly for this reason that *An American Dilemma* is an optimistic book, and *Asian Drama* a pessimistic one. He once said how kindred American aspirations and ideals, and the "American creed", were to his own beliefs, and how he could identify with these ideals when writing the book on the black problem; and how, in contrast, when he visited an Indian textile factory, the thin, half-naked brown bodies struck him as utterly alien.'[25]

It is easy to suppose that these half-starved, wretched and ignorant masses could not possibly conform, either as producers or consumers, to the behavioural assumption of orthodox neo-classical economics that 'people would act *economically*; when the opportunity of an advantage was presented to them they would take it'.[26] This has been termed the 'Economic Principle' by Hicks,[27] and denying it is the hallmark of much of development economics—together with the assertion that some ethereal and verbally sanitised entity (such as 'government', 'planners', or 'policy-makers') which is both knowledgeable and compassionate can overcome the defects of these stupid or ignorant producers and consumers and compel them to raise their living standards through various *dirigiste* means. As Myint has noted, the seemingly scientific language in which are couched these judgements questioning the validity of Western behavioural assumptions in other cultures is illusory:

'If one were to tell the politicians of the underdeveloped countries that their people are lazy, stupid, lacking in initiative and adaptability, one would be branded as an enemy; but if one were to rephrase these prejudices in another way and say that the people lack entrepreneurial capacity, one would be welcomed for giving "scientific" support for economic planning'.[28]

There is by now a vast body of empirical evidence from different cultures and climates which shows that uneducated peasants act economically as producers and consumers.[29] They respond to changes in relative prices much as neo-classical economic theory predicts. The 'Economic Principle' is not unrealistic in the Third World.

Nor has experience proved the conventional technological assumptions of neo-classical theory (about the possibilities of substituting different inputs in production) to be unrealistic. The degree to which inputs of different factors and commodities can be substituted in the production of the national product is not much different in developed or developing countries.[30] Furthermore, it cannot be assumed that Third World labourers (and consumers) have such peculiar preferences that, when they become richer, by however small an amount and from however lowly a base, they will not also seek to increase their 'leisure'; putting it the other way round, for them as for workers in the developed world the cost of 'sweat' rises the harder and longer they have to work. No less than their Western counterparts, they are unlikely to be in 'surplus' in any meaningful economic sense.

Nor are the so-called institutional features of the Third World, such as their strange social and agrarian structures or their usurious informal credit systems, necessarily a handicap to growth.[31] Far from asserting that these institutions inhibit efficiency, conventional neoclassical theory is now seeking to show the precise sense in which they may promote it and is discovering that they are not as irrational and uneconomic as so many *dirigistes* claim. They are likely to represent an efficient, second-best adaptation to the risks and uncertainties inevitable in the relevant economic environment. In the absence of other means of eliminating or alleviating the risks, the destruction of these traditional institutions could actually do more harm than good.[32]

Imperfect Markets Superior to Imperfect Planning

Nor has experience proved the irrelevance of neo-classical allocation theory; quite the contrary. The centralised planning which *dirigistes* have sought to promote has the same intellectual basis as the efficient allocation of resources through the market mechanism extolled by neo-classical economics. As Myint has noted: 'Both accept the optimum allocation of resources as their theoretical norm and their disagreements are about the *practical* means of fulfilling this norm'.[33] This book has given reasons, rooted both in the experience of developing countries and in theory, why, of the only feasible alternatives—a necessarily imperfect planning mechanism and a necessarily imperfect market mechanism—the latter is likely to perform better in practice. Finally, it is neo-classical economics which has provided the justification for *rational dirigisme,* by showing that there are methods of 'planning' through the price mechanism which may be both feasible and desirable.[34]

It is true, however, that economic theory is unable to offer a rigorous account of the *process* of development, the so-called dynamic aspects which much concern some *dirigistes*. But neither have the latter succeeded in supplying an alternative theoretical framework for studying and influencing the dynamic processes. Their arguments for *dirigisme* based on so-called 'dynamic aspects' usually turn out to be either incoherent or merely handwaving.[35] More importantly, the belief that neo-classical economics is particularly unsuitable for analysing dynamic processes in developing (as contrasted with developed) countries is unlikely to be valid. The fundamental method of neo-classical economics is to compare alternative equilibrium states of the economy. But, like perfect competition, the equilibria are only notional—yet not for that reason to be despised. There has been much discussion of the notion of equilibrium in economic analysis, and many have concluded that it is irrelevant for understanding the workings of actual economies.

This Paper cannot enter into these more theoretical debates. But, paradoxically, with its neglect of the adjustment process between two equilibria (at least in its most readily usable 'comparative statics' form) and its emphasis on the flexibility of the prices of both commodities and factors of production, neo-classical economics is likely to be more applicable to developing than to developed countries. For, unlike in richer countries, economic agents in poor ones will have few 'reserves' to fall back upon and will thus have to adjust speedily to a change in their economic environment by swiftly altering terms on which they are willing to exchange economic commodities. Though this may not always be desirable, it does mean that the simple stories derived from the comparative statics method are not irrelevant. It is in the developed countries that economic agents, endowed with fairly large reserves in the form either of past savings or of entitlements provided by the welfare state, can postpone the required price adjustments in a changing economic environment. The so-called fixed-price markets for goods and factors in developed countries which allegedly call for a revision of neo-classical theory are thus unlikely to be widespread in most developing countries.

Moreover, there now exists a quite large number of what may be termed analytical economic histories (the only type of truly dynamic analysis available), of which the various studies of trade and industrialisation are most notable in allowing us to form judgements about the policies likely to foster development.[36] Yet there are people who will not find this sufficient in their search for the Holy Grail of the 'necessary and sufficient conditions for development'.[37] It should be obvious that economics cannot hope to provide such conditions. What the experience of developing countries does show is that, other things equal, the most important advice that economists can currently offer is that of Stewart and Streeten's so-called Price Mechanist: 'Get the prices right'.[38]

Unlamented Demise of 'Development Economics'

It is in the political and administrative aspects of *dirigisme* that powerful practical arguments can be advanced against the *Dirigiste Dogma*. The political and administrative assumptions underlying the feasibility of various forms of *dirigisme* derive from those of modern welfare states in the West. These, in turn, reflect the values of the Enlightenment. It has taken nearly two centuries of political evolution for those values to be internalised and reflected (however imperfectly) in the political and administrative institutions of Western societies. In the Third World, an acceptance of the same values is at best confined to a small class of Westernised intellectuals. Despite their trappings of modernity, many developing countries are closer in their official workings to the rapacious and inefficient nation-states of 17th- or 18th-century Europe, governed as much for the personal aggrandisement of their rulers as for the welfare of the ruled. It is instructive to recall that Keynes, who so many *dirigistes* invoke as a founding father of their faith, noted in *The End of Lassez-Faire:*

'But above all, the ineptitude of public administrators strongly prejudiced the practical man in favour of *laissez-faire*—a sentiment which has by no means disappeared. Almost everything which the State did in the 18th century in excess of its minimum functions was, or seemed, injurious or unsuccessful.'[39]

It is in this context that anyone familiar with the actual administration and implementation of policies in very many Third World countries, and not blinkered by the *Dirigiste Dogma,* should find that oft-neglected work, *The Wealth of Nations,* both so relevant and so modern. For in most of our modern-day equivalents of the inefficient 18th-century state, not even the minimum governmental functions required for economic progress are always fulfilled. Yet the *dirigistes* have been urging a myriad new tasks on Third World governments which go well beyond what Keynes considered to be a sensible agenda for *mid-20th-century* Western polities:

'The most important *Agenda* of the State relate not to those activities which private individuals are already fulfilling, but to those functions which fall outside the sphere of the individual, to those decisions which are made by *no one* if the State does not make them. The important thing for governments is not to do things which individuals are doing already, and to do them a little better or a little worse; but to do those things which at present are not done at all'.[40]

This is a far cry from that 'enlightened discrimination' towards foreign trade, transnational companies, technology, and the meeting of basic needs currently being touted as desirable for developing countries.[41] In these deeply ideological times, it may be vain to hope to steer a middle course between *laissez-faire* and the *Dirigiste Dogma.* In the light of the foregoing, however, and the repeated trouncing of development economics, the author, for one, cannot join Hirschman in lamenting its fall. The major conclusion of this book is that the demise of development economics is likely to be conducive to the health of both the economics and the economies of developing countries.

Notes

1. Nurkse [43, 44], Myrdal [40], Hirschman [22], Balogh [3], Rosenstein-Rodan [47], Chenery [10], Prebisch [45], Singer [54], and Streeten [56] are notable amongst many others who would consider themselves to be non-neo-classicals and whose writings have been influential in providing various elements of the *Dirigiste Dogma.* There has, however, always been some opposition to these views: Haberler [17, 18], Viner [61], Bauer and Yamey [5], Schultz [48].

2. Keynes [25], p. 26. Nor is 'the phrase *laissez faire* to be found in the works of Adam Smith, of Ricardo or of Malthus. Even the idea is not present in a dogmatic form in any of these authors' (p. 20). 'This is what the economists are *supposed* to have said. No such idea is to be found in the writings of the greatest authorities' (p. 17). 'Some of the most important work of Alfred Marshall—to take one instance—was directed to the elucidation of the leading cases in which private interest and social interest are *not*

harmonious. Nevertheless, the guarded and undogmatic attitude of the best economists has not prevailed against the general opinion that an individualistic *laissez-faire* is both what they ought to teach and what in fact they do teach' (p. 27).

3. *Ibid.*, p. 17.
4. A. Hirschman [23].
5. *Ibid.*
6. The title of an influential neo-Marxist work by A. Emmanuel [15].
7. The title of a well-known collection of papers by Lord Balogh [3].
8. V.K.R.V. Rao [46].
9. J. Tinbergen [60].
10. W. Leontief [29], H. Chenery *et al.* [11].
11. F.H. Hahn [19].
12. I.M.D. Little and J.A. Mirrlees [33, 34], P. Dasgupta-S. Marglin-A. Sen [14], A.H. Harberger [20], Little, Scitoviky, Scott [35].
13. Sen [53] provides a lucid survey of the issues.
14. A.K. Sen [52].
15. P. Streeten and S. Lall [59], for instance.
16. Little [31], p. 80.
17. A 'contingent commodity', for instance, would be 'ballbearings' for delivery on 16 September 1995, where the future price is conditional upon whether or not industrial production in Indonesia is 20 per cent above average that month.
18. Rosenstein-Rodan [47], T. Scitovsky [49], Hirschman [22], Chenery [10].
19. Many externalities can be dealt with by suitable taxes and subsidies; and, in an open economy, the potential danger of decreasing-cost industries becoming monopolistic it reduced by foreign competition.
20. Arrow [2] cites the example of the lighthouse keeper who knows exactly 'when each ship will need its services, and ... abstract from indivisibility (since the light is either on or not). Assume further that only one ship will be within range of the lighthouse at any moment. Then exclusion is perfectly possible; the keeper need only shut off the light when a non-paying ship is coming into range. But there would be only one buyer and one seller and no competitive forces to drive the two into a competitive equilibrium. If in addition the costs of bargaining are high it may be most efficient to offer the service free' (p. 15).
21. Lipsey and Lancaster [30].
22. Two sets of applications of this theory are in Little and Mirrlees [33], and W.M. Corden [13].
23. Seers [51].
24. Myint [39], p. 70.
25. Streeten [58], p. 425.
26. Hicks [21], p. 43.
27. *Ibid.*
28. Myint [39], p. 71.
29. For references to numerous empirical studies, Nugent and Yotopoulos [42].
30. Morawetz [38]; Behrman [6].
31. Myrdal [41] emphasises the deleterious effects of these institutional factors on economic development in South Asia. Also, Madan [36] for an anthropological critique of Myrdal, and Lal [28] for an economic explanation of the origins and economic functions of caste.

32. Braverman and Stiglitz [9], Bardhan [4], Braverman and Srinivasan [8] on the agrarian structure; Lal [26] for a survey of the literature on industrial wage structures; and Binswanger and Rosenzweig [7] on rural wage structures.

33. Myint [39], p. 73.

34. Lal [26] for an application to India, and Scott, MacArthur. Newberry [50] for Kenya.

35. Thus, for instance, Hirschman has emphasised two seemingly unorthodox dynamic effects. The first are so-called backward and forward linkages of investments; the second is the so-called 'hiding hand' which turns apparently economically-disastrous projects into successes! These backward and forward linkages are, however, simply other names for the ubiquitous interdependence of production found in any moderately complex economy. It is doubtful, however, that the existence of these 'linkages' provides any special reasons for *dirigisme* (Little and Mirrlees [33]). The 'hiding hand' is equally unconvincing, and resorting to it would exclude the possibility of discriminating *ex ante* between good and bad projects, which is clearly absurd!

36. The OECD, World Bank and NBER studies cited earlier. Also, ILO [24] on the Philippines; Galenson (ed.) [16] on Taiwan; and a series of studies edited by Ed. Mason for the Harvard Institute of Development on Korea. Collier and Lal [12] on Kenya, and Lal [28] on India, seek to provide explicit analytical economic histories of these countries, primarily on the evolution of labour incomes and labour institutions.

37. This seems to be what Stewart and Streeten [55] are seeking.

38. Stewart and Streeten [55].

39. Keynes [25], p. 12.

40. *Ibid.*, pp. 46–7.

41. Streeten [57]. As Little [32] has rightly remarked: 'Of course, such a position always puts the critic at some disadvantage, because he seldom wants to advocate *laissez-faire*, and the policies described will usually contain some elements that he would himself advocate—for example, export taxes or hard case-by-case bargaining in the case of mineral exploitation. Nevertheless, the picture of "enlightened discrimination" drawn by Streeten seems to me to come too close to Indian policy over the past twenty years, and too close to maximum surveillance and control for it to be likely to do anything but retard growth without any offsetting benefit. There is a mass of evidence, in works already cited and elsewhere, that discrimination is seldom very enlightened'.

References

[1] A. N. Agarwala and S. P. Singh (eds.): *The Economics of Underdevelopment*, Oxford University Press, London, 1958.

[2] K.J. Arrow: "Political and Economic Evaluation of Social Effects and Externalities," in J. Margolis (ed.), *The Analysis of Public Output*, NBER, Columbia, New York, 1970.

[3] T. Balogh: *Unequal Partners*, 2 vols., Blackwells, Oxford, 1963.

[4] PK. Bardhan: "Interlocking Factor Markets and Agrarian Development: A Review of Issues," *Oxford Economic Papers*, March 1980.

[5] P.T. Bauer and B.S. Yamey: *The Economics of Underdeveloped Countries*, Cambridge, 1957.

[6] J.R. Behrman: "Review Article on Hollis Chenery: Structural Change in Development Policy," *Journal of Development Economics*, June 1982.

[7] H. Binswanger and M. Rosenzweig: "Contractual Arrangements, Employment and Wages in Rural Labour Markets – A Critical Review," mimeo, *Studies in Employment and Rural Development* No. 67, World Bank, Washington DC, June 1981, to be published as an introduction to a book of ADC/ICRISAT papers by Yale University Press.

[8] A. Braverman and T.N. Srinivasan: "Credit and Share Cropping in Agrarian Societies," *Journal of Development Economics*, 1982.

[9] A. Braverman and J. Stiglitz: Sharecropping and the Interlinking of Agrarian Markets," *American Economic Review*, September 1982.

[10] H. Chenery: "The Interdependence of Investment Decisions," in A. Abramowitz (ed.), *The Allocation of Economic Resources*, Stanford, 1959.

[11] H. Chenery *et al.*: *Structural Change and Development Policy*, Oxford, 1979.

[12] P. Collier and D. Lal: *Poverty and Growth in Kenya*, World Bank Staff Working Paper No. 389, 1980.

[13] W.M. Corden: *Trade Policy and Economic Welfare*, Oxford, 1974.

[14] P. Dasgupta, S. Marglin and A.K. Sen: *Guidelines for Project Evaluation*, UNIDO, New York, 1972.

[15] A. Emmanuel: *Unequal Exchange*, Monthly Review Press, New York, 1972.

[16] W. Galenson (ed.): *Economic Growth and Structural Change in Taiwan*, Cornell, 1979.

[17] G. Haberler: "Critical Observations on Some Current Notions in the Theory of Economic Development," *L'Industria*, No. 2, 1957, reprinted in G. Meier (ed.) [37].

[18] G. Haberler: *A Survey of International Trade Theory*, Princeton Special Papers in International Economics, 1961.

[19] F.H. Hahn: "On Optimum Taxation," *Journal of Economic Theory*, February 1973.

[20] A.C. Harberger: *Project Evaluation – Selected Essays*, Chicago, 1972.

[21] J.R. Hicks: *Causality in Economics*, Blackwells, Oxford, 1979.

[22] A.O. Hirschman: *The Strategy of Economic Development*, Yale, 1958.

[23] A. O. Hirschman: *Essays in Trespassing – Economics to Politics to Beyond*, Cambridge, 1981.

[24] ILO: *Sharing in Development*, ILO, Geneva, 1974.

[25] J.M. Keynes: *The End of Laissez-Faire*, Hogarth Press, London, 1926.

[26] D. Lal: "Theories of Industrial Wage Structures: A Review," *Indian Journal of Industrial Relations*, Vol. 15, No. 2, 1979; reprinted in World Bank Reprint Series No. 142.

[27] D. Lal: *Prices for Planning – Towards the Reform of Indian Planning*, Heinemann, London, 1980.

[28] D. Lal: *Cultural Stability and Economic Stagnation – India c. 1500 BC–1980 AD*, mimeo, draft manuscript, London, 1981.

[29] W. Leontief: *The Structure of the American Economy*, Oxford, 1941.

[30] R.G. Lipsey and K. Lancaster: "The General Theory of the Second Best," *Review of Economic Studies*, Vol. 26, 1956–57.

[31] I.M.D. Little: *A Critique of Welfare Economics*, Oxford, 1950.

[32] I.M.D. Little: "The Developing Countries and the International Order," in R.C. Amarcher, G. Haberler, and T.D. Willett (eds.): *Challenges to a Liberal International Economic Order, American Enterprise Institute*, Washington DC, 1979.

[33] I.M.D. Little and J.A. Mirrlees: *Manual of Industrial Project Analysis, Vol. II: Social Cost-Benefit Analysis*, OECD Development Centre, Paris, 1969.

[34] I.M.D. Little and J.A. Mirrlees: *Project Appraisal and Planning for Developing Countries*, Heinemann, London, 1974.

[35] I.M.D. Little, Tibor Scitovsky, and Maurice Scott: *Industry and Trade in Some Developing Countries*, Oxford University Press, 1970. There are separate case studies of India, Pakistan, Brazil, Mexico, the Philippines, and Taiwan in this OECD series, all published by the Oxford University Press.

[36] T.N. Madan: "Review of Asian Drama," *Economic and Political Weekly*, February 1969.

[37] G. Meier (ed.): *Leading Issues in Economic Development*, Oxford, 1970.

[38] D. Morawetz: "Elasticities of Substitution in Industry: What Do We Learn from Econometric Estimates?" *World Development*, January 1976.

[39] H. Myint: "Economic Theory and Development Policy," *Economica*, May 1967, reprinted in Meier (ed.) [37].

[40] G. Myrdal: *Economic Theory and Underdeveloped Regions*, Vora and Co., Bombay, 1958. (This is an expanded version of his 1956 Bank of Cairo lectures entitled: *Development and Underdevelopment – A Note on the Mechanism of National and International Economic Inequality.*)

[41] G. Myrdal: *Asian Drama*, Penguin Books, 1968.

[42] J. Nugent and P. Yotopoulos: *Economics of Development: Empirical Investigations*, Harper and Row, New York, 1976.

[43] R. Nurkse: *Problems of Capital Formation in Underdeveloped Countries*, Oxford, 1953.

[44] R. Nurkse: *Equilibrium and Growth in the World Economy*, Harvard University Press, 1961.

[45] R. Prebisch: *The Economic Development of Latin America and Its Principal Problems*, United Nations, New York, 1950.

[46] V.K.R.V. Rao: "Investment, Income, and the Multiplier in an Underdeveloped Economy," *Indian Economic Review*, February 1952; reprinted in Agarwala and Singh (eds.) [1].

[47] P.N. Rosenstein-Rodan: "Problems of Industrialisation of Eastern and South-Eastern Europe," *Economic Journal*, June–September 1943.

[48] T. Schultz: *Transforming Traditional Agriculture*, Yale, 1964.

[49] T. Scitovsky: "Two Concepts of External Economies," *Journal of Political Economy*, April 1954.

[50] M.F.G. Scott, D.M. Newberry, and J.A. MacArthur: *Project Appraisal in Practice*, Heinemann, London, 1976.

[51] D. Seers: "The Limitations of the Special Case," *Bulletin of the Oxford University Institute of Economics and Statistics*, May 1963, reprinted in Meier (ed.) [37].

[52] A.K.Sen: "Personal Utilities and Public Judgements: Or What's Wrong With Welfare Economics?" *Economic Journal*, September 1979; Comment by Y.K. Ng and Reply by Sen in *Economic Journal*, June 1981.

[53] A.K. Sen: "The Welfare Basis of Real Income Comparisons – A Survey." *Journal of Economic Literature*, March 1979.

[54] H. Singer: "The Distribution of Gains Between Borrowing and Investing Countries," *American Economic Review*, May 1950.

[55] F. Stewart and P. Streeten: "New Strategies for Development: Poverty, Income Distribution and Growth," *Oxford Economic Papers*, March 1976; reprinted as Chapter 8 in Streeten [204].

[56] P. Streeten: *The Frontiers of Development Studies*, Macmillan, 1972.

[57] P. Streeten: "Changing Perceptions of Development," *Finance and Development*, September 1977.

[58] P. Streeten: *Development Perspectives*, Macmillan, 1981.

[59] P. Streeten and S. Lall: *Foreign Investment, Transnationals and Developing Countries,* Macmillan, 1977.

[60] J. Tinbergen: *Statistical Testing of Business-Cycle Theories I: A Method and Its Application to Investment Activity, League of Nations,* Geneva, 1939.

[61] J. Viner: *International Trade and Economic Development,* Oxford, 1953.

Kiren Aziz Chaudhry,
"The Myths of the Market and the Common History of Late Developers" (1993)*

Introduction: Market as Teleology in the 1990s

The pervasive role of the state in developing countries is a truism: indeed, development economics was founded on the belief that the peculiar nature of market failures in late developers portended a large role for the state.[1] In Gerschenkron's formulation, the entrepreneurial classes of late developers lacked the requisite investment capital and skills to compete with their more advanced international rivals. Government intervention in planning, financing, and managing industrialization was a special institutional response to economic backwardness.[2]

The overall consensus on the necessary (and positive) role of the government in LDCs (late developing countries) in promoting growth and equity came under attack in the 1980s.[3] In the contemporary critique of etatisme, economic stagnation and chaos are viewed as by-products of an intrusive, excessively bureaucratizied state that upholds monopolies, prevents competition, and deliberately creates and profits from shortages and bottlenecks. If in the past it was difficult to reconcile the image of a strong and powerful government with conditions in the developing world, where informal markets, ill-defined property rights, shortages, and weak sectoral links are the norm, this dissonance has now been laid to rest. Citing failures of most planning and etatiste experiments, the new orthodoxy in development economics emphasizes the importance of "state shrinking," liberalization, and "the market" in overcoming economic crises and fostering long-term growth.[4]

At first glance, policy changes in developing countries appear to vindicate the new orthodoxy. The economic recession of the 1980s triggered economic liberalization and privatization programs in most developing countries, fueling the popular view that capitalism and democracy have been globally recognized as the tonic for underdevelopment. Yet the orthodoxy fails to explain the severe difficulties confronting almost all economic liberalization programs.[5] It furnishes few clues to understanding the texture of crises in the Third World or in the command economies of Eastern Europe and the successor states of the Soviet Union.[6]

The reification of "the market" as a neutral and natural institution, apolitical and ahistorical—as an end in itself rather than a means to promote social and individual welfare—has become common in academic and policy circles. The emerging revisionist history of the developing world presents a remarkably simplified and flawed view of why governments in late developers intervened in their economies to begin with, as much as it distorts the sources of current liberalization programs.

The conceptual and factual flaws of the neoliberal position have been explored in the literature on the dismantling of the welfare state, and they have drawn public comment from political leaders and financiers.[7] Yet they have not been adequately scrutinized by scholars and practitioners specializing in the developing world. Of course critiques of etatisme—whether in its Keynsian, socialist, or developmentalist permutations—are nothing new:[8] development economists have long recognized the problematic nature of state intervention in the developing world. The paradigm that gained currency in the mid-1980s, however, diverged radically from the debates that had been central to the political economy of development. Longstanding questions about how to reconcile the twin goals of growth and equity were replaced with the spartan certainties of monetarist economics.[9] Trickle-down theories long discredited in development economics were held out as the answer to distributional dilemmas, and crude modernization theory was resuscitated to forecast the ultimate convergence of economic and political systems across the globe.[10] The politics of economic organization were explicitly removed from the agenda[11] and replaced with formulas that upheld price liberalization, "speed," and "thoroughness" as the exclusive determinants of successful reform.[12]

This essay critically examines key aspects of the new orthodoxy in development economics. It focuses on two points. First, the neoliberal-liberal construct rests an abstract, stylized view of what market economies are and where they come from. As a result, it cannot answer the critical question of why late developers failed to create functioning national markets to begin with, I argue that it was often the institutional weakness of the state and its aborted attempts to create unified national markets that led to the interventionist regimes so roundly condemned by the neoliberals. *At base, government ownership is more often a response to the administrative weakness of the state in developing countries rather than a reaction to the private sector's inability to provide the skills and capital necessary for bulky investments.*

In contrast to the neoliberal ascendancy, which discounts the central role of the state in creating markets, I argue that state and market building are mutually dependent and potentially conflictual processes, shaped by historically constituted domestic and international factors. The difficulties encountered by late developers in constructing effective national legal and regulatory institutions suggest that economic liberalization alone will not produce the efficient market systems held out by neoliberal reformers.[13]

Neoliberals disregard the political nature of the institutions that undergird market economies.[14] Markets are conscious constructs—in the same vein that command economies are deliberate arrangements—in that they are based, by design or default, on political principles (who gets what, why, and how)[15] and on choices of how individual resources, rights, aspirations, and possibilities are reconciled with collective ones. The assumption that markets are "neutral" and "natural" obscures the political choices that are embedded in the institutions that govern the market.[16] Regulatory and extractive institutions embody the *political* and economic interests of dominant coalitions; they reflect the outcome of wrenching political conflicts. In the construction of market economies, tensions between unreconcilable private and collective interests need to be recognized, evaluated, and woven into underlying principles about the goals of development.[17] Explicit political struggles and political choices underlie the legal and regulatory institutions that define the way that markets work. The neoliberal-liberal tendency has been to reduce the politics of market reform to "political will." To prescribe "the market" as a panacea for late developers is to neglect political choices left unmade by the decision to have a "market economy." Even a cursory review of established market economies shows that they can embody a dizzying variety of incentives for labor, capital, and consumers that represent the outcome of political struggles.

Second, the new orthodoxy in development economics neglects the role of changes in the international economy in both fostering the shift away from etatisme and in circumscribing the realm of national economic policy in late developers. The neoliberal account of why economic liberalism has gained a near universal following in LDCs has strong evolutionary undertones emphasizing the pivotal role of the demonstration effect, economic stagnation, the emergence of a "competent bourgeoisie," and "learning."[18] Recognizing the importance of changes in international financial markets in fostering economic liberalization highlights unique aspects of both the domestic and international context in which late developers are trying to construct national market economies. Prior links to the international economy influenced the structure and functions of the state in late developers, with important implications for their ability to manage a market economy. Access to large volumes of international capital flows in the 1970s enhanced the absolute level of state intervention in LDCs, but it undermined those specific institutions that would become critical to creating market economies in the 1980s. These funds enhanced the economic role of the state as producer and creditor, but weakened the very institutional and political capacities necessary for creating functioning market economies.

Moreover, the neoliberal perspective does not account for the special obstacles facing late developers in trying to create market economies in a period of growing international economic interdependence. Contemporary efforts to construct market economies are in some ways uniquely difficult, for the "market" that late, late developers are "transiting" to is a truly global one, in which capital is highly mobile. Even advanced industrial states with entrenched regulatory bureaucracies can no longer pursue policies that assume national markets are separated from international economic forces. In late developers where the process of dislodging domestic barriers to the construction of national markets is incomplete, internationalization virtually forecloses the possibility of constructing effective regulatory institutions to govern a national market economy. Opening up to international economic forces under conditions of arrested nation building and institutional stagnation creates a much more complex set of contingencies than those recognized by the neoliberals. Rather than the formulaic outcomes anticipated by neoliberal reformers, liberalizing countries will carry the dual imprint of the international economic context in which reforms were undertaken and the confluence of domestic institutional and political factors that marked the initiation of liberalization policies.

In the first part of this essay, I examine domestic barriers to the construction of national market economies. I explore the particular conditions under which etatiste solutions emerged in late developers, stressing the role institutional and administrative failures and political conflicts in generating etatiste outcomes. Building on this discussion I then show how changes in the global economy in both the 1970s and the 1980s have influenced efforts to construct national market economies. I emphasize the special challenges faced by deeply divided late developers in trying to construct national market economies at a time when global economic forces are exerting centrifugal pressures on national regulatory institutions even in established market economies. The twin pressures of reconstructing domestic regulatory and extractive institutions, on the one hand, and forestalling political opposition to reforms, on the other, are generating a dangerous cycle of juridical, economic, and political fragmentation that is very unlikely to produce the efficient market economies promised by neoliberal reformers.

II. Internal Processes: The Failure of Regulatory Institutions and Etatisme in Late Developers

It is perhaps necessary to begin by restating the most basic tenet of the institutional economists: functioning national markets cannot exist without legal, administrative, and regulatory institutions maintained by the state.[19] Self-regulating labor and commodity markets do not automatically emerge in the absence of state action. Instead, they are conscious institutional constructs rooted in historical trajectories and based on evolving political choices. To create competitive markets, it is not enough to smash the state bureaucracy that owns, controls, or regulates goods and services; rather, the instruments of the state must be redeployed to perform the much more difficult task of indirect regulation and administration. Commonly recognized in the literature on regulation in advanced countries, this point has somehow escaped the notice of the current advocates of the free market in the Third World.[20]

Furthermore, the absence of state regulation results not in unbridled competition—the uncertainties of this condition are unacceptable to entrepreneurs themselves—but rather in collaborative agreements among producers that either provide informal rules to govern competition or directly create monopolistic conglomerates. Unregulated markets develop their own form of organization to stem uncertainty and introduce some level of predictability into commercial transactions. In the absence of state regulation, these agreements evolve into pacts that neglect the consumer and reflect only the preferences of merchants and entrepreneurs.[21]

The unregulated market, in short, does regulate itself—but not in the ways that the neoliberals predict. Adam Smith, the political economist, recognized this. It is another thing altogether that he rightly recoiled from the blunt solution that occurred to him at the time:

People of the same trade seldom meet together for merriment and diversion, but the conversation ends in a conspiracy against the public, or in some contrivance to raise prices. It is impossible indeed to prevent such meetings by any law which either could be executed, or would be consistent with liberty and justice.[22]

The minimal role of government in protecting collectively held resources (like air),[23] defining the institutional context within which labor and business bargain, protecting consumers,[24] and preventing the emergence of monopolies is accepted by the more sophisticated defenders of free market economies.[25] Recent research has shown that, rather than reflecting the interpretive and political preferences of theorists,[26] the pervasiveness of state in LDCs coexists with regulatory and administrative capacities of a specific, narrow character. Governments in the developing world rarely posses the qualities associated with Adam Smith's "watchman state" and often do not even command a monopoly on the legitimate use of violence. Thus, although most developing countries are directly involved in production and distribution, their capacities to regulate, define, and enforce property rights, dispense law, tax, and collect information are strictly circumscribed or nonexistent. To make the transition to a market economy successfully, these capacities become absolutely necessary. Understanding how these capacities evolve or fail to evolve is crucial to understanding both initial patterns of government intervention in the economy and the current crisis in the Third World as well as in the command economies of Eastern Europe, the former Soviet Union, and China, where attempts to liberalize the national economy have either repeatedly failed or created chaos.

Examining the way that this process unfolded in England and continental Europe on the eve of the Industrial Revolution highlights the role of political authority in creating markets.[27] Historically, the state has had an interest in creating national markets to reduce transaction costs, free up surplus, and literally create a tax base in the emerging urban economy.[28] Earlier, through mercantilist policies, the state protected domestic accumulation of capital. In the experience of the first developers, property rights, guaranteed by law and enforced through the courts and the police, were traded for revenue in agreements that became embedded in the constitutional pact.[29] At various times, different social and economic groups opposed or supported regulations designed to create competition and enforce pricing mechanisms. Indeed, once domestic markets have expanded beyond the "transparent" transactions described by Braudel, producers and capitalists themselves develop an avid interest in regulation providing stability, predictability, and standardization and facilitating information sharing and investment.[30]

The first regulation against unregulated market forces came, not surprisingly, in the labor markets on the eve of the Industrial Revolution.[31] As Polanyi has argued, in contrast to both long-distance trade and the early version of the putting-out system, both of which thrived in the context of restrictive urban guilds and structural barriers to labor mobility and migration, the creation of national markets required the removal of such obstacles through the legislative acts of the state.

In Europe, this was a long and drawn out process, which was manifested in the destruction of the guild system, the erosion of the privileges of the nobility, the termination of barriers to rural-urban migration, and the displacement of rural labor.[32] Substantial variation existed in different cases, depending on the organizational characteristics of business in the precapitalist era. Contrast, for example, the relatively smooth transition in eighteenth-century England, where guilds were weak, with the enormous barriers to the expansion of domestic markets into the hinterland of France and Italy, where highly organized urban guilds forestalled this development through sanctions and barriers to entry enforced by the city administration.[33]

Recognizing that there was nothing "natural" or automatic about the rise of the market mechanism in early developers, where the expansion of the central state coincided with the creation of national markets, pushes us to reexamine the conventional account of the role of the state in the Third World economies from a different angle that stresses the social and political rigidities that governments must overcome to forge national markets. Perhaps wishfully imagining that these capacities exist in LDCs, economists have paid scant attention to the process by which precapitalist monopolies, such as guilds, merchant associations, and agricultural monopolies, are eroded or to the particularly difficult process of regulating and undercutting monopolies and monopsonies upheld through partnerships between foreign companies and local businessmen. Although economists recognize that over time, national markets tend to generate monopolies and create systematic social inequalities, they neglect completely the role of state institutions in breaking down precapitalist arrangements that thwart the initial expansion of competitive market forces. Rather than being relegated to economic history, these themes should be the focus of any economist working on the political economy of late developers.

In the development economics tradition, the assumption underlying both the statist and the laissez-faire perspective was that a functioning market existed as a ready alternative state-directed or state-owned industrialization programs.[34] The less sophisticated supporters of the neoliberal orthodoxy, in particular, embrace the view that markets exist in an administrative, social, and institutional vacuum.[35] Hobbled by corrupt bureaucracies, the argument goes, markets are prevented from performing their effortless miracles in efficient allocation. Take out the disingenuous and stifling state, through deregulation, divestiture, liberalization, and privatization, and "market forces" will emerge full blown to replace it. Unfortunately, some variant of this assumption is shared by the classical school of development economics. The notion that direct state participation in the economy is a special burden for developing countries not only assumes that markets, with all their legal, regulatory, and administrative characteristics, exist but also that state control is administratively more difficult than the alternative of creating and regulating national markets. But is this true?

Historical accounts of etatisme in late developers suggest the opposite. There is evidence that under conditions of administrative weakness it is harder to create and regulate functioning national markets in goods, labor, and finance than it is for government to manage the bulk of production itself. At a practical level, creating and regulating markets requires myriad financial, legal, and civil institutions, with stable and firm long-term commitments to regulate the actions of producers, importers, and labor, enforce contracts, and ensure the free exchange of information among economic groups.[36] Market relations based on competition for profits and prices are inherently conflictual, involving shifting interests among producers, importers, labor, consumers, and the government. To create and regulate markets, the government must, at a minimum, provide the legal context within which disputes between competing actors are resolved. The state must also ensure that groups capable of sabotaging the expansion of markets are not bypassed in the bargaining process. To sustain itself in this role, the government itself must become a primary repository of information on the private sector.[37] This information need not underpin a unitary and moribund vision of the future that eclipses individual initiative, as Hayek suggested. On the contrary, it enables the central authority to tax and regulate and to supply entrepreneurs with information that reduces uncertainty, cuts transaction costs, and secures private sector confidence in making investment decisions. In short, the state's information reservoir reduces transaction costs for private actors at the same time that it equips political authorities with the tools to provide incentives and disincentives for economic actors in concert with collective social goals.

In cases where the government becomes the primary employer and producer and assumes the role of setting prices, its task is simplified to monitoring the activities of corporations and agencies that it owns and manages.[38] Direct state participation in the economies of developing countries serves as an administrative shortcut. At a purely administrative level, the involvement of the state as a producer, direct employer, and lender in countries lacking a regulatory infrastructure is simpler than, and, thus preferable to, the much more elusive alternative of creating and regulating a market economy. Thus it is not surprising to find that major attempts to reform the private sector in developing countries end with nationalization.[39] *The most intrusive economic policies of late developers often grow out of these failures to create acceptably functioning markets, signaling the administrative ineffectiveness of regulatory and extractive institutions in late developers.*

Even in cases where explicit ideological objections to private property and capitalism were strong, nationalization, collectivization, and outright confiscation were responses to administrative and regulatory failures. Episodes of the socialist experiment in the Peoples' Republic of China and the former Soviet Union illustrate this point with some forcefulness. Although it is not conventional to include them in the category of late, late developers, these two cases were chosen for detailed discussion for a number of important reasons. They represent the quintessential "strong state" command economy model. Unlike most late, late developers, where socialist or capitalist ideology had little to do with the extent of state intervention in the economy, there were clear ideological reasons for the Bolsheviks and the Communists to eliminate private property and market relations. Certainly, coming out of mass social revolutions, they had a clear mandate to do so. Yet, as we shall see, the state in both cases tried and failed to create functioning national markets and only then took the decision to nationalize all economic sectors.

The case of the Soviet Union during the later stages of the New Economic Policy (NEP) is a particularly instructive one. Immediately after the revolution, deep ambiguities emerged in the position of the leadership concerning the role of private property. In summer 1917, Lenin, at least, was convinced that socialism was not an immediate possibility in the Soviet Union. The problem, as he saw it, was to create a unified national market and to prevent capitalists from sabotaging the revolution by using their power, money, and organization against it.[40] This goal was to be achieved through administrative means. Lenin fully recognized that the distributional aims of the revolutionary regime could be met in a number of different ways and early on advocated taxation over confiscation: "Confiscation alone leads nowhere, as it does not contain the element of organization, of accounting for proper distribution. Instead of confiscation, we could easily impose a fair tax."[41] War Communism (1918–21) was a response to the immediate threat of mass starvation and the uncertainties of a completely dysfunctional market, the hallmarks of which were inflation, profiteering, and hoarding. Under these desperate conditions, private trade and speculation were forbidden for practical reasons: markets do not work in conditions of absolute scarcity. It is now widely recognized that War Communism, abandoned in 1921 for the market-oriented NEP, was neither a peculiarly Soviet phenomenon nor a conscious step to nationalize industry and agriculture as a prelude to eliminating private property.

NEP's restoration of market relations conceded agriculture to private producers and almost immediately confronted the Bolsheviks with problems of regulation. Wherever the truth lies in the scholarly debates on the collectivization of Soviet agriculture, there is ample evidence that the politically unbearable wide price differentials, hoarding, and shortages that became commonplace during the NEP years were the result of an inability to cope with these regulatory tasks.[42] Initial regulatory failures generated increasingly rash attempts to control prices, which only fueled the black markets and kindled consumer discontent.[43] The point is that economic policy flowed willy-nilly from the desperate need to achieve practical and political goals, not from some overarching ideological blueprint.[44] There were many ways to achieve the distributional goals of the new revolutionary state, and it would be difficult to attribute actual trends to the grand designs of the leadership of the Soviet Union between 1917 and 1926. It was only after failing to solve the problems of a fragmented and unregulated national economy through regulation that the government began to take over wholesale and retail trade. To be sure, the "great push" for industrialization and the search for sources of capital were important in ending NEP, but these alternative ways of constructing a functioning economy were only explored after NEP itself had failed: The immediate problem was supplying urban consumers, that is living up to the revolutionary pact. The rural and urban bourgeoisie that emerged from the NEP period was seen as a political threat not because it was "weak" but precisely because it was beyond administrative control and repeatedly threatened to undermine the redistributive aims of the state.

Terror was the last resort of an administratively dysfunctional and politically desperate state. The decision to end NEP embodied a particular choice between individual and collective utilities, between short- and long-term visions of the political economy after it became clear that NEP could not provide a viable solution to the fundamental disequilibrium between the urban and rural sectors. There is little evidence that collectivization and nationalization, incremental as both were, represented an end in themselves to the Soviet leadership.[45] Had the administrative and organizational means been available, it is not at all clear that other means would not have been used; certainly, they were openly discussed.[46]

If the Soviet case opens a crack in the edifice of the conventional view of state intervention in socialist countries, the Chinese case threatens to topple it entirely. The inflation of the 1940s had been critical in discrediting the Nationalists and the fear of a dysfunctioning market was the centerpiece of the Communists' demon-riddled imagination as the foremost political problem they faced upon assuming power. The Nationalists had already seized large industries, most of which had been foreign-owned, with the result that 67 percent of industrial capital was already under state control.[47] Since the "commanding heights" fell to them when they assumed power, insight into the economic vision of the Communists can be gleaned by examining their policy toward the rest of the private sector. To do this is to recognize that the problems that the Communists confronted between 1949 and 1953, when a free market operated in the countryside, were rooted in the administrative weakness of the state. At the time, China lacked a unified market; even the most basic infrastructure of a unified market, such as uniform weights and measures, did not exist.[48] Merchants took advantage of shortages and made concerted efforts to subvert the new regime through direct sabotage, spying, fraud, and artificially induced inflation.[49] Vacillating between the need to centralize and a deep distrust of overcentralization, the state responded brutally in 1952 with the *wu-san* (five anti) movement against the bourgeoisie in which 450,000 businessmen were investigated for bribery, tax evasion, fraud, theft, and hoarding.[50] The *san-fan* (three anti) campaign severed links between the merchants and bureaucrats by punishing government officials for corruption and collaboration. The real clamp-down on the rural private sector came in 1953,[51] and in 1954 the "Directive on Strengthening Market Control and the Transformation of Private Merchants" was issued, with mixed results. Finally, in December 1955, failures to control prices and consumer discontent pushed the state to form state monopolies for grains and to close all private wholesale firms. Even in the urban areas the state's inability to regulate and control private merchants led to new laws that fixed the retail areas and forced joint accounting upon merchants with the hope that concentration would simplify administrative and regulatory burdens.[52] Such concentration has its parallels in capitalist economies, where large firms facilitate rent gathering. Indeed, policy during this whole era was an attempt to transform the structure of the private sector for regulatory and extractive purposes.[53] According to the leadership, "Such plans facilitated an increased accumulation of wealth for the state, as the state could then draw more taxes from the firms."[54]

The argument here is not that state control of the "commanding heights" of the economy in China and the USSR was a topic of debate and vacillation but that the confiscation of light industry, wholesale trade, retailing, and rural markets was an incremental affair, born of the state's inability to create and regulate national markets. The resulting failure to achieve the distributional and social aims to which the revolutionary regimes were committed drew governments into the intrusive policies now so vehemently condemned by the neoliberals.[55]

III. Internal Processes: The Conflicting Goals of State Building and Capitalist Growth

Conflicts between private sector elites capable of evading regulation and administratively weak governments are even more apparent in late, late developers with heterogeneous divided societies. In these countries, many of which came into being through decolonization or global military conflicts, the aim of creating national markets often clashed directly with the pressing goal of national integration. Although contemporary accounts of failed attempts to liberalize because of opposition from consumers and labor abound, the assumptions embraced by economists kept them from appreciating the interest that political and economic elites may have in forestalling the creation of functioning national markets. Creating markets is politically dangerous. Functioning markets provide opportunity and mobility that undercut lineage and traditional rights of privilege and threaten the position of elites in developing societies. Markets create inequalities in wealth that may not match existing patterns of income distribution, status, power, and entitlements. Markets dislocate groups in both the political and the economic realm.[56]

In many countries, due to a variety of historical circumstances, the private sector on the eve of independence was dominated by an ethnic, sectarian, or regional group different from those that controlled political power. In these cases, the most intrusive policies of the state were aimed not at supplementing private capital to promote international competitiveness but at creating a national bourgeoisie that would support the state if not mirror the ethnic, religious, sectarian, and tribal characteristics of the new political and military leadership. *The "weak bourgeoisie" hypothesis, which codifies the idea that the state was a substitute for an underdeveloped capitalist class, obscures the extent to which the promotion of the old bourgeoisie often conflicted with the broader and more pressing political goals of state building and national integration in late developers.* In some cases, such as the Turkish one, the haute bourgeoisie of Jews, Armenians, Greeks, and Europeans that had become entrenched through the successive capitulations of the declining Ottoman Empire were seen as a threat to Attaturk's nationalist mission and were deliberately weeded out and replaced with a Turkish bourgeoisie.[57] The Egyptian, Syrian, Iraqi, Yemeni, Lebanese, and Saudi cases show similar patterns, as do several African countries, including Nigeria or Kenya. The expulsion of the Indian merchant community in Uganda in 1972 was one of the most violent examples.[58]

Far from being an archaic or culturally specific phenomenon confined to the Middle East and Africa, the tension between national integration and economic development is very much alive today in all parts of the globe. The example of Malaysia illustrates the continuing relationship between national integration and economic policy even in a country marked by relatively stable political institutions and relatively peaceful ethnic relations. The Malay-dominated government has long explicitly tried to create a Bumiputra business elite to compete with the entrenched Chinese and Indian private sector.[59] The new economic policy of 1971 aimed to increase the Bumiputra share of commercial and industrial capital to 30% of the total within twenty years. The state's aim of creating a class of Malay entrepreneurs led the government to offer loans, equity placement, scholarships, and employment. These policies actually led to the creation of state-owned companies, which were slated to employ, and later be bought by, the Bumiputras.[60] Then, in 1986, large-scale privatization of state-owned industries began, and preferential policies resulted in the 108-fold increase in Bumiputra corporate equity holdings, compared to the 24-fold increase for other ethnic groups.[61] Thus both the creation of state-owned enterprises and their subsequent privatization were designed to begat an economically powerful private sector that mirrored the ethnicity of the political leadership and was expected to form a stable base of support. The link between the political goal of nation building and economic policy is clear.

In cases where a substantial private sector existed, the political motives for nationalization were strong not just because the old commercial classes often achieved their dominance under colonial tutelage but also because these classes opposed the new and highly unstable political leadership by bringing their economic resources to bear on the incumbency of fragile regimes in the post-independence period. Across East Africa, the Middle East, South Asia, and parts of East and Southeast Asia, highly insular commercial communities used primordial ties to thwart the state's attempts to create competitive national markets, infiltrate illegal markets, tax, and undercut precapitalist or foreign monopolies.

The governments of many developing countries confronted the task of creating domestic markets in commodities and labor at short notice, immediately following the abrupt withdrawal of colonial powers and with the explicit intent of replacing trade with domestic manufactured goods. Evidence from cases as diverse as India, Pakistan, Iraq, and Egypt suggests that governments in late developers became directly involved in the economy by nationalizing foreign and domestic assets and financial institutions after long and frustrating failures to tax, redistribute, and regulate the behavior of private actors following decolonization or during the systemic crises of the 1930s and World War II. These exogenous shocks mark the juncture at which the policies most harshly criticized by the economic liberals were initiated. Through trade and exchange rate regimes, relationships to the international economy were defined with the explicit goal of creating an integrated, self-sufficient national economy.

Later the populist agendas of the Nassers, the Bhuttos, and the Qasims demanded redistribution and regulation of wages and prices, which, in theory, could have been effected with a strong regulatory and administrative apparatus by taxing and regulating private industry, commerce, and agriculture without directly taking over productive assets. In many cases, nationalization and direct controls on the private sector can best be explained not by private sector weakness but by the inordinate strength and cohesion of private elites and their ability to thwart the government's regulatory policies. The import substitution programs adopted by most developing countries in the 1950s and 1960s involved the state in directly planning and controlling domestic investment, prices, and so on. Unlike export-led industrialization, import substitution programs do not require governments to hold down domestic wages.[62] Regimes with weak domestic legitimacy often designed elaborate redistributive policies based on directly controlling the means of production and fixing wages. Similarly, prices for basic necessities were often directly controlled through state ownership. Import substitution required highly intrusive regulation that enabled weak administrative apparatuses to manipulate the economy directly but constrained the ability of business to respond quickly to new opportunities. These systems of licensing, preferential finance, and price manipulation became perverted over time as the instruments of economic control were increasingly used to serve the political ends of incumbent regimes.[63]

To summarize, the dirigisme of late developers is best understood as a response to twin crises—one administrative, the other political—encountered at the initial stages of creating a unified national economy. The administrative and institutional weakness of state bureaucracies generated solutions that substituted production, distribution, and redistribution for the more difficult task of extraction and regulation. Unable to erode subnational barriers, construct national financial institutions, dislodge oligopolistic groups, and create a uniform legal system, the government entered directly into the economy. The second kind of crisis was largely a political one, involving conflict between the goals of state building and capitalist growth. In divided societies with foreign or minority bourgeoisies, the goal of capitalist growth conflicted with the broader postindependence mandate of guaranteeing popular welfare, incorporating newly enfranchised groups into the political economy or living up to revolutionary pacts. In practice, these tensions translated into efforts to create a national bourgeoisie that would support the new political leadership in collaboration with the bureaucracy. In political terms, creating a unified national economy meant eliminating the political and economic strength of the old capitalist classes, many of which either did not support new political elites or belonged to regional, sectarian, tribal, or racial minorities. Political leaders equipped with administratively weak bureaucracies revised existing property rights by directly appropriating private holdings. The starkness of these "solutions" and the violence that often accompanied them accurately reflected the political and administrative weakness of the leadership and the bureaucracy. For, having lost the political battle to craft effective institutions to create and govern a national economy, the governments of many late developers substituted direct production and distribution for bureaucracies that taxed, regulated, and dispensed law.

IV. National Markets and Junctures in the International Economy

The complex interplay of political and administrative prerogatives sketched above focused on the special domestic obstacles to the creation of national market economies in late developers. To appreciate fully the texture of the difficulties confronting current attempts to construct market economies, it is necessary to recognize the special characteristics of the international context in which they are being undertaken. For, just as the creation of national market economies requires the erosion of subnational barriers and the construction of national institutions with singular jurisdiction over a territory, it also requires a level of insulation from international economic forces. As Richard Cooper observed more than two decades ago, the pursuit of national economic policies requires markets fragmented at the national border.[64] National market economies are territorially based institutional constructs that match the administrative reach of a single political authority. National market economies are best viewed as "clubs" that deliver excludable public goods to political communities within well-defined "borders."[65] Moreover, most economic policies become ineffective in economies that are completely permeable by transnational flows of labor and capital. Under such conditions, national institutions lack the ability to determine the distribution of public goods, tax, and regulate.

The international economic environment in which contemporary liberalization policies are being implemented is more thoroughly interdependent than ever before.

This process of economic internationalization began with the oil shock of 1973 and accelerated through the 1980s with the deregulation of banking in major financial centers. Changes in communications and technology facilitated the unprecedented integration of international capital markets and greatly enhanced the power of firms as international actors.[66] Efforts to construct national market economies at a moment of such high levels of internationalization must overcome a very special set of constraints.

I have already suggested that liberalization, decentralization, and deregulation are global phenomena that represent a response to the expansion and tight organization of international capital in the 1980s and 1990s.[67] Clusters of countries had very different experiences of this systemic change, depending on a host of historically constituted factors.[68] The common domestic effects of these changes in advanced industrial countries have included an overall convergence in fiscal and monetary policies,[69] a decline in the power of organized labor, albeit from radically different levels, and a growing rift between domestically and internationally based capital.[70] Aside from the widely recognized regulatory problems generated by transnational industrial corporations, the globalization of capital also curtails the overall ability of all governments to tax, regulate, and gather information.[71] The internationalization of capital recalls, in a different context, Huntington's observation concerning lags between economic change and the development of political institutions.[72] Internationalization exerts new pressures on institutions by opening up a rift between the political sphere, which is still nationally based, and the economic realm. Even advanced industrial states are unable to control large swaths of their alleged economies. Institutional arrangements for international regulation have been very slow to emerge, except in selected fields, such as patent and copyright law, where they are often ineffective.

If global changes in technology, production, and markets exert significant pressure on advanced industrial states, transforming domestic coalitions and production methods, their influence on late developers is both more dramatic and qualitatively different, due to a variety of institutional, political, and economic factors. For many developing countries, internationalization came in two waves, with the influx of wealth in the decade between 1973 and 1983 giving way to a massive outflow of liquid capital from the developing world in the 1980s and 1990s.

Changes in global financial markets were important in precipitating economic liberalization programs in a large number of developing countries as well as in Eastern European countries with close links to the international economy. The decade between 1973 and 1983 was distinguished by an enormous inflow of wealth to many developing countries in the form of aid, loans, oil revenues, labor remittances, and investment.[73] The bulk of external capital flows accrued directly to the state and fostered highly statist economic policies. In the 1980s, capital flows to the developing world fell dramatically. From an inflow of $33 billion in 1978, net transfers on debt for LDCs in 1989 were an astonishing *outflow* of $42 billion.[74] From a 1980 high of $243 billion, oil revenues for major exporters fell to $67 billion in 1988.[75] Direct foreign investment, which had actually declined from 1981 to 1986, surpassed all other forms of lending as a source of foreign capital to developing countries in 1988.[76]

Similarly, with the end of the Cold War, the facility with which developing countries could barter allegiance in exchange for cash dwindled, and competition for plummeting levels of aid, foreign investment, and loans became fierce.[77] Although policies adopted under the rubric of economic restructuring are diverse enough to belie generalization, with the exception of those countries where import substitution regimes were already in the process of being dismantled in favor of export-led strategies, such as Turkey, India, and Egypt, most liberalization and privatization programs in the 1980s were attempts to attract foreign investment to replace aid, labor remittances, and international loans, which had provided the developing world with foreign exchange in the 1970s.[78]

The first wave coincided with high levels of etatisme, fed by state access to international capital flows; the second generated severe pressures for the state to withdraw from the economy through economic liberalization and privatization. The dimensions of these systemic changes are similar to those that precipitated earlier shifts to and from "inward" and "outward" oriented strategies, including the change from primary export regimes to import substitution (ISI) and from ISI to export-led strategies. Each juncture followed a broad change in the international economy: the crisis of the 1920s and 1930s, the oil shocks of the 1970s, the debt crisis, and the liquidity crisis that began in the mid-1980s. Rather than being the result of an ideological conversion to open economies, economic liberalization and deregulation in the developing world are responses to changes in the global economy, the first common effect of which was a dramatic decline in their access to international capital flows.

The ability of different countries to respond effectively to the new constraints and opportunities of internationalization depends not simply on the policies they implement but on the character of their interaction with the international economy in the preceding period. Both "waves" of internationalization, with the opportunities and costs they presented, profoundly affected institutional development in late developers. The role of external capital inflows in retarding and undermining the very institutions, norms, and social changes that are critical to the creation of domestic market economies is increasingly recognized in the comparative politics literature.[79] One of the key insights to be found in studies comparing Latin American and Asian NICs (newly industrialized countries) has been the importance of the strength and coherence of bureaucratic institutions *prior* to the period in which they gain access to such inflows.[80] In LDCs, state bureaucracies responded to the influx of capital in the 1970s by undercutting regulatory and extractive institutions and augmenting the role of the state in direct production and distribution.[81] State-controlled foreign loans, aid, and oil revenues saved governments from having to tax their population directly. They gave administratively weak governments tools to govern the economy without developing extractive and regulatory capacities and provided funds to ameliorate political conflict through the distribution of gifts, subsidies, loans, and state contracts. Even in countries where the sources of external capital, such as labor remittances or private borrowing, were privately controlled, the institutional response of the state was to shrink regulatory institutions and pursue the most politically convenient regulatory strategies possible.[82] Access to unprecedented amounts of foreign exchange had identifiable effects on specific state capacities. These funds enhanced the economic role of the state as producer and creditor but weakened the very institutional and political capacities necessary for creating functioning market economies. Thus while the external capital inflows of the 1970s and early 1980s enhanced the state's role in production, distribution, and redistribution they simultaneously undermined the evolution and impaired the capacities of exactly those public and private institutions necessary for the creation of national market economies.[83]

By the mid-1980s, as sources of external funding dried up and debts became due, most LDCs were hit by severe economic crises for which they were singularly unprepared. In many cases, extractive and regulatory institutions had atrophied; accounting procedures in the private sector were primitive; and formal links among members of the commercial-industrial class and labor were weak. In institutional terms, the task facing governments in the recession was nothing less than a thorough reform of the public and private sectors. This entailed forging national regulatory, legal, and extractive institutions and their ancillary information gathering and enforcement agencies and creating legal, accounting, and disclosure requirements for private business elites who had yet to experience the burdens of regulation. In many cases, the hiatus of regulation, conflict, and political debate in the 1970s coincided with the intensification of primordial and regional divisions.[84] The second "wave" of internationalization, in short, came to many developing countries in the form of a foreign exchange crisis that forced them to liberalize their economies at a domestic juncture when the institutions necessary for managing the transition were particularly weak. These domestic conditions coincided with a systemic process of economic internationalization that undercut the overall effectiveness of national regulatory institutions. The confluence of these two trends suggests a particularly difficult transition for liberalizing late developers.

V. From the Global to the Local: National Fragmentation and the Rise of Illiberal Politics

As I have argued above, economic liberalization programs in many countries were initiated in response to fiscal crises prior to the construction of effective regulatory and extractive institutions that would undergird a market economy. Liberalization under these conditions undercuts the effectiveness of administrative institutions at the national level without replacing them with new ones. In practice, the "state shrinking" that accompanied economic liberalization and the policies embodied in structural adjustment programs meant the government's abrogation of basic goods and services, including, in some cases, the maintenance of law and order. This abrogation had profound implications for domestic politics, which, in turn would limit the realm of economic policy. Dirigisme was not simply a relatively stable mechanism for governing the national economy; it also upheld domestic social and political coalitions. In its implementation, economic liberalization not only nullified the instruments of economic management but, in many cases, also undid the coalitions that undergirded the etatiste construct.

Clearly, it is too early to make definitive judgments about outcomes. Still, it is possible to outline major trends, if only in a speculative fashion. Liberalization in the context of economic internationalization has resulted in the fragmentation of administrative, legal, and political jurisdictions within already constituted "national" economies. Often, these changes have occurred in a piecemeal fashion through ordinary political processes. Together, however, they add up to profound institutional change at the national level. Even in advanced industrial states, fragmentation cuts at the administrative basis of the territorial national state, destroying the institutional infrastructure through which large national economies reduced transaction costs and enforced regulation at an earlier period. In the United States, for example, under the guise of the "new federalism," key regulatory functions have devolved to the state, district, and municipal level. As Reich has observed, taxation, redistribution, and regulation are becoming increasingly local,[85] spawning a cycle of competitive bidding among jurisdictions that undercuts the bargaining power or labor, consumers, and environmental groups.

In many late developers, institutions that embody and rely on a fragmentation of markets at the national level and have singular jurisdiction over the territorial state were not dismantled in the same way because they had not taken form to begin with. These processes of institutional atrophy at the national level have culminated in a rather dramatic redrawing of politics in late developers, which has generated intense conflicts over the elements of political identity and the composition of political community. The institutional effects of economic liberalism coupled with internationalization have produced a decidedly illiberal politics in many parts of the globe, including the former Soviet Union, Eastern Europe, Africa, Europe, and the United States.

In cases where the process of national integration was arrested or had just begun, the political effects of dismantling the institutions that govern the incipient national economy have included the emergence of smaller administrative jurisdictions that often coincide with radically different economic endowments, different ethnic, religious, or linguistic groups, or some combination thereof. Economic crises in these circumstances are likely to lead not just to a more localized administration but to a redefinition of the political and geographical units to match different local visions of survival chances in the international economy. Just as earlier efforts to construct national market economies became entwined in the process of national integration and state-building, current attempts to create market economies reconstruct ascriptive social cleavages that are often expressed in the language of primordial identities. The atrophy of preexisting economic allocative networks reveal coincidences of regional, ethnic, and religious divisions with different kinds of industrialization or different prospects for economic success in the global economy. Examples of this phenomenon include the differential growth rates of the coastal and inland regions in China, contrasting patterns of industrialization in Czech and Slovak territories, and regional disparities between northern and southern Italy. Similar processes are at work in the intensified religious strife in India[86] and the regional conflict in Pakistan. Obviously, meaningful market reforms are impossible under these conditions.

In many LDCs, liberalization packages have dramatically increased poverty and skewed income distribution by eliminating whole sectors of economic activity and by removing state services and employment, liberalizing prices, and withdrawing subsidies to the urban poor. In countries where the state never performed its "watchman" functions to begin with, the realm of political authority is eroding fast, fueling what Jowitt has called "movements of rage": a profound redrawing of political boundaries along definitely illiberal lines.[87] Fundamentalist movements in Algeria,

Tunisia, Egypt, and elsewhere have gained mass followings by providing the services and "welfare nets" withdrawn by governments as part of liberalization programs. This recreation of an urban "moral economy" against the form of capitalism that liberalization has produced is reflected both in the rhetoric and in the services that these groups now provide in crowded urban areas. Between prayers, the Islamicists build and staff schools, repair streets, and collect garbage.[88]

Dismantling administrative institutions and patterns of economic organization that held together national economies through the intervention of the state has the potential to generate radically different visions of the future among groups with different resource, geographical, and cultural endowments. In many countries with deeply divided societies and very different subnational endowments, and especially in the former Leninist systems, states have literally fragmented in response to these pressures. Others, particularly in Africa and Western Asia, show signs of following suit. To the extent that low transportation costs and the rapid flow of capital, goods, and information makes small enclave economies with high levels of reliance on international trade a viable form of political organization, economic internationalization encourages this fragmentation. These possibilities challenge the concepts of self-sufficiency, autonomy, and national security that undergirded the dominant model of economic development in the Third World in the aftermath of World War II. Needless to say, these smaller political units are ultimately weaker partners to the foreign investors they seek to attract.[89]

In the past, the decision to create national market economies was made and unmade in late developers. Even revolutionary socialist regimes repeatedly revised the laws governing the private sector.[90] Unlike early developers, where pressures from emerging urban groups coincided with the centers's expanding fiscal appetite, social support for market reform in contemporary LDCs is conspicuous by its absence and is opposed both by entrepreneurial classes accustomed to high levels of protection and by labor and consumers. Only in cases where a small but powerful group of industrial elites with links to multinationals exist, such as found in Brazil, Argentina, and Mexico, is there a strong constituency for opening up to international markets.[91] As a result, most governments turn from the reforms early on, whereas those that manage to initiate the first disruptive stage of market reform do so with the support of formidable repressive apparatuses.[92] Many countries, including Turkey, Egypt, Chile, and Brazil, initiated liberalization programs over a decade earlier, only to backtrack.[93]

The current wave of liberalization is different. The integration of global capital markets creates unique pressures and opportunities for LDCs by tightly circumscribing the realm of national economic policy. This is not to suggest, as some have, that the national governments have become obsolete[94] but that the mobility of capital in a credit-hungry world simply removes some options from the policy menu of developing countries. The accommodation between liberalizing LDCs and the global economy will, no doubt, reflect the diversity of economic endowments in late, late developers. Existing levels of institutional development and national integration will be critical in determining their ability to make successful and sustained transitions to market systems within the global economy. The issues confronting radical liberalization programs in LDCs include basic domestic political choices about the distribution of property rights, income, and wealth that are intimately linked to their position in, and ability to control, the impact of global economic forces.

The global mobility of capital, combined with the credit crunch and conditionality, increasingly presents LDCs with the stark choices of total autarchy or unprotected inclusion in the international economy. Precisely because they pay little attention to the complexities of institution building, neoliberal economists believe that the dislocations of liberalization are temporary. Recent trends, however, raise the specter of rapidly eroding political authority. Lacking regulatory and extractive capacities and therefore the resources to provide basic services and stripped of their direct control over prices and wages, it is unclear exactly what the basis of state legitimacy will be once the process is complete.

VI. Conclusion

The subdiscipline of a development economics was based on powerful insights about the economic challenges facing late developers. Increasingly, these insights were lost through the wide acceptance of what Hirschman called the "monoeconomics" claim.[95] This essay has focused on the more problematic assumptions that the neoliberal ascendancy embraces concerning the sources of dirigisme in late, late developers, the nature of market economies, and how they emerge.

Understanding the difficulties of constructing market economies cannot be divorced from an account of the difficulties of state building and national integration in late developers. Market economies cannot exist without effective legal, regulatory, and extractive national institutions that have jurisdiction over a given territory. These institutions only dislodge and then prevent the reemergence of subnational barriers to exchange but also deliver excludable goods that require insulation from international economic forces.

Infirm regulatory and extractive institutions were critical in fostering high levels of etatisme in late developers even in times when the international system was biased toward the maintenance of national borders within a system of recognized nation-states. Especially in deeply divided societies where ascriptive and economic cleavages overlapped, political elites used dirigisme to achieve gains in national integration and to forge national economies. This account highlighted the highly political nature of economic organization showing how efforts to construct market economies often conflicted with the goal of state building and national integration in late developers.

Taking the institutional underpinnings of market economies seriously means that a host of complex historically constituted national and international factors must be brought to bear on our appreciation of the constraints faced by liberalizing late developers today. This discussion has emphasized the part of systemic crises in fostering the contemporary shift to liberalization and the role of international capital flows prior to the 1980s in undermining the very national institutions necessary for the creation of national market economies. Links between domestic economic institutions and the global economy reveal why the numerous social, institutional and political prerequisites for market economies do not exist in the developing world.

Current attempts to construct market economies are occurring in an international context that puts special constraints on the construction of national regulatory and extractive institutions. The globalization of the economy makes national economies permeable and undercuts the effectiveness of national regulatory regimes. At the same time, superpower rivalries no longer serve as a barrier to redrawing political borders. Undoing etatiste mechanisms for governing the economy without replacing them with effective alternatives encourages economic, administrative, and even political fragmentation. The administrative burdens of creating market economies after long interludes of etatisme characterized by hiatuses in economic regulation are politically disruptive in all countries, whether they involve transitions from socialist redistributive regimes, state capitalism, or distributive patrimonial systems.

To the extent that the outcomes are contested, the construction of such institutions will face myriad political and social obstacles similar to those that fostered high levels of state intervention to begin with. The speed and thoroughness advocated by neoliberal reformers should be evaluated against the long-term process of reconstruction and redeploying these institutions in an international context that is eroding such institutions and norms even in constituted national market economies.

The enormous influence of neoliberal economics on policy in the Second and Third worlds, in the advanced industrial countries, and in the institutions that mediate relationships between them is undeniable. In the wake of the experiment, the notion that economics is a universal, transportable science separable from a historically grounded political and social life is itself being critically reviewed.[96] As it stands, the neoliberal argument for liberalization centers on the "goods" of the market, namely, competition, growth, and efficiency. The critical link—between the policies (where the pain is) and a functioning market economy (where the "goods" are)—is missing. In fact, neoclassical economics is silent on the issue of how networks of self-regulating factor and commodity markets emerge. Coming out of an intellectual tradition that jettisoned its political economy component early on, the discipline is particularly ill-equipped to explore the complexities of market formation in late, late developers.[97]

The idea that the "market" is an end in itself was generated in Reagan's America and Thatcher's Britain as part of their attack on the welfare state.[98] The subsequent deployment of "the market" as an ideology presented "efficiency" as a supreme societal goal in itself; it clocked the politics of the market in the language of neutrality. The export of this rather remarkable view of the relationship between politics and economic policy to the Third World was made virtually effortless by the collapse of the Soviet Union and Eastern Europe. The feverish enthusiasm of international banks, donors, and agencies in promoting liberalization is not unrelated to the beliefs and interests of conservative political coalitions that have dominated politics in advanced capitalist countries for over a decade. Nor is the irony of their missionary zeal lost on decision makers in LDCs, who no doubt recall the long period between 1950 and 1980 in which these very institutions trumpeted the pivotal role of the state in economic development.

Apart from recognizing the by now obvious obstacles to constructing functioning market economies, it is critical that economists and "development practitioners" recognize the political nature of the current economic transition: no system of exchange encapsules a code for social organization. The market embodies no telos and has no self-contained blueprint on how societies should reconcile conflicts between individual and public goods. No matter how blatantly etatisme failed, the long, painful, and discontinuous process of redefining values in LDCs in the wake of the collapse of the Soviet Union and dramatic changes in global financial markets cannot be telescoped by a simpleminded application of market rationality. Rather, we should strain to understand the institutional, social, political, and, ultimately, moral contexts that circumscribe the realm of economic policy in the developing world.

Notes

1. For a detailed discussion of the variants in this position see Miles Kahler, "Orthodoxy and Its Alternatives: Explaining Approaches to Stabilization and Adjustment," in Joan M. Nelson, ed., *Economic Crisis and Policy Choice: The Politics of Adjustment in the Third World* (Princeton, NJ: Princeton University Press, 1990), 33–62.

2. Alexander Gerschenkron, Economic *Backwardness in Historical Perspective: A Book of Essays* (Cambridge, MA: Belknap Press of Harvard University Press, 1962).

3. R.P. Misra, "The Changing Perception of Development Problems," and Paul Streeten, "Development Ideas in Historical Perspective," in R.P. Misra and M. Honjo, eds., *Changing Perceptions on Development Problems,* United Nations Center for Regional Development, Regional Development Series, Vol. 1 (Hong Kong: Maruzen Asia, 1981), 7–38 and 39–68, respectively.

4. See, for example, Hernando De Soto, *The Other Path: The Invisible Revolution in the Third World* (New York: Harper & Row, 1989); P.T. Bauer, *Dissent on Development: Studies and Debates in Development Economics* (Cambridge, MA: Harvard University Press, 1972); Deepak Lal, *The Poverty of "Development Economics"* (Cambridge, MA: Harvard University Press, 1985); Beta Balassa et al., *Toward Renewed Economic Growth in Latin America* (Washington, DC: Institute for International Economics, 1986). Ian M. D. Little, *Economic Development: Theory, Policy and International Relations* (New York: Basic Books, 1982), esp. 29–77; Bela Belassa, "The Lessons of East Asian Development: An Overview," *Economic Development and Cultural Change* 36, no. 3 (April 1988, suppl.: S273–S290); Janos Komai, "The Reproduction of Shortage" and "Comments on the Present State and the Prospects of Hungarian Economic Reform," in *Contradictions and Dilemmas: Studies on the Socialist Economy and Society* (Cambridge: MIT Press, 1986).

5. For a review of these difficulties and a critique of some of the assumptions made by the neoliberals, see Tony Killick and Simon Commander, "State Divestiture as a Policy Instrument in Developing Countries," *World Development* 16, no. 12 (1988): 1465–79 and Tariq Banuri, "Introduction," in Tariq Banuri, ed., *Economic Liberalization, No Panacea: The Experience of Latin America and Asia* (Oxford: Clarendon, 1991), 1–29.

6. Building on the work of Karl Polanyi and Douglass North, the essays in Victor Nee and David Stark's edited volume *Remaking the Economic Institutions of Socialism: China and Eastern Europe* (Stanford, CA: Stanford University Press, 1989), analyze these reforms in detail. See especially Victor Nee, "Peasant Entrepreneurship and the Politics of Regulation," 169–207 and his coauthored piece with David Stark, "Toward an Institutional Analysis of State Socialism," 1–31.

7. See, for example, Robert Teitelman, 'The Revolt Against Free-Market Finance," *Institutional Investor* 26, no. 7 (June 1992): 37–44.

8. See, for example, Robert Bates, *Markets and States in Tropical Africa: The Political Basis of Economic Policies* (Berkeley: University of California Press, 1981); Robert Bates, "Governments and Agricultural Markets in Africa," in Robert Bates, ed., *Toward a Political Economy of Development: A Rational Choice Perspective* (Berkeley: University of California Press. 1988), 331–58.

9. The new ascendancy produced prescriptions for successful development based on novel uses of history and method, reinterpreting the "lessons" of the East Asian NICs (newly industrialized countries) at will. Consider, for example, the following quote:

> The conclusion is reached that outward-oriented countries succeeded in rapidly expanding their exports and reaching higher growth rates than inward-oriented countries in both periods. This conclusion is supported by a statistical analysis of exports and economic growth. The favorable effects of exports on economic growth are explained by reference to gains from resource allocation according to comparative advantage; the exploitation of economies of scale and increased capacity utilization; improvements in technology; and increases in domestic savings and foreign direct investment under an outward-oriented development strategy.

From Bela Balassa, *New Directions in the World Economy* (Washington Square, NY: New York University Press, 1989), 27. Contrast this view with the arguments made in the political economy literature on the NICs: Gustav Ranis, "The Role of Institutions in Transition Growth: The East Asian Newly Industrializing Countries," *World Development* 17, no. 9 (1989): 1443–53; Alice Amsden, *Asia's Next Giant: South Korea and Late Industrialization* (Oxford: Oxford University Press, 1989); Stephan Haggard and Tun jen-Cheng, "State and Foreign Capital in the East Asian NICs," and Peter Evans, "Class, State and Dependence in East Asia: Lessons for Latin Americanists," both in Fredric C. Deyo, *The Political Economy of the New Asian Industrialism* (Ithaca, NY: Cornell University Press, 1987); and Tun jen-Cheng, "Political Regimes and Development Strategies: South Korea and Taiwan," in Gary Gereffi and Donald Wyman, eds., *Manufacturing Miracles: Paths of Industrialization in Latin America and East Asia* (Princeton, NJ: Princeton University Press, 1990), 139–78.

10. Francis Fukuyama, *The End of History and the Last Man* (New York: Free Press, 1991).

11. As Jeffrey Sachs put it, "The main debate in economic reform should therefore be about the means of transition, not the ends." Sachs, "Poland and Eastern Europe: What Is to Be Done?" in Andras Koves and Paul Marer, eds., *Foreign Economic Liberalization: Transformations in Socialist and Market Economies* (Boulder, CO: Westview, 1991), 235.

12. See Bela Balassa, "Policy Choices in the Newly Industrializing Countries," and Jeffrey Sachs, "Poland and Eastern Europe: What Is to Be Done?" in Andras Koves and Paul Marer, eds. *Foreign Economic Liberalization,* 71–80 and 235–46, respectively.

13. For a detailed account of key institutional and political prerequisites for the construction of market economies, see Kiren A. Chaudhry, "Economic Liberalization and the Lineages of the Rentier State," *Comparative Politics,* forthcoming 1993.

14. Some neoliberals concede the importance of institutions, yet they do not recognize complex social and political struggles that institutions embody any more than they appreciate the role of changes in the international economy in influencing their formation. Thus, in explaining the "shock therapy" he designed for Poland in 1990, Jeff Sachs confidently tells us how the stabilization program presupposes the creation of a new legal system and a secure system of property rights within one year. See Jeffrey Sachs, "Poland and Eastern Europe: What Is to Be Done?" in Koves and Marer, eds., *Foreign Economic Liberalization,* 236.

15. John Zysman, in *Governments, Markets and Growth: Financial Systems and the Politics of Industrial Change* (Ithaca, NY: Cornell University Press, 1983), 11–80.

16. Recently, neoliberal economists and even the IMF and the World Bank have begun to recognize the importance of institutions. Yet even these accounts present a mechanistic view of institutions, which fails to appreciate their intrinsically political character. See, for example, Jan S. Prybyla, "The Road From Socialism: Why, Where, What and How," *Problems of Communism*, 40 (January–April 1991): 1–17.

17. Amaryta Sen, "The Profit Motive," in *Resources, Values and Development* (Oxford: Blackwell, 1984), 90–112; Robert Bates, "Toward a Political Economy of Development," in Bates, ed., *Toward a Political Economy of Development*, 239–44; and Fred Hirsch, *Social Limits to Growth* (Cambridge, MA: Harvard University Press, 1976).

18. These arguments and their supporters are summarized in Raymond Vernon, ed., *The Promise of Privatization: A Challenge for U.S. Policy* (New York: Council on Foreign Relations, 1988), "Introduction," 1–22.

19. Douglass C. North, *Structure and Change in Economic History* (New York: Norton, 1981). For a descriptive account of how an unregulated market economy with genuine shortages works, see Michael Kelly's account of Baghdad in 1991, "Mob Town," *The New York Times Magazine*, February 14, 1993.

20. For an excellent review of the issues involved in the debate on regulation in the United States, for example, see the essays in Roger G. Noll ed., *Regulatory Policy and the Social Sciences* (Berkeley: University of California Press, 1985); for a sophisticated critique of the British neoliberals that encompasses the philosophical, political, and economic aspects of the current debate, see Dieter Helm, "The Economic Borders of the State," Alan Ryan, "Value-Judgments and Welfare," Amartya Sen, "The Moral Standing of the Market," and Christopher Allsopp, "The Macro-economic Role of the State," all in Dieter Helm, ed., *The Economic Borders of the State* (Oxford: Oxford University Press, 1989).

21. Yair Aharoni, *The Evolution and Management of State Owned Enterprises* (Melrose, MA: Ballinger, 1986) 69 and 105, and Mitchel Abolafia, "Self Regulation as Market Maintenance: An Organizational Perspective," in Roger Noll, ed., *Regulatory Policy and the Social Sciences*, 312–43.

22. Adam Smith, *An Inquiry into the Nature and Causes of the Wealth of Nations*, vol. 1, edited by Edwin Cannan (London: Methuen, 1950), 130.

23. Hirsch, *Social Limits to Growth*.

24. See Laura Nader and Claire Nader, "A Wide Angle on Regulation: An Anthropological Perspective," 146–48, and Carol MacLennan's "Comment," both in Roger Noll, ed., *Regulatory Policy and the Social Sciences*.

25. On the distinction between laissez-faire and capitalist markets, see Deepak Lal, *The Poverty of "Development Economics."*

26. Joel S. Migdal, *Strong Societies and Weak States: State-Society Relations and State Capabilities in the Third World* (Princeton, NJ: Princeton University Press, 1988), 3–45.

27. Karl Polanyi, *The Great Transformation: The Political and Economic Origins of Our Time* (Boston: Beacon, 1957), esp. chaps. 5–6.

28. Fernand Braudel, *The Wheels of Commerce: Civilization and Capitalism, 15–18th Centuries*, vol. 2 (New York: Harper & Row, 1979), 26–231.

29. North, *Structure and Change*.

30. On this point, see Abolafia's excellent essay, "Self Regulation as Market Maintenance," in Roger Noll, ed., *Regulatory Policy and the Social Sciences*, 312–43.

31. Polanyi, *The Great Transformation*.

32. The grand coalition that managed to override the objections of the feudal elite to prevail in this process, according to widely accepted interpretations of European history, was the crown and the bourgeoisie. Barrington Moore, *Social Origins of Dictatorship and Democracy: Lord and Peasant in the Making of the Modern World* (Boston: Beacon, 1966), 413–32.

33. David Landes, *The Unbound Prometheus: Technological Change and the Industrial Revolution in Western Europe from 1750 to the Present* (London: Cambridge University Press, 1987 [1969]), 134.

34. This is true, for example, in Robert Bates's early work, *States and Markets*.

35. The work of De Soto, Bela Belassa, and Jeffrey Sachs exemplifies this perspective. See note 4 above.

36. The particular importance of institutions in understanding the economies of the developing world is succinctly presented in Mustapha Nabli and Jeffrey Nugent, "The New Institutional Economics and Its Applicability to Development," and also see Douglass North's discussion of property rights and institutional development in "Institutions and Economic Growth: an Historical Introduction," both in *World Development* 17, no. 9 (1989): 1333–47 and 1319–32, respectively.

37. See Pranab Bardhan, "The New Institutional Economics and Development Theory: A Brief Critical Assessment," *World Development* 17, no. 9 (1989): 1389–95.

38. In particular, as Van de Walle has noted in his survey of issues related to privatization, information costs are higher for state regulation than for state ownership. Nicolas Van de Walle, "Privatization in Developing Countries: A Review of the Issues," *World Development* 17, no. 5 (1989): 607.

39. Ibid., 602–3.

40. "Transform reactionary bureaucratic regulation into revolutionary democratic regulation by simple decrees providing for the summoning of the congress of employees, engineers, directors and shareholders, the introduction of uniform accountancy, control by the workers' unions, etc." Lenin, quoted in Alec Nove, *An Economic History of the U.S.S.R.* (London: Penguin, 1982 ed.), 42.

41. Quoted in Nove, *An Economic History,* 44.

42. See James R. Millar and Alec Nove, "A Debate on Collectivization: Was Stalin Really Necessary?" *Problems of Communism* 25 (July–August 1976): 49–62.

43. Nove, *An Economic History,* 139.

44. See Moshe Lewin, "The Immediate Background of Soviet Collectivization," in Lewin, *The Making of the Soviet System: Essays in the Social History of Interwar Russia* (New York: Pantheon, 1985), 91–120.

45. Stephen Cohen, "Bolshevism and Stalinism," in Robert C. Tucker, ed., *Stalinism: Essays in Historical Interpretation* (New York: Norton, 1977), 3–29.

46. For a discussion of the contours of this debate, see Stephen Cohen, *Bukharin and the Bolshevik Revolution: a Political Biography, 1888-1938* (Oxford: Oxford University Press, 1980 [1973]).

47. On foreign investment, see Carl Riskin, China's *Political Economy: The Quest for Development since 1949* (Oxford: Oxford University Press, 1987), 19–22.

48. Dorothy J. Solinger, *Chinese Business Under Socialism: The Politics of Domestic Commerce in Contemporary China, 1949-1980* (Berkeley: University of California Press, 1984), 140; and Vivienne Shue, *Peasant China in Transition: The Dynamics of Development Toward Socialism, 1949-1956* (Berkeley: University of California Press, 1980), 15–40, 195–245.

49. Solinger, *Chinese Business,* 143.

50. Franz Schumann, *Ideology and Organization in Communist China* (Berkeley: University of California Press, 1966), 322–64.

51. See Solinger, *Chinese Business,* 153, esp. n. 123.

52. The incremental nature of this transformation is described in detail in Ezra F. Vogel, *Canton Under Communism: Programs and Politics in a Provincial Capital, 1949–1968* (Cambridge, MA: Harvard University Press, 1969), 125–77. See also Solinger, *Chinese Business,* 181.

53. Kenneth G. Lieberthal, *Revolution and Tradition in Tientsin, 1949–1952* (Stanford, CA: Stanford University Press, 1980), 78–96, 125–52.

54. Solinger, *Chinese Business,* 182, quoted from *DGB,* January 4 and 17, 1956.

55. As Mao put it in 1947, the revolution was aimed "not at wiping out capitalism in general, the upper petty bourgeoisie or the middle bourgeoisie. In view of China's economic backwardness, even after the country-wide victory of the revolution, it will still be necessary to permit the existence for a long time of a petty bourgeoisie and middle bourgeoisie. … This capitalist sector will still be an indispensable part of the whole national economy." Quoted in Carl Riskin, *China's Political Economy,* 39.

56. Although it is widely acknowledged, following Marx that functioning markets create self-perpetuating economic and social inequalities, the tenor of reports from experts on the current transition in Eastern Europe and the Soviet Union have stressed the equalizing effects of markets when they initially replace distributive or redistributive arrangements. See Ivan Szelenyi, "Eastern Europe in an Epoch of Transition: Toward a Socialist Mixed Economy?" in Nee and Stark, eds., *Remaking the Economic Institutions of Socialism,* 208–32.

57. Cylar Keyder, "Looking for the Missing Bourgeoisie," in *State and Class in Turkey: A Study in Capitalist Development* (New York: Verso, 1987).

58. The best and most comprehensive overall treatment of this subject is Paul Kennedy's *African Capitalism: The Struggle for Ascendancy* (Cambridge: Cambridge University Press, 1988), see especially chaps. 1–4.

59. A discussion of investment and tax laws is found in Fong Chan Onn, *New Economic Dynamo: Structures and Investment Opportunities in the Malaysian Economy* (London: Allen & Unwin, 1986); see also James V. Jesudason, *Ethnicity and the Economy: The State, Chinese Business, and Multinationals in Malaysia* (Singapore: Oxford University Press, 1989).

60. Fong Chan Onn, *The Malaysian Economic Challenge in the 1990s: Transformation for Growth* (Singapore: Longman, 1989), 75–77.

61. Ibid.

62. David Felix, "Import Substitution and Late Industrialization: Latin America and Asia Compared," *World Development* 17, no. 9 (1989): 1455–69.

63. This pattern is found in most LDCs but is illustrated in detail in De Soto's *The Other Path.*

64. Richard Cooper, "Economic Interdependence and Foreign Policy in the Seventies," *World Politics* 24, no. 2 (January 1972): 159–81.

65. This distinction between "market" and "club" is presented by Casella as follows: "…they emphasize the difference between (i) issues that do not require explicit coordination and can be solved through the functioning of a price system in a free market (once property rights are defined) and (ii) issues which instead demand some explicit form of collective decision-making." This clearly shows the difference, for example, between an international market for wheat and a national market economy, undergirded by authoritative

institutions that deliver "excludable public goods." Alessandra Casella, "On Markets and Clubs: Economic and Political Integration of Regions with Unequal Productivity," *American Economic Association Papers and Proceedings,* May 1992: 115–21.

66. Susan Strange, "States, Firms and Diplomacy," *International Affairs* 68, no. 1 (January 1992): 1–15.

67. Jeffry A. Frieden, "Invested Interests: The Politics of National Economic Policies in a World of Global Finance," *International Organization* 45, no. 4 (Autumn 1991): 425–51; Peter Gourevitch, *Politics in Hard Times: Comparative Responses to International Economic Crises* (Ithaca, NY: Cornell University Press, 1986); Ethan Barnaby Kapstein, "Between Power and Purpose: Central Bankers and the Politics of Regulatory Convergence," *International Organization* 46, no. 1 (Winter 1992); Michael C. Webb, "International Economic Structures, Government Interests, and International Coordination of Macroeconomic Adjustment Policies," *International Organization* 45, no. 3 (Summer 1991); and Susan Strange, "States, Firms and Diplomacy," *International Affairs* 68, no. 1 (January 1992).

68. For a study about the effects of international Interdependence on the state's role in the domestic economy, see Peter Evans, "Transnational Linkages and the Economic Role of the State: An Analysis of Developing and Industrialized Nations in the Post-World War II Period," in Peter Evans, Dietrich Rueschemeyer, and Theda Skocpol, eds., *Bringing the State Back In* (Cambridge and New York: Cambridge University Press, 1985), 192–94.

69. See Kapstein, "Between Power and Purpose: Central Bankers and the Politics of Regulatory Convergence"; and Michael Webb, "International Economic Structures, Government Interests and International Coordination of Macroeconomic Adjustment Policies," *International Organization* 45, no. 3 (Summer 1991): 309–42.

70. Jeffry Frieden, "Invested Interests."

71. Hugh Ault and David Bradford, "Taxing International Income: An Analysis of the U.S. System and Its Economic Premises," in Assaf Razin and Joel Slemrod, eds., *Taxation in the Global Economy* (A National Bureau of Economic Research Project Report) (Chicago: University of Chicago Press, 1990), 16, 19, 38. See also Joel Slemrod. "Tax Principles in an International Economy," in Michael Boskin and Charles McLure, Jr., eds., *World Tax Reform* (San Francisco: International Center for Economic Growth, 1990), 11–25.

72. Samuel P. Huntington, *Political Order in Changing Societies* (New Haven, CT: Yale University Press, 1966).

73. Barbara Stallings, "The Role of Foreign Capital in Economic Development," in Gary Gereffi and Donald Wyman, eds., *Manufacturing Miracles,* 55–89.

74. For the 1978 figure, see *World Debt Tables, 1982–83,* at xii; for the 1988 figure, see *World Debt Tables, 1990–91,* at 126.

75. Includes value of fuel exports from Algeria, Ecuador, Gabon, Indonesia, Kuwait, Libya, Nigeria, Saudi Arabia, United Arab Emirates, and Venezuela. IBRD, *World Tables,* 1991.

76. IBRD, *World Development Report,* 1991, 95.

77. Laura D'Andrea Tyson, "Debt Crisis and Adjustment Responses in Eastern Europe: A Comparative Perspective," in Ellen Comisso and Laura D'Andrea Tyson, *Power Purpose and Collective Choice: Economic Strategy in Socialist States* (Ithaca, NY: Cornell University Press, 1986), 63–110.

78. For example, this is the view held by Raymond Vernon. See his "Introduction: The Promise and the Challenge," in Raymond Vernon, ed., *The Promise of Privatization,* 1–22.

79. See, for example, Peter Evans, "Transnational Linkages and the Economic Role of the State"; Peter Evans and John Stephens, "Development and the World Economy," in Neil Smelser, ed., *The Handbook of Sociology* (Newbury Park, CA: Sage, 1988); and Kiren A. Chaudhry "Economic Liberalization."

80. Peter Evans, "Class, State and Dependence in East Asia: Lessons for Latin American-ists," in Deyo, *The Political Economy*, 203–26; and Albert Fishlow, "Some Reflections on Comparative Latin American Economic Performance and Policy," in Tariq Banuri, ed., *Economic Liberalization, No Panacea: The Experiences of Latin America and Asia*, 149–70.

81. Kiren Aziz Chaudhry, "The Price of Wealth: Business and State in Labor Remittance and Oil Economies," *International Organization* 43, no. 1 (Winter 1989): 101–45.

82. Ibid.

83. For a detailed discussion, see Chaudhry, "Economic Liberalization."

84. See Susan Woodward, "Orthodoxy and Solidarity: Competing Claims and Interna-tional Adjustment in Yugoslavia," in Comisso and Tyson, eds., *Power, Purpose*, 329–70, esp. 338, 340, 343, 345, 353, 357, 366; and Joan M. Nelson, "The Politics of Economic Transformation: Is Third World Experience Relevant in Eastern Europe?" *World Poli-tics* 45, no. 3 (April 1993): 433–63.

85. Robert B. Reich, *The Work of Nations: Preparing Ourselves for 21st-century Capitalism* (New York: Alfred A. Knopf, 1991).

86. See Praful Bidwai, "Bringing Down the Temple: Democracy at Risk in India," *The Nation* 256, no. 3. (January 25, 1993).

87. Ken Jowitt, *New World Disorder: The Leninist Extinction* (Berkeley: University of Cali-fornia Press, 1992), chap. 7.

88. For some descriptive accounts, see John Esposito, *The Islamic Threat: Myth or Reality?* (New York: Oxford University Press, 1992).

89. These links are explored in depth in Kiren Chaudhry and Elaine Thomas, "Cities of the Future: International Economics and Primordial Politics" (Manuscript, Department of Political Science, UC Berkeley, 1992). See also Kiren A. Chaudhry, "From the Global to the Local: Liberal Economics, Illiberal Politics," Proposal submitted to the SSRC, 1993.

90. See Benjamin Cohen and Gustav Ranis, "The Second Postwar Restructuring," in Ranis, ed., *Government and Economic Development* (New Haven, CT: Yale University Press, 1971), 231–468 for a discussion of the first such "liberal" shift in LDCs.

91. Pierre Ostiguy, "Privatization Processes: The Latin American Experience in Perspec-tive" (Manuscript, UC Berkeley, May 1991).

92. The experiences of African, Turkish, Indian, Egyptian, Algerian, Tunisian, Libyan, and Latin American countries have been far from encouraging. See Atul Kohli, "Politics of Economic Liberalization in India," *World Development* 17, no. 3, (1989): 305–28; John Staatz et al., "Cereals Market Liberalization in Mali," *World Development* 17, no. 5 (1989): 703–18; Pan Yotopoulos, "The (Rip) Tide of Privatization: Lessons from Chile," *World Development* 17, no. 5 (1989): 683–702; Henry Bienen and John Waterbury, "The Political Economy of Privatization in Developing Countries," *World Development* 17, no. 5 (1989): 617–32; Peter Heller and Christian Schiller, "The Fiscal Impact of Privati-zation, with Some Examples from Arab Countries," *World Development* 17, no. 5 (1989): 757–67; William Glade, "Privatization in Rent-Seeking Societies," *World Development* 17, no. 5 (1989): 673–82; Jon Marks's reports on Algeria include "Algeria Breaks with the Past," *Middle East Economic Development* (MEED), 14 April 1989; "In-fighting Leads to PM's Dismissal," *MEED*, 22 September 1989; "Setting the Course for Reform," *MEED*, 29 September 1989; and "Reform Gets Only Qualified Support," *MEED*, 15 December

1989; Angus Hindley, "Gaddafi Keeps a Check on Reform," *MEED*. 17 November 1989; Roger Leeds, "Malaysia: Genesis of a Privatization Transaction," *World Development* 17, no. 5 (1989): 741–56; and Elliot Berg, "The Liberalization of Rice Marketing in Madagascar," *World Development* 17, no. 5 (1989): 719–28.

93. Joseph Ramos, "Stabilization and Adjustment Policies in the Southern Cone, 1974–1983," *CEPAL Review*, no. 25 (August 1984): 107–21.

94. Christos Pitelis, "Beyond the Nation-State: The Transnational Firm and the Nation-State' *Capital and Class* 43 (Spring 1991): 131–52.

95. Albert Hirschman, "Rise and Decline of Development Economics," in Hirschman, *Essays in Trespassing: Economics to Politics and Beyond* (New York: Cambridge University Press, 1981), 1–24.

96. One text that makes this purpose explicit is William Lazonick, *Business Organization and the Myth of the Market Economy* (Cambridge: Cambridge University Press, 1991).

97. The question of what market economies are and how they emerge has long been the preserve of economic historians and political economists. The contributors to the debate, most notably Polanyi, Braudel, Smith, Wallerstein, and Marx, have widely divergent ideas on the issue, which are connected to their very different conceptions of the emergence and indeed, the nature of modern capitalism. Nevertheless, all agree on one critical point: market economies are something other than either the human propensity to truck and barter, or marketplaces, or simple capitalist exchange.

98. Hector E. Schamis, "Reconceptualizing Latin American Authoritarianism in the 1970s: From Bureaucratic-Authoritarianism to Neoconservatism," *Comparative Politics* 23, no. 2 (January 1991): 201–20.

Hernando de Soto, "The Mystery of Capital" (2001)*

Why has the genesis of capital become such a mystery?

And why have the rich nations of the world not explained to other nations how indispensable a formal property system is to capital formation?

Walk down most roads in the Middle East, the former Soviet Union, or Latin America, and you will see many things: houses used for shelter; parcels of land being tilled, sowed, and harvested; merchandise being bought and sold. Assets in developing and former communist countries primarily serve these immediate physical purposes. In the West, however, the same assets also lead a parallel life as capital outside the physical world. They can be used to put in motion more production by securing the interests of other parties as "collateral" for a mortgage, for example, or by assuring the supply of other forms of credit and public utilities.

Why can't buildings and land elsewhere in the world also lead this parallel life? Why can't the enormous resources in developing and former communist countries, which my colleagues at the Institute for Liberty and Democracy (Lima) and I estimate at $9.3 trillion of dead capital, produce value beyond their "natural" state? My reply is, dead capital exists because we have forgotten (or perhaps never realized) that converting a physical asset to generate capital—using your house to borrow money to finance an enterprise, for example—requires a very complex process. It is not unlike the process that Albert Einstein taught us whereby a single brick can be made to release a huge amount of energy in the form of an atomic explosion. By analogy, capital is the result of discovering and unleashing potential energy from the trillions of bricks that the poor have accumulated in their buildings.

Clues from the Past

To unravel the mystery of capital, we have to go back to the seminal meaning of the word. In medieval Latin, "capital" appears to have denoted head of cattle or other livestock, which have always been important sources of wealth beyond the basic meat, milk, hides, wool, and fuel they provide. Livestock can also reproduce themselves. Thus, the term "capital" begins to do two jobs simultaneously, capturing the physical

---

dimension of assets (livestock) as well as their potential to generate surplus value. From the barnyard, it was only a short step to the desks of the inventors of economics, who generally defined "capital" as that part of a country's assets that initiates surplus production and increases productivity.

Great classical economists such as Adam Smith and, later, Karl Marx believed that capital was the engine that powered the market economy. In The Wealth of Nations, Smith emphasized one point that is at the very heart of the mystery we are trying to solve: for accumulated assets to become active capital and put additional production in motion, they must be fixed and realized in some particular subject "which lasts for some time at least after that labour is past. It is, as it were, a certain quantity of labour stocked and stored up to be employed, if necessary, upon some other occasion." What I take from Smith is that capital is not the accumulated stock of assets but the potential it holds to deploy new production. This potential is, of course, abstract. It must be processed and fixed into a tangible form before we can release it—just like the potential nuclear energy in Einstein's brick.

This essential meaning of capital has been lost to history. Capital is now confused with money, which is only one of the many forms in which it travels. It is always easier to remember a difficult concept in one of its tangible manifestations than in its essence. The mind wraps itself around "money" more easily than "capital." But it is a mistake to assume that money is what finally fixes capital. Money facilitates transactions, allowing us to buy and sell things, but it is not itself the progenitor of additional production.

Potential Energy in Assets

What is it that fixes the potential of an asset so that it can put additional production into motion? What detaches value from a simple house and fixes it in a way that allows us to realize it as capital?

We can begin to find an answer by using our energy analogy. Consider a mountain lake. We can think about this lake in its immediate physical context and see some primary uses for it, such as canoeing and fishing. But when we think about this same lake as an engineer would by focusing on its capacity to generate electrical energy, by means of a hydroelectric plant, as an additional value beyond the lake's natural state as a body of water, we suddenly see the potential created by the lake's elevated position. The challenge for the engineer is finding out how he can create a process that allows him to convert and fix this potential into a form that can be used to do additional work.

Capital, like energy, is a dormant value. Bringing it to life requires us to go beyond looking at our assets as they are to actively thinking about them as they could be. It requires a process for fixing an asset's economic potential into a form that can be used to initiate additional production.

Although the process that converts the potential energy in the water into electricity is well known, the one that gives assets the form required to put in motion more production is not known. This is so because that key process was not deliberately set up to create capital but for the more mundane purpose of protecting property ownership. As the property systems of Western nations grew, they developed, imperceptibly, a variety of mechanisms that gradually combined into a process that churned out capital as never before.

Hidden Conversion Process of the West

In the West, this formal property system begins to process assets into capital by describing and organizing the most economically and socially useful aspects about assets, preserving this information in a recording system—as insertions in a written ledger or a blip on a computer disk—and then embodying it in a title. A set of detailed and precise legal rules governs this entire process. Formal property records and titles thus represent our shared concept of what is economically meaningful about any asset. They capture and organize all the relevant information required to conceptualize the potential value of an asset and so allow us to control it.

Any asset whose economic and social aspects are not fixed in a formal property system is extremely hard to move in the market. How can the huge amounts of assets changing hands in a modern market economy be controlled, if not through a formal property process? Without such a system, any trade of an asset, say a piece of real estate, requires an enormous effort just to determine the basics of the transaction: Does the seller own the real estate and have the right to transfer it? Can he pledge it? Will the new owner be accepted as such by those who enforce property rights? What are the effective means to exclude other claimants? This is why the exchange of most assets outside the West is restricted to local circles of trading partners.

Developing and former communist countries' principal problem is clearly not the lack of entrepreneurship: the poor have accumulated trillions of dollars of real estate during the past forty years. What the poor lack is easy access to the property mechanisms that could legally fix the economic potential of their assets so that they could be used to produce, secure, or guarantee greater value in the expanded market.

Why has the genesis of capital become such a mystery? Why have the rich nations of the world, so quick with their economic advice, not explained how indispensable formal property is to capital formation? The answer is that the process within the formal property system that breaks down assets into capital is extremely difficult to visualize. It is hidden in thousands of pieces of legislation, statutes, regulations, and institutions that govern the system. Anyone trapped in such a legal morass would be hard-pressed to figure out how the system actually works. The only way to see it is from outside the system—from the extralegal sector—which is where my colleagues and I do most of our research.

The formal property systems of the West produce six effects that allow their citizens to generate capital.

(1) *Fixing the economic potential of assets.* Capital is born by representing in writing—in a title, a security, a contract, and other such records—the most economically and socially useful qualities about the asset as opposed to the visually more striking aspects of the asset. This is where potential value is first described and registered. The moment you focus your attention on the title of a house, for example, and not on the

house itself, you have automatically stepped from the material world into the conceptual universe where capital lives.

The proof that formal property is pure concept comes when a house changes hands: nothing physically changes. Property is not the house itself but an economic concept about the house, embodied in a legal representation that describes not its physical qualities but rather economically and socially meaningful qualities we humans have attributed to the house (such as the ability to use it for a variety of purposes—for example, to generate funds for investment in a business without having to sell the house—by providing security to lenders in the form of liens, mortgages, easements, or other covenants). In advanced nations, this formal property representation functions as the means to secure the interests of other parties and to create accountability by providing all the information, references, rules, and enforcement mechanisms required to do so.

Legal property thus gave the West the tools to produce surplus value over and above its physical assets. Whether anyone intended it or not, the legal property system became the staircase that took these nations from the universe of assets in their natural state to the conceptual universe of capital where assets can be viewed in their full productive potential.

(2) *Integrating dispersed information into one system.* The reason capitalism has triumphed in the West and sputtered in the rest of the world is because most of the assets in Western nations have been integrated into one formal representational system. This integration did not happen casually. Over decades in the nineteenth century, politicians, legislators, and judges pulled together the scattered facts and rules that had governed property throughout cities, villages, buildings, and farms and integrated them into one system. This "pulling together" of property representations, a revolutionary moment in the history of developed nations, deposited all the information and rules governing the accumulated wealth of their citizens into one knowledge base. Before that moment, information about assets was far less accessible. Every farm or settlement recorded its assets and the rules governing them in rudimentary ledgers, symbols, or oral testimony. But the information was atomized, dispersed, and not available to any one agent at any given moment.

Developing and former communist nations have not created unified formal property systems. In all of these countries I have studied, I have never found just one legal system but instead dozens and hundreds, managed by all sorts of organizations, some legal, others extralegal, ranging from small entrepreneurial groups to housing organizations. Consequently, what people in those countries can do with their property is limited to the imagination of the owners and their acquaintances. In Western countries, where property information is standardized and universally available, what owners can do with their assets benefits from the collective imagination of a larger network of people.

It may surprise the Western reader that most of the world's nations have yet to integrate extralegal property agreements into one formal legal system. For Westerners today, there supposedly is only one law—the official one. Diverse informal property arrangements, however, were once the norm in every nation—the West's reliance on integrated property systems is a phenomenon of at most the last two hundred years. The reason it is so hard to follow the history of the integration of widespread property systems is that the process took place over a very long time.

(3) *Making people accountable.* The integration of all property systems under one formal property law shifted the legitimacy of the rights of owners from the political context of local communities to the impersonal context of law. Releasing owners from restrictive local arrangements and bringing them into a more integrated legal system facilitated their accountability.

By transforming people with real property interests into accountable individuals, formal property created individuals from masses. People no longer needed to rely on neighborhood relationships or make local arrangements to protect their rights to assets. They were thus freed to explore how to generate surplus value from their own assets. But there was a price to pay: once inside a formal property system, owners lost their anonymity while their individual accountability was reinforced. People who do not pay for goods or services they have consumed can be identified, charged interest penalties, fined, and embargoed, and can have their credit ratings downgraded. Authorities are able to learn about legal infractions and dishonored contracts; they can suspend services, place liens against property, and withdraw some or all of the privileges of legal property.

Respect in Western nations for property and transactions is hardly encoded in their citizens' DNA; it is rather the result of having enforceable formal property systems. Formal property's role in protecting not only ownership but also the security of transactions strongly encourages citizens in advanced countries to respect titles, honor contracts, and obey the law. Legal property thus invites commitment.

The lack of legal property thus explains why citizens in developing and former communist nations cannot make profitable contracts with strangers and cannot get credit, insurance, or utilities services: they have no property to lose. Because they have no legal property, they are taken seriously as contracting parties only by their immediate family and neighbors. People with nothing to lose are trapped in the grubby basement of the precapitalist world.

(4) *Making assets fungible.* One of the most important things a formal property system does is transform assets from a less accessible condition to a more accessible condition, so that they can do additional work. Unlike physical assets, representations of assets are easily combined, divided, mobilized, and used to stimulate business deals. By uncoupling the economic features of an asset from its rigid, physical state, a representation makes the asset "fungible"—able to be fashioned to suit practically any transaction.

By describing all assets in standard categories, an integrated formal property system enables the comparison of two architecturally different buildings constructed for the same purpose. This allows one to discriminate quickly and inexpensively between similarities and differences in assets without having to deal with each asset as if it were unique.

Standard property descriptions in the West are also written to facilitate the combination of assets. Formal property rules require assets to be described and characterized in a way that not only outlines their singularities but also points out their similarities to other assets, thus making potential combinations more obvious.

Through the use of standardized records, one can determine how to exploit a particular asset most profitably.

Representations also enable one to divide assets without touching them. Whereas an asset such as a factory may be an indivisible unit in the real world, in the conceptual universe of formal property representation it can be subdivided into any number of portions. Citizens of advanced nations are thus able to split most of their assets into shares, each of which can be owned by different persons, with different rights, to carry out different functions.

Formal property representations can also serve as movable stand-ins for physical assets, enabling owners and entrepreneurs to simulate hypothetical situations in order to explore other profitable uses of their assets. In addition, all standard formal property documents are crafted in such a way as to facilitate the easy measurement of an asset's attributes. By providing standards, Western formal property systems have significantly reduced the transaction costs of mobilizing and using assets.

(5) *Networking people.* By making assets fungible, by attaching owners to assets, assets to addresses, and ownership to enforcement, and by making information on the history of assets and owners easily accessible, formal property systems converted the citizens of the West into a network of individually identifiable and accountable business agents. The formal property process created a whole infrastructure of connecting devices that, like a railway switchyard, allowed the assets (trains) to run safely between people (stations). Formal property's contribution to mankind is not the protection of ownership: squatters, housing organizations, mafias, and even primitive tribes manage to protect their assets quite efficiently. The property system's real breakthrough is that it radically improved the flow of communications about assets and their potential. It also enhanced the status of their owners.

Western legal property also provides businesses with information about assets and their owners, verifiable addresses, and objective records of property values, all of which lead to credit records. This information and the existence of integrated law make risk more manageable by spreading it through insurance-type devices as well as by pooling property to secure debts.

Few seem to have noticed that the legal property system of an advanced nation is the center of a complex web of connections that equips ordinary citizens to form ties with both the government and the private sector, and so to obtain additional goods and services. Without the tools of formal property, it is hard to see how assets could be used for everything they accomplish in the West.

(6) *Protecting transactions.* One important reason why the Western formal property system works like a network is that all the property records (titles, deeds, securities, and contracts that describe the economically significant aspects of assets) are continually tracked and protected as they travel through time and space. Public agencies are the stewards of an advanced nation's representations. They administer the files that contain all the economically useful descriptions of assets, whether land, buildings, chattels, ships, industries, mines, or airplanes. These files will alert anyone eager to use an asset about things that may restrict or enhance its utilization, such as encumbrances, easements, leases, arrears, bankruptcies, or mortgages. In addition to public record-keeping systems, many other private services (escrow and closing organiza-

tions, appraisers, etc.) have evolved to assist parties in fixing, moving, and tracking representations so they can easily and securely produce surplus value.

Although they are established to protect the security of both ownership and transactions, it is obvious that Western systems emphasize the latter. Security is principally focused on producing trust in transactions so that people can more easily make their assets lead a parallel life as capital. The Western emphasis on the security of transactions allows citizens to move large amounts of assets with very few transactions. In most developing countries, by contrast, the law and official agencies are trapped by early colonial and Roman law, which tilt toward protecting ownership. They have become the custodians of the wishes of the dead.

Conclusion

Much of the marginalization of the poor in developing and former communist nations comes from their inability to benefit from the six effects that formal property provides. The challenge these countries face is not whether they should produce or receive more money but whether they can understand the legal institutions and summon the political will necessary to build a property system that is easily accessible to the poor.

The French historian Fernand Braudel found it a great mystery that at the inception of Western capitalism, it served only a privileged few, just as it does elsewhere in the world today:

> The key problem is to find out why that sector of society of the past, which I would not hesitate to call capitalist, should have lived as if in a bell jar, cut off from the rest; why was it not able to expand and conquer the whole of society? ... [Why was it that] a significant rate of capital formation was possible only in certain sectors and not in the whole market economy of the time?

I believe the answer to Braudel's question lies in restricted access to formal property, both in the West's past and in developing and former communist countries today. Local and foreign investors do have capital; their assets are more or less integrated, fungible, networked, and protected by formal property systems. But they are only a tiny minority—those who can afford the expert lawyers, insider connections, and patience required to navigate the red tape of their property systems. The great majority of people, who cannot get the fruits of their labor represented by the formal property system, live outside Braudel's bell jar.

The bell jar makes capitalism a private club, open only to a privileged few, and enrages the billions standing outside looking in. This capitalist apartheid will inevitably continue until we all come to terms with the critical flaw in many countries' legal and political systems that prevents the majority from entering the formal property system.

The time is right to find out why most countries have not been able to create open formal property systems. This is the moment, as Third World and former communist nations are living through their most ambitious attempts to implement capitalist systems, to lift the bell jar.

References

Fernand Braudel, *The Wheels of Commerce* (New York: Harper and Row, 1982).
Adam Smith, *The Wealth of Nations* (1776; reprint, London: Everyman's Library, 1977).

4

Globalization and the Information Technology Revolution

The phenomenon of globalization—usually defined as increased trade, finance, and information flows across state borders—has profoundly influenced national markets since the late 1970s. The information technology (IT) revolution has been central in facilitating globalization and also has had an impact of its own on political–economic systems. Yet scholars and observers differ widely on precisely how national varieties of capitalism or market systems have been affected by these global trends. The major analytical cleavage in this issue area is between those who observe and predict convergence in national political economies in response to globalization and the IT revolution and those who predict lasting variation in political–economic systems and continued divergence. These two perspectives differ on how market institutions respond to external pressures and the role of government in mediating the effects on national market institutions.

One dominant framework asserts that national political–economic systems are vulnerable to IT and other flows associated with globalization and that these external pressures are so great that all countries begin to converge in their responses. Scholars, businesspeople, and journalists have argued that footloose capital, the nature of information flows, and an increased emphasis on transnational economic and social networks have constrained the ability of governments to shape their national political–economic institutions and policies in an era of globalization.[1] **Thomas Friedman** argues, with entertaining imagery, that globalization brings with it the pressure for all countries to adapt to the democratization of technology, finance, and information. He contends that countries (and, at the microlevel, corporations) that fail to respond to the pressures of rapidly growing technology, finance, and information flows will fall irretrievably behind their peers. In Friedman's view, there is no longer an alternative to free market capitalism in responding to these external pressures. In pursuing capitalism, moreover, countries must conform to the "golden straitjacket" that comes with integration into the global economy. As a result of both the IT revolution and globalization, therefore, nations converge in terms of government policy. Although some market-institutional national differences are retained, economic convergence in the pursuit of growth and development, according to Friedman, hamstrings governments to such a degree that it also drives some degree of political convergence. Friedman has more recently articulated the view that various components of the IT revolution and globalization—such as outsourcing, open source software, off-shoring, and supply chaining, for example—act as flattening pressures that continue to drive convergence.[2]

Unlike analysts such as Friedman who argue that IT flows reduce the state's power in the international economy, **Abraham Newman and John Zysman** believe that the state continues to play a critical role in creating digital markets and in managing the sociopolitical consequences of the IT revolution. In their view, the national foundations of distinctive political economies and corporate strategies persist in an increasingly global market. Institutional innovation rooted in national structures continues and, furthermore, reverberates through the global economy, facilitated by IT. They employ **Karl Polanyi's** metaphor of a great transformation to articulate a market-institutional perspective on the political economy of the digital era. Like Polanyi's analysis of the Industrial Revolution in England, Newman and Zysman believe that the IT revolution brings with it a fundamental shift in the rules of society that in turn affect the way political economy operates.

Newman and Zysman argue that, as during the Industrial Revolution, the state is actively involved in constructing markets for information. Governments have removed barriers to digital markets and built new rules and infrastructure for them, enabling the creation of the fictitious commodity of information. Governments have also intervened to mediate the advent of the IT revolution, and these state actions are not neutral; rather they affect the very nature of the transformation and its sociopolitical impacts. The state has developed new market rules for society to embed markets in social norms and manage the new social externalities and political–economic dislocations that arise as a result of the IT revolution. Newman and Zysman look at both microlevel firm–industry dynamics and macrolevel societal bargains in the context of political economy to demonstrate that governments have a range of policy instruments open to them in intervening to create and sustain markets. The different choices that governments make, in response to various economic and social groups, are filtered by political configuration and in turn reinforce and shape national political–economic systems.

Susan Strange addresses the role of the state in a globalizing world. She represents the convergence and state-weakening logics highlighted previously, arguing that national governments have lost an enormous part of the authority that they used to have over their political economies and that this leads to fewer differences among the national varieties of capitalism. These phenomena are the results of the global integration of markets, the accelerating pace of technological change, and the increased need to raise capital on global financial markets. In her view, markets have come to be masters over states, and states are increasingly unable to perform even the bare minimum functions as laid out by **Adam Smith** and the liberal school.

Robert Gilpin reaches the opposite conclusion, explaining how both the extent and consequences of economic globalization have been exaggerated and that the nation-state remains the major actor in both national and international affairs. Gilpin sees more varied outcomes than does Strange, and he attributes this lasting differentiation to (1) the fact that the impact of globalization varies by issue and (2) the fact that the policy latitude that states have to reduce their vulnerability to these effects varies by national size and economic power. In other words, we should expect not convergence in national political–economic responses to globalization but rather the persistence of variety and even divergence in economic policy and market institutions.

The convergence-versus-divergence debate is a central issue in contemporary political economy, as states, markets, and societal actors deal with the changes that come with globalization and the IT revolution. Several of the authors we have already encountered in this volume also weigh in on this issue. **David Landes,** building on his historical perspective, argues that the empirical evidence is against the convergence school: the gap between rich countries and poor countries is simply not closing in reality. **Peter Hall and David Soskice** point out that their varieties of capitalism framework can explain persistent differences in political economy even in the age of globalization; indeed, their expectation over time is continued national divergence. They explicitly consider the IT revolution and liberalization associated with globalization as drivers of political–economic changes and take head on the convergence perspective often associated with globalization. This convergence perspective, they argue, sees firms as essentially similar across all nations, a viewpoint their varieties of capitalism approach explicitly rejects.

In their view, firms develop different strategies to cope with and adjust to the challenges associated with globalization, which in turn aggregate into varying national political–economic responses and outcomes. These microdifferences are reinforced at a macrolevel, through the phenomenon of comparative institutional advantage and its impact on innovation. Hall and Soskice argue that, based on their institutional makeup, liberal market economies (LMEs) are more suited to radical or breakthrough innovation and coordinated market economies (CMEs) are more suited to incremental innovation. These two types of political economy thus adapt to the challenges of globalization and IT revolution in different ways; there is variation in the national pattern of specialization and adaptation, which are rational responses to the market institutional frameworks.[3] Because of comparative institutional advantage, nations adjust and prosper by building on their institutional differences and hence continue to maintain the varieties of political–economic systems.

Notes

1. See, for example, Manuel Castells, *The Rise of Network Society* (Cambridge: Blackwell, 1996); and Walter B. Wriston, *The Twilight of Sovereignty: How the Information Revolution Is Transforming Our World* (New York: Macmillan, 1992). Notes.
2. Thomas Friedman, *The World Is Flat: A Brief History of the Twenty-first Century* (New York: Farrar, Straus and Giroux, 2005).

3. Peter A. Hall and David Soskice, eds., *Varieties of Capitalism: The Institutional Foundations of Comparative Advantage* (Oxford: Oxford University Press, 2001), 36–41 and this volume, pp. 314–318.

Thomas L. Friedman,
The Lexus and the Olive Tree (1999)*

5: Microchip Immune Deficiency

SOONER OR LATER, ALL TYRANNIES CRUMBLE
Those That Keep Putting Their Customers
On Hold Tend to Crumble Sooner.

—ad in *The Washington Post* announcing Star Power, a new phone,
cable and Internet service provider competing with Bell Atlantic

You can never feel like you've won
You can never break even
You can never get out of the game

—motto for doing business on the Internet

E or be eaten

—motto for adapting your company to the Internet

Now, some people will say, "Well, these changes in how people communicate, invest and see the world that made globalization possible are all well and good for developed societies, but what about the rest of the world? How can you talk about globalization being global when the vast majority of humanity still lives in villages without telephones, and has never touched a computer or sent an E-mail message?"

It is true that globalization today is not global, in the sense that we are still a long, long way away from a world in which everyone is online (although some 300,000 new users join the Internet each week). But globalization is global in the sense that almost everyone now is feeling—directly or indirectly—the pressures, constraints and opportunities to adapt to the democratizations of technology, finance and information that are at the heart of the globalization system. As Chen Yuan, the deputy governor of the Central Bank of China, once remarked to me:

"Every country has a part that is underdeveloped. Even in the United States you can drive south from Washington to Virginia and still find some mountainous areas

---

with remote villages. But you cannot say that this area is not in the process of globalization. China is the same."

Indeed it is. If there is a place that should have been beyond the frontiers of globalization, it is the village of Gujialingzi, a tiny hamlet in northeastern China, north of North Korea. I went there in the winter of 1998 with a team of international monitors to observe village elections in rural China. But I actually had an ulterior motive for going. I wanted to see what globalization looked like from beyond the frontier—from outside the system, as it were—and I discovered something fundamental on this trip: I couldn't get there. I couldn't get beyond the frontier. I couldn't get outside the system, which now extended deep into even the villages of northeastern China. When our monitoring team arrived in Gujialingzi, we found virtually all the voting-age adults gathered in the schoolyard. They were assembled to hear the two candidates for village chief deliver their campaign speeches. This place was dirt poor; in fact, the school rooms had dirt floors. The Chinese province within which it is located, Jilin, is in the heart of the former industrial belt of China, which is fast becoming a rust belt, because the state-owned industries there are not globally competitive and increasingly the Beijing government can't afford to subsidize these factories, or the social benefits they normally provide. Maybe that was why when the two candidates for village chief rose and delivered their campaign speeches in Gujialingzi they sounded as if they were running for mayor of an old steel-mill town in central Ohio.

The first to speak was the incumbent chief, Li Hongling. Here is an excerpt from his remarks: "Villagers, how are you? Let me remind you I am forty-seven years old, a member of the Communist Party with a junior high school education. I want to do something good for the village. As you know, I helped this village recover from the Cultural Revolution. Everywhere you can see my sweat. I visit everyone's home. I get ideas from you. I have never used the village's money to host a banquet. I have tried to handle everything legally. I promise to improve our elementary school and raise our incomes. If elected I vow that I will get our vegetables to the township more quickly. I will also improve the spirit of the village. We need more trees, and also fiber-optic cable so everyone can have a telephone. Under the leadership of the Party branch, I will correct all my shortcomings. This is my contract with you."

After polite applause, his challenger, Liu Fu, took the podium. He went right for the gender vote: "First let me say that tomorrow is Women's Day and I want to express my congratulations to all the women. I am fifty-one years old, with a junior high education. I own my own bean curd business. I love this village. I love you all. Your poverty is my shame. Under the guidance of the Party I will turn a new chapter here. I promise to reduce gambling and pornography in the village and create more channels for making money. I won't be arrogant. I will reduce the village budget to save your money. I won't take any bribes, and even if my superior comes from the city, I won't take him for a banquet. We have too many official banquets. I have not been to a banquet or drunk one drop of alcohol in ten years. I will guard the money of the masses. No cadres from the village will be allowed to travel to the township on village money. I will bring technology here. I promise to give everyone the technology for making bean curd. I will drill more wells. The Cultural Revolution wasted ten years of our lives. We have to think now of better ideas for how to prosper. I will be very nonideological. As Deng Xiaoping said: 'Black cat, white cat. It doesn't matter. All that matters is that it catches mice.' I will improve our school. Knowledge is important. If you are ignorant you cannot build a socialist economy. And I will take care of all the bachelors here who do not have the income to find a wife. I will make you rich! Let's march together."

While the villagers voted and waited for the results to be announced, I did some exit polling, asking villagers at random which speech they liked most. The village butcher in a blue Mao cap stepped forward from a crowd and freely unburdened himself of his views: "When [the challenger] said he had never been to a restaurant, I believe him. There should be no more banquets for superiors who come to town. We end up paying for that."

Another villager then chimed in: "They are making government smaller in Beijing. They must do that here too. ... And he's right, we have to have a fiber-optic cable in here. We have no phones."

How do you know about fiber optics? I asked the villager.

"I don't know." He shrugged. "I just heard about it."

I got a similar response at a neighboring village, Heng Dao, where we also went to listen to campaign speeches. The incumbent, Jiang Ying, told his villagers: "I have tried to be very pragmatic in leading the village on the road to wealth. Our annual income is now 2,300 yuan per year. The budget is much smaller and during my tenure we've gotten many cadres off the village payroll. If elected, we need to introduce more science and technology into agriculture, get more enterprises here and speed up procedures for generating wealth ... [because] the whole world is turning into one big market for merchandise."

I asked him where he got such ideas. The village has only one phone. He answered: "I read newspapers. I listen to radio. ... We have a window-frame factory here. Right now we only sell locally, but we were told that if we improve the quality, we can sell abroad, make more money."

So globalization isn't global, eh?

Don't believe it for a second. Tip O'Neill was wrong. All politics isn't local—not anymore. All politics is now global. Not every country may feel itself part of the globalization system, but every country is directly or indirectly being shaped and affected by this system. And that is why it is not a historical accident that East Germany, the Soviet Union, Asian capitalism, Brazilian state-owned industries, Chinese communism, General Motors and IBM all either collapsed or were forced to radically restructure at roughly the same time. They all got hit with the same basic disease that brought down the Berlin Wall and all the other walls that defined the Cold War. They all got hit with a disease I call Microchip Immune Deficiency Syndrome, or MIDS. Microchip Immune Deficiency Syndrome is the defining political disease of the globalization era. It can strike any company or country, large or small, East or West, North or South. If I were writing the entry in a medical dictionary for Microchip Immune Deficiency Syndrome, it would read as follows:

"MIDS: A disease that can afflict any bloated, overweight, sclerotic system in the post–Cold War era. MIDS is usually contracted by countries and companies that fail to inoculate themselves against changes brought about by the microchip, and the democratizations of technology, finance and information—which created a much faster, more open and more complex marketplace, with a whole new set of efficiencies. The symptoms of MIDS appear when a country or company exhibits a consistent inability to increase productivity, wages, living standards, knowledge use and competitiveness, and becomes too slow to respond to the challenges of the Fast World. Countries and companies with MIDS tend to be those run on Cold War corporate models—where one or a few people at the top hold all the information and make all the decisions, and all the people in the middle and the bottom simply carry out those decisions, using only the information they need to know to do their jobs. The only known cure for countries and companies with MIDS is 'the fourth democratization.' This is the democratization of decision-making and information flows, and the deconcentration of power, in ways that allow more people in a country or company to share knowledge, experiment and innovate faster. This enables them to keep up with a marketplace in which consumers are constantly demanding cheaper products and services tailored specifically for them. MIDS can be fatal to those companies and countries that do not get appropriate treatment in time. (See entries for *Soviet Union, East Germany* and *Pan Am*.)"

At some level there is nothing new about the basic concept of MIDS. Market economies have thrived over centuries by brutally killing off those firms that are less efficient, less able to adapt to new technologies and less able to remain in touch with the changing demands of consumers and to meet those demands with the minimum use of labor and capital. But what the democratizations of technology, finance and information did was put this process into hyperspeed in the 1980s, requiring companies and countries to move much faster in order to avoid contracting MIDS. Think of it as a three-stage evolution:

It began in the era before microprocessors and microchips made possible the personal computer and before the personal computer made possible the democratizations of technology, finance and information. This was an era that began with the end of World War I and lasted until the late 1970s. It was a time when both governments and corporations could be more lumbering and less efficient, because everyone was operating in a more protected game. As Alan Greenspan once described this restrictive Cold War system in a speech:

"Adjustments were slower. International trade comprised a far smaller share of domestic economies. Tariff walls [restricted] competition, and capital controls often constrained cross-border currency flows. In retrospect, [this] economic environment appeared less competitive, more tranquil and certainly less threatening to those with only moderate or lesser skills. Indeed, before computer technology automated many repetitive tasks, the unskilled were able to contribute significant value-added and earn a respectable wage relative to the skilled. In this less demanding world, governments were able to construct social safety nets and engage in policies intended to redistribute income."

To be sure, added Greenspan, average standards of living were less than they could have been in this walled-up Cold War system, and the choice of products in the market was far less sensitive to changing consumer tastes than in today's microchip-based environment. The huge barriers to entry from one business to another guaranteed that change evolved much more leisurely, and it took much longer for a country or company to get into trouble. Even though both labor and product costs in those days were higher and less flexible than they needed to be, a significant portion of every society today looks back on this slower, less competitive Stone Age with a warm glow of nostalgia.

The most egregious example of this more controlled economic environment was the centrally planned, centrally controlled, top-down-directed economy of the Soviet Union. The purpose of the Soviet economy was not to meet the demands of consumers, but to reinforce the control of the central government. So all information flowed up and all orders flowed down. At a Soviet company that made bed frames the managers were paid by the central government not according to how many bed frames they sold, but on the basis of how much steel they consumed. The number of bed frames sold is a measure of consumer satisfaction. The amount of steel produced and used is a measure of state power. In the Cold War, the Soviet Union was only interested in the latter. And as long as the Cold War lasted, and the pace of change and information flows were controlled, the Soviets could get away with such an absurd system.

I will never forget a trip I took with Secretary of State Baker in 1992 to visit Chelyabinsk-70, the Soviet nuclear-bomb-designing complex located east of the Urals—a place so secret it was never registered on official Soviet maps. This was Russia's Los Alamos, home to its top nuclear scientists. What I remember most, though, was that we stayed overnight in nearby Sverdlovsk, at the October Hotel, and when I got in the elevator I noticed that the buttons read: 1, 3, 4, 5, 6, 7, 8, 9, 2. Someone forgot the second-floor button and then just tacked it on later. When you pressed the 2 button you went to the second floor—even though it was in the 10 spot. This was a hotel in the Soviet Union's most sophisticated military industrial complex! Only in a divided, chopped up, slowed-down, regulated Cold War system could the Russians get away with an elevator with the floor buttons out of sequence.

IBM in the 1970s and 1980s was a lot like Gosplan, the Soviet central planning system, with the top telling the bottom what the right products should be and what the customers should want. I once asked John Chambers, president of Cisco Systems, what it was like working for IBM in its Gosplan days. Chambers said that when he was at IBM in the early 1980s, it supposedly had an "open door" policy, whereby any employee could raise any question with any executive at any level and if he didn't like the answer he got he could go to the next higher level. "I tried that once," recalled Chambers, "and one of my friends in the company took me aside and said to me, 'You got away with it this time, but don't do it again.' At one point I told one of my superiors that the product line they were pushing would not be accepted by our customers and we would have to use up an enormous amount of resources to move it, but he didn't want to hear it. He said to me, 'I have my bonus riding on that, so go out and sell a lot of them.' "

IBM was safe as long as the barriers to entry into something as complex as the computer business were so high that the big, slow firms could be protected from mistakes, even failure, for a long time. And countries such as the Soviet Union were safe as long as the barriers to information were so high—and the awareness by its own people of competing lifestyles was so low—that the big, slow Kremlin could be protected from its mistakes, even failures, for a long time.

... And then came the 1980s.

The second stage in the evolution of MIDS as a disease came about with the destruction of this slow-moving world. At both the corporate and government levels, the democratizations of technology, finance and information started to converge in the late 1980s and created amazing new efficiencies and economies of scale in the marketplace, as well as a whole new place to do business, called cyberspace. This transformation became known as the Information Revolution. It will be seen in time as one of those great leaps forward in technology that occur every one hundred years, such as the discovery of electricity, which triggered a fundamental break from the previous era.

There are many ways to sum up what the Information Revolution and the three democratizations did to the marketplace. But for me it comes down to two simple concepts: First, it greatly lowered the barriers to entry into almost every business, by radically lowering the costs for new entrants. And, by doing so, it radically increased competition and the speed by which a product moved from being an innovation to being a commodity. Second, by lowering the barriers around companies, the Information Revolution also brought them closer to their customers, giving consumers much greater power to communicate their choices and to move quickly from companies that won't deliver them to companies that will.

Let's look at this in detail. The three democratizations lowered the barriers to entry because with a single personal computer, credit card, phone line, modem, color printer, Internet link, Web site and Federal Express delivery account, anyone could sit in the basement and start his or her own publishing house, retail outlet, catalogue business, global design or consulting firm, newspaper, advertising agency, distribution business, brokerage firm, gambling casino, video store, bank, bookstore, auto sales market or clothing showroom. And it could be done overnight at very low cost, and the company could become a global competitor by the next morning. You could be living on a block with three bookstores—Barnes & Noble, Crown Books and Borders—and practically overnight you could be giving them all a run for their money by creating "Borderless Books" in cyberspace by the name of Amazon.com. Amazon.com was created out of the democratization of technology (home computers for all), the democratization of finance (credit cards for all) and the democratization of information (the Internet for all) to become not just a neighborhood bookstore tailored to the specific buying habits of a community, but a twenty-four-hour-a-day bookstore, where you can shop anytime and the whole store is dedicated just to you.

When this sort of thing starts to happen across the American economy and across the world, it means that any product or service can be transformed, much more quickly, from being an innovation—that only one or two players can produce and that has a high-value-added component and fat profit margins—to being a commodity. A commodity is any product, service or process that can be provided by any number of firms, and the only distinguishing feature among these firms is who can do it cheapest. Having your product or service turned into a commodity is no fun, because it means your profit margins will become razor thin, you will have dozens of competitors and all you can do is make that product or service cheaper and sell more of it than the next guy, every day, or die.

In the walled-up Cold War system this process of going from innovation to commoditization happened at 10 miles per hour, because the barriers to entry into businesses were generally much higher and the barriers countries could erect around their economies were also much higher. In the globalization world, with the barriers now lowered or removed, this process is happening at 110 miles per hour. And as we evolve to an economy that will be increasingly defined by the Internet, the move from innovation to commoditization is going to reach Net speed, which is as fast as the speed of light. It isn't for nothing that Webheads like to say that competition on the Internet is like "Darwinism on steroids."

This is because the Internet offers the closest thing to a perfectly competitive market in the world today, explained Edward Yardeni, chief economist for Deutsche Bank. In the model of perfect competition, he noted, "there are no barriers to entry, no protection from failure for unprofitable firms, and everyone (consumers and producers) has easy and free access to all information. These just happen to be the three main characteristics of Internet commerce. ... The Internet lowers the cost of comparison shopping to zero. Increasingly, the consumer can easily and quickly find the lowest price for any good or service. In the cyber-economy, the low-cost producer will offer the lowest price and provide this information at no cost to any and all potential customers anywhere on the planet." In the low-tech economy, notes Yardeni, the cost of searching for the lowest price was relatively high. You had to climb over all sorts of walls and travel all sorts of distances to get the best deal, and this gave a built-in advantage to local or well-established companies and stores. Now manufacturers, service providers and retailers anywhere in the world can bid for business anywhere in the world, and consumers can seek out the lowest price anywhere in the world. In the past, companies made money by depending on the consumer's lack of information and lack of the technology to track it down. The Internet changes that forever. Any business that thinks it can survive by maintaining an information imbalance between buyers and sellers is fooling itself.

That's why it is going to be wonderful to be a consumer in the age of the Internet and it's going to be hell on wheels to be a seller or manufacturer. To some extent, every successful product business is going to have to become a service business. That is, every product business needs to learn to use technology to cut its costs, streamline its operations and speed up its innovation cycle so that it can play to that other feature of the Information Revolution—the ability of consumers to demand products tailored to their own personal needs. Human beings are collections of skin and bones, not digits, and therefore they will always crave, and pay a little more for, the human touch and the service or product tailored just for them. Therefore, every company now needs to use the Internet not just to improve its own business operations as an end in itself, but so that it will have more time, energy and money to tailor more products to more customers, because it is the tailored product and the personal touch that can never be commoditized. Therefore, the tailored product and human touch will always be able to earn a premium return.

Look at the brokerage business. You may think that being a stockbroker is a high-value-added service, which should pay a handsome salary. But when fifty online Internet brokerage sites suddenly appear in cyberspace and enable all your clients to buy and sell stocks for a fraction of what Merrill Lynch charges, and also give them market analyses online for free, your stockbroker's basic trading job has just been turned into a commodity. If you want to survive as a broker you are going to have to learn to use technology to understand the individual needs and demands of your customers better, learn to market them a wider array of products than just stocks and bonds and, finally, get smarter as a broker so that you can offer them real value-added service in the form of advice and judgment. Merrill Lynch will have to charge less and less for stock transactions, now that the barriers to entry into its business have collapsed with online brokerage. But it can survive if it can provide high-touch, personal advice for navigating the global market place. *That* people will always pay for.

When the barriers to entry to your business start to fall this dramatically, you simply never know where your next competitor might come from. Because when the walls fall we are all increasingly in one another's business. Let me give a real-life example of this new world: One day I was flipping through a newsmagazine and I saw an ad for a new Sony digital camera system. So the first thing I said to myself was: "Wait a minute, did that ad say *Sony*? Sony was never in the camera and film business. I thought they made stereos, Walkmans and CDs." Well, yes, they do. But what is a CD? It is just a round piece of plastic coded with digits that are read by a light beam and turned into music. When you look at it that way, Sony is in the digits business, and with its digital know-how Sony can be in any business that can be converted into digits. Which brings me back to the ad for Sony's digital Mavica camera. The ad contained three pictures: The first was of the camera, which takes snapshots like your old Instamatic, only it records them digitally. Above the camera, the ad copy read: "This is your camera." Next to the camera was a 3.5-inch Sony floppy diskette. Above this diskette was written the words: "This is your film." And next to the diskette was a computer with a picture of a baby on the screen. Above the computer were the words: "This is your post office."

Now think about this ad and what it was saying. It was saying that someone back at Sony headquarters woke up one morning and said to themselves, "Hey, what are we? We're just a big factory for digitizing stuff. It happens that all these years we've been digitizing music. But, hey, what the heck, if we can digitize anything, why don't we digitize your baby pictures too? Why don't we be Sony *and* Kodak? Because with our digital camera you can take digital pictures, store them on a diskette, edit them on a computer and then just print them out on your own printer." Then someone down in Sony's shipping and receiving office said, "Hey, while we're digitizing these baby pictures, we could also be E-mailing them around the world. Because once they are digitized our customers can edit them on their computers and then send them on modems to the grandparents on different continents. So we can be Sony. We can be Kodak. And we can be Federal Express—all at the same time."

After seeing that ad, I said to myself: "I wonder how the folks at Kodak feel about this?" But then I was listening to the radio and heard an ad for Kodak, promoting all its new online computerized photo technology. Kodak seemed to be talking as though it had turned itself into a personal computer company, which also developed film. That made me wonder how the folks at Compaq and Dell felt about Kodak talking like a computer company. But then I saw some ads for Compaq and Dell, and they were both boasting that they weren't just selling computers anymore—those are a commodity. They were now selling "business solutions" through computers, for whatever problem your company or country needed to solve. They each were presenting themselves as business consulting firms, who happen to sell computers.

Indeed, Compaq's ads often didn't even show pictures of their computers, they just said: "Compaq—better answers." Well, that made me wonder about a friend of mine who worked for PricewaterhouseCoopers. I had seen advertisements for his firm—an accounting-consulting giant—which said the firm was now providing business solutions and better answers, not just preparing tax returns. So I asked my friend if he was worried about competition from Compaq and Dell in the business-consulting world? My friend told me that his firm wasn't afraid of the PC companies, but they were worried about the fact that Goldman Sachs, the investment bank, was now offering tax-saving solutions, in the form of newly tailored tax derivatives. PricewaterhouseCoopers now has to worry that investment bankers are going to move into its tax-consulting business. My friend suggested I read something on the subject, so I figured I'd go over to Borders Books and try to find some literature, but my wife said she never goes to the bookstore anymore, because we have Amazon.com—"borderless books"—right in our basement now. So I went downstairs and clicked up Amazon.com and found that not only was it a bookstore, but it was also selling CDs. So I said to myself, "Hey, wasn't that Sony's business?"

This led me to wonder what all of this would mean for the marketing of this book you're reading. So I went up to New York and addressed the sales force of Farrar, Straus and Giroux, the publishers of the hardcover edition, and I was seated next to Mark Gates, one of the company's top sales reps. We started talking about the book business and Gates was clearly upset. Why? He told me: "I just went into Brooks Brothers to look for a suit. So I go into the suit department and I see on one of the tables a stack of Michael Jordan's latest book, *For the Love of the Game*. It's on sale in the Brooks Brothers men's department, displayed on a pile of suits! So I go over to the salesman and say to him: 'You're not a bookstore. How would you like it if I told my bookstores they should start selling suits?' He laughed. He was a little embarrassed, but then he says to me: 'Have you looked at your electricity bill lately? Consolidated Edison has a special on for the Christmas holidays. They are offering the Jordan book at forty percent off and you can just charge it to your electric bill and they will mail it to you!' I really got depressed. I am forty-six years old. I don't plan to retire for nineteen years. But I'm asking myself now whether I will have any accounts in nineteen years. In my heart of hearts, I don't think so. All the lines are getting blurred now."

The New York Times ran a headline around this time which really stuck in my mind. It was about how AT&T was branching out into all sorts of new business, and the headline read: "AT&T: Ma Everything." Everyone today seems to be either becoming a niche, boutique player or Ma Everything. Everyone now is in everyone else's business.

No wonder then that the first to get hit with Microchip Immune Deficiency Syndrome in this era were the most top-heavy, overweight, slow systems like the Soviet Union and IBM, who, in a world without walls, completely lost touch with its customers and simply couldn't keep up with the speed of change in the marketplace at large. Next to catch the virus were the next closest things to Soviet central planning—the heavily state-controlled economies of Latin America, the most bloated welfare systems of Canada and Western Europe and the most overly centralized, slow-moving corporations of North America. By the late 1990s, the MIDS virus had spread to Asia and struck the top-heavy, state-directed economies of Indonesia, Malaysia, Thailand, China and even South Korea and Japan.

"I always felt that it was surely no accident that communism, planning ministries and corporate conglomerates all ran into great difficulties in the same era," Deputy Treasury Secretary Larry Summers once remarked to me, "because with the PC and the microchip it became much more efficient to empower individuals who could get more information and make more decisions themselves rather than having a single person at the top trying to direct everything."

The Buck Starts Here

The latest stage in this MIDS evolution is the one we are now in. It is the era of globalization in which governments and companies are either restructuring themselves in order to take advantage of the three democratizations, or failing to do so and finally succumbing to MIDS. It is in this stage that we see the fourth democratization—that of decision-making and the deconcentration of power and information—being used as the main technique to ward off or recover from MIDS.

To understand what I mean by the democratization of decision-making and the deconcentration of power and information, think again of the most extreme case, the former Soviet Union. Because the Soviet system was built for the sole purpose of control, it centralized all the main functions of leadership. It centralized decision-making—all decisions were made at the top and the top told you what to think, what to make, what to aspire to and what to like. It centralized information—all information flowed to the top and only the top few people had a complete picture of what was going on. And it centralized strategy—all strategic decisions about where the country was headed were made at the top.

What the democratization of decision-making and deconcentration of power does is to take a centrally controlled system like this, loosen it up and redefine the center so that decision-making and information flow both top-down and bottom-up. Each successful company or country will reorganize its center a little bit differently, depending on its marketplace, geography, population and level of development. Dell Computer now centralizes all of its billing, inventory management and distribution of computers for its European operations by having them flow through a single call center in Ireland. It is centralizing certain functions not for the purpose of control but to take advantage of new cost-saving efficiencies. At the same time, Dell has decentralized a lot of other decision-making to its individual sales and service centers in each European country, because each of these centers is closer to its customers, can tailor its services to their particular needs and tastes and can quickly adapt to any changes.

In today's hyperspeed, enormously complex globalization system, most of the information needed to answer most of the problems now rests in the hands of people on the outer edges of organizations, not at the center. And if your country or company has not democratized decision-making and deconcentrated power to enable these people to use and share their knowledge, it is going to be at a real disadvantage. As Warren Bennis, in his book *Organizing Genius,* puts it: "None of us is as smart as all of us."

One way to summarize this shift is to think of the sign that used to sit on the desk of every American leader or executive. It said: "The Buck Stops Here." That was a plausible motto during the Cold War since all information flowed to the top so that all decisions could flow down from the top, and the marketplace was slow enough to wait for one person. But today the best CEOs will be those who understand that their job is to chart the broad corporate strategies, to establish the broad corporate culture, to get the balls rolling on the right paths and then let those closest to the customers and to the rapidly changing marketplace manage those balls on their own.

Therefore the sign on the desk of the successful CEO in the era of globalization will not be "The Buck Stops Here." It will be "The Buck Starts Here." I, the boss, set the broad strategies, I keep everyone connected on the same path, I get the balls rolling, but you, the employees, gather the information, share it and make as many of the decisions as you can, quickly and close to the market.

6: The Golden Straitjacket

"We're still very much in a straitjacket for the next year or two. The new government will have to be quite careful."

—Umar Juoro, economic adviser to former Indonesian Prime Minister B.J. Habibie, describing to *The New York Times* how little room to maneuver the Indonesian government has on the economic front, because if it does anything rash it will get hammered by the IMF and the global markets. October 23, 1999.

While I was on that trip monitoring elections in Chinese villages and my interpreter and I were wandering through the village of Heng Dao, we dropped in on a farmer-turned-mechanic who had geese and pigs in the front yard, but a stereo and color television inside his brick hut. My interpreter, a Chinese student who was studying in America, noticed something I never would have—that there didn't seem to be any loudspeaker around. During Mao's day the Communist Party installed loudspeakers in the "brigades," as small villages were known, and used them to blare out propaganda and other messages exhorting the workers. We asked our host what happened to it.

"We took it down last year," the villager said of the loudspeaker. "No one wanted to listen to it anymore. We have stereo and TV now." What the villager didn't say was that he didn't need to hear the message from Beijing and the Communist Party anymore, because he knew what it was and it wasn't the teachings of Chairman Mao. The only message coming from them was much simpler: "You're on your own. Get a job. Send money."

A few months earlier I had been in Thailand, watching Thailand's crony capitalist economy going into a tailspin. I had arranged to interview Sirivat Voravetvuthikun, a Thai real estate developer who had gone bankrupt in the Thai economic crash. He and his wife had become the poster children for the Thai crash, because they had decided to go into the sandwich-selling business to make ends meet. This once-wealthy couple rented out some vacant space in downtown Bangkok, set up a sandwich-making operation with many of their former employees and started

delivering fresh ham-and-cheese around the streets of Bangkok. Sirivat arrived at
our interview carrying a yellow picnic box strapped around his neck like a sandwich
vendor at an American baseball game. What I remembered most about our conversation, though, was the absence of bitterness in his voice, and the much more pungent
air of resignation. His message was that Thailand had messed up. People knew it.
They would now have to tighten their belts and get with the program and there wasn't
much else to say. Wasn't he mad? I asked. Didn't he want to burn down some government building in anger at being wiped out?

No, Sirivat explained to me: "Communism fails, socialism fails, so now there is only
capitalism. We don't want to go back to the jungle, we all want a better standard of living, so you have to make capitalism work, because you don't have a choice. We have to
improve ourselves and follow the world rules. … Only the competitive survive. It will
probably require a national unity government, because the burden is so big."

A few months after this I attended a lecture in Washington by Anatoly Chubais,
the architect of Russia's failed economic reforms and privatization. Chubais had come
to Washington to make a last-ditch appeal to the IMF for more aid to Russia, but at
the time the still-communist-dominated Russian Duma, or parliament, was resisting
the IMF's conditions. The Duma was also regularly denouncing Chubais as a traitor
and foreign agent for submitting to IMF demands that Russia radically reform its
economy along real free-market lines. I asked Chubais how he answered his critics,
and he told me: " 'O.K.,' I tell them, 'Chubais is a spy for the CIA and IMF. But what
is your substitute? Do you have [any alternative] workable ideas?' " Chubais said he
never gets any coherent answer, because the communists have no alternative.

I was in Brazil a few months later, where I interviewed Fabio Feldmann, the former
environmental secretary of São Paulo and a federal deputy in the Brazilian parliament, who was campaigning for reelection in São Paulo. His office was a beehive of
campaign workers, awash in posters and other campaign paraphernalia. Feldmann
is a liberal, and I asked him about the nature of the political debate in Brazil today.
He responded: "The [ideological] left in Brazil have lost their flag. The challenge of
the federal government is jobs and employment. You have to generate *and* distribute
income. And what is the program of the left? They don't have proposals to generate
income, only to distribute it."

What are these stories telling us? Once the three democratizations came together
in the late 1980s and blew away all the walls, they also blew away all the major ideological alternatives to free-market capitalism. People can talk about alternatives to
the free market and global integration, they can demand alternatives, they can insist
on a "Third Way," but for now none is apparent. This is very different from the first
era of globalization. During the nineteenth and early twentieth centuries, when the
Industrial Revolution and global finance capitalism roared through Europe and
America, many people were shocked by their Darwinian brutality and "dark Satanic
mills." They destroyed old orders and hierarchies, produced huge income gaps and
put everyone under pressure, but they also produced sharply rising standards of living
for those who could make a go of it. This experience triggered a great deal of debate
and revolutionary theorizing, as people tried to find ways to cushion workers from
the crudest aspects of free-market capitalism in that day. As Karl Marx and Friedrich
Engels described this era in *The Communist Manifesto:* "Constant revolutionizing of

production, uninterrupted disturbance of all social conditions, everlasting uncertainty and agitation distinguish the bourgeois epoch from all earlier ones. All fixed, fast-frozen relations, with their train of ancient and venerable prejudices and opinions, are swept away, all new-formed ones become antiquated before they can ossify. All that is solid melts into air, all that is holy is profaned, and man is at last compelled to face with sober senses, his real conditions of life, and his relations with his kind."

Eventually, people came along who declared that they could take these destabilizing, brutalizing swings out of the free market, and create a world that would never be dependent on unfettered bourgeois capitalists. They would have the government centrally plan and fund everything, and distribute to each worker according to his needs and expect from each worker a contribution according to his abilities. The names of these revolutionary thinkers were Engels, Marx, Lenin and Mussolini, among others. The centrally planned, nondemocratic alternatives they offered—communism, socialism and fascism—helped to abort the first era of globalization as they were tested out on the world stage from 1917 to 1989.

There is only one thing to say about those alternatives: *They didn't work.* And the people who rendered that judgment were the people who lived under them. So with the collapse of communism in Europe, in the Soviet Union and in China—and all the walls that protected these systems—those people who are unhappy with the Darwinian brutality of free-market capitalism don't have any ready ideological alternative now. When it comes to the question of which system today is the most effective at generating rising standards of living, the historical debate is over. The answer is free-market capitalism. Other systems may be able to distribute and divide income more efficiently and equitably, but none can generate income to distribute as efficiently as free-market capitalism. And more and more people now know that. So, ideologically speaking, there is no more mint chocolate chip, there is no more strawberry swirl and there is no more lemon-lime. Today there is only free-market vanilla and North Korea. There can be different brands of free-market vanilla and you can adjust your society to it by going faster or slower. But, in the end, if you want higher standards of living in a world without walls, the free market is the only ideological alternative left. One road. Different speeds. But one road.

When your country recognizes this fact, when it recognizes the rules of the free market in today's global economy, and decides to abide by them, it puts on what I call the Golden Straitjacket. The Golden Straitjacket is the defining political-economic garment of this globalization era. The Cold War had the Mao suit, the Nehru jacket, the Russian fur. Globalization has only the Golden Straitjacket. If your country has not been fitted for one, it will be soon.

The Golden Straitjacket first began to be stitched together and popularized in 1979 by British Prime Minister Margaret Thatcher—who, as the original seamstress of the Golden Straitjacket, will go down in history as one of the great revolutionaries of the second half of the twentieth century. That Thatcherite coat was soon reinforced by Ronald Reagan in the United States in the 1980s, giving the straitjacket, and its rules, some real critical mass. It became a global fashion with the end of the Cold War, once the three democratizations blew away all the alternative fashions and all the walls that protected them. The Thatcherite–Reaganite revolutions came about because popular majorities in these two major Western economies concluded that the old government-directed economic approaches simply were not providing sufficient levels of growth. Thatcher and Reagan combined to strip huge chunks of economic decision-making power from the state, from the advocates of the Great Society and from traditional Keynesian economics, and hand them over to the free market.

To fit into the Golden Straitjacket a country must either adopt, or be seen as moving toward, the following golden rules: making the private sector the primary engine of its economic growth, maintaining a low rate of inflation and price stability, shrinking the size of its state bureaucracy, maintaining as close to a balanced budget as possible, if not a surplus, eliminating and lowering tariffs on imported goods, removing restrictions on foreign investment, getting rid of quotas and domestic monopolies, increasing exports, privatizing state-owned industries and utilities, deregulating capital markets, making its currency convertible, opening its industries, stock and bond markets to direct foreign ownership and investment, deregulating its economy to promote as much domestic competition as possible, eliminating government corruption, subsidies and kickbacks as much as possible, opening its banking and telecommunications systems to private ownership and competition and allowing its citizens to choose from an array of competing pension options and foreign-run pension and mutual funds. When you stitch all of these pieces together you have the Golden Straitjacket.

Unfortunately, this Golden Straitjacket is pretty much "one size fits all." So it pinches certain groups, squeezes others and keeps a society under pressure to constantly streamline its economic institutions and upgrade its performance. It leaves people behind quicker than ever if they shuck it off, and it helps them catch up quicker than ever if they wear it right. It is not always pretty or gentle or comfortable. But it's here and it's the only model on the rack this historical season.

As your country puts on the Golden Straitjacket, two things tend to happen: your economy grows and your politics shrinks. That is, on the economic front the Golden Straitjacket usually fosters more growth and higher average incomes—through more trade, foreign investment, privatization and more efficient use of resources under the pressure of global competition. But on the political front, the Golden Straitjacket narrows the political and economic policy choices of those in power to relatively tight parameters. That is why it is increasingly difficult these days to find any real differences between ruling and opposition parties in those countries that have put on the Golden Straitjacket. Once your country puts it on, its political choices get reduced to Pepsi or Coke—to slight nuances of taste, slight nuances of policy, slight alterations in design to account for local traditions, some loosening here or there, but never any major deviation from the core golden rules. Governments—be they led by Democrats or Republicans, Conservatives or Labourites, Gaullists or Socialists, Christian Democrats or Social Democrats—that deviate too far from the core rules will see their investors stampede away, interest rates rise and stock market valuations fall. The only way to get more room to maneuver in the Golden Straitjacket is by enlarging it, and the only way to enlarge it is by keeping it on tight. That's its one virtue: the tighter you wear it, the more gold it produces and the more padding you can then put into it for your society.

No wonder so much of the political debate in developed countries today has been reduced to arguments over minor tailoring changes in the Golden Straitjacket, not radical alterations. When it came to economics, how much of a difference was there really between Bill Clinton and Bob Dole in the 1996 American presidential election? On broad economic issues, very little. Clinton essentially said, "We're in this Golden Straitjacket, but I have a way we can put a little more padding in the elbows and enlarge the middle a bit." And Dole said in effect, "No, no, you can't loosen the middle at all. Keep it on tight and we'll put a little less padding in the elbows." But they were really discussing the buttonholes on a jacket neither of them intended to alter very much—and they were hardly alone. In the 1997 British election campaign Tony Blair vowed in essence that if he won, "We'll keep the Golden Straitjacket on as tight as the Tories, but we'll add some padding to the shoulders and the chest," while his opponent, Conservative John Major, seemed to retort, "Don't you dare touch a thread on that jacket. Margaret Thatcher designed it to be snug and by God that's the way it should stay." No wonder Paddy Ashdown, the leader of Britain's Liberal Party, looked at Tony Blair and John Major during the 1997 British election, listened to their respective platforms and then declared that there was not a whit of difference between them. Ashdown sneered that Blair and Major were engaged in "synchronized swimming."

With the fall of the Cold War walls, and the rise of the Golden Straitjacket, I see a lot of synchronized swimming when I travel the world these days. Before the 1998 German elections, in which Social Democrat Gerhard Schroeder defeated Christian Democrat Helmut Kohl, the Associated Press quoted Karl-Josef Meiers of the German Society for Foreign Affairs as saying of the two German candidates: "You can forget the labels right and left. They're all sitting in the same boat." Korea's Lee Hong Koo learned firsthand about life in the Golden Straitjacket when he served as his country's Prime Minister in the mid-1990s. "In the old days we used to say, 'History dictated this or that,'" Lee remarked to me one day. "Now we say that 'market forces' dictate this and you have to live within [those forces]. It took us time to understand what had happened. We didn't realize that the victory of the Cold War was a victory for market forces above politics. The big decisions today are whether you have a democracy or not and whether you have an open economy or not. Those are the big choices. But once you've made those big choices, politics becomes just political engineering to implement decisions in the narrow space allowed you within this system." Lee was raised in Korea's long-dominant Grand National Party. But after Korea's economic meltdown in 1997–98, when the country found it had to put on the Golden Straitjacket much more snugly if it was to continue to thrive and attract foreign investment, the Korean public spurned the veteran, old-style Korean politicians and elected longtime liberal human rights advocate Kim Dae Jung as President, from the opposition National Congress for New Politics. But Kim asked Lee to go to Washington to be his ambassador anyway. As Lee told me: "It would have been unthinkable in the past that someone like myself, who was a presidential candidate from my party and former Prime Minister and party chairman, would go to Washington as an ambassador from another party, like President Kim's. But now, with what Korea has to do to get out of this economic crisis, the differences between me and Mr. Kim are insignificant. We don't have a lot of choices." How do you say "same boat" or "synchronized swimming" in Korean?

Manmohan Singh was India's Finance Minister when his country decided in 1991 to abandon decades of statist, quasi-socialist economics and don the Golden Straitjacket. Sitting in his office in the Indian Parliament in the summer of 1998, he spoke to me of the loss of control he felt once India embarked on this route.

"We learned that there were advantages to having access to international capital markets, [but] the government's ability to deliver and control shrank the more it opened to the world. If you are operating in a globalized economy, perceptions of other participants matter much more—whether they are right or wrong. Then you have to take those perceptions and make them an important input into your decision-making. … We have a world where our fates are linked, but [India's specific] concerns and aspirations don't get taken into account. It brings a lot more anxiety. If you are operating an exchange-rate policy, or monetary policy, your policies become an adjunct of what Alan Greenspan does. It reduces your degree of freedom, even in fiscal policies. In a world in which capital is internationally mobile, you cannot adopt rates of taxation that are far from the rates that prevail in other countries and when labor is mobile you also can't be out of line with others' wages. It has reduced the amount of maneuverability. … I have a friend from a neighboring country who also became a finance minister. The day he got his job I called to congratulate him. He said, 'Don't congratulate me. I am only half a minister. The other half is in Washington.' "

Not every country puts on the Golden Straitjacket all the way—some just go partway or a little at a time (India, Egypt). Some put it on and take it off (Malaysia, Russia). Some try to tailor it to their specific culture and wear a few of the buttons unfastened (Germany, Japan and France). Some think they can resist its pinch altogether because they have a natural resource such as oil (Iran, Saudi Arabia). And some are so poor and isolated, with a government able to force people to accept being poor, that they can get away with dressing their people not in a Golden Straitjacket, but in a plain old straitjacket (North Korea, Cuba, Sudan, Afghanistan). But over time, this Golden Straitjacket is becoming harder and harder for countries to avoid.

Often, when I make this point to non-Americans, I get some version of the following reaction: "Don't tell us we have to put on a straitjacket and plug into the global markets. We have our own culture, our own values, and we will do it our own way at our own pace. Your thesis is way too deterministic. Why can't we all just get together and agree on a different, less restrictive model?"

To which I answer the following: "I am not saying that you have to put on the straitjacket. And if your culture and social traditions are opposed to the values embodied in that jacket, I certainly sympathize with that But I am saying this: Today's global market system, the Fast World and the Golden Straitjacket were produced by large historical forces that have fundamentally reshaped how we communicate, how we invest and how we see the world. If you want to resist these changes, that is your business. And it should be your business. But if you think that you can resist these changes without paying an increasingly steep price, without building an increasingly high wall and without falling behind increasingly fast, men you are deluding yourself."

Here's why: The democratizations of finance, technology and information didn't just blow away all the walls protecting alternative systems—from Mao's little red book to *The Communist Manifesto* to the welfare states of Western Europe to the crony capitalism of Southeast Asia. These three democratizations also gave birth to a new power source in the world—what I call the Electronic Herd.

The Electronic Herd is made up of all the faceless stock, bond and currency traders sitting behind computer screens all over the globe, moving their money around from mutual funds to pension funds to emerging market funds, or trading on the Internet from their basements. And it also consists of the big multinational corporations who now spread their factories around the world, constantly shifting them to the most efficient, low-cost producers. This herd has grown exponentially thanks to the democratizations of finance, technology and information—so much so that today it is beginning to replace governments as the primary source of capital for both companies and countries to grow. Indeed, as countries increasingly have to run balanced budgets to fit into the Golden Straitjacket, their economies become ever more dependent on the Electronic Herd for growth capital. So to thrive in today's globalization system a country not only has to put on the Golden Straitjacket, it has to join this Electronic Herd. The Electronic Herd loves the Golden Straitjacket, because it embodies all the liberal, free-market rules the herd wants to see in a country. Those countries that put on the Golden Straitjacket and keep it on are rewarded by the herd with investment capital. Those that don't put it on are disciplined by the herd—either by the herd avoiding or withdrawing its money from that country.

Moody's Investors Service, Duff & Phelps Credit Rating Co. and Standard & Poor's are the bloodhounds for the Electronic Herd. These credit-rating agencies prowl the world, constantly sniffing over countries. They are supposed to bark loudly when they see a country slipping out of the Golden Straitjacket (although sometimes Moody's and S&P also lose the scent or get caught up in euphorias, as in Southeast Asia, and don't bark until it's too late).

This interaction among the Electronic Herd, nation-states and the Golden Straitjacket is at the center of today's globalization system. I first realized this in February 1995, on the eve of President Clinton's first visit to Canada. I was covering the White House at the time, and in preparation for the President's trip I was keeping an eye out for articles in the *Financial Times* and other papers to see what the Canadians might be talking about in advance of their first visit from the "Man from Hope." I was intrigued to find that they weren't talking about the U.S. President at all. Instead, they were talking about the visit that had just been made to Canada by the "Man from Moody's." Canada's Parliament at the time was debating the country's budget. A team from Moody's had just come to Ottawa and read the riot act to the Canadian Finance Ministry and legislators. The Moody's team told them that if they did not get their deficit-to-GDP ratio more in line with international norms and expectations, Moody's would downgrade their triple-A credit rating, and therefore Canada and every Canadian company would have to pay higher interest rates to borrow abroad. To underscore that point Canada's Finance Ministry issued a statement declaring: "The sheer magnitude of Canada's foreign debt in relation to the size of the economy means that Canada has become excessively vulnerable to the volatile sentiments of global financial markets. We have suffered a tangible loss of economic sovereignty." For those Canadians who might not have gotten the point, Finance Minister Paul Martin put it more bluntly: "We are in hock up to our eyeballs." No, the Canadians were not the least bit interested in the Man from Hope. It was the Man from Moody's, and the Electronic Herd, who had their undivided attention.

Where did this herd come from and how did it become a force so formidable that it could intimidate and enrich nation-states every bit as much as a superpower could?

Abraham Newman and John Zysman,
How Revolutionary Was the Digital Revolution? (2006)*

19: Transforming Politics in the Digital Era

With the rise of digital technology, advanced democracies are in the process of transitioning from industrial to knowledge-based economies. The combination of binary knowledge expression, immense processing power, and digital networks has created the basis for a fundamental shift in economic and political organization domestically and internationally. This digital era holds tremendous opportunity for society and the global economy as new markets, business models, and means of organization emerge. At the same time, however, innovation has an intensely destabilizing effect for broad societal bargains, such as the notion of property, as well as real competitive position, as new entrants take advantage of technology to challenge incumbents. Our concern is how politics shapes this technologically instigated shift in society and the economy.

Borrowing from Karl Polanyi, we employ the metaphor of a second great transformation to drive a discussion about the political economy of the digital era.[1] By great transformation, we mean a fundamental and basic shift in the rules of society that alters the way economy and polity operate. There is one classic example: the great transformation that began in England in the sixteenth century. In this case, the commodification of land, labor, and money by the state defined the establishment of a market society. Before that transformation, markets were more of an adjunct to society. Those early markets, created by traders and burghers, were in a secondary position to landowners. For landlord, peasant, and burgher, position in a politically defined social community defined access to opportunities and to earning income. When the market system was endorsed by the state, it stood these relations on their head. Land and labor became commodities to be bought and sold in the market. Social position could move in relation to what was captured in the market.

Although some technological fanatics have naively downplayed the importance of politics, it is our contention that political actors—government, business interests, and public interest groups—serve an integral role in the evolution of the digital transformations transpiring across the globe. Counter to claims that technology vitiates

---

state power in the international economy, we believe that the state has a critical role to play. Just as in the classic example, governments are actively involved in creating a market for the fictitious commodity of information. The crux of this essay is to use the metaphor of the great transformation to demonstrate how politics shapes and influences the digital era. Governments have acted to mediate the transformation: promoting the technological infrastructure necessary for the digital era, establishing the fictitious commodity of information through intellectual property, and embedding digital markets in social norms. Far from being a neutral intervention, state actions influence the character of the transformation, including its political effects. At the same time, governments have confronted well-organized interest groups that have played an active role in shaping policy outcomes.

This chapter analyzes the politics of the digital transformation in four parts. The first section describes the scope and scale of the technological change in more depth. This is followed by a brief presentation of the naive technologist view that relegates politics to a peripheral role. The third section uses the lens of the great transformation to explore in more detail the means by which the state interacts with digital world. The fourth section offers a set of policy strategies that governments may employ to resolve digital challenges. The fifth section highlights the dynamics of the political process that influence government policy and then presents some thoughts for future research.

The Renewable Revolution

Just as the Industrial Revolution grew out of a revolution in tools and power, the core of the information technology sector is the creation and production of a new tool set, which Steve Cohen, Brad DeLong and John Zysman have termed tools for thought (Cohen, DeLong, and Zysman 2000, 7–8). These tools manipulate, organize, transmit, and store information in digital form, thereby creating a set of information services and products that allow the application of information to industrial as well as machine processes (Weiner 1954). The digital transformation and the tools for thought can be broken down into three fundamental elements:

- *The concept.* Information technology begins with the notion of information as something that can be expressed in binary form (Weiner 1954, 1965; Shannon 1993). Data ranging from supermarket purchases to fingerprints can be represented in digital code.
- *The equipment.* Software consists of written programs, including procedures and rules, that guide how equipment processes information. The hardware, or equipment, that executes the processing instructions has evolved from vacuum tubes through individual silicon transistors to integrated circuits implemented on silicon wafers and may evolve into still other physical manifestations.
- *The networks.* Data networks interlink the processing nodes of individual computers, and the network of networks creates a digital community and society.

Tools for thought create the capabilities to process and distribute digital data, multiplying the scale and speed with which thought and information can be applied. Information Technology (IT) affects economic activity in which information sensing, organizing, processing, or communication is important—in short, every single economic activity.

What seems most significant is that information technology represents not one but a sequence of revolutions. It is a continued and enduring unfolding of digital innovation sustaining a long process of industrial adaptation and transition. The IT revolution is a recurrent one:

> In the 1960s Intel Corporation co-founder Gordon Moore projected that the density of transistors on a silicon chip—and thus the power of a chip—would double every eighteen months. Moore's law, as it came to be called, has held. Today's chips have 256 times the density of those manufactured in 1987—and 65,000 times the density of those of 1975. This continued and continuing every-eighteen-month doubling of semiconductor capability and productivity underpins the revolution in information technology. The increase in semiconductor density means that today's computers have 66,000 times the processing power, at the same cost, as the computers of 1975. In ten years computers will be more than 10 million times more powerful than those of 1975—at the same cost. We now expect—routinely—that today's $1,000 personal computer ordered over the Internet will have the power of a $20,000 scientific workstation of five years ago. And what was once supercomputing is now run-of-the-mill. The past forty years have seen perhaps a billion-fold increase in the installed base of computing power. (Cohen, DeLong, and Zysman 2000, 13–14)

The conventional economic explanation of a leading sector is that the original innovation creates a set of opportunities, somewhat like distributing money on the ground. The original technological revolution loses force as the most valuable opportunities are picked up and implemented. The notion argued in this chapter is, of course, that the revolution is renewed—if not with each cycle of Moore's law, certainly with the radical increases in computing power generated every few years. An original transistor, a single bit, bears little relationship to a 16 kilobit integrated memory chip. A gigabyte chip with a billion transistors is another thing altogether, and it is seven Moore cycles, less than two decades, along the road from the 16k. And Moore's law has at least several more cycles to run. The technological revolution is renewed every decade. The currency is redistributed on the ground as the bills themselves get larger. The fundamental question, then, is how these resources will be distributed.

Putting the State on the Sidelines

With the creation of the Internet, the U.S. and European governments effectively laid the foundation for self-regulating groups. For those early "net" pioneers, it seemed as though the government was an interloper in a system run by technologists for technologists. These technological enthusiasts argued that the architecture of the Internet made it impossible to regulate. The famous claim made by the early Internet advocate John Gilmore that "the Net interprets censorship as damage and routes around it" epitomized the beliefs of many technologists.[2] They viewed cyberspace as beyond the reach of state controls. National governments would be forced to cede much of their regulatory authority to the cybercommunity, eroding traditional notions of sovereignty (Post and Johnson 1996).

The digital era posed a dual challenge to the state. First, IT reduced the costs associated with conducting international business, part of a phenomenon popularly labeled globalization (Weber 2001). Firms that took advantage of digital technology to expand their geographic reach in turn limited the efforts of public officials to manage their economies. Stringent domestic regulations, it was believed, encouraged footloose capital to relocate to more hospitable institutional environments, forcing governments around the globe to engage in a race to the bottom in economic intervention (Tonnelson 2000). State autonomy supposedly fell victim in the digital era to firm mobility (Ohmae 1993).

Second, the decentralized, non-hierarchical character of digital networks was viewed as incompatible with the rigid, inflexible governance tools available to the state. As Virginia Haufler has argued in the case of information privacy, "The decentralized, open, global character of one of the main transmission sources for personal information—the Internet—makes it difficult to design and implement effective regulations through top-down, government-by-government approaches" (2001, 82). The governance problems raised by digital technologies threatened to further erode state autonomy, as nonstate actors were empowered to resolve major societal disputes (Rosenau and Singh 2002). Operating from this perspective, Debora Spar describes a cyberworld of state regulation displaced by industry self-regulation:

> Fundamentally, I argue, governments cannot set the rules of cyberspace. That is because cyberspace, unlike governments, slips seamlessly and nearly unavoidably across national boundaries. ... With governments pushed effectively to the sidelines, firms will have to write and enforce their own rules, creating private networks to facilitate and protect electronic commerce. (1999, 82)

Politicians in the United States relied heavily on the private sector to navigate the first years of the digital era. A chorus of business lobbies argued that government regulation would crush this vital infant industry. The role of the government, if any, was to get out of the way of the sector's development. The Clinton administration did not stray far from these demands, insisting that the government should not interfere with the development of information technology. The administration believed that private sector self-regulatory mechanisms would guarantee the successful construction of information markets. In their 1997 Framework for Global Electronic Commerce, President Clinton and Vice President Gore asserted that "the Administration ... will encourage the creation of private fora to take the lead in areas requiring self-regulation such as privacy, content ratings, and consumer protection and in areas such as standards development, commercial code, and fostering interoperability." Echoing the U.S. view, Europe's then Commissioner for Telecommunications, Martin Bangemann, suggested that business should take the lead in developing an "International Charter for Electronic Commerce" that would rely heavily on "market-led, industry-driven self-regulatory models" (Commission of the European Communities 1998).[3]

Of course, the early notions that the Internet should be free of government, like the mythical Wild West, ignored the fact that western settlements required a local sheriff; they required governments. When the Internet was transferred to the commercial world, those requirements for legal structure in the operation of the network became more evident, more urgent, and the rule making for the Internet became, at least in part, rule making for the economy. The issues were no longer simply technical ones of how to operate the network or communicate across this global network of networks. Suddenly, all the questions of an operating marketplace had to be addressed; appropriate domestic and international rules had to be defined for domains from privacy to taxation. The results of these decisions have real distributional and societal consequences. And states were not about to abdicate this responsibility to private actors. In fact, despite the decentralized, international character of digital networks, governments have played an instrumental role in shaping the character of forming digital societies.

The emergence and evolution of the digital era has not been the product of purely neoliberal strategies, on the one hand, nor of purely interventionist strategies, on the other hand. Governments acted simultaneously to subsidize infrastructure development, extract themselves from direct market control, and forge new rules to promote economic transactions. Framing the role of the state in ideological terms confounds the multitudinous and seemingly contradictory strategies governments undertook. Like all markets, cybermarkets require definitions of property, exchange, and competitive market structure. And all of this requires rules.

The Role of the State in the Digital Transformation

The drama of the great transformation itself was the shift from a traditional society, in which markets fitted within social order and economic activity bowed to the confines of social rules, to a market society, in which land, labor, and capital became commodities moving in response to price signals from the market. That transition was the product of a series of political battles that redefined England, including the enclosures, the Poor Laws, and the repeal of the Corn Laws. Enclosures transformed community public lands into private farming lands, beginning the creation of a market for land. The series of Poor Laws, culminating in the elimination of the Speenhamland system in 1834, created a labor market. The 1834 Poor Law Reform broke the link for survival between individual and local community, making the individual worker's well-being dependent on wages obtained in the labor market. The repeal of the Corn Laws in 1846 opened British agricultural markets, limiting trade protection so that lower-cost grain could feed the emerging industrial workforce. That political decision marked a shift in power from the landed classes to the emerging industrial bourgeoisie (K. Polanyi 1944).

In the contemporary era, as during the Industrial Revolution, the state has played a vital role in the construction of the digital economy through policies of deregulation, market making, and reregulation.[4] This effort has focused around two central questions. First, what are the rules that should underpin new digital markets? As digital technologies diffuse, businesses in industries ranging from financial services to telecommunications search for market advantage. At the same time, these innovations have the potential to disrupt the current distribution of power within a sector and across polities. Incumbents simultaneously see lucrative market potential and economic disruption in digital advances. Market rules, drafted and enforced by the state, fundamentally shape the distribution of economic gains and modulate the extent of the transformation domestically and internationally.

The second question confronting state authorities concerns the implications of new market rules for society more generally. As the digital economy is constructed, decisions about market rules inherently structure information flows, influencing the character of the political community. The state must manage the social externalities that arise in parallel to the digital economy.

The role of the state in the digital debate has a peculiar form, in that the rules of digital information, hence of a digital polity, are embedded not only in convention or in the law, but in the computer code itself (Lessig 1999). Just as highway architecture dictates where you can get on and off the freeway, computer architecture and the code implementing applications dictate what is and isn't possible in a digital era. In the early years of the Internet, the open, user-controlled architecture led to the sense of cyberspace as a domain outside the control of governments or physical communities. Hence Stewart Brand's infamous remark that "information wants to be free" reflected the particular architecture of the early Internet. But that early Internet was only one potential architecture; other, more controlled or more restricted networks are also possible. Digital information wants nothing at all; it flows where the network architecture permits. And network architecture is a product of the code writers. To say that we must regulate the code, hence the code writers, is not to say that there is a single technologically dictated outcome. Although politics is always about values and outcomes, about who gets what, for such choices to have meaning in a digital world they must inevitably be embedded in code and respect the technological logic of the tools for thought. Law and code then interact to establish the rules of the digital era.

At the dawn of the digital era, governments have played a critical part in the creation of the fictitious commodity of information. In this effort, they have used public policy to build the infrastructure for and remove barriers to the new market. Government legislation has shaped the way that information technology has interacted with production patterns, influencing the success of emerging business models and modes of industrial organization. At the same time, state initiatives have been instrumental in navigating the complex political fights that surround the digital transformation.[5] Government legislation is critical in order to embed the new markets in social norms and to limit the inevitable pushback by the losers of the new era. In short, the character of the digital era has been modulated by government interventions. The following section highlights several pathways by which the state has shaped the digital transformation. Chief among these are establishing the digital infrastructure and removing barriers to market evolution, constructing the commodity of information, and embedding new markets in social norms.

Building the Digital Infrastructure and Removing Barriers to New Market Evolution

In Polanyi's England, the government promoted enclosure at the same time it repealed protections that hindered the market's development. Similarly, in the digital era, governments have simultaneously developed the infrastructure for and removed barriers to commodified information markets. In the United States, the creation of the Internet was the product of both purposive intervention—government action by the Defense Department's Advanced Research Projects Agency (DARPA)—and aggressive deregulation and reregulation.

Seeking to promote communication among scientific researchers, DARPA funded the creation of the underlying conception and protocols of the Internet in what was called ARPANET (Hafner and Lyon 1998). This Internet prototype refined the technology necessary to transmit data through packets of information, providing the fundamental architecture of the current Internet. In contrast to telephone lines, which traditionally used switches to directly connect the receiver to the sender, packet switching decomposes information into its components and sends them through the network before recombining them at their destination. The government managed ARPANET through the National Science Foundation, then prepared it for transfer to commercial use.

The government laid the groundwork for the digital era through regulatory reform as well as infrastructure investment. The aggressive introduction of competition in the telecommunications sector, highlighted by but not confined to the break-up of AT&T, unleashed user-led and consumer-based innovation in data networks. Inexpensive local flat-rate fees, for example, gave consumers the ability to experiment with data networking at relatively minimal cost. That opened the way to user-generated networks and facilitated the radical and rapid spread of Internet technology (Hafner and Lyon 1998).

The European story likewise displays these twin roles of the state. Simplified, one part of the story is the deregulation of the telecommunications system led by the European Commission. The Commission created national coalitions for Europe-wide rules that would compel the transformation of state administrations responsible for post and telegraph into regulated companies in at least partly competitive markets.[6] The other side of the story is an array of directed state actions intended to develop and diffuse digital technology. The foundations of the World Wide Web were developed at the Center for Nuclear Research (CERN) in Geneva, Switzerland. A pan-European nuclear physics lab, CERN faced the dilemma of bringing together a geographically very dispersed European nuclear physics community. An information systems scholar from CERN, in response to this organizational demand, developed the architecture of the World Wide Web based on a language for constructing Web pages, the protocol for transmitting these pages, and a browser system for reading the transmitted information. This last innovation resulted in the highly accessible browser system that has facilitated the rapid diffusion of the Web (Gribble 2004).

Government intervention has continued, but taken on a different flavor, with the state-sponsored transition to high-speed broadband connectivity. The reason the original consumer use of the Internet expanded so suddenly was that it could be deployed over the existing telephone infrastructure. However, new uses of the Internet, such as downloading music or playing videos, require a different infrastructure. That infrastructure is loosely called broadband, a term that typically refers to anything faster than telephone lines, whether a network of fiber or DSL technology. The fact that the next-generation consumer network requires an infrastructure other than the traditional copper-wire phone system has posed new policy problems.

Although there is international agreement on the need for rapid deployment of broadband, the policies to accomplish that rapid deployment vary radically by country. The question remains whether this build-out should be a purely private decision of local providers or should be encouraged and subsidized by the government. The answers around the world are quite varied. Korea, for example, is a story of stunning penetration of broadband services into the society. Of the 16 million Korean households, 78 percent have broadband access, compared to roughly 20 percent in the United States.[7] A conscious decision was made to subsidize the broadband build-out by redirecting funds from wireless spectrum auctions. In total, the Korean government has spent nearly $3 billion on broadband diffusion. This effort has been carried out through an aggressive campaign, including direct subsidies, loan programs, and research and development funding. The government has even adjusted its housing ratings system so that units with broadband systems may be priced at a higher rate.[8] In the United States, by contrast, we have left the effort to a competition amongst the cable TV companies, phone companies offering DSL services, and potentially even power companies offering access over electricity lines. The result is less overall coverage but more diversity in network forms. In both the United States and Korea, government policy has been instrumental in shaping the technological infrastructure for information markets, albeit in very different ways.

Commodifying Information

Cyber law has for the most part focused on creating a market world in cyberspace. The concept of intellectual property (IP), though not new, plays a particularly critical role in this effort and in the digital era more broadly. We know that property is always a legal fiction involving the specification of enforceable rules about what a person can have, hold, and dispose of. Hence, in a fundamental way, property and its rules of use are always a political creation.

We also know that physical property and intellectual property have different characteristics. In the case of tangible goods with a physical existence, the rules of property set the terms of use and disposition. Since physical property cannot be simultaneously shared, some rules of use and disposal are necessary, whether those rules constitute private property or not. With the great transformation in England, the enclosure movement closed off common public lands, converting them into private holdings. By contrast, intellectual property is a nonexcludable good—its use by one does not preclude use by another. Hence, intellectual property as economic property, that is, something one is willing to buy because one cannot have its use without payment, is an entirely political creation, a fictitious commodity. The very "good" is a product of a rule. Thus the rules of intellectual property are in a digital era absolutely central.

Digital technology radically changes the logic of control and distribution of intellectual property. Whatever the cost of developing intellectual property, be it a movie or a software product, the marginal cost of precise reproduction and distribution is almost zero. Since media products are so immediately affected, it is evident why media companies have driven the reformulation of intellectual property law to permit them to recreate control over the distribution of their products.

The most blatant example of the effort to recreate traditional notions of property in the digital era is the Digital Millennium Copyright Act (DMCA) of 1998 (Kemp, this volume). Content providers ranging from Hollywood to the publishing industry lobbied to rebuild walls around their intellectual property preserves. The DMCA contained two critical provisions. First, it created criminal penalties for the circumvention of encryption programs, which hide the underlying software code from the user, preventing the reproduction and distribution of the purchased product. Second, the DMCA outlaws the manufacturing or sale of code-breaking software. The digital nature of the media, however, does not just recreate past IP protection. Regulating code has broader implications for society more generally. The notion of "fair use," which allows the holder of intellectual property to make that information available in a noncommercial manner, has been severely curtailed. A digital recording or book, for example, may be encrypted so that it can never be duplicated, eliminating the consumer's ability to share a purchase with friends or colleagues, even though that practice is fully legal. Digital rights management software may stop the consumer from duplicating downloaded music, preventing the customer from listening to the recording on multiple personal entertainment devices—another legal practice. Implanting intellectual property protection into the product through encryption systems permits perfect control over use, replication, and distribution.[9]

The digital era allows new forms of intellectual property to be created. For example, many types of data can now be easily packaged and sold. Expressed in digital form, information becomes a commodity that can be transmitted, manipulated, stored, and sold as an object. Argued most generally, in a digital era commodified explicit knowledge becomes pervasive. As knowledge, including digital instructions for physical control, becomes explicit and expressible in useful ways, the possibility and importance of protecting that knowledge as property increases. As patent offices recognize the legitimacy of business model patents, processes increasingly expressed in digital form have become property. Patent disputes over the eBay auction or the Amazon checkout strategy provide troubling examples of how previously shared knowledge may become commodifiable through law. The process of establishing a checkout procedure on the Web, rather than the intellectual property behind the book being purchased, receives proprietary protection (Preston 2004).[10] The seemingly inexorable expansion of the protectable is the issue.

Intellectual property rules inevitably affect more than just the media industries or the business possibilities of sectors that use digitized information and programs. Intellectual property has always been about balancing the need to reward those who generate knowledge against the desire for widespread distribution and use. Digital technology makes more information more easily accessible; offsetting that, technology and law create new boxes to control that information. The texture of social and political debate is powerfully influenced by who owns and can use content generated by others. The political community is thus shaping and shaped by the rules of intellectual property.

Embedding Markets in Social Norms

The digital era has radically altered the types and amount of information in the economy as well as the ability of actors to transmit and use that information. With data cheaply passing over digital networks, long-nourished business dreams become reality. Yet the question arises: who will capture the benefits of these innovations, and what threats do they pose to society? Government stands at the crossroads of the digital era, constructing the rules that underpin these emerging markets and mitigating negative social externalities. As in the case of the Industrial Revolution, the immensity of the technological change creates tremendous instability and displacement, which could derail the transformation. The state then steers Polanyi's "self-regulating market" so as to assure its viability. What is new about the digital state is less some technologically augmented or vitiated state authority than the ability of the state to influence the resolution of fundamental societal bargains that have been reopened by changes in information technology.

Two debates appear most critical. The first is privacy—that which permits us to remain in our personal domains, secluded from the view of others. The second debate concerns speech—that which we can say and debate in the public arena. These debates began in the marketplace over how to use information to economic advantage and spilled over into society, addressing how our communities and political processes will be organized. The state's failure to address these conflicts risks derailing the transformation and therefore demands government attention. Although the state has long been seen as the number 1 enemy of civil rights such as privacy and free speech, the digital transformation has ironically positioned the state as a critical defender of these very freedoms. As businesses augment their power to collect data and control the dissemination of information, new private sector threats emerge. Although fears concerning potential government abuse persist, the state also has the capacity to construct the rules to mitigate individual exploitation, formulating a consumer protection regime for the digital world.

The rules and norms associated with the collection, processing, and exchange of personal information, which come under the banner of privacy, are essential to the digital world. With the rise of digital technologies, both the quantity and the quality of personally identifiable information have shifted. As each credit card purchase, Web visit, and mobile phone log creates a new bit of data, behavior becomes easily tracked. New moments of personal life become monitorable. From the Webcam in the taxi to emerging genetic tests, these technologies erode the barriers between the knowable and the unknowable. They also permit the networking of previously discrete data. Information-intensive sectors, such as telecommunications, banking, and health care, are the first to rely on this wealth of personal information to customize products, rationalize costs, and minimize fraud. The supermarket club card typifies this line of innovation. With each swipe, the company is better able to target customers and lock in loyalty. The shift in a range of service industries, from marketing products to marketing customers, further demonstrates this trend. Where once an insurance firm marketed homeowner policies, it now attempts to understand individual customer needs across a wide array of company products. Reversing the logic of traditional credit cooperatives or risk-pooling efforts, complex individuation offers firms the ability to profit from extreme differentiation.

The opportunities inherent in personal information processing threaten to erode personal privacy, however. As digital technology expands the quantity and quality of personal information available, individuals lose the capacity to control information flows. The boundary between public knowledge and private secrets shifts, leaving less and less room for the private. What worries privacy advocates most is the networking of formally discrete personal information for third-party economic gain. Information privacy deals fundamentally with an individual's ability to control what is known about him or her, and not just what is published about him or her. And therefore, it addresses at root how individuals construct their identity. If credit data banks cement early risky consumer behavior into a widely distributed consumer report, it is difficult for individuals to be free of the negative data profile. In short, a major concern of the digital age is the inability to forget, a fundament of most healthy societies. Similarly, one could imagine car insurance firms using mobile phone logs to track commuting patterns and potentially changing rates of individuals traveling through high-risk areas. The flip side of customization and risk reduction is potential discrimination against those who are most vulnerable.[11]

As the amount of information held by the private sector rises, the possibility also exists that governments will look to private sector data warehouses to enhance public sector surveillance needs. A scandal involving JetBlue vividly illustrates the potential harm that lies in the linkage between private sector firms collecting information and government bureaucracies hoping to advance security interests. In this case, the airline transferred millions of personal customer files to a defense department contractor, who linked the airline data to commercial databanks in order to construct risk profiles.[12] Far from an isolated incident, governments across the globe are looking to private sector data files such as telephone or ISP records to monitor citizens' behavior. As the line between public and private enforcement breaks down, traditional checks against government abuse are neutralized. The traditional fear of a government-dominated Orwellian world is replaced by the specter of public-private partnerships of control.[13]

Such partnerships can operate in both directions. If the JetBlue scandal is a case of personal information gathered by a company being made available to the state, public policy has also compelled companies to make private information available to other business actors. For example, in attacking music downloading, the Recording Industry Association of America entered a series of lawsuits. To obtain the information on which the suits were based, the trade association required access to the records of the ISPs. The law as now written, the DMCA, compels the ISP to provide access to that information on the basis of suspicion of IP violations, without court authorization or review. This constitutes the creation of a private posse enforcing its will in civil courts.

Such threats have not gone unnoticed by state authorities. Since the 1970s, with the proliferation of computer technology, lawmakers have recognized the danger inherent in the collection and storage of personal information. In response, nations across the industrial world have adopted data privacy legislation. These rules have varied considerably, with the United States focusing on public sector data usage and Europe constructing comprehensive regulatory institutions for the public and private sectors (Bennett 1992; Regan 1995). As data processing has left the confines of a small number of government agencies in the mainframe era, the comprehensive structure has shown itself better suited at dealing with the explosion of data collection inherent in the digital era. In European countries, for example, it is difficult for private sector companies to routinely share personal information with government security agencies. Data protection rules often prevent the collection of detailed information by firms, limiting the amount of information available for sharing. Recent disputes between the United States and Europe over data privacy issues, ranging from telecommunications information to airline passenger flight records, demonstrate the importance of national government policy in the development of very distinct information societies (Newman 2005).

Like notions of privacy, questions concerning free speech have been reopened by the emergence of digital technologies. Though they receive fewer headlines than the economically more potent cases of property or privacy, speech issues lie at the cornerstone of modern political communities. By defining what can be said to whom, free speech rules shape an individual's ability to express himself or herself, maintain social networks, and organize politically. Free speech is invariably included in the catalog of basic democratic rights as the most critical right held by opponents of established power. Yet free speech is far from uncontroversial. By altering patterns of communication and the capacity to transmit content, digital technology has transformed global debates about free speech. With the rise of international Internet connectivity, a resident of the United States can as easily transmit information to a fellow netizen in Europe as to a local neighbor. As a result, differing cultural norms concerning criminal speech have come into conflict with one another. Most common among these are forms of obscenity, hate speech, and political protests. As digital connectivity permits citizens from one nation easy access to the media of another, jurisdictional conflicts emerge ("Recent Developments" 1999).

Technology has changed not only patterns of communication, but also the ability to control content. As previously described in the discussion of intellectual property, digital goods are naturally non rival and replicable at no marginal cost. This has challenged traditional business models, spurring industry to use digital tools to increase the controllability of content. Through legislation and code, content providers have attempted to minimize the amount of IP available in the digital commons. This "second enclosure" restricts the fair use of information and in turn limits the free flow of ideas essential to free speech (Boyle 2003). It becomes much more difficult for activists to circulate news updates, for example, when they have to pay distribution fees to use digital information. The state is left in the delicate position of determining which types of content individuals should be allowed to share.

Potentially just as important for free speech have been policies concerned with harmful content. A distinct feature of modern society is the belief that certain information is dangerous and should be controlled through public policy. European governments, including Germany and France, have applied existing content laws to the digital era—for example, banning the sale of Nazi paraphernalia on the Internet. The firms selling such products are often located in countries with different laws. As a result, the application of content laws can take on an extraterritorial flair (Beesom and Hansen 1997). Far from a technologically driven race to the bottom in standards, firms playing in international markets have been confronted by the projection of national rules through digital networks.

At the same time that governments have moved to control content, they have also actively participated in the dissemination of information technology. Access is no doubt a precursor for communication and participation. In the United States, the E-Rate program was established, which subsidized broadband technology access in schools and rural communities (Newman 2003). Similarly, as discussed previously, the Korean government has been active in subsidizing the rollout of broadband technology. Though access is a critical component in overcoming the digital divide, the dissemination of digital technology should not be strictly equated with the promotion of free speech. Governments can promote technology diffusion while at the same time controlling (or supporting companies to control) the manner in which it is used (Boas, 2006).

Government Efforts to Mediate the Transformation

Given the continued importance of the state in the political economy of the global digital era, it is important to consider how state intervention shapes markets and societies. We identify three basic strategies that states have adopted in response to the challenges posed by information technology. First, governments may intervene to promote competition in the new marketplace, as technological change disrupts existing business strategies. States intervene to secure fair ground rules for the fights between dominant players and new entrants. These rules may emphasize equal market access, level regulatory playing fields, and transparency. The European Union convergence effort in the communications regime typifies this policy strategy. As media including telecommunications, radio, cable, and satellite compete head-to-head with one another for core digital products, market disruptions result from regulatory legacies. Telecommunications companies, for example, face very different regulatory burdens when entering new markets than cable companies: universal service requirements mandate that telephone companies guarantee access to underserved communities, a cost not faced by cable companies looking to compete in broadband markets. The convergence process attempts to smooth over these regulatory differences and create a comprehensive regime for the digital communications industry. This strategy of getting the market rules right privileges procedural neutrality and long-term market competition over attempts to shield specific national champions.

In the second policy strategy, governments intervene to reassert incumbent market power. Digital innovations have the potential to upset existing business dynamics in a sector, threatening powerful industry groups. Policies in this strain attempt to shore up the predigital distribution of resources and prevent political coalitions from shifting. The DMCA offers the prototypical example of this form of state intervention. It criminalized the development and use of devices that may be used to break encryption systems. Technological solutions to intellectual property rights questions received legal support, consolidating the entertainment industry's effort to reassert property rules in the digital environment. Despite intense lobbying efforts by new entrants from the information technology sector to curb the legislation, the government attempted to reassure the entertainment industry as a critical interest group. Similar international efforts have been carried out by advanced countries vis-à-vis the developing world. The WTO's Agreement on Trade Related Aspects of Intellectual Property Rights (TRIPS) and World Intellectual Property Organization (WIPO) agreements further insulate the intellectual property warehouses of incumbent players. The agreements provide firms with international commitments and credible enforcement mechanisms to protect their intellectual property globally. Potentially viewed as a reactionary strategy, the second approach steers the political character of the digital transformation in favor of existing power centers.

A third strategy likewise attempts to shape the substantive character of emerging digital markets. Instead of bolstering existing interest constellations, however, the state recasts the balance of power in favor of public interests. The citizen consumer is empowered in the new digital environment, receiving increased control over information resources. Most easily identified with the mission of consumer advocates, this third strategy attempts to promote the public interest more broadly and to prevent digital innovations from further concentrating power in the hands of economic and government elites. Often motivated by political fears that individuals will reject new technologies and thereby stall economic development, this approach emphasizes state safeguards that protect and assure citizens. The EU data privacy directive provides an important international example. With the explosion of personal information in the digital age, the directive provides individuals with a clear level of control over industry and government data processing. Before a company or a bureaucracy may transmit personal information to a third party, it must obtain consent from the individual in question. If an organization fails to obtain consent, it can be punished by the data protection agency. Though they do not eliminate the commodification of personal information, the European regulations reset the default position in favor of consumers. Governments, by promoting the third, potentially populist or progressive option, channel the transformation so as to rebalance societal relationships prioritizing citizen concerns.

The Politics of State Regulation of Digital Technologies

The digital era has reopened fundamental societal debates and in turn brought on a reexamination of the role of the state in the emerging political economy. As firms use digital technologies to create advantage or position in their markets, old political economy bargains are undermined. Often new entrants see opportunity in the technological disruption, incumbents struggle to hold on to old business models, and public interest groups fight to maintain or expand consumer rights. Amidst the commotion, governments begin to formulate policy strategies that inevitably impact the distribution of business opportunities.

The dynamics of these political debates are complex. In addition to the state, business lobbies and public interest groups struggle within a given political institutional environment to construct the emerging rules of the digital economy. In order to understand the variation in policy results across countries and internationally, it is vital to identify the roots of business sector and public interest preferences. In short, we contend that the organization of economic and public interest sectors influences their preference formation and their stake in digital debates.

Several caveats about business and public interests are important to keep in mind, as we examine the preferences of various political actors. Business interests may be driving the process of reformulating rules for a digital age, but there is no unified business position. There is certainly no "digital sectoral" interest, let alone a class interest. Firms have different preferences and positions on the same issues; competitors in networks seek to turn the rules to their advantage; and companies building and using different technologies, or at different positions in the market, have quite distinct needs.

But there is more to the story. The business interests of financial institutions depend not only on market problems alone, but also on the corporate organization of the firms themselves (Newman 2005). This organization is partly a business choice and partly a result of regulation. Integrated financial institutions, such as France has, do not depend on customer information markets to gather the information they need to market to their customers. French financial institutions rely instead on their internal warehouse of information to target customer needs. By contrast, the highly fragmented character of financial services in the United States reinforces demands for a market in personal information. So interests may be definable, but they cannot be read off a market map in any simple way.

Similarly, public interest groups have been at the forefront of many digital policy debates across the globe. But their level of engagement, their policy goals, and their lobbying strategies differ dramatically across countries. Compare the work of the most active public interest groups in the United States, such as the Electronic Privacy and Information Center and the Electronic Freedom Foundation, to that of their counterparts in Europe, such as data protection or consumer protection bureaus. Though the goals appear identical, guaranteeing a social agenda for an information society, the logic of their tactics (e.g., class action suits and media scandals versus negotiated technocratic bargains) vary and are in a very real sense shaped by their institutional settings.

Not only do their tactics differ, but the capacity of players to influence legislative debates varies across policy landscapes. In the United States, broader public interests are represented in only a limited way in the struggles over digital rules. Certainly, the narrow business story of the emergence of electronic commerce and the tools to conduct commerce using networks has become entangled with the broader political struggle over fundamental values, goals, and processes and jurisdiction. But at least in the United States—to oversimplify—it is a story of business seeking new rules to implement digital technologies, with public interest groups seeking to influence the character of those rules.[14] More often than not, groups defending general principles, such as privacy or consumer protection on the network, enter the fights in response to business-initiated or -proposed rule changes. None have mobilized effectively on a mass basis and, as a result, there is no digital equivalent of the environmentalist movement.

The U.S. debate is driven by markets and market actors and therefore has the flavor of business dominating the political debate. Elsewhere, public interest voices are fitted differently into the political system, either through a formal institutional position or through political parties. This positioning may force trade associations to respond to legislative agendas pushed by consumer interests. Two examples prove illustrative. The role of the Green Party in Germany has radically altered the place of consumer groups. This small party, a member of the governing coalition between 1998 and 2005, has successfully raised consumer protection to a cabinet responsibility. At the level of the European Union, consumer interests have been institutionalized in the consumer protection directorate, elevating public interest demands within European policy debates. As a result, industry finds itself in the position of responding to positions placed on the table by consumer advocates, who at the same time often have the sympathetic ears of the European Commission or national governments (Young and Wallace 2000).

These differences force us to at least open the basic question of how political groups form and how their interests are defined. Because business now operates globally, with markets and products crossing borders, these domestic battles for values and principles, from privacy through to the right to expression, will have to be fought again and again—and the terrain of the political battlefield will be much more varied and complex. Political strategies will now involve cross-national coalitions and deals in international institutions to settle what were once exclusively domestic decisions. Indeed, the creation of interests in the whole array of digital cases emphasizes that interest groups are never mechanical functions of markets or institutional structures, but rather the product of political struggles.

Conclusion

Information and how it is used provide the very substance of communities, polities, and markets. Communities can be conceived and indeed expressed as the character and flow of communications amongst members, polities as systems of decisions based on information, and markets as architectures for exchange based on information. Consequently, even technical rules about digital technology and the digital market are directly and simultaneously decisions about the very nature of the community and the polity.

It is clear that new deals are being struck, but the content of these deals is not compelled in any consistent way by the digital tools and networks themselves. Rather, the state finds itself struggling to manage digitally inspired conflicts fueled by business and public interest groups. As technology reopens debates, governments have varying policy tools at their disposal and confront distinct policy legacies. One should, therefore, expect to see different government approaches to basic digital fights. Not only will proposed government solutions vary, but these proposals will be filtered by each country's unique political configuration. The cross-national diversity of policy debates will reflect not only market conditions and problems, but also, and more fundamentally, the distinct organization of the public and private sector lobbies involved. Owing to the transnational character of digital markets, these varying state positions will naturally shape international negotiations.

The state has played a fundamental role in the emergence and development of the digital era. As in the case of the great transformation, government policy has created the infrastructure for the fictitious commodity of information. Through deregulation, market making, and reregulation, public policy has constructed the rules for the new market and managed conflicts that threatened to derail the digital transformation. These efforts have had important political consequences for the character of the contemporary era. Given the differing ways governments have dealt with the various challenges posed by this digital transformation, several distinct information societies will no doubt emerge.

Notes

1. All due deference to Karl Polanyi (1944).

2. See John Gilmore as quoted in Peter Lewis, "Limiting a Medium without Boundaries: How Do You Let the Good Fish through the Net while Blocking the Bad?" *New York Times,* January 15, 1996. See also Barlow 1996. Manuel Castells (1996) makes a more nuanced argument that the rise of complex networks has limited the power of the state.

3. For a more general discussion of the role of self-regulation in the early years of the Internet, see Marsden 2000.

4. For a detailed analysis of the various roles the state can play in modern political economy, see Levy 2006.

5. For the important role states have played in resolving international disputes posed by digital technologies, see Drezner 2004.

6. For a discussion of the political development of telecommunications liberalization, see Cowhey 1990a.

7. Assif Shameen, "Korea's Broadband Revolution," *Chief Executive,* April 2004, http://www.chiefexecutive.net (accessed December 5, 2005).

8. See Tim Richardson, "South Korea Broadband in League of Its Own," *The Register,* October 14, 2002, http://www.theregister.co.uk (accessed December 5, 2005).

9. For a discussion of the DMCA as well as its implications for fair use, see Samuelson 1999; Nimmer 2000.

10. Available at http://www.nwc.com/showArricle.jhtml?articleID=20300119 (accessed December 5, 2005).

11. See Ron Lieber, "Banks Now Get Daily Reports on Their Customers," *San Francisco Chronicle,* August 4, 2003.

12. *New York Times,* "Two US Agencies Investigate JetBlue over Privacy Issues," September 23, 2003.

13. For a review of privacy concerns in a digital age, see Newman and Bach 2004.

14. There are exceptions, of course. One is the present debate about the effort to restrict telemarketing calls in the United States, which has mobilized a broad constituency. But even this issue, which receives almost universal popular support, has faced a harrowing road to implementation, including multiple court injunctions that threaten to derail a consumer-friendly outcome.

References

Barlow, John Perry. 1996. *Declaration of the Independence of Cyberspace.* http://www.eff.org/~barlow/Declaration-Final (accessed November 12, 2005).

Beesom, Ann, and Chris Hansen. 1997. "Fahrenheit 451.2: Is Cyberspace Burning?" White paper for the American Civil Liberties Union, March 17.

Bennett, Colin J. 1992. *Regulating Privacy: Data Protection and Public Policy in Europe and the United States.* Ithaca, NY, Cornell University Press.

Boas, Taylor C. (2006) "Weaving the Authoritarian Web: The Control of Internet Use in Nondemocratic Regimes." In John Zysman and Abraham Newman (eds.), *How Revolutionary Was the Digital Revolution? National Responses, Market Transitions, and Global Technology.* Stanford, CA: Stanford University Press. 361–378.

Boyle, James. 2003. "The Second Enclosure Movement and the Construction of the Public Domain." *Law and Contemporary Problems* 66: 33–74.

Castells, Manuel. 1996. *The Rise of the Network Society.* Cambridge: Blackwell.

Cohen, Stephen S., J. Bradford DeLong, and John Zysman. 2000. "Tools for Thought: What Is New and Important about the 'E-conomy'?" Berkeley Roundtable on the International Economy Working Paper 138, University of California, Berkeley.

———. 1998. *Globalization and the Information Society: The Need for Strengthened International Co-ordination.* Brussels: European Communities.

Cowhey, Peter. 1990. "The International Telecommunications Regime: The Political Roots of High Technology Regimes." *International Organization* 44:169–199.

Drezner, Daniel. 2004. "The Global Governance of the Internet: Bringing the State Back In." *Political Science Quarterly* 119: 477–498.

Gribble, Cheryl. 2004. "History of the Web Beginning at CERN," July 13. http://www.hitmill. com/internet/web_history.html (accessed December 13, 2005).

Hafner, Katie, and Matthew Lyon. 1998. *Where Wizards Stay Up Late: The Origins of the Internet.* New York: Touchstone.

Haufler, Virginia. 2001. *Public Role for the Private Sector: Industry Self-regulation in a Global Economy.* Washington, DC: Carnegie Endowment for International Peace.

Kemp, Brodi. (2006) "Copyright's Digital Reformulation." In John Zysman and Abraham Newman (eds.), *How Revolutionary Was the Digital Revolution? National Responses, Market Transitions, and Global Technology.* Stanford, CA: Stanford University Press. 379–390.

Lessig, Lawrence. 1999. "Internet Regulation through Architectural Modification." *Harvard Law Review* 112(May): 1634–1657.

Levy, Jonah. 2006. *The State after Statism: New State Activities among the Affluent Democracies.* Cambridge, MA: Harvard University Press.

Marsden, Christopher. 2000. *Regulating the Global Information Society.* New York: Routledge.

Newman, Abraham. 2003. "When Opportunity Knocks: Economic Liberalization and Stealth Welfare in the United States." *Journal of Social Policy* 32: 179–197.

———. 2005. "Creating Privacy: The International Politics of Personal Information." Ph.D. diss., University of California, Berkeley.

Newman, Abraham L., and David Bach. 2004. "Privacy and Regulation in a Digital Age." In Brigitte Preissl, Harry Bouwman, and Charles Steinfeld (eds.), *E-life after the Dot Com Bust.* Heidelberg: Physica Verlag.

Nimmer, David. 2000. "A Riff on Fair Use in the Digital Millenium Copyright Act." *University of Pennsylvania Law Review* 148: 673–742.

Ohmae, Kenichi. 1993. "The Rise of the Region State," *Foreign Affairs* 72: 78–87.

Polanyi, Karl. 1944. *Great Transformation: The Political and Economic Origins of Our Time.* Boston, MA: Beacon Press.

Post, David, and David Johnson. 1996. "Law and Borders: The Rise of Law in Cyberspace." *Stanford Law Review* 48: 1367. http://www.firstmonday.org/issues/issue1/law/index. html (accessed December 13, 2005).

Preston, Ron. 2004. "Software Patents Abused." *Network Computing,* May 13.

"Recent Developments in the Law: The Law of Cyberspace." 1999. *Harvard Law Review* 112: 1574–1704.

Regan, Priscilla. 1995. *Legislating Privacy.* Raleigh: University of North Carolina Press.

Richardson, Tim. 2002. "South Korea Broadband in League of Its Own." Register, October 14, 2002. http://www.theregister.co.uk (accessed November 11, 2005).

Rosenau, James, and J.P. Singh. 2002. *Information Technologies and Global Politics: The Changing Scope of Power and Governance.* Albany: State University of New York Press.

Samuelson, Pamela. 1999. "Intellectual Property and the Digital Economy: Why the Anti-circumvention Regulations Need to be Revisited." *Berkeley Technology Law Journal* 14: 519–566.

Shameen, Assif. 2004. "Korea's Broadband Revolution," *Chief Executive*, April. http://www.chiefexecutive.net (accessed November 11, 2005).

Shannon, Claude Elmwood. 1993. "A Mathematical Theory of Communication." In N.J.A. Sloane and Aaron D. Wyner (eds.), *Claude Elmwood Shannon: Collected Papers*. New York: IEEE Press.

Spar, Debora. 1999. "Lost in (Cyber)space: The Private Rules of Online Commerce." In A. Claire Cutler, Virginia Haufler, and Tony Porter (eds.), *Private Authority in International Affairs*. Albany: SUNY Press.

Tonnelson, Alan. 2000. *The Race to the Bottom*. Boulder, CO: Westview Press.

Weber, Steven. 2001. *Introduction to Globalization and the European Political Economy*. New York: Columbia University Press.

Weiner, Norbert. 1954. *The Human Use of Human Beings: Cybernetics and Society*. Boston: Da Capo Press.

_____. 1965. *Cybernetics, or Control and Communication in the Animal and the Machine*. Cambridge: MIT Press.

Young, Alisdair R., and Helen Wallace. 2000. *Regulatory Politics in the Enlarging European Union: Weighing Civic and Producer Interests*. Manchester: Manchester University Press.

Susan Strange,
The Retreat of the State (1996)*

1: The Declining Authority of States

Today it seems that the heads of governments may be the last to recognise that they and their ministers have lost the authority over national societies and economies that they used to have. Their command over outcomes is not what it used to be. Politicians everywhere talk as though they have the answers to economic and social problems, as if they really are in charge of their country's destiny. People no longer believe them. Disillusion with national leaders brought down the leaders of the Soviet Union and the states of central Europe. But the disillusion is by no means confined to socialist systems. Popular contempt for ministers and for the head of state has grown in most of the capitalist countries—Italy, Britain, France and the United States are leading examples. Nor is the lack of confidence confined to those in office; opposition parties and their leaders are often no better thought of than those they wish to replace. In the last few years, the cartoonists and the tabloid press have been more bitter, less restrained critics of those in authority in government than at any other time this century. Although there are exceptions—mostly small countries—this seems to be a worldwide phenomenon of the closing years of the twentieth century, more evident in some places than others, but palpable enough to suggest that some common causes lie behind it.

This book is written in the firm belief that the perceptions of ordinary citizens are more to be trusted than the pretensions of national leaders and of the bureaucracies who serve them; that the commonsense of common people is a better guide to understanding than most of the academic theories being taught in universities. The social scientists, in politics and economics especially, cling to obsolete concepts and inappropriate theories. These theories belong to a more stable and orderly world than the one we live in. It was one in which the territorial borders of states really meant something. But it has been swept away by a pace of change more rapid than human society had ever before experienced.

For this reason I believe the time has come to reconsider a few of the entrenched ideas of some academic colleagues in economics, politics, sociology and international relations. The study of international political economy has convinced me that we have to rethink some of the assumptions of conventional social science, and especially of

* From: *The Retreat of the State: The Diffusion of Power in the World Economy*. Copyright © Cambridge University Press 1996. (pp. 3–14) Reprinted with the permission of Cambridge University Press.

the study of international relations. These concern: firstly, the limits of politics as a social activity; secondly, the nature and sources of power in society; thirdly, the necessity and also the indivisibility of authority in a market economy; and fourthly, the anarchic nature of international society and the rational conduct of states as the unitary actors within that society. The first and second are assumptions commonly taken for granted in political science. The third is an assumption of much liberal, or neo-classical economic science. And the last is an assumption of much so-called realist or neo-realist thinking in international relations. Each of these assumptions will be examined more closely later in the book.

But first it may help to outline briefly the argument of the book as a whole. That will show the context in which these more fundamental questions about politics and power arise and have to be reconsidered. The argument put forward is that the impersonal forces of world markets, integrated over the postwar period more by private enterprise in finance, industry and trade than by the cooperative decisions of governments, are now more powerful than the states to whom ultimate political authority over society and economy is supposed to belong.

Where states were once the masters of markets, now it is the markets which, on many crucial issues, are the masters over the governments of states. And the declining authority of states is reflected in a growing diffusion of authority to other institutions and associations, and to local and regional bodies, and in a growing asymmetry between the larger states with structural power and weaker ones without it.

There are, to be sure, some striking paradoxes about this reversal of the state-market balance of power. One, which disguises from many people the overall decline of state power, is that the *intervention* of state authority and of the agencies of the state in the daily lives of the citizen appears to be growing. Where once it was left to the individual to look for work, to buy goods or services with caution in case they were unsafe or not what they seemed to be, to build or to pull down houses, to manage family relationships and so on, now governments pass laws, set up inspectorates and planning authorities, provide employment services, enforce customer protection against unclean water, unsafe food, faulty buildings or transport systems. The impression is conveyed that less and less of daily life is immune from the activities and decisions of government bureaucracies.

That is not necessarily inconsistent with my contention that state *power* is declining. It is less effective on those basic matters that the market, left to itself, has never been able to provide—security against violence, stable money for trade and investment, a clear system of law and the means to enforce it, and a sufficiency of public goods like drains, water supplies, infrastructures for transport and communications. Little wonder that it is less respected and lacks its erstwhile legitimacy. The need for a political authority of some kind, legitimated either by coercive force or by popular consent, or more often by a combination of the two, is the fundamental reason for the state's existence. But many states are coming to be deficient in these fundamentals. Their deficiency is not made good by greater activity in marginal matters, matters that are optional for society, and which are not absolutely necessary for the functioning of the market and the maintenance of social order. Trivialising government does not make its authority more respected; often, the contrary is true.

The second paradox is that while the governments of established states, most notably in North America and western Europe, are suffering this progressive loss of real authority, the queue of societies that want to have their own state is lengthening. This is true not only of ethnic groups that were forcibly suppressed by the single-party government of the former Soviet Union. It is true of literally hundreds of minorities and aboriginal peoples in every part of the world—in Canada and Australia, in India and Africa, even in the old so-called nation-states of Europe. Many—perhaps the majority—are suppressed by force, like the Kurds or the Basques. Others—like the Scots or the Corsicans—are just not strong enough or angry enough to offer a serious challenge to the existing state. Still others such as the native Americans, the Aboriginals, the Samis or the Flemish are pacified by resource transfers or by half-measures that go some way to meet their perceived need for an independent identity. Only a few, such as the Greenlanders, the Slovaks or Slovenes or the unwanted, unviable Pacific island-states, have succeeded in getting what they wanted—statehood. But once achieved, it does not seem to give them any real control over the kind of society or the nature of their economy that they might have preferred. In short, the desire for ethnic or cultural autonomy is universal; the political means to satisfy that desire within an integrated world market economy is not. Many, perhaps most, societies have to be content with the mere appearance of autonomy, with a facade of statehood. The struggle for independence has often proved a pyrrhic victory.

The final paradox which can be brought as evidence against my basic contention about the hollowness of state authority at the end of this century is that this is a western, or even an Anglo-Saxon phenomenon, and is refuted by the Asian experience of the state. The Asian state, it is argued, has in fact been the means to achieve economic growth, industrialisation, a modernised infrastructure and rising living standards for the people. Singapore might be the prime example of a strong state achieving economic success. But Japan, Korea, Taiwan are all states which have had strong governments, governments which have successfully used the means to restrict and control foreign trade and foreign investment, and to allocate credit and to guide corporate development in the private sector. Is it not premature—just another instance of Eurocentrism therefore—to assume the declining authority of the state?

There are two answers to this third paradox. One is that all these Asian states were exceptionally fortunate. They profited in three ways from their geographical position on the western frontier of the United States during the Cold War. Their strategic importance in the 1950s and after was such that they could count on generous military and economic aid from the Americans, aid which was combined with their exceptionally high domestic savings and low patterns of consumption. The combination gave a head start to rapid economic development. Secondly, and also for strategic reasons, they could be—almost had to be—exempted from the pressure to conform to the norms of the open liberal economy. They were allowed, first formally and then informally, to limit foreign imports and also to restrict the entry of the foreign firms that might have proved too strong competitors for their local enterprises. At the same time, they were given relatively open access first to the large, rich US market for manufactures, and later, under some protest, to the European one. And thirdly, the technology necessary to their industrialisation was available to be bought on the market, either in the form of patents, or in the person of technical advisors from Europe and

America or through corporate alliances which brought them the technology without the loss of managerial control.

Now, I would argue, these special dispensations are on the way out, and not only because the Cold War is over. The Asian governments will be under increasing pressure from Washington to adopt more liberal non-discriminatory policies on trade and investment. And they will also be under pressure from within to liberalise and to allow more competition, including foreign competition, for the benefit of consumers and of other producers. In short, the exceptionalism of the Asian state during the Cold War has already been substantially eroded, and will continue to be so. As it has been at other times, and in other places, there will be contests for control over the institutions and agencies of government in most of the Asian countries. There will be contests between factions of political parties, between vested interests both in the private sectors and in the public sector. There will be power struggles between branches of the state bureaucracy. Both the unity and the authority of government is bound to suffer.

The Neglected Factor—Technology

The argument in the book depends a good deal on the accelerating pace of technological change as a prime cause of the shift in the state-market balance of power. Since social scientists are, not, by definition, natural scientists, they have a strong tendency to overlook the importance of technology which rests, ultimately, on advances in physics, in chemistry and related sciences like nuclear physics or industrial chemistry. In the last 100 years, there has been more rapid technological change than ever before in human history. On this the scientists themselves are generally agreed. It took hundreds—in some places, thousands—of years to domesticate animals so that horses could be used for transport and oxen (later heavy horses) could be used to replace manpower to plough and sow ground for the production of crops in agriculture. It has taken less than 100 years for the car and truck to replace the horse and for aircraft to partly take over from road and rail transport. The electric telegraph as a means of communication was invented in the 1840s and remained the dominant system in Europe until the 1920s. But in the next eighty years, the telegraph gave way to the telephone, the telephone gave way to radio, radio to television and cables to satellites and optic fibres linking computers to other computers. No one under the age of thirty or thirty-five today needs convincing that, just in their own lifetime, the pace of technological change has been getting faster and faster. The technically unsophisticated worlds of business, government and education of even the 1960s would be unrecognisable to them. No fax, no personal computers, no accessible copiers, no mobile phones, no video shops, no DNA tests, no cable TV, no satellite networks connecting distant markets, twenty-four hours a day. The world in which their grandparents grew up in the 1930 or 1940s is as alien to them as that of the Middle Ages. There is no reason to suppose that technological change in products and processes, driven by profit, will not continue to accelerate in future.

This simple, everyday, commonsense fact of modern life is important because it goes a long way to explaining both political and economic change. It illuminates the changes both in the power of states and in the power of markets. Its dynamism, in fact, is basic to my argument, because it is a continuing factor, not a once-for-all change.

For the sake of clarity, consider first the military aspects of technical change, and then the civilian aspects—although in reality each spills over into the other. In what are known as strategic studies circles, no one doubts that the development of the atom bomb in the middle of the twentieth century, and later of nuclear weapons carried by intercontinental missiles, has brought about a major change in the nature of warfare between states. Mutual assured destruction was a powerful reason for having nuclear weapons—but equally it was a good reason for not using them. After the paradoxical long peace of the Cold War, two things began to change. The expectation that, sooner or later, nuclear war would destroy life on the planet began to moderate. And confidence began to wane that the state could, by a defensive strategy, prevent this happening. Either it would or it wouldn't, and governments could do little to alter the probabilities. Thus, technology had undermined one of the primary reasons for the existence of the state—its capacity to repel attack by others, its responsibility for what Adam Smith called 'the defence of the realm'.

At the same time technology has had its effect on civilian life. Medical technology has made human life both longer and more comfortable. Electrical technology has liberated millions of women from the drudgery that imprisoned previous generations in the day-long labour of preparing food, keeping the family's clothes clean and mended, and houses clean and warm. As washing machines, vacuum cleaners, dishwashers, central heating and refrigerators and freezers spread down the income levels, more people had more to lose from inter-state conflict. Comfort bred conservatism in politics. Moreover, the new wealth was being acquired by the Germans and the Japanese who had actually been defeated in World War II. Acquiring territory was no longer seen as a means to increase wealth. Losing territory did not mean the state became poorer or weaker. Gaining market shares in the world outside the territorial borders of the state, however, did enable formerly poor countries like Japan, Taiwan or Hong Kong to earn the foreign exchange with which to buy capital goods, foreign technology and the necessary resources of energy and raw materials. As John Stopford and I have argued, competition for world market shares has replaced competition for territory, or for control over the natural resources of territory, as the 'name of the game' between states (Stopford and Strange, 1991; Strange in Rizopoulos (ed.), 1990). In this new game, the search for allies among other states goes on, but not for their added military capabilities. It is for the added bargaining power conferred by a larger economic area.

Moreover, the search for allies is not confined to other states or inter-governmental organisations. It is supplemented by a search for allies among foreign-owned firms. These firms may be persuaded, in exchange for access to the national market, to raise the finance, apply their technology, provide the management and the access to export markets—in short, to take all the steps necessary to locate production of goods or services within the territory of the host state. In most developing or ex-socialist countries, the prospect of new jobs and extra export earnings brought by such investments have become powerful reasons for a change of attitude toward the so-called 'multinationals'.

The Second Neglect—Finance

Not the least of the TNC's [transnational corporations] attractions to host states is its ability to raise finance both for the investment itself and—even more important—for the development of new technology. Another key part of the argument of this book is that, besides the accelerating pace of technological change, there has been an escalation in the capital cost of most technological innovations—in agriculture, in manufacturing and the provision of services, and in new products and in new processes. In all of these, the input of capital has risen while the relative input of labour has fallen. It is this increased cost which has raised the stakes, as it were, in the game of staying up with the competition. This is so whether we look at competition from other firms who are also striving for larger market shares, or whether we look at governments trying to make sure that the economies for whose performance they are held responsible stay up with the competition in wealth-creation coming from other economies. Thus, to the extent that a government can benefit from a TNC's past and future investments without itself bearing the main cost of it, there are strong reasons for forging such alliances.

But the escalating costs of technological change are also important for a more fundamental reason, and not just because it explains the changing policies of host states to TNCs. It has to do with change in the world system. The cost of new technology in the production structure has added to the salience of money in the international political economy. It is no exaggeration to say that, with a few notable exceptions, scholars in international relations for the past half-century have grossly neglected the political aspects of credit-creation, and of changes in the global financial structure.[1] In much theorising about international relations or even international political economy there is no mention at all of the financial structure (as distinct from the international monetary order governing the exchange relations of national currencies). Briefly, the escalating capital costs of new technologies could not have been covered at all without, firstly, some very fundamental changes in the volume and nature of credit created by the capitalist market economy; and secondly, without the added mobility that in recent years has characterised that created credit. The *supply* of capital to finance technological innovation (and for other purposes) has been as important in the international political economy as the *demand* from the innovators for more money to produce ever more sophisticated products by ever more capital-intensive processes of production.

These supply and demand changes take place, and take effect, in the market. And it is markets, rather than state–state relations that many leading texts in international political economy tend to overlook. Much more emphasis is put on international monetary relations between governments and their national currencies. To the extent that attention is paid at all to the institutions creating and marketing credit in the world economy, they are held to be important chiefly for the increased volatility they may cause to exchange rates, or to the impact they may have on the ability of governments to borrow abroad to finance development or the shortfall between revenue and spending, or between export earnings and import bills.

More significant in the long run, however, when it comes to evolving better theories to explain change in the international political economy is the accompanying neglect of the three-way connections between the supply side of international finance (credit), the demand side from firms, and the political intervention of governments as regulators of banking and financial markets and as borrowers or lenders, at home and abroad. There are theories to explain each of the three, but no unifying theory to explain their mutual connections.

For example, it may be asked why so many firms come to financial markets to raise money. It may be to finance a merger or takeover of another firm, to finance the development or application of a new technology or for expansion into a new market. The body of literature known as theories of the firm has produced some answers. One of the best-known is Ray Vernon's product-cycle theory. Although it is now recognised that this theory as first proposed in the late 1960s was over-influenced by the recent experience of US firms setting up affiliates in Europe, and was in any case a rather simplified model of actual corporate behaviour, it did nevertheless have a powerful central idea in it. Briefly, the product cycle begins with the firm introducing a new product or developing a new process in its home market. But when the temporary monopoly rent from the innovation is undercut by its competitors, it starts to export the product to new markets where there is still little or no competition. When that monopoly rent is also undercut by competing exporters, the firm extends the cycle by producing inside the foreign market at lower cost and with greater efficiency. Ploughing back all these monopoly rents into the next technological innovation starts another product cycle (Vernon, 1966).

Since Vernon's pioneering idea, there have been other elaborations of the theory of transnational production. One of the best-known is Dunning's self-styled eclectic theory which adds in, as complicating variables, the possible advantages a firm may have in the way it organises production and marketing, the possible advantages—such as cheap labour or access to raw materials—of alternative locations (Dunning, 1988). Both Vernon and Dunning shared with economic theorists a concern with the firm's interest in lowering transaction costs by internalising transactions that otherwise could be effected at arm's length in the market. More politically perceptive of the realities behind corporate behaviour was Hymer's idea that lowering cost was often less important to firms than keeping control (Hymer, 1976).

The point is that such theories helped to explain, at least in part, the demand side for credit. What is needed to complement them is some theory that explains the matching of supply to demand, the expansion of new sources and forms of credit to keep pace with the demand. While there are descriptive accounts galore of the evolution of Eurocurrency markets in the 1960s and 1970s, and of syndicated bank loans to developing countries in the 1970s, and of junk bonds and securitisation in the 1980s, the theoretical explanation of periods of credit expansion has not been well developed. The historians have observed that such periods of expansion often—but not always—lead to booms and bubbles, followed by slumps and crashes. And, of course, economists have developed theories of business cycles and long waves though generally these are couched in rather abstract fashion.

Not only do the demand theories and the supply theories fail to come together, both tend to assume a kind of political vacuum, in which nothing changes in the behaviour of governments to each other and to the operators—industrial, commercial and financial, in the market economy. For example, historians are well aware that financial inflation—excessive creation of credit—is apt to accompany the conduct of war—civil or international. Yet neither the theories of international production nor of banking and credit take account of the dynamics of international relations, any more than the latter take into account the behaviour of firms or financial markets.

Awareness of this failure of inter-connection between bodies of theory relating to political and economic change customarily treated by social scientists in isolation from each other has powerfully motivated the writing of this book. My exploration of the phenomenon of diffuse authority over the global political economy is necessarily sketchy and incomplete. Yet by drawing attention to both the theoretical lacunae in social science and to the empirical evidence of the increasing exercise of non-state authority, my hope is that further work will be inspired to develop at both the theoretical and the empirical level.

Politics, Power and Legitimacy

There are three premises underlying the argument in this book. Each relates directly to—indeed, challenges—some of the conventional assumptions of economics, social and political science and international relations. The first premise is that politics is a common activity; it is not confined to politicians and their officials. The second is that power over outcomes is exercised impersonally by markets and often unintentionally by those who buy and sell and deal in markets. The third is that authority in society and over economic transactions is legitimately exercised by agents other than states, and has come to be freely acknowledged by those who are subject to it.

The first two premises require some excursion into matters of theory. As they are essential to the whole argument, they will be dealt with first, in chapters 2 and 3 respectively. General readers may be inclined to skip these two chapters as being overly academic, especially if they already find themselves broadly in sympathy with the main thrust of my argument. However, if they have doubts about it, they may be interested to see where and why my understanding of the nature of power and of politics diverges from the conventional.

In subsequent chapters, dealing with recent changes in international political economy, readers will encounter three general propositions about the patterns of legitimate authority now developing in the international political economy towards the end of the twentieth century. One is that there is growing asymmetry among allegedly sovereign states in the authority they exercise in society and economy. In international relations, back to Thucydides, there has always been some recognition of a difference between small states and great powers, in the way each behaves to others and in the options available to them in their relations with other states. But there has been a tendency all along to assume a certain uniformity in the nature and effectiveness of the control which each state has over social and economic relations within their respective territorial boundaries. The attributes of domestic sovereignty, in other words, were assumed automatically to go with the regulation accorded each state by its peers. Now, I shall argue, that assumption can no longer be sustained. What was regarded as an exceptional anomaly when in 1945 the United States conceded two extra votes in the UN General Assembly for the Soviet Union—one for the 'sovereign' republic of the Ukraine and one for Byelorussia—now hardly attracts comment. The micro-states of Vanuatu and the Republic of San Marino are admitted to the select circle of member-states of the United Nations. But no one really believes that recognition of their 'sovereignty' is more than a courteous pretence. It is understood that there is only a difference of degree between these and many of the smaller and poorer members of the international society of states who are established occupants of seats in the UN.

The second proposition is that the authority of the governments of all states, large and small, strong and weak, has been weakened as a result of technological and financial change and of the accelerated integration of national economies into one single global market economy. Their failure to manage the national economy, to maintain employment and sustain economic growth, to avoid imbalances of payments with other states, to control the rate of interest and the exchange rate is not a matter of technical incompetence, nor moral turpitude nor political maladroitness. It is neither in any direct sense their fault, nor the fault of others. None of these failures can be blamed on other countries or on other governments. They are, simply, the victims of the market economy.

The third proposition complements the second. It is that some of the fundamental responsibilities of the state in a market economy—responsibilities first recognised, described and discussed at considerable length by Adam Smith over 200 years ago—are not now being adequately discharged by anyone. At the heart of the international political economy, there is a vacuum, a vacuum not adequately filled by inter-governmental institutions or by a hegemonic power exercising leadership in the common interest. The polarisation of states between those who retain some control over their destinies and those who are effectively incapable of exercising any such control does not add up to a zero-sum game. What some have lost, others have not gained. The diffusion of authority away from national governments has left a yawning hole of non-authority, ungovernance it might be called.

Note

1. The notable exceptions include Cerny, 1993; Porter, 1994; Veseth 1990; Wachtel, 1986; Frieden, 1987; Moffitt, 1983; Calleo, 1982. I should add that we all owe big debts to the economic historians such as Kindleberger, Cipolla, Feis and de Cecco, and more recently Cain and Hopkin; to the practitioners such as Volcker and Gyoten, and, not least to journalists such as the late Fred Hirsch and Yoichi Funabashi.

References

Calleo, D. 1982, *The Imperious Economy*. Cambridge MA: Howard University Press.
Cerny, Philip 1989, *The Changing Architecture of Politics: Structure, Agency, and the Future of the State*. London: Sage.
Dunning, John 1988, *Explaining International Production*. London: Harper and Collins.
Frieden, Jeffry 1987, *Banking on the World: The Politics of American International Finance*. New York: Harper & Row.
Moffitt, M. 1984, *The World's Money: International Banking from Bretton Woods to the Brink of Insolvency*. London: Joseph.

Porter, Michael 1990, *The Competitive Advantage of Nations.* New York: Free Press.

Rizopoulos, N. 1990, *Sea-Changes: American Foreign Policy in a World Transformed.* New York: Council on Foreign Relations.

Stopford, John and Strange, Susan 1991, *Rival States, Rival Firms Competition for World Market Shares.* Cambridge: Cambridge University Press.

Vernon, Raymond 1966, "International Investment and International Trade in the Product Cycle," *Quarterly Journal of Economics,* **80**: 190–207.

Veseth, Michael 1990, *Mountains of Debt – Crisis and Change in Renaissance Florence, Victorian Britain and Post-war America.* Oxford: Oxford University Press.

Wachtel, Howard 1986, *The Money Mandarins: The Making of a New Supranational Economic Order.* New York: Pantheon Books.

Robert Gilpin,
Global Political Economy (2001)*

Chapter Fourteen: The Nation-State
in the Global Economy

The idea that the nation-state has been undermined by the transnational forces of economic globalization has appeared in writings on the international system and on the international economy. Many writings have argued that international organizations (IOs) and nongovernmental actors are replacing nation-states as the dominant actors in the international system. Books that have made this claim include those with such dramatic titles as *The Retreat of the State, The End of Geography*, and the *End of Sovereignty?*[1] Daniel Yergin and Joseph Stanislaw maintain that the market has wrested control from the state over the commanding heights of the economy and that the economic role of the nation-state is just about at an end.[2] Other writers believe a global economy has emerged or is emerging in which distinct national economies no longer exist and national economic policies are no longer possible.[3] This chapter disagrees with such views and argues that the nation-state continues to be the major actor in both domestic and international affairs.

At the beginning of the twenty-first century, the nation-state is clearly under serious attack from both above and below, and there is no doubt that there have been very important changes. Within many nations, the politics of identity and ethnic conflict is challenging the integrity of states, as ethnic and regional groups seek independence or at least greater autonomy.[4] Yet it is important to understand that the Kurds, Palestinians, and many other groups all want nation-states of their own; they do not wish to eliminate nation-states but to divide present nation-states into units that they themselves can control. It is also accurate to say that economic globalization and transnational economic forces are eroding economic sovereignty in important ways. Nevertheless, both the extent of globalization and the consequences of economic globalization for the nation-state have been considerably exaggerated. For better or for worse, this is still a state-dominated world.

As Vincent Cable of the Royal Institute of International Affairs (London) has noted, it is not easy to assess globalization's implications for the nation-state.[5] Although the economic role of the state has declined in certain significant ways, it has expanded

* *Global Political Economy: Understanding the International Economic Order.* © 2001 Princeton University Press. (pp. 362–76) Reprinted by permission of Princeton University Press.

in others and, therefore, it is inaccurate to conclude that the nation-state has become redundant or anachronistic. As Cable says, the situation is "much messier" than that. The impact of the global economy on individual nations is highly uneven, and its impact varies from issue to issue; finance is much more globalized than are services and industrial production. While globalization has reduced some policy options, the degree of reduction is highly dependent on national size and economic power; the United States and Western Europe, for example, are much less vulnerable to destabilizing financial flows than are small economies. Indeed, the importance of the state has even actually increased in some areas, certainly with respect to promoting international competitiveness through support for R & D, for technology policy, and for other assistance to domestic firms.

Economic globalization is much more limited than many realize, and consequently, its overall impact on the economic role of the state is similarly limited. Moreover, although economic globalization has been a factor in whatever diminishment of the state may have occurred, ideological, technological, and international political changes have had an even more powerful influence. Furthermore, many and perhaps most of the social, economic, and other problems ascribed to globalization are actually due to technological and other developments that have little or nothing to do with globalization. Even though its role may have diminished somewhat, the nation-state remains preeminent in both domestic and international economic affairs. To borrow a phrase from the American humorist Mark Twain, I would like to report that the rumors of the death of the state "have been greatly exaggerated."[6]

The Limited Nature of Economic Globalization

In one sense, globalization has been taking place for centuries whenever improvements in transportation and communications have brought formerly separated peoples into contact with one another. The domestication of the horse and camel, the invention of the sailing ship, and the development of the telegraph all proved powerful instruments for uniting people, although not always to their liking. For thousands of years, ideas, artistic styles, and other artifacts have diffused from one society to another and have given rise to fears similar to those associated with economic globalization today. Nevertheless, it is important to discuss the economic globalization that has resulted from the rapid economic and technological integration of national societies that took place in the final decades of the twentieth century, especially after the end of the Cold War. This recent global economic integration has been the result of major changes in trade flows, of the activities of multinational corporations, and of developments in international finance.

Despite the increasing significance of economic globalization, the integration of the world economy has been highly uneven, restricted to particular economic sectors, and not nearly as extensive as many believe. As a number of commentators have pointed out, there are many ways in which the world is less integrated today than it was in the late nineteenth century. This should remind us that although the technology leading to increased globalization may be irreversible, national policies that have been responsible for the process of economic globalization have been reversed in the past and could be reversed again in the future.

As the twenty-first century opens, the world is not as well integrated as it was in a number of respects prior to World War I. Under the gold standard and the influential doctrine of laissez-faire, for example, the decades prior to World War I were an era when markets were truly supreme and governments had little power over economic affairs. Trade, investment, and financial flows were actually greater in the late 1800s, at least relative to the size of national economies and the international economy, than they are today. Twentieth-century changes appear primarily in the form of the greatly increased speed and absolute magnitude of economic flows across national borders and in the inclusion of more and more countries in the global economy. Yet, economic globalization is largely confined to North America, Western Europe, and Pacific Asia. And even though these industrial economies have become much more open, imports and investments from abroad are still small compared to the size of the domestic economies. For example, American imports rose from 5 percent of the total U.S. production in 1970 to just 13 percent in 1995, even though the United States was the most globalized economy.

Although trade has grown enormously during the past half century, trade still accounts for a relatively small portion of most economies; moreover, even though the number of "tradables" has been increasing, trade is still confined to a limited number of economic sectors. The principal competitors for most firms (with important exceptions in such areas as motor vehicles and electronics) are other national firms. The largest portions of foreign direct investment flows are invested in the United States, Western Europe, and China; a very small portion of the investment in sectors other than raw materials and resources has been invested in most less developed countries. International finance alone can be accurately described as a global phenomenon. Yet, even the globalization of finance must be qualified, as much of international finance is confined to short-term and speculative investment.

The most important measure of the economic integration and interdependence of distinct economies is what economists call the "law of one price." If identical goods and services in different economies have the same or nearly equal prices, then economists consider these economies to be closely integrated with one another. However, evidence indicates that the prices of identical goods around the world differ considerably whether measured by *The Economist* magazine's Big Mac index or by more formal economic measures.[7] When the law of one price is applied to the United States, it is clear that American prices differ greatly from those of other countries, especially Japan's. Price differentials in the cost of labor around the world are particularly notable, and there are large disparities in wages. All of this clearly suggests that the world is not as integrated as many proclaim.

The significant and sizable decline in migration is one of the major differences between late-nineteenth-century globalization and globalization of the early twenty-first century. During the past half century, the United States has been the only country to welcome large numbers of new citizens. Although Western Europe has accepted a flood of refugees and "guest workers," the situation in those countries has been and remains tenuous; few have been or will be offered citizenship. The globalization of labor was considerably more advanced prior to World War I than afterward. In the late nineteenth century, millions of Europeans crossed the Atlantic to settle as permanent residents in North America; West Europeans also migrated in significant numbers to such "lands of recent settlement" as Australia, Argentina, and other temperate-zone regions. There were large migrations of Indians and Chinese to Southeast Asia, Africa, and other tropical regions. All these streams of migration became powerful determinants of the structure of the world economy.[8] In the early twenty-first century, labor migration is no longer a major feature of the world economy, and even within the European Union, migration from one member nation to another is relatively low.

Barriers to labor migration are built by policies intended to protect the real wages and social welfare of the nation's citizens, and the modern welfare state is based on the assumption that its benefits will be available only to its own citizens.[9] Some reformers in industrialized countries have constructed an ethical case that national wealth should be shared with the destitute around the world, but to my knowledge, even they have not advocated elimination of the barriers to international migration in order to enable the poor to move to more wealthy countries and thus decrease international income disparities. I find it remarkable that in the debate over globalization, little attention has been given to the most important factor of production; namely, labor and labor migration. For the billions of people in poor countries, national borders certainly remain an important feature of the global economy.

Alleged Consequences of Economic Globalization

The conjuncture of globalization with a number of other political, economic, and technological developments transforming the world makes it very difficult to understand economic globalization and its consequences. Among far-reaching economic changes at the end of the twentieth century have been a shift in industrialized countries from manufacturing to services and several revolutionary technological developments associated with the computer, including emergence of the Internet and information economy. The skills and education required by jobs in the computer age place unskilled labor in the industrialized countries at a severe disadvantage in their wages and job security.

Although some economic and technological developments associated with the computer, including the rapid advances in telecommunications, have certainly contributed to the process of globalization, and globalization in some cases has accentuated these economic and technological changes, the two developments are not synonymous. In fact, the contemporary technological "revolution" has been a far more pervasive and, in many ways, a much more profound development than is globalization, at least thus far. For example, the most important development currently altering individual lives is the incredible revolution in the biological sciences, such as biological engineering. Yet this important development in human affairs has nothing whatsoever to do with globalization as it is commonly conceived.

Many of the problems alleged to be the result of economic globalization are really the consequence of unfortunate national policies and government decisions. Environmentalists rage against globalization and its evils; yet, most environmental damage is the result of the policies and behaviors of national governments. Air, water, and soil pollution result primarily from the lax policies of individual nations and/or from their poor enforcement procedures. The destruction of the Amazon forest has been caused principally by the Brazilian government's national development policies; in the United States, forest clear-cutting is actually promoted by generous government subsidies to logging companies. Land-hungry peasants in Southeast Asia are permitted to destroy forests to acquire cultivable land. Small farmers in France, the United States, and elsewhere blame globalization for their economic plight, but small farms are victims of economic/technological changes that have increased the importance of economies of scale in agriculture. Unfortunately, large farms and agribusinesses are now best suited to take full advantage of such economic/technological changes. The American agricultural sector, especially the large farms, even benefit from generous government subsidies. It would be easy to expand the list of problems generally attributed to globalization that have really been caused by technological changes, by national government policies, or by other wholly domestic factors.

In Western Europe, globalization is frequently blamed for many of the problems that have emerged from the economic and political integration of the region. Both globalization and regionalism are characterized by lowered economic barriers, restructuring of business, and other economic/social changes; it is easy, therefore, to see why some have conflated the two developments into one. Yet, globalization and regionalism are different, especially in the goals that each is seeking to achieve.

The tendency to blame globalization for many vexing problems of modern life is due in part to nationalistic and xenophobic attitudes on the political right and an anticapitalist mentality on the political left. Nationalistic attitudes have been expressed by Ross Perot, Patrick Buchanan, and American organized labor; the latter long ago gave up the slogan "workers of the world unite" in favor of their own parochial interests. The leftist criticism of capitalism runs deep in some peoples and countries and within advanced capitalist economies, most notably France. The antagonism toward capitalism is directed at the principal representatives of the capitalist system in the modern world: the United States, large multinational firms, and such international economic institutions as the International Monetary Fund and World Trade Organization. When I note these criticisms, I myself do not intend to endorse such excesses of capitalism as rampant commercialism, enormous disparities in wealth and privilege, advertising's creation of "wants," or the worship of wealth as the measure of all things. Capitalism is a system based on self-interest that is too frequently made manifest in outright greed. Despite capitalism's serious flaws, the evils of today's world will not be solved by attacks on globalization. One may say about capitalism what Winston Churchill is reputed to have said about democracy, that it is the worst of all social systems except for all the others.

Elsewhere in this book and in another of my books, *The Challenge of Global Capitalism,* I have addressed many of the negative consequences alleged to have been caused by globalization and have argued that most of the charges against globalization are wrong, misleading, or exaggerated.[10] Domestic and international income disparities, the problems of unskilled workers, and the alleged "race to the bottom" in modern welfare states in general should not be attributed to economic globalization. In almost all cases, such other factors as technological changes, national policies, or the triumph of conservative economic ideologies carry primary responsibility for these developments. Those particularly concerned about income inequalities among national societies should recognize that globalization in the form of exports from

industrializing to industrialized countries has actually greatly benefited the industrializing countries; furthermore, very few countries have developed in this century
without active participation in the global economy.

Effectiveness of Macroeconomic Policy

Since the end of World War II, and especially since governments accepted Keynesian
economics in the early postwar era, national governments in the advanced industrialized economies have been held responsible for national economic performance. States
were assigned the tasks of promoting national economic stability and steering their
economies between the undesirable conditions of recession and inflation. Through
macroeconomic policies, the state has been able to control, at least to some extent,
the troubling vicissitudes of the market. However, the argument that the power of the
state over economic affairs has significantly declined implies that national governments can no longer manage their economies. While it is true that macroeconomic
policy has become more complicated in the highly integrated world economy of the
twenty-first century, these policies do still work and can achieve their goals at least
as well as in the past. What better example than the Federal Reserve's very successful
management of the American economy in the mid-to-late 1990s! Moreover, today as
in the past, the principal constraints on macroeconomic policy are to be found at the
domestic rather than at the international level.

Macroeconomic policy consists of two basic tools for managing a national economy: fiscal policies and monetary policies. The principal instruments of fiscal policy
are taxation and government expenditures. Through lowering or raising taxes and/or
increasing or decreasing national expenditures, the federal government (Congress
and the Executive) can affect the national level of economic activities. Whereas a
federal budget deficit (spending more than tax receipts) will stimulate the economy,
a budget surplus (spending less than tax receipts) will decrease economic activities.
Monetary policy works through its determination of the size and velocity of a nation's
money supply. The Federal Reserve can stimulate or depress the level of economic
activities by increasing or restricting the supply of dollars available to consumers and
producers. The principal method employed by the Federal Reserve to achieve this
goal is to determine the national level of interest rates; whereas a low interest rate
stimulates economic growth, a high rate depresses it.

Many commentators argue that the effectiveness of monetary policy has been significantly reduced by increased international financial flows. If, for example, a central bank lowers interest rates to stimulate the economy, investors will transfer their
capital to other economies with higher interest rates and thus counter the intended
stimulus of lower rates. Similarly, if a central bank increases interest rates in order
to slow the economy, investment capital will flow into the economy, counter the
intended deflationary effects of higher rates, and stimulate economic activities. In
all these ways, economic globalization is believed to have undermined the efficacy of
fiscal and monetary policy. Therefore, some consider national governments no longer
able to manage their economies.

To examine this contention, it is helpful to apply the logic of the "trilemma" or
"irreconcilable trinity." Every nation is confronted by an inevitable trade-off among

the following three desirable goals of economic policy: fixed exchange rates, national autonomy in macroeconomic policy, and international capital mobility. A nation might want a stable exchange rate in order to reduce economic uncertainty and stabilize the economy. Or it might desire discretionary monetary policy to avoid high unemployment and steer the economy between recession and inflation. Or a government might want freedom of capital movements to facilitate the conduct of trade, foreign investment, and other international business activities. Unfortunately, a government cannot achieve all three of these goals simultaneously. It can obtain at most two. For example, choosing a fixed and stable exchange rate along with some latitude for independent monetary policies would mean forgoing freedom of capital movements, because international capital flows could undermine both exchange rate stability and independent monetary policies. On the other hand, a country might choose to pursue macroeconomic policies to promote full employment, but it then would have to sacrifice either a fixed exchange rate or freedom of capital movement.

Such an analysis tells us that although economic globalization does constrain government policy options, it does not impose a financial straitjacket on national macroeconomic policies. Whether an individual nation does or does not have the capacity for an independent macroeconomic policy is itself a policy choice. If a nation wants the capability to pursue an independent macroeconomic policy, it can achieve that goal by abandoning either fixed exchange rates or capital mobility. Different countries do, in fact, make different choices. The United States, for example, prefers independent monetary policy and freedom of capital movements and therefore sacrifices exchange rate stability; members of the European Economic Monetary Union (EMU), on the other hand, prefer fixed exchange rates and have created a common currency to achieve this goal. Some other countries that place a high value on macroeconomic independence—China, for example—have imposed controls on capital movements.

Different domestic economic interests also have differing preferences. Whereas export businesses have a strong interest in the exchange rate, domestic-oriented businesses place a higher priority on national policy autonomy. Investors prefer freedom of capital movement, whereas labor tends to be opposed to such movement, unless the movement should mean increased investment in their own nation. Economic globalization in itself does not prevent a nation from using macroeconomic policies for managing its economy.

The mechanisms employed to conduct monetary policy have not been seriously affected by globalization. Although various central banks operate differently from one another, an examination of the ways in which the American Federal Reserve (the Fed) steers the American economy is instructive and reveals that, at least in the American case, globalization has had only minimal effects.

Through its power to increase or decrease the number of dollars available to consumers and producers (liquidity), the Fed is able to steer the overall economy. The level of national economic activity is strongly influenced by the size of the nation's money supply; an increase in the money supply stimulates economic activities and a decrease slows down economic activity. The Fed has three basic instruments to influence the nation's supply of money. The first directly affects the money supply; the other tools work indirectly through the banking system.

The Fed's primary means for management of the economy is "open market operations," conducted through the Open Market Desk of the Federal Reserve Bank of New York. Through sale or purchase of U.S. government bonds directly to the public, the Fed can influence the overall level of national economic activity. If, for example, the Fed wants to slow the economy, it sells U.S. Government bonds. This takes money or liquidity out of the economy. If, on the other hand, the Fed wants to stimulate the economy, it uses dollars to purchase U.S. Government bonds and thus increases the money or liquidity in the economy.

The Fed can also change the discount rate, which is the interest rate on loans that the Fed makes directly to the nation's commercial banks. The Fed, for example, loans money to banks whose reserves fall below the Fed's reserve requirements (see below); this may happen if a bank has made too many loans or is experiencing too many withdrawals. By lending to private banks and increasing the reserves of those banks, the Fed enables banks to make more loans and thus to increase the nation's money supply. Whereas raising the discount rate decreases loans and money creation, lowering of the discount rate increases loans and money creation. These changes in turn have a powerful influence on the overall level of economic activity.

Another tool that the Fed has available is its authority to determine the reserve requirements of the nation's banks. Reserve requirements specify the minimal size of the monetary reserves that a bank must hold against deposits subject to withdrawal. Reserve requirements thus determine the amount of money that a bank is permitted to lend and, thereby, how much money the bank can place in circulation. Through raising or lowering reserve requirements, the Fed sets a limit on how much money the nation's banks can inject into the economy. However, this method of changing the money supply is used infrequently because changed reserve requirements can be very disruptive to the banking system.

Globalization and a more open world economy have had only minimal impact on the Fed's ability to manage the economy. Yet the effectiveness of open market operations has probably been somewhat reduced by growth of the international financial market, and the purchase or sale of U.S. securities by foreigners certainly affects the national money supply. In the late 1990s, it was estimated that approximately $150 billion was held overseas. However, the effect of that large amount is minimized by the size of the more than $8 trillion domestic economy. Also, the American financial system (like that of other industrialized countries) exhibits a "home bias"; that is to say, most individuals keep their financial assets in their own currency. It is possible, however, that central banks in smaller and weaker economies find that their ability to manage their own money supply has been decreased, as was exemplified by the 1997 Asian financial crisis.

One should note that the continuing power of the Fed over the banks and the money supply through control of the interest rate has been challenged by the development of the credit card and other new forms of money. These credit instruments have decreased, at least somewhat, the effectiveness of the Fed's use of this instrument to control the economy. Still more problematic for the Fed is the increasing use of e-money in Internet commerce. In effect, these developments mean that the monopoly of money creation once held by the Fed and the banking system is being diluted. Through use of a credit card and/or participation in e-commerce, an individual or business can create money. Yet, at some point e-money and other novel forms of money must be converted into "real" or legal tender, and, at that point the Fed retains control of the creation of real money. Thus, although the monetary system has become much more complex, the Fed still has ultimate control over that system and through it, the overall economy.

Although the power of central banks over interest rates and the money supply has been somewhat diminished, as long as cash and bank reserves remain the ultimate means of exchange and of settlement of accounts, central banks can still retain control over the money supply and hence of the economy. In fact, even if everyone switched to electronic means of payment but credit issuers still settled their balances with merchants through the banking system (as happens with credit cards now), central banks would still retain overall control. However, one day, e-money could displace other forms of money. If and when this develops, financial settlements could be carried out without going through commercial banks, and central banks would lose their ability to control the economy through interest rates. Such a development could lead to the "denationalization" of money. However, it seems reasonable to believe that some public authority would still be needed to control inflation and monitor the integrity of the computer system used for payments settlements.

With respect to *reserve requirements,* intense competition among international banks has induced some central banks to reduce reserve requirements in order to make the domestic banking industry more competitive internationally. Japanese banks, for example, have long been permitted by the government to keep much smaller reserves than American banks. One of the major purposes of the Basle Agreement (1988), was to make reserve requirements more uniform throughout the world. Rumor has it that this agreement was engineered by the Fed to decrease the international competitiveness of Japanese and other foreign banks vis-à-vis American international banks. Whatever the underlying motive, the agreement has been described as a response to financial globalization, and the establishment of uniform international reserve requirements has largely reestablished their effectiveness as instruments of policy.

The most important constraints on macroeconomic policy are found at the domestic level. If an economy were isolated from the international economy, fiscal policy would be constrained by the cost of borrowing. If a national government were to use deficit spending to stimulate its economy, the resulting budget deficit would have to be financed by domestic lenders. In that situation, an upper limit would be placed on government borrowing, because as the budget deficit and the costs of servicing that deficit rose, bond purchasers would become more and more fearful that the government might default on its debt and/or use monetary policy to inflate the money supply and thus reduce the real value of the debt. Increased risk as debt rises causes lenders to stop lending and/or to charge higher and higher interest rates; this then discourages further borrowing by the government. Also, another important constraint on monetary policy in a domestic economy is the threat of inflation; this threat places an upper limit on the ability of a central bank to stimulate the economy by increasing the money supply and/or lowering the interest rate. At some point, the threat of inflation will discourage economic activity. In short, there are limits on macroeconomic policy that have nothing whatsoever to do with the international economy—and these domestic constraints existed long before anyone had heard the term "globalization."

Economic globalization has made the task of managing an economy easier in some ways and more difficult in others. On the one hand, globalization has enabled governments to borrow more freely; the United States in the 1980s and 1990s borrowed heavily from Japanese and other foreign investors in order to finance a federal budget deficit and a high rate of economic growth. However, this debt-financed growth strategy, as Susan Strange pointed out first in *Casino Capitalism* (1986) and again in *Mad Money* (1998), is extraordinarily risky and can not continue forever. Fearing collapse of the dollar, investors could one day flee dollar-denominated assets for safer assets denominated in other currencies.[11] The consequences of such flight could be devastating for the United States and for the rest of the world economy. Thus, although economic globalization has increased the latitude of governments to pursue expansionary economic policies through borrowing excessively abroad, such serious financial crises of the postwar era as the Mexican crisis in 1994–1995, the 1997 East Asian financial crisis, and the disturbing collapse of the Russian ruble in August 1998 demonstrate the huge and widespread risks associated with such a practice.

Economic globalization and the greater openness of domestic economies have also modified the rules of economic policy. Certainly, the increasing openness of national economies has made the exercise of macroeconomic policy more complex and difficult. This does not mean that a national government can no longer guide the economy around the dangerous shoals of inflation and recession, but it does mean that the risk of shipwreck has grown.

The Need for a Historical Perspective

The globalization thesis lacks a historical perspective. Those individuals who argue that globalization has severely limited economic sovereignty appear to believe that governments once possessed unlimited national autonomy and freedom in economic matters. Their argument assumes that nation-states have enjoyed unrestricted ability to determine economic policy and manage their economies and that governments were free because they were not subordinate to or encumbered by transnational market forces. As proponents of the globalization thesis contrast economic policy in the twenty-first century to this imagined past, they conclude that nation-states, for the first time ever, have become constrained by the increased integration of national economies through trade, financial flows, and the activities of multinational firms. In effect, having assumed that states once had complete economic freedom, these individuals misperceive the reality of the fundamental relationship between the state and the economy. When viewed from a more accurate historical perspective, the relationship of state and market in the contemporary era is neither particularly startling nor revolutionary.

In the decades prior to World War I, national governments had little effective control over their economies. Under the classical gold standard of fixed exchange rates, governments were more tightly bound by what Barry Eichengreen has called "golden fetters" than they are in the early-twenty-first century world of flexible rates. Moreover, as Nobel Laureate Arthur Lewis has noted, prior to World War I the economic agenda of governments everywhere was limited to the efforts of central banks to maintain the value of their currencies.[12] As Keynes pointed out in *The Economic Consequences of the Peace* (1919), national economic policy did not concern itself with the welfare of the "lower orders" of society.[13] This minor and highly constrained role of the state in the economy changed dramatically with World War I and subsequent economic and political developments.

Throughout the twentieth century, the relationship of state and market indeed changed significantly as governments harnessed their economies for total war and to meet their citizens' rising economic expectations. The world wars of the twentieth century, the Great Depression of the 1930s, and the immense economic demands of the Cold War elevated the state's role in the economy. During periods of intense concern about security, national governments used new tools to manage their economies and began to exercise unprecedented control over their economies. The Great Depression, the rise of organized labor, and the sacrifices imposed on societies by World War II led Western governments to expand their activities to guarantee the welfare of their citizens. For some years, the perceived success of the communist experiment also encouraged governments to help Keynes's "lower orders," and after World War II, governments in every advanced economy assumed responsibility for promotion of full employment and provision of a generous and high level of economic welfare.

Conclusion

The argument that the nation-state is in retreat is most applicable to the United States, Western Europe, and perhaps Japan. The end of the Cold War represented the end of a century and a half of rapid economic development and political/military conflict. Since the American Civil War (1861–1865), the Franco-Prussian War (1870–1871), and the Russo-Japanese War (1904–1905), the forces of nationalism, industrialization, and state-creation had driven the industrialized powers of Europe, the United States, and Japan. World War I, World War II, and the Cold War forged the modern nation-state as an economic and war-making machine. During these decades of interstate rivalry, the economy was often harnessed to the needs of the national war machine. This bellicose epoch appears to have ended, and the industrialized countries may be retreating to their more modest late nineteenth-century status. Yet, one must ask whether the forces of nationalism, industrialization, and state-creation might not be causing a repeat of the tragic Western experience in the developing economies of Asia, Africa, and elsewhere! Thus far, there is little evidence to suggest that these countries will avoid repeating the mistakes made by the industrialized world.

Notes

1. Richard O'Brien, *Global Financial Integration: The End of Geography*; Walter B. Wriston, *The Twilight of Sovereignty: How the Information Revolution Is Transforming Our World* (New York: Scribner's, 1992); Joseph A. Camilleri and Jim Falk, *End of Sover-*

eignty? The Politics of a Shrinking and Fragmenting World (Brookfield, Vt.: Elgar, 1992); Susan Strange, *The Retreat of the State: The Diffusion of Power in the World Economy* (New York: Cambridge University Press, 1996).

2. Daniel Yergin and Joseph Stanislaw, *The Commanding Heights: The Battle Between Government and the Marketplace That Is Remaking the Modern World* (New York: Simon and Schuster, 1998).

3. Paul Hirst and Grahame Thompson, *Globalization in Question: The International Economy and the Possibility of Governance* (London: Polity Press, 1996), 1.

4. Vincent Cable, "The Diminished Nation-State: A Study in the Loss of Economic Power," in *What Future for the State? Daedalus* 124, no. 2 (spring 1995): 44–46.

5. Ibid., 38.

6. Mark Twain was a nineteenth-century American author whose obituary was mistakenly published before his death, leading Twain to comment that rumors of his death were greatly exaggerated.

7. Charles Engel and John H. Rogers, "Regional Patterns in the Law of One Price: The Roles of Geography versus Currencies," in Jeffrey A. Frankel, ed., *The Regionalization of the World Economy* (Chicago: University of Chicago Press, 1998), 153.

8. W. Arthur Lewis, *The Evolution of the International Economic Order* (Princeton: Princeton University Press, 1978).

9. James Mayall, *Nationalism and International Society* (Cambridge: Cambridge University Press, 1990), Chapter 5.

10. A very effective critique of the antiglobalist position is found in Geoffrey Garrett, "Global Markets and National Politics," *International Organization* 52, no. 4 (autumn 1998): 787–824.

11. Susan Strange, *Casino Capitalism* (Oxford: Blackwell, 1986); and *Mad Money: From the Author of Casino Capitalism* (Manchester, U.K.: Manchester University Press, 1998).

12. Barry Eichengreen, *Golden Fetters: The Gold Standard and the Great Depression* (New York: Oxford University Press, 1992); and W. Arthur Lewis, *Growth and Fluctuations, 1870–1913* (London: Allen and Unwin, 1978).

13. John Maynard Keynes, *The Economic Consequences of the Peace* (London: Macmillan, 1919).

Suggestions for Further Reading

The Classics

Jeremy Bentham. *Jeremy Bentham's Economic Writings*. 3 vols., edited by W. Stark. London: George Allan and Unwin, 1952.

Robert Heilbroner. *The Worldly Philosophers: The Lives, Times, and Ideas of the Great Economic Thinkers*. New York: Simon & Schuster, 1999.

Karl Marx, *Capital: An Abridged Edition*. Edited by David McLellan. Oxford: Oxford University Press, 1999.

John Stuart Mill. *Principles of Political Economy*. London: Longmans, Green, 1909.

Jerry Z. Muller. *The Mind and the Market: Capitalism in Modern European Thought*. New York: Alfred A. Knopf, 2002.

David Ricardo. *On the Principles of Political Economy and Taxation*. London: John Murray, 1821.

Adam Smith. *The Theory of Moral Sentiments*. Cambridge: Cambridge University Press, 2002.

The Liberal Paradigm

Milton Friedman and Rose Friedman. *Free to Choose: A Personal Statement*. New York: Harcourt Brace Jovanovich, 1980.

Friedrich Hayek. *The Constitution of Liberty*. Chicago: University of Chicago Press, 1960.

Carl Menger. *Principles of Economics*. New York: New York University Press, 1981.

George J. Stigler, ed. *Chicago Studies in Political Economy*. Chicago: University of Chicago Press, 1988.

Ludwig von Mises. *Socialism: An Economic and Sociological Analysis*. Indianapolis: Liberty Fund, 1981.

Economic Sociology

Nicole W. Biggart, ed. *Readings in Economic Sociology*. Oxford: Blackwell, 2002.

Paul DiMaggio, ed. *The Twenty-first-Century Firm: Changing Economic Organization in International Perspective*. Princeton: Princeton University Press, 2001.

Frank Dobbin, ed. *The New Economic Sociology: A Reader*. Princeton: Princeton University Press, 2004.

Neil Fligstein. *The Transformation of Corporate Control.* Cambridge: Harvard University Press, 1990.

Mark Granovetter. "Economic Action and Social Structure: The Problem of Embeddedness." *American Journal of Sociology* 91 (1985): 481–510.

Victor Nee and Richard Swedberg, eds. *The Economic Sociology of Capitalism.* Princeton: Princeton University Press, 2005.

Walter W. Powell and Paul J. DiMaggio, eds. *The New Institutionalism in Organizational Analysis.* Chicago: University of Chicago Press, 1991.

Neil J. Smelser and Richard Swedberg, eds. *The Handbook of Economic Sociology.* 2nd ed. Princeton: Princeton University Press, 2005.

Harrison White. *Markets from Networks: Socioeconomic Models of Production.* Princeton: Princeton University Press, 2002.

The New Institutional Economics

Masahiko Aoki. *Toward a Comparative Institutional Analysis.* Cambridge: MIT Press, 2001.

Ronald Coase. "The Nature of the Firm." *Economica* 4 (1937): 386–405.

Claude Menard, ed. *The International Library of New Institutional Economics.* 7 vols. Cheltenham: Edward Elgar, 2004.

Claude Menard and Mary M. Shirley, eds. *Handbook of New Institutional Economics.* Dordrecht: Springer, 2005.

Douglass C. North. *Institutions, Institutional Change and Economic Performance.* Cambridge: Cambridge University Press, 1990.

_____. "Market and Other Allocation Systems in History: The Challenge of Karl Polanyi." *Journal of European Economic History* (Winter 1977): 703–16.

_____. "The New Institutional Economics." *Journal of Institutional and Theoretical Economics* 142 (1986): 230–37.

Oliver Williamson. *The Mechanisms of Governance.* New York: Oxford University Press, 1996.

_____. "The New Institutional Economics: Taking Stock, Looking Ahead." *Journal of Economic Literature* 38 (September 2000): 595–613.

Oliver E. Williamson and Scott E. Master. *Transaction Cost Economics.* 2 vols. Aldershot: Edward Elgar, 1995.

Historical Perspectives

Alfred Chandler. *The Visible Hand: The Managerial Revolution in American Business.* Cambridge: Belknap Press, 1977.

Jared Diamond. *Guns, Germs and Steel: The Fates of Human Societies.* New York: W.W. Norton, 1997.

Patrice Higonnet, David S. Landes, and Henry Rosovsky, eds. *Favorites of Fortune: Technology, Growth, and Economic Development since the Industrial Revolution.* Cambridge: Harvard University Press, 1991.

Eric J. Hobsbawm. *Industry and Empire: An Economic History of Britain since 1750.* London: Weidenfeld and Nicolson, 1968.

David Landes. *The Unbound Prometheus: Technological Change and Industrial Development in Western Europe from 1750 to the Present.* London: Cambridge University Press, 1969.

Thomas K. McCraw, ed. *Creating Modern Capitalism: How Entrepreneurs, Companies, and Countries Triumphed in Three Industrial Revolutions.* Cambridge: Harvard University Press, 1997.

Clive Trebilcock. *The Industrialization of the Continental Powers: 1780–1914.* London: Longman, 1981.

Thorstein Veblen. *Imperial Germany and the Industrial Revolution.* New York: Viking Press, 1939.

Political Science and Political Economy

Peter Evans. *Embedded Autonomy: States and Industrial Transformation.* Princeton: Princeton University Press, 1995.

Peter Hall. *Governing the Economy: The Politics of State Intervention in Britain and France.* New York: Oxford University Press, 1986.

Peter Katzenstein, ed. *Between Power and Plenty: Foreign Economic Policies of Advanced Industrial States.* Madison: University of Wisconsin Press, 1978.

Atul Kohli. *State-Directed Development: Political Power and Industrialization in the Global Periphery.* Cambridge: Cambridge University Press, 2004.

Charles Lindblom. *Politics and Markets: The World's Political-Economic Systems.* New York: Basic Books, 1977.

Harold Wilensky. *Rich Democracies: Political Economy, Public Policy, and Performance.* Berkeley: University of California Press, 2002.

John Zysman. *Governments, Markets and Growth: Financial Systems and the Politics of Industrial Change.* Ithaca: Cornell University Press, 1983.

Market Reform in Advanced Industrial Countries

Herbert Kitschelt et al., eds. *Continuity and Change in Contemporary Capitalism.* Cambridge: Cambridge University Press, 1999.

Marc K. Landy, Martin A. Levin, and Martin Shapiro, eds. *Creating Competitive Markets: The Politics of Regulatory Reform.* Washington, DC: Brookings Institution Press, 2007.

Jonah Levy, ed. *The State after Statism: New State Activities in the Age of Liberalization.* Cambridge: Harvard University Press, 2006.

Raghuram G. Rajan and Luigi Zingales. *Saving Capitalism from the Capitalists: Unleashing the Power of Financial Markets to Create Wealth and Spread Opportunity.* New York: Random House, 2003.

Vivien A. Schmidt. *The Futures of European Capitalism.* Oxford: Oxford University Press, 2002.

Wolfgang Streeck and Kathleen Thelen, eds. *Beyond Continuity: Institutional Change in Advanced Political Economies.* Oxford: Oxford University Press, 2005.

Kozo Yamamura and Wolfgang Streeck. *The End of Diversity? Prospects for German and Japanese Capitalism.* Ithaca: Cornell University Press, 2003.

Market Transition in Eastern Europe and China

Alice H. Amsden, Jacek Kochanowicz, and Lance Taylor. *The Market Meets Its Match: Restructuring the Economies of Eastern Europe.* Cambridge: Harvard University Press, 1994.

Anders Åslund. *Building Capitalism: The Transformation of the Former Soviet Bloc.* Cambridge: Cambridge University Press, 2002.

Timothy Frye. *Brokers and Bureaucrats: Building Market Institutions in Russia.* Ann Arbor: University of Michigan Press, 2000.

Doug Guthrie. *Dragon in a Three-Piece Suit: The Emergence of Capitalism in China.* Princeton: Princeton University Press, 1999.

Jean C. Oi and Andrew G. Walder, eds. *Property Rights and Economic Reform in China.* Stanford: Stanford University Press, 1999.

Adam Przeworski. *Democracy and the Market: Political and Economic Reforms in Eastern Europe and South America.* Cambridge: Cambridge University Press, 1991.

Gerard Roland. *Transition and Economics: Politics, Markets, and Firms.* Cambridge: MIT Press, 2000.

Edward Steinfeld. *Forging Reform in China: The Fate of State-Owned Industry.* Cambridge: Cambridge University Press, 1998.

Kellee Tsai. *Back-Alley Banking: Private Entrepreneurs in China.* Ithaca: Cornell University Press, 2002.

David Woodruff. *Money Unmade: Barter and the Fate of Russian Capitalism.* Ithaca: Cornell University Press, 1999.

Dali Yang. *Remaking the Chinese Leviathan: Market Transition and the Politics of Governance in China.* Stanford: Stanford University Press, 2004.

Market Development in Developing Countries

Pranab Bardhan. *Scarcity, Conflicts, and Cooperation: Essays in the Political and Institutional Economics of Development.* Cambridge: MIT Press, 2005.

Robert H. Bates, ed. *Toward a Political Economy of Development: A Rational Choice Perspective.* Berkeley: University of California Press, 1988.

Kiren Chaudhry. *The Price of Wealth: Economies and Institutions in the Middle East.* Ithaca: Cornell University Press, 1997.

Christopher Clague, ed. *Institutions and Economic Development: Growth and Governance in Less-Developed and Post-Socialist Countries.* Baltimore: Johns Hopkins University Press, 1997.

John Harriss, Janet Hunter, and Colin M. Lewis, eds. *The New Institutional Economics and Third World Development.* London: Routledge, 1995.

Elhanan Helpman. *The Mystery of Economic Growth.* Cambridge: Belknap Press, 2004.

Albert O. Hirschman. *The Strategy of Economic Development.* New Haven: Yale University Press, 1958.

Dani Rodrick. "Institutions for High-Quality Growth: What They Are and How to Acquire Them." *Studies in Comparative International Development* 35 (Fall 2000): 3–31.

Amartya Sen. *Development as Freedom.* New York: Anchor Books, 2000.

World Bank. *World Development Report 2002: Building Institutions for Markets.* Oxford: Oxford University Press, 2002.

Globalization and the Information Technology Revolution

Suzanne Berger and Ronald Dore, eds. *National Diversity and Global Capitalism*. Ithaca: Cornell University Press, 1996.

Manuel Castells and Gustavo Cardoso, eds. *The Network Society: From Knowledge to Policy*. Washington, DC: Center for Transatlantic Relations, Johns Hopkins University, 2006.

Benjamin Cohen. *The Future of Money*. Princeton: Princeton University Press, 2004.

Paul N. Doremus, William W. Keller, Louis W. Pauly, and Simon Reich. *The Myth of the Global Corporation*. Princeton: Princeton University Press, 1998.

Jeffry Frieden. *Global Capitalism: Its Fall and Rise in the Twentieth Century*. New York: W.W. Norton, 2006.

Thomas Friedman. *The World Is Flat: A Brief History of the Twenty-first Century*. New York: Farrar, Straus and Giroux, 2005.

Mauro Guillen. *The Limits of Convergence: Globalization and Organizational Change in Argentina, South Korea, and Spain*. Princeton: Princeton University Press, 2001.

Robert O. Keohane and Helen V. Milner, eds. *Internationalization and Domestic Politics*. Cambridge: Cambridge University Press, 1996.

Michael M. Weinstein, ed. *Globalization: What's New?* New York: Columbia University Press, 2005.

Linda Weiss. *The Myth of the Powerless State*. Ithaca: Cornell University Press, 1998.

Index

N

O

U

V

CPSIA information can be obtained at www.ICGtesting.com
Printed in the USA
LVOW10s0752300814

401375LV00004B/12/P